Personal Finance

Students

Log on to the Online Learning Center
persfinance07.glencoe.com

Integrated Academics

To reinforce and improve academic skills in math, language arts, history, geography, economics, social studies, science, and art:

- Academic Connection
- Go Figure Financial Math
- Section Assessment activities
- Academic Skills
- Your Financial Figures

New Student Edition Features

To connect you with real-world personal finance:

- WebQuest unit projects
- Ask Standard & Poor's
- S&P's Global Financial Landscape
- S&P's Put on Your Financial Planner's Cap
- *BusinessWeek* Finance File
- *BusinessWeek* Online
- Document Detective
- TechByte

Reading Skills and Assessments

- Reading Strategies
- Focus on Reading
- New chapter assessments
- Project-based learning

Online Learning Center

- Chapter Study Organizers
- Chapter feature activities
- WebQuest projects
- Go Figure Math
- Practice Tests
- Online resources
- Vocabulary puzzles and games

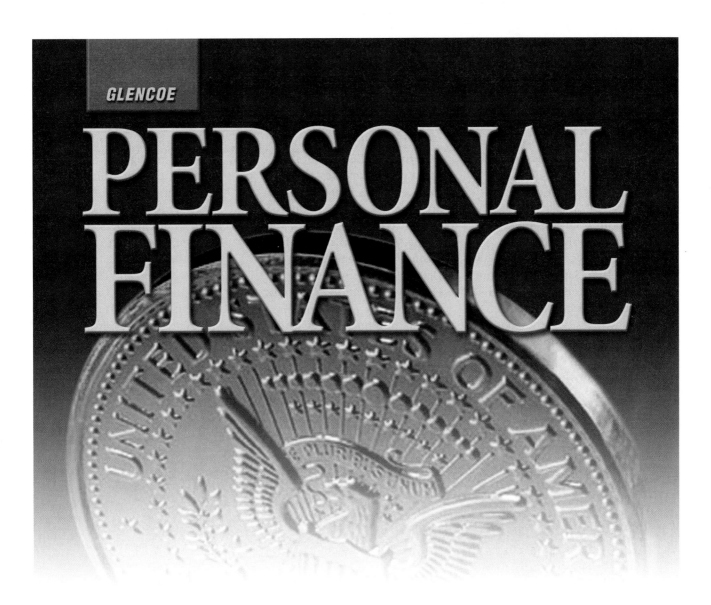

PERSONAL FINANCE

GLENCOE

Jack R. Kapoor
Professor of Business and Economics
Business and Services Division
College of DuPage
Glen Ellyn, Illinois

Les R. Dlabay
Professor of Business
Department of Economics and Business
Lake Forest College
Lake Forest, Illinois

Robert J. Hughes
Professor of Business
Dallas County Community Colleges
Dallas, Texas

About the Authors

Jack R. Kapoor

Jack R. Kapoor is professor of business and economics in the Business and Services Division at College of DuPage, where he has taught since 1969. He received his Bachelor of Arts in Business Administration and Master of Science in International Business from San Francisco State College. He received his Doctor of Education from Northern Illinois University. Dr. Kapoor was awarded the Business and Services Division's Outstanding Professor Award for 1999–2000.

Les R. Dlabay

Les R. Dlabay teaches in the Department of Economics and Business at Lake Forest College. He received his Bachelor of Science in Accounting from University of Illinois, his Master of Business Administration in Business Management from DePaul University, and his Doctor of Education in Business and Economic Education from Northern Illinois University. He is a founding member of the Illinois Consumer Education Association.

Robert J. Hughes

Robert J. Hughes teaches business, management, and finance courses at Dallas County Community Colleges. He received his Bachelor of Arts in Business Administration from Southern Nazarene University and his Master of Business Administration and Doctor of Education from the University of North Texas. Dr. Hughes has taught at the high school, community college, and four-year university levels for 36 years. He received the Excellence in Teaching Award at Richland College and has 15 years of experience teaching personal finance courses.

Glencoe

The *McGraw·Hill* Companies

Printed in the United States of America.

Send all inquiries to:

Glencoe/McGraw-Hill
21600 Oxnard Street, Suite 500
Woodland Hills, California 91367-4906

ISBN-13: 978-0-07-869800-2 (Student Text)
ISBN-10: 0-07-869800-6 (Student Text)

ISBN-13: 978-0-07-869789-0 (Teacher Annotated Edition)
ISBN-10: 0-07-869789-1 (Teacher Annotated Edition)

6 7 8 9   027   13 12 11 10 09 08

Reviewers

Rosella Bannister
Jump$tart Personal Finance
   Clearinghouse
Ann Arbor, Michigan

Janet Barnes
Hazelwood West High School
Hazelwood, Missouri

Thelma Brooks
Educational Consultant
Columbus, Ohio

Edlena Carmon
Marion Franklin High School
Columbus, Ohio

Sharon Clemons
Thomas Worthington High
   School
Worthington, Ohio

John E. Clow, Ph.D.
State University of New York
Oneonta, New York

Joe Cook
Southeast Career Center
Columbus, Ohio

Diane W. Culpepper
Winter Park Tech
Winter Park, Florida

Joy Davis
Delaware Area Career Center
Delaware, Ohio

Laneita Dunphy
Montclair High School
Montclair, New Jersey

Ernestine Gordon
Montclair High School
Montclair, New Jersey

Georgia Hoover
Dublin Scioto High School
Dublin, Ohio

Paul Jussila
South Windsor High School
South Windsor, Connecticut

Mike Kelly
Hazelwood East High School
St. Louis, Missouri

Jason Lee
Olympia High School
Orlando, Florida

Diane Manley
St. Louis, Missouri

Greg Moore
Columbus, Ohio

Jeff Noyes
Minnetonka High School
Minnetonka, Minnesota

Verta Parks
Marion Franklin High School
Columbus, Ohio

Kevin Richberg
Montclair High School
Montclair, New Jersey

Verlin Samples
Hamilton Local
Columbus, Ohio

James C. Scharer
Fremont Ross High School
Fremont, Ohio

Natalie Schaublin
Westerville North High
   School
Westerville, Ohio

Ken Schnitzer
Montclair High School
Montclair, New Jersey

Julie Smith
Southeast Career Center
Columbus, Ohio

Betty Tobler
St. Louis Public Schools
St. Louis, Missouri

Mark Van Hoy
Hazelwood West High School
Hazelwood, Missouri

Patty Wamble
Cape Central High School
Cape Girardeau, Missouri

Elizabeth Watt
North Education Center
Columbus, Ohio

Ken Watts
Montclair High School
Montclair, New Jersey

Polly White
Wawasee High School
Syracuse, Indiana

Tamara Wickline
Dublin Coffman High School
Dublin, Ohio

Susie Wright
Walnut Ridge High School
Columbus, Ohio

Glenn Zipfel
Christian Brothers High
   School
St. Louis, Missouri

Welcome to *Personal Finance*

Each day you are surrounded by new choices for shopping, watching television, and other activities. You also have many choices about how to spend your money. *Personal Finance* can help you make the right decisions. You will develop financial literacy through integrated academics, real-world examples, and practical advice. By learning how to make informed decisions related to spending, saving, borrowing, and investing, you can build a solid foundation for your financial security now and in the future.

Brief Table of Contents

Table of Contents

UNIT 2 Banking and Credit 118

UNIT 4   Protecting Your Finances   376

Understanding the Unit

The 15 chapters of *Personal Finance* are divided into four units. Each unit opens with a *BusinessWeek* Finance File feature and WebQuest activity and concludes with a finance simulation application that gives you a chance to apply what you have learned.

Previewing the Unit

Unit-Opener Photo
The unit-opener photo illustrates a concept that is related to the unit. Ask yourself: "How does the photo relate to the content of the unit?"

WebQuest This unit activity is continued in each chapter in the unit as it introduces you to a unit topic and directs you to the Online Learning Center to research and complete this Web-based project.

BusinessWeek Finance File Each unit opens with an excerpt from a real *BusinessWeek* article about an aspect of the unit material. The feature directs you to the Online Learning Center to read the complete article and do an application activity.

Closing the Unit

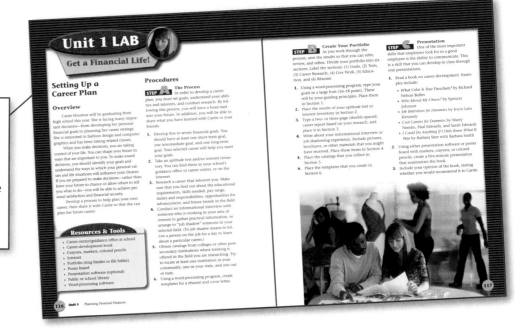

Get a Financial Life! Unit Lab Simulation
This unit simulation provides hands-on experience that expands your understanding of finance as you apply what you have learned to a real-world project.

Understanding the Chapter

Each unit of *Personal Finance* includes three to four chapters. Each chapter focuses on an aspect of finance that will apply to your everyday financial management.

Previewing the Chapter

Chapter-Opener Photo The chapter-opener photo focuses on the chapter topic as you get ready to read. You might ask yourself: "How does this photo relate to the chapter title?"

In the Real World A brief scenario introduces a chapter concept so you can relate it to the real world as you get ready to begin the chapter.

Chapter Objectives The objectives help you preview the most important things you will learn as you study the chapter.

Ask Standard & Poor's Get expert financial advice from Standard & Poor's as this feature answers real-world questions about everyday personal finance.

Reading Strategies The reading strategies listed in the Reading Strategies box at the beginning of each chapter can help you to read actively. Also, notice them in the margins as you read.

Using the Section

Each chapter of *Personal Finance* is divided into two to four sections. Each section introduces and develops material in organized segments.

Photographs and Figures Throughout each section, relevant photographs, and useful charts and graphs illustrate and reinforce the content. Captions with questions guide you.

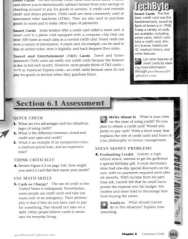

Focus on Reading
- **Read to Learn** lists the concept you will learn in the section.
- **Main Idea** explains the main concepts that you will learn.
- **Key Terms** list the major terms presented in each section. You will also see them highlighted as you read each chapter.

Section Assessment The section-ending assessments help you review, apply, and respond to what you have read.

Understanding the Features

Special features in each chapter are designed to interest you and to promote your understanding of the chapter topics. Features incorporate activities, such as critical-thinking questions, that help you to integrate what you have learned and apply it.

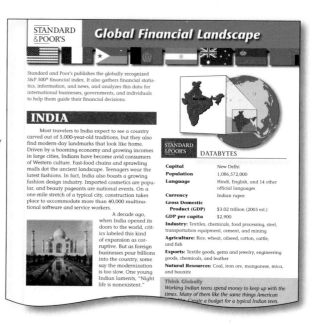

STANDARD &POOR'S
Global Financial Landscape

Standard and Poor's publishes the globally recognized S&P 500® financial index. It also gathers financial statistics, information, and news, and analyzes this data for international businesses, governments, and individuals to help them guide their financial decisions.

INDIA

Most travelers to India expect to see a country carved out of 5,000-year-old traditions, but they also find modern-day landmarks that look like home. Driven by a booming economy and growing incomes in large cities, Indians have become avid consumers of Western culture. Fast-food chains and sprawling malls dot the ancient landscape. Teenagers wear the latest fashions. In fact, India also boasts a growing fashion design industry. Imported cosmetics are popular, and beauty pageants are national events. On a one-mile stretch of a typical city, construction takes place to accommodate more than 40,000 multinational software and service workers.

A decade ago, when India opened its doors to the world, critics labeled this kind of expansion as corruptive. But as foreign businesses pour billions into the country, some say the modernization is too slow. One young Indian laments, "Night life is nonexistent."

STANDARD &POOR'S DATABYTES

Capital	New Delhi
Population	1,086,572,000
Language	Hindi, English, and 14 other official languages
Currency	Indian rupee
Gross Domestic Product (GDP)	$3.02 trillion (2003 est.)
GDP per capita	$2,900

Industry: Textiles, chemicals, food processing, steel, transportation equipment, cement, and mining

Agriculture: Rice, wheat, oilseed, cotton, cattle, and fish

Exports: Textile goods, gems and jewelry, engineering goods, chemicals, and leather

Natural Resources: Coal, iron ore, manganese, mica, and bauxite

Think Globally
Working Indian teens spend money to keep up with the times. Many of them like the same things American ... Create a budget for a typical Indian teen.

Global Financial Landscape
The S&P's Global Financial Landscape feature presents interesting financial profiles of different countries with a DataByte snapshot of the country's statistics by Standard & Poor's.

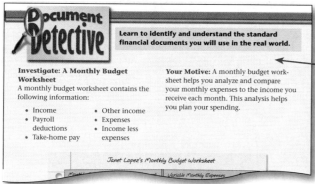

Document Detective

Learn to identify and understand the standard financial documents you will use in the real world.

Investigate: A Monthly Budget Worksheet
A monthly budget worksheet contains the following information:

- Income
- Payroll deductions
- Take-home pay
- Other income
- Expenses
- Income less expenses

Your Motive: A monthly budget worksheet helps you analyze and compare your monthly expenses to the income you receive each month. This analysis helps you plan your spending.

Janet Lopez's Monthly Budget Worksheet

Document Detective This feature is a guide to understanding the financial documents you will use in everyday finance. Questions reinforce your understanding.

Careers in Finance The *Careers in Finance* feature provides insight through profiles of real people working in the world of finance. Information on the education and skills needed for the career is provided. A chapter-related, critical-thinking question follows.

Careers in Finance

PERSONAL BANKER **Jason Lee**
National Bank

Working as a personal banker for National Bank, Jason develops, manages, and expands customer relationships. His challenge is to recognize the needs of the customers and match them to the services offered by his branch. His clients range from high school students, who are opening their first savings and checking accounts, to businesspeople, who are seeking very precise financial products and services. Jason enjoys working with a wide variety of customers and gains satisfaction from helping them reach their financial goals.

SKILLS: Communication, customer-service, computer, interpersonal, math, sales, cross-selling, and second language skills

PERSONAL TRAITS: Good judgment, likes working with people, tactful, detail oriented, ability to adapt to a flexible schedule in a high-volume environment

GO FIGURE FINANCIAL MATH

UNIT PRICING

Synopsis: Knowing the unit price of an item can help you determine the best buy.

Example: The brand of peppermint mouthwash that Claudia likes is offered in two sizes, 12 ounces for $2.89 and 16 ounces for $3.39. Which is the better buy?

Formula: $\dfrac{\text{Total Price}}{\text{Unit of Measurement}} = \text{Unit Price}$

Solution: $\dfrac{\$2.89}{12 \text{ oz.}} = \$0.24/\text{oz.}$

$\dfrac{\$3.39}{16 \text{ oz.}} = \$0.21/\text{oz.}$

The 16-ounce size is the better buy at 21 cents per ounce.

YOU FIGURE

You are considering buying soft drinks for your sister's birthday party. The market is offering a six-pack of 12-ounces for $2.99 and a liter bottle for $1.29. Which is the better buy? (Hint: One liter equals 33.8 ounces.)

Go Figure This feature provides a financial math formula related to chapter discussions, and then gives you a chance to use it in the *You Figure* application.

To the Student

TechByte

Using Software There are many software products on the market today designed to help you keep track of your personal finances. One of the first and most popular is Quicken®. Features allow you to track and pay bills and see if you have enough money to cover upcoming bills. You can also schedule bill payments and deposits.

@ Describe the information given on the Quicken monthly view screen by reading information through **persfinance07.glencoe.com**.

TechByte Technology is today's number-one trend. This feature highlights the wide range of technological applications that enhance personal finance today. An exercise directs you to the book's Online Learning Center at **persfinance07.glencoe.com**.

S&P's Put on Your Financial Planner's Cap Real scenarios provide problems you can solve as you think like a financial planner.

Put on Your Financial Planner's Cap

If you were planning an investment for yourself, would you choose an annuity? Why or why not?

Savvy Saver Lists of interesting tips and facts about personal finance help you save money.

$avvy Saver

Get a Good Credit Rating
1. Open a savings account and make regular deposits.
2. Apply for a department store or gasoline credit card and use it responsibly.
3. Pay all loans and credit card bills on time.
4. Open a checking account and do not bounce checks.
5. Never let anyone use your credit card.

Academic Connection

HISTORY

The first credit card, a travel and entertainment card, was issued in 1950 by Diners Club. Card holders could charge meals in 27 restaurants in New York City. Eight years later, the first bank credit card was issued. By 1965, about 5 million credit cards were in circulation. Fast forward to 2004, and U.S. consumers held more than 1.8 billion credit cards. Credit cards make buying easier—but give less incentive to save. *Do you think that credit cards have caused people to have more debt? Explain why or why not in two sentences.*

Academic Connection Integrate finance with your academic subjects as you complete brief activities.

Common CENTS

One Is Enough

When you turn 18, you may start receiving applications for credit cards. Be a smart consumer and compare interest rates, annual fees, and any other fees. Decide which credit card best suits your needs and apply for that one. Toss any other applications you get into the trash. *Why should you get the best (or lowest) interest rate for a credit card?*

Common Cents Quick finance facts related to the chapter topics are reinforced with a critical-thinking application.

Understanding Assessments

At the end of each chapter, the *Review and Activities* section presents a chapter summary with a key terms activity, recall-and-review questions, real-world applications, and activities that help you integrate a variety of academics with finance.

Chapter Summary The Chapter Summary is a list of chapter highlights to help you review and remember. Each highlight is related to a chapter objective.

Communicating Key Terms Review the financial key terms you learn throughout the chapter by applying them in written context.

Academic Skills Reinforce the connection between a variety of academic subjects as you relate and apply them to finance.

Your Financial Figures Solve a financial problem presented as a real-life scenario as you calculate the answer and use software.

Real-World Application Make the connection with real-world finance as you solve a problem.

Internet Connection This activity helps you develop your Internet research skills. Resources can be found through the book's Online Learning Center at **persfinance07.glencoe.com.**

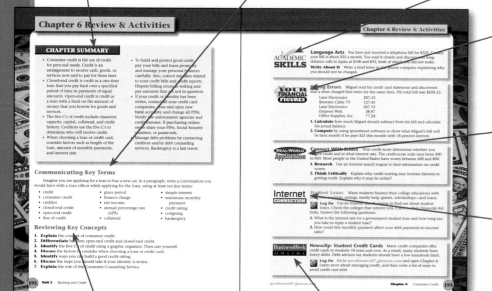

Reviewing Key Concepts Review questions are correlated to the chapter objectives to help you check your understanding of the text through defining terms, describing processes, and explaining concepts.

***BusinessWeek* Online** Go to the Student Center of the book's Online Learning Center, and you will find a complete chapter-related article to read.

Application Activity and Portfolio

At the end of each chapter's text, *What's Your Financial ID?* provides a special self-assessment, quiz, or other profile activity.

Your Financial Portfolio ends each chapter with an exercise to demonstrate your knowledge of personal finance topics.

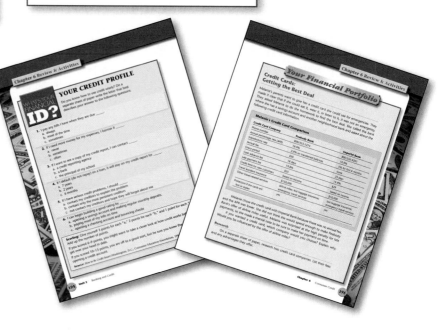

To the Student

Focus on Reading

Top 10 Reasons to Become a Better Reader

10. Give yourself more choices in life. Reading well opens the door to a wider variety of interesting career options.

9. Empower yourself through the written word. Teach yourself sailing, computer skills, the latest techniques in skateboarding. Discover how to create your own Web site.

8. Improve your chances of getting into and graduating from an institution of higher learning. On average, a person who gets a postsecondary education makes three times more money than a high school dropout!

7. Increase your chances of getting a job when you look for one. That is important, considering that the average person will hold 11 different jobs over his or her lifetime.

6. Advance more quickly in your chosen career. In many positions, people with strong reading skills are ten times as likely to receive training from their employer as those with limited reading skills.

5. Make the country economically stronger. More people reading well means more people contributing to the progress and prosperity of the country.

4. Save money and gain confidence in many real-life situations. For example, you will be able to pass your driver's test and read the lease for your first apartment.

3. Be more civic minded. People who read well are more likely to vote and to participate in democratic elections and in civic life.

2. Once learned, never forgotten. Reading is a lifelong skill, like riding a bicycle—once you learn, you will never forget!

1. Enjoy life more! Reading well can not only help you get ahead and stay ahead in life—it's fun!

To the Student

Reading Strategies

Reading Strategies

How can you get the most from your reading?
Effective readers are active readers. Get involved with the text. Think of your textbook as a tool that helps you learn more about the world around you. The material is a form of nonfiction writing—it describes real-life ideas, people, events, and places. Use the reading strategies listed in the *Reading Strategies* box at the beginning of each chapter along with strategies in the margins to help you read actively.

Before You Read

PREDICT

Make educated guesses about what the section is about by combining clues in the text with what you already know. Predicting helps you anticipate questions and stay alert to new information.

Ask yourself:
- What does this section heading mean?
- What is this section about?
- How does this section tie in with what I have read so far?
- Why is this information important in understanding the subject?

As You Read

RELATE

Draw parallels between what you are reading and the events and circumstances in your own life.

Ask yourself:
- What do I know about the topic?
- How do my experiences compare to the information in the text?
- How could I apply this information to my own life?
- Why is this information important in understanding the subject?

As You Read

QUESTION

Ask yourself questions to help clarify the reading as you go along.

Ask yourself:
- Do I understand what I have read so far?
- What is this section about?
- What does this mean?
- Why is this information important in understanding the subject?

After You Read

REACT

React to what you are reading. Form opinions and make judgments about the section while you are reading—not just after you have finished.

Ask yourself:
- Does this information make sense?
- What can I learn from this section?
- How can I use this information to start planning for my financial future?
- Why is this information important in understanding the subject?

To the Student

More Reading Strategies

Use this menu for more reading strategies to help you get the most from your reading.

Before You Read

Set a purpose
- Why are you reading the textbook?
- How does the subject relate to your life?
- How might you be able to use what you learn in your own life?

Preview
- Read the chapter title to preview the topic.
- Read the subtitles to see what you will learn about the topic.
- Skim the photos, charts, graphs, or maps. How do they support the topic?
- Look for key terms that are boldfaced. How are they defined?

Draw from your background
- What have you read or heard concerning new information on the topic?
- How is the new information different from what you already know?
- How will the information that you already know help you understand the new information?

As You Read

Predict
- Predict events or outcomes by using clues and information that you already know.
- Change your predictions as you read and gather new information.

Connect
- Think about people, places, and events in your own life. Are there any similarities with those in your textbook?
- Can you relate the textbook information to other areas of your life?

Question
- What is the main idea?
- How do the photos, charts, graphs, and maps support the main idea?

Visualize
- Pay careful attention to details and descriptions.
- Create graphic organizers to show relationships that you find in the information.

Notice Comparison and Contrast Sentences
- Look for clue words and phrases that signal comparison, such as *similarly, just as, both, in common, also,* and *too.*
- Look for clue words and phrases that signal contrast, such as *on the other hand, in contrast to, however, different, instead of, rather than, but,* and *unlike.*

Notice Cause-and-Effect Sentences
- Look for clue words and phrases, such as *because, as a result, therefore, that is why, since, so, for this reason,* and *consequently.*

Notice Chronological Sentences
- Look for clue words and phrases, such as *after, before, first, next, last, during, finally, earlier, later, since,* and *then.*

After You Read

Summarize
- Describe the main idea and how the details support it.
- Use your own words to explain what you have read.

Assess
- What was the main idea?
- Did the text clearly support the main idea?
- Did you learn anything new from the material?
- Can you use this new information in other school subjects or at home?
- What other sources could you use to find more information about the topic?

Unit 1

Planning Personal Finances

Internet Project

One Life to Plan

Financial planners help people plan for paying for college or retirement, and then show them how to save to reach those goals. Life planners assist clients to pinpoint what they want out of life, and then use financial planning to help people achieve it. In this project, you will weigh the pros and cons of each career and decide which one might best suit you.

Log on to persfinance07.glencoe.com. Begin your WebQuest by reading Task 1. Then continue working on your WebQuest as you study Unit 1.

Section	1.2	2.2	3.2	4.1
Page	25	52	71	96

FINANCE FILE

Which Adviser Knows the Way?

Almost anyone can claim to be a financial planner or investment adviser. If you're looking for an adviser for the first time—you need to figure out how much and what kind of advice you need. If all you want are some suggestions for your IRA or your investment portfolio, you could get that through Charles Schwab or Fidelity Brokerage Services for a fee of about $250.

But there's more to your financial well-being than stocks and bonds. Do you have a debt-management problem? Do you have enough insurance, and is your estate in order?

And what about credentials? Certified Financial Planner (CFP) is the most recognized designation. CFPs have comprehensive education and must pass a ten-hour certification exam and have at least three years' experience before qualifying.

The irony is that most people seek advisers to relieve the burden of managing their finances themselves. But it's a burden in itself to make sure you've got the right adviser.

— *By Lewis Braham*
with Amy Borrus

Write About It   Why should you know how to plan your personal finances even if you can hire a financial planner?

Log On   To read the complete *BusinessWeek* article and do the *BusinessWeek* Extension activity to help you learn more about financial and life planning, go to **persfinance07.glencoe.com**.

CHAPTER 1

Personal Financial Planning

$ What You'll Learn

hen you have completed this chapter, you will be able to:

Section 1.1
- Define personal financial planning.
- Name the six steps of financial planning.
- Identify factors that affect personal financial decisions.

Section 1.2
- Explain opportunity costs associated with personal financial decisions.
- Identify eight strategies for achieving financial goals at different stages of life.

Reading Strategies

To get the most out of your reading:

Predict what you will learn in this chapter.

Relate what you read to your own life.

Question what you are reading to be sure you understand.

React to what you have read.

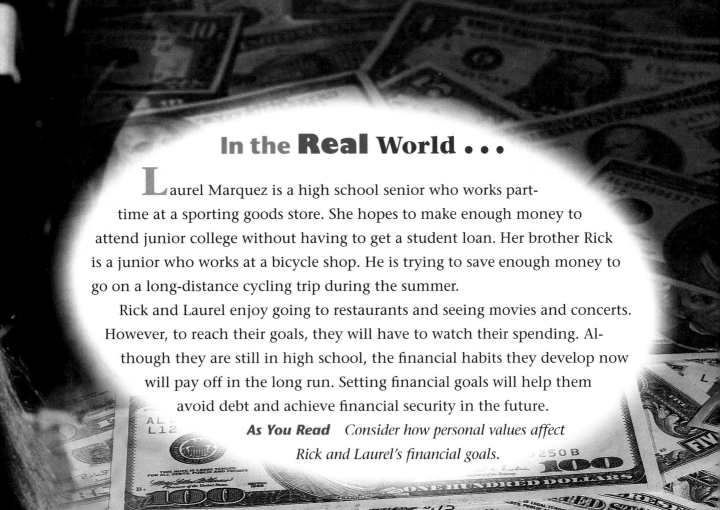

In the **Real** World . . .

Laurel Marquez is a high school senior who works part-time at a sporting goods store. She hopes to make enough money to attend junior college without having to get a student loan. Her brother Rick is a junior who works at a bicycle shop. He is trying to save enough money to go on a long-distance cycling trip during the summer.

Rick and Laurel enjoy going to restaurants and seeing movies and concerts. However, to reach their goals, they will have to watch their spending. Although they are still in high school, the financial habits they develop now will pay off in the long run. Setting financial goals will help them avoid debt and achieve financial security in the future.

As You Read *Consider how personal values affect Rick and Laurel's financial goals.*

ASK STANDARD &POOR'S

The Money Plan

Q: I am a high school student. I do not have money for investments or buying property. So what difference does it make how I spend my money now?

A: You will not always be a student. Learning to save and use money wisely now will help you know how to achieve financial security in the future. While you are in high school, financial planning can help you decide how to spend, save, and invest your money for special purchases or activities that matter to you. You may even be able to buy stock!

Ask Yourself What item do you think you could buy if you saved some money for several months? Explain why this would be financial planning.

 Go to **persfinance07.glencoe.com** to complete the Standard & Poor's Financial Focus activity.

Financial Decisions and Goals

Focus on Reading

Read to Learn
- How to define personal financial planning.
- How to name the six steps of financial planning.
- How to identify factors that affect personal financial decisions.

Main Idea
The financial planning process can help you reach your financial goals.

Key Terms
- personal financial planning
- goals
- values
- opportunity cost
- liquidity
- service
- good
- economics
- economy
- supply
- demand
- Federal Reserve System
- inflation
- consumer
- interest

Before You Read

PREDICT

List three of your financial goals.

Personal Financial Decisions
What are the benefits of financial planning?

What is personal finance? It is everything in your life that involves money. **Personal financial planning** is arranging to spend, save, and invest money to live comfortably, have financial security, and achieve goals. Everyone has different financial goals. **Goals** are the things you want to accomplish. For example, getting a college education, buying a car, and starting a business are goals. Planning your personal finances is important because it will help you to reach your goals, no matter what they are. It is up to you to make and follow a financial plan.

Some of the benefits of planning are:

- You have more money and financial security.
- You know how to use money to achieve your goals.
- You have less chance of going into debt you cannot handle.
- You can help your partner and support your children, if you have a family.

Whether you are spending, saving, or investing money, planning can help you to make big or small financial decisions. The financial planning process has six steps to help you reach your goals.

STEP 1: Determine Your Current Financial Situation

To figure out your current financial situation, make a list of items that relate to your finances:

- Savings
- Monthly income (job earnings, allowance, gifts, and interest on bank accounts)
- Monthly expenses (money you spend)
- Debts (money you owe to others)

A good way to estimate your expenses is to keep a careful record of everything you buy for one month. You can use a small notebook to track your expenses. When you have determined your financial situation, you will be able to start planning.

STEP 2: Develop Your Financial Goals

To develop clear financial goals, think about your attitude toward money and ask yourself some questions: Is it more important to spend your money now or to save for the future? Would you rather get a job right after high school or continue your education? Do your personal values affect your financial decisions? **Values** are the beliefs and principles you consider important, correct, and desirable. Different people value different things.

Needs and Wants Another important aspect of developing financial goals is knowing the difference between your needs and your wants. A *need* is something you must have to survive, such as food, shelter, and clothing. A *want* is something you desire or would like to have or do. For example, if you live in an area where the winter is cold, you need a coat. So you may want a leather jacket, but other less expensive coats would also keep you warm.

Only you can decide what specific goals to pursue. For example, you might want to save money. So, you could save $50 every month or 15 percent of every paycheck.

STEP 3: Identify Your Options

It is impossible to make a good decision unless you know all your options. Generally, you have several possible courses of action. Suppose that you are saving $50 a month. You might have these options:

- **Expand the current situation.** You may decide to increase the amount of money you save every month to $60.
- **Change the current situation.** You could invest in stocks instead of putting your money into a savings account.
- **Start something new.** You could use the $50 to pay off your debts.
- **Continue the same course of action.** You may choose not to change anything.

However, in each case, be aware that the costs of your decision may outweigh the benefits.

► MONEY MATTERS Your values affect your spending habits. *Why might people shop at vintage clothing stores or swap meets?*

TechByte

Using Software There are many software products on the market today designed to help you keep track of your personal finances. One of the first and most popular is Quicken®. Features allow you to track and pay bills and see if you have enough money to cover upcoming bills. You can also schedule bill payments and deposits.

@ Describe the information given on the Quicken monthly view screen by reading information through **persfinance07.glencoe.com**.

STEP 4: Evaluate Your Alternatives

In this step, you evaluate your alternatives as part of the financial planning process. Use the many sources of financial information that are available. (See **Figure 1.1.**) Look at your situation in life, your present financial situation, and your personal values. Consider the consequences and risks of each decision you make.

Sources of Financial Information It is important to keep up-to-date with social and economic conditions because they can affect your financial situation. For example, a company that manufactures the latest technology or designs the trendiest clothes may be a good investment. On the other hand, if you learn that the company is being sued, would you invest in it?

Consequences of Choices When you choose one option, you eliminate other possibilities. You cannot choose all options. Suppose that you want to become a full-time college student. You also want the income you would earn at a full-time job. In choosing to pursue your education, you give up the opportunity to work full time, at least for the moment. An **opportunity cost**, or a trade-off, is what is given up when making one choice instead of another. The opportunity cost of going to college would be the benefit of having a full-time job.

Figure 1.1   **Get the Facts**

Information on financial planning can come from many sources:

1 **Financial Specialists:** accountants, bankers, financial planners, insurance agents, tax attorneys, and tax preparers

2 **Technology:** computer software and the Internet

However, choosing involves more than knowing what you might give up. It also involves knowing what you would gain. For example, by going to college, you could gain a higher-paying job.

Understanding Risks   If you decide to ride your bicycle on a very busy city street, you are taking a risk of having an accident. When you make a financial decision, you also accept certain financial risks. Some types of financial risks include:

- **Inflation Risk**—If you wait to buy a car until next year, you accept the possibility that the price may increase.
- **Interest Rate Risk**—Interest rates go up or down, which may affect the cost of borrowing or the profits you earn when you save or invest.
- **Income Risk**—You may lose your job due to unexpected health problems, family problems, an accident, or changes in your field of work.
- **Personal Risk**—Driving for eight hours on icy mountain roads may be hazardous. The risk may not be worth the money you would save on airfare.
- **Liquidity Risk**—**Liquidity** is the ability to easily convert financial assets into cash without loss in value. Some long-term investments, such as a house, can be difficult to convert quickly.

As You Read

RELATE

What are your financial goals? Which goals are needs and which goals are wants?

3 **The Media:** books, magazines, newsletters, newspapers, radio, and television

4 **Financial Institutions:** banks, credit unions, insurance and investment companies, and savings and loan associations

5 **Education:** high school and college courses and seminars

STEP 5: Create and Use Your Financial Plan of Action

A plan of action is a list of ways to achieve your financial goals. If your goal is to increase your savings, a plan of action could be to cut back on spending. If you want to increase your income, you might get a part-time job or work more hours at your present job. You could use the extra money you earn to pay off debts, save money, purchase stocks, or make other investments.

STEP 6: Review and Revise Your Plan

Financial planning continues as you follow your plan. As you get older, your finances and needs will change. That means that your financial plan will have to change too. You should reevaluate and revise it every year.

Developing Personal Financial Goals
What should you consider to set financial goals for yourself?

Why do so many people have money problems? The main reason is that they do not plan how they will use their money. You can avoid money problems by planning with some clear financial goals in mind.

Types of Financial Goals

Two factors will influence your planning for financial goals. The first factor is the time frame in which you would like to achieve your goals. The second factor is the type of financial need that inspires your goals.

Time Frame of Goals   Goals can be defined by the time it takes to achieve them:

- **Short-term goals** take one year or less to achieve (such as saving to buy a computer).
- **Intermediate goals** take two to five years to achieve (such as saving for a down payment on a house).
- **Long-term goals** take more than five years to achieve (such as planning for retirement).

Start with short-term goals that may lead to long-term ones. Some goals, such as having money for the holidays or other special occasions, occur every year. Other goals, such as buying a car, may come up only occasionally. What are some of your short-term, intermediate, and long-term financial goals?

Common CENTS

Pay Yourself First
When you receive your paycheck, pay yourself first. This means that before you pay bills or buy anything, you should put something into your savings account—even a small amount. Think of it as paying yourself. Try saving a percentage of your take-home pay or allowance—1 percent the first month, 2 percent the second month, and so forth. Then sit back and watch your money grow. *If your take-home pay is $860 a month and you save the percentages listed above for 12 months, how much would you have?*

Careers in Finance

PERSONAL BANKER **Jason Lee**
National Bank

Working as a personal banker for National Bank, Jason develops, manages, and expands customer relationships. His challenge is to recognize the needs of the customers and match them to the services offered by his branch. His clients range from high school students, who are opening their first savings and checking accounts, to businesspeople, who are seeking very precise financial products and services. Jason enjoys working with a wide variety of customers and gains satisfaction from helping them reach their financial goals.

SKILLS: Communication, customer-service, computer, interpersonal, math, sales, cross-selling, and second language skills

PERSONAL TRAITS: Good judgment, likes working with people, tactful, detail oriented, ability to adapt to a flexible schedule in a high-volume environment

EDUCATION: Associate degree or bachelor's degree with a major in business administration or economics

ANALYZE Banking services are increasingly offered via ATMs, the telephone, or online. Explain why personal bankers are still in demand.

 To learn more about career paths for personal bankers, visit **persfinance07.glencoe.com**.

Goals for Different Needs The need to have your hair cut at a salon is different from the need to buy a new car. A haircut is a **service**, or a task that a person or a machine performs for you. A new car is a **good**, or a physical item that is produced and can be weighed or measured. You might buy a soda every day. You might buy a new car every five or six years. How you establish and reach your financial goals will depend on whether a goal involves the need for consumable goods (such as a soda), durable goods (such as a car), or intangible items (such as an education):

- **Consumable goods** are purchases that you make often and use up quickly. Food and products, such as shampoo and conditioner, are in this category. Although the cost of such items may not equal the cost of a car, the costs of consumable goods add up.
- **Durable goods** are expensive items that you do not purchase often. Most durable goods, such as cars and large appliances, will last three years or more when used on a regular basis.
- **Intangible items** cannot be touched but are often important to your well-being and happiness. Examples of intangibles include your personal relationships, health, education, and free time. Intangibles are often overlooked but can be expensive.

As You Read

QUESTION

Think about consumable goods, durable goods, and intangibles. Over the long term (ten years or more), which category do you think has the highest cost?

Learn to identify and understand the standard financial documents you will use in the real world.

Investigate: A Monthly Budget Worksheet

A monthly budget worksheet contains the following information:

- Income
- Payroll deductions
- Take-home pay
- Other income
- Expenses
- Income less expenses

Your Motive: A monthly budget worksheet helps you analyze and compare your monthly expenses to the income you receive each month. This analysis helps you plan your spending.

Janet Lopez's Monthly Budget Worksheet

Monthly Income	Amount	Variable Monthly Expenses	Amount
Wages (before taxes)	$3,500	Utilities (gas, electric)	$75
Allowance	0	Telephone/Cell phone	65
Other income	35	Groceries	135
Payroll Deductions		Clothing	75
		Credit card	150
Federal tax	$ 700	Donations	25
Social Security tax	268	Gasoline	85
State tax	175	Personal items	45
Local tax	35		
Other	0		
Total Take-Home Income	$ 2,357		
Fixed Monthly Expenses		**Discretionary Monthly Expenses**	
Savings	$ 100	Movies	$ 15
Rent/Mortgage	750	Hobbies	35
Car loan	425	Restaurants	55
Vehicle and apartment or house insurance	125	Other	155
Life and health insurance	55		
Cable TV/Internet access	95		
		Total Expenses	$ 2,465
		Income Less Expenses	- $ 108

Key Points: You create a budget by determining your take-home income. Take-home income is the difference between your wages and deductions. Taxes, union dues, and health insurance are wage deductions. Expenses are also listed. Some expenses are fixed. They do not change. Variable expenses change each month. Discretionary expenses do not include expenses for basic needs.

Find the Solutions

1. Explain the difference between fixed expenses and variable expenses.
2. List other possible expenses that are not listed on this worksheet.
3. Decide if Janet has enough monthly income for monthly expenses.
4. Explain why utilities are a variable expense.
5. Suggest ways this budget can be balanced.

Guidelines for Setting Goals

How can you make good financial decisions? You must identify your goals. Then identify the time frame for achieving each goal and the type of need. However, these factors will change as you go through life. The financial goals you set as a student will be different from the goals you may have if you marry or have children. **Figure 1.2** shows examples of financial goals and activities related to various life situations.

When setting your financial goals, follow these guidelines:

1. Your financial goals should be realistic.
2. Your financial goals should be specific.
3. Your financial goals should have a clear time frame.
4. Your financial goals should help you decide what type of action to take.

Academic Connection

LANGUAGE ARTS

Look at Figure 1.2 and consider setting some financial goals for yourself. *Think of three goals. Write them down, explaining how each meets the four guidelines.*

Figure 1.2 **Financial Goals and Activities for Various Life Situations**

Life Situation	Financial Goals and Activities
Young single adult	• Obtain career training. • Become financially independent. • Obtain health insurance. • Develop a savings plan. • Carefully manage your use of credit.
Young couple with no children	• Create an effective financial record-keeping system. • Obtain adequate health and life insurance. • Implement a budget. • Carefully manage your use of credit. • Develop a savings and investment program.
Couple with young children	• Purchase a home. • Obtain adequate health and life insurance. • Start a college fund. • Make a will and name a guardian for your children.
Single parent with young children	• Obtain adequate health, life, and disability insurance. • Make a will and name a guardian for your children. • Establish an emergency fund.
Middle-aged, single adult	• Contribute to a tax-deferred retirement plan. • Evaluate and select appropriate investments. • Accumulate an adequate emergency fund. • Review will and estate plans.
Older couple with no children at home	• Plan retirement housing, living expenses, and activities. • Obtain health insurance for retirement. • Review will and estate plans.

Economic Conditions Your financial needs and goals change at different stages of life.

What are some goals you will have ten years from now that you do not have today?

Influences on Personal Financial Planning

What factors can influence your personal financial planning?

Many factors will influence your day-to-day decisions about finances. The three most important factors are:

- Life situations
- Personal values
- Economic factors

Life Situations and Personal Values

As you enter adulthood, you will experience many changes. You may go to college, start a new career, get married, have children, or move to a new city. These new life situations will affect your financial planning. Your personal values also influence your financial decisions.

For example, Angela just graduated from high school and will be going to college in the fall. She will move out of her parents' house and live in the college dorm. Angela is beginning a new and exciting stage in her life. She values independence, and so she plans to move to an apartment with a roommate in her sophomore year. She will experience more personal freedom, but with her independence will also come more financial responsibility.

Economic Factors

Economic factors across the country and around the world can affect personal finances. They play a role in day-to-day financial planning and decision making for most people. **Economics** is the study of the decisions that go into making, distributing, and using goods and services. The **economy** consists of the ways in which people make, distribute, and use their goods and services. To understand economics and the economy, you need to be aware of the market forces, financial institutions, global influences, and economic conditions that affect global as well as personal decisions.

Market Forces The forces of supply and demand determine the prices of products, or goods and services, you purchase. **Supply** is the amount of goods and services available for sale. **Demand** is the amount of goods and services people are willing to buy. When there is a high demand for an item, such as a popular toy, or when a company cannot manufacture enough of a certain product to keep up with the demand, the price of the product rises. When there is little demand for a product, or when a company produces more than it can sell, the price of the product drops.

Financial Institutions Most people do business with financial institutions, which include banks, credit unions, savings and loan associations, insurance companies, and investment companies. Financial institutions provide services that increase financial activity in the economy. For example, they handle savings and checking accounts, provide loans, sell insurance, and make investments for their clients.

STANDARD & POOR'S
Global Financial Landscape

Standard and Poor's publishes the globally recognized S&P 500® financial index. It also gathers financial statistics, information, and news, and analyzes this data for international businesses, governments, and individuals to help them guide their financial decisions.

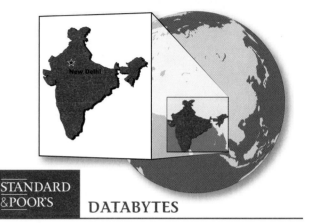

INDIA

Most travelers to India expect to see a country carved out of 5,000-year-old traditions, but they also find modern-day landmarks that look like home. Driven by a booming economy and growing incomes in large cities, Indians have become avid consumers of Western culture. Fast-food chains and sprawling malls dot the ancient landscape. Teenagers wear the latest fashions. In fact, India also boasts a growing fashion design industry. Imported cosmetics are popular, and beauty pageants are national events. On a one-mile stretch of a typical city of India, construction takes place to accommodate more than 40,000 multinational technology and service workers.

A decade ago, when India opened its doors to the world, critics labeled this kind of expansion as corruptive. But as foreign businesses pour billions into the country, some say the modernization is too slow. One young Indian laments, "Night life is nonexistent."

STANDARD & POOR'S
DATABYTES

Capital	New Delhi
Population	1,086,572,000
Language	Hindi, English, and 14 other official languages
Currency	Indian rupee
Gross Domestic Product (GDP)	$3.02 trillion (2003 est.)
GDP per capita	$2,900

Industry: Textiles, chemicals, food processing, steel, transportation equipment, cement, and mining

Agriculture: Rice, wheat, oilseed, cotton, cattle, and fish

Exports: Textile goods, gems and jewelry, engineering goods, chemicals, and leather

Natural Resources: Coal, iron ore, manganese, mica, and bauxite

Think Globally
Working Indian teens spend money to keep up with the times. Many of them like the same things American teens like. Create a budget for a typical Indian teen.

Among the various government agencies that regulate the financial activities of financial institutions, the Federal Reserve System has a significant responsibility in the U.S. economy. The **Federal Reserve System**, or the Fed, is the central banking organization of the United States. Its primary role in the U.S. economy is the regulation of the money supply. The Fed controls the money supply by determining interest rates and by buying or selling government securities. Its decisions affect the interest rate you earn on your savings, the interest rate you pay when you borrow money, and to some extent the prices of the products you buy.

Global Influences You and the money you spend are part of the global marketplace, which is another economic factor that can affect financial planning. Look at the items in your home or classroom and you will discover that many of the products were made in other countries.

The economy of every nation is affected by competition with other nations. Each country wants consumers in other countries to buy their products. When other countries sell more goods to the United States than U.S. companies can sell in those markets, more money leaves the United States than enters it. Then less money is available for spending and investing, and interest rates may rise. These global influences also affect financial decisions.

Economic Conditions Current economic conditions also affect your personal financial decisions. **Figure 1.3** shows how economic conditions can influence financial planning. There are three important economic conditions:

1. Consumer prices
2. Consumer spending
3. Interest rates

- **Consumer Prices** Over time the prices of most products go up. This rise in the level of prices for goods and services is called **inflation**. During times of rapid inflation, it takes more money to buy the same amount of goods and services. For example, if the rate of inflation is 5 percent, then a computer that cost $1,000 a year ago would now cost $1,050 if the computer price increased at the inflationary rate.

  The main cause of inflation is an increase in demand without an increase in supply. For example, if people have more money to spend because of pay increases or borrowing, but the same amounts of goods and services are available, then prices will rise.

  Inflation can be especially hard on certain groups, such as retired people whose income may not increase. The inflation rate affects consumer prices and varies from year to year. In the early 1960s, the annual inflation rate was between 1 and 3 percent. In the late 1970s and early 1980s, the inflation rate climbed to 10–12 percent each year. More recently it slowed to 2–4 percent each year.

- **Consumer Spending** A **consumer** is a person who purchases and uses goods or services. You are a consumer whenever you buy anything—a CD, books, clothes, lunch, or even a haircut. Consumer spending affects the economy by helping to create and maintain jobs. When people buy more goods or services, companies have to hire extra employees to meet the demand. This situation leads to a higher rate of employment, making more jobs available. More people work, and they have more money to spend. However, when consumers buy fewer goods and services, companies have to produce less and lay off workers. Then unemployment rises, making jobs harder to find.

Figure 1.3 **Economic Conditions and Financial Planning**

Economic Condition	What It Measures	How It Influences Financial Planning
Consumer prices	The value of a dollar; changes in inflation	If consumer prices increase faster than wages, the value of the dollar decreases—a dollar buys less than it did before. Consumers tend to buy fewer goods and services. Lenders charge higher interest rates.
Consumer spending	Demand for goods and services by individuals and households	Increased consumer spending usually creates more jobs and higher wages. Reduced consumer spending causes unemployment to increase.
Interest rates	Cost of money, cost of credit when you borrow, and the return on your money when you save or invest	Higher interest rates make borrowing money more expensive and make saving more attractive. When interest rates increase, consumer prices tend to increase.
Money supply	The dollars available for spending in our economy	The Federal Reserve System (Fed) sometimes adjusts interest rates in order to increase or decrease the amount of money circulating in the economy. If the Fed lowers interest rates, the money supply increases. If the Fed raises interest rates, the money supply decreases.
Unemployment	The number of people without jobs who are willing and able to work	Low unemployment increases consumer spending. High unemployment reduces consumer spending.
Gross domestic product (GDP)	Total dollar value of all the goods and services produced in a country in one year	The GDP provides an indication of how well people are living in a country.

Economic Conditions Economic conditions you cannot control will affect your financial planning.

Choose an economic condition listed above, and explain how it affects your life today.

- **Interest Rates**   Like everything else, money has a price, and this price is called interest. **Interest** is the price that is paid for the use of another's money. Interest rates also affect the economy. When you deposit your paycheck in a savings account, the interest you receive is money the bank or another financial institution pays you for the use of your money. The bank, in turn, uses your money to make loans to people who want to purchase items such as houses, automobiles, and new businesses. Borrowers who receive the loans must pay a fee, or interest to the bank or lending institution.

Interest rates represent the cost of money. When consumers increase their savings and investments, the supply of money that is available for others to borrow grows, and interest rates go down. When consumers borrow more money, the demand for money increases, and interest rates go up.

Interest rates on loans also rise during times of inflation. Interest rates will affect your financial planning, whether you save, invest, or obtain loans. The amount of earnings you receive from your savings account or the interest you pay on a loan depend on the current interest rates. Interest rates are just one facet of the economic factors that influence your personal financial planning.

Section 1.1 Assessment

QUICK CHECK

1. What are the six steps used to create a financial plan?
2. What is the relationship between the timing of your goals and the type of good or service that you want?
3. What are two economic factors that affect financial decisions? How might these factors influence your financial planning?

THINK CRITICALLY

4. Why is it important to distinguish between your needs and your wants?

USE COMMUNICATION SKILLS

5. **Left to Chance?**   You are talking to a friend who says that she never sets any financial goals and that her financial success or failure happens by luck.

Role-Play   With a partner, role-play a response to your friend's philosophy. Explain how planning, more than luck, determines financial success or failure.

SOLVE MONEY PROBLEMS

6. **Financial Planning Process**   Rosa and her best friend, Linda, live in Chicago and want to drive cross-country next year. Both work part-time and earn $97 a week after taxes. They need to save at least $500 each to pay for the trip. They plan to visit Rosa's aunt, who lives in Albuquerque, and Linda's brother in Los Angeles.

Write About It   Help Rosa and Linda apply the six steps of the financial planning process to reach their goal. Write a six-step plan for them.

Opportunity Costs and Strategies

Personal and Financial Opportunity Costs

What are personal and financial opportunity costs?

As discussed in Section 1.1, whenever you make a choice, you have to give up, or trade off, some of your other options. When making your financial decisions and plans, consider both the personal and financial opportunity costs carefully.

Personal Opportunity Costs

Like financial resources, your personal resources—your health, knowledge, skills, and time—require management. Do you eat a lot of junk food and avoid exercise? Do you get enough sleep each night? The decisions you make about your health now can have consequences as you get older.

In much the same way, the financial decisions you make today will affect your financial health in the future. For example, suppose that you and your friends have tickets to a sold-out concert this Thursday night. On Thursday afternoon your algebra teacher announces an important test for Friday. You must decide whether you will go to the concert, study for the test, or somehow do both. The opportunity cost of going to the concert might be getting a good grade on the test. You have to decide how to use your time to meet your needs, to achieve your goals, and to satisfy your values.

Financial Opportunity Costs

You also must make choices about how you spend money. For example, would you buy the $129 pair of sneakers you saw at the mall or save that money? You cannot do both, because most people have a limited amount of money. To help make choices, consider the **time value of money**, which is the increase of an amount of money due to earned interest or dividends. If you decide to save or invest the $129 instead of buying the sneakers, that money could be worth more later because you would earn interest or dividends on it.

▲ **TIMING YOUR FUN** Managing your time by making trade-offs is as important as managing your money. *How can you use your time more efficiently when studying so you will also have time to do things you enjoy?*

On the other hand, perhaps your sneakers are worn out. In that case, your current needs would determine that trading off interest earnings is worthwhile.

Every time you spend, save, or invest money, think about the time value of that money as an opportunity cost. For example, if you start early in life to save money for retirement, you will probably be able to live comfortably in the future.

Calculating Interest You can calculate the time value of your savings by figuring out how much interest you will earn. To do this, you need to know the principal, the annual interest rate, and the length of time your money will be in an account.

For a savings account, the **principal** is the original amount of money on deposit. (For a loan, the principal is the amount that you borrow.) When you open a savings account, the bank or financial institution identifies the interest rate for your account. This is usually given as an annual percentage so that you know how much you will earn each year. By comparing interest rates at several financial institutions, you can figure out which one will make your money grow the fastest.

You can figure out how much interest your money will earn in the first year by multiplying the principal by the annual interest rate.

As You Read

RELATE

Is it important to start planning your financial future and monitoring your costs at your age now? Why or why not?

ANNUAL INTEREST

Synopsis: Interest is extra money earned from money in an account.

Example: You just deposited $1,000 in a savings account. The bank will pay you 3 percent annual interest. How much interest will you earn if you keep your money in the bank for one year?

Formula: Principal × Annual Interest Rate = Interest Earned for One Year

Solution: $1,000 × .03 = $30

You will earn $30 in interest.

YOU FIGURE

What if your sister deposited $50 for one year at the same interest? How much would she have?

Future Value of a Single Deposit **Future value** is the amount your original deposit will be worth in the future based on earning a specific interest rate over a specific period of time. Figure out how much your savings will earn and grow by multiplying the principal by the annual interest rate and then adding that interest amount to the principal.

You can determine the future value for two years, three years, and so on. Each year, interest is earned on your principal and on previously earned interest.

To calculate the interest earned for the second year, add interest earned in the first year to the principal. Then take that amount and multiply it by the annual interest rate.

Future value computations are also called *compounding*. With compounding, your money increases faster over time. If you make deposits now, your money will have more time to increase.

GO FIGURE | FINANCIAL MATH

THE FUTURE VALUE OF A SINGLE DEPOSIT

Synopsis: When you earn interest from money you deposit in the bank, your balance increases over time.

Example: You just deposited $1,000 in a savings account that will pay you 3 percent (.03) annual interest. You earned $30 in interest after the first year. How much will you earn after two years?

Formula: (Principal + Previously Earned Interest) × Annual Interest Rate = Interest Earned for the Second Year

Solution: ($1,000 + $30) × .03 = $30.90

You will earn $30.90 in interest. Add this earned interest to your previous amount ($1,030 + $30.90 = $1,060.90). The future value of your original $1,000 deposit will be $1,060.90 after two years.

YOU FIGURE

What if you decided to deposit more money, say, $1,500? With 3 percent annual interest, how much would you have after three years?

Future value tables simplify the process of figuring out the effect of compounding. Many online future value calculators are available. The table in Part A of **Figure 1.4** shows the future value of a single deposit of $1. To use the table, find the annual interest rate that your money is earning. Then see what the future value is at Year 5, Year 6, and so on. Multiply the future value figure by the amount of your deposit. For example, if you deposit $1 in a 7 percent account, at the end of Year 7, you would have $1.61:

$$\$1 \times 1.606 = \$1.606$$

Future Value of a Series of Deposits   Some savers and investors like to make regular deposits into their savings. A series of equal regular deposits is sometimes called an **annuity**. Use Part B of the chart in Figure 1.4 (future value of a series of equal yearly deposits) to find out the future value of $1,000 a year at 5 percent annual interest for six years. At the end of the six years, you would have $6,802:

$$\$1,000 \times 6.802 = \$6,802$$

Present Value of a Single Deposit   You can also calculate the **present value**, which is the amount of money you would need to deposit now in order to have a desired amount in the future. For example, if you want to have $1,000 in five years for a down payment on a car, and your savings account pays 5 percent annual interest, how much money will you need to deposit now to accumulate $1,000? Part C of Figure 1.4 will help you find the answer. Find Year 5 in the left column, and look across to the 5 percent interest-rate column. The value given is 0.784. Multiply this value by the amount of money you want to have in five years:

$$\$1,000 \times 0.784 = \$784$$

You need to deposit $784 now to have $1,000 in five years.

Present Value of a Series of Deposits   You can also use present value calculations to determine how much you would need to deposit so you can take a specific amount of money out of your savings account for a certain number of years. If you want to take $400 out of your account each year for nine years, and your money is earning interest at 8 percent a year, how much money would you need to deposit now? Part D of Figure 1.4 will help you find the answer. Find Year 9 in the left column and look across to the 8 percent interest-rate column. The value given is 6.247. Multiply this value by the amount of money that you want to take out every year:

$$\$400 \times 6.247 = \$2,498.80$$

You need to deposit $2,498.80 now to be able to take out $400 each year for nine years. This calculation is used for retirement.

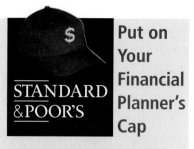

Figure 1.4 — Future and Present Value Tables

A. Future Value of a Single Deposit of $1

Year	Annual Interest Rate				
	5%	6%	7%	8%	9%
5	1.276	1.338	1.403	1.469	1.539
6	1.340	1.419	1.501	1.587	1.677
7	1.407	1.504	1.606	1.714	1.828
8	1.477	1.594	1.718	1.851	1.993
9	1.551	1.689	1.838	1.999	2.172
10	1.629	1.791	1.967	2.159	2.367

B. Future Value of a Series of Equal Annual Deposits

Year	5%	6%	7%	8%	9%
5	5.526	5.637	5.751	5.867	5.985
6	6.802	6.975	7.153	7.336	7.523
7	8.142	8.394	8.654	8.923	9.200
8	9.549	9.897	10.260	10.637	11.028
9	11.027	11.491	11.978	12.488	13.021
10	12.578	13.181	13.816	14.487	15.193

C. Present Value of a Single Deposit

Year	5%	6%	7%	8%	9%
5	0.784	0.747	0.713	0.681	0.650
6	0.746	0.705	0.666	0.630	0.596
7	0.711	0.665	0.623	0.583	0.547
8	0.677	0.627	0.582	0.540	0.502
9	0.645	0.592	0.544	0.500	0.460
10	0.614	0.558	0.508	0.463	0.422

D. Present Value of a Series of Equal Annual Deposits

Year	5%	6%	7%	8%	9%
5	4.329	4.212	4.100	3.993	3.890
6	5.076	4.917	4.767	4.623	4.486
7	5.786	5.582	5.389	5.206	5.033
8	6.463	6.210	5.971	5.747	5.535
9	7.108	6.802	6.515	6.247	5.995
10	7.722	7.360	7.024	6.710	6.418

Time Is Money   Future value tables can save you time and reduce errors when you compute interest over a long period of time. Present value tables can help you figure out how much you need to deposit now in order to have a certain amount of money in the future.

How much money will you have if you save $2,000 a year for ten years at 9 percent interest?

Achieving Your Financial Goals
What strategies can you use to reach your financial goals?

Throughout your life you will have many different financial needs and goals. By learning to use your money wisely now, you will be able to achieve many of those goals.

Financial planning involves choosing a career, and then learning how to protect and manage the money you earn. By using eight strategies, you can avoid many common money mistakes:

1. **Obtain**—Obtain financial resources by working, making investments, or owning property. Obtaining money is the foundation of financial planning because you will use that money for all other financial activities.

2. **Plan**—The key to achieving your financial goals and financial security is to plan how you will spend your money.

3. **Spend Wisely**—Many people spend more than they can afford. Other people buy things they can afford but do not need. Spending less than you earn is the only way to achieve financial security.

4. **Save**—Long-term financial security starts with a savings plan. If you save on a regular basis, you will have money to pay your bills, make major purchases, and cope with emergencies.

5. **Borrow Wisely**—When you use a credit card or take out another type of a loan, you are borrowing money. Borrowing wisely—and only when necessary—will help you achieve your financial goals and avoid money problems.

6. **Invest**—People invest for two main reasons: to increase their current income and to achieve long-term growth. To increase current income, you can choose investments that pay regular dividends or interest. To achieve long-term growth, you might choose stocks, mutual funds, real estate, and other investments that have the potential to increase in value in the future.

◀ **RISKY BUSINESS** Accidents can happen when you least expect them. *What are some ways to manage the financial risks associated with sports accidents?*

7. **Manage Risk**—To protect your resources in case you are ever seriously injured, get sick, or die, you will need insurance coverage. Insurance will protect you and those who depend on you.

8. **Plan for Retirement**—When you start to plan for retirement, consider the age at which you would like to stop working full time. You should also think about where you will want to live and how you will want to spend your time: at a part-time job, doing volunteer work, or enjoying hobbies or sports.

Developing and Using a Financial Plan

A good personal financial plan includes assessing your present financial situation, making a list of your current needs, and deciding how to plan for future needs. You can design a plan on your own, hire a financial planner, or use a good money-management software program. Making your financial plan work takes time, effort, and patience, but you will develop habits that will give you a lifetime of satisfaction and security.

WebQuest

One Life to Plan
Learn about how financial counselors help people get out of debt and plan for the future—just one aspect of a financial planner's job.

@ To continue with Task 2 of your Web-Quest project, visit **persfinance07.glencoe.com**.

Section 1.2 Assessment

QUICK CHECK

1. What are the opportunity costs associated with financial decisions?
2. What is the time value of money?
3. What are the eight strategies you can apply to achieve your financial goals?

THINK CRITICALLY

4. Using the concept of the time value of money, write an argument in favor of shopping for a good interest rate.

USE MATH SKILLS

5. **Saving Strategies**   Tanya wants to open her own pet-grooming business after she graduates from high school. However, after doing research, she realizes that she needs to save $18,000 for the start-up capital for her business. Tanya plans to make a series of deposits of $3,000 every year for five years. She estimates that she will earn an annual interest rate of 5 percent on her savings.

Calculate   Using the tables in Figure 1.4, calculate what amount Tanya will have available in five years to start her business. How much more money will she need to save?

SOLVE MONEY PROBLEMS

6. **Saving Versus Spending**   Omar received $1,525 in gifts when he graduated from high school. His parents want him to save the money for college, but Omar wants to buy new clothes, a watch, some CDs, and a video game. He also needs new tires because the ones on his car are badly worn. Omar asks you for advice. How should he spend his graduation money?

Analyze   Working in a small group, discuss what Omar should do with his money. Consider the various financial opportunity costs and the time value of money.

CHAPTER SUMMARY

- Personal financial planning means managing your money (spending, saving, and investing) so that you can achieve financial independence and security.
- The six steps of financial planning are: (1) Determine your current financial situation; (2) develop financial goals; (3) identify alternative courses of action; (4) evaluate alternatives; 5) create and use your financial plan of action; and (6) review and revise your plan.

- The most important factors that influence personal financial planning are your life situations, your personal values, and outside economic factors.
- For all your financial decisions, you must make choices and give up something. These opportunity costs, or trade-offs, can be personal or financial.
- The eight strategies for achieving your financial goals and avoiding money problems are: Obtain, plan, spend wisely, save, borrow wisely, invest, manage risk, and plan for retirement.

Communicating Key Terms

Find an article on unemployment, inflation, interest rates, or the value of the U.S. dollar. Use 8 to 12 of the terms below and write three paragraphs relating the information in the article to personal financial planning.

- personal financial planning
- goals
- values
- opportunity cost
- liquidity
- service
- good
- economics
- economy
- supply

- demand
- Federal Reserve System
- inflation
- consumer
- interest
- time value of money
- principal
- future value
- annuity
- present value

Reviewing Key Concepts

1. **Explain** personal financial planning and its importance.
2. **Describe** the six strategies of financial planning.
3. **Describe** the factors that affect personal financial decisions.
4. **Explain** opportunity costs and how they might affect your personal financial decisions.
5. **List** eight strategies for achieving financial goals.

ACADEMIC SKILLS

Language Arts The prices of new electronic gadgets usually come down over time.

Write About It Write a paragraph explaining why this might occur. Also explain how those prices might affect your financial planning if you want to buy certain items.

YOUR FINANCIAL FIGURES

Current Interest Rates Find out from a bank or other financial institution the current interest rate on a standard savings account. Find out what other savings plans are available and their interest rates.

1. **Calculate** by using the interest rate on regular savings accounts to find out the future value of your account after eight years if you deposit $1,600 in it every year.
2. **Compute** by using spreadsheet software to calculate and compare the future values of your series of deposits based on the different interest rates offered for other savings plans.

REAL-WORLD Application

Connect with Global Economics Your brother works for a company that makes components for DVD players. The company has started to outsource some of its component assembly work to a country where employees' wages are much lower than in the United States. As a result, the company can sell components at lower prices. However, your brother's employer has started to lay off employees at its U.S. plants. Your brother believes he will have a job for two more years, but after that, he is not sure.

1. **Research** Use the Internet or library to research the trend to outsource manufacturing of electronic products in countries such as China.
2. **Think Critically** Your brother comes to you and asks if you think he should look for another job now. What would you say to him?

Internet CONNECTION

Interest Rates and Inflation Inflation (how much your money will buy) and interest rates (how much your money will earn if saved) are connected—and both of these economic factors should be considered in your financial planning, particularly for long-term goals.

 Log On Use an Internet search engine. Type "inflation and interest rates." Answer the following questions:

1. If inflation is low, how does that affect interest rates?
2. If inflation is high, how does that affect interest rates?

Newsclip: Internet Planning If your knowledge about personal finance is limited, being Web and tech savvy will help you learn more. Finance is a frequent topic on the news and is easy to research.

Log On Go to persfinance07.glencoe.com and open Chapter 1. Learn more about financial decisions and strategies. Write a list of ways you can learn more about finance.

YOUR SPENDING PROFILE

Being a saver or a spender is part of your personality. Here is a chance to test your financial personality.

If someone gave you $200, what would you do with it? Read the options below and choose three. Write the number of points for each of the three choices on a separate piece of paper. Then add up your points.

_____ Take my closest friends out to eat and to the movies (5 points)

_____ Spend $50 on fun items and save the rest (3 points)

_____ Put the money toward my next car payment (1 point)

_____ Buy new clothes for school (3 points)

_____ Hit the nearest record store and buy several CDs (5 points)

_____ Buy a CD player (3 points)

_____ Get a cell phone (5 points)

_____ Buy a savings bond (1 point)

_____ Put it in a savings account for future education (1 point)

_____ Buy the hottest new concert tickets (5 points)

What do your choices say about you?

Big saver: If you scored 3–5, you are willing to give up things today so you can buy something you want more tomorrow.

Middle of the roader: If you scored 7–11, you know how to use your money for current needs while keeping an eye on the future.

Big spender: If you scored 13–15, you like to spend money!

Your Financial Portfolio

Getting Your Own Wheels

Are you dreaming of buying your own car? Olivia Johnson is. So far she has saved $3,000. Olivia has her eye on a used car that costs $9,000. Olivia figures she can afford a monthly car payment of no more than $200. Using the interest-rate table below, Olivia calculates the monthly payment needed to repay her car loan by multiplying the amount of the loan by the interest factor. She wants to pay off her loan in three years.

Olivia's Loan Story

Cost of car	$9,000.00
Less the down payment	– 3,000.00
Amount of loan	$6,000.00

Interest Rate of 8%

Months	Interest Factor
12 (one year)	0.08698
24 (two years)	0.04522
36 (three years)	**0.03133**
48 (four years)	0.02441

Multiply loan amount by interest factor (0.03133) for 36 months

$6,000 X 0.03133 = $187.98

Olivia will pay $187.98 a month if she decides to borrow $6,000 for three years.

Calculate

Now look in your local newspaper for a car you would like to buy. How much will it cost? Suppose you can afford 25 percent of the total price for a down payment. How much money will you need to borrow to pay the complete cost of the car you want? On a separate sheet of paper, calculate how much money you will need for your monthly car payment. Calculate what your monthly payment will be if you paid off your loan in 1, 2, 3, or 4 years. (1) What is the total amount you will pay for your car if you pay it off in 1, 2, 3, or 4 years? (2) How much interest will you pay on your loan? (3) Which payment plan would enable you to pay the least amount of money for your car? (4) Which payment plan would have the lowest payments?

CHAPTER 2

Finances and Career Planning

$ What You'll Learn

When you have completed this chapter, you will be able to:

Section 2.1
- Identify the personal issues to consider when choosing and planning your career.
- Explain how education and training affect career advancement.
- Discuss the factors that influence employment.

Section 2.2
- Describe effective strategies to obtain employment.
- Identify sources of career opportunities.
- Identify the financial and legal issues to consider when looking for employment.

Reading Strategies

To get the most out of your reading:

Predict what you will learn in this chapter.

Relate what you read to your own life.

Question what you are reading to be sure you understand.

React to what you have read.

In the **Real** World . . .

George Leonard is not sure what career to pursue. Since graduating from high school, he has held jobs at a sandwich shop, a bookstore, and an animal park. George learned about small businesses while he was working. As a result, he has decided that he would like to run his own business one day—perhaps a pet store.

Jessica Rodriguez, a high school junior, loves movies. She watches classic films and edits her own short features on the computer. She hopes to work in the film industry.

George and Jessica are not exactly sure what their careers will be, but they realize they will need to make informed decisions.

As You Read *Consider how education and training might affect careers and job opportunities.*

ASK STANDARD &POOR'S

Planning for Life

Q: Career plans are for people who do not know what they want. I know already that I want a high-paying job. So why should I bother thinking about career planning?

A: Money is just one motivation for work. You need to consider many other factors as well. Career planning considers your personal values, goals, and interests—the basics for any career decision. Since you will probably spend the majority of your life working, consider the old adage: "Choose a career you love, and the money will follow."

Ask Yourself What job would you love to do?

 Go to **persfinance07.glencoe.com** to complete the Standard & Poor's Financial Focus activity.

Planning Your Career

Choosing a Career

What is the difference between a job and a career?

Some people find true satisfaction in their work, while others work just to make money. Like many people, you may decide to get a **job**—work that you do mainly to earn money. On the other hand, you may decide to prepare for a career. A **career** is a commitment to work in a field that you find interesting and fulfilling. Ensuring that your career will fulfill your personal and financial goals requires planning.

Career Decision Trade-Offs

Your choice of career will affect the amount of money you make, the people you meet, and how much spare time you have. Some people work just to maintain a **standard of living**, a measure of quality of life based on the amounts and kinds of goods and services a person can buy. They also work to pay for the hobbies and activities they enjoy. Others pursue careers that provide them with both money and personal fulfillment. They select careers that reflect their interests, values, and goals.

Choosing a career will involve trade-offs, or opportunity costs. Many people devote most of their time and energy to their work. As a result, their family lives and personal satisfaction may suffer. Recent **trends**—developments that mark changes in a particular area—indicate that some people are making career decisions, such as declining a promotion, that allow them to spend more time with their families or to enjoy their hobbies and interests.

You may select a career that is challenging and offers you the chance to grow, even if it does not earn you a large salary. On the other hand, you may choose to work in a job that is less satisfying but offers more money. You may look for part-time work or work situations with flexible hours so that you will have more time to spend with your family. You could also decide to give up the security of working for someone else to take on the challenge of running your own business.

The more you know about your own interests, values, needs, and goals, the better you will be able to choose a career that will provide a balance between personal satisfaction and financial rewards.

◀ **WEIGHING YOUR OPTIONS** Choosing a career involves trade-offs. Some parents will decline a job with a higher salary for a job that offers a flexible schedule. *What other trade-offs might a parent have to make?*

Career Training and Skill Development

Obtaining as much education as possible will help you meet your financial goals. The more you know, the greater your chances are for success. Having a college degree does not guarantee that you will reach your goals and make a lot of money. However, acquiring more education increases your **potential earning power**, which is the amount of money you may earn over time. Your field of study will also affect your salary. Some careers, such as law and medicine, generally offer higher salaries than others, such as education and the fine arts.

Education is not the only ingredient for success in your job or career. By developing certain habits, you will become an asset to any employer. For example, most successful people are able to work well with others. They always strive to do their best. They do not allow conflict with other employees or changes in their duties to affect the quality of their work. They are creative when it comes to solving problems. They communicate well. They understand themselves and other people. These basic qualities and skills make success more likely in most job situations. How do you measure up to this checklist for success? If you think that you might fall short in some areas, what might you do to improve?

As You Read

RELATE

Imagine yourself 15 years from now. Will you have a career or a job? Would that career or job fulfill personal and financial goals?

Personal Factors

You can take special tests to learn more about your own abilities, interests, and personal qualities. These tests—called *aptitude tests* and *interest inventories*—may give you an edge in choosing a career. You can usually find out more about such tests in your school's guidance office. If you would rather test yourself, you can find test materials in public libraries, bookstores, and on the Internet.

What Do You Do Best? **Aptitudes** are the natural abilities that people possess. For example, you may have a beautiful singing voice, excel at math, or be able to solve puzzles easily. These are all natural aptitudes. Try taking an aptitude test to find out what you do best.

What Do You Enjoy? **Interest inventories** are tests that help you identify the activities you enjoy the most. They match your interests, likes, and dislikes with various kinds of work. For example, someone who enjoys nature and the outdoors could become a science teacher, nature photographer, or landscape designer. A person who likes to make things could study to become a carpenter, clothes designer, architect, or engineer. List some of your interests. What types of careers can you think of that would match your interests?

The Right Fit Aptitude tests and interest inventories may not lead you to the ideal career. They can only point you in the right direction. Another important issue to consider is your personality. For example, do you enjoy large parties, or would you rather stay at home and read a book? Do you like to take chances, or do you prefer to play it safe? Do you work well under pressure, or do you need time to do a job?

The goal is to find a job or career that gives you the right balance between financial rewards and personal satisfaction. Some people adapt easily to any work environment. Others are always looking for something better. Because your work situation will never stop changing, the key to success is to remain flexible.

Stages of Career Planning

Before you make any decisions about your career, you should review your situation. Changes in your personal life and in society will affect your work life, and the reverse is also true. **Figure 2.1** shows the stages of career planning, changes, and advancement. If you are getting ready to enter the workforce, you will probably start at Stage 1. That stage will involve determining your personal and career interests.

The diagram in Figure 2.1 is only one plan of action. Your progress will depend on your opportunity costs, the choices that are available to you, and your career area. If you are unsure about your direction, talk to people in your field of interest. Ask them what they like and dislike about their work and how they got into the field. Answers to these questions can help you with your career planning.

Academic Connection

SCIENCE

The world around us is constantly changing, and the field of science is expanding to keep up with it. There are many careers in the science field, such as cancer research, environmental science, pharmaceutical research, and genetic engineering. *Choose three careers, one science-related, and find out the educational requirements and average salaries for them. Which of the three jobs pays more? Do you think salary should affect your choice of career?*

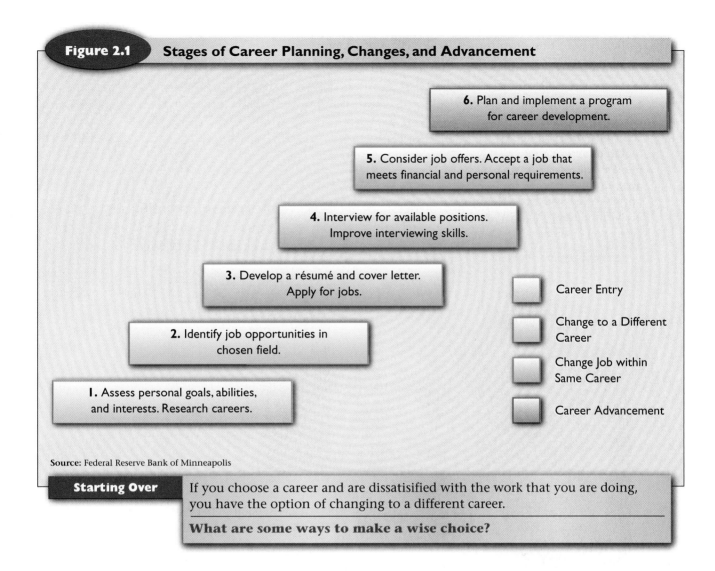

Figure 2.1 Stages of Career Planning, Changes, and Advancement

6. Plan and implement a program for career development.

5. Consider job offers. Accept a job that meets financial and personal requirements.

4. Interview for available positions. Improve interviewing skills.

3. Develop a résumé and cover letter. Apply for jobs.

2. Identify job opportunities in chosen field.

1. Assess personal goals, abilities, and interests. Research careers.

Career Entry

Change to a Different Career

Change Job within Same Career

Career Advancement

Source: Federal Reserve Bank of Minneapolis

Starting Over If you choose a career and are dissatisfied with the work that you are doing, you have the option of changing to a different career.

What are some ways to make a wise choice?

External Factors and Opportunities

Why should you consider external influences when thinking about your career?

Before you begin your job search, you should think about how external factors such as social influences, economic factors, and trends might affect your career. These factors directly affect the job market and the opportunities that are available to you. When you consider your career options, you not only need to focus on your skills, training, and experience, you also need to view the "big picture" on a national and global scale. You may have no control over these particular factors, but you can make some personal decisions based on real-world influences.

Social influences include factors such as demographic trends and geographic trends. Economic conditions include factors such as interest rates, inflation, and consumer demand. Industry trends are affected by factors such as foreign competition and the changing and expanding uses of technology.

Figure 2.2   Developing a Career Plan of Action

If you want your career to start off on the right foot, you need a plan of action. You need to know where you are, where you want to go, when you want to arrive, and how you are going to get there.

1 Personal and Career Interests Make a list of things you enjoy doing. Think about how you could turn an activity like that into a career.

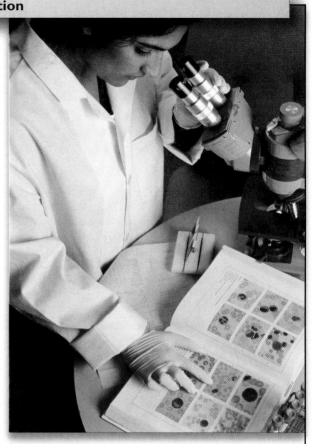

2 Career Skills Think about work experiences you have already had. Which ones did you like? Which ones did not go so well? What skills did you learn?

3 Career Training and Education What kind of education or training do you need for the career you want?

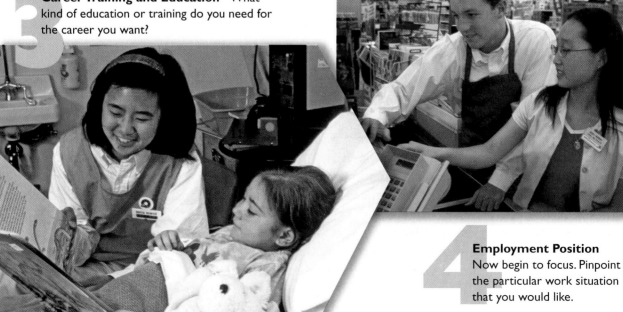

4 Employment Position Now begin to focus. Pinpoint the particular work situation that you would like.

Social Influences

Demographic trends are tendencies of people grouped by age, gender, ethnicity, education, or income that change over time. These developments can affect your employment opportunities. Several demographic trends have affected the job market:

- More working parents, which expands the supply of jobs in child care and food services
- More leisure time, which boosts interest in health, physical fitness, and recreational products
- More elderly people in the overall population, which produces a greater need for workers in retirement facilities, health care, and travel services
- Greater demand for ongoing employment training, which increases career opportunities for teachers and trainers

Geographic trends are tendencies of people moving from one area of the country to another as financial centers shift location. In recent years, some of the fastest-growing job markets have included cities in Florida, Nevada, Arizona, Arkansas, New Jersey, and California.

Geographic location also influences earning level. Remember to consider differences in earning levels as you decide where to look for employment. Big cities, such as San Francisco, New York, and Chicago, usually offer higher salaries, but the cost of living (the cost of food, housing, transportation, and other expenses) is also higher in such areas. If you accept a high-paying position in a big city, you may actually have a lower standard of living than you would in an area where income levels and the cost of living are lower.

Economic Factors

High interest rates, price increases, or decreased demand for certain goods and services can reduce career opportunities. The job market changes as the economy does, and so the demand for certain types of jobs changes. For example, in the 1990s many companies were looking for people to work in the computer and technology fields. As a result, there were a lot of jobs from which to choose, and salaries were high. As we moved into the 21st century, however, the demand for workers in those industries decreased, and salaries either stayed the same or came down. You cannot control the effects of economic factors on employment trends, so be aware of what jobs are currently in high demand.

In addition, economic factors affect some businesses more than others. For example, high interest rates may reduce employment in housing-related industries, such as construction and real estate, because people are less likely to buy houses when interest rates are high. Being aware of current economic trends will help you to choose a career so that you can achieve your financial goals.

Common CENTS

Career Center
At your school's career center, you will find a variety of free information that can help you with college choices, résumé preparation, job opportunities, and career counseling. *How can researching different careers that interest you help your financial planning for the future?*

As You Read

QUESTION

What other employment opportunities might be influenced by demographic and geographic trends?

Trends in Industry and Technology

Changes in industry and technology also affect the job market. In recent years, the need for workers in manufacturing has decreased as a result of several trends. First, increased competition from other countries has reduced demand for American-made products. Second, automation has taken over many tasks that used to be done by factory workers.

Perhaps you would like a career in the field of electronics technology. You know that your skills are valuable, but you also know that constant technological advances can quickly outdate products and jobs. As a result, you must accept some financial uncertainty.

STANDARD &POOR'S

Global Financial Landscape

Standard and Poor's publishes the globally recognized S&P 500® financial index. It also gathers financial statistics, information, and news, and analyzes this data for international businesses, governments, and individuals to help them guide their financial decisions.

JAPAN

Traditionally, the domain of Japanese women has been the home and children. However, when the first equal-opportunity law was passed in Japan in the mid-1980s, many women began to shun marriage for the workplace. In fact, in the past decade, the number of unmarried women ages 25 to 29 has grown from 40 to 54 percent. As a result, the birthrate in Japan dropped steadily during that time. Japanese leaders fear that there will be a decrease in population and consequent labor shortages in the future. In response to this potential problem, policymakers have suggested that companies provide better job opportunities *and* child-care programs to the female workforce. That way Japanese women can opt for marriage and having children as well as successful careers.

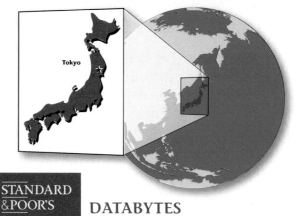

STANDARD &POOR'S

DATABYTES

Capital	Tokyo
Population	127,508,000
Language	Japanese
Currency	yen
Gross Domestic Product (GDP)	$3.567 trillion (2003 est.)
GDP per capita	$28,000

Industry: Motor vehicles, electronic equipment, machine tools, steel, and non-ferrous metals

Agriculture: Rice, sugar, beets, vegetables, fruit, pork, and fish

Exports: Motor vehicles, semiconductors, office machinery, and chemicals

Natural Resources: Mineral resources and fish

Think Globally
What trend in Japan might affect job opportunities there? Why?

While opportunities have dwindled in some areas of the economy, opportunities in other areas have grown. **Service industries**, which are businesses that provide services for a fee, offer employment potential in coming years. There are numerous careers in these industries:

- Computer or telecommunications technology—systems analysts, Web-site developers, service technicians
- Health care—medical assistants, physical therapists, home-health workers
- Business services—employee benefit managers, trainers
- Social services—child-care workers, elder-care coordinators
- Hospitality services—travel agents, food service managers
- Management—employment service workers, recruiters
- Education—elementary, secondary, postsecondary, and adult education teachers
- Financial services—insurance agents, investment brokers

Whatever career area you choose, having knowledge of a variety of computer programs and the Internet will be essential.

Section 2.1 Assessment

QUICK CHECK

1. What are three characteristics of successful people? Describe how each characteristic might be an asset at school or work.

2. How can you learn more about your own abilities, interests, and personal qualities as they relate to career planning?

3. What are three factors that influence employment opportunities?

THINK CRITICALLY

4. Why do you think that the increase in the number of working parents has contributed to a higher demand for food services?

USE COMMUNICATION SKILLS

5. New Career Choices Service industries will offer some of the greatest potential for jobs in coming years.

> **Analyze** With a partner, conduct a survey of five students and identify their most popular career choices.

SOLVE MONEY PROBLEMS

6. Geographic Influences Tyrell has worked his way up from sales associate to department supervisor for a large suburban discount store. Now he has been offered a higher position in Atlanta. Currently, Tyrell earns about $18,000 annually, which covers the cost of food, housing, transportation, and other living expenses. With the new job, his salary would increase 20 percent, but the cost of living in Atlanta is much higher than it is in the suburbs. By doing some research, he found that the rent for a one-bedroom apartment averages $800 per month, and the round-trip train ride to work will cost about $4 per day. Food will probably cost $65 per week.

> **Calculate** Assuming Tyrell works five days a week and 52 weeks a year, help him calculate what his living expenses would total per year if he moved to Atlanta.

Employment and Career Development

Focus on Reading

Read to Learn

- How to describe effective strategies to obtain employment.
- How to identify sources of career opportunities.
- How to identify the financial and legal issues to consider when looking for employment.

Main Idea

Learn effective strategies to help you get the job or career that meets your personal and financial goals.

Key Terms

- internship
- cooperative education
- networking
- informational interview
- résumé
- cover letter
- cafeteria-style employee benefits
- pension plan
- mentor

Before You Read

PREDICT

What are some strategies you think might be effective in obtaining employment experience?

Employment Search Strategies

What are steps to take when searching for a job?

Meg filled out dozens of job applications but never received a call for an interview. Douglas went to many interviews and found a challenging and satisfying job. What were the differences between these two people? The answer has to do with how well they communicated the value of the experience they already had and how effectively they used proven employment strategies.

Obtaining Employment Experience

Many young people who are entering the world of work worry that they do not have enough experience. They may be overlooking the importance of various kinds of work-related training:

- Part-time work
- Volunteer work
- Internships and cooperative education
- Class projects or after-school activities

Part-Time Work   Summer and part-time jobs can provide valuable experience. If you have been a camp counselor during the summer, you may decide that you really enjoy working with children and would like to get a job in a day-care center. Perhaps you are a cashier at a drugstore after school and on weekends. You may want to pursue a career in pharmacology or business administration.

Many companies use temporary workers to fill various positions. Working as a "temp" is a good way to gain experience and learn more about a particular field. For the same reasons, part-time and temporary work can be worthwhile for people who are changing careers.

Volunteer Work   You can learn new skills, develop good work habits, and make professional contacts by volunteering. Many nonprofit community organizations and some government agencies include volunteers on their staffs. You might collect funds for a disaster relief project or build houses with Habitat for Humanity. Volunteering can help you develop skills that you can apply to other work situations. Where could you volunteer in your community?

Internships and Cooperative Education An internship may give you the experience you need to obtain employment. An **internship** is a position in which a person receives training by working with people who are experienced in a particular field. Sometimes it can lead to permanent employment. You also get a chance to practice your application and interviewing skills.

Cooperative education programs allow students to enhance classroom learning with part-time work related to their majors and interests. For example, you would take your high school classes in the morning, and in the afternoon you would work at a local business to apply the workplace skills you learned in class.

Class Projects or After-School Activities Class assignments and school activities can be sources of work-related experience. They can help you gain valuable career skills such as:

- Managing, organizing, and coordinating people
- Public speaking
- Goal setting, planning, and supervising
- Financial planning and budgeting
- Conducting research

Career Information Sources

You need up-to-date information to make the best career decisions. Many sources of information are available to you.

Libraries Most school and public libraries offer a variety of references on careers. Start with such guides as the *Occupational Outlook Handbook*, the *O*NET Dictionary of Occupational Titles*, and Occupational Outlook Quarterly Online.

◄ **VOLUNTEER** Volunteering for a local or national nonprofit organization can provide work-related experience. *What types of skills might you gain by helping to clean up a city park?*

Document Detective

Learn to identify and understand the standard financial documents you will use in the real world.

Investigate: An IRS Form W-4

A Form W-4 asks you for the following:

- Your name and address
- Your marital status
- Number of allowances
- Additional withholdings
- Signature and date

Your Motive: By properly filling out a Form W-4, you will ensure that the appropriate amount of tax is deducted from your paychecks. Withholding too little from your pay can result in penalties when you file your yearly income tax return.

Personal Allowances Worksheet (Keep for your records.)

A Enter "1" for **yourself** if no one else can claim you as a dependent . . . . A _____

B Enter "1" if:
- You are single and have only one job; or
- You are married, have only one job, and your spouse does not work; or
- Your wages from a second job or your spouse's wages (or the total of both) are $1,000 or less. } . . . B _____

C Enter "1" for your **spouse**. But, you may choose to enter "-0-" if you are married and have either a working spouse or more than one job. (Entering "-0-" may help you avoid having too little tax withheld.) . . . . C _____

D Enter number of **dependents** (other than your spouse or yourself) you will claim on your tax return . . . . D _____

E Enter "1" if you will file as **head of household** on your tax return (see conditions under **Head of household** above) . E _____

F Enter "1" if you have at least $1,500 of **child or dependent care expenses** for which you plan to claim a credit . . F _____
(**Note.** Do **not** include child support payments. See **Pub. 503**, Child and Dependent Care Expenses, for details.)

G **Child Tax Credit** (including additional child tax credit):
- If your total income will be less than $54,000 ($79,000 if married), enter "2" for each eligible child.
- If your total income will be between $54,000 and $84,000 ($79,000 and $119,000 if married), enter "1" for each eligible child plus "1" **additional** if you have four or more eligible children. . . . . G _____

H Add lines A through G and enter total here. (**Note.** This may be different from the number of exemptions you claim on your tax return.) ► H _____

For accuracy, complete all worksheets that apply.
- If you plan to **itemize or claim adjustments to income** and want to reduce your withholding, see the **Deductions and Adjustments Worksheet** on page 2.
- If you have **more than one job** or are **married and you and your spouse both work** and the combined earnings from all jobs exceed $35,000 ($25,000 if married) see the **Two-Earner/Two-Job Worksheet** on page 2 to avoid having too little tax withheld.
- If **neither** of the above situations applies, **stop here** and enter the number from line H on line 5 of Form W-4 below.

- - - - - - - - - - - - - - - - - - - **Cut here and give Form W-4 to your employer. Keep the top part for your records.** - - - - - - - - - - - - - - - - - - -

Form **W-4**

Department of the Treasury
Internal Revenue Service

Employee's Withholding Allowance Certificate

► Whether you are entitled to claim a certain number of allowances or exemption from withholding is subject to review by the IRS. Your employer may be required to send a copy of this form to the IRS.

OMB No. 1545-0010

20--

1 Type or print your first name and middle initial Last name		2 Your social security number
Home address (number and street or rural route)	3 ☐ Single ☐ Married ☐ Married, but withhold at higher Single rate. **Note.** If married, but legally separated, or spouse is a nonresident alien, check the "Single" box.	
City or town, state, and ZIP code	4 If your last name differs from that shown on your social security card, check here. You must call 1-800-772-1213 for a new card. ► ☐	

5 Total number of allowances you are claiming (from line **H** above **or** from the applicable worksheet on page 2) | 5 _____

6 Additional amount, if any, you want withheld from each paycheck . . . . | 6 $ _____

7 I claim exemption from withholding for 2005, and I certify that I meet **both** of the following conditions for exemption.
- Last year I had a right to a refund of **all** federal income tax withheld because I had **no** tax liability **and**
- This year I expect a refund of **all** federal income tax withheld because I expect to have **no** tax liability.
If you meet both conditions, write "Exempt" here . . . . ► | 7 _____

Under penalties of perjury, I declare that I have examined this certificate and to the best of my knowledge and belief, it is true, correct, and complete.

Employee's signature
(Form is not valid unless you sign it.) ►   Date ►

| 8 Employer's name and address (Employer: Complete lines 8 and 10 only if sending to the IRS.) | 9 Office code (optional) | 10 Employer identification number (EIN) |

For Privacy Act and Paperwork Reduction Act Notice, see page 2.   Cat. No. 10220Q   Form **W-4** (20--)

Key Points: Employers are required to have each employee complete an IRS Form W-4 to determine the tax withholding. The number of dependents (people you are financially responsible for) you claim on Form W-4 determines the amount of tax withheld from your paychecks. The tax rate varies by the number of dependents you claim. The more dependents, the less you pay in taxes. Because your tax situation may change, review your withholdings each year.

Find the Solutions

1. What is the purpose of the Form W-4?
2. On line 6, you may elect to withhold additional money from your pay. Why would someone choose to do this?
3. How could a person be exempt from having withholdings taken from his or her pay?
4. Why is it necessary for the employee to sign the form?
5. Can a married person withhold at the same rate as a single person?

Mass Media Most newspapers feature business and employment sections with articles on job hunting and career trends.

The Internet Log on to the Internet for a wealth of information about jobs and employment. You will find tips and suggestions on everything from filling out applications to job interviewing.

School Guidance Offices Visit your school guidance office for materials and advice on career planning. Take advantage of any placement services your school may offer.

Community Organizations Almost every community has business and civic groups that can help you in your career search. Attending their meetings gives you an opportunity to meet local businesspeople.

Professional Organizations Many professions have organizations dedicated to sharing information. The *Encyclopedia of Associations* can help you find organizations representing careers that interest you.

Contacts Family, friends, coworkers, teachers, professors, and former employers are the people you already know who can help you to prepare for your career. Even people whom you do not know can assist you in a job search. That is why it is never too late to begin networking. **Networking** is a way of making and using contacts to get job information and advice. The contacts you make may not be people who can hire you, but they may know someone who can.

They may be able to arrange an **informational interview**, which is a meeting with someone who works in your area of interest who can provide you with practical information about the career or company you are considering.

Identifying Job Opportunities
What sources can you use to find an employment opportunity?

If you are going to find employment that is right for you, you need to know where to look for job openings. Explore sources such as job advertisements, job fairs, and employment agencies.

Job Advertisements

All newspapers have classified ads that include job listings. Although most advertise only jobs that are available locally, some major newspapers, such as *The Wall Street Journal,* list jobs from a wide geographic area.

The Internet is a valuable source for job opportunities. If you are interested in working for a particular company, you can use a search engine to find its Web site and learn more about it. Sometimes you can also find that company's list of current job openings. In addition to company Web sites, the Internet offers job-search Web sites with job advertisements, advice, and résumé services.

Job Fairs

At a job fair, recruiters from local and national companies set up tables or booths where you can discuss job opportunities and submit your résumé. To make the most of a job fair, be prepared to make your best impression on several recruiters in a short amount of time. They may call you for an in-depth interview at a later date.

Employment Agencies

Employment agencies are businesses that match job hunters with employers. Most often the company that hires you pays the employment agency fee. In some cases, you pay the fee, or you and your new employer share the cost. Do not get involved with agencies that ask you to pay a fee without promising you a job in return. The government also supports employment services. To find out more about them, contact your state's employment service or department of labor.

Other Ways to Find a Job

Your ability to find a job is limited only by your imagination and energy. Remember that finding a job is a job in itself. There are also other ways to find a job:

- **Visit**—Visit specific companies where you would like to work and ask to speak to someone who might help you.
- **Call**—Check your local telephone directories for the names of businesses in your field of interest, and contact them.
- **Network**—Talk to people with similar interests who have already graduated from your school. They may be able to help you focus your career search.

▶ **ANOTHER APPROACH**
One way to find a job is to write a letter to a company that interests you. *What might be some of the benefits of contacting companies even if they are not advertising a job opening?*

Applying for a Job
What are the steps involved in the job application process?

As You Read

QUESTION

Why would a skills résumé be a better choice for a recent high school graduate?

This morning the personnel director of a company to whom Christopher had sent his résumé and cover letter many weeks ago called him. In two days, he has an appointment for a job interview. He is excited, but he knows that he has a lot to do to prepare.

Making the best possible presentation of your skills and experience is the key to landing a job. Your résumé is your most important tool. A **résumé** is a one- or two-page summary of your education, training, experience, and qualifications. It provides prospective employers with an overview of the special contribution you may be able to make to their companies.

The two basic types of résumés are the chronological résumé and the skills résumé. The chronological résumé provides a year-by-year (or longer periods) outline of your education, work experience, and related information. This format is useful for job hunters who have continuous work experience. A skills résumé highlights your skills and abilities in specific categories, such as communications, supervision, or research. If you are a recent graduate or are changing careers, a skills résumé might be the better choice for you.

When you send your résumé to an employer by regular mail, e-mail, or fax, you will want to include a cover letter. A **cover letter** is the personal letter that you present along with your résumé. While the résumé serves as an overall summary of your qualifications, a cover letter tells a potential employer why you are interested in a particular job and why you think that it would be worthwhile for him or her to interview you. See **Figure 2.3** on page 46 for examples of a chronological résumé and a skills résumé, and **Figure 2.4** on page 47 for a sample cover letter.

The interview is a formal meeting with your potential employer that allows you to express why you think you are the best person for the job. If you are granted an interview, you should obtain as much information as you can about the company or industry before your interview. Possible resources include the library, the Internet, and informal interviews with people who are familiar with that company or industry. Here are some typical questions an employer might ask:

- What education and training qualify you for this job?
- Why are you interested in working for this company?
- Other than past jobs, what experiences have helped prepare you for this job?
- What are your major strengths? Major weaknesses?
- What do you plan to be doing five or ten years from now?

Most interviewers will end the interview by telling you when you can expect a response. While you are waiting, send that person a note reiterating your interest and expressing your thanks for the opportunity to interview. You may also want to recall your performance during the interview and think about how you might improve.

Figure 2.3 Types of Résumés

Chronological Résumé

CHAD BOSTWICK
2348 University Drive
Apartment 212
Jasper, Missouri 54321

Phone: 315-555-7659
E-mail: chbos@internet.com

CAREER OBJECTIVE:

Seeking an entry-level position in medical or healthcare administration.

EXPERIENCE:
November 20-––Present

PATIENT ACCOUNT CLERK
University Hospital,
Jasper, Missouri
• Researched overdue accounts.
• Created collection method for faster accounts receivable turnover.
• Assisted in training billing clerks.

January–August 20--

SALES DATA CLERK
Jones Medical Supply Company,
Benton, Kansas
• Maintained inventory records.
• Processed customer records.

EDUCATION:

B.S. in business administration and healthcare marketing, 20--
University of Western Missouri, Jasper, Missouri.

CAMPUS ACTIVITIES:

Newsletter editor, University of Western Missouri chapter of Financial Management Association, 20--.

HONORS:

College of Business Community Service Award, University of Western Missouri, May 20--.

COMPUTER SKILLS:

Microsoft® Windows®, Microsoft Office®, Peachtree Complete® Accounting.

Skills Résumé

Phone: 203-555-6710
E-mail: nanfrank@internet.com

NANCY FRANK
670 Dove Circle
Apartment 5B
Reston, Maine 01267

CAREER OBJECTIVE:

Seeking a human resources position in which supervisory, communication, and research experience can be used to train new and existing company employees.

ACHIEVEMENTS:

SUPERVISORY EXPERIENCE
• Developed and implemented training programs.
• Coordinated conference committees.

COMMUNICATION EXPERIENCE
• Created training manuals.
• Wrote press releases.

RESEARCH EXPERIENCE
• Investigated training problems of large industrial organizations.

COMPUTER SKILLS
• Mastered Microsoft® Windows®, Microsoft Office®.

EMPLOYMENT HISTORY:

• Assistant to director of human resources, Arkond Incorporated, Harper, Maine, June 20-–Present.
• Copy writer, Ashton Marketing Services, Benton, Maine, January 20-– May 20--.
• Research associate for Representative Henry Lake, Benton, Maine, June 20-– December 20--.

EDUCATION:

High School Diploma (College Preparatory Program), James Madison High School, Reston, Maine

Getting to Know You Your résumé should give a clear overview of your education, training, experience, and qualifications.

What are some experiences that you would describe in your résumé?

Figure 2.4 **Cover Letter**

JERRY HOPKINS
5678 Collins Road
West Barrington, New York 14332

Phone: 914-555-4556
E-mail: jhopkins@internet.com

May 23, 20--

Ms. Hanna Cabral
Human Resources Director
Global Translation Services
3400 Superior Boulevard
Jamestown, New York 13456

Dear Ms. Cabral:

Based on my background and studies in international relations, I am writing to express my interest in the position of associate translator available with your organization. Brenda Kelly, a member of your accounting department, recommended that I contact you. My studies have included courses in global business practices as well as an internship with the exporting department of an electronics company.

My language skills have allowed me to handle customer relations activities with international customers. My ability to work in a cross-cultural environment would provide your organization with a person who can adapt to varied business settings. As a result of my work with companies in other countries, I would be able to meet the diverse needs of your clients.

The enclosed résumé will provide additional information about my qualifications.

I would appreciate the opportunity to meet with you and discuss the ways that my training and background will allow me to contribute to the continued success of your organization. I will call your office on June 1 to determine whether you can arrange a time to see me.

Sincerely,

Jerry Hopkins

Jerry Hopkins
Enclosure

The Introduction Your cover letter should be simple, informative, and free of errors.

What information could you include in your letter that would set you apart from other applicants?

Considering a Job Offer

What factor would be most important to you when considering a job offer?

You may go on several interviews and experience disappointment. Sooner or later, however, someone will say, "We'd like you to work for us." But before you accept an offer, you have to consider several factors. Find out all you can about the company, the job itself, the working environment, the salary, and any other benefits.

The Work Environment

As you go on interviews, you will notice differences in workplaces. The pace and pressure will vary. Even the way people behave when they are at work will depend on the company.

Ask about official company policies. How does the company handle pay increases? How does it measure the quality of employees' work? How does it decide which employees to promote?

Factors Affecting Salary

Your beginning salary will depend on your education and experience, the size of the company, and the average salary for the job you are considering. To make sure that you are starting with a fair salary, talk to people with similar jobs at other companies or look for related information on the Internet.

Raises and promotions are a direct result of how well you do your job. Once you have accepted a job offer and started to work, meet regularly with your supervisor. Ask for feedback on your performance and any suggestions for improvement. Let your supervisor know that you are interested in increased responsibility. Meeting—or exceeding—your supervisor's expectations should bring the reward of a raise. If it does not, you might want to look for another job.

Measuring Employee Benefits

You should also evaluate the types of benefits the company offers besides a paycheck. Pay particular attention to health care, retirement benefits, and the specific needs of your family.

▲ **WORK CULTURE** The pace and pressure of work differ from company to company. *What type of pace might be most appropriate for your personality and work habits?*

Careers in Finance

CASHIER

Mark Leeds
Burlington Coat Factory

Mark has always wanted a job that balances his attention to detail with his ability to work with customers. Working as a cashier for Burlington Coat Factory, Mark is responsible for providing outstanding service and a friendly environment to each customer. His duties include handling money, totaling bills, making change, and giving receipts. He also handles returns, exchanges, and gift certificates. Mark likes interacting with people and also appreciates that his schedule is flexible. If something comes up, he can usually trade shifts with another cashier. Sales, holidays, and a varied work schedule provide diversity in the activity and intensity of a cashier's job.

SKILLS: Communication, dexterity, computer, and math

PERSONAL TRAITS: Detail oriented, honest, likes working with people, tactful, neat, and able to work weekends, holidays, and evenings

EDUCATION: High school diploma or equivalent, on-the-job training

ANALYZE What types of factors might a cashier examine before accepting a job?

 To learn more about career paths for cashiers, visit **persfinance07.glencoe.com**.

Meeting Employee Needs Changes in society have brought about changes in the types of benefits that employees receive. Today single-parent families and households in which both parents work are common. Businesses have responded to these changes in a variety of ways.

Cafeteria-style employee benefits are programs that allow workers to choose the benefits that best meet their personal needs. A married employee with children may want more life and health insurance, whereas a single parent may also be interested in child-care services.

Because people today live longer, retirement programs are more important than ever. In addition to Social Security benefits, some companies contribute to a **pension plan**, which is a retirement plan that is funded at least in part by an employer. The features of pension plans vary among several basic types. Some plans provide you with a fixed amount of money at retirement. If a business uses a profit-sharing plan, it makes an annual contribution to a retirement fund each year. The money in this fund builds up until you reach retirement age. A third type of pension plan is a 401(k). You set aside a portion of your salary from each paycheck to go into your 401(k) fund. Your employer may match a percentage of your contribution.

Comparing Benefits You can compare the dollar value of employee benefits in several ways. The market value of a benefit is what the benefit would cost if you had to pay for it yourself. For example, the market value of free health insurance is what it would cost you to buy the same insurance. Also, the market value of one week's (five days') paid vacation is one week's salary.

Taxes should also play a part in your decisions about employment benefits. There are two types of employment benefits: tax-exempt and tax-deferred. A tax-exempt benefit is a benefit that is not taxable. For example, medical insurance paid by an employer is tax exempt. For example, if your employer pays $2,000 for your medical insurance, it equals $2,500 before taxes (for the 25 percent tax bracket). A free life insurance policy for an employee is an example of a tax-exempt benefit.

A tax-deferred benefit is a benefit for which you will have to pay income tax sometime in the future, most likely after you retire. A 401(k) plan is an example of a tax-deferred benefit.

Your Rights as an Employee
Why should you know your legal rights as an employee?

As an employee, you have certain legal rights, which can also affect your financial situation. You also have certain legal rights during the hiring process:

- An employer cannot refuse to hire a woman or terminate her employment because she is pregnant. A female employee who stops working because she is pregnant must be given full credit for previous service and for any retirement benefits.
- An employer cannot discriminate against a person for any reason related to age, race, color, religion, gender, marital status, national origin, or any mental or physical disabilities.
- In some cases, an employer must pay the minimum wage set by the government as well as a certain amount for overtime work.
- An employer must pay for unemployment insurance, contribute to Social Security, and provide for workers' compensation funds in case of a work-related injury or illness.

Long-Term Career Development
What steps can you take to help make your career a success?

A job is for today, but a career can last a lifetime. As you enter the world of work, ask yourself: Will you always enjoy the work that you do today? Will you be successful in the career you select? You cannot predict the future, but you can develop skills and attitudes that will increase your chances of being satisfied with your work in years to come. Here are some basic guidelines to follow for career success:

◀ **YOUR RIGHTS** An employer cannot discriminate against a person during the hiring process for any reason related to age, race, color, religion, gender, marital status, national origin, or any mental or physical disabilities. *What would you do if your legal rights were not honored?*

- Make a point of improving your communication skills—both written and oral.
- Do your best to get along with your coworkers.
- Remain flexible and open to new ideas.
- Develop good work habits.
- Use lists, short-term and long-term goals, note cards, and other time-management techniques. When you have a task to complete, do it as well as you can.
- Be aware that problems may arise, and be ready to take action when they do.
- Be creative in solving your own problems.
- Be willing to learn new techniques and technologies.

Training Opportunities

Advances in technology are changing the world of work at a rapid pace. Many careers that people have today did not exist just a few years ago. These changes will surely continue. A key to your ongoing success will be your ability to keep up with changes in technology and to adapt to the global economy. Remember that you will always be learning new skills and ideas.

How can you make sure that your skills remain up to date? Many companies offer regular training programs, encourage attendance at professional seminars, or help pay for college courses. Read as much as possible on your own. Take advantage of the wealth of information on business, economic, and social trends on the Internet and in newspapers, magazines, and professional journals. Talk with others in your field. Informal meetings with coworkers and associates from other companies can be a valuable source of new information.

Figure 2.5   Stages of Career Development

Stage	Tasks	Concerns
Pre-entry and career exploration	• Assess personal interests. • Obtain necessary training. • Find an entry-level job.	• Matching interests and abilities to job • Dealing with disappointment
Career growth	• Obtain experience, develop skills. • Concentrate on an area of specialization. • Gain respect of colleagues.	• Developing career contacts • Avoiding career burnout
Advancement and mid-career adjustment	• Continue to gain experience and knowledge. • Seek new challenges and expanded responsibility.	• Finding continued satisfaction • Maintaining sensitivity toward colleagues and subordinates
Late career and preretirement	• Make financial and personal plans for retirement.	• Determining professional involvement after retirement • Planning participation in community activities

New Horizons   Each stage of career development brings new tasks and new concerns.

Why might you decide to seek new challenges and responsibilities during the mid-career adjustment stage?

Career Paths and Advancement

As time goes by, you will experience changes in your personal interests, values, and goals. Outside factors, such as economic conditions and social trends, will also affect you. These changes will influence your career choices and other financial decisions that you make. You will probably go through a series of career stages, such as those shown in **Figure 2.5,** and experience specific tasks and concerns with each one.

One way to make sure that your career develops in the right direction is to gain support from someone with more experience and knowledge. A **mentor** is an experienced employee who serves as a teacher and counselor for a less-experienced person. A mentor can give you one-on-one training and help you to meet other knowledgeable people. He or she can also provide you with emotional support during difficult times at work. Many organizations have formal mentoring programs. Some of the best mentors are retired people who are eager to share a lifetime of knowledge and experience.

In addition, you may know a small number of people who can provide opportunities and guidance on a personal basis. Mentors can be role models, or they can be professionals outside your career area who take an interest in your career. They can make suggestions, inform you of opportunities, introduce you to key people, and help guide you through your career. Besides mentors, you probably know other people, friends and/or family, who can serve as role models and supporters as you travel your career path.

One Life to Plan
Learn more about life planners and how you can apply what they do for people to your own life right now.

 To continue with Task 3 of your Web-Quest project, visit **persfinance07.glencoe.com**.

Changing Careers

Most workers change jobs several times over the course of their lives. Some seek a better position within the same field. Others move to new careers. There are various signs that it is time to move on:

- You feel bored or depressed at work.
- Your job adversely affects you physically or emotionally.
- You receive a series of poor performance evaluations.
- You have little opportunity to obtain a raise or promotion.
- You have a poor relationship with your supervisor or coworkers.

At some point you may find yourself out of a job through no fault of your own. This situation can cause emotional and financial stress. While you are looking for another job, continue to eat, sleep, and exercise as usual. Stay involved in family and community activities. You may find new career contacts anywhere. Improve your skills through personal study, classes, or volunteer work. Think about opportunities with nonprofit or government organizations.

Whether looking for a new job or your first job, always consider how the financial and personal costs and benefits of your career choice will affect your needs and goals.

After You Read

REACT

Do you think the skills needed to embark on a career are the same as those needed to simply get a job? How are they the same? How are they different?

Section 2.2 Assessment

QUICK CHECK

1. What are three ways through which you might obtain employment experience?
2. What factors will affect your salary?
3. What are two methods that you might use to grow and develop your career?

THINK CRITICALLY

4. Compare the advantages and disadvantages of using the career information sources discussed in this section.

USE MATH SKILLS

5. **Employee Benefits** Gustavo has received a promising job offer from XYZ Company. He would earn $25,000 a year. In addition, he would receive two weeks of paid vacation, five paid personal days, and five sick days. He would also receive a free health insurance plan that has an equivalent market value of approximately $5,000.

Calculate If you consider the dollar value of employee benefits, how much will Gustavo's employment package be worth if he accepts this job offer?

SOLVE MONEY PROBLEMS

6. **Measuring Employee Benefits** Suzanne is a single mother who works full time and pays a sitter to take care of her two children. She recently moved to another state and found a new job. The company offers a variety of employee benefit plans. Suzanne needs to determine which benefits will be best for her family.

Write About It Based on the information in the section on measuring employee benefits, what possibilities might Suzanne have? What will she have to consider in making her decision? Write a one-page report to help Suzanne make her decision.

CHAPTER SUMMARY

- Personal issues to consider when choosing a career include your aptitudes, interests, personality, and current personal situation.
- The more education and training you have, the greater your potential earning power will be. Also, the field of study you select will affect your salary.
- Employment opportunities are affected by social influences, such as demographic trends, geographic trends, and economic factors, as well as industry and technology trends.
- Gain experience through part-time work, volunteer work, internships, cooperative education, and class projects.

- To evaluate career opportunities, use sources such as the Internet, libraries, newspapers, school guidance offices, community organizations, and networking with people working in the field you choose.
- Financial issues to consider when looking for employment are your starting salary, opportunities for promotions and raises, benefits, and the cost of living. Legal issues to consider relate to the work environment of the company, its adherence to laws regarding discrimination, minimum wage unemployment insurance, Social Security, and workers' compensation.

Communicating Key Terms

Using 8 to 12 of the terms below, write an article for a class or school newspaper on the primary influences that will affect your personal career choice.

- job
- career
- standard of living
- trends
- potential earning power
- aptitudes
- interest inventories

- demographic trends
- geographic trends
- service industries
- internship
- cooperative education
- networking
- informational interview

- résumé
- cover letter
- cafeteria-style employee benefits
- pension plan
- mentor

Reviewing Key Concepts

1. **List** some of the personal issues you will need to consider when planning your career.
2. **Describe** factors that affect your potential earning power.
3. **Explain** how current demographic trends might influence your choice of career.
4. **List** some ways you might obtain job-related experience.
5. **Identify** sources of information to find out more about the career in which you are interested.
6. **Explain** your rights as an employee.

Language Arts   Review the information about the factors involved in choosing a career. Choose a career you would be interested in pursuing.

Write About It   Write a short essay about why you chose this career. Be sure to discuss some of the personal issues that influenced you.

Cost of Living   Use an Internet search engine to find a Web site that compares the cost of living in cities in the United States. If you were offered a salary of $35,000 in Columbus, Ohio, what salary would you need to maintain the same standard of living in Chicago, Illinois? In Richmond, Virginia? In San Diego, California?

1. **Analyze and Calculate**   (a) What are the differences among the cities in percent increases and decreases? (b) Use the cost of living information and real estate Web sites to find out the reason for the difference in costs of housing, insurance, and utilities.
2. **Compute** by using spreadsheet software to calculate and compare the proportional differences in costs of living among the cities.

Connect with Communication Skills   You are applying for summer jobs. Look through the sources described in this chapter and prepare a list of employers to whom you will submit your résumé and cover letter.

1. **Write About It**   For each job, prepare a résumé and cover letter. Next, work with a partner to role-play an interview. Interview each other using the résumés and cover letters as a basis.
2. **Think Critically**   How will you change your résumé and cover letter to emphasize your specific skills?

Career Information Updates   Forecasts about careers with the greatest potential can help you narrow your choices.

@ Log On   Go to persfinance07.glencoe.com for a link to a Web site for nationwide career information developed by the U.S. Department of Labor. Click on Résumé Tutorial to find directions about what to include in your résumé. Answer the following questions:

1. What are most employers looking for when they read your résumé?
2. What can you do to make your résumé stand out from other résumés?

Newsclip: Career Edge   Students who develop strong job-search skills have a career advantage. They develop clear career direction. They also communicate and promote their competitive edge to employers.

@ Log On   Go to persfinance07.glencoe.com and open Chapter 2. Learn more about career strategies. Write a paragraph about how you can boost your chances of getting hired.

FIND YOUR PERSONALITY TRAITS

Learning more about your own personality will help you choose the best career for you. Read the characteristics below that describe people's personalities. On a separate piece of paper, write down the five traits that best describe you, then answer the question that follows the list of characteristics.

Personality Traits

outgoing	ambitious	patient
studious	kind	thoughtful
neat	strong	intelligent
quiet	trustworthy	respectful
playful	warm	happy
energetic	persistent	spontaneous
serious	organized	worried
easygoing	rebellious	sensitive
caring	stubborn	sociable
loyal	responsible	creative
confident	fair	talkative
cheerful	calm	inquisitive
dependable	brave	funny
generous	helpful	athletic
shy	imaginative	competitive

Activity

Keeping in mind the five traits that best describe your personality, what kind of work do you think would suit you? For example, if you are persistent, outgoing, assertive, energetic, and confident you might enjoy working in sales. If you are creative, imaginative, inquisitive, and intelligent you might enjoy a career in writing. List the jobs or careers that you think fit best with your personality.

Your Financial Portfolio

Applying for a Job

Mark Cortez was interested in working at his neighborhood grocery store as a clerk. He wanted to work part-time after school and on weekends to earn money for his personal expenses. He filled out the application at the store and was called back for an interview. Mark interviewed with the store manager and got the job.

Complete

Before you interview for a job, you will probably have to fill out an application. Take time to practice "the art" of completing application forms. Always fill out a job application as neatly and accurately as possible. Write "N/A" in any blank for which an answer is not required. N/A means "Not Applicable" and tells the employer that you saw the question, but it does not apply to you. Fill out the application on a separate sheet of paper, being sure to fill it out completely. Use a pencil before you complete the application in ink, or use a rough copy. Were there any questions that you could not answer? If so, list those questions and see if you can find answers to them elsewhere.

Analyze

What would a neatly prepared application tell a prospective employer about you?

APPLICATION FOR EMPLOYMENT
SUPERIOR MARKETS

DIRECTIONS: Please use a pen and print. Answer all sections completely and accurately.

NAME			SOCIAL SECURITY NUMBER
LAST Cortez	FIRST Mark	MIDDLE A.	032 – XX – XXXX

HOME ADDRESS

NUMBER 134	STREET North Avenue	CITY Indianapolis	STATE IN	ZIP 46268

TELEPHONE # (317) 555-2492	ALTERNATE #

POSITION APPLIED FOR	SPECIFY DAYS AND HOURS AVAILABLE	PAY DESIRED
Clerk	evenings and weekends	negotiable

EDUCATION

	NAME AND ADDRESS OF SCHOOL	COURSE	DATE LEFT
MIDDLE SCHOOL	Valley Middle School Indianapolis, IN 46266	N/A	June 6, 20--
HIGH SCHOOL	Northwest High School Indianapolis, IN 46244	N/A	N/A
VOCATIONAL SCHOOL	N/A	N/A	N/A
COLLEGE OR UNIVERSITY	N/A	N/A	N/A
OTHER	N/A	N/A	N/A

LAST EMPLOYMENT

NAME OF COMPANY	ADDRESS	SUPERVISOR	JOB	PAY
Cameron's Business Supply	1217 Sheldon Ave Indianapolis, IN 46244	Jill Lambert	Clerk	$6.50/hr

DATE BEGAN	DATE LEFT	REASON FOR LEAVING
June 20--	September 20--	Summer position only

Additional qualifications applicant has to offer for consideration. These may include job-related interests, experiences, or volunteer activities.
Volunteer one night a week to help deliver meals-on-wheels, on weight-lifting team, and run track at school.

The facts set forth on my application are true and complete.

DATE October 8, 20-- SIGNATURE *Mark A. Cortez*

CHAPTER 3
Money Management Strategy

 What You'll Learn

When you have completed this chapter, you will be able to:

Section 3.1
- Discuss the relationship between opportunity costs and money management.
- Explain the benefits of keeping financial records and documents.
- Describe a system to maintain personal financial documents.

Section 3.2
- Describe a personal balance sheet and cash flow statement.
- Develop a personal balance sheet and cash flow statement.

Section 3.3
- Identify the steps of creating a personal budget.
- Discuss the advantage of increasing your savings.

Reading Strategies

To get the most out of your reading:

Predict what you will learn in this chapter.

Relate what you read to your own life.

Question what you are reading to be sure you understand.

React to what you have read.

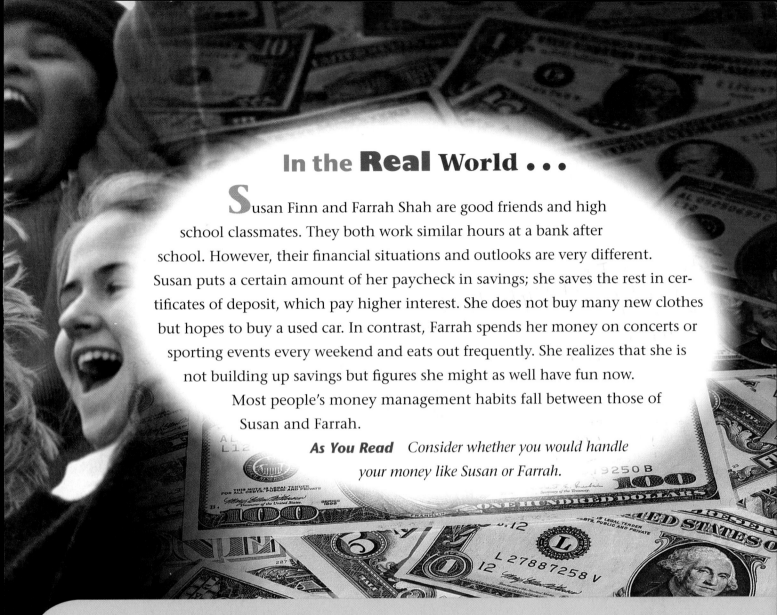

In the **Real** World . . .

Susan Finn and Farrah Shah are good friends and high school classmates. They both work similar hours at a bank after school. However, their financial situations and outlooks are very different. Susan puts a certain amount of her paycheck in savings; she saves the rest in certificates of deposit, which pay higher interest. She does not buy many new clothes but hopes to buy a used car. In contrast, Farrah spends her money on concerts or sporting events every weekend and eats out frequently. She realizes that she is not building up savings but figures she might as well have fun now.

Most people's money management habits fall between those of Susan and Farrah.

As You Read *Consider whether you would handle your money like Susan or Farrah.*

ASK STANDARD &POOR'S

Money When You Need It

Q: Do I need an emergency fund even though I work part time, live at home, and have no bills?

A: There is no guarantee that your job will always be there for you. If you become sick or injured, you may have to take time off from work. Even if you have disability insurance, it may pay only a fraction of what you earn. If you own a car, you may have unexpected repair bills. Emergency funds are for those unexpected things.

Ask Yourself How much of your monthly income do you think you should put into your emergency fund?

 Go to **persfinance07.glencoe.com** to complete the Standard & Poor's Financial Focus activity.

Organizing Financial Records

Focus on Reading

Read to Learn
- How to discuss the relationship between opportunity costs and money management.
- How to explain the benefits of keeping financial records and documents.
- How to describe a system to maintain personal financial documents.

Main Idea
Organizing your personal financial records can help you make informed decisions about your spending.

Key Terms
- money management
- safe-deposit box

Before You Read
PREDICT

Do you think it is necessary to keep organized copies of your financial records? Why or why not?

Opportunity Costs and Money Management

How do opportunity costs affect managing your money?

Every time you make a decision, you choose one thing and reject another. This is true no matter how major or minor the decision may be. Perhaps you decide to go to the movies instead of reading a book for your English homework assignment. On a Saturday afternoon, you may choose to play with the neighbor's dog instead of watching television or playing with your Xbox. Every decision you make represents a trade-off, or opportunity cost.

Trade-offs are especially common when it comes to making decisions about money management. **Money management** is planning how to get the most from your money. Good money management can help you keep track of where your money goes so that you can make it go farther. In order to manage your money well, you probably consider financial trade-offs. For example, you may consider whether you should spend your paycheck on clothes or put some of it in the bank to earn interest. You might also wonder if you should shop around for a CD or MP3 player at a lower price or if doing that is a waste of time.

Trade-offs can be very hard to resolve because you might think of good reasons for making either choice. In the first example, the first option would increase the amount you can spend now. However, depositing some money would contribute to your long-term financial security. In the second example, you might be able to save some money by checking prices at other stores downtown or at a different mall, but you would also be using up something you can never replace—your time.

How can you be sure of making the right decisions when you are faced with tough opportunity costs? You may never be sure, but you can become a better judge of your options. Consider the factors that influence your decision making by compiling a mental list of your options. Then consider how those options fit your values, your current financial situation, and your goal of effective money management.

By considering your values, your goals, and the state of your bank account, you can make better spending decisions. For example, if your goal is to save as much money as you can for college, then you might borrow a book from a library rather than buy it from a bookstore. On the other hand, if your goal is to put aside only a certain amount of your paycheck each month, you might be able to buy the book with the money you have left.

As You Read

RELATE

Have you ever wondered what happened to a sum of money you had? Explain the circumstances.

Benefits of Organizing Your Financial Documents

Why is it important to have a system to organize your financial documents?

The first step in effective money management is to organize your personal financial documents. The category of "personal financial documents" includes a variety of materials, such as bank statements and paycheck stubs. (The receipt for the shirt you bought is also a document.) These documents tell you how much money you have.

Personal financial documents also include records that are not directly related to your day-to-day use of money. Automobile ownership titles, birth certificates, and tax forms are personal financial documents. Together, these records present a clear picture of your finances.

Creating an organized system for handling your personal financial documents has several advantages. Most obviously, a system helps you quickly find any document you may need in a hurry. Organizing your documents also helps you:

- Plan and measure your financial progress.
- Handle routine money matters, such as paying bills on time.
- Determine how much money you will have now and in the future.
- Make effective decisions about how to save money.

Where to Keep Your Financial Documents

Why should you keep your financial documents in a specific place?

You can keep your financial documents in different places—in a home file, in a safe-deposit box, or on a computer. See **Figure 3.1** on page 62 for a list of the types of financial documents you might keep in these places. To organize your documents as effectively as possible, you may want to use all three. Each method has advantages and disadvantages, depending on the types of documents being kept.

▼ **HALF OFF** Some people like to wait until an item they want goes on sale before they buy it. *When might this be a wise money management strategy? When might it make more sense to go ahead and buy the item, even if it is not on sale?*

Figure 3.1   Where to Keep Your Financial Records

Home File

1. Personal and Employment Records (Social Security number, employee benefit information, current résumé)

2. Money Management Records (current budget, balance sheet, cash flow statement, list of financial goals, copies of documents in safe-deposit box)

3. Financial Services Records (checkbook, canceled checks, bank statements, location and number of safe-deposit box)

4. Tax Records (W-2 forms, paycheck stubs, copies of income tax returns)

5. Consumer Records (receipts for major purchases, automobile service and repair records, owner's manuals for cars and major appliances, warranties)

6. Housing Records (lease, if renting; property tax records; home repair and improvement receipts)

7. Insurance Records (original insurance policies; list of insurance premium amounts and due dates; medical information, such as health history, prescription drug information)

8. Investment Records (records of stock, bond, and mutual fund purchases and sales, list of investment certificate numbers, brokerage statements, dividend records)

9. Estate Planning and Retirement Records (will, pension plan information, IRA statements, Social Security information)

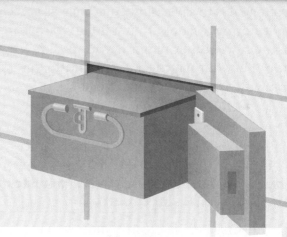

Safe-Deposit Box

Birth certificates, mortgage loan papers, title deeds, copy of will, certificates of deposit, checking and savings account numbers, automobile title(s), insurance policy numbers, valuable collectibles

Home Computer

Current and past budgets, summaries of checks written and other banking transactions, tax records, résumé

Safe and Sound   A home file, safe-deposit box, or personal computer will enable you to organize your financial documents.

Name at least three personal financial documents that you might store in a home file.

Home Files

A home file is one place to keep financial documents. This type of file is simple to set up and does not take up much space. You can use a file drawer, several folders, or even a cardboard box. Whatever method you use, your home file should be simple so that you have quick access to your documents.

You may already have the beginnings of a home filing system. For example, you may have been keeping a savings account passbook in the back of a bureau drawer since you were ten years old, or maybe you have an accordion file folder where you store all your receipts. To make good use of a home filing system, sort through all your personal financial records and arrange them according to the type of each document. Next, label all folders or boxes. Train yourself to file your receipts and other financial papers as soon as possible after receiving them.

What types of financial documents should you keep in a home file? If you have a checking account, keep your bank statements so that you can determine how much money you have in your account or verify your checkbook against the statements. However, do not keep hard-to-replace documents, such as a car title or paperwork related to a mortgage loan, in a home file. A cardboard box does not protect against fire, water, or theft.

Safe-Deposit Boxes

You should keep important documents such as car titles and mortgage loan papers locked away in a **safe-deposit box**—a small, secure storage compartment that you can rent in a bank, usually for $100 a year or less. Other items commonly kept in safe-deposit boxes include rental agreements, birth certificates, adoption papers, a list of insurance policies, stock certificates, and valuable collectibles, such as coins or stamps.

Safe-deposit boxes are usually kept in a locked, fireproof room that is accessible only while the bank is open for business. Each box has two individual locks. You, the holder of the box, have one key; the bank keeps the other key. The box can be opened only when both keys are used together.

Safe-deposit boxes offer more security for your valuables than your home file because at a bank loss from fire and other disasters is extremely rare. Moreover, the financial institution that owns the box usually (though not always) has insurance to cover such losses. Nevertheless, it is probably a wise idea to keep copies at home of all the financial records in your safe-deposit box.

As an alternative, some people use home fire-safe boxes that lock. These "safes" are an inexpensive way to protect against loss due to fire but not due to theft.

As You Read

QUESTION

Why might it be necessary to have easy access to auto repair records, bank statements, and receipts for purchases such as clothes or video games?

TechByte

Net Worth Calculator
Your net worth is the difference between your assets (the things you own that have value) and your liabilities (short-term and long-term debts you are working to pay off). Figuring out your net worth from time to time will help you evaluate the progress you are making toward your financial goals.

 Calculate your net worth through **persfinance07.glencoe.com**.

Home Computers

Rental agreements and canceled checks cannot be stored on a home computer. However, if you have a personal computer, it can be a great place to keep certain types of financial records. It is also a good tool to use for planning your financial future.

You can use a software program specifically designed to keep a running summary of checks you have written. You enter any checks, and the program automatically calculates the new balance in your account. Some programs also facilitate payments online. By tracking your monthly spending on a computer, you can see at a glance how much money you are spending, and you can easily compare your expenses from one month to the next. You can also generate personal financial documents and statements from the information you have organized by using software.

Section 3.1 Assessment

QUICK CHECK

1. How will organizing your financial documents help you manage your money?
2. What steps would you take to create a home filing system?
3. What are the advantages of using a safe-deposit box to store your personal financial documents?

THINK CRITICALLY

4. List three examples of money-related opportunity costs you have faced in the last two months. Write a sentence explaining what decision you made for each one and why.

USE COMMUNICATION SKILLS

5. **Organizing Financial Records** To become a member of an Internet DVD library, Maritza has to put down a deposit of $100, using her credit card. When and if Maritza chooses to discontinue her membership, the library will refund her deposit only if she has returned all her rented DVDs, has paid the annual membership fee, and has presented her membership agreement.

Write About It Write a list of some places Maritza might store the agreement to ensure her claim to the deposit.

SOLVE MONEY PROBLEMS

6. **Financial Documents** Martin is sitting in his bedroom surrounded by dozens of papers—gas receipts for his car, a checkbook, a couple of unopened and unpaid bills, paycheck stubs from his work at a day-care center, and much more. He wants to organize his financial documents in a shoebox, but he is completely overwhelmed by the amount of paper.

Analyze Help Martin prioritize this job. Give him some suggestions about breaking it down into parts, starting with the most important tasks. For example, tell Martin to begin by categorizing his documents by the type of each document.

Section 3.2

Personal Financial Statements

Personal Balance Sheet

How can a personal balance sheet help you find out your current worth?

Most of the documents mentioned in the previous section are issued by banks, federal and state governments, and businesses. However, such documents reveal only part of your financial picture. For a complete look at your financial situation, you should create a personal balance sheet and a cash flow statement. These reports are known as personal financial statements. A **personal financial statement** is a document that provides information about an individual's current financial position and presents a summary of income and spending.

Personal financial statements can help you:

- Determine what you own and what you owe.
- Measure your progress toward your financial goals.
- Track your financial activities.
- Organize information that you can use when you file your tax return or apply for credit.

To evaluate your financial situation, you first need to create a balance sheet. A **personal balance sheet**, also called a net worth statement, is a financial statement that lists items of value owned, debts owed, and a person's net worth. Your **net worth** is the difference between the amount that you own and the debts that you owe. Net worth is a measure of your current financial position. To create a personal balance sheet, follow these steps. **Figure 3.2** on page 66 shows an example of a personal balance sheet.

STEP 1: Determine Your Assets

Assets are any items of value that an individual or company owns, including cash, property, personal possessions, and investments. To determine your assets, you need to consider four categories of wealth. **Wealth** is an abundance of valuable material possessions or resources. The categories include: liquid assets, real estate, personal possessions, and investment assets.

Focus on Reading

Read to Learn
- How to describe a personal balance sheet and cash flow statement.
- How to develop a personal balance sheet and cash flow statement.

Main Idea

A personal balance sheet and cash flow statement can help you to analyze your financial situation.

Key Terms
- personal financial statement
- personal balance sheet
- net worth
- assets
- wealth
- liquid assets
- real estate
- market value
- liabilities
- insolvency
- cash flow
- income
- take-home pay
- discretionary income
- surplus
- deficit

Before You Read

PREDICT

What information do you think might be on a cash flow statement?

Figure 3.2   **A Personal Balance Sheet**

Melinda and Carroll Durbin
Personal Balance Sheet as of October 31, 20--

Assets		
Liquid Assets		
Checking account balance	$1,450	
Savings account balance	550	
Total liquid assets		$2,000
Real Estate		
Market value of house		105,000
Personal Possessions		
Market value of car	$4,250	
Furniture and appliances	2,500	
Electronic equipment	2,000	
Collectibles	750	
Total personal possessions		9,500
Investment Assets		
Retirement accounts	$15,000	
Stock investments	3,300	
Total investment assets		18,300
Total Assets		$134,800
Liabilities		
Current Liabilities		
Medical bills	$1,250	
Credit card balances	2,300	
Total current liabilities		$3,550
Long-Term Liabilities		
Mortgage	$92,500	
Student loan	3,500	
Car loan	2,500	
Total long-term liabilities		98,500
Total Liabilities		$102,050
Net Worth (assets minus liabilities)		$32,750

True or False?   The Durbins' personal balance sheet indicates that they have a positive net worth of $32,750.

Does this net worth figure reflect their true financial situation? Explain your answer.

Liquid Assets   The first category is called liquid assets. **Liquid assets** are cash and items that can be quickly converted to cash. The money in your savings and checking accounts is a liquid asset. For example, if Bharat has $500 in his savings account and $35 in cash, his liquid assets are worth $535 ($500 + $35 = $535). This money is immediately available for Bharat to spend. He may be able to convert other assets into cash, but the process is not quite as easy or as fast.

Real Estate   The second category of wealth is **real estate**, land and any structures that are on it, such as a house or any other building that a person or family owns. The amount recorded on the real estate portion of your balance sheet is the property's **market value**, or the price at which property would sell. Suppose that the Louis family owns a house and a cottage with market values at $135,000 and $84,000, respectively. They would list the sum of those figures—$219,000—under the heading "Real Estate" on their balance sheet.

▼ PLAY TIME Many people save favorite toys or other items from childhood. *Which items do you have that might be valuable? How can you find out?*

Personal Possessions Personal possessions—cars and any other valuable belongings that are not real estate—make up the third category. For example, Joyce might choose to list her new $800 electric guitar, her television, her skis, and several pieces of fine jewelry. Note that the emphasis is on "valuable"; old clothes and used CDs do not count.

You may list personal possessions on the balance sheet at their original cost, but you will get a better idea of your financial situation by recording their current market value. For example, Joyce's television is worth less now than it was when she purchased it five years ago. In contrast, collectible items, such as old baseball cards and comic books, may increase in value over time. Although determining current values for some items may be difficult, doing so will give you a more accurate picture of your net worth. You may have to look up comparable items in newspaper classified ads or visit thrift stores. You can also check Web sites where people buy and sell such items.

NET WORTH

Synopsis: Calculating your net worth will help you get an accurate measure of your current financial situation.

Example: What is Janine's net worth if her assets are worth $3,000 and her liabilities total $700?

Formula: Assets − Liabilities = Net Worth

Solution: $3,000 − $700 = $2,300

Janine's net worth is $2,300.

YOU FIGURE

You own a bike that is worth $250, a watch that is worth $60, and a stereo that is worth $400. You owe your older brother $70 for some concert tickets he bought for you, and you owe $120 to a department store. What is your net worth?

Investment Assets The fourth category of wealth is investment assets. Investment assets include retirement accounts and securities such as stocks and bonds. Set aside such assets for long-term financial needs, such as paying for college, buying a house, or retirement.

STEP 2: Determine Your Liabilities

When you prepare a personal balance sheet, you must also record your **liabilities**, or the debts that you owe. Suppose that Marlene borrows $200 from her mother to buy a new printer for her computer. She would record the printer as an asset, but she would also have to record $200 as a liability on her personal balance sheet.

Current Liabilities Current liabilities are short-term debts that have to be paid within one year. Most medical bills, cash loans, and taxes fall under this heading.

Long-Term Liabilities Long-term liabilities are debts that do not have to be fully repaid for at least a year. Car loans, student loans, and mortgage loans are examples of long-term liabilities. Note that the term "liabilities" includes only money that you will owe for longer than a month. For example, a telephone bill does not qualify as a liability.

STEP 3: Calculate Your Net Worth

Once you know the amounts of your assets and liabilities, you can calculate your net worth. To determine your net worth, subtract your liabilities from your assets; the difference is your net worth.

It is important to understand the meaning of net worth. If the Romano family has a net worth of $62,300, that does not mean they have $62,300 to spend. Much of their wealth may be in stocks, real estate, and personal possessions, which cannot be easily converted to cash. Net worth is only an indication of your general financial situation.

As You Read

RELATE

Using the formula in the Go Figure box, calculate your net worth.

Although you may have a high net worth, you can still have trouble paying your bills. This is especially true when most of your assets are not liquid and you do not have enough cash to meet your expenses. That can happen if you purchase a more expensive car than you can afford or spend all of your savings to buy a house.

If you are unable to pay all your debts, you may experience insolvency. **Insolvency** is a financial state that occurs if liabilities are greater than assets. Suppose that Brad owes $4,000 and that his assets—a ten-year-old car and an old computer—are worth $1,800. Even if Brad sold all his assets and put his whole $1,500 paycheck toward paying his debts, he would still be insolvent.

STEP 4: Evaluate Your Financial Situation

You can use a balance sheet to track your financial progress. Update your balance sheet, or make a new one, every few months to chart changes over time. Is your net worth increasing? Good! Keep doing what you are doing to make that happen. Is it decreasing or just holding steady? Then you might make changes. As a rule, you can increase your net worth by increasing your savings, increasing your investments, reducing your expenses, and/or reducing your debts.

Careers in Finance

FINANCIAL ADVISOR **Elaine Hawkins**
AXA Financial, Inc.

Elaine has always been good at coming up with solutions to difficult or complicated problems, so handling finances comes naturally to her. In her capacity as a financial advisor, Elaine visits with a wide variety of clients and helps them understand their financial needs. She also helps them create a plan for reaching their goals through financial planning, investment services, and risk management. At a time when people are unsure of the soundness of Social Security and may be financially unprepared for retirement, Elaine is able to provide them with options and comfort. Elaine gains work through word of mouth and enjoys building and assisting a network of friends and acquaintances.

SKILLS: Finance, math, communication, business, and problem-solving skills

PERSONAL TRAITS: Entrepreneurial, social, tactful, and goal oriented

EDUCATION: Bachelor's degree or higher in law, accounting, banking, or management; certification as a Certified Financial Planner or Chartered Financial Consultant

ANALYZE What are some financial goals that a financial advisor could help you reach?

@ To learn more about career paths for financial advisors, visit *persfinance07.glencoe.com.*

Cash Flow Statement: Income Versus Expenses

What kind of information do you get from creating a cash flow statement?

The money that actually goes into and out of your wallet and bank accounts is called **cash flow**. It is divided into two parts: cash inflow and cash outflow. Cash inflow is the money you receive, or your **income**. That may include a paycheck from a job, an allowance from your parents, or interest earned in your savings account. Cash outflow includes all of the money you spend.

A cash flow statement is simply a summary of your cash flow during a particular period, usually a month or a year. This summary gives you important information and feedback on your income and spending patterns. To create a cash flow statement, such as the one shown in **Figure 3.3,** follow these steps:

1. Record your income.
2. Record your expenses.
3. Determine your net cash flow.

Figure 3.3   Cash Flow Statement

Amy Grossman	Cash Flow Statement for Month Ending July 31, 20--
Income (Cash Inflow)	
Take-home pay	$450
Allowance	100
Savings account interest	12
Total income	$562
Expenses (Cash Outflow)	
Fixed expenses (cable TV, train commuter tickets, etc.)	$ 80
Variable expenses (recreation, clothing, take-out food)	320
Total expenses	$400
Net Cash Flow	$162

Money Supply   Amy's cash flow statement indicates that her net cash flow is $162.

How might she increase her net cash flow?

STEP 1: Record Your Income

List all of your sources of income during a given month, and record the amounts as your cash inflow. Make sure that you record the exact amount. Most paychecks include various deductions for federal and state taxes. These taxes are withheld from the total amount of money you have earned, or your gross pay. Your **take-home pay**, or net pay, is the amount of income left after taxes and other deductions are taken out of your gross pay. For example, Joshua earns $1,000 a month, but he does not receive the entire amount. After taxes, his take-home pay is $700. Your take-home pay plus your interest earnings on investments and savings is your cash *inflow*.

Some financial experts evaluate the strength of a person's income by measuring **discretionary income**—the money left over after paying for the essentials, such as food, clothing, shelter, transportation, and medication. You can spend this amount at your discretion, or according to your wants. The higher your discretionary income, the better off you are.

STEP 2: Record Your Expenses

Expenses can be fixed or variable. Fixed expenses are those that are more or less the same each month. Cable television charges, rent, and bus fare for commuting to work or school are all examples of fixed expenses. Variable expenses may change from month to month. Food and clothing are variable expenses. During some months you may need to buy new sweaters and pants, but during other months, you may not buy any clothing. Electricity, medical costs, and recreation are also examples of variable expenses. The total of your fixed and variable expenses is your cash *outflow*.

One Life to Plan
Learn about different kinds of investments that a financial planner would suggest for a young person planning for college and then beginning a career.

@ To continue with Task 4 of your WebQuest project, visit **persfinance07.glencoe.com**.

GO FIGURE — FINANCIAL MATH

NET CASH FLOW

Synopsis: Computing your net cash flow will help you determine your financial health.

Example: What is Jason's net cash flow if his income for the month is $1,500 and his expenses add up to $1,350?

Formula: Income − Expenses = Net Cash Flow

Solution: $1,500 − $1,350 = $150.

Jason has a positive net cash flow of $150.

YOU FIGURE

You work 12 hours a week, 3 weeks a month, at a part-time job after school. You get $8 an hour. You pay $40 a month for gas, $60 a month for entertainment (CDs, movies, etc.), and $25 a month toward paying off your new skis. What is your net cash flow?

STEP 3: Determine Your Net Cash Flow

You can determine your net cash flow by subtracting your expenses from your income.

Because Jason's net cash flow is positive, he has a **surplus**—extra money that can be spent or saved, depending on a person's financial goals and values. A cash surplus can be placed in an emergency fund savings account for unexpected expenses or to pay living costs if you do not receive a salary. You might also place cash surplus in savings and investment plans.

If Jason's net cash flow were negative, however, he would have a deficit. A **deficit** is the financial situation that occurs when more money is spent than is earned or received.

A current and accurate cash flow statement can provide the foundation for preparing and implementing your spending, savings, and investment plans.

Figure 3.4   Evaluating Your Financial Progress

Ratio	Calculation	Example	Meaning
Debt ratio	Liabilities divided by net worth	$25,000 ÷ $50,000 = 0.5	Compares your liabilities to your net worth. A low debt ratio is desirable.
Liquidity ratio	Liquid assets divided by monthly expenses	$10,000 ÷ $4,000 = 2.5	Indicates number of months you would be able to pay your living expenses in case of a financial emergency, such as the loss of your job. The higher the liquidity ratio, the better.
Debt-payments ratio	Monthly credit payments divided by take-home pay	$540 ÷ $3,600 = 0.15 = 15%	Indicates how much of a person's earnings goes to pay debts (excluding a home mortgage). Most financial experts recommend a debt-payments ratio of less than 20 percent.
Savings ratio	Amount saved each month divided by gross monthly income	$600 ÷ $5,000 = 0.12 = 12%	Most financial experts recommend a savings ratio of at least 10 percent.

Expert Advice   You can check your financial progress by figuring different ratios.

Suppose that you earned $2,200 gross monthly income and you were paid twice a month. What would be your savings ratio if you saved approximately $60 from each paycheck? Would you be saving enough?

Your Financial Position
How do you calculate your net worth by using personal financial statements?

When your net cash flow changes, so does your net worth. Every time you create a deficit by spending more than you earn, your net worth decreases. To make up for the deficit, you can either borrow money (increasing your liabilities) or draw from your savings (decreasing your assets). In either case, your net worth declines.

On the other hand, if you end a month with a surplus, your net worth will probably go up. You can choose to save the money, adding to your assets, or you can use it to pay off previous debts and reduce your liabilities. Whichever path you select, your net worth will increase. As a general rule, if you have a surplus cash flow, your net worth increases; if you have a deficit, your net worth decreases.

However, net worth does not give you a completely accurate picture of your finances. You can use your balance sheet and cash flow statement to determine your financial situation in other ways as well. See **Figure 3.4** for details.

Section 3.2 Assessment

QUICK CHECK

1. How do you calculate your net worth when preparing a balance sheet?
2. How should you record your income on a cash flow statement?
3. If your personal financial statements indicate that you have a deficit, what might you do to change your financial situation?

THINK CRITICALLY

4. List the three most valuable items that you own that would fall into the category of personal possessions.

USE MATH SKILLS

5. **Finding the Net** Tameka's income for the month of January was $2,375. Her fixed expenses during that same month were $750, and her variable expenses totaled $1,750.

Calculate What was Tameka's net cash flow during the month of January? Be sure to indicate whether she had a surplus or a deficit.

SOLVE MONEY PROBLEMS

6. **Spending Wisely** Larry's personal balance sheet shows $1,200 in credit card debts; a savings account of $550; and personal property amounting to $3,700 in rare stamps. Recently he was promoted at his part-time job. Because of that and because he made an effort to reduce his expenses, he had a positive cash flow of $600 last month. He asks what you think he should do with the surplus cash.

Present Evaluate Larry's possible choices and come up with a specific plan of action for his use of the surplus.

Budgeting for Financial Goals

Focus on Reading

Read to Learn
- How to identify the steps of creating a personal budget.
- How to discuss the advantage of increasing your savings.

Main Idea
Learn to budget and achieve financial goals by increasing your savings.

Key Terms
- budget
- consumer price index (CPI)
- budget variance

Before You Read

PREDICT

What is your definition of a budget, and what are the advantages of using one?

Preparing a Practical Budget

What is so important about having a budget?

A **budget** is a plan for using money to meet wants and needs. Having a budget is necessary for successful financial planning. By using a budget, you will learn how to live within your income and how to spend your money wisely. You will also develop good money management skills that will help you reach your financial goals.

STEP 1: Set Your Financial Goals

As discussed in Chapter 1, your financial goals are the things you want to accomplish with your money. What you do with your money today will affect your ability to achieve your financial goals in the future. To meet those financial goals, you will need to plan your savings, your spending, and your investments.

How should you set your financial goals? That depends on your lifestyle, your values, and your hopes for the future. The type of job you choose will determine your income and your ability to save to reach your financial goals. For example, perhaps you would like to get a pilot's license after you graduate from college. When setting your financial goals, you will need to take into account the cost of the lessons and the amount of time it will take to obtain the license.

It is important to make your financial goals as specific as possible. Having a definite time frame can also help you achieve your goals. You can separate your goals into short-term, intermediate, and long-term goals.

STEP 2: Estimate Your Income

When you have set your goals, you can begin working on a budget that is practical for you. Start by recording your estimated income for the next month. Include all sources of income that you know you will be receiving, such as your take-home pay and income on investments and savings. Do not include money you may or may not get, such as bonuses and gifts.

Estimating income is easier in some cases than in others. For example, because Ryan always works 12 hours each week, he gets paid the same amount every month. In contrast, Rachel works irregular hours at two part-time jobs. During some weeks, she earns only $75, but there are weeks when her earnings are more. Rachel should estimate her income based on her best guess about what will happen in the coming month. She might make her estimate a little lower than she thinks it will actually be. That will help her avoid overspending.

In another example, in **Figure 3.5** on page 76, the Thompsons have estimated that their income for next month will be $3,550. Estimate your income and record that amount, using a similar budget form. Remember that a budget should always be a written document.

STEP 3: Budget for Unexpected Expenses

The Thompsons have decided to put aside a little money each month for unexpected expenses and savings to reach their financial goals. Every month they place $100 in an emergency fund. One of their financial goals is to save three to six months' worth of living expenses in case someone in the family becomes unemployed, needs medical attention, or encounters some other financial problem. They keep their emergency fund in a separate savings account that will earn interest.

The Thompsons are also trying to meet three other financial goals, some short-term, others long-term. They deposit money in their vacation fund each month, hoping that they will soon have enough to take a trip to Jamaica. They also have a college fund for their young children and an investment fund to buy stocks. They put $150 into these other special savings accounts each month, bringing their total monthly savings to $250.

STEP 4: Budget for Fixed Expenses

The Thompsons then list all their monthly expenses. They start by listing their fixed expenses, or those that do not change from month to month. That includes their mortgage, automobile and student loan payments, and insurance premiums. Their budgeted total for fixed payments totals $1,200.

STEP 5: Budget for Variable Expenses

Planning for variable expenses—those that vary from month to month—is not as easy as budgeting for fixed expenses. Such items as medical costs are often unexpected. Heating and cooling costs can vary with the season. You should make your best guesses based on costs from previous months. When in doubt, guess high. The Thompsons budgeted $2,100 for these variable expenses.

Academic Connection

HISTORY

By 1865, approximately one-third of all circulating currency was counterfeit. As a result, the Department of the Treasury established the United States Secret Service in an effort to control counterfeiting. Just as it is important that the government manages the distribution of currency and tracks down counterfeiters, it is important that you properly manage your money. *Why is setting financial goals such an essential part of good money management?*

As You Read

RELATE

Do you think you should have an emergency fund? How large do you think your fund should be?

Figure 3.5 The Monthly Budget

Step 1:
Set Financial
Goals

Financial Goals: Pay off car loan, save for college, take vacation trip, and increase investments

Step 6:
Record What You Spend

	Budgeted Amounts	Actual Amounts	Variance
Step 2: Estimate Your Income			
Income:			
Salary and interest income	$3,550	$3,550	–
Outflows:			
Step 3: Budget for Unexpected Expenses and Savings			
Unexpected Expenses and Savings			
Emergency fund savings	100	100	–
Vacation savings	30	30	–
College savings	70	70	–
Investment savings	50	50	–
Total savings	250	250	–
Step 4: Budget for Fixed Expenses			
Fixed Expenses			
Mortgage	700	700	–
Automobile loan	200	200	–
Student loan	150	150	–
Insurance premiums	150	150	–
Total fixed expenses	1,200	1,200	–
Step 5: Budget for Variable Expenses			
Variable Expenses			
Food	500	600	−100
Clothing	250	250	–
Utilities	250	250	–
Entertainment	200	150	+50
Medical	250	250	–
Transportation	450	450	–
Personal allowances	200	225	−25
Total variable expenses	2,100	2,175	−75
Total outflow	**$3,550**	**$3,625**	**−$75**

Step 7:
Review Spending and Saving Patterns

Keeping Track You can use this sample monthly budget form to keep track of your own income and expenses so you can manage your finances and reach goals.

In this sample, how might the Thompsons' budget be affected if they had to buy a second automobile?

How can you determine reasonable expense levels? Financial experts publish guidelines that tell what percentage of income should go for various expenses. The U.S. Department of Labor produces the **consumer price index (CPI),** which is a measure of the changes in prices for commonly purchased goods and services in the United States. Comparing the CPI to your actual budget can indicate when you are spending too much on various items. A third source of information is your friends and relatives. If you eat out more often than your friends do or buy more clothes than your siblings buy, your budget may be in trouble.

STEP 6: Record What You Spend

Your budget is prepared, but your work is still incomplete. You must begin to keep track of your actual income and expenses. Remember, many budgeted items are only guesses. Your old car may continue to run through the month. However, maybe it will break down next week and need $400 worth of repairs. To find out how practical your budget is, you will need to keep track of your expenses during an entire month and then revise your budget if necessary.

In **Figure 3.5,** the Thompsons have used a second column to record the actual amounts they spent. Some of their expenses were what they had expected, and some were not. Your spending will not always work out as planned. The **budget variance** is the difference between the budgeted amount and the actual amount that you spend. This figure can be either a surplus or a deficit. It is a surplus if you spend less money than you had expected, and it is a deficit if you spend more. Budget variances can also occur in the income category. Earning more than you anticipated creates a surplus, whereas earning less results in a deficit.

Although the Thompsons have no budget variance on the income side, they have a surplus in their expense section. They spent $50 less than they had expected they would spend on entertainment. However, they spent more than they had budgeted in the other variable expense categories, creating a deficit in those categories. The overall result was a total monthly deficit of $75.

STEP 7: Review Spending and Saving Patterns

Budgeting is a continual process. You may need to review your budget each month and consider making changes based on the nature of your expenses.

Reviewing Financial Progress If you fall behind on bill payments, or if you are left with a lot of money at the end of the month, you may need to revise your budget. Even if your budget generally seems to be on target, it is a good idea to prepare an occasional budget summary to review your progress. (See **Figure 3.6** on page 78.)

As You Read

QUESTION

Prepare a written monthly budget according to Steps 1 to 7. How well does your budget match your financial goals?

Figure 3.6 **A Budget Summary**

You can prepare an annual budget summary to compare your actual spending with the amounts that you have budgeted. Completing an annual budget summary will be vital to both successful short-term money management and long-term financial security.

1 **Create** your own monthly budget document.

2 **Record** what you spend in each category of your budget during a period of several months.

3 **Highlight** areas where your spending consistently goes over your budget. Also highlight areas where you have spent less than you budgeted. This will help you identify the changes you need to make in your budget.

Revising Goals and Adjusting Your Budget If you always have deficits, ask yourself where you can cut your expenses. Review your spending patterns carefully to see where the shortfalls occur. Could you rent videos instead of going to the movie theater every week? Could you take a bag lunch to school instead of buying cafeteria food? Perhaps you do not really need a car to get around. Doing without it might sometimes be inconvenient, but it certainly would be cheaper.

To decide which expenses to cut, you might take another look at your financial goals. Which purchases fit into your overall plan for the future? The answer can help you in deciding what to cut. How quickly are you progressing toward your objectives? Are your goals changing or outdated? It may be necessary to revise your goals to meet your needs.

How to Budget Successfully
How can you plan a good budget?

Simply preparing a budget will not solve your financial problems, nor will keeping track of every expense down to the last penny. You have to follow a practical spending plan to make it work.

Money management experts agree that a budget should have several important characteristics:

1. **A good budget is carefully planned.** Your estimates cannot be wild guesses, and your spending categories must cover all expenses.
2. **A good budget is practical.** If your first full-time job pays you $1,500 a month, do not expect to buy an expensive sports car soon.
3. **A good budget is flexible.** As you experience changes in your life—marriage, children, or retirement—you will need to adapt your budget accordingly. You will also encounter unexpected expenses and unexpected shifts in income. Your budget should be easy to revise when life changes such as these occur.
4. **A good budget must be written and easily accessible.** Use a notebook, folder, or computer to store your budget. Do not try to keep the information in your head or on loose scraps of paper. The odds are you will forget or lose the information.

Ways to Increase Your Savings
Why is it important to have a savings plan?

Increasing your savings is the key to establishing a sound financial future. The more you save, the better you will be able to handle unexpected emergencies and the sooner you will be able to meet your financial goals. If you save large amounts, it may be possible for you to retire comfortably and to send your children to college. Best of all, money that is saved earns interest income.

Put on Your Financial Planner's Cap

STANDARD &POOR'S

Your client has just started his first full-time job and needs to revise his budget to reflect the new income. What expense categories will you suggest to change?

However, learning to save is not easy. Many people are tempted to buy whatever they want, whenever they want it. Moreover, when income is low, saving anything at all can be especially hard. From 1996 to 2001, Americans saved an average of only 31 cents for every ten dollars they earned. Fortunately, you can improve your savings rate by using several savings strategies.

STANDARD &POOR'S

Global Financial Landscape

Standard and Poor's publishes the globally recognized S&P 500® financial index. It also gathers financial statistics, information, and news, and analyzes this data for international businesses, governments, and individuals to help them guide their financial decisions.

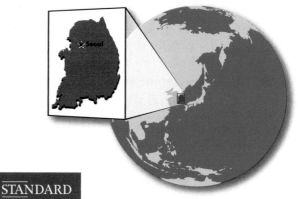

SOUTH KOREA

In the last half-century, South Korea has grown into one of the world's leading high-tech economies. This success is due in large part to the Korean peoples' willingness to spend great amounts of time and money on education. Fierce competition to attend the country's best colleges and universities has developed. As a result, there is an extremely high demand for private tutoring, "cram schools," pre-testing services for college entrance exams, and educational sites on the Internet. Children as young as two can receive 20 minutes of weekly instruction in Korean, English, and math. This type of extra schooling does not come cheap. In a single year, Koreans pay more than $25 billion for after-school instruction. Parents may spend as much as $36,000 on each child per year, as Koreans compete for a position in the global landscape.

STANDARD &POOR'S DATABYTES

Capital	Seoul
Population	47,939,000
Languages	Korean, English
Currency	South Korean won
Gross Domestic Product (GDP)	$855.3 billion (2003 est.)
GDP per capita	$17,700

Industry: Electronics, automobile production, chemicals, shipbuilding, steel, and textiles

Agriculture: Rice, root crops, barley, vegetables, cattle, and fish

Exports: Electronic products, machinery and equipment, motor vehicles, steel, ships, and textiles

Natural Resources: Coal, tungsten, graphite, and molybdenum

Think Globally

Why do you think education has been such an important part in South Korea's growth into a high-tech economic leader?

Learn to identify and understand the standard financial documents you will use in the real world.

Investigate: A Personal Balance Sheet
A personal balance sheet contains the following information:

- Your assets with a value for each
- Your liabilities with a value for each
- Amount of your net worth

Your Motive: A balance sheet shows your financial health at a given point in time. Updating your personal balance sheet from time to time will help you keep track of your financial situation.

Tanisha Brigg's Personal Balance Sheet

Assets	Amount
Cash/Checking & Savings	$3,000
Securities (stocks, bonds, etc.)	15,000
Real estate/home	125,000
Other real estate	0
Automobiles	18,000
Personal property	23,000
Personal loans	5,000
Insurance cash values	15,000
Total Assets	**$204,000**
Liabilities	
Loans	$3,500
Credit card debt	6,500
Current monthly bills	2,500
Mortgage	145,000
Unpaid taxes	4,500
Other debt	2,300
Total Liabilities	**$164,300**
NET WORTH	**$39,700**

Key Points: A balance sheet lists the items of value that you own, the debts that you owe, and your net worth. Personal financial statements such as a personal balance sheet can help you determine what you own and what you owe; measure your progress toward your financial goals; track your financial activities; and organize information for taxes and credit applications.

Find the Solutions

1. What are Tanisha's assets?
2. What are Tanisha's liabilities?
3. According to the balance sheet, what is Tanisha's current net worth?
4. Why might a bank be interested in a person's net worth?
5. How do you figure net worth?

▶ **SAVE** Bringing your lunch to school or work is one way to spend less money than you would by eating out. *On an average day, how much money do you spend on food? How might you save in this area?*

Pay or Save?
Be a smart consumer and pay off your credit card bills before you put money away in a savings account. The interest rate charged on credit cards is usually higher than the interest you can earn from your savings account. *How do you determine the interest rate on your credit card?*

Pay Yourself First

One method you can adopt is to set aside a fixed amount as savings before you sit down to pay your bills. For example, Tyronne considers his savings as a fixed expense. He writes himself a check for $75 before he pays his bills; then he sends the check for immediate deposit into his savings account. As an alternative to writing a check each month, many banks will automatically deduct a certain amount from your checking account each month and deposit that in your savings account. Tyronne has set a specific dollar amount, but you can also set aside a percentage of your monthly income.

Payroll Savings

Your employer may offer a similar option called a payroll savings deduction. A payroll savings deduction is a portion of your earnings that is automatically taken out of your paycheck and put into your savings or retirement account.

For example, Teresa has authorized her employer to deduct $50 from each paycheck. Although that arrangement reduces her take-home pay to $750, she knows she is on her way to meeting her financial goals.

Spending Less to Save

A third way to save is to start small. Make an effort to spend less each day. If you read a magazine in the library rather than buying it in a store, count out the purchase price of the magazine and place it in a jar. If you go to the $4.50 matinee movie instead of the $7.75 evening show, pat yourself on the back and pay the jar the $3.25 difference. Before long you will have enough cash to start a savings account or make a substantial deposit into an existing one.

How you save, though, is less important than the action of saving. The earlier you start, the better. Even small amounts of savings can grow quickly and help you reach your financial goals.

Section 3.3 Assessment

QUICK CHECK

1. What are some practical ways to budget for variable expenses?
2. If you continually experience budget deficits, how can you decide which expenses to cut?
3. What are three methods you might use to increase your savings?

THINK CRITICALLY

4. List three of your variable expenses. Estimate the amounts for each of these expenses for one month.

USE COMMUNICATION SKILLS

5. **No Cuts!** Tara complains that she cannot seem to get ahead financially. Every time she receives a paycheck, it seems to disappear. She also points out that all her expenses, such as her phone bill, car payment, and subscriptions to several magazines, are absolutely necessary.

Write About It Write a paragraph persuading Tara that cutting some of her expenses is not only possible but is also necessary if she wants to meet her financial goals.

SOLVE MONEY PROBLEMS

6. **Budgets** Hiroko earns $2,000 a month. Her monthly expenses are about $1,850, leaving $150 for savings. She now has $1,000 in her emergency savings account and another $300 in an account for a new computer. Hiroko has been offered a job that will pay her an extra $200 a month, but she will need to buy a car to travel to the new job.

Analyze What financial factors should Hiroko consider as she decides whether to accept the job?

CHAPTER SUMMARY

- There are opportunity costs, or trade-offs, in all decisions. When you make a decision about how to manage your money, you remove the option to use the money in a different way.
- Organizing your financial documents makes it easier to plan and measure progress, handle routine money matters, know how much money is available, and make effective decisions.
- You can organize financial documents in home files, a safe-deposit box, and on a computer.
- A personal balance sheet helps determine your net worth, so you can manage your money to meet your financial goals. A personal cash flow statement helps determine the amount of cash you receive and how you spend it.

- On a personal balance sheet, list the value of all your assets, along with all your liabilities. On a personal cash flow statement, record your income and expenses. Then subtract your expenses from your income to determine your net cash flow.
- To create a budget: (1) Set financial goals; (2) estimate your income; 3) budget for unexpected expenses and savings; 4) budget for fixed expenses; (5) budget for variable expenses; (6) record what you spend; and (7) review your spending and saving patterns.
- Savings are the key to a sound financial future. Savings enable you to handle unexpected emergencies.

Communicating Key Terms

Your best friend has asked you to explain how much he needs to save from each paycheck to buy a digital camera that costs $350. Use 8 to 12 of the terms below to write an explanation.

- money management
- safe-deposit box
- personal financial statement
- personal balance sheet
- net worth
- assets
- wealth
- liquid assets
- real estate
- market value
- liabilities
- insolvency
- cash flow
- income
- take-home pay
- discretionary income
- surplus
- deficit
- budget
- consumer price index (CPI)
- budget variance

Reviewing Key Concepts

1. **List** at least three examples from your own experience of opportunity costs.
2. **Explain** the benefits of keeping and organizing financial records and documents.
3. **Identify** documents to store in home files, safe-deposit boxes, or on a computer.
4. **Describe** what you learn from a balance sheet and personal cash flow statement.
5. **List** the steps in preparing a personal balance sheet and a personal cash flow statement.
6. **Identify** the steps in preparing a personal budget.
7. **Explain** how you can use your budget to identify ways to increase your savings.

ACADEMIC SKILLS

Social Studies Many people have difficulty saving money for a variety of reasons. Research some typical roadblocks to saving money.

Write About It Write a paragraph explaining at least three reasons and how you would counsel them if they asked you for help.

YOUR FINANCIAL FIGURES

Saving for a Club Trip The school Spanish Club is sponsoring a trip to Mexico that will cost $1,000 per student. Your parents will contribute $300, but you need to save the remaining $700 over the next four months. You currently work seven hours a week babysitting for $10 per hour. The following are your monthly expenses:

Variable Expenses (clothes, CDs, movie tickets, etc.) $180
Fixed Expenses (school fees, bus pass) $65

1. **Calculate** your total monthly earnings and expenses.
2. **Compute** by using spreadsheet software to calculate how much you need to earn and/or reduce your expenses to meet your goal.

REAL-WORLD Application

Connect with Mathematics You want to save $2,000 for college by working over the summer. You can find a job that will pay you for 40 hours per week at regular rates plus an average of 10 hours per week at overtime rates at 1.5 times. You can work for 10 weeks. You figure that you need $150 per week to pay miscellaneous variable expenses.

1. **Calculate** How much will you need to earn per hour to save at least $2,000 in addition to meeting your weekly expenses?
2. **Think Critically** Is $150 in weekly expenses a realistic estimate? What are you not including?

Internet CONNECTION

How Much Is Enough? You have started a job at an annual salary of $32,000. Your take-home pay is about 2/3 of your gross salary.

Log On Use an Internet search engine to find Web sites that discuss what proportion of your salary you should spend on fixed expenses. Answer the following questions:

1. What percentage of your take-home pay should be fixed expenses?
2. What percentage of your take-home pay should be discretionary income?

BusinessWeek ONLINE

Newsclip: Ways to Save Best-selling personal finance authors advise finding ways to save by cutting small luxuries and saving money from summer jobs.

Log On Go to persfinance07.glencoe.com and open Chapter 3. Read the article. Then make a record of expenses. Ask yourself: What are your spending and saving habits?

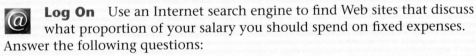

MONEY MANAGEMENT QUIZ

Imagine you were living on your own. How would you handle your money? On a separate sheet of paper, take this money management quiz.

1. I would create a budget for my income and expenses.
   a. Always
   b. Sometimes
   c. Never

2. I would pay the rent or mortgage payment and utility bills on time.
   a. Always
   b. Sometimes
   c. Never

3. I would keep three months of my living expenses in reserve for emergencies.
   a. Always
   b. Sometimes
   c. Never

4. I would save 10 percent of my take-home pay.
   a. Always
   b. Sometimes
   c. Never

5. I would set money aside for large expenses.
   a. Always
   b. Sometimes
   c. Never

6. I would save to buy what I want.
   a. Always
   b. Sometimes
   c. Never

7. I would use credit only when I have money to cover the charge.
   a. Always
   b. Sometimes
   c. Never

8. I would balance my checkbook every month.
   a. Always
   b. Sometimes
   c. Never

How did you score? Give yourself 2 points for each "Always," 1 point for each "Sometimes," and 0 points for each "Never."
If you scored 12–16, you are practicing good money management skills.
If you scored 6–11, with a little more effort you could improve your money management skills.
If you scored 0–5, it is time to start developing money management skills.

Your Financial Portfolio

What Is Your Net Worth?

Roberto plans to go to Europe next summer with the school band. He probably will be able to save enough money by working all year at his part-time job. However, he is prepared to sell some of his possessions if he needs to, so he made a list of his assets and liabilities to determine his net worth.

Roberto's Balance Sheet as of December 31, 20--	
Liquid Assets	
Checking account balance	$150
Savings accounts	635
Total liquid assets	$785
Personal Possessions	
Market value of automobile	$2,300
Stereo, TV, and video equipment	1,600
Computer	1,350
Watch	330
Total personal possessions	$5,580
Investment Assets	
Savings bonds	$ 600
Total investment assets	600
Total Assets	**$6,965**
Liabilities	
Balance due on car loan	$1,527
Total Liabilities	**$1,527**
Net Worth	**$5,438**

Calculate

Determine your net worth. In your workbook or on a separate sheet of paper, list your assets, personal possessions, and liabilities (what you owe). Are you surprised that your net worth is as much (or as little) as it is? How much would you like your net worth to be in ten years? When you retire?

Consumer Purchasing and Protection

$ What You'll Learn

When you have completed this chapter, you will be able to:

Section 4.1
- Determine the factors that influence buying decisions.
- Explain a research-based approach to buying goods and services.
- Identify strategies for making wise buying decisions.

Section 4.2
- Identify ways to solve consumer problems.
- Describe the legal alternatives for consumers.

Reading Strategies

To get the most out of your reading:

Predict what you will learn in this chapter.
Relate what you read to your own life.
Question what you are reading to be sure you understand.
React to what you have read.

In the **Real** World . . .

For more than a year, Carla Jackson has been saving money for a down payment to buy a car. Now that she has enough, she is not sure what to do. Used cars sold by private owners are the most affordable, but Carla would like to have a warranty. While auto dealers offer financing, they do not sell the model that she wants. Everyone seems to have a different opinion about where to buy a car, and Carla is unsure about what to believe. In addition, when she decides where to buy the car, Carla is faced with other dilemmas: How much money should she put down? If the car ends up being a "lemon," how can she protect her investment?

As You Read *Consider the safest strategy for a consumer who is making a major purchase and what protection he or she can expect.*

ASK STANDARD &POOR'S

Comparison Shopping

Q: I would like to purchase a new stereo. Is it really that important for me to comparison shop?

A: Prices and quality can be very different from one store to another. Particularly with expensive items, it is worthwhile to compare prices on similar items to see if one store has a lower price than the others. If you write down the manufacturer and style information, you can do a lot of this "legwork" by phone or by looking at store advertisements or by doing research on the Internet.

Ask Yourself What is the benefit of comparison shopping?

 Go to persfinance07.glencoe.com to complete the Standard & Poor's Financial Focus activity.

Focus on Reading

Read to Learn
- How to determine the factors that influence buying decisions.
- How to explain a research-based approach to buying goods and services.
- How to identify strategies for making wise buying decisions.

Main Idea
Understanding the factors that influence your buying decisions will help you get the best value for your money.

Key Terms
- down payment
- cooperative
- impulse buying
- open dating
- unit pricing
- rebate
- warranty
- service contract

Before You Read

PREDICT

How could learning about consumer purchasing benefit you now and in the future?

Consumer Purchasing

Factors That Influence Buying Decisions
What influences you to make a purchase?

You may enjoy shopping and do it often, or you might go to the mall only if you need to buy something. In either case, wise buying decisions will help you get the most out of the products you buy now and will enable you to meet your long-term financial goals. To get the most for your money, you need to recognize the factors that affect your buying habits. **Figure 4.1** shows some of the economic, social, and personal factors that influence the purchases you make.

The following example shows several of these factors at work. Jessica is thinking about buying a new backpack. Economic factors will play an important role in her decision. She will be more likely to spend her money on a backpack that is well made but not too expensive and can be repaired easily if it rips. Social factors may also affect Jessica's choice. She may be more likely to buy a certain brand if it is in style and if she could use it for her hobby, painting. In addition, personal factors may be at work. Jessica will have to determine how much of her income she can spend on the backpack.

Trade-Offs and Buying Decisions

To make the most of your buying power, consider trade-offs. Suppose that you buy a sound system with a credit card instead of waiting until you have saved enough money to pay cash for it. You get the pleasure of having the sound system now. However, you may pay a higher price in the long run because of fees and interest the credit card company charges for use of the card.

Perhaps you choose a jacket because it is the cheapest one available. Within a few days, you may discover that it is poorly made or difficult to repair. You may save time by ordering a sweater from a catalog or online. However, if you decide that you do not want it, you may have to pay postage to return it to the mail-order company. You might not get your money back for the initial shipping and handling charges. Keep in mind that buying decisions always involve trade-offs, so you will be prepared to make wise choices.

Researching Consumer Purchases

How do you research a product you want to buy?

As You Read

RELATE

What are the economic, social, and personal factors that would influence you if you were going to buy a car?

By taking time to do research and evaluating products you want to buy, you can get more value for your money. By following a research-based approach to buying goods and services, you can buy a high-priced item, such as a treadmill or a gym membership, more intelligently. In addition, you will gain useful practice in making ordinary purchasing decisions about low-cost items, such as toothpaste. A research-based approach to buying has four phases:

1. Before you shop
2. Weighing alternatives
3. Making the purchase
4. After the purchase

PHASE 1: Before You Shop

Before you can begin to construct the walls of a house, you need to lay its foundation. In the same way, before you begin to shop, you need to do some background work. A good start to successful shopping involves three steps: identifying your needs, gathering information, and becoming aware of the marketplace. Completing these steps will enable you to get what you really want.

Figure 4.1 **Influences on Consumer Buying Decisions**

Economic Factors	Social Factors	Personal Factors
• Prices • Interest rates • Product quality • Supply and demand • Convenience • Product safety • Brand name • Maintenance costs • Warranty	• Lifestyle • Interests • Hobbies • Friends • Culture • Advertisements • Media (magazines, radio, television, newspapers)	• Gender • Age • Occupation • Income • Education • Family size • Geographic region • Ethnic background • Religion

Making a Difference Economic, social, and personal factors influence consumer buying decisions.

How might a family's size and income affect the type of house the family buys?

Identify Your Needs   Suppose that your VeryKool jeans are worn out, and you would like to buy a new pair. You think that your problem is a "need for a new pair of VeryKool jeans," when the actual problem is a "need for new jeans." Some people always buy Brand A when Brand B sells for the same price. They may not even consider Brand C, which is cheaper than either A or B, and which also serves their needs. If you define your needs clearly, you will be more likely to make the best buying decisions.

Gather Information   For example, suppose that Sarah loses her watch on a white-water rafting trip. She might be able to borrow a watch from a friend for a day or two, but eventually she will need to buy a new watch. To begin her research, she should gather information on the different models and prices of watches.

Information for buying decisions usually falls into three categories: costs, options, and consequences. Sarah might ask questions related to cost, such as "What do watches cost at different stores?" Her options will depend on the brands that the manufacturers produce and on where those brands are available. Sarah will also have to consider consequences—how the purchase will affect her budget.

Figure 4.2   **Sources of Consumer Information**

You can gather information to help with purchasing decisions from a number of different sources. Make sure they are reliable, complete, relevant, and impartial.

2 **Ads and packaging** can tell you a lot about a product, so be sure to read the labels.

1 **People** you know might be able to provide insight on a product's performance, quality, and average price.

Some people do not spend enough time gathering and evaluating information. Others do so much research that they become confused and frustrated. Simple, routine purchases probably do not require much more research than your own experience can provide. For more expensive items, ask people you know for recommendations.

Other resources include product advertising and labeling, media sources, consumer publications, such as *Consumer Reports*, government agencies, or the Internet. **Figure 4.2** illustrates some of these resources. As you research and gather information, take notes on what you learn. Having a written record of the information you collect can be helpful in making comparisons later.

Be Aware of the Marketplace Knowledge is power. Research provides sources for the item you want to buy. In addition, you will be able to identify the brands and features from which you can choose, average prices for an item, and where you can obtain reliable information about similar products. Also, familiarize yourself with some common myths about sales, returns, and credits in **Figure 4.3** on page 94.

3 Reports issued by the media and independent testing organizations on the quality of products and services are usually valuable, easily available, and inexpensive.

4 Web sites for companies, magazines, newspapers, and government agencies have product information and shopping suggestions.

Figure 4.3 | **Common Consumer Myths**

The National Association of Consumer Agency Administrators recently identified a list of common consumer myths. These include:

"I can return my car within three days of purchase." While many people would say that this statement is true, there is no such time period.

"It says right here that I've won; it must be true." Fake prize notifications continue to become more convincing. Some consumers actually go to company offices to try to pick up their prizes.

"If I lose my credit cards, I'm liable for purchases." Federal laws limit charges on lost or stolen cards to $50. Most major credit card companies will not even charge you the $50 if you make a reasonable effort to notify the company quickly of lost or stolen cards.

"An auto lease is just like a rental; if I have problems with the car or problems paying, I can just bring it back." Most leases require payments for the duration of the contract. Early termination of the contract can often result in various additional charges.

"You can't repossess my car; it's on private property." While state laws vary, the general rule is that repossession cannot occur if it involves force or entry into a dwelling. However, vehicles in driveways and unlocked garages are usually fair game.

Source: "Ten Top Consumer Law 'Urban Myths,'" National Association of Consumer Agency Administrators, Two Brentwood Commons, Suite 150, 750 Old Hickory Blvd, TN 37207; (615) 371-6125 or 866-SAY-NACAA; Web site: www.nacaa.net.

Fact or Fiction? There are some typical myths that consumers believe about sales, returns, and credit.

How do such myths affect you as a consumer?

PHASE 2: Weighing the Alternatives

Every consumer decision may be approached in several effective ways. Instead of buying an item, for example, you might decide to rent it, borrow it, or do without it. You also have alternatives to spending cash for a product. You might take advantage of special deals that allow you to delay payment, or you might choose to pay with a credit card.

Identify What Is Important to You As you evaluate alternatives, decide which characteristics of the product—such as features, performance, or design—are important to you. As you research the available brands, you will recognize the characteristics that most closely match your needs. You can judge a potential purchase by considering the following factors:

- Your personal values
- Available time for research
- Amount of money you have to spend
- Convenience of buying the item immediately
- Pros and cons of a particular brand

For example, as Sarah considers the selection of watches in a department store, she decides that a light-up dial and an alarm are two features that she would use. In terms of performance, she prefers a model that can withstand rugged outdoor activities. She wants a watch that has big numbers and a stainless steel wristband.

Compare Prices The price of an item is an important consideration. Prices can vary for all types of products. For example, Sarah's watch may cost as little as $15 or as much as $500. Differences in price may be related to quality, but price does not always equal quality. When the quality and quantity are basically the same for an item such as aspirin, sugar, or salt, the lowest-priced item is probably the wisest choice.

When prices and quality vary, you have two options. If you can afford all choices, you can buy the highest-quality item. If you cannot afford all choices, you should consider buying the item that gives you the best value per dollar.

Do Comparison Shopping Comparison shopping means you compare prices and features of similar items at different stores. Many people consider comparison shopping a waste of time. However, it can be very useful under certain circumstances:

- You are buying complex or expensive items, such as a computer or a mountain bike.
- You are buying items you purchase often, such as shampoo or school supplies.
- You are using the Internet, print advertisements, or mail-order catalogs.
- Different sellers are offering different prices and services.
- Product quality or price varies greatly.

$avvy Saver

Shopping for Clothes

1. Look at the sale items first.
2. Choose clothes that you can mix and match or wear over several seasons.
3. Shop at outlet malls and discount stores, from sale catalogs, and on the Internet.
4. Wait for end-of-season clearance sales.
5. Buy only items you are sure you will wear.

▶ **BEST BUYS** Timing your purchases to get the best buys is not limited to clothes. *Why do you think that September, October, and November are the best months to buy apples?*

PHASE 3: Making the Purchase

After you have completed the research and evaluation process, some other activities and decisions may be appropriate. These include negotiating the price (if possible), deciding whether to use credit or cash, and determining the real price of the product.

Negotiate the Price   Certain purchases, such as real estate or cars, may involve price negotiation. To negotiate, research information about the product and the buying situation. Be sure that you are dealing with the person, such as the owner or store manager, who has authority to give you a lower price or additional features.

Decide on Credit or Cash   When making a purchase, you usually have two options—pay credit or cash. You need to consider the costs and benefits of each one.

Credit is an arrangement to buy something now and pay for it later. It is a type of loan. To repay the loan, you make monthly payments that often include additional fees or interest. The advantage of paying cash is that you do not have to pay these extra fees or make continuing payments. However, because the cash is no longer in your bank account, you lose the opportunity to earn interest on it. In addition, the money is no longer available for emergencies.

Before deciding to use credit, evaluate its costs, such as interest rates and fees. These costs will differ depending on various factors:

- Source of the loan (e.g., parents, bank, or credit card company)
- Type of credit account
- Payment period
- Amount of **down payment**—a portion of the total cost of an item that must be paid at the time of purchase

One Life to Plan
Learn about personal inventories and how you can use them to match yourself to the right job, which will be part of your financial plan.

@ To continue with Task 3 of your WebQuest project, visit persfinance07.glencoe.com.

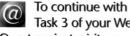

Know the Real Price Sometimes you may discover that what appears to be a bargain is not such a good deal after extra costs are added to the price. Stores may charge you a fee for installation or delivery. Find out exactly what the purchase price includes and get all costs and conditions in writing.

PHASE 4: After the Purchase

After making a purchase, you may have other costs or tasks. A car, for example, will require additional maintenance and ownership costs, such as gasoline and insurance. You may have to learn how to operate it correctly to improve its performance and to avoid major repairs. If your car requires repair service, you should follow a process similar to the one you used when you bought the car—investigate, evaluate, and negotiate a variety of servicing options.

In some cases, you may be dissatisfied with a purchase and want to return or replace it. When that happens, you need to know how to handle your complaints effectively. The next section of this chapter explains how to resolve consumer complaints.

Remember that the purchasing process is an ongoing activity. You should rethink and reevaluate your decisions. The information that you gather before you shop, along with your previous buying experiences, will help you make decisions in the future. Also, be sure to consider changes in your needs, lifestyle, values, goals, and financial resources.

Smart Buying Strategies

How can you make an informed purchase decision?

People have a variety of buying styles. For example, Gordon looks for ways to save on the brands he buys regularly. Anita and Roger buy the lowest-priced brands or look for bargains.

▶ SMART SHOPPING To get the best buys, do research about products and do comparison shopping. *What is comparison shopping?*

Whatever your style, several strategies can help you get the most value for your dollar—timing of purchases, store selection, brand comparison, information research, price comparison, and warranty evaluation.

Timing Purchases

You are more likely to find a bargain at certain times of the year. Stores traditionally offer reduced prices for seasonal clothing, such as swimsuits, overcoats, and other items, about midway through a particular season. You can also find reduced prices at back-to-school sales, spring sales, and other special sales. Timing your purchases to take advantage of sales can result in big savings.

The law of supply and demand can also affect the timing of purchases. For example, if you wait a few months before buying a popular new CD or DVD, the price may be lower than it was when it first came out because the demand for the item has decreased. When businesses want to reduce the supply of a product, they have clearance sales.

Figure 4.4 **Types of Retailers**

	Benefits	Limitations
Traditional Stores		
Department stores	• Wide variety of products grouped by department	• Possible inexperience or limited knowledge of sales staff
Specialty stores	• Wide selection of a specific product line; knowledgeable sales staff	• Prices generally higher; location and shopping hours may not be convenient
Discount stores	• Convenient parking; low prices	• Self-service format; minimal assistance from sales staff
Contemporary Retailers		
Convenience stores	• Convenient location; long hours; fast service	• Prices generally higher than those of other types of retail outlets
Factory outlet	• Brand-name items; low prices	• May offer only "seconds" or "irregulars"; few services; returns may not be allowed
Hypermarket	• Full supermarket combined with general merchandise discount store	• Clerks not likely to offer specialized service or product information
Warehouse, Superstore	• Large quantities of items at discount prices	• May require membership fee; limited services; inventory items may vary

Shop Around Consumers have a choice of many different types of stores, each of which has pros and cons.

How can competition among stores benefit consumers?

Store Selection

The quality and variety of goods as well as the price at a store may influence your decision to shop there. Store selection may affect the value of the products you purchase. You may also choose a retail store because of its hours, location, reputation, policies, and services such as parking and delivery. **Figure 4.4** provides an overview of the major types of retailers—businesses that sell directly to consumers.

Over the years, several alternatives to store shopping have emerged. One alternative is the **cooperative**, a nonprofit organization owned and operated by its members for the purpose of saving money on the purchase of goods and services. Because a cooperative buys large amounts of goods, it can lower prices for its members. The main drawback to cooperatives is that they offer few customer services.

Another alternative to store shopping is direct selling, which includes mail order, TV home shopping, and online shopping. An advantage of these types of shopping is the convenience of not having to leave home. Online shopping sometimes offers lower prices, and you may find excellent product information on the Internet. The possible disadvantages of online direct selling are paying for shipping and handling, and difficulty in returning purchases.

Brand Comparison

Most items are sold under a number of well-known brand names that identify the products and their manufacturers. National-brand products are widely advertised and available in many stores. Although they are usually more expensive than non-brand products, national brands usually offer consistent quality or value for your money.

A store-brand, or generic, product is usually sold by one chain of stores and carries the name of that chain on its label. Examples of these products include paper, canned goods, and dairy foods. Because store-brand products are often made by the same companies that make national-brand products, their quality is good. However, because they do not carry a brand-name label, they are less expensive.

When you compare brands, remember to consider price and quality. Plan what you are going to buy before you shop and take a list of what you need. Displays may attract your attention and lead to **impulse buying**, which is purchasing items on the spur of the moment. Impulse buying may be fun, but it can cost you more. Also, you may buy products that you do not really need.

▶ **HONEST BRANDING** Some food labels claim that the product is considered "low in fat" or "light." Foods must meet government criteria to be labeled with such terms. *Why do you think this type of regulation is necessary?*

Label Information Research

Labels on product packages typically include a great deal of advertising. However, federal laws also require labels to present factual information. For example, food labels must indicate the common name of the product, the name and address of the manufacturer or distributor, the net weight of the product, and a list of the ingredients in decreasing order of weight.

In addition, labels on almost all processed foods must have nutritional information, such as the number of calories in one serving and the specific amounts of nutrients and food substances in the product. Some foods are advertised as being "low in fat" or "light," "low in sodium," or "high in fiber." Foods must meet government criteria to be labeled with such terms. Manufacturers can include health claims on product packages only if they have scientific evidence to support the claims.

To help consumers determine the freshness of some foods, manufacturers print dates on the labels. **Open dating** is a labeling method that indicates the freshness, or shelf life, of a perishable product, such as milk or bread. Labels indicate open dating with phrases such as "Use before May 25, 2008" or "Not to be sold after October 8."

Product labels for appliances, such as refrigerators and washing machines, include information about operating costs, which identify the most energy-efficient models.

Price Comparison

Unit pricing is the use of a standard unit of measurement to compare the prices of packages that are different sizes. For example, Claudia went to the drugstore to buy a bottle of mouthwash and noticed that her favorite brand comes in two sizes at different prices. The best way for her to determine which one is the better buy is to use unit pricing. Most grocery stores and drugstores display the unit pricing information for the products they sell. If a store does not provide this information, you can calculate the unit price by dividing the price of the item by the unit of measurement (weight, volume, or quantity). For example, an 8-ounce can of frozen orange juice that costs $1.60 has a unit price of 20 cents per ounce.

When you know how to calculate the unit price, you can compare the unit prices for various sizes, brands, and stores. Keep in mind that the package with the lowest unit price may not be the best buy for your situation. For example, a 10-pound bag of potatoes might have the lowest unit price; but if you do not eat potatoes often, they may spoil before you can use them.

Two common ways to save money are to take advantage of discount coupons and manufacturers' rebates. By using discount coupons, you save money on products at the time you purchase them. A **rebate** is a partial refund of the price of a product. To obtain a rebate, you usually have to submit a form, the original receipt, and the package's UPC symbol, or bar code.

UNIT PRICING

Synopsis: Knowing the unit price of an item can help you determine the best buy.

Example: The brand of peppermint mouthwash that Claudia likes is offered in two sizes, 12 ounces for $2.89 and 16 ounces for $3.39. Which is the better buy?

Formula: $\dfrac{\text{Total Price}}{\text{Unit of Measurement}} = \text{Unit Price}$

Solution: $\dfrac{\$2.89}{12 \text{ oz.}} = \$0.24/\text{oz.}$

$\dfrac{\$3.39}{16 \text{ oz.}} = \$0.21/\text{oz.}$

The 16-ounce size is the better buy at 21 cents per ounce.

YOU FIGURE

You are considering buying soft drinks for your sister's birthday party. The market is offering a six-pack of 12-ounces for $2.99 and a liter bottle for $1.29. Which is the better buy? (Hint: One liter equals 33.8 ounces.)

When comparing prices, the following guidelines can be very helpful:

- More convenience (location, hours, sales staff) usually means higher prices.
- Ready-to-use products (frozen prepared dinners, preassembled toys) usually have higher prices.
- Large packages are usually the best buy; use unit pricing to compare brands, sizes, and stores.
- Buying items "on sale" may not always mean that you save money; the sale price at one store may be higher than the regular price at another store.

Warranty Evaluation

Many products come with a guarantee of quality called a warranty. A **warranty** is a written guarantee from the manufacturer or distributor that states the conditions under which the product can be returned, replaced, or repaired. Federal law requires sellers of products that cost more than $15 (and that have a warranty) to make the warranty available to customers before purchase. The warranty is often printed directly on the package.

Types of Warranties Warranties are divided into two basic types: implied and express. *Implied warranties* are unwritten guarantees that cover certain aspects of a product or its use. An implied warranty of merchantability guarantees that a product is fit for its intended use. For example, a toaster will toast bread, or a CD player will play CDs.

Investigate: A Warranty

A warranty for a product contains the following information:
- Name of the seller or manufacturer
- Name of product
- Terms of the warranty
- Instructions for how to get service

Your Motive: Before making a purchase, you should read the product's warranty to understand exactly what protections the manufacturer offers you. A warranty is an assurance from the seller to the buyer that a product will perform as promised, or it will be replaced or repaired.

FREE FLOW® ONE-YEAR LIMITED WARRANTY

FREE FLOW® plumbing fixture, faucets, and fittings are warranted to be free of defects in material and workmanship for one year from date of installation.

Free Flow will, at its election, repair, replace, or make appropriate adjustments where Free Flow inspection discloses any such defects occurring in normal usage within one year after installation. Free Flow is not responsible for removal or installation costs.

To obtain warranty service, contact Free Flow either through your dealer, plumbing contractor, home center or e-tailer, or by writing to Free Flow, Attn: Customer Service Department, 2525 Highland Drive, Glenview, WI 53044, USA.

IMPLIED WARRANTIES INCLUDING THAT OF MERCHANTABILITY AND FITNESS FOR A PARTICULAR PURPOSE ARE EXPRESSLY LIMITED IN DURATION TO THE DURATION OF THIS WARRANTY. FREE FLOW DISCLAIMS ANY LIABILITY FOR SPECIAL, INCIDENTAL, OR CONSEQUENTIAL DAMAGES. Some states/provinces do not allow limitations on how long an implied warranty lasts, or the exclusion or limitation of special, incidental, or consequential damages so these limitations and exclusions may not apply to you. This warranty gives you specific legal rights. You may also have other rights, which vary from state/province to state/province.

This is our exclusive written warranty.

Notes:
1. There may be variation in color fidelity between catalog images and actual plumbing fixtures.
2. Free Flow reserves the right to make changes in product characteristics, packaging, or availability at any time without notice.

Copyright © 2006.

Key Points: A warranty usually covers defects in materials and workmanship, and promises that the product will work properly under normal circumstances. It does not usually cover defects that occur due to the user's carelessness or inappropriate use of the product. It also explains how a buyer can resolve any problems.

Find the Solutions

1. For how many years are Free Flow fixtures covered by this warranty?
2. If you purchased a Free Flow faucet in November of 2006 and installed it in August of 2007, when would the warranty expire?
3. What will Free Flow do if a product is defective?
4. Who is responsible for the cost of removing a defective faucet and replacing it?
5. If a faucet is replaced under this warranty, will it be the same model faucet?

Express warranties, which are usually written, come in two forms. A full warranty states that a defective product will be fixed or replaced at no charge during a reasonable amount of time. A limited warranty covers only certain aspects of the product, such as parts. This type may also require the buyer to pay a portion of the shipping or repair charges.

When you buy a product, you may be offered a **service contract**, which is a separately purchased agreement by the manufacturer or distributor to cover the costs of repairing the item. Service contracts are sometimes called *extended warranties*, but they are not really warranties. You have to pay extra to obtain a service contract. Such contracts are generally offered on large, expensive items, such as cars and home appliances. Sometimes service contracts are not worth the cost.

Smart shoppers know when to buy, where to buy, what to buy, how much to pay, and how to make sure that the products they buy will perform as advertised. In the next section, you will learn some additional rules for smart shoppers: how to resolve consumer complaints and how to use the law to ensure that your rights as a consumer are protected.

As You Read

QUESTION

What research should you do if you are considering buying a used car with a limited warranty? What do you need to consider if a service contract is offered?

Section 4.1 Assessment

QUICK CHECK

1. What are three economic factors that influence what people buy?
2. Suppose that you are considering buying a pair of in-line skates. What steps might you take before you shop and as you weigh your alternatives?
3. What are at least five strategies followed by smart shoppers.

THINK CRITICALLY

4. Create a scenario in which someone is considering a purchase. Discuss the economic, social, and personal factors that will affect this buying decision.

USE MATH SKILLS

5. **Cat Food Costs**   Gilda would do anything for Luna, her 11-year-old cat. Until recently, she had been paying an animal hospital $22.50 every two weeks for a 10-pound bag of vitamin-enriched organic cat food designed for older cats. On Wednesday, Gilda called a local pet store.

The store stocks food similar to the one she buys at the animal hospital, but it is not organic. The store sells 25-pound bags for $59.55 and 50-pound bags for $99.50.

   Calculate   Using the formula for unit pricing, calculate the best buy among the three different-sized bags of cat food. Would the lowest-priced cat food be the best choice? Why or why not?

SOLVE MONEY PROBLEMS

6. **Getting the Best Buy**   Marta loves shopping for holiday gifts for her friends and family. This year she started looking for gifts early, in June. She hopes that the extra time will allow her to find the perfect gift for everyone on her shopping list. By shopping early, she might get some good buys.

   Write About It   Using the information in the section on smart buying strategies, explain how Marta can shop wisely to make the best choices for gifts and get good bargains.

Resolving Consumer Complaints

Sources of Consumer Complaints

What are some examples of consumer complaints?

When you purchase a product, you do not expect to have any problems with it, especially if you have done research and considered the alternatives. Unfortunately, every purchase involves some degree of risk.

Most customer dissatisfaction results from products that are defective or of poor quality. Consumers also complain about unexpected costs, deceptive pricing, and unsatisfactory repair service. Another source of consumer complaints is **fraud**—dishonest business practices that are meant to deceive, trick, or gain an unfair advantage.

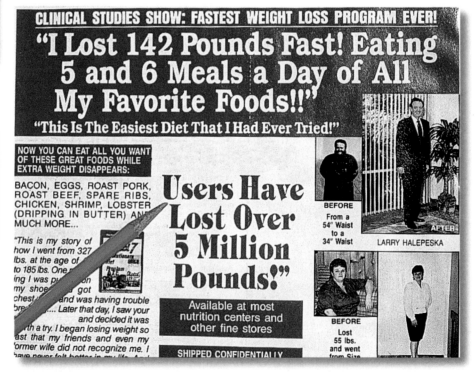

CLINICAL STUDIES SHOW: FASTEST WEIGHT LOSS PROGRAM EVER!

"I Lost 142 Pounds Fast! Eating 5 and 6 Meals a Day of All My Favorite Foods!!"

"This Is The Easiest Diet That I Had Ever Tried!"

NOW YOU CAN EAT ALL YOU WANT OF THESE GREAT FOODS WHILE EXTRA WEIGHT DISAPPEARS:

BACON, EGGS, ROAST PORK, ROAST BEEF, SPARE RIBS, CHICKEN, SHRIMP, LOBSTER (DRIPPING IN BUTTER) AND MUCH MORE...

"This is my story of how I went from 327 lbs. at the age of ... to 185 lbs. One ... ing I was p... on my shoe... got chest... and was having trouble bre... Later that day, I saw your ... and decided it was ...th a try. I began losing weight so ...ast that my friends and even my ...ormer wife did not recognize me. I have never felt better in my life..."

Users Have Lost Over 5 Million Pounds!"

Available at most nutrition centers and other fine stores

SHIPPED CONFIDENTIALLY

BEFORE
From a 54" Waist to a 34" Waist
AFTER
LARRY HALEPESKA

BEFORE
Lost 55 lbs. and went from Size...

▲ **BUYER BEWARE** Many advertisements appeal to the emotions of consumers. *How might this ad influence someone to buy the product?*

Common Types of Fraud

Every year millions of consumers become victims of unethical people who use dishonest business practices to trick or cheat buyers. Experts estimate that fraud costs consumers tens of billions of dollars annually.

As a consumer, you must be aware of various types of fraud. Telephone and mail scams may offer you phony free prizes, travel packages, work-at-home schemes, and investment opportunities. Fraudulent diet products and other remedies attract consumers with phrases such as "scientific breakthrough" or "miraculous cure." The best way to protect yourself from consumer fraud is to recognize it before you become a victim—and to report it if you see it happening.

Resolving Differences Between Buyers and Sellers

What is the best way to resolve a dispute over goods or services?

If you are dissatisfied with a product or service and decide to make a complaint, remember to document the process. Keep a file of receipts, names of people you talk to, dates of attempted repairs, copies of letters you write, and any fees that you have had to pay. Resolving complaints with a business can be handled in five different ways.

▼ BACK TO THE STORE
If you have a problem with a product and want to resolve it, remember to document each step you take. *What types of records should you keep?*

As You Read

RELATE

Have you ever been dissatisfied with a purchase? What did you do?

Return to the Place of Purchase

Most consumers can resolve their complaints at the original place of purchase. Most businesses care about having a reputation for honesty and fairness and will usually do what is necessary to settle reasonable complaints. Remember to bring sales receipts and other relevant information. Also, keep calm and avoid yelling or threatening the salespeople or managers. Explain the problem as clearly as possible, and ask them to help you resolve it.

STANDARD &POOR'S

Global Financial Landscape

Standard and Poor's publishes the globally recognized S&P 500® financial index. It also gathers financial statistics, information, and news, and analyzes this data for international businesses, governments, and individuals to help them guide their financial decisions.

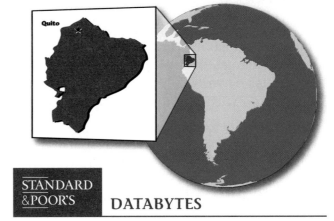

Quito

ECUADOR

In 2000, Ecuador became the first country in Latin America to adopt U.S. currency and discontinue using its own—a practice called *dollarization.* Although most nations have their own money, dollarization in Ecuador's case was a last-ditch effort to save the country's collapsing economy. It was hoped that trading Ecuadorian money for the American dollar would improve the country's financial situation. It has—but to greater and lesser degrees. For example,  the exchange has lowered inflation but has spurred wage increases only slightly. (Ecuador's minimum wage has grown from $50 to $120 a month.) For now dollarization has set up a stable economic foundation for growth. It was "a life raft," sums up one Ecuadorian economist. "We didn't have many options."

STANDARD &POOR'S

DATABYTES

Capital	Quito
Population	12,558,000
Languages	Spanish and Quechua
Currency	U.S. dollar
Gross Domestic Product (GDP)	$45.4 billion (2003 est.)
GDP per capita	$3,200

Industry: petroleum, food processing, textiles, and metal work

Agriculture: *bananas, coffee, cacao, rice; cattle; balsa wood; and fish*

Exports: petroleum, bananas, shrimp, coffee, and cacao

Natural Resources: petroleum, fish, and timber

Think Globally

Do you think consumers in Ecuador can resolve purchase complaints as suggested in this chapter? Why or why not?

Contact Company Headquarters

If you cannot resolve your problem at the local store or business, contact the company's headquarters. Sending a complaint letter such as the one shown in **Figure 4.5** can be effective. To find a company's address, check the *Consumer's Resource Handbook.* Your library may have other useful references as well. Company Web sites are also good sources. If you would rather talk to someone in the company's customer service department but do not know the telephone number, call 1-800-555-1212, the information number. Your library may also carry a directory of toll-free numbers. Some companies print their toll-free customer-service numbers on their packages.

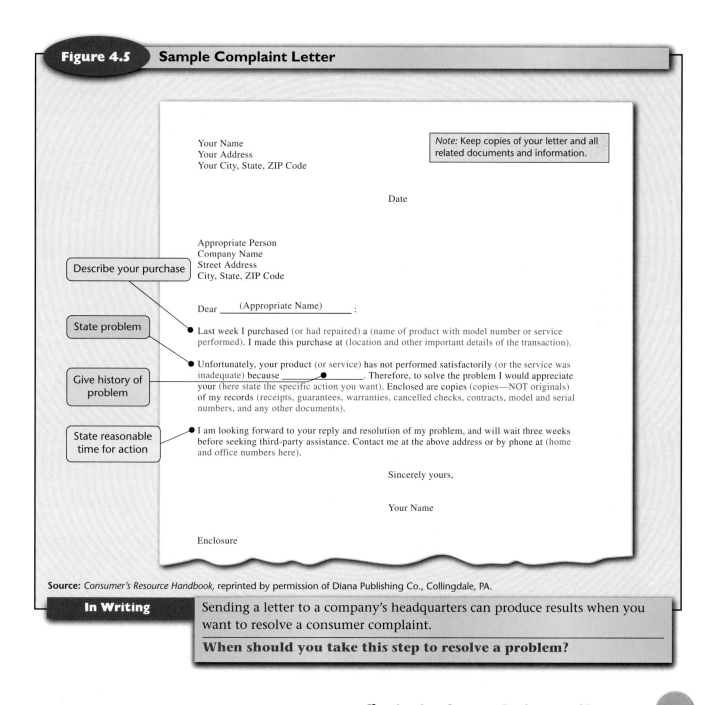

Figure 4.5 **Sample Complaint Letter**

Your Name
Your Address
Your City, State, ZIP Code

Note: Keep copies of your letter and all related documents and information.

Date

Appropriate Person
Company Name
Street Address
City, State, ZIP Code

Describe your purchase

Dear _____(Appropriate Name)_____ :

State problem

Last week I purchased (or had repaired) a (name of product with model number or service performed). I made this purchase at (location and other important details of the transaction).

Give history of problem

Unfortunately, your product (or service) has not performed satisfactorily (or the service was inadequate) because _____. Therefore, to solve the problem I would appreciate your (here state the specific action you want). Enclosed are copies (copies—NOT originals) of my records (receipts, guarantees, warranties, cancelled checks, contracts, model and serial numbers, and any other documents).

State reasonable time for action

I am looking forward to your reply and resolution of my problem, and will wait three weeks before seeking third-party assistance. Contact me at the above address or by phone at (home and office numbers here).

Sincerely yours,

Your Name

Enclosure

Source: *Consumer's Resource Handbook,* reprinted by permission of Diana Publishing Co., Collingdale, PA.

In Writing Sending a letter to a company's headquarters can produce results when you want to resolve a consumer complaint.

When should you take this step to resolve a problem?

Consumer Agency Assistance

If the company is not providing the answers you seek, get help from various consumer, business, and government organizations. These groups include national organizations that deal with issues such as nutrition and automobile safety. Local organizations also handle complaints, do surveys, and provide legal assistance.

Among the best-known consumer agencies is the Better Business Bureau, a network of offices around the country sponsored by local business organizations. These bureaus deal with complaints against local merchants. However, the merchants are under no obligation to respond to those complaints. Therefore, the bureaus are most useful before you buy a product. They can tell you about the experiences other consumers have had with a certain store or company.

Government Agencies A large network of local, state, and federal government agencies is also available. These agencies handle all types of problems, from false advertising to illegal business activities. One federal agency is the Food and Drug Administration, which sets safety standards for food, drugs, chemicals, cosmetics, and household and medical devices. The Consumer Product Safety Commission, another federal agency, helps protect consumers against unsafe products. If you do not know which consumer protection agency to choose, contact your U.S. representative locally or in Washington, D.C.

Dispute Resolution

Dispute resolution programs offer other ways to settle disagreements about a product. Working out a complaint may involve **mediation**—the attempt by a neutral third party to resolve a conflict between a customer and a business through discussion and negotiation. However, a decision made in mediation is not legally binding. Sometimes manufacturers and industry organizations use the arbitration process to resolve consumer complaints. **Arbitration** is a process whereby a conflict between a customer and a business is resolved by an impartial third party whose decision is legally binding.

Settling a dispute through one of these methods can be quicker, less expensive, and less stressful than going to court. Sources for dispute resolution programs in your area include:

- Local or state consumer protection agencies
- State attorney general's office
- Small claims courts
- Better Business Bureau
- trade associations
- local bar associations.

If these dispute resolution methods do not produce the results you want, you may choose to take legal action.

Legal Options for Consumers
What are your legal rights?

As You Read

QUESTION

What are the alternative measures available to consumers before they resort to the legal system?

First, try to settle your dispute by going to the place of business, contacting the company's headquarters, or getting help from a consumer agency. However, if you are still unhappy with the outcome, your final alternative is the legal system.

Small Claims Court

Every state has a court system to settle minor disagreements. A **small claims court** is a court that deals with legal disputes that involve amounts below a certain limit. The amount varies from state to state, ranging from about $500 to $10,000. Cases usually do not involve juries or lawyers, so the cost of this type of legal action is relatively low. The decision of the judge is final.

When you present your case, you should be calm and polite and stick to the point. Submit your own evidence, such as receipts, contracts, and photographs. You may use witnesses who can testify on your behalf and support your claim. The process takes a few weeks.

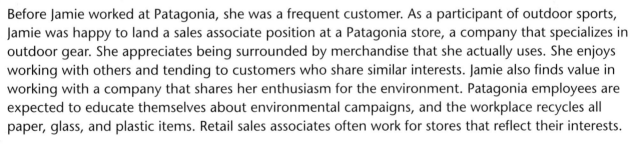

Careers in Finance

RETAIL SALES ASSOCIATE

Jamie Jefferson
Patagonia

Before Jamie worked at Patagonia, she was a frequent customer. As a participant of outdoor sports, Jamie was happy to land a sales associate position at a Patagonia store, a company that specializes in outdoor gear. She appreciates being surrounded by merchandise that she actually uses. She enjoys working with others and tending to customers who share similar interests. Jamie also finds value in working with a company that shares her enthusiasm for the environment. Patagonia employees are expected to educate themselves about environmental campaigns, and the workplace recycles all paper, glass, and plastic items. Retail sales associates often work for stores that reflect their interests.

SKILLS: Sales, communication, cooperation

PERSONAL TRAITS: Positive, neat, detail-oriented, shares company's vision for outdoor activities and responsibilities, able to lift heavy objects and stand for long periods of time

EDUCATION: High school diploma or equivalent, sales experience

ANALYZE How do you think a company such as Patagonia trains employees to respond to customer complaints?

 To learn more about career paths for retail sales associates, visit persfinance07.glencoe.com.

▲ **FORMAL COMPLAINTS** To resolve a consumer complaint, sometimes you must take your case to small claims court. *How is a small claims court different from a trial court?*

Class-Action Suits

Sometimes many people have the same complaint. For example, several people may have been injured by a defective product or overcharged by a utility company. Such a group may qualify for a class-action suit. A **class-action suit** is a legal action on behalf of all the people who have suffered the same injustice. These people are called a "class" and are represented by one lawyer or a group of lawyers working together.

If a situation qualifies for a class-action suit, all parties must be notified of the suit. An individual may decide to file a separate lawsuit instead. If the court rules in favor of the class action, the money awarded is divided among the claimants or put into public funds.

Other Legal Alternatives

If you do not want to go to small claims court or join in a class-action suit, you may seek the services of a lawyer. Get a referral for a lawyer from someone you know. You can also find the names of lawyers in newspapers, in the yellow pages of the phone book, or by calling a local branch of the American Bar Association (ABA), a professional organization of lawyers. It is important to make sure that the lawyer you choose has experience in handling your type of case. You should also ask about fees and payment policies. Lawyers can be expensive. You may decide that your problem is not worth the time and expense.

TechByte

Lawyering Up If you have not been able to resolve a consumer complaint by talking with the company's customer service representative, you can take some legal steps on your own without the help of a lawyer. But if you still cannot resolve the issue, you may need to search for a lawyer to help you.

@ List two things you can do to resolve a complaint. Then list steps for finding a good lawyer after reading information through **persfinance07 .glencoe.com**.

If the cost of lawyers and other legal services is too high for you, you may seek help from a **legal aid society**, a network of community law offices that provide free or low-cost legal assistance. Supported by public funds, these offices provide a variety of legal services. Not everyone is eligible for help from a legal aid society. Your income must fall below a certain amount to qualify, which varies from state to state.

If you do not qualify to use the legal aid society, and hiring a private attorney is out of your budget, you might visit a legal clinic. In many cases, such businesses can offer basic assistance with advice and filing paperwork. In addition, some private attorneys offer their services at reduced rates and work part time in legal clinics.

Many tools are available to protect your rights. However, they will not be valuable, unless you use them. You will have fewer consumer problems if you do business only with companies that have good reputations. You should avoid signing contracts and other documents you do not understand, and watch out for offers that seem too good to be true.

After You Read

REACT

What legal remedies are available for settling consumer disputes?

Section 4.2 Assessment

QUICK CHECK

1. What are some typical consumer complaints?
2. What are five methods of resolving consumer complaints?
3. What are some of the advantages and disadvantages of taking a consumer dispute to small claims court?

THINK CRITICALLY

4. Write a brief paragraph describing a product or service with which you were dissatisfied, and explain what the problem was. Did you complain? If so, what specific steps did you take, and what was the outcome?

USE COMMUNICATION SKILLS

5. **Too Good to Be True?** You recently received a letter offering a four-day vacation trip to Hawaii for only $350. The price includes transportation, a hotel room, and meals. To reserve a space, you must send $175. The offer sounds too good to be true, and you suspect that it is fraudulent.

Discuss With your classmates, brainstorm various types of fraud. Discuss ways to avoid becoming a victim of fraud.

SOLVE MONEY PROBLEMS

6. **Resolving Consumer Complaints** Eduardo and Ana recently bought a new dining room table that they saw advertised on a furniture manufacturer's Web site. When the table arrived and they opened the box, they discovered long, deep scratches on the top of the table. The manufacturer is located thousands of miles from where they live. The box had no directions about how they could return the product.

Write About It Describe the steps Eduardo and Ana should take to resolve their situation and get either a refund or a new table.

Chapter 4 Review & Activities

- Buying decisions are influenced by several factors: economic factors, such as prices, brand names, quality, and maintenance costs; social factors, such as lifestyle and culture; and personal factors, such as age, occupation, and family size.
- A research-based approach to buying involves identifying needs, gathering information, becoming aware of the marketplace, weighing alternatives, and making the purchase. The purchase may involve negotiation, plus you will need to determine whether to pay cash or use credit.

- Make buying decisions by using the following strategies: time your purchases, select stores, compare brands, check labels, compare prices, and evaluate warranties.
- To solve consumer problems, return to the place of purchase, contact the company that manufactured the disputed product, obtain help from a consumer agency or dispute resolution program, or initiate legal action.
- Legal alternatives available to consumers include lawsuits in small claims court, joining in a class-action suit, hiring a lawyer, and obtaining assistance from a legal aid society.

Communicating Key Terms

A neighbor who has just moved to the United States is buying several large appliances. He is having some difficulty understanding some of the advertising information on the products. Write simple explanations of eight of the terms below that you think he may be having trouble understanding.

- down payment
- cooperative
- impulse buying
- open dating
- unit pricing
- rebate
- warranty

- service contract
- fraud
- mediation
- arbitration
- small claims court
- class-action suit
- legal aid society

Reviewing Key Concepts

1. **List** the economic, social, and personal factors that influence a decision to buy an article of clothing.
2. **Describe** the research-based steps for buying a personal computer.
3. **Explain** why some of the strategies for making wise purchases may be more important than others, depending on the item being purchased.
4. **Identify** methods to resolve consumer complaints.
5. **Describe** the advantages and disadvantages of small claims court and joining a class-action suit.

ACADEMIC SKILLS

Language Arts Many consumers are attracted to name brands because they are recognized through advertising. However, generic or store brands have become popular alternatives.

Write About It Write a paragraph explaining three reasons for buying a brand-name product and three reasons for buying a store brand instead.

Back to School You have $130 to spend at August "back-to-school" sales. The tennis shoes you really want cost $105 plus 7 percent sales tax. Online, the shoes cost $95.99, with 11 percent shipping charges but no sales tax. Based on experience, you think the shoes' price will be one-third less by mid-October.

1. **Calculate** (a) How much will the shoes cost in October? Compare that total price to the current store and online prices. (b) What trade-offs do you incur by waiting to buy the shoes? (c) How do those trade-offs compare to having more money now for other purchases?
2. **Compute** by using spreadsheet software the total costs of the shoes in stores now, online now, and in stores in October.

Connect with Social Studies In late 2004, a pain medication called Vioxx was removed voluntarily from the market by its manufacturer, Merck, Inc., due to a risk of heart-related problems. Merck lost a great deal of income and its stock price went down significantly.

Research Use library and Internet sources to find out about Merck's voluntary removal of Vioxx and the potential for class-action lawsuits against the company. Investigate the Federal Food and Drug Act and other laws aimed at protecting citizens and summarize your findings

Shopping Online Many people limit their online purchases to books, CDs, and airplane tickets. Based on this chapter, explain why you would or would not buy the following items online:

 Log On Use an Internet search engine to find Web sites selling the items listed:

1. Expensive tennis shoes
2. An iPod
3. A dress or suit for the prom
4. Flowers for your mother
5. The latest CD from your favorite band
6. Four CDs from your favorite bands

Newsclip: Continuous Shopping Consumer spending has been on the rise since 2001. Despite unemployment rates, higher oil prices, and terrorist threats, Americans continue to shop.

Log On Go to persfinance07.glencoe.com and open Chapter 4. List reasons consumers continue to spend. Ask your teenage friends what they buy and want. Make a list.

WHAT'S YOUR FINANCIAL **ID?**

ARE YOU A SMART SHOPPER?

With so many places to shop and a wide variety of products to buy, it takes skill and practice to get the most from your money. On a separate sheet of paper, test your shopping know-how.

1. When I want something, I
   a. go to the nearest store that has it and buy it.   (1 point)
   b. locate where I can buy it at the lowest cost today and buy it.   (2 points)
   c. wait for the item to go on sale.   (3 points)

2. I like to
   a. buy what looks good to me at the time.   (1 point)
   b. look at consumer guides to help me choose the best buy.   (2 points)
   c. compare all the brands and decide which offers the most value.   (3 points)

3. When buying an item in the drugstore, I
   a. always buy name brands.   (1 point)
   b. always buy generic brands.   (2 points)
   c. calculate the best price per weight or unit and buy accordingly.   (3 points)

4. When shopping for clothes, I
   a. buy what strikes my fancy.   (1 point)
   b. only buy what's on sale.   (2 points)
   c. only buy what I know I will wear.   (3 points)

5. I use coupons whenever I can.
   a. Never   (1 point)
   b. Sometimes   (2 points)
   c. Always   (3 points)

6. When eating out, I
   a. order what I want, regardless of cost.   (1 point)
   b. sometimes am more concerned about cost but sometimes order expensive dishes.   (2 points)
   c. always look at prices and order accordingly.   (3 points)

7. Whenever I can, I borrow books and DVDs from the library.
   a. Never   (1 point)
   b. Sometimes   (2 points)
   c. Always   (3 points)

8. When buying CDs or DVDs, I
   a. get what I want as soon as it comes out.   (1 point)
   b. try to wait for a sale but get what I want if I really want it.   (2 points)
   c. wait for a sale.   (3 points)

If you scored:

21–24: You are a smart shopper. However, be sure you treat yourself occasionally.
16–20: You sometimes make choices that cost more, but you are usually aware of them.
Less than 16: Try to practice a few more smart shopping skills and see how much you save.

Your Financial Portfolio

Your Budget

David wants a $2,500 laptop computer. At his part-time job at Computer Warehouse, he earns $7 an hour and works an average of 16 hours a week. For ten weeks in the summer, he works 40 hours a week. He also makes money on the side by setting up and troubleshooting computers. By keeping track of his expenses, he has figured his monthly budget.

   If David sticks to his budget, in a year's time he can save $3,630 ($302.50 × 12 = $3,630). That would be more than enough to buy the computer he wants.

Average Monthly Income	
Income:	
Monthly take-home pay from Computer Warehouse	$502.50
Income from setting up and troubleshooting computers	50.00
Other income	20.00
Total Income	**$572.50**
Average Monthly Expenses	
Expenses:	
Fixed Expenses	
Online services	$ 20.00
Car loan and insurance	135.00
Variable Expenses	
Entertainment and personal	90.00
Gifts and contributions	25.00
Total Expenses	**$270.00**

(Total Income − Total Expenses = Savings)
($572.50 − 270.00 = $302.50)
David can save $302.50 a month.

Calculate

   What is your budget? A budget can help you see where you are spending your money and assist you in determining how long it will take to save for a special purchase. In your workbook or on a separate sheet of paper, calculate your income and expenses for one month. How much can you save in one month? What is the cost of your desired purchase? How long will it take you to save for what you want?

Unit 1 LAB

Get a Financial Life!

Setting Up a Career Plan

Overview

Carrie Houston will be graduating from high school this year. She is facing many important decisions—from developing her personal financial goals to planning her career strategy. She is interested in fashion design and computer graphics and has been taking related classes.

When you make decisions, you are taking control of your life. You can shape your future in ways that are important to you. To make sound decisions, you should identify your goals and understand the ways in which your personal values and life situations will influence your choices. If you are prepared to make decisions—rather than leave your future to chance or allow others to tell you what to do—you will be able to achieve personal satisfaction and financial security.

Develop a process to help plan your own career; then share it with Carrie so that she can plan her future career.

Resources & Tools

- Career center/guidance office at school
- Career-development book
- Crayons, markers, colored pencils
- Internet
- Portfolio (ring binder or file folder)
- Poster board
- Presentation software (optional)
- Public or school library
- Word-processing software

Procedures

STEP A

The Process
In order to develop a career plan, you must set goals, understand your abilities and interests, and conduct research. By following this process, you will have a head start into your future. In addition, you will be able to share what you have learned with Carrie or your friends.

1. Develop five to seven financial goals. You should have at least one short-term goal, one intermediate goal, and one long-term goal. Your selected career will help you meet your goals.
2. Take an aptitude test and/or interest inventory. You can find these in your school's guidance office or career center, or on the Internet.
3. Research a career that interests you. Make sure that you find out about the educational requirements, skills needed, pay range, duties and responsibilities, opportunities for advancement, and future trends in the field.
4. Conduct an informational interview with someone who is working in your area of interest to gather practical information, or arrange to "job shadow" someone in your selected field. (To *job shadow* means to follow a person on the job for a day to learn about a particular career.)
5. Obtain catalogs from colleges or other post-secondary institutions where training is offered in the field you are researching. Try to locate at least one institution in your community, one in your state, and one out of state.
6. Using a word-processing program, create templates for a résumé and cover letter.

STEP B — Create Your Portfolio

As you work through the process, save the results so that you can refer, review, and refine. Divide your portfolio into six sections. Label the sections: (1) Goals, (2) Tests, (3) Career Research, (4) Live Work, (5) Education, and (6) Résumé.

1. Using a word-processing program, type your goals in a large font (16–18 point). These will be your guiding principles. Place them in Section 1.
2. Place the results of your aptitude test or interest inventory in Section 2.
3. Type a two- or three-page (double-spaced) career report based on your research, and place it in Section 3.
4. Write about your informational interview or job shadowing experience. Include pictures, brochures, or other materials that you might have received. Place these items in Section 4.
5. Place the catalogs that you collect in Section 5.
6. Place the templates that you create in Section 6.

STEP C — Presentation

One of the most important skills that employers look for in a good employee is the ability to communicate. This is a skill that you can develop in class through oral presentations.

1. Read a book on career development. Examples include:
   - *What Color Is Your Parachute?* by Richard Nelson Bolles
   - *Who Moved My Cheese?* by Spencer Johnson
   - *Job Interviews for Dummies* by Joyce Lain Kennedy
   - *Cool Careers for Dummies* by Marty Nemko, Paul Edwards, and Sarah Edwards
   - *I Could Do Anything If I Only Knew What It Was* by Barbara Sher with Barbara Smith
2. Using either presentation software or poster board with markers, crayons, or colored pencils, create a five-minute presentation that summarizes the book.
3. Include your opinion of the book, stating whether you would recommend it to Carrie.

Unit 2

Banking and Credit

 **Internet Project**

Your Own Home

Buying your first home takes a lot of planning and preparation. In this project, you will write a plan designed to help you to purchase your first home when you are an adult. Since you have several years to accomplish this goal, you have time to save some money for a down payment, establish a good credit rating, choose a home, apply for a mortgage, and negotiate a price.

 Log on to persfinance07.glencoe.com. Begin by reading Task 1. Then continue on your WebQuest as you study Unit 2.

Section	5.1	6.2	7.3
Page	135	170	223

FINANCE FILE

Consumer Debt: The Deeper the Hole, the Better for Business

When is bad debt good business? Public collection agencies that specialize in the purchase of unpaid credit-card obligations and other bills are expected to get a lift as the consumer starts to show signs of overload.

Consumers have borrowed a bundle in recent years—over $2 trillion in credit card and auto debt, according to the Federal Reserve. Add mortgages and the figure jumps to nearly $10 trillion. The average U.S. household is deeper in the hole than it was four years ago, carrying debt of about $9,200, up from $7,200.

Since household income isn't keeping pace with debt growth, more consumers are getting close to the edge. Credit card charge-offs, or the bad debt that banks write off the books, were expected to hit a record $65 billion in 2004, up from $57.3 billion in 2003, according to the *Nilson Report*. Such debts will increase to $2.8 trillion by 2010.

Ultimately, collection companies make their money from bad-debt portfolios by working out reasonable solutions with borrowers. Zaro [CEO of Cavalry Investments] says: "If you don't help them, you don't help yourself."

—*By Mara Der Hovanesian*

Write About It How do you think consumers can reduce their credit debt?

Log On To read the complete *BusinessWeek* article and do the *BusinessWeek* Extension activity to help you learn more about handling credit and avoiding debt, go to **persfinance07.glencoe.com**.

CHAPTER 5

Banking

 What You'll Learn

When you have completed this chapter, you will be able to:

Section 5.1
- Identify types of financial services.
- Describe the various types of financial institutions.

Section 5.2
- Compare the costs and benefits of different savings plans.
- Explain features of different savings plans.
- Compare the costs and benefits of different types of checking accounts.
- Explain how to use a checking account effectively.

Reading Strategies

To get the most out of your reading:

Predict what you will learn in this chapter.

Relate what you read to your own life.

Question what you are reading to be sure you understand.

React to what you have read.

In the **Real** World . . .

When Lynn Podesta was hired for her first job, she decided to open a bank account. She went to local branches and picked up brochures that explained interest rates, fees for services, locations of ATMs, and online services. Lynn was surprised to find out that each bank had different benefits and costs. Some banks charged for ATM usage and teller services. She also found a bank that offered a free checking account if her paychecks were deposited directly. Lynn felt that it was important to start an account. Using a debit card would allow her to shop without carrying cash, and having an account would help her establish credit. Getting to know banking would not be too difficult, and she would have advantages.

As You Read *Consider how you can use basic banking services to your advantage.*

ASK STANDARD &POOR'S

Savings Account

Q: I make only $75 a week at my part-time job and use most of it for movies, food, and CDs. Because I make so little, do I really need to put my money in a bank?

A: Since you have a small amount of money to take care of, you may not need a bank. However, $75 a week is a large sum to spend on entertainment. You should open a savings account and try to save at least $10 a week. After three months you would have $130, and after a year you would have more than $500.

Ask Yourself Why is it a good idea to start a savings account now?

 Go to **persfinance07.glencoe.com** to complete the Standard & Poor's Financial Focus activity.

Section 5.1

Financial Services and Institutions

Focus on Reading

Read to Learn

- How to identify types of financial services.
- How to describe the various types of financial institutions.

Main Idea

Understanding the features of financial services and institutions will help you choose options that best meet your needs.

Key Terms

- direct deposit
- automated teller machine (ATM)
- debit card
- point-of-sale transaction
- commercial bank
- savings and loan association (S&L)
- credit union

Before You Read

PREDICT

What might be the differences between commercial banks, savings and loans, and credit unions?

How to Manage Your Cash

What are your cash needs?

Banking in America began in 1791, soon after the United States declared independence. Congress established the nation's first central bank with eight branches. Today, with more than 11,000 banks, 2,000 savings and loan associations, and 12,000 credit unions in the United States, you have a wide array of financial services from which to choose. A trip to the bank may be a visit to an automated teller machine (ATM) in the mall or a quick look at your savings account balance on the Internet. Your choice of financial services will depend on your daily cash needs and your savings goals. (See **Figure 5.1.**)

Daily Cash Needs

Your daily cash needs may include buying lunch, going to the movies with friends, filling the car with gasoline, or paying for other routine activities. Of course, you can carry cash, or currency—bills and coins—to pay for these items. You can also use a credit card or go to an ATM, also known as a cash machine.

As you decide which method to use for your everyday cash needs, consider the pros and cons of each one. For example, ATMs may charge a fee for each use. If you pay a $1 fee each time you take out cash, say, twice a week, you will spend $104 on fees each year.

In addition to your short-term cash needs, you need to consider your long-term financial goals. Resist the temptation to overspend and avoid buying on impulse or overusing credit cards. Try not to dip into your savings to pay current bills. Put extra money you have to work for you—in a savings account or an investment plan.

Sources of Quick Cash

Regardless of how well you plan, you may sometimes need more cash than you have available. You have two options: Use your savings or borrow the money. Remember that either choice requires a trade-off. Although you will have immediate access to the funds you need, long-term financial goals—such as paying for college, buying a car, or starting a business—may be delayed.

Types of Financial Services
Which financial services would benefit you?

In order to stay competitive in today's marketplace, banks and other financial institutions have expanded the range of services that they offer. These services can be divided into three main categories:

- Savings
- Payment services
- Borrowing

Savings

Safe storage of funds for future use is a basic need for everyone. Money that is going to be left in a financial institution for months or years is called a *time deposit*. Some examples of time deposit funds include money that you keep in any type of savings account and certificates of deposit or CDs. Having a savings acount is essential for any personal finance plan.

Figure 5.1 **Financial Services**

Financial Services for Short-Term Needs

- Daily purchases
- Living expenses
- Emergency fund

Daily Cash Needs	Savings	Checking	Credit Cards
• Check cashing • Automated teller machines (ATMs) • Prepaid cards	• Regular savings account • Money market account	• Regular checking account • Online payments • Automatic preauthorized payments • Payment by phone • Cashier's checks • Money orders	

Financial Services for Long-Term Needs

- Major purchases
- Long-term financial security

Savings	Credit Services	Investment Services	Other Services
• Certificates of deposit (CDs) • U.S. Savings Bonds	• Cash loans for cars, education • Home loans	• Mutual funds • Financial advice	• Tax preparation • Insurance • Budgeting

Planning Ahead You may think that you need only cash and checking services at this time in your life.

Why would it be a good idea to save a small amount regularly?

Careers in Finance

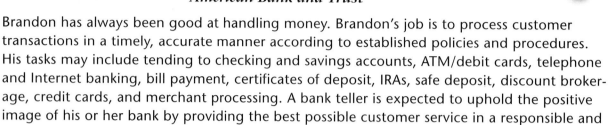

BANK TELLER **Brandon Lewis**
American Bank and Trust

Brandon has always been good at handling money. Brandon's job is to process customer transactions in a timely, accurate manner according to established policies and procedures. His tasks may include tending to checking and savings accounts, ATM/debit cards, telephone and Internet banking, bill payment, certificates of deposit, IRAs, safe deposit, discount brokerage, credit cards, and merchant processing. A bank teller is expected to uphold the positive image of his or her bank by providing the best possible customer service in a responsible and professional manner.

SKILLS: Communication, problem-solving, decision-making, retail sales, and cash-handling skills, as well as proficiency with office machines

PERSONAL TRAITS: Personable, courteous, outgoing, team oriented, and able to remain calm under pressure

EDUCATION: High school diploma or equivalent; associate degree or higher degree

ANALYZE Why would a bank teller's job require selling skills? Provide examples.

 To learn more about career paths for bank tellers, visit **persfinance07.glencoe.com**.

Payment Services

Transferring money from a personal account to businesses or individuals for payments is a basic function of day-to-day financial activity at a bank. The most commonly used payment service is a checking account. Money that you place in a checking account is called a *demand deposit* because you can withdraw the money at any time, or on demand.

Borrowing

Most people use credit at some time during their lives. If you need to borrow money, financial institutions offer many options. You can borrow money for a short term by using a credit card or taking out a personal cash loan. If you need to borrow for a longer term, say, for the purpose of buying a house or car, you may apply for a mortgage or auto loan. Chapter 6 discusses the types and costs of credit.

Other Financial Services

Financial institutions may also offer a variety of services, such as insurance protection; stock, bond, and mutual fund investment accounts; income tax assistance; and financial planning services.

Electronic Banking Services

How can you use electronic banking services?

When Jeff's older brother was in high school, he had to get to his bank by 3 P.M. on Friday, or he would have to wait until 9 A.M. on Monday to cash his paycheck. Today Jeff's bank is open for longer periods on weekdays as well as on Saturdays. For more convenience, Jeff can use the bank's electronic services 24 hours a day. He can check the status of his account or make a transaction from an ATM, by telephone, or online. Other online services allow customers to get up-to-date account information with personal financial management software to view details about a home loan or a line of credit and to check the amount of interest paid.

Security is the number one issue for online customers. The way to ensure online security is to use a security code, or password, and a customer identification name or number.

Direct Deposit

Many businesses offer their employees **direct deposit**, an automatic deposit of net pay to an employee's designated bank account. Instead of a paper paycheck, employees receive a printed statement that lists deductions and information about their earnings. Direct deposit saves time, money, and effort—and offers a safe way to transfer funds.

As You Read

RELATE

Would you use electronic banking services? Why or why not?

▼ **CASH AT HAND** Follow simple rules of ATM etiquette when using this banking convenience. If you are in line, stand at least a few feet away from the person who is using the machine. When you are at the machine, protect the screen as you enter your PIN and other information. *Why are these practices important?*

Automatic Payments

Utility companies, lenders, and other businesses allow customers to use an automatic payment system. With your authorization, your bank will withdraw the amount of your monthly payment or bill from your bank account. Make sure you have enough money in your account for the payment. Arrange your payments according to when you receive your paycheck. Check your bank statements each month to make sure the payments were made correctly.

Automated Teller Machines (ATMs)

A cash machine, or **automated teller machine (ATM)**, is a computer terminal that allows a withdrawal of cash from an account. You can also make deposits and transfer money from one account to another. ATMs are located in banks, shopping malls, grocery stores, and even sports arenas.

To use an ATM for banking, you must apply for a card from your financial institution. This card is called a **debit card**, which is a cash card that allows you to withdraw money or pay for purchases from your checking or savings account. The card also allows you to access the machine for other purposes. Some financial institutions may charge a small fee for the use of the card. Unlike a credit card, a debit card enables you to spend only the money that you have in your account.

When you use your debit card, the ATM computer will ask you to enter your personal identification number (PIN). Never give this number to any business or individual, or for online transactions. Memorize it and keep a written record in a safe place. Never keep your PIN with your debit card. If your card is lost or stolen along with your PIN, anyone could withdraw money from your account.

ATM Fees The fees that some financial institutions charge for the convenience of using an ATM can add up over time. You may feel that the benefit is worth the cost. However, you might consider these suggestions:

► PLASTIC PAYMENT Debit cards are convenient, cashless ways to make purchases. *What might be one drawback of using a debit card?*

- Compare ATM fees before opening an account. Get a list of fees in writing.
- Use your bank's ATM machines to avoid the additional fees that other banks charge when you use their machines.
- Consider using traveler's checks, credit cards, personal checks, and prepaid cash cards when you are away from home.

Lost Debit Cards   If you lose your debit card, or if it is stolen, notify your bank immediately. Most card issuers will not hold you responsible for stolen funds. Check with your card issuer. However, some institutions require you to notify them within two days of losing your card. If you wait longer, you may be held responsible for up to $500 for its unauthorized use for up to 60 days. Beyond that time, your liability may be unlimited.

Plastic Payments

Although cash and checks are very common methods of paying for goods and services, various access cards are also available.

Point-of-Sale Transactions   A **point-of-sale transaction** is a purchase by a debit card of a good or service at a retail store, a restaurant, or elsewhere. Financial institutions offer two types of cards for these transactions—online and offline. An online card works like an ATM card. You have to use your PIN to authorize the payment, and the money is transferred from your account instantly. Charges made with an offline card do not require a PIN, and the funds to cover the payment are deducted from your account within a day or two.

Stored-Value Cards   Prepaid cards that you can use for bus or subway fares, school lunches, long-distance phone calls, or library fees are popular. Some of these cards, such as phone cards, are disposable. Others, called *stored-value cards*, are reloadable or rechargeable, which means that money can be added to the card.

Electronic Cash   Some companies are working to develop electronic money. They plan to create electronic versions of all existing payment systems—paper money, coins, credit cards, and checks. The day may come when you will not handle currency at all.

Opportunity Costs of Financial Services
What are the trade-offs when you choose financial services?

When you are making decisions about saving and spending, try to find a balance between your short-term needs and your future financial security. Also, consider the opportunity costs, or trade-offs, of each choice you make as you select financial services. Ask several questions.

- Is a higher interest rate on a certificate of deposit worth giving up liquidity, which is the ability to easily convert your resources into cash without a loss in value?
- Would you trade the convenience of getting cash from the ATM near your office for lower ATM fees?
- Is it worth opening a checking account that has no fees—but does not earn interest—if you have to keep a minimum balance of $500?

Remember to consider the value of your time in addition to the money you are saving. Reevaluate your choices occasionally. You may find a new financial institution that offers you more of the services you need or offers less expensive services.

Types of Financial Institutions
What are the differences between financial institutions?

After you have identified the services you want, you can choose from among many types of financial institutions. You may select an institution that offers a wide range of services or one that specializes in certain services. **Figure 5.2** provides some tips for selecting a financial institution. Many institutions provide the option of cyber-banking, or banking via the Internet. Some banks operate exclusively on the Internet.

Figure 5.2   **Selecting a Financial Institution**

When you are ready to choose a financial institution, plan so that you will have the services you need and will not have to pay for those you will not use. Do your banking homework.

Stop by the bank. Pick up brochures about the bank's services. While there, speak to a customer service representative about the bank's services.

Take the brochures home. Study them and discuss the features with your parents.

Federal Deposit Insurance Corporation

When you consider a financial institution consider its safety record. During the Great Depression of the 1930s, many banks failed. The people and businesses that had made deposits in these institutions lost their money. In 1933, the federal government created the Federal Deposit Insurance Corporation (FDIC) to protect deposits in banks. The FDIC insures each account in a federally chartered bank up to $100,000 per account. The FDIC also administers the Savings Association Insurance Fund (SAIF) for savings and loan associations. Like the FDIC, the SAIF insures deposits up to $100,000. All federally chartered banks must participate in the FDIC program. Banks that are not federally chartered may choose to enroll in the program.

Deposit Institutions

Most people use deposit-type institutions to handle their banking needs. These institutions include commercial banks, savings and loan associations, mutual savings banks, and credit unions.

Commercial Banks   A **commercial bank** is a for-profit institution that offers a full range of financial services, including checking, savings, and lending. Commercial banks serve individuals and businesses. These banks are authorized to conduct business through a charter, or license, granted by either the federal government or a state government.

Go online. Get complete information on the institution's benefits, fees, and charges.

Open your accounts. Use checking and savings accounts to start managing your money.

▲ **CONVENIENCE** Many people use commercial banks because these banks offer a full range of financial services. *What might be some benefits of using a large commercial bank?*

Savings and Loan Associations A **savings and loan association (S&L)** is a financial institution that traditionally specialized in savings accounts and mortgage loans but now offers many of the same services as commercial banks. Services include checking accounts, business loans, and investment services. S&Ls have either a federal or a state charter.

Mutual Savings Banks Mutual savings banks specialize in savings accounts and mortgage loans. Some offer personal and automobile loans as well. The interest rates on loans from a mutual savings bank may be lower than those that a commercial bank charges. In addition, mutual savings banks sometimes pay a higher interest rate on savings accounts.

Credit Unions A **credit union** is a nonprofit financial institution that is owned by its members and organized for their benefit. Traditionally, its members have some common bond, such as membership in a labor union, college alumni association, or employment by the same company. Most credit unions offer a full range of services, including checking accounts, loans, credit cards, ATMs, and investment services. Credit union fees and loan rates may be lower than those at commercial banks.

Non-Deposit Institutions

Financial services are also available at institutions such as life insurance companies, investment companies, finance companies, and mortgage companies.

Life Insurance Companies Though the main purpose of life insurance companies is to provide financial security for dependents, many insurance policies also contain savings and investment features. In addition, some insurance companies offer retirement planning services. You will learn more about life insurance in Chapter 14.

Investment Companies These firms combine your money with funds from other investors in order to buy stocks, bonds, and other securities. The investment company then manages these combined investments, which are called *mutual funds*. Chapter 10 discusses more about mutual funds.

Finance Companies Finance companies make higher-interest loans to consumers and small businesses that cannot borrow elsewhere because they have below-average credit ratings.

Mortgage Companies   Mortgage companies specialize in loans for the purchase of homes. Chapter 7 discusses the finances of housing.

Comparing Financial Institutions

What should you know to choose a financial institution?

When you compare banks and other financial institutions, you should ask these questions to help choose the best one:

- Where can you get the highest rate of interest on your savings?
- Where can you obtain a checking account with low (or no) fees?
- Will you be able to borrow money from the institution—with a credit card or another type of loan—when you need it?
- Do you need an institution that offers free financial advice?
- Is the institution FDIC- or SAIF-insured?
- Does the institution have convenient locations?
- Does it have online banking services?
- Does it have any special banking services that you might need?

As You Read

QUESTION

Under what circumstances might you be better off with each of these institutions: a commercial bank, a savings and loan association, a mutual savings bank, or a credit union?

Section 5.1 Assessment

QUICK CHECK

1. What are three main categories of services offered by financial institutions?
2. What are the types of electronic banking services that are available?
3. Which institutions fall under the category of deposit institutions? Which are classified as non-deposit institutions?

THINK CRITICALLY

4. Name some financial services you use now. How might your needs for services change in the next five years?

USE MATH SKILLS

5. **Wise Use of ATMs**   Margaret uses an ATM three times a week. It is not her bank's machine, but it is convenient to the store where she works. For every transaction, Margaret pays a fee of $1.50.

 Calculate   What is Margaret's annual expense for the use of this ATM?

SOLVE MONEY PROBLEMS

6. **Choosing a Financial Institution**
   Dakota is thinking about changing banks. He has a part-time job at a supermarket. Sometimes he works late hours, and he would like the convenience of being able to make deposits and withdrawals at any time. He needs cash for food and gas, and he writes only two checks a month—to his music CD club account and to his credit card company. Soon he will need to take out a loan to buy a car. He also wants to put aside some money to pay for technical school.

   Write About It   Help Dakota select the type of financial institution that offers the features that would be most useful to him and write a list for him.

Focus on Reading

Read to Learn
- How to compare the costs and benefits of different savings plans.
- How to explain features of different savings plans.
- How to compare the costs and benefits of different types of checking accounts.
- How to use a checking account effectively.

Main Idea
Recognizing the types of savings plans and payment methods that financial institutions offer can help you use money wisely.

Key Terms
- certificate of deposit (CD)
- money market account
- rate of return
- compounding
- annual percentage yield (APY)
- overdraft protection
- stop-payment order
- endorsement
- bank reconciliation

Before You Read

PREDICT

What is the difference between a CD and a money market account?

Savings Plans and Payment Methods

Types of Savings Plans
What are some savings program options?

To achieve your financial goals, you will need a savings program. Various types of savings programs include regular savings accounts, certificates of deposit, money market accounts, and U.S. Savings Bonds. (See **Figure 5.3.**)

Regular Savings Accounts

Regular savings accounts, traditionally called *passbook accounts*, are ideal if you plan to make frequent deposits and withdrawals. They require little or no minimum balance and allow you to withdraw money on demand. The trade-off for this convenience is that the interest you earn will be low compared with other savings plans.

You may receive a passbook that records deposits and withdrawals, but typically, you will get a monthly or quarterly statement in the mail. Commercial banks, savings and loan associations, and other financial institutions offer regular savings accounts. At credit unions they may be called *share accounts*.

Certificates of Deposit

A **certificate of deposit (CD)** is a savings alternative in which money is left on deposit for a stated period of time to earn a specific rate of return. This period of time is called the *term*. The date when the money becomes available to you is called the *maturity date*. This savings plan is a relatively low-risk way to invest your money. It offers a higher interest rate than a regular savings account pays, but you will have to accept a few trade-offs.

To earn the higher interest rate paid by CDs, you must accept three key limitations. First, you may have to leave your money on deposit for one month to five or more years. Second, you probably will pay a penalty if you take the money out before the maturity date. Third, financial institutions require that you deposit a minimum amount to buy a certificate of deposit. This amount is usually larger than the balance a regular savings account requires.

CD Investment Strategies Here are some tips for investing in CDs:

- Find out where you can get the best rate. You can put your savings in a bank anywhere in the United States. You can use the Internet to find out what rates banks offer all over the country.
- Consider the economy as you decide what maturity date to choose. You may want to buy a long-term CD if interest rates are relatively high. Then, if interest rates go down because of changes in the economy, your money will continue to earn the higher rate.
- Never let a financial institution "roll over" a CD. For example, if your one-year CD matures, and you do nothing, the bank will redeposit that money in another one-year CD. You may decide to roll over, however, if you know that you will get the best rate possible.
- Consider when you will need the money. If you plan to use the money in two years to help pay for college, then buy a CD with a term of two years or less.
- If you have enough funds to have several accounts, you might consider creating a CD portfolio, which includes CDs that mature at different times. For example, you could have $1,000 in a three-month CD, $1,000 in a six-month CD, and $1,000 in a one-year CD. This way, you would be able to withdraw money at different times and still get better interest rates than you would with a passbook savings account.

Figure 5.3 **Savings Alternatives**

Type of Account	Benefits	Drawbacks
Regular savings accounts	• Low minimum balance • Ease of withdrawal • Insured	• Low rate of return
Certificates of deposit (CDs)	• Guaranteed rate of return for time of CD • Insured	• Possible penalty for early withdrawal • Minimum deposit
Money market accounts	• Good rate of return • Some check writing • Insured	• Minimum balance • No interest and possible service charge if below a certain balance
U.S. Savings Bonds	• Low minimum deposit • Guaranteed by the government • Free from state and local taxes	• Lower rate of return when cashed in before bond reaches maturity date

So Many Choices Each type of savings plan has pros and cons that you should consider.

Which type(s) would be best for a person who wants to save frequently but with small amounts?

Money Market Accounts

A **money market account** is a savings account that requires a minimum balance and earns interest that varies from month to month. The rates float, or go up and down, as market rates change. Although the interest rate of a money market account is usually higher than that of a regular savings account, a money market account also requires a higher minimum balance, typically $1,000. You may have to pay a penalty if your balance goes below the minimum amount. You can write a limited number of checks to make large payments or to transfer money to other accounts. The FDIC insures money market accounts up to $100,000.

U.S. Savings Bonds

Another savings option is purchasing a U.S. Savings Bond (also called a *Patriot Bond)*. For example, when Meagan graduated high school in 2005, her aunt gave her a U.S. Savings Bond as a gift. Her aunt paid $250 for the bond, but it has a face value of $500. This means that if Meagan keeps the bond long enough until the designated maturity date, it will eventually earn enough interest to be worth $500 or even more.

▲ **MEETING GOALS** Most people save for many years to go to college. *Why might certificates of deposit and U.S. Savings Bonds be good investments for someone who is saving for a long-term goal such as college?*

You can purchase Series EE Savings Bonds from the federal government in amounts that range from $25 to $5,000 (face values of $50 to $10,000, respectively). The government limits total purchases per year to $15,000 ($30,000 face value) per person. You may buy savings bonds from banks or through the governments' Web site. The Federal Reserve sends bond certificates within 15 business days.

The maturity date, or the date a bond reaches its face value, depends on the date it was bought and the interest rate the bond is earning. For some bonds, the rate changes every six months. Because interest rates vary, no official maturity date exists for Series EE Savings Bonds. Bonds purchased after April 1997 and cashed after less than five years are subject to a three-month penalty—that is, you will not receive any interest for the last three months before you cash it. For example, if you cash a bond after 18 months, you receive only 15 months' worth of interest.

A Series EE Savings Bond continues to earn interest for 30 years if you do not cash it in. The longer you hold it, the more it is worth. Its value may be more than the face value if it is held past maturity.

Meagan kept her bond for ten years. In 2004, she decided to cash it in to help her make a down payment on a condominium. She found out that it was worth a little more than $450. Your bond's worth will depend on current interest rates and on the month and year in which the bond was issued.

Taxes on Savings Bonds The interest you earn on Series EE Bonds is exempt from, or free of, state and local taxes. You do not pay federal taxes on the interest earnings until you cash in the bond. Once a Series EE Bond has reached maturity, you can choose to defer federal taxes further by exchanging it for a Series HH Bond. Low- and middle-income families who use the money from redeemed Series EE Bonds to pay for higher education pay no taxes on the interest.

Your Own Home
Learn about saving for a down payment on your first home and how to choose a bank that fits your needs.

@ To continue with Task 2 of your Web-Quest project, visit **persfinance07.glencoe.com**.

Evaluating Savings Plans
How should you evaluate a savings plan?

Your selection of a savings plan will be influenced by several factors. You should consider the rate of return, inflation, tax considerations, liquidity, restrictions, and fees.

Rate of Return

Earnings on savings can be measured by the rate of return, or yield. The **rate of return** is the percentage of increase in the value of your savings from earned interest. For example, when Emisha put the $75 she earned from babysitting on New Year's Eve into a regular savings account last year, she earned $3 in interest. Therefore, her rate of return was 4 percent. To calculate the rate of return, she divided the total interest by the amount of her deposit ($3 ÷ $75 = .04 or 4 percent).

Compounding The yield on your savings will usually be greater than the stated interest rate. **Compounding** is the process in which interest is earned on both the principal—the original amount you deposited—and on any previously earned interest. It is a multistep process for computing interest. First, the interest on the principal is computed. That interest is added to the principal. The next time interest is computed, the new, larger balance is used. Compounding may take place every year, every quarter, every month, or even every day.

How much interest would your account earn in one year if the interest were compounded monthly? To make this calculation, first multiply the principal by the annual interest rate. Divide that figure by 12, the number of months in a year. This is the interest you would earn after the first month. To calculate the interest earned for the second month, add any interest earned in the first month to the principal. Then take that amount and multiply it by the annual interest rate. Next divide that number by 12. This is your interest earned in the second month. After you have repeated this calculation for all 12 months, add the monthly interest totals. The sum of the monthly interest amounts is the interest your account would earn in one year if the interest were compounded monthly.

GO FIGURE   FINANCIAL MATH

INTEREST COMPOUNDED MONTHLY

Synopsis: Savings accounts that pay interest monthly can end up earning more interest than an account that pays once a year.

Example: You deposit $100 in a savings account. The bank is paying you 4 percent annually, which is compounded monthly. How much interest will you earn for the year?

Formula: Find the interest earned for the first month:

A. $\dfrac{\text{Principal} \times \text{Annual Interest Rate}}{12} = \text{Interest Earned for First Month}$

B. $\dfrac{(\text{Principal} + \text{Previously Earned Interest}) \times \text{Annual Interest Rate}}{12} = \text{Interest Earned for a Given Month}$

Solution:

Month	Calculation
1	($100.00 × 4%) ÷ 12 = $0.33
2	($100.33 × 4%) ÷ 12 = $0.33
3	($100.66 × 4%) ÷ 12 = $0.34
4	($101.00 × 4%) ÷ 12 = $0.34
5	($101.34 × 4%) ÷ 12 = $0.34
6	($101.68 × 4%) ÷ 12 = $0.34
7	($102.02 × 4%) ÷ 12 = $0.34
8	($102.36 × 4%) ÷ 12 = $0.34
9	($102.70 × 4%) ÷ 12 = $0.34
10	($103.04 × 4%) ÷ 12 = $0.34
11	($103.38 × 4%) ÷ 12 = $0.34
12	($103.72 × 4%) ÷ 12 = $0.35

At the end of the year, you will have $104.07 ($100.00 + $4.07 = $104.07). You earned $4.07 in compounded interest for the year.

YOU FIGURE

How much interest would this account earn if interest was paid once for the whole year?

RATE OF RETURN

Synopsis: A compounded rate of return (percentage) is more than the stated year's rate.

Example: You deposit $100 in a savings account. The bank is paying you 4 percent annually, compounded monthly. After one year, the account has earned $4.07 in interest. What would your rate of return be for one year?

Formula: $\dfrac{\text{Total Interest Earned}}{\text{Original Deposit}} = \text{Rate of Return}$

Solution: $\dfrac{\$4.07}{\$100} = 0.0407 = 4.07\%$

Your rate of return is 4.07 percent.

YOU FIGURE

What would be your rate of return for one year if the account earned $5.14 in interest on a deposit of $100?

The more frequently your balance is compounded, the greater your yield, or rate of return, will be. For example, if you deposited $100 in an account with a 4 percent annual interest rate that is compounded annually (once a year), after one year you will earn $4 ($100 × .04 or 4% = $4). Your rate of return is 4 percent. If you put that same $100 in an account that is compounded monthly at an annual interest rate of 4 percent, your rate of return will be higher.

Remember, your rate of return is the total interest earned divided by the amount of your original deposit. The difference may not seem like much, but compounding can have a great impact on large amounts of money that are held in savings accounts for long periods.

Truth in Savings   According to the Truth in Savings law (Federal Reserve Regulation DD), financial institutions have to inform you of the following information:

- Fees on deposit accounts
- Interest rate
- Annual percentage yield (APY)
- Terms and conditions of the savings plan

The **annual percentage yield (APY)** is the amount of interest that a $100 deposit would earn, after compounding, for one year. The interest is based on the annual stated interest rate and the frequency of compounding for a 365-day period. In the previous **Go Figure** example, the APY is 4.07 percent. The higher the APY is, the better the return. The APY helps you determine the amount you can expect to earn on your money. Because the APY is stated as a percentage and as an annual rate, it you can compare savings plans that have different rates and compounding frequencies.

Document Detective

Learn to identify and understand the standard financial documents you will use in the real world.

Investigate: A Checking Account Bank Statement

A checking account bank statement contains the following information:

- Balance, or amount, in the account at the beginning of a time period
- Deposits made to the account
- Deductions made from the account
- Ending balance at the end of the time period

Your Motive: You need to keep track of deductions and deposits in your check register as you write checks and deposit money. The monthly statement is the bank's record of that activity. It is important that your records and the bank's records are the same so your account will not get overdrawn.

SMITHVILLE BANK N.A.

Tom Jones
21 First Street
Smithville, Florida 55523

ACCOUNT SUMMARY	Statement Date: 02/24/05
Balance forwarded from 01/23/05	$41,452.80
Checks	6,310.00
Interest added	50.59
Ending balance	**$35,193.39**

ELECTRONIC CREDITS

Date	Description	
2/24/05	INTEREST PAID	$50.59

CHECKS AND OTHER DEBITS			DAILY BALANCE SUMMARY	
Date	Check#	Amount	Date	Balance
01/27/05	1043	$70.00	1/27/05	$41,382.80
02/18/05	1044	100.00	02/10/05	38,942.80
02/12/05	1045	3,600.00	02/12/05	35,342.80
02/10/05	1046	2,440.00	02/18/05	35,242.80
02/19/05	1047	100.00	02/19/05	35,142.80
			02/24/05	35,193.39

Key Points: If there is a difference between your records and the bank's records, you need to resolve the problem with your bank. If the bank thinks you have less money than you do, your checks may "bounce," or be rejected and go unpaid, causing the bank to charge you penalty fees.

Find the Solutions

1. What time period does this statement cover?
2. From this statement, what do you think is the meaning of the word *credits*?
3. From this statement, what do you think is the meaning of the word *debits*?
4. On 02/10/05, the balance in this account changed. Why?
5. There is a line on this statement that reads "Checks 6,310.00." What does this mean?

Inflation

You should compare the rate of interest you earn on your savings with the rate of inflation. If you open a savings account that offers 3 percent interest, and the inflation rate rises to 6 percent, your money will lose value and buying power. Usually, however, the interest rates offered on savings accounts increase if the rate of inflation increases. The biggest problem with inflation occurs if you are locked into a lower interest rate for a long period.

Tax Considerations

Like inflation, taxes reduce the interest earned on savings. For example, Karim was glad to find a savings account that would pay 5 percent interest. However, he was not happy when he filled out his tax return and had to pay taxes on that interest. He decided to look into tax-exempt and tax-deferred savings plans for some of his money.

Liquidity

Check the savings plans you are considering to determine whether they charge a penalty or pay a lower rate of interest if you withdraw your funds early. If you need to be able to withdraw your money easily, put your money in a liquid account—even if it earns lower interest. On the other hand, if you are saving for long-term goals, a high interest rate is more important than liquidity.

Restrictions and Fees

Be aware of any restrictions on savings plans, such as a delay between the time when interest is earned and when it is actually paid into your account. Also check for fees for making deposits and withdrawals. Find out about any service charges you may have to pay if your balance drops below a certain amount, or if you do not use your account for a certain period. These fees and service charges can add up.

Types of Checking Accounts

What are the different kinds of checking accounts?

Checking accounts can be divided into three main categories: regular, activity, and interest-earning accounts.

Regular Checking Accounts

Regular checking accounts usually do not require a minimum balance. However, if the account does require a minimum balance, and your account drops below that amount, you will have to pay a monthly service charge. A $10 charge every month can take a bite out of your funds. Some institutions will waive a service charge if you keep a certain balance in your savings account.

STANDARD &POOR'S

Put on Your Financial Planner's Cap

A previously unknown relative has died and left your friend $50,000. Would you recommend that she open a checking account, a savings account, or another type of account? Why or why not?

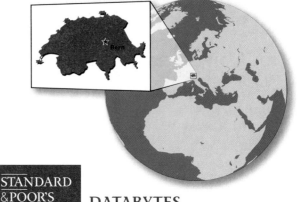

Standard and Poor's publishes the globally recognized S&P 500® financial index. It also gathers financial statistics, information, and news, and analyzes this data for international businesses, governments, and individuals to help them guide their financial decisions.

SWITZERLAND

Say "Switzerland," and people often think of rich chocolate, cozy alpine villages, and cuckoo clocks. Switzerland also boasts its most famous industry—banking. Once called the crossroads of Europe, the country of Switzerland has been one of the world's most important financial centers for centuries. Its government's neutrality during times of war and the skill of its bankers attract depositors by the millions. Above all, clients—from the ordinary to the rich—appreciate the banks' secrecy. Numbers, not names, identify each customer. "Serious money is safe and private in a Swiss bank in Switzerland," promises one ad. However, a new Swiss federal law now prohibits complete secrecy. Deposits of questionable or criminal origin must be reported to the authorities.

STANDARD &POOR'S
DATABYTES

Capital	Bern
Population	7,341,000
Languages	German, French, Italian, and Romanisch
Currency	Swiss franc
Gross Domestic Product (GDP)	$239.8 billion (2003 est.)
GDP per capita	$32,800

Industry: Banking, machinery, chemicals, watches, textiles, and precision instruments

Agriculture: Grains, fruits and vegetables, and meat

Exports: Machinery, chemicals, metals, watches, and agricultural products

Natural Resources: Hydropower potential, timber, and salt

Think Globally
If you were planning to open a checking or savings account in Switzerland or the United States what three types of accounts would you consider?

Activity Accounts

If you write only a few checks each month and are unable to maintain a minimum balance, this type of checking account may be right for you. The financial institution will charge a fee for each check you write and sometimes a fee for each deposit. In addition, a monthly service fee will be charged. However, you do not need to maintain a minimum balance.

Interest-Earning Checking Accounts

Interest-earning checking accounts are a combination of checking and savings accounts. These accounts pay interest if you maintain a minimum balance. If your account balance goes below the limit, you may not earn any interest, and you may also have to pay a service charge.

Evaluating Checking Accounts
What factors should you consider when choosing a checking account?

How do you decide which type of checking account will meet your needs? You will need to weigh several factors: restrictions, fees and charges, interest, and special services.

Restrictions

The most common restriction is the requirement that you keep a minimum balance. Other restrictions may include the number of transactions allowed and the number of checks you may write in a month.

Fees and Charges

You may pay a monthly service charge as well as fees for check printing, overdrafts, and stop-payment orders.

Interest

Interest rates, frequency of compounding, and the way in which interest is calculated all affect an interest-bearing checking account.

Special Services

Checking account services include ATMs and banking by telephone and online. As a checking account customer, you may also receive **overdraft protection**—an automatic loan made to an account if the balance will not cover checks written. The institution will charge interest on that loan, but the amount may be less than the fee for overdrawing your account. Your bank may also offer an overdraft protection service that transfers money from your savings to your checking account.

The Check Clearing for the 21st Century Act, or "Check 21," took effect as of October 28, 2004. The Act allows banks to dispense with original paper checks. Banks can now transmit electronic images of checks through the check-clearing process. If you want to receive your cancelled paper check, the bank will provide a substitute check, such as a printout of an electronic image, for a fee.

Academic Connection

HISTORY

In response to financial hardship caused by the Great Depression, the Emergency Banking Act of 1933 called for a four-day bank holiday during which time all banks were assessed by federal inspectors. Within those four days, roughly two-thirds of the nation's banks were declared financially secure and were reopened, restoring Americans' faith in banking institutions. *Research the Great Depression and write a short paragraph explaining why you think the Emergency Banking Act helped restore faith in banking institutions.*

Finding the Best Savings Account

1. Shop around to find the bank that offers the highest interest rates.
2. Ask if you must deposit a minimum amount.
3. Find out if the bank pays less on small accounts.
4. Ask the bank how often it credits interest to your account.
5. Ask if you will receive simple interest or compound interest.

Using a Checking Account
How do you open and use a checking account?

After you select the type of checking account that best fits your needs, you need to know how to use it effectively.

Opening a Checking Account

Before you open a checking account, decide whether you want an individual or joint account. An individual account has one owner; a joint account has two or more. Personal joint accounts are usually "or" accounts, which means that only one of the owners needs to sign a check. You sign a signature card at the bank so that your signature on a check can be verified.

Writing Checks

Before you write a check, write the date, the number of the check, the name of the party who will receive the payment, and the exact amount in your check register. A check register is a small booklet that you use to record activity in your account. You receive it with your supply of blank checks. Record all checks that you write, deposits, ATM withdrawals, debit card charges, interest earned (if any), any fees, and other transactions. Be sure to keep a current balance of the money you have by deducting from or adding to your balance the amount of any check transaction. **Figure 5.4** shows a sample check register.

Figure 5.4   Check Register

NUMBER	DATE	DESCRIPTION OF TRANSACTION	PAYMENT/DEBIT (-)	√ T	FEE (IF ANY) (-)	DEPOSIT/CREDIT (+)	BALANCE $ 418 00
106	7/15	Bob's Service Station	$ 25 00		$	$	-25 00
		oil change					393 00
107	7/15	Cutler Enterprises	14 00				-14 00
		magazine subscription					379 00
108	7/16	Motor Vehicles Department	160 00				-160 00
		renewal					219 00
109	7/18	Jack's Music	34 00				-34 00
		gift					185 00

Keeping Track   This sample check register shows how to keep track of checks as you write them.

What other amounts should you record in your check register?

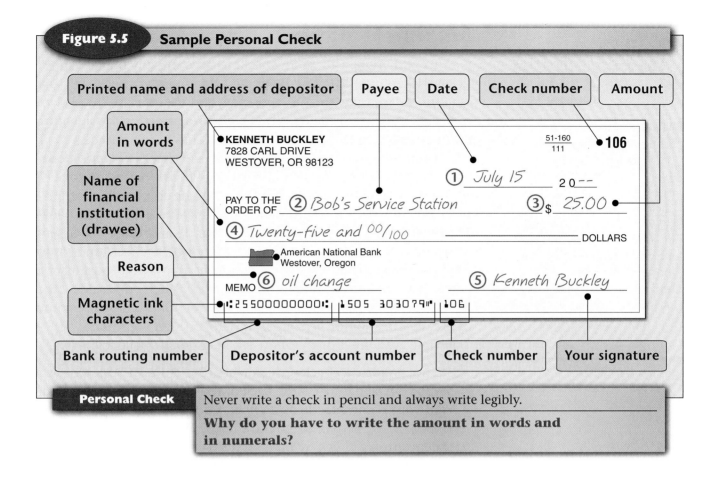

Figure 5.5 Sample Personal Check

Printed name and address of depositor	Payee	Date	Check number	Amount

Amount in words

Name of financial institution (drawee)

Reason

Magnetic ink characters

KENNETH BUCKLEY
7828 CARL DRIVE
WESTOVER, OR 98123

$\frac{51\text{-}160}{111}$ • **106**

① *July 15* 20--

PAY TO THE ORDER OF ② *Bob's Service Station* ③ $ *25.00*

④ *Twenty-five and* ^{00}/$_{100}$ _____ DOLLARS

American National Bank
Westover, Oregon

MEMO ⑥ *oil change* ⑤ *Kenneth Buckley*

⑈:25500000000⑈ ⑈505 303079⑈ 106

Bank routing number | Depositor's account number | Check number | Your signature

Personal Check Never write a check in pencil and always write legibly.

Why do you have to write the amount in words and in numerals?

Figure 5.5 illustrates the correct way to write a check. Follow these steps when you write a check:

1. Write the current date.
2. Write the name of the party (payee) who will receive the check.
3. Record the amount of the payment in numerals.
4. Write the amount in words.
5. Sign the check in the same way you signed your signature card at the bank.
6. Make a note of the reason for the payment. This is a good place to record an account number if the payment is for a credit card or service, such as electricity or cable television.

If you make a mistake when writing a check, do not erase the error. Write a new check, tear up the old check, and write the word *Void* in your check register. If the mistake is small, you may be able to correct the check and write your initials next to the correction.

If a check is lost or stolen, or if you want to take back your payment for a business transaction, you may ask the bank to issue a stop-payment order. A **stop-payment order** is a request that a bank or other financial institution not cash a particular check. Fees for this service can range from $10 to $20 or more.

Making Deposits

To add money to your checking account, fill out a deposit ticket. Tickets usually include room to list four or five checks and any amount of cash that you are depositing. Endorse, or sign, the back of each check you want to deposit. The **endorsement** is the signature of the payee, the party to whom the check has been written.

There are also different ways to endorse a check. A *blank endorsement* is the most simple. You or the check holder signs the back of the check. A *restrictive endorsement* requires the check holder's signature and a restriction on how the paper may be used by the bank. The most common expression used is "For deposit only." This is an instruction that restricts the bank to applying the check amount to the holder's account. A *special endorsement* allows you to transfer a check to an organization or another person. When you endorse the check, you write the words *pay to the order of,* followed by the name of the organization or person, and then you sign your name.

Here are some tips to follow when endorsing a check:

- Do not endorse a check until you are ready to cash or deposit it.
- Write your signature on the back of the check at the top left end.
- Sign your name exactly as it appears on the front of the check.
- Use a pen so that your signature cannot be erased.
- If depositing a check by mail, write "For deposit only" above your signature.

Check Clearing

Check clearing is a system that ensures that the money you deposited in the account is available for withdrawal. For example, if you deposit a check for $50 into your account, your bank usually holds that $50 until it clears with the bank on which it was drawn. During this time you cannot withdraw that money. By law, institutions are limited to holding funds from checks drawn on local banks to no more than two business days, and from checks drawn on non-local banks to no more than five business days. Check-clearing rules vary by bank, so ask your bank about its rules.

Keeping Track of a Checking Account

Each month your bank will send you a statement that shows your checking account activity for the month.
Your bank statement will list:

- Deposits
- Checks you have written (charged against your account)
- ATM withdrawals
- Debit card charges (identified by the business or organization to whom you made the payment)
- Interest earned
- Fees

Reconciliation The balance reported on the bank statement may be different from the balance in your check register. You might have written checks that have not yet cleared your bank, or maybe you deposited money into your account after the bank prepared your statement.

To determine your true balance, you can fill out a bank reconciliation form. A **bank reconciliation** is a report that accounts for the differences between the bank statement and a checkbook balance. This process is called *balancing your checkbook*. To balance, or reconcile, your account, follow several steps (a simplified version of a reconciliation form is shown in **Figure 5.6**).

Figure 5.6   **Bank Account Reconciliation**

❖ *American National Bank*
WESTOVER, OREGON

Kenneth Buckley
7828 Carl Drive
Westover, OR 98123

FDIC

Account Number: 303079
Statement Date: 7/15/--

Balance Last Statement	Deposits & Other Credits		Checks & Other Debits		Balance This Statement
	No.	Amount	No.	Amount	
00.00	2	700.00	5	482.00	218.00

Description	Checks & Other Debits	Deposits & Other Credits	Date	Balance
Balance Forward				00.00
Deposit		500.00	7/01	500.00
Check 101	273.00		7/04	227.00
Check 102	27.00		7/07	200.00
Check 103	50.00		7/08	150.00
Deposit		200.00	7/10	350.00
Check 104	100.00		7/14	250.00
Check 105	32.00		7/14	218.00

PLEASE EXAMINE YOUR STATEMENT AT ONCE. IF NO ERROR IS REPORTED IN 10 DAYS THE ACCOUNT WILL BE CONSIDERED CORRECT AND VOUCHERS GENUINE. ALL ITEMS ARE CREDITED SUBJECT TO FINAL PAYMENT.

BANK RECONCILIATION FORM

PLEASE EXAMINE YOUR STATEMENT AT ONCE. ANY DISCREPANCY SHOULD BE REPORTED TO THE BANK IMMEDIATELY.

1. In your checkbook, record any transactions appearing on this statement but not yet listed.

2. List any checks still outstanding in the space provided to the right.

3. Enter the balance shown on this statement here. | 218 | 00 |

4. Enter deposits recorded in your checkbook but not shown on this statement. | — | — |

5. Total lines 3 and 4 and enter here. | 218 | 00 |

6. Enter total checks outstanding here. | 69 | 00 |

7. Subtract line 6 from line 5. This adjusted bank balance should agree with your checkbook balance. | 149 | 00 |

CHECKS OUTSTANDING	
Number	Amount
106	25 00
107	14 00
108	30 00
TOTAL	69 00

Balancing Your Checkbook   The adjusted bank balance should agree with your checkbook register.

Why should you reconcile your checking account with each new statement?

1. Compare the checks you have written during the month with those that are listed on the bank statement as paid, or cleared. List all outstanding checks—checks you wrote but have not cleared. Subtract the total amount of outstanding checks from the balance on the bank statement.

2. Determine whether any recent deposits are not on the bank statement. If so, add the amounts of those deposits to the bank statement balance.

3. Subtract fees and charges listed on the statement from your checkbook balance.

4. Add interest earned to your checkbook balance.

Then compare the balance in your check register and the adjusted bank balance on the reconciliation form. They should be the same. If the balances do not match, check your math, and make sure all checks and deposits are entered in your check register and on the statement. If there is a bank error, report it.

Other Payment Methods

You may make payments by other methods besides using a personal check. A certified check is a personal check with a guaranteed payment. The financial institution deducts the amount from your account when it certifies the check. You can also purchase a cashier's check or money order from a financial institution. You pay the amount of the check or money order plus a fee. Travelers checks allow you to obtain cash in a country's currency when you are away from home.

▶ **TRAVELING MONEY**
Travelers checks are one option for students who need to carry money while traveling in foreign countries. Most banks, hotels, and stores will accept this currency. *Why are travelers checks preferred over regular cash when traveling?*

You sign each check once when you purchase the checks and a second time when you cash them. If you lose a check or it is stolen, it can be replaced with proof of purchase. Prepaid travelers cards allow travelers to get local currency from ATMs throughout the world.

After You Read

REACT

What is a bank reconciliation? Why is it important?

Financial Institutions and Your Money

How Do Banks Make Money?

The amount of deposits held by a bank affects its ability to loan money. Banks make money by making loans. The amount of money that banks can lend is affected by the reserve requirement set by the Federal Reserve. The reserve requirement is 3 percent to 10 percent of a bank's total deposits, including your deposit. For example, when a bank gets a deposit of $100, the bank can then lend out $90. That $90 goes back into the economy, paying for goods or services, and may end up deposited in another bank. That bank can then lend out $81 of that $90 deposit, and that $81 goes into the economy to pay for goods or services, and is then deposited into another bank that proceeds to lend out a percentage of it. Thus, banking your money benefits you as well as others in the economic system.

Section 5.2 Assessment

QUICK CHECK

1. What are some of the costs and benefits of a certificate of deposit?
2. What factors can you use to evaluate a savings plan?
3. What are regular, activity, and interest-earning checking accounts?

THINK CRITICALLY

4. Why do you think a law was passed to standardize the ways in which financial institutions inform consumers of the terms and conditions of savings plans?

USE COMMUNICATION SKILLS

5. **The Banking Business** Banks advertise to attract customers.

Present a Poster Choose one or more features of savings or checking accounts and create a poster advertising those features in a way that will inform people and invite them to become customers.

SOLVE MONEY PROBLEMS

6. **Checking Account Choices** Matthew Delarosa has just moved to a new town and is about to open a checking account. He pays for all his monthly expenses—rent, phone, car payment, credit card bills, dry cleaning, and insurance—by check.

Write About It With a partner, examine the features of the different types of checking accounts and write a paragraph to help Matthew decide which type would be best for him.

CHAPTER SUMMARY

- The three primary types of financial services are savings; payment services; and borrowing.
- Commercial banks, savings and loan associations, mutual savings banks, and credit unions are financial institutions that accept secure deposits and provide transfer and lending services. Life insurance companies and investment companies accept customers' funds, provide financial security for dependents, and invest and manage funds. Finance companies and mortgage companies offer loans.
- Bank savings plans offer the lowest interest rates with the greatest liquidity. Higher interest rates are available on certificates of deposit (CDs); money must be on deposit for a specified time.

- Money market accounts and U.S. Savings Bonds are less liquid than bank savings accounts, but may provide greater returns.
- To evaluate a savings plan, look at its features, such as its rate of return compared with inflation, tax considerations, liquidity, and restrictions and fees.
- Regular, activity, and interest-earning are the three categories of checking accounts. Some of these require minimum balances and/or fees for transactions. Some pay interest on deposits.
- To use a checking account, write checks carefully, endorse checks you deposit, and reconcile your checkbook against bank statements.

Communicating Key Terms

Write the copy for a promotional brochure for a commercial bank, explaining what the bank offers its customers. Use at least eight of the terms below in your brochure copy.

- direct deposit
- automated teller machine (ATM)
- debit card
- point-of-sale transaction
- commercial bank

- savings and loan association (S&L)
- credit union
- certificate of deposit (CD)
- money market account
- rate of return

- compounding
- annual percentage yield (APY)
- overdraft protection
- stop-payment order
- endorsement
- bank reconciliation

Reviewing Key Concepts

1. **Explain** two advantages and two disadvantages of online banking.
2. **Identify** the services offered by the different financial institutions.
3. **Explain** why a large, nationally chartered bank may be the safest place to deposit your money.
4. **Discuss** how you benefit when interest is compounded monthly as opposed to annually.
5. **Explain** the circumstances under which a person should choose a regular checking account, activity checking account, or interest-bearing checking account.
6. **List** the steps to take to use a checking account effectively.

ACADEMIC
SKILLS

Economics Explain at least three ways to reduce ATM fees charged to your account. Also describe the trade-offs involved in each action.

Write About It Create a list with your explanations.

**YOUR
FINANCIAL
FIGURES**

Checking Account Minimum Balances Bank X offers a checking account with a minimum balance of $300, but does not charge fees nor give interest. Bank Y's minimum balance is $50, but it charges a fee of $25 if you have more than 35 transactions per month, including deposits. Both banks pay 2 percent interest on regular savings accounts and 3 percent on certificates of deposit with terms of 24 months.

1. **Describe** (a) Someone for whom Bank A's offer is the best deal. (b) Someone for whom Bank B's offer is the best deal.
2. **Compute** by using spreadsheet software bank statements that compare returns from Bank A and Bank B for the people profiled.

**REAL-WORLD
Application**

Connect with Business and Government Check 21 is a federal law that lets banks handle more checks electronically, which should make check processing faster, more efficient, and less expensive. Before Check 21 became effective in late 2004, banks physically moved paper checks from one bank to another. If you used to receive your cancelled checks after they cleared your bank, you now receive a picture of the front and back of your checks instead.

1. **Research** Use library and online sources to find out more about Check 21.
2. **Think Critically** Who do you think benefits the most from this change? The least?

Internet
CONNECTION

Banking Online Many banks offer online banking, but it does not appeal to everyone.

 Log On Go to the Web site of a bank that you or your family uses and find out if it offers Internet banking. Answer the following questions:

1. How can you be sure the site is secure?
2. What transactions can you perform with an online account?

BusinessWeek
O N L I N E

Newsclip: Teen Savings Banks offer many savings options to teenagers. A teen can open a savings/passbook account or a CD (certificate of deposit).

Log On Go to persfinance07.glencoe.com and open Chapter 5. Read about the different types of available savings options. Then answer this question: When is it the right time to save, and what types of savings accounts are available?

WHAT'S YOUR FINANCIAL ID?

BASIC BANKING QUIZ

How much do you know about basic bank services and terms? Take this quiz before you read the chapter and retake it after studying the chapter to see how much you have learned. Write your answers on a separate sheet of paper.

1. A bank CD is a _____ .
a. cash deposit
b. compact disc
c.   certificate of deposit
d.   compact deposit

2. To borrow money from the bank, you need to ask for a _____.
a. loan   c.
b. money market account
safe-deposit box
d.   transfer

3. You can store valuables in the bank's vault if you have _____.
a. permission
b. a money market account
c.   a safe-deposit box
d.   an ATM card

4. You keep money in a bank account to _____ .
a. keep it safe
b. earn interest
c.   learn financial responsibility
d.   all of the above

5. The total amount of money in your bank account is called _____.
a. the statement
b. the interest
c.   the balance
d.   peanuts

6. The amount of money your bank account earns depends on the _____ .
a. type of account you have
b. balance in your account
c.   interest rate
d.   all of the above

7. When you make a purchase and have the funds taken directly from your checking account, you use a _____ .
a. credit card
b. note from your mother
c.   debit card
d.   driver's license

8. To set up a savings plan that requires a low minimum balance and allows you to withdraw funds at any time, you would _____ .
a. buy a CD
b. buy a U.S. Savings Bond
c.   put the money under your mattress
d.   open a savings account

Your Financial Portfolio

Comparison Shopping for Banking Services

Sean is ready to open some bank accounts and is looking for the bank that best suits his needs. He is deciding between the local bank and the credit union where he works.

Sean's Savings Search

Name of Institution	Kensington Bank	Acme Credit Union
Savings		
Annual interest rate	1.8%	2.5%
Minimum balance required	$100	none
Certificate of Deposit (CD) interest rate for 6 months	5.20%	5.40%
Checking		
Monthly service charge	$8.50	$6.00
Minimum balance for "free" checking	$3,000	$1,000
Fees for ATM	Free	no ATMs
Cost of checks	$10.00	$8.75
Overdraft protection	yes	none
Banking hours	Mon.–Sat. 9–6, Closed Sun.	Mon.–Fri. 9–6, Closed Sat. and Sun.

Sean decided to open a checking account at the bank because he needs the convenience of using the ATM. He opened a savings account at the credit union because it pays higher interest. When he has enough money, he will also purchase a CD at the credit union.

Compare

In your workbook or on a separate sheet of paper, list the banking services that are important to you. Then call or visit several banks in your area and compare services, costs, and interest rates that are available to you. What services are most important to you? Which bank would you choose? Explain why.

CHAPTER 6
Consumer Credit

 What You'll Learn

When you have completed this chapter, you will be able to:

Section 6.1
- Explain the meaning of consumer credit.
- Differentiate between closed-end credit and open-end credit.

Section 6.2
- Name the five C's of credit.
- Identify factors to consider when choosing a loan or credit card.
- Explain how to build and protect your credit rating.

Section 6.3
- Discuss how to protect yourself from fraud and identity theft.

Section 6.4
- Identify ways to manage debt problems.

Reading Strategies

To get the most out of your reading:

Predict what you will learn in this chapter.
Relate what you read to your own life.
Question what you are reading to be sure you understand.
React to what you have read.

In the **Real** World . . .

When Jillian graduated high school and went to a local college in Atlanta, she received an offer for a credit card and applied for it. She was excited when she made her first charge for a new outfit. After purchasing more clothes on credit, she reached her card limit. So she applied for two more credit cards, each with an annual interest rate of 21 percent. Then she began to charge groceries and furniture because it was easier than paying cash. Jillian continued to use credit but did not notice her balances until they grew to $9,500. Then she realized it would take years to pay them off and knew she needed to learn more about handling credit.

As You Read   *Consider ways Jillian could manage her credit more effectively.*

ASK STANDARD &POOR'S

Credit Payments

Q: My brother is going to college and has three credit cards with balances totaling $5,000. He is having trouble paying the minimum monthly payments. What should I tell him?

A: He needs a plan to pay down these debts. Have him contact the credit card companies and tell them that he wants to pay the debt and maintain good credit. They may accept payments of interest only for a few months while he finds ways to increase his income or cut spending.

Ask Yourself Why would communicating with a debtor (the credit card company) benefit someone who is behind in payments?

 Go to **persfinance07.glencoe.com** to complete the Standard & Poor's Financial Focus activity.

What Is Consumer Credit?

Using Consumer Credit Wisely
Why is having good credit important?

When you borrow money or charge an item to a credit card, you are using credit. **Credit** is an arrangement to receive cash, goods, or services now and pay for them in the future. **Consumer credit** is the use of credit for personal needs. It is also an indicator of consumer spending and demand. A common form of consumer credit is a credit card account issued by a financial institution. Merchants may also provide financing for products that they sell. Banks may directly finance purchases through loans and mortgages. A financial institution, merchant, or individual can be a **creditor**—an entity that lends money. Good credit is valuable. Having the ability to borrow funds allows us to buy things we would otherwise have to save for years to afford: homes, cars, or a college education. Credit is an important financial tool, but it can also be dangerous, leading people into debt beyond their ability to repay. That is why using credit wisely is a valuable financial skill.

Today consumer credit is a major force in the American economy, and the use of credit is a basic factor in personal and family financial planning (see **Figure 6.1**). Sometimes using credit is necessary, and it can be an advantage. However, paying for an item through credit also involves responsibility and risks.

Credit Uses and Misuses
When is it appropriate to use credit?

You can probably think of many good reasons for using credit. For example, maybe you can buy something on credit now for less money than it will cost to pay in cash later. If you live in an area that lacks good public transportation, you may need a vehicle to travel. But when is it appropriate to use credit? If you cannot afford a high monthly payment, it probably is not a good idea to borrow money to buy an expensive sports car when all you need is simple and reliable transportation.

Using credit may increase the amount of money you can spend now, but the cost of credit decreases the amount of money you will have in the future. That is because you will be paying back the money you borrowed along with any charges for borrowing that money.

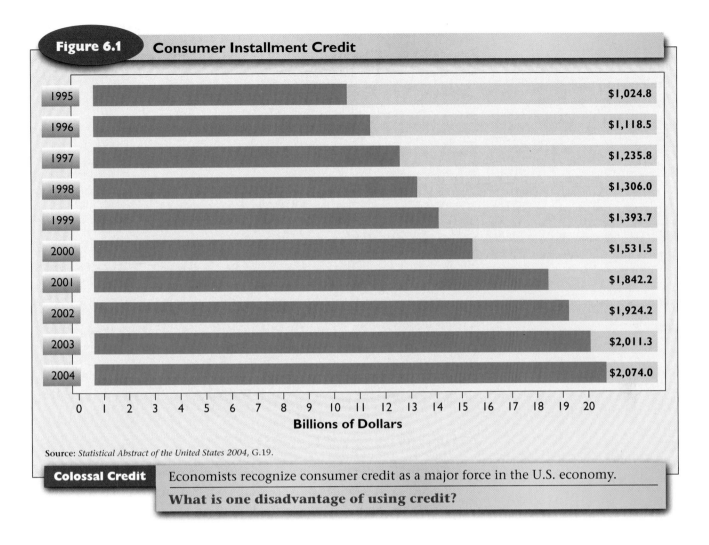

Figure 6.1 Consumer Installment Credit

Year		Amount
1995		$1,024.8
1996		$1,118.5
1997		$1,235.8
1998		$1,306.0
1999		$1,393.7
2000		$1,531.5
2001		$1,842.2
2002		$1,924.2
2003		$2,011.3
2004		$2,074.0

Billions of Dollars

0 1 2 3 4 5 6 7 8 9 10 11 12 13 14 15 16 17 18 19 20

Source: *Statistical Abstract of the United States 2004*, G.19.

Colossal Credit Economists recognize consumer credit as a major force in the U.S. economy.

What is one disadvantage of using credit?

Factors to Consider Before Using Credit

What should you know before using credit?

Imagine you want to finance—give or get money for—a used vehicle. Before you decide to finance a major purchase by using credit, consider:

- Do you have the cash you need for the down payment?
- Do you want to use your savings instead of credit?
- Can you afford the item?
- Could you use the credit in some better way?
- Could you put off buying the item for a while?
- What are the costs of using credit?

When you buy something on credit, you also agree to pay the fee that a creditor adds to the purchase price. For example, if you do not pay your credit card bill in full every month, you will be charged interest on the amount that you have not paid. Interest is the price that is paid for the use of another's money. It can be a periodic charge for the use of credit. Think carefully before you decide to use credit. Make sure the benefits of making the purchase now outweigh the costs of credit.

As You Read

RELATE

Did you ever use credit to buy something you could not afford?

► **THINK FIRST** Everyone likes to have nice things, but using credit unwisely can lead to problems. *What should you consider before using credit?*

Advantages of Credit

The main advantage of using consumer credit is that it lets you enjoy goods and services now, perhaps when your funds are low, and pay for them later. Credit cards allow you to combine several purchases, making just one monthly payment.

If you are making hotel reservations, renting a car, or shopping by phone or online, you will probably need a credit card. Using credit gives you a record of your expenses. Shopping and traveling without carrying a lot of cash is safer.

Finally, if you use credit wisely, other lenders will view you as a responsible person.

Disadvantages of Credit

Always remember that credit costs money. Perhaps the greatest disadvantage of using credit is the temptation to buy more than you can afford. Using credit to buy goods or services you cannot afford can lead to serious trouble. If you fail to repay a loan, or a credit card balance, you can lose your good credit reputation. You may also lose some of your income and property, which may be taken from you in order to repay your debts.

Using credit does not increase your total purchasing power, nor does it mean that you have more money. It just allows you buy things now for which you must pay later. If your income does not increase, you may have difficulty paying your bills. Therefore, you should always approach credit with caution and avoid using it for more than your budget allows.

As You Read

QUESTION

Why is it important to protect your good reputation as a borrower?

Types of Credit

Why will you need more than one type of credit?

There are two basic types of consumer credit: closed-end credit and open-end credit. You may use both types during your lifetime because each has advantages and disadvantages.

Closed-End Credit

Closed-end credit is credit as a one-time loan that you will pay back over a specified period of time in payments of equal amounts. Closed-end credit is used for a specific purpose and involves a definite amount of money.

A mortgage—a long-term loan extended to someone who buys property—is a common use of closed-end credit. Vehicle loans and installment loans for purchasing furniture or large appliances are also examples of closed-end credit. These types of loans usually carry lower interest rates than open-end credit carries.

For example, when the Petersons were ready to move out of their apartment, they decided to buy a three-bedroom house and apply for a mortgage from a bank. They signed a written agreement that indicated how much their monthly payments would be, how many payments they would make, and the cost of the credit over the life of the loan. The bank will hold the title to the house until the Petersons have completed their payments.

Suppose that you want to buy a sofa and loveseat to furnish your living room. You might apply for an installment loan from a furniture company. You would sign a contract promising to repay the balance, plus interest, in equal installments over a specified period.

Open-End Credit

What does open-end credit mean? **Open-end credit** is credit as a loan with a certain limit on the amount of money you can borrow for a variety of goods and services. A **line of credit** is the maximum amount of money a creditor will allow a credit user to borrow. Department store credit cards and bank credit cards, such as Visa or MasterCard, are examples of open-end credit. After a credit card company has approved your application for credit and you have received the card, you can use it to make as many purchases as you wish, as long as you do not exceed your line of credit. You are then billed periodically for at least partial payment of the total amount you owe.

Sources of Consumer Credit

What are some sources of consumer credit?

Many sources of consumer credit are available, including commercial banks and credit unions. **Figure 6.2** summarizes the major sources of consumer credit. Study and compare the differences to determine which source might best meet your needs and requirements.

Figure 6.2 **Sources of Consumer Credit**

Credit Source	Type of Loan	Lending Policies
Commercial Banks	Single-payment loan Personal installment loans Passbook loans Check-credit loans Credit card loans Second mortgages	• Seek customers with established credit history • Often require collateral or security • Prefer to deal in large loans, such as vehicle, home improvement, and home modernization, with the exception of credit card and check-credit plans • Determine repayment schedules according to the purpose of the loan • Vary credit rates according to the type of credit, time period, customer's credit history, and the security offered • May require several days to process a new credit application
Consumer Finance Companies	Personal installment loans Second mortgages	• Often lend to consumers without established credit history • Often make unsecured loans • Often vary rates according to the size of the loan balance • Offer a variety of repayment schedules • Make a higher percentage of small loans than other lenders • Maximum loan size limited by law • Process applications quickly, frequently on the same day the application is made
Credit Unions	Personal installment loans Share draft-credit plans Credit card loans Second mortgages	• Lend to members only • Make unsecured loans • May require collateral or cosigner for loans over a specified amount • May require payroll deductions to pay off loan • May submit large loan applications to a committee of members for approval • Offer a variety of repayment schedules
Life Insurance Companies	Single-payment or partial payment loans	• Lend on cash value of life insurance policy • No date or penalty on repayment • Deduct amount owed from the value of the policy benefit if death or other maturity occurs before repayment
Federal Savings Banks (Savings and Loan Associations)	Personal installment loans (generally permitted by state-chartered savings associations) Home improvement loans Education loans Savings account loans Second mortgages	• Will lend to all creditworthy individuals • Often require collateral • Loan rates vary depending on size of loan, length of payment, and security involved

Seeking Customers Consumer credit is available from several types of sources.

Which sources seem to offer the widest variety of loans?

Loans

A loan is borrowed money with an agreement to repay it with interest within a certain amount of time. If you were considering taking out a loan, your immediate thought might be to go to your local bank. However, you might want to explore some other options first.

Inexpensive Loans   Parents or other family members are often the source of the least expensive loans—loans with low interest. They may charge only the interest they would have earned on the money if they had deposited it in a savings account. They may even give you a loan without interest. Be aware, however, that loans can complicate family relationships.

Medium-Priced Loans   Often you can obtain medium-priced loans—loans with moderate interest—from commercial banks, savings and loan associations, and credit unions. Borrowing from credit unions has several advantages. Credit unions provide personalized service, and they are usually willing to be patient with borrowers who can provide good reasons for late or missed payments. As you learned in Chapter 5, you must be a member of a credit union in order to get a loan from one.

Expensive Loans   The easiest loans to obtain are also the most expensive. Finance companies and retail stores that lend to consumers will frequently charge high interest rates, ranging from 12 to 25 percent. Banks also lend money to their credit card holders through cash advances—loans that are billed to the customer's credit card account. Most cards charge higher interest for a cash advance and charge interest from the day the cash advance is made. As a result, it is much more expensive to take out a cash advance than to charge a purchase to a credit card.

Home Equity Loans   A home equity loan is a loan based on your home equity—the difference between the current market value of your home and the amount you still owe on the mortgage. Unlike interest on most other types of credit, the interest you pay on a home equity loan is tax-deductible. Use these loans only for major items such as education, home improvements, or medical bills. If you miss payments on a home equity loan, the lender can take your home. For more information about home equity loans, see Chapters 7 and 17.

Credit Cards

Credit cards are extremely popular. The average cardholder has more than nine credit cards, including bank, retail, gasoline, and telephone cards. Cardholders who pay off their balances in full each month are often known as convenience users. Cardholders who do not pay off their balances every month are known as borrowers.

▼ QUICK CASH Using a debit card can be a convenient way to get cash any time you need it. *How is a debit card different from a credit card?*

Most credit card companies offer a **grace period**, a time period during which no finance charges will be added to your account. A **finance charge** is the total dollar amount you pay to use credit. Generally, if you pay your balance before the due date stated on your monthly bill, you do not have to pay a finance charge. Borrowers who carry balances beyond the grace period pay finance charges.

The cost of a credit card depends on the type of credit card you have and the terms set forth by the lender. As a cardholder, you may have to pay interest or other finance charges. Some credit card companies charge cardholders an annual fee, usually about $20. However, many companies have eliminated annual fees. If you are looking for a credit card, be sure to shop around for one with no annual fee. **Figure 6.3** gives some other helpful hints for choosing a credit card.

Figure 6.3   **Choosing and Using a Credit Card**

When you choose a credit card, it pays to shop around. Follow these suggestions to find the card that best meets your needs and to use it wisely:

1. Department stores and gasoline companies are good places to obtain your first credit card.

2. Bank credit cards are offered through banks and savings and loan associations. Annual fees and finance charges vary widely, so shop around.

3. If you plan on paying off your balance every month, look for a card that has a grace period and carries no annual fee or a low annual fee. You might have a higher interest rate, but you plan to pay little or no interest anyway.

4. Watch out for creditors that offer low or no annual fees but instead charge a transaction fee every time you use the card.

5. If you plan to carry a balance, look for a card with a low monthly finance charge. Be sure that you understand how the finance charge is calculated.

6. To avoid delays that may result in finance charges, follow the card issuer's instructions as to where, how, and when to make bill payments.

7. Beware of offers of easy credit. No one can guarantee to get you credit.

8. If your card offers a grace period, take advantage of it by paying off your balance in full each month. With a grace period of 25 days, you actually get a free loan when you pay bills in full each month.

9. If you have a bad credit history and have trouble getting a credit card, look for a savings institution that will give you a secured credit card. With this type of card, your line of credit depends on how much money you keep in a savings account that you open at the same time.

10. Travel and entertainment cards often charge higher annual fees than most credit cards. Usually, you must make payment in full within 30 days of receiving your bill, or no further purchases will be approved on the account.

11. Be aware that debit cards are not credit cards but simply a substitute for a check or cash. The amount of the sale is subtracted from your checking account.

12. Think twice before you make a telephone call to a 900 number to request a credit card. You will pay from $2 to $50 for the 900 call and may never receive a credit card.

Sources: American Institute of Certified Public Accountants; U.S. Office of Consumer Affairs; Federal Trade Commission.

Critical Thinking   Before you enter the world of credit, you need to understand the various options that are available to you.

Which of these factors would be most important in your choice of a credit card?

Debit Cards Do not confuse credit cards with debit cards. A debit card allows you to electronically subtract money from your savings or checking account to pay for goods or services. A credit card extends credit and delays payment. Debit cards are most commonly used at automated teller machines (ATMs). They are also used to purchase goods in stores and to make other types of payments.

Smart Cards Some lenders offer a credit card called a *smart card*. A smart card is a plastic card equipped with a computer chip that can store 500 times as much data as a normal credit card. Smart cards can store a variety of information. A smart card, for example, can be used to buy an airline ticket, store it digitally, and track frequent flyer miles.

Travel and Entertainment (T&E) Cards Travel and Entertainment (T&E) cards are really not credit cards because the balance is due in full each month. However, most people think of T&E cards—such as American Express cards—as credit cards because users do not pay for goods or services when they purchase them.

TechByte

Smart Cards The first basic credit card was the BankAmericard, issued by Bank of America in 1958. Today a variety of cards are available, including smart cards, which combine a credit card, driver's license, healthcare ID, medical history, and other features.

@ List other features of smart cards by reading more information through **persfinance07 .glencoe.com**.

Section 6.1 Assessment

QUICK CHECK

1. What are two advantages and two disadvantages of using credit?
2. What is the difference between closed-end credit and open-end credit?
3. What is an example of an inexpensive loan, a medium-priced loan, and an expensive loan?

THINK CRITICALLY

4. Review Figure 6.3 on page 160. How might you select a card that best meets your needs?

USE MATH SKILLS

5. **Cash or Charge?** The use of credit in the United States is widespread. Nevertheless, some people use credit cards and take out loans only in an emergency. Their philosophy is that if they do not have cash to pay for something, they should not take on a debt. Other people believe credit is necessary for everyday living.

Write About It What is your view on the issue of using credit? Do you plan to obtain a credit card? Would you prefer to pay cash? Write a short essay that explains the role of credit cards and loans in your philosophy of money management.

SOLVE MONEY PROBLEMS

6. **Evaluating Credit** Garrett, a high school senior, wanted to get his girlfriend a special birthday gift. A local electronics store had one-day special discounts on stereos, with no payments required until after six months. With income from his part-time job, Garrett felt that he could incorporate the expense into his budget. His mother and sister tried to discourage him from buying the stereo.

Analyze What should Garrett do in this situation? Explain your reasoning.

Focus on Reading

Read to Learn
- How to name the five C's of credit.
- How to identify factors to consider when choosing a loan or credit card.
- How to explain how to build and protect your credit rating.

Main Idea
You should consider the costs of credit and your own credit standing when applying for credit.

Key Terms
- net income
- annual percentage rate (APR)
- collateral
- simple interest
- minimum monthly payment
- credit rating

Before You Read

PREDICT
What is your definition of credit?

The Costs and Methods of Obtaining Credit

Can You Afford a Loan?
What is a loan?

A loan is money that you borrow and must repay. Loans cost money to the borrower in the form of interest. Taking out a loan can be a substantial financial burden. Before you take out a loan, you need to be sure that you can afford it. Will you be able to meet all your usual expenses plus the monthly loan payments you will have to make? You can answer this question in several ways.

One way is to add up all your basic monthly expenses and then subtract the total from your take-home pay. If the difference is not enough to make a monthly loan payment and still have a little left over, you cannot afford the loan.

A second way is to consider what you might give up to make the monthly loan payment. For example, perhaps you are putting some of your monthly income into a savings account. Would you be willing to use that money to make loan payments instead? If not, would you consider cutting back on unnecessary but fun activities, such as going to movies or eating out? Are you prepared to make this trade-off?

Although you cannot measure your credit capacity exactly, you can use the debt payments-to-income ratio formula to decide whether you can safely take on the responsibility of credit.

Debt Payments-to-Income Ratio

The debt payments-to-income ratio is the percentage of debt you have in relation to your net income. **Net income** is the income you receive (take-home pay, allowance, gifts, and interest). Experts suggest that you spend no more than 20 percent of your net income on debt payments. For example, if your net income is $1,000 per month, your monthly debt payments should total no more than $200. Monthly debt payments include credit card and loan payments. You can calculate your debt payments-to-income ratio by dividing your total monthly debt payments (not including housing payments) by your monthly net income.

DEBT PAYMENTS-TO-INCOME RATIO (DPR)

Synopsis: Computing your monthly net income will help you calculate how much to spend on debt payments. Your debt payments-to-income ratio (DPR) will also determine your monthly budget.

Example: Suppose that your monthly net income is $1,200. Your monthly debt payments include your student loan payment and a gas credit card, and they total $180. What is your debt payments-to-income ratio?

Formula: $\dfrac{\text{Monthly Debt Payments}}{\text{Monthly Net Income}} =$

Debt Payments-to-Income Ratio (DPR)

Solution: $\dfrac{\$180}{\$1,200} = 0.15 = 15\%$

YOU FIGURE

What is your debt payments-to-income ratio if your debt payments total $342 and your net income is $1,000 per month?

Twenty percent is the most you should spend on debt payments, but 15 percent is much better. The higher figure does not take into account emergency expenses, and it is based on an average family's average expenses. If you are a young adult who is just beginning to experiment with credit, play it safe and stay below the 20 percent limit.

The Cost of Credit
What does it cost to apply for credit?

If you are thinking of taking out a loan or applying for a credit card, your first step should be to figure out how much the loan will cost you and whether you can afford it. Then you should shop for the best credit terms. Two key factors will be the finance charge and the annual percentage rate (APR).

The Finance Charge and the Annual Percentage Rate (APR)

The finance charge is the total dollar amount you pay to use credit. In most cases, you will have to pay finance charges to a creditor on any unpaid balance.

The finance charge is calculated using the annual percentage rate. The **annual percentage rate (APR)** is the cost of credit on a yearly basis, expressed as a percentage. For example, an APR of 18 percent means that you pay $18 per year on each $100 you owe. Every organization that extends credit of any kind must state the true APR that it charges its customers. This makes it easy to compare the cost of credit at several businesses or among several different credit cards.

STANDARD &POOR'S

Put on Your Financial Planner's Cap

If you were a financial planner, what is the first thing you would say to a client who was in serious credit card debt?

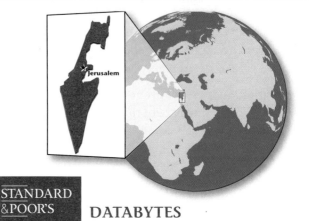

Standard and Poor's publishes the globally recognized S&P 500® financial index. It also gathers financial statistics, information, and news, and analyzes this data for international businesses, governments, and individuals to help them guide their financial decisions.

ISRAEL

Israel's economy operates on borrowed money from institutions such as the World Bank and the International Monetary Exchange or from foreign nations. However, because of ongoing political conflicts and an economic slump, the country's credit rating dropped. When countries or individuals carry excessive debt, lenders view them as credit risks. However, tight security and an upbeat global market set the stage for Israel's financial recovery. Israeli exports grew by 20 percent. Incentives such as tax-free "holidays" encouraged the development of new companies. Even tourism has grown. In fact, the country made its biggest economic gain in 2004. One news headline described the country and its turn-around: "Israel: A Bunch of Blooms in the Desert."

STANDARD &POOR'S DATABYTES

Capital	Jerusalem
Population	6,707,000
Languages	Hebrew, Arabic, and English
Currency	new Israeli shekel
Gross Domestic Product (GDP)	$120.6 billion
GDP per capita	$19,700

Industry: High-technology projects, wood and paper products, potash and phosphates, and food

Agriculture: Citrus, vegetables, cotton, and beef

Exports: machinery and equipment, software, cut diamonds, agricultural products, and chemicals

Natural Resources: Copper, phosphates, bromide, potash, and clay

Think Globally

Would you invest in an international stock from Israel? Why or why not?

To determine the total amount of finance charges that you will pay on $100 borrowed, look at **Figure 6.4.** Find the APR at the top of the chart and the number of payments at the left side of the chart. The point at which they meet is the total amount you will pay in finance charges for each $100 borrowed.

For example, find the column showing an APR of 8 percent. Follow it down until it meets the row showing 24 monthly payments. You will see that if you borrow $100 at an APR of 8 percent for two years (24 months), you will pay $8.55 in finance charges. Under the Truth in Lending Act, the creditor must inform you, in writing and before you sign any agreement, of the finance charge and the APR.

Figure 6.4 — Annual Percentage Rate Table for Monthly Payments

Number of Monthly Payments	Annual Percentage Rate—APR (Finance Charge per $100 Borrowed)				
	7.0%	7.5%	8.0%	8.5%	9.0%
6	$2.05	$2.20	$ 2.35	$ 2.49	$ 2.64
12	$3.83	$4.11	$ 4.39	$ 4.66	$ 4.94
18	$5.63	$6.04	$ 6.45	$ 6.86	$ 7.28
24	$7.45	$8.00	$ 8.55	$ 9.09	$ 9.64
30	$9.30	$9.98	$10.66	$11.35	$12.04

Finding the Finance Charge

If you borrow money and do not pay it back right away, you will probably have to pay a finance charge.

What is the finance charge that you would pay if you borrowed $100 for 18 months at an APR of 9 percent?

Tackling the Trade-Offs

When you select your financing, you will have to make trade-offs. You will have to choose among various features, including the length of the loan, the size of monthly payments, and the interest rate. Here are some of the major trade-offs you should consider.

Term Versus Interest Costs   Many people choose longer-term financing because they want smaller monthly payments. However, the longer the term (the period of time) of a loan at a given interest rate, the greater the amount you will pay in interest charges. Compare the following credit arrangements on a $6,000 loan:

	APR	Term of Loan	Monthly Payment	Total Finance Charge	Total Cost
Creditor A	14%	3 years	$205.07	$1,382.52	$7,382.52
Creditor B	14%	4 years	163.96	1,870.08	7,870.08

How do these choices compare? The answer depends partly on what you need. The lower-cost loan is available from Creditor A. If you are looking for lower monthly payments, you could repay the loan over a longer period of time. However, you would have to pay more in total costs. A loan from Creditor B provides smaller monthly payments but adds about $488 to your total finance charge.

Lender Risk Versus Interest Rate   You may prefer financing that requires a minimum down payment, a portion of the total cost of an item that is required at the time of purchase. Another option is to take out a loan that features low fixed payments with a large final payment. Keep in mind that the lender's goal is to minimize risk, or make sure that you pay back the loan in full. Consumers who want these types of features have to accept the trade-off of a more expensive loan.

SIMPLE INTEREST ON A LOAN

Synopsis: Simple interest, compounded annually, is a percentage of the amount borrowed. The amount borrowed is called principal. Compound interest may be computed daily, monthly, or yearly.

Example: Janelle's cousin agreed to lend her $1,000 to purchase a used laptop computer. She has agreed to charge only 5 percent simple interest, and Janelle has agreed to repay the loan at the end of one year. How much interest will she pay for the year? Use the formula below to help compute Janelle's loan interest.

Formula: Principal × Interest Rate × Amount of Time = Simple Interest

Solution: $1,000 × .05 or 5% × 1 = $50 interest

YOU FIGURE

You just bought a used car for $3,500 from your aunt. She agreed to let you make payments for 3 years with simple interest at 6 percent. How much interest will you pay?

To reduce lender risk and increase your chance of getting a loan at a lower interest rate, consider the following options:

- **Variable Interest Rate**   A variable interest rate is based on changing rates in the banking system. This means that the interest rate you pay on your loan will vary from time to time. If you have a loan with a variable interest rate and overall interest rates rise, the rate on your loan is adjusted accordingly. Therefore, the lender may offer you a lower beginning interest rate than you would have with a fixed-rate loan.

- **A Secured Loan**   You will probably receive a lower interest rate on your loan if you pledge collateral. **Collateral** is a form of security to help guarantee that the creditor will be repaid. It indicates that if you lost your source of income, you could repay your loan with the collateral, such as your savings, or by selling some of your property. If you do not pay back the loan, the lender may have the legal right to take whatever you pledged as collateral.

- **Up-Front Cash**   Many lenders believe that you have a higher stake in repaying a loan if you make a large down payment. Thus, you may have a better chance of getting the other loan features you want.

- **A Shorter Term**   The shorter the period of time (or term) for which you borrow, the smaller the chance that something will prevent you from repaying your loan. This lowers the risk to the lender. Therefore, you may be able to borrow at a lower interest rate if you accept a shorter-term loan, but your monthly payments will be higher.

Careers in Finance

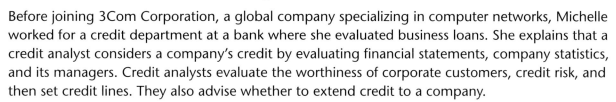

CREDIT ANALYST **Michelle Molyneux**
3Com Corporation

Before joining 3Com Corporation, a global company specializing in computer networks, Michelle worked for a credit department at a bank where she evaluated business loans. She explains that a credit analyst considers a company's credit by evaluating financial statements, company statistics, and its managers. Credit analysts evaluate the worthiness of corporate customers, credit risk, and then set credit lines. They also advise whether to extend credit to a company.

SKILLS: Time-management, accounting, judgment, investigative, analytical, communication, some foreign language, and interpersonal skills

PERSONAL TRAITS: Curiosity, a desire to know the big picture, and an international perspective

EDUCATION: High school diploma or equivalent; bachelor's degree in accounting or finance

ANALYZE People can get into debt by mistaking needs and wants. List your needs, such as clothing and food. Then list your wants, such as luxury items or recreation. Describe how a credit analyst might rate your credit worthiness, based on your needs and wants.

 To learn more about career paths for credit analysts visit **persfinance07.glencoe.com**.

Calculating the Cost of Credit

To assess your trade-offs, you can also compare loans and credit cards by calculating the interest to find the cost of credit. The most common method of calculating interest is the simple interest formula. Other methods, such as simple interest on the declining balance and add-on interest, are variations of this formula.

Simple Interest **Simple interest** is the interest computed only on the principal, the amount that you borrow. It is based on three factors: the principal, the interest rate, and the amount of time for which the principal is borrowed. To calculate the simple interest on a loan, multiply the principal by the interest rate and by the amount of time (in years) for which the money is borrowed. (See the Go Figure box on page 166.)

Simple Interest on the Declining Balance When a simple interest loan is paid back in more than one payment, the method of computing interest is known as the declining balance method. You pay interest only on the amount of principal that you have not yet repaid. The more often you make payments, the lower the interest you will pay. Most credit unions use this method.

As You Read

RELATE

Why should you pay more than the monthly minimum balance on a credit card debt?

x

Add-On Interest With the add-on interest method, interest is calculated on the full amount of the original principal, no matter how often you make payments. When you pay off the loan with one payment, this method produces the same APR as the simple interest method. However, if you pay in installments, your actual rate of interest will be higher than the stated rate. Interest payments on this type of loan do not decrease as the loan is repaid. The longer you take to repay the loan, the more interest you will pay.

Cost of Open-End Credit The Truth in Lending Act requires that open-end creditors inform consumers as to how the finance charge and the APR will affect their costs. For example, they must explain how they calculate the finance charge. They must also inform you when finance charges on your credit account begin to accrue so that you know how much time you have to pay your bills before a finance charge is added.

Cost of Credit and Expected Inflation Inflation reduces the buying power of money. Each percentage point increase in inflation means a decrease of about 1 percent in the quantity of goods and services you can buy with the same amount of money. Because of this, lenders incorporate the expected rate of inflation when deciding how much interest to charge.

Remember the earlier example in which Damon borrowed $1,000 from his aunt at the bargain rate of 5 percent for one year? If the inflation rate was 4 percent that year, his aunt's actual rate of return on the loan would have been only about 1 percent (5 percent stated interest minus 4 percent inflation rate). A professional lender that wanted to receive 5 percent interest on Damon's loan might have charged him 9 percent interest (5 percent interest plus 4 percent—anticipated inflation rate).

The Minimum Monthly Payment Trap On credit card bills and for other forms of credit, the **minimum monthly payment** is the smallest amount you can pay and remain a borrower in good standing. Lenders often encourage you to make the minimum payment because it will then take you longer to pay off the loan. However, if you are paying only the minimum amount on your monthly statement, you need to plan your budget more carefully. The longer it takes for you to pay off a bill, the more interest you pay. The finance charges you pay on an item could end up being more than the item is worth.

For example, suppose that Natasha is buying new books for college. She spends $500 on textbooks, using a credit card that charges 19.8 percent interest per year, and she makes only the minimum monthly payment of $21.67. Based on that payment amount, it will take Natasha approximately two and one-half years to pay off the loan. Interest charges of $150 will be added to the cost of her purchase.

Applying for Credit

Why does a lender need to know about your credit history to extend credit?

When you are ready to apply for a loan or a credit card, you should understand the factors that determine whether a lender will extend credit to you.

The Five C's of Credit

When a lender extends credit to consumers, it takes for granted that some people will be unable or unwilling to pay their debts. Therefore, lenders establish policies for determining who will receive credit. Most lenders build such policies around the "five C's of credit": character, capacity, capital, collateral, and credit history.

Character: Will You Repay the Loan? Creditors want to know what kind of person to whom they will be lending money. They want to know that you are trustworthy and stable. They may ask for personal or professional references, and they may check to see whether you have a history of trouble with the law. Some questions a lender might ask to determine your character are:

- Have you used credit before?
- How long have you lived at your present address?
- How long have you held your current job?

Capacity: Can You Repay the Loan? Your income and the debts you already have will affect your ability to pay additional debts. If you already have a large amount of debt in proportion to your income, lenders probably will not extend more credit to you.

Common CENTS

One Is Enough
When you turn 18, you may start receiving applications for credit cards. Be a smart consumer and compare interest rates, annual fees, and any other fees. Decide which credit card best suits your needs and apply for that one. Toss any other applications you get into the trash. *Why should you get the best (or lowest) interest rate for a credit card?*

◀ **LOOK BEFORE YOU LEAP**
Before taking out a loan, you should sit down and figure out your finances. *What is perhaps the most important point you should consider?*

A creditor may ask several questions about your income and expenses:

- What is your job, and how much is your salary?
- Do you have other sources of income?
- What are your current debts?

Capital: What Are Your Assets and Net Worth? You may recall from Chapter 3 that assets are any items of value that you own, including cash, property, personal possessions, and investments. Your capital is the amount of your assets that exceed your liabilities, or the debts you owe. Lenders want to be sure that you have enough capital to pay back a loan. That way, if you lost your source of income, you could repay your loan from your savings or by selling some of your assets. A lender might ask:

- What are your assets?
- What are your liabilities?

Collateral: What If You Do Not Repay the Loan? Creditors look at what kinds of property or savings you already have, because these can be offered as collateral to secure the loan. If you fail to repay the loan, the creditor may take whatever you pledged as collateral. A creditor might ask:

- What assets do you have to secure the loan (a vehicle, your home, or furniture)?
- Do you have any other assets (bonds or savings)?

Credit History: What Is Your Credit History? Lenders will review your credit history to find out whether you have used credit responsibly in the past. They will probably obtain a copy of your credit report from a credit bureau. Some questions a creditor might ask about your credit history are:

- Do you pay your bills on time?
- Have you ever filed for bankruptcy?

The information gathered from your application and the credit bureau establishes your credit rating.

A **credit rating** is a measure of a person's ability and willingness to make credit payments on time. The factors that determine a person's credit rating are income, current debt, information about character, and how debts have been repaid in the past. If you always make your payments on time, you will probably have an excellent credit rating. If not, your credit rating will be poor, and a lender probably will not extend credit to you. A good credit rating is a valuable asset that you should protect.

Creditors use different combinations of the five C's to reach their decisions. Some creditors set unusually high standards, and others simply do not offer certain types of loans. Creditors also use various rating systems. Some rely strictly on their own instincts and experience. Others use a credit scoring or statistical system to predict whether an applicant is a good credit risk. When you apply for a loan, the lender is likely to evaluate your application by asking questions such as those included in the checklist in **Figure 6.5** on page 172.

Your Own Home
Learn how to establish and maintain good credit so you can get a mortgage when the time comes to buy your first home.

@ To continue with Task 3 of your WebQuest project, visit **persfinance07.glencoe.com**.

As You Read

QUESTION

Why does a lender need to know about your credit history to extend credit?

Learn to identify and understand the standard financial documents you will use in the real world.

Investigate: A Credit Card Statement

A credit card statement lists this information:
- Payments made
- New balance
- Your available credit
- Transactions for the month
- Minimum payment due

Your Motive: Understanding how to read your credit card statement is important so you can track where you spend your money each month. You can also verify that the transactions on the statement are accurate.

 CREDIT CARD STATEMENT

Previous Balance	Payments and Credits	New Charges	New Balance	Credit Line
$100	$100	$40.60	$40.60	$5,000

Statement Date 02/03/--

Payment Date 02/28/--

FOR CUSTOMER SERVICE CALL OR WRITE 1-800-555-4553 P.O. BOX 23 SIOUX FALLS, SD

SEND PAYMENTS TO: BANKCENTER P.O. BOX 6575 GOLDEN, NEVADA 88777

6593-5800-0086-1905	Cash Advance Limit $500	Available Credit Line $4,900	Available Cash Line* $500

Sale Date	Post Date	Reference Number	Type of Activity	Location	Amount
01/05	01/07	24036215006661	Daisy Market	Clover, IL	4.30
01/08	01/10	24692165008000	Chloe's Coffee	Fielding, CT	2.30
01/13	01/13	74046585013013	PAYMENT RECEIVED--THANK YOU		100.00
01/18	01/20	24036215019664	Real Music	Clover, IL	15.50
02/02	02/03	242753050337531	Books 'n' News	Montclair, MO	13.90
02/01	02/03	242753950329000	Nick's Candy	Montclair, MO	4.60

DAYS IN BILLING PERIOD: 40		Purchases	Cash Advance		
Balance Subject to Interest Charge >		0.00	.00	Payment Due:	20.00
Periodic Rate >		.0000%	.0000%	Amount Over Credit Limit:	.00
ANNUAL PERCENTAGE RATE >		0.00%	0.00%	Amount Past Due	.00
				MINIMUM AMOUNT DUE:	20.00

Key Points: A credit card statement is sent to you each month. It lists all the purchases you have made using your credit card and the amount of each purchase. It also lists the payments you made during the month. In addition, it indicates how much money you can still borrow from the credit card.

Find the Solutions

1. How many charges or transactions were completed on this statement?
2. How much more can you charge on the credit card?
3. What is the new balance listed on the statement?
4. What is the minimum payment to be paid?
5. What is the due date of the next payment?

Figure 6.5   **Credit Application Information**

- Amount of loan requested

- Proposed use of the loan

- Your name and birth date

- Social Security and driver's license numbers

- Present and previous street addresses

- Present and previous employers and their addresses

- Present salary

- Number and ages of dependents

- Other income and sources of other income

- Have you ever received credit from us?

- If so, when and at which office?

- Checking account number, institution, and branch

- Savings account number, institution, and branch

- Name of nearest relative not living with you

- Relative's address and telephone number

- Your marital status

Who Are You?   A potential lender will require you to answer a number of specific questions on a credit application.

Why do you think that a creditor would want to know the names and addresses of your present and previous employers?

Credit and Equal Opportunity

You should also know what factors a lender cannot consider, according to the law. The Equal Credit Opportunity Act (ECOA) gives all credit applicants the same basic rights. It states that a lender may not use race, nationality, age, sex, marital status, and certain other factors to discriminate against you.

Age   The Equal Credit Opportunity Act (ECOA) is very specific about how a person's age may be used as a factor in credit decisions. A creditor may request that you state your age on an application, but if you are old enough to sign a legal contract (usually 18 or 21 years old, depending on state law), a creditor may not turn you down or decrease your credit because of your age. Creditors may not close your credit account because you reach a certain age or retire.

Public Assistance   You may not be denied credit because you receive Social Security or public assistance. However, certain information related to this source of income can be considered in determining your creditworthiness.

Housing Loans   The ECOA also covers applications for mortgages or home improvement loans. In particular, it bans discrimination against you based on the race or nationality of the people in the neighborhood where you live or want to buy your home, a practice that is called *redlining*.

What If Your Application Is Denied?

If your credit application is denied, the ECOA gives you the right to know the reasons. If the denial is based on a credit report from a credit bureau, you are entitled to know what specific information in the report led to the denial. After you receive this information, you can contact the credit bureau and ask for a copy of your credit report. The bureau cannot charge a fee for this service as long as you ask to see your files within 60 days of notification that your credit application has been denied. You are entitled to ask the bureau to investigate any inaccurate or incomplete information and correct its records. (See **Figure 6.6.**)

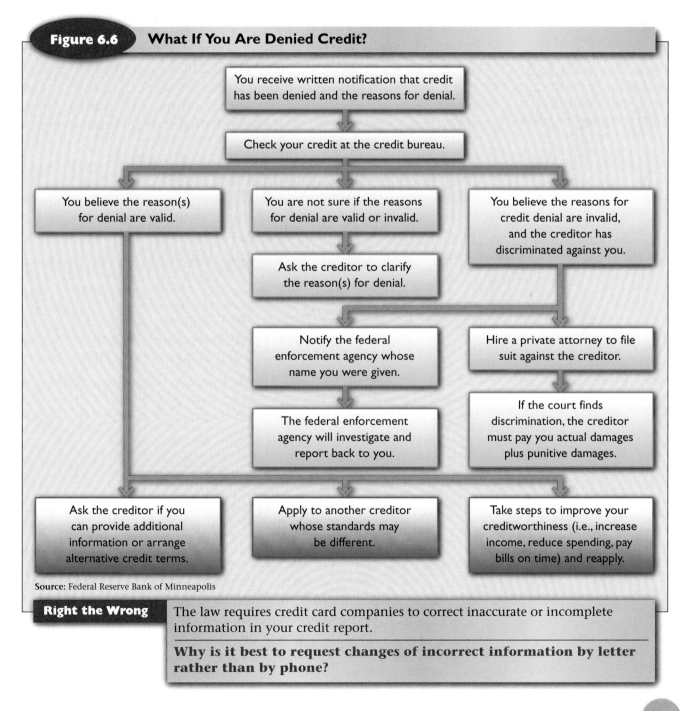

Figure 6.6   **What If You Are Denied Credit?**

You receive written notification that credit has been denied and the reasons for denial.

Check your credit at the credit bureau.

You believe the reason(s) for denial are valid.

You are not sure if the reasons for denial are valid or invalid.

You believe the reasons for credit denial are invalid, and the creditor has discriminated against you.

Ask the creditor to clarify the reason(s) for denial.

Notify the federal enforcement agency whose name you were given.

Hire a private attorney to file suit against the creditor.

The federal enforcement agency will investigate and report back to you.

If the court finds discrimination, the creditor must pay you actual damages plus punitive damages.

Ask the creditor if you can provide additional information or arrange alternative credit terms.

Apply to another creditor whose standards may be different.

Take steps to improve your creditworthiness (i.e., increase income, reduce spending, pay bills on time) and reapply.

Source: Federal Reserve Bank of Minneapolis

Right the Wrong   The law requires credit card companies to correct inaccurate or incomplete information in your credit report.

Why is it best to request changes of incorrect information by letter rather than by phone?

Your Credit Report
Why is your credit report important?

When you apply for a loan, the lender will review your credit history closely. The record of your complete credit history is called your credit report, or credit file. Your credit records are collected and maintained by credit bureaus. Most lenders rely heavily on credit reports when they consider loan applications. **Figure 6.7** provides information on building and protecting your credit history.

Credit Bureaus

A credit bureau is an agency that collects information on how promptly people and businesses pay their bills. The three major credit bureaus are Experian, Trans Union, and Equifax. Each of these bureaus maintains more than 200 million credit files on individuals, based on information they receive from lenders. Several thousand smaller credit bureaus also collect credit information about consumers. These firms make money by selling the information they collect to creditors who are considering loan applications.

Credit bureaus get their information from banks, finance companies, stores, credit card companies, and other lenders. These sources regularly transmit information about the types of credit they extend to customers, the amounts and terms of the loans, and the customers' payment habits. Credit bureaus also collect some information from other sources, such as court records.

Your Credit File

A typical credit bureau file contains your name, address, Social Security number, and birth date as well as other information:

- Your employer, position, and income
- Your previous address
- Your previous employer
- Your spouse's name, Social Security number, employer, and income
- Homeowner or renter status
- Checks returned for insufficient funds

In addition, your credit file contains detailed credit information. Each time you use credit to make a purchase or take out a loan of any kind, a credit bureau is informed of your account number and the date, amount, terms, and type of credit.

Your file is updated regularly to show how many payments you have made, how many payments were late or missed, and how much you owe. Any lawsuits or judgments against you may appear as well. Federal law protects your rights if the information in your credit file is incorrect.

Figure 6.7 **Ways to Build and Protect Your Credit**

☑ Open a checking or savings account, or both.
☑ Apply for a local department store credit card.
☑ Take out a small loan from your bank.
☑ Make payments on time.

Be aware that a creditor must:

1. Evaluate all applicants on the same basis.
2. Consider income from part-time employment.
3. Consider the payment history of all joint accounts, if this accurately reflects your credit history.
4. Disregard information on accounts if you can prove that it does not affect your ability or willingness to repay.

Be aware that a creditor cannot:

1. Refuse you individual credit in your own name if your are creditworthy.
2. Require your spouse to cosign a loan. Any credit-worthy person can be your cosigner if one is required.
3. Ask about your family plans or assume that your income will be interrupted to have children.
4. Consider whether you have a telephone listing in your name.

Source: Reprinted by permission of the Federal Reserve Bank of Minneapolis.

Firm Foundation If you want a good credit rating, you must use credit wisely.

Why is it a good idea to apply for a local department credit card or a small loan from your bank?

Fair Credit Reporting

Fair and accurate credit reporting is vital to both creditors and consumers. In 1971, the U.S. Congress enacted the Fair Credit Reporting Act, which regulates the use of credit reports. This law requires the deletion of out-of-date information and gives consumers access to their files as well as the right to correct any misinformation that the files may include. The act also places limits on who can obtain your credit report.

Who Can Obtain a Credit Report?

Your credit report may be issued only to properly identified persons for approved purposes. It may be supplied in response to a court order or by your own written request. A credit report may also be provided for use in connection with a credit transaction, underwriting of insurance, or some other legitimate business need. Friends, neighbors, and other individuals cannot be given access to credit information about you. In fact, if they even request such information, they may be subject to a fine, imprisonment, or both.

The credit bureaus contend that current laws protect a consumer's privacy, but many consumer organizations believe that anyone with a personal computer and a modem can easily access credit bureau files.

You may obtain a copy of your credit report free of charge if you have been denied credit. Current law also allows anyone using credit to obtain one free credit report per year.

▲ **EQUAL PLAYING FIELD**
Part of the American dream is to own a home. *What federal law ensures that all applicants for mortgages or home improvement loans will be treated equally?*

Time Limits on Unfavorable Data

Most of the information in your credit file may be reported for only seven years. However, if you have declared personal bankruptcy, that fact may be reported for ten years. A credit reporting agency cannot disclose information in your credit file that is more than seven or ten years old unless you are being reviewed for a credit application of $75,000 or more, or unless you apply to purchase life insurance of $150,000 or more.

Incorrect Information

Credit bureaus are required to follow reasonable procedures to make sure that the information in their files is correct. Mistakes can and do occur, however. If you think that a credit bureau may be reporting incorrect data from your file, contact the bureau to dispute the information. The credit bureau must check its records and change or remove the incorrect items. If you challenge the accuracy of an item on your credit report, the bureau must remove the item unless the lender can verify that the information is accurate.

If you are denied credit, insurance, employment, or rental housing based on the information in a credit report, you can get a free copy of your report. Request it within 60 days of the denial.

Legal Action

You have a legal right to sue a credit bureau or creditor that has caused you harm by not following the rules established by the Fair Credit Reporting Act. If the agency or the user is found guilty, the consumer may be awarded actual damages, court costs, and attorneys' fees. In the case of willful noncompliance, punitive damages in the form of money may also be awarded by the court. The action must be brought within two years of the occurrence or within two years after the discovery of material and willful misrepresentation of the information.

An unauthorized person who obtains a credit report under false pretenses may be fined up to $5,000, imprisoned for one year, or both. The same penalties apply to anyone who willfully provides credit information to someone not authorized to receive it.

Section 6.2 Assessment

QUICK CHECK

1. What are some ways to determine whether you can afford a loan?
2. What are the five C's of credit?
3. What are at least three steps you can take to maintain a good credit rating?

THINK CRITICALLY

4. Summarize ways you can lower lender risk to increase your chances of getting a loan at a lower interest rate?

USE MATH SKILLS

5. **Debt Payments-to-Income Ratio**
   Kim Lee is trying to decide whether she can afford a loan she needs so she can go to chiropractic school. Right now, Kim lives at home and works in a shoe store earning a gross income of $820 per month. Kim also pays $95 on several credit card debts each month. The loan she needs for chiropractic school will cost her an additional $120 per month.

Calculate Help Kim make her decision by calculating her debt payments-to-income ratio with and without the college loan. (Remember the 20 percent rule.)

SOLVE MONEY PROBLEMS

6. **Equal Credit Opportunity Act**
   Eleanor Davis is a single woman. Although she has a good income and uses credit wisely, she has been denied a loan to buy a house and does not know why. She believes that she may have been discriminated against or that there may be some incorrect information on her credit report.

Write About It Using the information in this section on applying for credit, discuss Eleanor's rights and options for finding out why she was denied credit.

Focus on Reading

Read to Learn
- How to protect yourself from fraud and identity theft.

Main Idea
You must take action to protect your credit if you discover billing errors, have purchase disputes, or experience identity theft.

Key Term
- cosigning

Before You Read

PREDICT

How could you protect you credit?

Protecting Your Credit

Billing Errors and Disputes
What can you do to correct billing errors?

Have you ever received a bill for something you did not buy? Have you ever made a payment that was not credited to your account? If so, you are not alone. You may be a responsible consumer who pays bills promptly and manages personal finances carefully. Even so, mistakes can happen. If you want to protect your credit rating, your time, and your money, you need to know how to correct mistakes that may pop up in your credit dealings.

What can you do to dispute billing errors? Follow these steps if you think that a bill is wrong or want more information about it. First, notify your creditor in writing, and include any information that might support your case. (A telephone call is not sufficient and will not protect your rights.) Then pay the portion of the bill that is not in question.

Your creditor must acknowledge your letter within 30 days. Then within two billing periods (but not longer than 90 days), the creditor must either adjust your account or tell you why the bill is correct. If the creditor made a mistake, you do not have to pay any finance charges on the disputed amount. If no mistake is found, the creditor must promptly send you an explanation of the situation and a statement of what you owe, including any finance charges that accumulated and any minimum payments you missed while you were questioning the bill.

Protecting Your Credit Rating

According to law, a creditor may not threaten your credit rating or do anything to damage your credit reputation while you are negotiating a billing dispute. In addition, the creditor may not take any action to collect the amount in question until your complaint has been answered.

Defective Goods and Services

According to the Fair Credit Billing Act, if you purchase a defective item and the store will not accept a return, you may tell your credit card company to stop payment because you made a sincere attempt to resolve the problem.

▲ **PLAYING FAIR** Suppose that you buy something with your credit card, and it turns out to be defective. *If you try to get your money back and the store refuses your request, what might you do?*

Credit and Stolen Identity
How can someone steal your identity?

Imagine yourself saying: "I don't remember charging those items. I've never been in that store." Maybe you never charged those goods and services, but someone else did—someone who used your name and personal information to commit fraud. When impostors use your personal information for their own purposes, they are committing a crime, sometimes called "identity theft."

You may not even know that your identity has been stolen until you notice that something is wrong: You may get bills for a credit card account you never opened, or you may see charges to your account for things that you did not purchase. In addition, a thief may access your bank account and withdraw your money using your ATM information.

If you think that your identity has been stolen and that someone is using it to charge purchases or obtain credit in some other way, you can take action. See **Figure 6.8** on page 181 for information on what to do if your identity is stolen.

Protecting Your Credit from Theft or Loss

What should you do when you realize your credit has been stolen?

Some thieves will pick through your trash in the hope of coming across your personal information. You can prevent this from happening by tearing or shredding any papers that contain personal information before you throw them out.

If you believe that an identity thief has accessed your bank accounts, close the accounts immediately. If your checks have been stolen or misused, stop payment on them. If your debit card has been lost or stolen, cancel it and get another with a new Personal Identification Number (PIN). You may also need to close your account and open a new one as a precaution.

Lost credit cards are a key element in credit card fraud. To protect your card, you should take the following actions:

- Be sure that your card is returned to you after you make a purchase. Unreturned cards can sometimes find their way into the wrong hands.
- Keep a record of your credit card number. You should keep this record separate from your card.

Notify the credit card company immediately if your card is lost or stolen. Under the Consumer Credit Protection Act, the maximum amount that you must pay if someone uses your card illegally is $50. If you manage to inform the company before the card is used illegally, you have no obligation to pay at all. However, many credit card companies do not require the cardholder to pay even the maximum amount if the card is used.

Keeping Track of Your Credit

A big problem with credit or identity theft is that you may not know your credit has been stolen until you notice that something is wrong. As discussed in Section 6.2, you might get bills for a credit card account you never opened. Your credit report may include debts you never knew you had; a billing cycle may pass without you receiving a statement; or you may see charges on your bills for which you did not sign or did not authorize.

Steps to Protect Other Accounts   If you believe an identity thief has accessed your bank accounts, checking account, or ATM card, close those accounts immediately. When you open new accounts, insist on password-only access. If your checks have been stolen or misused, stop payment on them. If your ATM card has been lost, stolen, or otherwise compromised, cancel the card and get another one with a new PIN. Stay alert to new instances of identity theft. Notify the company or creditor immediately, and follow up in writing.

Figure 6.8 Dealing With Stolen Identity

If someone has stolen your identity, the Federal Trade Commission recommends that you take three actions immediately:

Contact the Credit Bureaus Tell them to flag your file with a fraud or security alert, including a statement that creditors should call you for permission before they open any new accounts in your name.

Contact the Creditors Contact the creditors for any accounts that have been tampered with or opened fraudulently. Follow up in writing.

File a Police Report Keep a copy of the police report in case your creditors need proof of the crime. If you are still having identity problems, stay alert to new instances of identity theft. You can also contact the Privacy Rights Clearinghouse.

Government Agency Protection   If you continue to experience identity-theft problems after taking these steps, contact the Privacy Rights Clearinghouse of the Federal Trade Commission (FTC), which provides information on how to network with other victims.

The U.S. Secret Service has jurisdiction over financial fraud cases. Although the service generally investigates cases that involve substantial monetary loss, your information may provide evidence of a larger pattern of fraud that requires its attention.

The Social Security Administration may issue you a new Social Security number if you are still having difficulties after trying to resolve problems resulting from identity theft. Unfortunately, however, there is no guarantee that a new number will resolve the problem.

The Federal Trade Commission cannot resolve individual problems for consumers, but it can act against a company if it sees a pattern of possible law violations. You can file a complaint with the FTC through a toll-free consumer help line; by mail; or at its Web site, using the online complaint from.

Protecting Your Credit Information on the Internet

The Internet is becoming almost as important to daily life as the telephone and television. Increasing numbers of consumers use the Internet for financial activities, such as investing, banking, and shopping.

When you make purchases online, make sure that your transactions are secure, that your personal information is protected, and that your "fraud sensors" are sharpened. Although you cannot control fraud or deception on the Internet, you can take steps to recognize it, avoid it, and report it. Here's how:

- Use a secure browser.
- Keep records of your online transactions.
- Review your monthly bank and credit card statements.
- Read the privacy and security policies of Web sites you visit.
- Keep your personal information private.
- Never give your password to anyone online.
- Do not download files sent to you by strangers.

Cosigning a Loan
Why would someone ask a friend or relative to cosign a loan?

If a friend or relative ever asks you to cosign a loan, think twice. **Cosigning** a loan means that you agree to be responsible for the loan payments if the other person fails to make them. When you cosign, you are taking a chance that a professional lender will not take. The lender would not require a cosigner if the borrower were considered a good risk.

As You Read

RELATE

Do you, your friends, or family members shop online? How do you or they make sure all transactions are secure?

If you cosign a loan and the borrower does not pay the debt, you may have to pay up to the full amount of the debt as well as any late fees or collection costs. The creditor can even collect the debt from you without first trying to collect from the borrower. The creditor can use the same collection methods against you that can be used against the borrower. If the debt is not repaid, that fact will appear on your credit record.

Complaining About Consumer Credit
When should you complain about a lender?

If you believe that a lender is not following the consumer credit protection laws, first try to solve the problem directly with the lender. If that fails, then you should use more formal complaint procedures. This section describes how to file a complaint with the federal agencies that administer consumer credit protection laws.

Consumer Credit Protection Laws

If you have a particular problem with a bank in connection with any of the consumer credit protection laws, you can get advice and help from the Federal Reserve System. You do not need to have an account at the bank to file a complaint. You may also take legal action against a creditor. If you decide to file a lawsuit, you should be aware of the various consumer credit protection laws described below.

Truth in Lending and Consumer Leasing Acts If a creditor fails to disclose information as required under the Truth in Lending Act or the Consumer Leasing Act, or gives inaccurate information, you can sue for any money loss you suffer. You can also sue a creditor that does not follow rules regarding credit cards. In addition, the Truth in Lending Act and the Consumer Leasing Act permit class-action lawsuits. A class-action suit is a legal action on behalf of all of the people who have suffered the same injustice.

As You Read

QUESTION

What is the Truth in Lending Act?

Equal Credit Opportunity Act (ECOA) If you think that you can prove that a creditor has discriminated against you for any reason prohibited by the ECOA, you may sue for actual damages plus punitive damages—a payment used to punish the creditor who has violated the law—up to $10,000.

Fair Credit Opportunity Act A creditor that fails to follow the rules that apply to correcting any billing errors will automatically give up the amount owed on the item in question and any finance charges on it, up to a combined total of $50. This is true even if the bill was correct. You may also sue for actual damages plus twice the amount of any finance charges.

Figure 6.9 Federal Agencies that Enforce Consumer Credit Laws

If you think you've been discriminated against by:	You may file a complaint with the following agency:
A retailer, nonbank credit card issuer, consumer finance company, state-chartered credit union or bank, and noninsured savings and loan institution	Consumer Response Center Federal Trade Commission (FTC) Washington, DC 20580
A national bank	Comptroller of the Currency Compliance Management Mail Stop 7–5 Washington, DC 20219
A Federal Reserve member bank	Board of Governors of the Federal Reserve System Director, Division of Consumer and Community Affairs Washington, DC 20551
Other insured banks	Federal Deposit Insurance Corporation Consumer Affairs Division Washington, DC 20429
Insured savings and loan institutions and federally chartered state banks	Office of Thrift Supervision Consumer Affairs Program Washington, DC 20552
The FHA mortgage program	Housing and Urban Development (HUD) Department of Health, Education and Welfare Washington, DC 20410
A federal credit union	National Credit Union Administration Consumer Affairs Division Washington, DC 20456

Protecting Your Rights The law gives you certain rights as a consumer of credit.

What types of complaints about a creditor might you report to these government agencies?

Fair Credit Reporting Act You may sue any credit bureau or creditor that violates the rules regarding access to your credit records or that fails to correct errors in your credit file. You are entitled to actual damages plus any punitive damages the court allows if the violation is proven to have been intentional.

Consumer Credit Reporting Reform Act The Consumer Credit Reporting Reform Act of 1997 places the burden of proof for accurate credit information on the credit bureau rather than on you. Under this law, the creditor must prove that disputed information is accurate. If a creditor or the credit bureau verifies incorrect data, you can sue for damages.

The Federal Reserve System has set up a separate office, the Division of Consumer and Community Affairs, in Washington to handle consumer complaints. This division also writes regulations to carry out the consumer credit laws, enforces these laws, and helps banks comply with these laws.

Your Rights Under Consumer Credit Laws

If you believe that you have been refused credit because of discrimination, you can take one or more of the following steps:

1. **Complain to the creditor.** Let the creditor know that you are aware of the law.
2. **File a complaint with the government.** You can report any violations to the appropriate government enforcement agency, as shown in **Figure 6.9.**
3. **If all else fails, sue the creditor.** You have the right to bring a case in a federal district court. If you win, you can receive actual damages and punitive damages of up to $10,000. You can also recover reasonable attorneys' fees and court costs.

Section 6.3 Assessment

QUICK CHECK

1. What should you do if you think that a bill is wrong or want more information about it? How should your creditor respond to your attempt to resolve the situation?
2. How can you protect yourself against credit card theft or loss?
3. How does the Fair Credit Reporting Act protect you?

THINK CRITICALLY

4. Recall the suggestions for protecting your credit information on the Internet. Predict the problems that could result from not following the guidelines.

USE COMMUNICATION SKILLS

5. **Cosigning a Loan** Suppose that a close friend has asked you to cosign a loan she needs to start up a children's clothing store. You would like to help if you can. However, your friend is currently unemployed, and you are concerned that she will not be able to repay the loan. After much thought, you decide not to cosign the loan.

Write About It Write a letter to your friend explaining why you have decided not to cosign her loan. In the letter, point out what the consequences to you will be if she is unable to repay the loan.

SOLVE MONEY PROBLEMS

6. **Putting a Stop to Fraud** Joel went to the ATM the other day to withdraw some cash. When he checked his receipt, he noticed that the balance on his savings account was $500 less than it should have been. After discussing the matter with a customer service representative at his bank, he realized that someone else had gained access to his account number and Personal Identification Number (PIN).

Role-Play Using what you have learned about protecting yourself from fraud, explain to Joel the steps he should take to stop any further damage from being done. Partner with another student to role-play the conversation.

Section 6.4

Focus on Reading

Read to Learn
• How to identify ways to manage debt problems.

Main Idea
If you experience the warning signs of debt problems, there are several options available to manage your finances.

Key Term
• bankruptcy

Before You Read

PREDICT
What corrective steps would you take if you were experiencing the debt troubles listed here?

Managing Your Debts

Signs of Debt Problems

How do you know when you are getting in financial trouble?

Carl Reynolds is in his early 20s. A recent college graduate, he has a steady job and earns an annual income of $40,000. With the latest model sports car parked in the driveway of his new home, it would appear that Carl has the ideal life.

However, Carl is deeply in debt. He is drowning in a sea of bills. Almost all of his income is tied up in debt payments. The bank has already begun foreclosure proceedings on his home, and several stores have court orders to repossess practically all of his new furniture and electronic gadgets. His current car payment is overdue, and he is behind in payments on all of his credit cards. If he does not come up with a plan of action, he will lose everything.

Carl's situation is all too common. Some people who seem to be wealthy are just barely keeping their heads above water financially. They may lack self-discipline and do not control their impulses. They use poor judgment or fail to accept responsibility for managing their money. Carl and others like him are not necessarily bad people. They simply have not thought about their long-term financial goals.

The Warning Signs

There are some warning signs of being in financial trouble. If you are experiencing two or more of these warning signs, it is time for you to rethink your priorities.

• You make only the minimum monthly payment on credit cards.
• You are having trouble making even the minimum monthly payment on your credit card bills.
• The total balance on your credit cards increases every month.
• You miss loan payments or often pay late.
• You use savings to pay for necessities such as food and utilities.
• You receive second or third payment due notices from creditors.
• You borrow money to pay off old debts.
• You exceed the credit limits on your credit cards.
• You have been denied credit because of a bad credit report.

Debt Collection Practices
Are debt collection practices regulated by laws?

When people are in debt and getting behind in payments, they may worry about debt collection agencies. Creditors will often turn their bad debts over to such companies. However, a federal agency protects certain legal rights of debtors in their dealings with these types of agencies.

The Federal Trade Commission enforces the Fair Debt Collection Practices Act (FDCPA). This act prohibits certain practices by debt collectors—businesses that collect debts for creditors. The act does not erase the legitimate debts that consumers owe, but it does control the ways in which debt collection agencies do business and deal with consumers in debt.

Financial Counseling Services
What are sources of financial counseling?

If you are having trouble paying your bills and need help, you have several options. You can contact your creditors and try to work out an adjusted repayment plan. In addition, you can contact a non-profit financial counseling program, such as the Consumer Credit Counseling Service, which operates nationwide.

Consumer Credit Counseling Service

The Consumer Credit Counseling Service (CCCS) is a nonprofit organization affiliated with the National Foundation for Consumer Credit (NFCC). Local branches of the CCCS provide debt counseling services for families and individuals with serious financial problems. The CCCS is not a charity, a lending institution, or a government agency. CCCS counseling is usually free. However, when the organization supervises a debt repayment plan, it sometimes charges a small fee to help pay administrative costs.

According to the NFCC, millions of consumers contact CCCS offices each year for help with their personal financial problems. To find an office near you, check the white pages of your local telephone directory under Consumer Credit Counseling Service, or call 1-800-388-CCCS. All information is kept confidential.

Credit counselors know that most individuals who are overwhelmed with debt are basically honest people who want to clear up their unmanageable indebtedness, the condition of being deeply in debt. Too often, such problems arise from a lack of planning or a miscalculation of earnings. The CCCS is concerned with preventing problems as much as it is with solving them. As a result, its activities are divided into two parts:

- Aiding families with serious debt problems by helping them manage their money better and setting up a realistic budget
- Helping people prevent indebtedness by teaching them the importance of budget planning, educating them about the pitfalls of unwise credit buying, and encouraging credit institutions to withhold credit from people who cannot afford it

Other Counseling Services

In addition to the CCCS, universities, credit unions, military bases, and state and federal housing authorities sometimes provide nonprofit credit counseling services. These organizations usually charge little to nothing for their assistance. You can also check with your bank or local consumer protection office to see whether it has a listing of reputable financial counseling services.

Declaring Personal Bankruptcy
Why do people declare personal bankruptcy?

What if an individual suffers from an extreme case of debt problems? Is there any relief? As a last resort, an individual can declare bankruptcy. **Bankruptcy** is a legal process in which some or all of the assets of a debtor are distributed among the creditors because the debtor is unable to pay his or her debts. Bankruptcy may also include a plan for the debtor to repay creditors on an installment basis. Declaring bankruptcy is a last resort because it severely damages your credit rating.

Cosmo Syste smells

Prakrit Singh illustrates the new face of bankruptcy. A 43-year-old freelance photographer from California, she was never in serious financial trouble until she began running up big medical costs. She reached for her credit cards to pay the bills. Because Prakrit did not have health insurance, her debt quickly mounted and soon reached $17,000—too much to pay off with her $25,000-a-year income. Her solution was to declare personal bankruptcy and enjoy the immediate freedom it would bring from creditors' demands.

In 1994, the U.S. Senate passed a bill that reduced the time and cost of bankruptcy proceedings. The bill strengthened creditor rights and enabled more individuals to get through bankruptcy proceedings without selling their assets. Today legislators have enacted new tougher bankruptcy law reforms that are intended to end perceived abuses of the current bankruptcy system.

As You Read

RELATE

What might cause you or someone you know to declare personal bankruptcy?

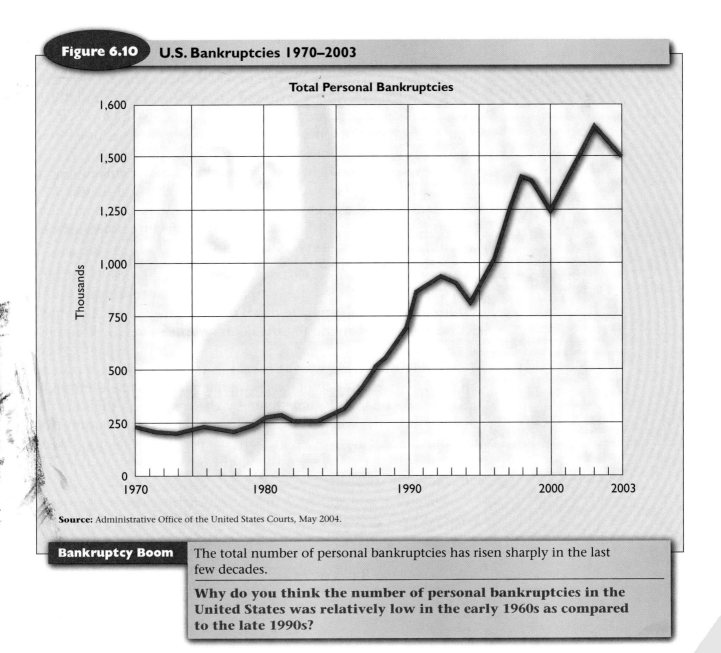

Figure 6.10 **U.S. Bankruptcies 1970–2003**

Total Personal Bankruptcies

Source: Administrative Office of the United States Courts, May 2004.

Bankruptcy Boom The total number of personal bankruptcies has risen sharply in the last few decades.

Why do you think the number of personal bankruptcies in the United States was relatively low in the early 1960s as compared to the late 1990s?

As You Read

QUESTION

How would filing for bankruptcy negatively impact a person's future?

The U.S. Bankruptcy Act of 1978

Figure 6.10 on page 189 illustrates the rate of personal bankruptcy in the United States. The vast majority of bankruptcies in the United States, like Prakrit Singh's, are filed under a part of the U.S. bankruptcy code known as Chapter 7. You have two choices in declaring personal bankruptcy:

- Chapter 7 (a straight bankruptcy)
- Chapter 13 (a wage-earner plan bankruptcy)

Both choices are undesirable, and neither should be considered an easy way to get out of debt.

Chapter 7 Bankruptcy In a Chapter 7 bankruptcy, an individual is required to draw up a petition listing his or her assets and liabilities. A person who files for relief under the bankruptcy code is called a debtor. The debtor submits the petition to a U.S. district court and pays a filing fee.

Chapter 7 is a straight bankruptcy in which many, but not all, debts are forgiven. Most of the debtor's assets are sold to pay off creditors. Certain assets, however, receive some protection. Among the assets usually protected are Social Security payments, unemployment compensation, and the net value of your home, vehicle, household goods and appliances, tools used in your work, and books.

The release from debt does not affect alimony, child support, certain taxes, fines, certain debts arising from educational loans, or debts that you fail to disclose properly to the bankruptcy court. Furthermore, debts arising from fraud, driving while intoxicated, or certain other acts or crimes may also be excluded.

Chapter 13 Bankruptcy In a Chapter 13 bankruptcy, a debtor with a regular income proposes a plan to the court for using future earnings or assets to eliminate his or her debts over a specific period of time. In such a bankruptcy, the debtor normally keeps all or most of his or her property.

During the period when the plan is in effect, which can be as long as five years, the debtor makes regular payments to a Chapter 13 trustee, or representative appointed by the court, who then distributes the money to the creditors. Under certain circumstances, the bankruptcy court may approve a plan that permits the debtor to keep all of his or her property even though he or she repays less than the full amount of the debts.

Using a Lawyer

Choosing a bankruptcy lawyer may be difficult. Some of the least reputable lawyers make easy money by handling hundreds of bankruptcy cases without considering individual needs. Recommendations from friends, family, or employee assistance programs are most useful.

Effects of Bankruptcy

People have varying experiences in obtaining credit after they file for bankruptcy. Some find the process more difficult, whereas others find it easier because they have removed the burden of prior debts or because creditors know that they cannot file another bankruptcy case for a certain period of time. Obtaining credit may be easier for people who file a Chapter 13 bankruptcy and repay some of their debts than for those who file a Chapter 7 bankruptcy and make no effort to repay any of their debts. Bankruptcy reports are kept on file in credit bureaus for ten years, a fact that is likely to make getting credit more difficult during that time. Therefore, you should take the extreme step of declaring bankruptcy only when you have no other options. Of course, the best way to solve your financial problems is to avoid them by maintaining good credit.

After You Read

REACT

What would be the best way to avoid credit problems and bankruptcy?

Section 6.4 Assessment

QUICK CHECK

1. What are some of the warning signs of debt problems?
2. What consumer credit counseling services are available?
3. What are the differences between declaring Chapter 7 and Chapter 13 bankruptcy?

THINK CRITICALLY

4. Consider your own financial situation and determine whether any of the warning signs of debt problems might apply to you or to someone you know. Analyze what you might do to correct them or how you might advise someone else.

USE MATH SKILLS

5. **Declaring Bankruptcy** Unfortunately, bankruptcy has increased.

   Calculate Using the graph in Figure 6.10 on page 189, determine the percent increase of total personal bankruptcies from 1990 to 2003. Do you think this figure will rise? Why?

SOLVE MONEY PROBLEMS

6. **Making Financial Decisions** Deanne is a customer service representative for a popular fitness club. Her income is modest, but that does not stop her from satisfying her most important desire—to travel. Deanne takes two vacations a year, and she has been all over the world. She has paid for most of her trips to faraway places with her credit card. However, when she received the bills for her last trip to India, reality hit hard. Her monthly debt payments are actually greater than her monthly net income.

   Write About It According to what you have learned in this section, what can Deanne do to solve her problem? Consider the options she might have, and write a plan.

Chapter 6 Review & Activities

CHAPTER SUMMARY

- Consumer credit is the use of credit for personal needs. Credit is an arrangement to receive cash, goods, or services now and to pay for them later.
- Closed-end credit is credit as a one-time loan that you pay back over a specified period of time in payments of equal amounts. Open-end credit is credit as a loan with a limit on the amount of money that you borrow for goods and services.
- The five C's of credit include character, capacity, capital, collateral, and credit history. Creditors use the five C's to determine who will receive credit.
- When choosing a loan or credit card, consider factors such as length of the loan, amount of monthly payments, and interest rate.

- To build and protect good credit, pay your bills and loans promptly and manage your personal finances carefully. Also, correct mistakes related to your credit bills and credit reports. Dispute billing errors in writing and pay amounts that are not in question.
- If your credit or identity has been stolen, contact all your credit card companies; close and open new bank accounts; and change all PINs. Notify law enforcement agencies and credit bureaus. If purchasing online, never share your PINs, Social Security numbers, or passwords.
- Manage debt problems by contacting creditors and/or debt counseling services. Bankruptcy is a last resort.

Communicating Key Terms

Imagine you are applying for a loan to buy a new car. In a paragraph, write a conversation you would have with a loan officer while applying for the loan, using at least ten key terms:

- credit
- consumer credit
- creditor
- closed-end credit
- open-end credit
- line of credit
- grace period
- finance charge
- net income
- annual percentage rate (APR)
- collateral
- simple interest
- minimum monthly payment
- credit rating
- cosigning
- bankruptcy

Reviewing Key Concepts

1. **Explain** the concept of consumer credit.
2. **Differentiate** between open-end credit and closed-end credit.
3. **Identify** the five C's of credit using a graphic organizer. Then rate yourself.
4. **Discuss** the factors to consider when choosing a loan or credit card.
5. **Identify** ways you can build a good credit rating.
6. **Discuss** the steps you should take if your identity is stolen.
7. **Explain** the role of consumer counseling services.

ACADEMIC **SKILLS**

Language Arts You have just received a telephone bill for $225. Usually your bill is about $35 a month. You read it closely and discover two long-distance calls to Japan at $100 and $92, both of which you did not make.

Write About It Write a brief letter to the phone company explaining why you should not be charged.

YOUR FINANCIAL FIGURES

Billing Errors Miguel read his credit card statement and discovered that a store charged him twice for the same item. His total bill was $658.22:

Lane Electronics	207.33
Brewster Cable TV	127.45
Lane Electronics	207.33
Empress Wok	38.87
Office Supplies, Inc.	77.24

1. **Calculate** how much Miguel should subtract from his bill and calculate his actual balance.
2. **Compute** by using spreadsheet software to show what Miguel's bill will be next month if he pays $25 this month with 18 percent interest.

REAL-WORLD *Application*

Connect With Ethics Your credit score determines whether you receive credit and at what interest rate. The credit-score scale runs from 300 to 850. Most people in the United States have scores between 600 and 800.

1. **Research** Use an Internet search engine to find information on credit scores.
2. **Think Critically** Explain why credit scoring may increase fairness in getting credit. Explain why it may be unfair.

Internet **CONNECTION**

Student Loans Many students finance their college educations with their own earnings, savings, family help, grants, scholarships—and loans.

@ **Log On** Use an Internet search engine to find out about student loans. Check the colleges that interest you. Click on their Financial Aid links. Answer the following questions:

1. What is the interest rate for a government student loan and how long can you take to repay a student loan?
2. How could this monthly payment affect your debt payments-to-income ratio?

BusinessWeek ONLINE

Newsclip: Student Credit Cards Many credit companies offer credit cards to students 18 years and over. As a result, many students have heavy debts. Debt advisers say students should have a low maximum limit.

@ **Log On** Go to persfinance07.glencoe.com and open Chapter 6. Learn more about managing credit, and then write a list of ways to avoid credit card debt.

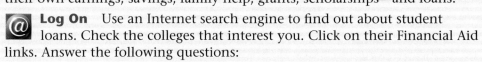

WHAT'S YOUR FINANCIAL ID?

YOUR CREDIT PROFILE

Do you know how to use credit wisely? On a separate sheet of paper write the letter that best describes your answer to the following questions.

1. I pay any bills I have when they are due _____.
   a. always
   b. most of the time
   c. sometimes

2. If I need more money for my expenses, I borrow it _____.
   a. never
   b. sometimes
   c. often

3. If I want to see a copy of my credit report, I can contact _____.
   a. a credit reporting agency
   b. a bank
   c. the principal of my school

4. If I default (do not repay) on a loan, it will stay on my credit report for _____.
   a. 7 years
   b. 2 years
   c. 6 months

5. If I have serious credit problems, I should _____.
   a. contact my creditors to explain the problem
   b. contact only the most persistent creditors
   c. not contact my creditors and hope they will forget about me

6. I can begin building a good rating by _____.
   a. opening a savings account and making regular monthly deposits.
   b. paying most of my bills on time
   c. opening a checking account and bouncing checks

Scoring: Give yourself 3 points for each "a," 2 points for each "b," and 1 point for each "c." Add up the number of points.

If you scored 6–9 points, you might want to take a closer look at how credit works before you get over your head in debt.

If you scored 10–13 points, you are off to a good start, but be sure you know the pitfalls of opening a credit account.

Source: *How to Be Credit Smart* (Washington, D.C., Consumer Education Foundation, 1994).

Your Financial Portfolio

Credit Cards: Getting the Best Deal

Melanie's parents want to give her a credit card she could use for emergencies. They made it clear that if she could eat it, wear it, or listen to it, it was not an emergency. They asked Melanie to do the homework to find the best deal. She called the bank where she has a savings account and another neighborhood bank and asked about the following credit card information.

Melanie's Credit Card Comparison

Credit Card Company	Peabody Bank	Imperial Bank
Phone number	800/555-1274	800/555-9201
Annual percentage rate (APR)	19.9%	10.9%
Introductory rate	2.9% on transferred balances	5% for first 6 months
Annual fee	$50	none
Grace period	18 days	25 days
Cash advance fee	19.8%	19.9%
Late payment fee	$25	$29
Credit limit for new customers	based on income	based on income
Travel accident insurance	$150,000	$10,000
Other travel-related services	airline miles; lost luggage insurance; emergency travel services	lost luggage insurance; emergency travel services
Protection if the cards are lost or stolen	yes	yes

Melanie chose the credit card with Imperial Bank because there was no annual fee, and the APR was lower. She did not think she would spend enough to make Peabody Bank's offer of airline miles useful. Melanie was surprised at the high penalty for late payments, so she made a mental note to be sure to make her payment on time.

If you wanted a credit card, which company would you choose? Explain why. Would you be influenced by the offer of airline miles?

Research

On a separate sheet of paper, research two credit card companies. List their fees and any advantages they offer.

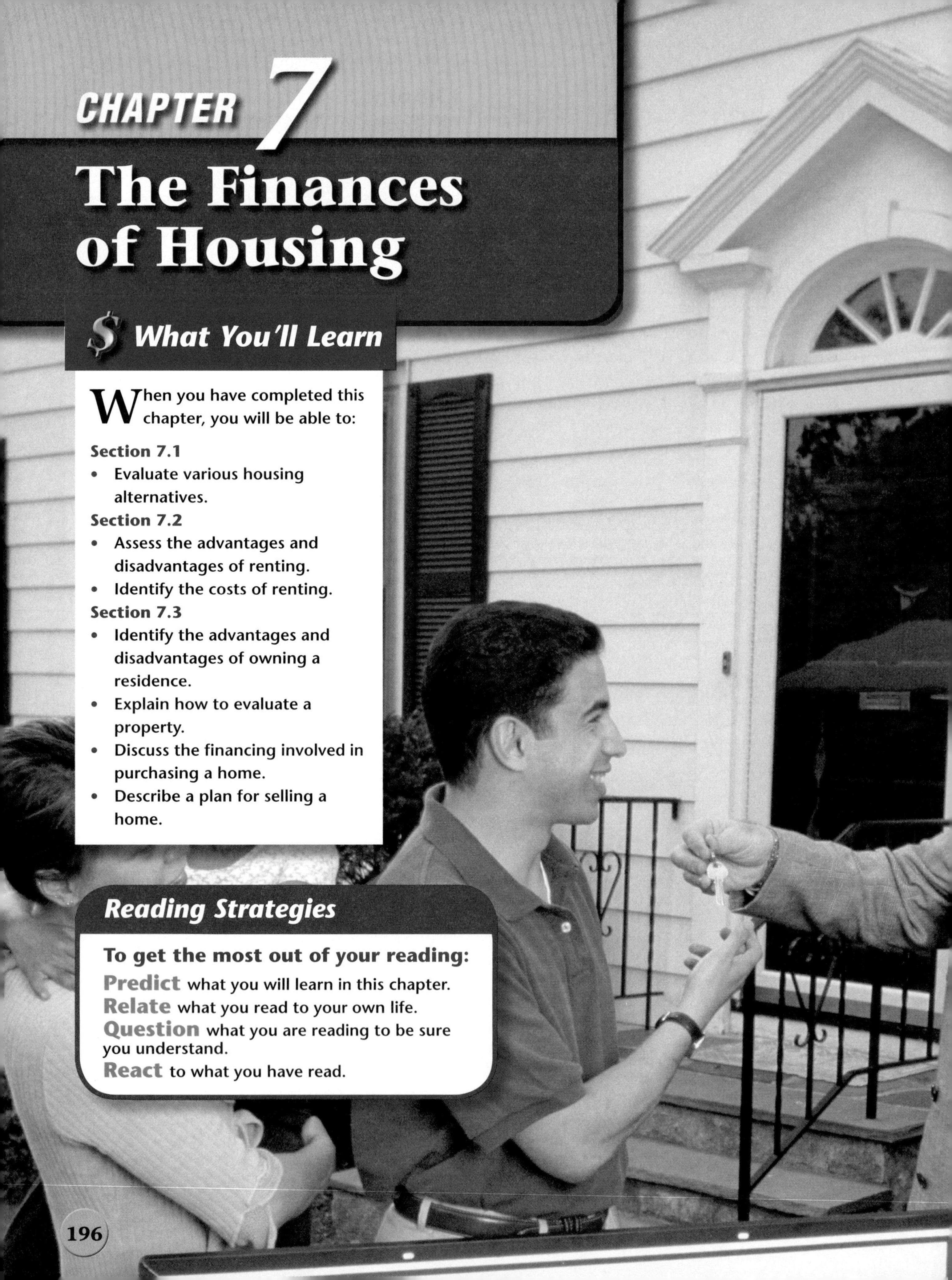

The Finances of Housing

$ *What You'll Learn*

When you have completed this chapter, you will be able to:

Section 7.1
- Evaluate various housing alternatives.

Section 7.2
- Assess the advantages and disadvantages of renting.
- Identify the costs of renting.

Section 7.3
- Identify the advantages and disadvantages of owning a residence.
- Explain how to evaluate a property.
- Discuss the financing involved in purchasing a home.
- Describe a plan for selling a home.

Reading Strategies

To get the most out of your reading:

Predict what you will learn in this chapter.
Relate what you read to your own life.
Question what you are reading to be sure you understand.
React to what you have read.

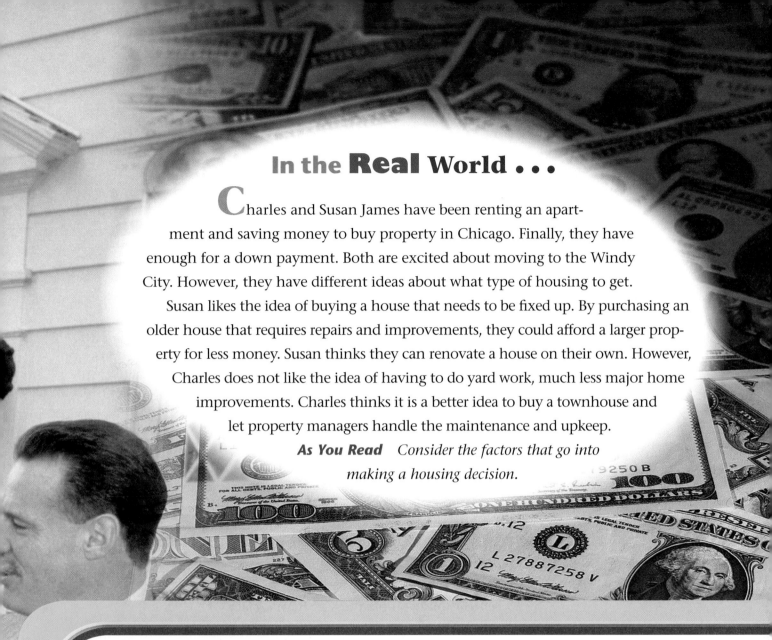

In the **Real** World . . .

Charles and Susan James have been renting an apartment and saving money to buy property in Chicago. Finally, they have enough for a down payment. Both are excited about moving to the Windy City. However, they have different ideas about what type of housing to get.

Susan likes the idea of buying a house that needs to be fixed up. By purchasing an older house that requires repairs and improvements, they could afford a larger property for less money. Susan thinks they can renovate a house on their own. However, Charles does not like the idea of having to do yard work, much less major home improvements. Charles thinks it is a better idea to buy a townhouse and let property managers handle the maintenance and upkeep.

As You Read *Consider the factors that go into making a housing decision.*

ASK STANDARD &POOR'S

Housing Options

Q: My older sister loves her new job and has decided that she would like to work for her company at least five years. Is this a good time for her to buy a house, or should she continue renting?

A: A home can be an excellent investment, but your sister will need to take some things into consideration before she makes this decision. For example, she will need to assess her finances to determine if she can afford to buy a house. She must also consider whether she wants to spend time maintaining a house; if not, it may be best for her to continue renting.

Ask Yourself What could be some advantages of owning a house?

 Go to **persfinance07.glencoe.com** to complete the Standard & Poor's Financial Focus activity.

Focus on Reading

Read to Learn
- How to evaluate various housing alternatives.

Main Idea
Knowing about housing options will help you spend your money wisely now and in the future.

Key Term
- mobility

Before You Read

PREDICT

Do you plan to own or rent a residence? Explain your choice.

Housing Options

Your Lifestyle and Choice of Housing
How does your lifestyle affect your choice of housing?

Finances play an important role in housing decisions. Whether you are renting a small apartment in a city or buying a house in the country, you will have to consider your financial situation. You can use your budget and the other personal financial statements discussed in Chapter 3 to determine how much you should spend for housing.

One major factor you will need to consider when making housing decisions is your lifestyle, which is the way you choose to spend your time and money. For example, when looking at your housing choices, you might consider if you like hosting big family gatherings. If so, you would probably want a large living room or family room. **Figure 7.1** lists types of housing for people in different life situations. Your lifestyle will determine several housing decisions:

- How close to work you want to live
- How long you plan to stay in one place
- How much privacy you would like to have

Opportunity Costs of Housing Choices
What are some opportunity costs to consider when purchasing a home?

A housing decision requires many trade-offs, or opportunity costs. For example, buying a handyman's special—a home that is priced lower because it needs repairs and improvements—may allow you to purchase a larger property for less money, but it also means that you will have to work on the house. Renting an apartment may give you more **mobility**, which is the ability to move easily from place to place. However, you will give up the tax advantages that homeowners enjoy. When you make choices about housing, you cannot look at only the benefits. You also have to consider what you will be giving up in terms of time, effort, or money.

Figure 7.1 Housing for Different Life Situations

Life Situation	Possible Types of Housing
Young single	• Rent an apartment or house because mobility is important and finances are low. • Buy a small home for tax advantages and possible increase in value.
Single parent	• Rent an apartment or house because time for maintenance is at a premium, playmates for children may be nearby, and finances are low. • Buy a home to build long-term financial security.
Young couple, no children	• Rent an apartment or house because mobility is important and finances are low • Buy a home to build long-term financial security.
Couple with children	• Rent an apartment or house because time for maintenance is at a premium and playmates for children may be nearby. • Buy a house to build long-term financial security and to provide more space and privacy.
Retired person	• Rent an apartment or house to meet financial, social, and physical needs. • Buy a home that needs little maintenance, offers convenience, and provides different services.

Rent or Buy? Different life situations will require different housing choices.

What might be a wise housing choice for a single parent? Explain your reasoning.

Renting versus Buying
Why would you rent a home if you could buy one?

One of the most basic considerations about housing is whether to rent or buy. Your decision will depend on your lifestyle and on financial factors.

Renting is a good choice for young adults who are beginning their careers. It also appeals to people who want or need mobility. Renting is also a good choice for people who do not want to devote time or money to maintenance. Because renting is often—though not always—cheaper than owning a home, it appeals to people whose funds are limited.

In contrast, owning property also has advantages. It is a wise choice for people who want a certain amount of stability in their lives. Buying a home also gives the owner privacy and some freedoms that may not be available to a renter. For example, you may not be allowed to have pets or large parties in an apartment, but you can do so in a house that you own. While ownership can be costly—at least in the short run—it offers financial benefits, such as tax advantages. In addition, the value of a house may increase, making the purchase of a home a good long-term investment. See **Figure 7.2** on page 200 for more information about renting and buying.

As You Read

RELATE

What opportunity costs are you willing to pay to obtain the home you would like?

Figure 7.2 **Evaluating Housing Alternatives**

	Advantages	Disadvantages
Renting an Apartment	• easy to move • low maintenance responsibility • low financial commitment	• no tax advantage • limitations on activities • less privacy
Renting a House	• easy to move • low maintenance responsibility • low financial commitment • more space	• higher utility expenses • some limitations on activities • no tax advantage
Owning a House	• pride of ownership • plenty of space • tax benefits	• financial commitment • high living expenses • limited mobility
Owning a Condominium	• pride of ownership • fewer maintenance costs or responsibilities than a house • tax benefits • access to recreation and businesses	• financial commitment • less privacy than in a house • need to get along with others • typically small and limited space • may be hard to sell
Owning a Mobile Home	• less expensive than other ownership options	• may be hard to sell • possible poor construction quality

On the Other Hand Choosing a type of housing is a decision that involves many trade-offs.

Find the three advantages or disadvantages on this list that seem most important to you now.

Housing Information Sources
Where can you research housing options?

Housing information is plentiful and often free. You can begin researching on your own, using a variety of sources:

- **Libraries**—The public library will probably have books and other basic resources on the subject.
- **Newspapers**—You can find articles on renting, buying, and other housing topics in the real estate section of a newspaper.
- **Internet**—The Internet can provide home buying tips, the latest mortgage rates, and information on available housing in your area and in other parts of the United States.

- **Friends and Family**—Friends and family can also be good sources of information on housing. They can share some of their own housing choices.
- **Real Estate Agents**—You might seek the services of an experienced real estate agent who is familiar with the local housing market.
- **Government Agencies**—You can also write to government agencies, such as the U.S. Department of Housing and Urban Development (HUD).

Any combination of these sources will provide the information you need to make wise housing decisions, whether you decide to rent or buy your home.

As You Read

QUESTION

What are some sources of housing information?

Section 7.1 Assessment

QUICK CHECK

1. What should you consider when you evaluate available housing alternatives?
2. When would buying a residence be a better choice than renting one?
3. What are at least three sources of housing information?

THINK CRITICALLY

4. Write a short paragraph explaining the probable housing needs of a family that consists of two working adults and three school-age children. Decide whether this family should rent or buy, and explain why you think so.

USE COMMUNICATION SKILLS

5. **Housing Options** Your uncle Manny's company has transferred him to your area, and he and his wife, Karen, will be moving within the next two months. Because Manny's work requires fairly frequent moves, he and Karen are not interested in purchasing a home at this time. Manny and Karen are both busy with their jobs, so they have little time to research a place to live. You have offered to do some background work to get them started.

Present Review the classified section of your local newspaper. Choose several houses and apartments for Manny and Karen that are about the same size and for rent, and prepare a chart that compares the prices, locations, and features of each option. Display it in class.

SOLVE MONEY PROBLEMS

6. **Housing and Lifestyle** Your cousin Lavani, who is 25 years old and single, tells you that she is thinking of buying a house. She has been at her job for eight months and loves it so far, but she has not made many friends yet. The house she is looking at is 10 miles from her workplace. Lavani says that the house needs a new roof, and the basement sometimes floods, but otherwise it is in good shape. She thinks that she will be able to afford it when she gets her first raise.

Analyze Help Lavani determine the opportunity costs of this potential purchase. Would buying the house be a good decision for Lavani? Explain your answer.

Renting a Residence

Selecting a Rental Unit
What should you know before signing a lease?

Focus on Reading

Read to Learn
- How to assess the advantages and disadvantages of renting.
- How to identify the costs of renting.

Main Idea
Knowing more about the advantages, disadvantages, and costs of renting will help you make the right choice.

Key Terms
- tenant
- landlord
- lease
- security deposit
- renters insurance

Before You Read

PREDICT

How would you begin a search for an apartment?

Are you interested in a "3-bdrm apt., a/c, w/w carpet, pvt back ent, $800 + utils, ref reqd"? This is not a secret code. It is just a short way of describing an apartment for rent listed in the classified ads of a newspaper. Decoded, the message reads: "Three-bedroom apartment for rent. It has air conditioning, wall-to-wall carpeting, and a private back entrance. The rent is $800, and the renter must also pay for utilities. The renter must provide references." The ability to read and understand such ads is one of the skills you will need if you are going to look for some type of rental housing.

When you rent the place where you live, you become a **tenant**— a person who pays for the right to live in a residence owned by someone else. Your **landlord** is the person who owns the property that is rented. You should consider the differences in the size, cost, and location of rental units when making a selection.

Size and Cost

Most people who rent live in apartments. These units may be located in a two-story house, in a high-rise building, or in an apartment complex. An apartment building contains a number of separate living units that can range in size from one room (an efficiency or studio) to three-bedroom or larger units.

HAMILTON TWP—2 bdrm 1 bath, off str prkg. quiet nghborhd. Use of cellar. $800 mo. 602-989-7767.	**SIERRAS**—2 bdrm 1 bath, beautiful view, quiet nghborhd. $700 mo. 612-999-7647.
PRINCETON—Close to campus. Pvt 1st flr, 1 bdrm. apt., wood flr., lndry. & prkg. No smkg/pets. $925/mo + utils. Avail 7/1 or 8/1. 1 yr lse. 616-433-8756.	**AUSTIN**—Close to stores. 1 bdrm. apt., wood flr., lndry. & prkg. No smkg/pets. $825/mo + 1st and last. Avail 10/2 or 11/2. 788-997-8211.
TRENTON—Historic dist. Attractive apt. Refinished wood fire, 1 large bdrm, lg liv rm, lg kit, yard. $850/mo. 677-547-6400.	**UPSTATE**—Affordable rental. Spacious apt. Refinished wood floor, 2 large bdrm, lg kit, din rm, bsmnt storage. $950/mo. 565-989-5466.

▲ **MEET THE PRESS** Newspaper ads are one way to find out about available rental units. *What information is usually included in an ad for a rental unit?*

If a unit features a patio and a bit of lawn, it may be called a *garden apartment*. Some apartments are located in complexes with on-site conveniences such as swimming pools, tennis courts, and laundry facilities.

A family or individual who needs more space than an apartment provides may prefer to rent a house. The trade-off for the extra space is usually higher rent. A single person with very few possessions might choose to rent a private room in a house. He or she may have to share common areas, such as the kitchen and bathroom.

Sources of Information

To find a rental unit, you can check the classified section of the local newspaper. Friends and coworkers are good sources of suggestions, too. You can also check with real estate and rental offices. **Figure 7.3** describes what to look for when selecting an apartment.

Figure 7.3 Selecting an Apartment

Location	Finances	Building	Layout and Facilities
• Near school or work • Near place of worship • Near shopping • Near public transportation • Near recreation: parks and museums	• Amount of monthly rent • Amount of security deposit • Cost of utilities • Length of lease	• Condition of building and grounds • Parking facilities • Recreation on premises • Security system • Condition of hallways, stairs, and elevators • Access to mailboxes	• Size and condition of unit • Type and controls of heating and cooling systems • Plumbing and water pressure • Type and condition of appliances • Condition of doors, locks, windows, closets, and floors

On Your Own Many considerations go into renting an apartment.

Which of the four broad categories above would be most important to you right now?

▶ **ON THE MOVE** Many people like to rent because it allows them to move easily to different places. *What types of individuals might find such mobility most attractive?*

As You Read

RELATE

How would you begin a search for an apartment?

Advantages of Renting

What are some of the advantages of renting?

The three main advantages of renting over buying a home are greater mobility, fewer responsibilities, and lower initial costs.

Mobility and Fewer Responsibilities

For many people, the appeal of renting is the mobility it offers. If you want to move, you can usually notify your landlord 30 days before you plan to leave, and he or she can find a new tenant. If you are offered a job in another town, you can move quickly and simply. This is also an advantage for growing families who need more space. If your landlord increases your rent beyond the amount you have budgeted, or if you decide that you want to live in a different community, making a change will be fairly easy if you rent an apartment.

Tenants do not have many of the responsibilities that homeowners have. Making major repairs and maintaining the property are the landlord's concern. Tenants do not have to worry about property taxes or property insurance. Of course, they must pay the rent and any utility bills on time, and keep their homes clean.

Low Initial Costs

A third advantage to renting is cost. Buying a house typically requires many thousands of dollars for the down payment and other costs. In contrast, you usually pay the equivalent of only one or two months' rent to move into a rental unit.

Disadvantages of Renting
What are some of the disadvantages of renting?

Renting is a good option for many people, but it has some disadvantages. Renting offers few financial benefits, and it can contribute to a more restrictive lifestyle. In addition, renting may involve various legal issues for tenants.

Financial and Lifestyle Restrictions

Although it has lower initial costs, renting may actually be more expensive than owning property in some cases. Certain financial benefits are available to homeowners but not to tenants. Homeowners, for example, are eligible for various tax deductions. They also benefit as the value of their property increases. Over time, homeowners pay back the money they borrowed to buy their home, eventually eliminating their monthly housing payments after many years. Tenants, on the other hand, must continue to pay housing costs each month for as long as they continue to rent. They are also subject to rent increases.

Tenants must accept certain limitations regarding their activities in the places they rent. For example, you might not be allowed to paint your walls without first getting permission from your landlord. Homeowners have more freedom to do what they want on their own property.

Legal Issues

If you decide to rent, you will probably have to sign a **lease**, a legal document that defines the conditions of the rental agreement between the tenant and the landlord (see **Figure 7.4** on page 206 for an example of a lease).

Never sign a lease without making sure that you understand and agree with what it says. Pay special attention to the amount and due date of the monthly rent and the length of the rental period. Also, check to see whether you have the right to sublet the property if you want to move out before the lease expires. To sublet is to have a person other than the original tenant take over the rental unit and payments for the remaining term of the lease. If you disagree with any of the terms of the lease, discuss those issues with the landlord before you sign the lease—not afterward. Sometimes landlords are willing to negotiate changes to the document.

A lease is designed to protect the rights of both the landlord and the tenant. The tenant is usually protected from rent increases during the lease term. In most states, the tenant cannot be locked out or forced to move without a court hearing. However, the lease gives the landlord the right to take legal action against a tenant who does not pay his or her rent or who damages the property.

Figure 7.4   **A Typical Lease Agreement**

Description of the property, including its address	RENTAL AGREEMENT OF PROPERTY

RENTAL AGREEMENT OF PROPERTY
AT 4744 LEMONA STREET, EAST TROY, WISCONSIN 53120

Description of the property, including its address

Names of owners and tenants

Parties in agreement are Blanca Romero and April Shullman. Blanca Romero has rented the second floor apartment to be used as a private residence, for his or her (one person) use only and for no other purpose, for a term of six months.

Dates during which the lease is valid

The term of this agreement will be from June 1, 20--, to November 30, 20--, at which time another six-month agreement will be drawn.

Amount of the security deposit

The rent will be $650 per month. There will be a security deposit of one and one-half months' rent, for a total of $975. The monies held as security will be held until such time that the tenant desires to move or until he/she is asked to vacate the premises. The security deposit along with any interest it accrues will be returned to the tenant, minus any monies held for repair of damages, rubbish removal, or cleaning to be done.

Amount and due date of monthly rent and penalties for late payment

Rent will be due from the tenant on the first of each month and not later than five days after the first of each month. A late penalty of 5% of the monthly rent will be assessed for any rent not paid by the end of the five-day grace period.

The tenant is personally responsible for paying the monthly expenses, including electric, telephone, and cable service. These expenses are not included in any monthly rent payment.

List of restrictions regarding pets, remodeling, activities, and so on

The tenant was advised that there is to be NO SMOKING in the apartment, while he/she is in residence at this address.

There will be no pets allowed at any time in the apartment while he/she resides here.

If the tenant or landlord decides that the tenant must vacate the apartment, a thirty (30) day notice must be given before the first of the month.

Tenant's right to sublet the rental unit

The tenant may not sublease (rent to another person) this property without the landlord's written permission.

The tenant must provide his/her own insurance on the contents of the apartment, such as furniture, jewelry, clothes, etc. The tenant will not hold the landlord or landlord's agent responsible in the event of a loss.

Conditions under which the landlord may enter the apartment

The tenant agrees to let landlord enter property at reasonable hours to inspect or repair the property. Landlord will notify the tenant 24 hours in advance and give the time and reason for the visit.

This place of residence shall be occupied by no more than one (1) person.

Charges to the tenant for damage or for moving out of the unit early or refusing to pay rent

At the expiration of tenancy, the tenant will surrender the premises to the landlord in as good condition as when received. The tenant will remove all rubbish from the premises. Failing to do so, the tenant will forfeit part of the security deposit in order for the landlord to pay for removal. If tenant breaks the lease for any reason, the landlord may keep the security deposit.

This agreement is between Blanca Romero and April Shullman. On this day, this agreement is signed by both parties.

Tenant _Blanca Romero_ Date _6/1/--_ Landlord _____ Date _6/1/--_

Making a Deal   A lease is a legal document extending protection to both tenant and landlord.

Which components of a lease are likely to be most negotiable?

The Cost of Renting

What are the factors affecting the cost of renting besides basic rent?

Several factors affect and determine the price of renting a home: location, living space, utilities, security deposit, and insurance.

Location

The amount of your monthly rent will depend on the location, or neighborhood, in which you choose to live (see **Figure 7.5**). You may decide that you are willing to live near the freeway if it costs less than living elsewhere. However, you may be willing to pay more for an apartment that is close to a park or work.

Living Space

The price of a rental unit will also depend on the amount of living space that you require. The least expensive choice might be a private room in a house, but you have to be willing to share common areas. Apartments, which are more expensive, often feature one to four bedrooms. Your most costly option might be to rent a townhouse or single-family house. You might consider living with one or more roommates to share expenses.

Common CENTS

On Your Own
Sharing an apartment or a house with a roommate is a great way to cut costs and can be fun. It is a good idea to have a trial period to make sure you get along before making a long-term commitment. *Why do you think sharing an apartment or a house will help you cut costs?*

Figure 7.5 **Finding and Living in Rental Housing**

Step 1: The Search
- Choose a location and a price that fits your needs.
- Compare costs and features among possible rental units.
- Talk to people who live in the apartment complex or the neighborhood where the units are located.

Step 2: Before Signing a Lease
- Be sure that you understand and agree with all aspects of the lease.
- Note the condition of the rental unit in writing; have the unit's owner sign it.

Step 3: Living in Rental Property
- Notify the owner of any necessary repairs.
- Respect the rights of neighbors.
- Obtain renters insurance to protect personal belongings.

Step 4: At the End of the Lease
- Leave the unit in good condition.
- Tell your landlord where to send your refunded security deposit.
- Ask that any deductions from your deposit be explained in writing.

Seeing Eye to Eye Renting involves more than just finding a desirable apartment.

How do these steps protect the rights of both tenant and landlord?

Utilities

You may also have to pay for utilities, such as electricity, gas, water, and trash. Before you sign a lease, be sure to ask your landlord if the rent payment includes any utilities.

Security Deposits

When you sign a lease, you may have to pay a **security deposit**, an amount of money paid to the owner of the property by a tenant to guard against any financial loss or damage that the tenant might cause. Security deposits usually equal one or two months' rent.

When you move out, your landlord must return the security deposit, minus any charges for damage you may have caused or for any unpaid rent. Most states require landlords to return the security deposit within one month. In California, however, it must be returned within three weeks.

Renters Insurance

Another expense is **renters insurance**, a type of insurance that covers the loss of a tenant's personal property as a result of damage or theft. Many tenants neglect to buy renters insurance, wrongly assuming that their possessions are covered by their landlord's insurance. Most tenants who buy it find the cost worth the peace of mind it brings.

Section 7.2 Assessment

QUICK CHECK

1. What are the three main advantages of renting a residence?
2. What are the disadvantages of renting a residence.
3. What are the costs of renting a residence?

THINK CRITICALLY

4. Explain which types of apartments would best suit two friends who plan to become roommates.

USE MATH SKILLS

5. **Sharing Costs**   Raji is currently paying $675 a month to rent a one-bedroom apartment. The cost of all utilities is included in the rent. However, he is thinking about renting a house with his friend Jon.

The monthly rent on the house is $900. Utilities will be $300 a month. Raji and Jon have agreed to split all costs evenly.

Calculate   How much would the move save or cost Raji each month and over the course of a year?

SOLVE MONEY PROBLEMS

6. **Lease Terms**   Jaycee is a college student who has a small apartment for which she pays $450 a month in rent. The lease she signed in August specified that no pets were allowed. However, while visiting her parents over winter break, Jaycee found a stray cat, and she would like to keep it.

Analyze   What options does Jaycee have? Consider all possibilities and rank them from most to least desirable.

Buying and Selling a Home

The Home-Buying Process
How do you buy a home?

Many people dream of owning a home. Buying a home, however, is a huge financial commitment. It will probably be the most costly purchase you will ever make. There are a number of steps that you will need to take to purchase a home. You will need to determine your home ownership needs, find and evaluate a property to purchase, price the property, obtain financing, and close the transaction.

STEP 1: Determine Your Home Ownership Needs
What are some of the benefits and drawbacks of owning a home?

To make an informed decision about whether to buy a home, you will need to consider the benefits and drawbacks of ownership. You will also need to consider the types of homes that are available and how much you can afford to spend.

Owning Your Residence: Benefits

While renters may be attracted to the idea of mobility, home-owners may enjoy a sense of stability and permanence. Home ownership also allows individual expression. You have more freedom to decorate and change your own home and to have pets. Many people find this type of flexibility very appealing.

As a homeowner, you will also gain financial benefits. You can deduct the interest charges on your loan payments from your federal income taxes each year. Your property taxes are also deductible. Moreover, the value of many homes rises steadily. Therefore, homeowners can usually sell their homes for a profit, depending on their **equity**, which is the value of the home less the amount still owed on the money borrowed to purchase it. In addition, once the borrowed money is paid off, homeowners have no further payments to make other than property taxes, homeowners insurance, and maintenance costs.

Focus on Reading

Read to Learn
- How to identify the advantages and disadvantages of owning a residence.
- How to explain how to evaluate a property.
- How to discuss the financing involved in purchasing a home.
- How to describe a plan for selling a home.

Main Idea
Understanding the processes involved with homeownership is necessary when you buy or sell a home.

Key Terms
- equity
- escrow account
- private mortgage insurance (PMI)
- mortgage
- points
- amortization
- fixed-rate mortgage
- adjustable-rate mortgage (ARM)
- home equity loan
- refinance
- closing
- title insurance
- deed
- appraisal

► **FREEDOM OF EXPRESSION** For many people, one of the most appealing advantages of home ownership is the ability to decorate or remodel freely. *Can you think of any situations in which homeowners are not completely free to change the look of their homes?*

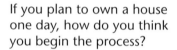

Before You Read

PREDICT

If you plan to own a house one day, how do you think you begin the process?

Owning Your Residence: Drawbacks

Of course, buying a home does not guarantee happiness. Home ownership can involve financial risk. Saving money for a down payment to buy a home is very difficult for many people. Moreover, the tax deductions may not make up for high loan payments. Property values do not always go up; in some cases, they may even decline.

A second drawback is limited mobility. A homeowner who wants to move must either sell his or her property or arrange to rent it to tenants. These processes can be slow and may result in financial loss.

Owning a home can involve high expenses. Homeowners must pay for all maintenance and repairs, such as fixing a leaky roof, cleaning out a flooded basement, putting up new wallpaper, and replacing or repairing broken appliances. The cost of taking good care of a home can be quite high, even if homeowners do most of the work themselves.

Types of Housing

Homes come in all shapes and sizes, providing housing alternatives for a range of budgets and lifestyles.

Single-Family Dwellings The most popular type of housing in the United States is the single-family house. A single-family house usually stands on a separate lot with a lawn and some outdoor living space. The home is not attached to any other buildings. Because a single-family dwelling provides the most privacy of any type of housing, it is often the most expensive.

Multiunit Dwellings This category of housing includes duplexes and townhouses. A duplex is a single building divided into living spaces for two families—or two units. A building divided into three units is a triplex. A townhouse is one of many single-family units attached to other units. For these types of housing, each unit has its own outside entrance.

Condominiums A condominium is one of a group of apartments or townhouses that people own instead of rent. Condominium owners pay a monthly fee to cover the cost of maintenance, repairs, improvements, and insurance for the building and its common spaces. The unit owners form a condominium association, which manages the housing complex. Common spaces, such as hallways, lawns, elevators, and recreational areas, belong to the association, not to individual owners.

Cooperative Housing Cooperative housing is another apartment-style living arrangement in which a building that contains a number of units is owned by a nonprofit organization. Members of the organization do not actually own the property. Members pay a monthly fee which covers their rent and the operating expenses of the organization.

Prefabricated Homes Prefabricated houses are manufactured and partially assembled at a factory. The pieces are then transported to a building site and put together there. Prefabricated homes are often cheaper than other single-family houses because the mass production of their pieces and partial assembly at the factory help keep costs down.

◀ **OPTIONS TO BUY**
Attractively designed prefabricated homes are a less costly alternative for housing. *Who might be interested in purchasing these homes? Why?*

Mobile Homes   Another type of manufactured home is known as a *mobile home*. Most mobile homes are not truly mobile because they are rarely moved from their original sites. Mobile homes are fully assembled in factories. They contain many of the features of larger houses, such as fully equipped kitchens, bathrooms, and even fireplaces. Some mobile-home owners purchase the land on which their houses are located. Spaces can also be rented in mobile-home parks where access to community recreation facilities is often included.

Compared with other housing choices, mobile homes are relatively inexpensive. However, they are not as well constructed or as safe as many other types of housing, and they usually do not increase in value at the same rate as single-family houses do.

Affordability and Your Needs

Selecting a type of dwelling is only one part of determining your home ownership needs. You will also need to consider the price of a home, its size, and its quality.

Price and Down Payment   To determine how much you can afford to spend on a home, you will need to examine your income, your savings, and your current living expenses. Can you afford to make a large down payment when you buy a home? A down payment is a portion of the total cost of an item that is required at the time of purchase. You will need to make monthly payments on a loan, pay property taxes, and buy homeowners insurance. The exact amounts will depend on interest rates and local economic conditions. Is your income enough to cover these costs as well as other current expenses?

Before you look for the home of your dreams, it is smart to know exactly what you can afford to pay. To determine how much you can afford to spend on a home and if you will be approved for a loan, talk to a loan officer at a mortgage company or other financial institution. Many companies and banks will prequalify loan applicants so that prospective home buyers will know in advance if they can get a mortgage loan. This service is usually provided without charge.

Size and Quality   Ideally, the home you buy will be big enough for your needs and will be in good condition. If you are a first-time buyer, though, you may not be able to get everything you want.

Trading Up   Most financial experts recommend buying what you can afford, even if you have to sacrifice the size and features you would love to have. As you advance in your career and your income increases, you may be able to "trade up" and purchase a home with some extra comforts. For example, eight years ago, Kanya bought a condominium that had only a tiny garden and one small bathroom. Last week she sold it, made a profit, and moved into a larger house, where she will be able to plant a vegetable and flower garden and enjoy the convenience of two full baths.

STEP 2: Find and Evaluate a Property to Purchase

Why is the location of your home important?

When you know what type of residence you would prefer and what you can afford, you will be able to start searching for a property to purchase.

Selecting a Location

The location of your home is very important. Ask yourself if you would rather live in a city, in the suburbs, or in a small-town or country setting. Perhaps you want a neighborhood with parks and trails that accommodate cyclists and runners. If you commute to work by bus, you will have to make sure that your house is close to the bus lines. The distance between home and work, the quality of the local school system, your interests and lifestyle, and other factors all help determine where you will want to live.

Careers in Finance

REAL ESTATE AGENT Carlos Garza
RealTime Real Estate, Inc.

Carlos has always had a knack for putting people at ease. This ability has proven very useful in his job as a real estate sales agent. Carlos is also very good at handling the complicated procedures involved in selling real estate. He sees his job as being a matchmaker between buyers and sellers. He works well with both sides, advising sellers on how to make homes more appealing to potential buyers and advising buyers on the suitability and value of the homes they visit. As a real estate agent, he relishes the challenge of making his clients happy and the satisfaction of closing a deal.

SKILLS: Sales, marketing, administration, time-management, communication, negotiation, math, and legal skills

PERSONAL TRAITS: Personable, highly disciplined, persistent, trustworthy, and self-starting

EDUCATION: High school diploma or equivalent; training through a real estate company or organization; and state license

ANALYZE If you were looking for a home to buy, what qualities, in addition to trustworthiness, would you look for in a real estate agent?

 To learn more about career paths for real estate agents, visit **persfinance07.glencoe.com.**

Document Detective

Investigate: Calculating a Mortgage Payment

A worksheet to calculate an affordable mortgage payment contains the following information:

- Your monthly income
- Your monthly expenses
- Difference between your monthly income and expenses

Your Motive: You may not realize all of the expenses you incur each month. Therefore, when considering purchasing a home, you must carefully calculate your cash flow to be sure you are not overestimating your ability to pay for expenses.

Name: LeBron	
Monthly Income (cash flow)	
Wages and salary	$5,500
Investment income	300
Other income	0
Total Monthly Income	**$5,800**
Monthly Expenses	
Groceries	$300
Car payments	350
Car maintenance	50
Gasoline	75
Clothing	125
Student loan payments	200
Medical expenses not covered by insurance	55
Automatic deposit, savings account	200
Retirement account	200
Credit card payments	350
Insurance payments (car, life, health, etc.)	550
Income taxes, including Social Security	1,925
Restaurants	50
Charitable contributions	25
Vacations	150
Entertainment	75
Other expenses	0
Total Monthly Expenses	**$4,680**
Affordable Mortgage Payment (Monthly Income – Expenses)	**$1,120**

Key Points: A mortgage payment for a house is usually the single largest monthly expense you will incur. It is important that you are able to pay it each month. By determining your monthly income and expenses, you will be able to calculate how much you can afford to pay each month for a mortgage.

Find the Solutions

1. What are some other possible expenses?
2. Why are income taxes monthly expenses?
3. Does LeBron have enough money to cover monthly mortgage payments and closing and other costs?
4. Should LeBron spend all of the money he has left after paying his monthly expenses on a mortgage payment?
5. What expenses would you be willing to cut if your mortgage payment was $1,500 per month? Why?

Local Zoning Laws Some communities have strict zoning laws, which are regulations that limit how property in a given area can be used. The existence of such laws may also affect your housing decisions. William wanted to live in an all-residential area, so he bought a duplex in a neighborhood where local zoning laws ban any commercial construction of stores or business buildings. In contrast, Alicia bought a condominium in a much less restrictive community because she wanted to be able to walk to nearby restaurants and businesses.

Hiring a Real Estate Agent

Real estate agents are people who arrange the sale and purchase of homes as well as other buildings and land. They are good sources of information about the location, availability, prices, and quality of homes. Potential home buyers often use real estate agents to help them find housing. The agents can also negotiate the purchase price between buyer and seller. They help buyers arrange financing for the purchase, and they can recommend lawyers, insurance agents, and home inspectors to serve the buyers' needs.

Real estate services are usually free to the buyer. The agents may represent the sellers, who pay them a commission of 3 to 6 percent when the property is sold. Some real estate agents also represent buyers. In this case, the agent may be paid by either the buyer or the seller.

As You Read

RELATE

How would you go about finding a real estate agent who suits you?

Conducting a Home Inspection

Before you make a final decision to buy property, it is important to get an evaluation of the house and land by a qualified home inspector. (See **Figure 7.6** on page 216.) When Josh Samuels called in a home inspector to check the house he wanted to buy, the inspector found cracks in the foundation, an overloaded electrical system, and problems with the water quality. Josh still wanted the house, and he was able to negotiate a lower price because he had the inspector's report. A home inspection costs money, but it can save you from problems and unplanned expenses in the future.

Some states, cities, and lenders require inspection documents. The mortgage company will usually conduct an appraisal to determine the fair market value of the property. An appraisal is not a detailed inspection. It is an estimation of the value of the property usually in comparison with other similar properties that have recently sold in the particular area.

STEP 3: Price the Property
What price should you offer to pay?

After you have checked out the property as thoroughly as possible, it is time to consider making an offer to the current owner. This is usually done through a real estate agent, unless the owner is acting as his or her own agent.

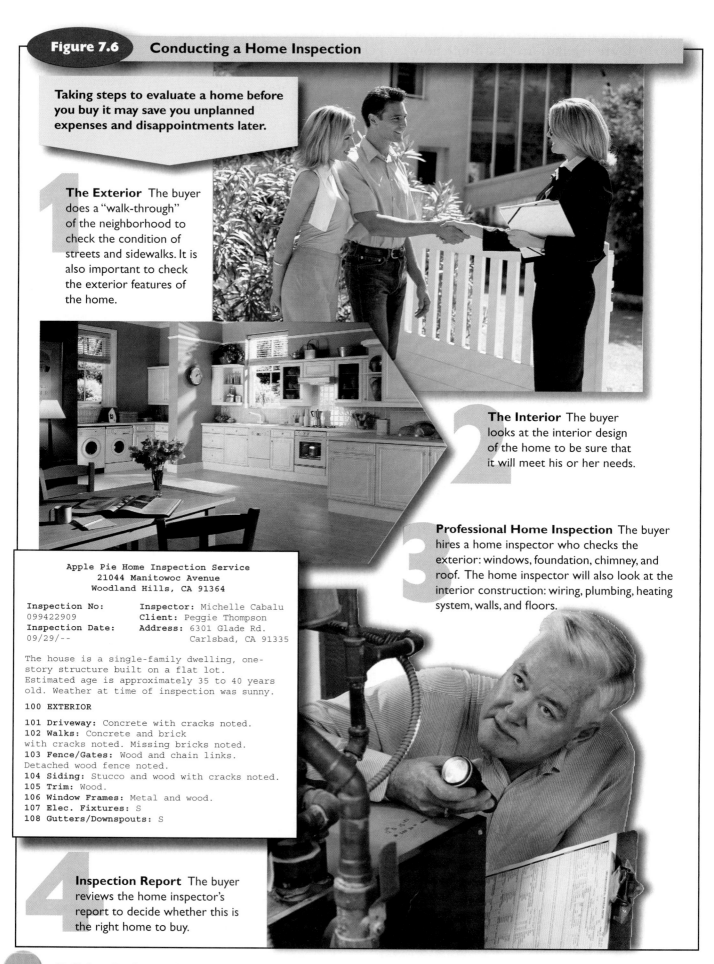

Figure 7.6 **Conducting a Home Inspection**

Taking steps to evaluate a home before you buy it may save you unplanned expenses and disappointments later.

1 The Exterior The buyer does a "walk-through" of the neighborhood to check the condition of streets and sidewalks. It is also important to check the exterior features of the home.

2 The Interior The buyer looks at the interior design of the home to be sure that it will meet his or her needs.

3 Professional Home Inspection The buyer hires a home inspector who checks the exterior: windows, foundation, chimney, and roof. The home inspector will also look at the interior construction: wiring, plumbing, heating system, walls, and floors.

Apple Pie Home Inspection Service
21044 Manitowoc Avenue
Woodland Hills, CA 91364

Inspection No: Inspector: Michelle Cabalu
099422909   Client: Peggie Thompson
Inspection Date: Address: 6301 Glade Rd.
09/29/--   Carlsbad, CA 91335

The house is a single-family dwelling, one-story structure built on a flat lot. Estimated age is approximately 35 to 40 years old. Weather at time of inspection was sunny.

100 EXTERIOR

101 **Driveway:** Concrete with cracks noted.
102 **Walks:** Concrete and brick with cracks noted. Missing bricks noted.
103 **Fence/Gates:** Wood and chain links. Detached wood fence noted.
104 **Siding:** Stucco and wood with cracks noted.
105 **Trim:** Wood.
106 **Window Frames:** Metal and wood.
107 **Elec. Fixtures:** S
108 **Gutters/Downspouts:** S

4 Inspection Report The buyer reviews the home inspector's report to decide whether this is the right home to buy.

Determining the Price of the Home

Every home that is for sale has a listing price—the price that the owner is asking for it. That price is not necessarily the price you will pay, however. You are free to make a lower offer. What should you offer? Here are some questions to consider:

- How long has the home been on the market? If a home is on the market for a while, the owner may accept a lower price.
- What have similar homes in the neighborhood sold for recently? If a listing price is too high, you should offer less.
- How tight is the housing market? In a "seller's market," homes are in high demand, and sellers can get the highest prices. In a "buyer's market," there is an abundant supply of homes for sale, and buyers can pay lower prices.
- Do the current owners need to sell in a hurry? If so, they may be willing to accept less than they feel the home is worth.
- How well does the home meet your needs? If a home fits your needs, you may be willing to pay more.
- How easily can you arrange financing? If interest rates are high, your payment will be higher.

Negotiating the Purchase Price

Once you have decided on a reasonable amount to offer, the real estate agent will communicate it to the seller, who may either accept or reject it. If your offer is accepted, congratulations! You will soon have a new home—and at a price you are willing to pay.

Sometimes the seller will not accept your offer if it is below the listing price. In that case, you will have to make a second, higher offer, or start looking for a different home. A seller may also make a counteroffer in response to your bid. Making a counteroffer means dropping the asking price. For example, Jian Wang offered $178,900 for a condominium that was listed at $186,000. The sellers rejected his offer but made a counteroffer of $184,500. Jian thought that the price was still too high, so he submitted a bid of $182,000. They eventually settled on a purchase price of $183,000.

When the buyer and seller agree on a price, they must sign a purchase agreement, or purchase contract, that states their intention to complete the sale. Most purchase contracts are conditional; that is, they take effect only if certain other events occur. For example, the contract may be valid only if the buyers can obtain financing, or only if they can sell their current home in a specified period of time.

At this point in the process, the buyer sometimes must pay the seller a portion of the purchase price, called *earnest money*. This money shows that the offer is serious. It is held in an escrow account until the sale is completed. An **escrow account** is an account where money is held in trust until it can be delivered to a designated party. The earnest money is applied toward the down payment.

MATH

An average homeowner stays in a home for about six years. With an 8 percent mortgage, the homeowner will sell the home, still owing over 90 percent of the mortgage. If this trend continued, the homeowner would *never* pay off a mortgage in his or her lifetime. *Imagine you have purchased a house for $97,000, with $9,700 down and a simple interest rate of 8 percent. How long would it take to pay off your mortgage if you paid $700 a month?*

STEP 4: Obtain Financing
What are the costs involved in purchasing property?

After you have decided to purchase a specific home and have agreed on a price, you will have to think about how you will pay for your purchase. First, you will have to come up with money for the down payment. Next, you will probably have to get a loan to help pay for the remainder of the purchase price. Finally, you will be responsible for fees and other expenses related to the settlement of the real estate transaction.

Determining Amount of Down Payment

As a general rule, the greater the portion of the total purchase price you can pay up front, the easier it will be to obtain a loan. Many lenders suggest that you put 20 percent or more of the purchase price as a down payment. For example, if the purchase price of the house is $100,000, you would need to make a down payment of $20,000. The most common sources of funds for down payments are personal savings accounts, sales of investments or other assets, or gifts or loans from relatives.

Private Mortgage Insurance   Lenders might accept lower down payments. However, if the down payment is less than 20 percent of the purchase price, some lenders will require you to obtain private mortgage insurance. **Private mortgage insurance (PMI)** is a special policy that protects the lender in case the buyer cannot make payments or cannot make them on time. Sometimes buyers will pay the cost of PMI up front, and sometimes they will agree to spread the cost over the life of the loan. When the borrower has paid between 20 to 25 percent of the purchase price, the insurance can be dropped.

Qualifying for a Mortgage

A **mortgage** is a long-term loan extended to someone who buys property. The buyer borrows money from a bank, credit union, savings and loan association, or mortgage company, which pays the full amount of the loan to the seller. In return, the buyer makes monthly payments to the lender. These monthly payments are usually made over a period of 15, 20, or 30 years. The home you buy serves as collateral, a type of guarantee that the loan will be repaid. If you fail to repay the mortgage or make regular payments, the lender can foreclose, or take possession of the property.

Financial Qualifications   To take out a mortgage, you need to meet certain criteria, just as you would to qualify for any other type of loan. Lenders look at your income, your debts, and your savings to decide whether you are a good risk. These figures are put into a formula to determine how much you can afford to pay.

As You Read

QUESTION

Lenders want to know how much money you owe. What other information do they look for?

▲ **THE TEST** Applying for a loan requires paperwork that will be examined by the lender to determine your eligibility for the loan. *Why is this process so important to the lender?*

Interest Rate Factors   The size of your mortgage will also depend on the current interest rate. The higher the rate, the more you will need to pay in interest each month. That means that less of your money will be available to pay off the purchase price. When interest rates rise, fewer people are able to afford the cost of an average-priced home. In contrast, low rates increase the size of the loan that you can receive.

For example, Bernadette qualifies for a monthly mortgage payment of $700. If interest rates are 7 percent, she will be able to take out a 30-year loan of $105,215. However, if interest rates increase to 12 percent, she will qualify for a 30-year loan of only $68,053. Both of these loans will carry the same monthly payment of $700. The differences can be quite surprising.

Paying Points

Different lenders may offer slightly different interest rates for mortgages. In addition, when you compare the cost of doing business with various lenders, you will have to consider other factors. If you want a lower interest rate, you may have to pay a higher down payment and **points**—extra charges that must be paid by the buyer to the lender in order to get a lower interest rate. Each point equals 1 percent of the loan amount. For example, suppose that a bank offers you a $100,000 mortgage with two points, or 2 percent. Since 2 percent of $100,000 is $2,000, you will have to pay an extra $2,000 when you get the loan to purchase your home.

Standard and Poor's publishes the globally recognized S&P 500® financial index. It also gathers financial statistics, information, and news, and analyzes this data for international businesses, governments, and individuals to help them guide their financial decisions.

SPAIN

Each year thousands of people from Britain make their way to Spain, seeking what their homeland does not offer—affordable housing. The average house in England costs more than 150,000 pounds (US $278,000). In comparison, a three-bedroom home not far from the beautiful Spanish coast costs less than 100,000 pounds (US $185,000). A roomy handyman's special can be found for under 20,000 pounds (US $37,000). Many of the British househunters may purchase a house to fit their pocketbooks, but there may be other motivations as well. Some buy Spanish property as an investment, and then lease the homes to renters. Others simply prefer the more stress-free life and agreeable climate of sunny Spain.

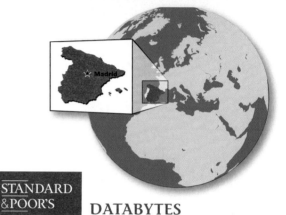

STANDARD
&POOR'S
DATABYTES

Capital	Madrid
Population	41,334,000
Languages	Castilian Spanish, Catalan, Galician, and Basque
Currency	euro
Gross Domestic Product (GDP)	$885.5 billion (2003 est.)
GDP per capita	$22,000

Industry: Textiles and apparel, food and beverages, metal manufacturing, and chemicals

Agriculture: Grain, vegetables, olives, wine grapes, beef, and fish

Exports: Machinery, motor vehicles, foodstuffs, and other consumer goods

Natural Resources: Coal, lignite, iron ore, and uranium

Think Globally
Would you buy a home in another country? Why or why not?

Comparing Points How does a high interest rate with no points compare to a low interest rate with points? A lower interest rate results in a lower monthly payment, but you pay more money up front.

If you keep your home for only a short time, you may lose money with the lower rate because the monthly savings will not add up to what you had to pay in points. If you keep the home for several years, however, your monthly savings will eventually make up for what you paid in points. As a rule, the longer you keep the home, the better off you are when paying the points in exchange for a lower interest rate.

The Loan Application Process

Most lenders charge home buyers a fee of between $100 and $300 to apply for a mortgage, which is added into the loan amount. To apply, the buyer must fill out forms, giving details of his or her income, employment, debts, and other information. The lender will verify this information by obtaining a buyer's credit report.

After a careful examination of the buyer's financial history and the size, location, and condition of the property, the lender decides to approve or deny the application. If it is approved, the purchase contract between seller and buyer becomes legally binding.

STANDARD &POOR'S

Put on Your Financial Planner's Cap

A client has $27,000 in savings and an excellent credit history. Assuming 20 percent down, what price should your client pay for a house?

Types of Mortgages
How do the various types of mortgages differ?

For most people, a mortgage is the greatest financial obligation of their lives. There are several types of mortgages. Depending on the terms of the loan, a homeowner will have to make monthly payments for many years.

The monthly payments on a mortgage are set at a level that allows amortization of the loan. **Amortization** is the reduction of a loan balance through payments made over a period of time. So the balance is reduced every time you make a payment. The amount of your payment is applied first to the interest owed and then to the principal, which is the original amount you borrowed. In the first years of the loan, only a small part of each monthly payment goes to reduce the principal. Most goes toward paying off the interest. Near the end of the loan period, almost all of each payment goes toward reducing the principal. By the end of the loan period, both the interest and the principal will be completely paid off.

It is possible to pay off a mortgage early. Paying a little extra each month and applying that amount to the principal will save interest charges over the long run. For example, paying $25 extra a month on a 30-year, 10 percent mortgage of $75,000 will save more than $34,000 in interest charges—and will repay the loan in about 25 years. Some lenders charge an extra fee for prepaying.

Fixed-Rate Mortgages

A **fixed-rate mortgage**, or conventional mortgage, is a mortgage with a fixed interest rate and a fixed schedule of payments. A fixed rate is an interest rate that does not change. For example, if the interest rate is 8.75 percent when the loan is granted, the homeowner will continue to pay 8.75 percent throughout the life of the loan, even if interest rates for new loans rise. Conventional mortgages typically run for a period of 15, 20, or 30 years. They offer peace of mind because monthly payments always remain the same.

Adjustable-Rate Mortgages

Fixed-rate loans guarantee a particular interest rate for the life of the loan. An **adjustable-rate mortgage (ARM)**, also known as a variable-payment mortgage, is a mortgage with an interest rate that increases or decreases during the life of the loan. The rate changes according to economic indicators, such as rates on U.S. Treasury securities, the Federal Home Loan Bank Board's mortgage rate index, or the lender's own cost-of-funds index. As a result, your loan payments may go up or down.

Your rates will change according to the terms of your agreement with the lender. Generally, if interest rates decline and stay low, an ARM will save you substantial amounts of money. However, if rates increase and stay high, an ARM may cost you a lot of money because your monthly payment will go up.

Evaluating Adjustable-Rate Mortgages Consider several factors when you evaluate adjustable-rate mortgages:

1. Determine the frequency of and restrictions on allowed changes in interest rates.
2. Consider the frequency of and restrictions on changes in the monthly payment.
3. Find out what index the lender will use to set the mortgage interest rate over the term of the loan.

Rate Caps Most adjustable-rate mortgages have a rate cap, which limits the amount the interest rate can rise or fall. Rate caps generally limit increases (or decreases) of the interest rate to one or two percentage points in a year—or no more than five points over the life of the loan.

Some ARMs also carry payment caps, which limit the size of monthly payments. That may seem like good protection for the buyer, but it has drawbacks. When interest rates rise while monthly payments remain the same, the payments will not cover the interest. As a result, the loan balance increases, and payments may have to be extended over a longer time.

Convertible ARMs Some lenders also offer convertible ARMs. Convertible ARMs permit a borrower to convert, or change, an adjustable-rate mortgage to a fixed-rate mortgage during a certain period of time. If you decide to make the change, your interest rate will be 0.25 to 0.50 percent higher than current rates for conventional 30-year mortgages. You will also have to pay a conversion fee, which is usually $500 or less.

Government Financing Programs The Federal Housing Administration (FHA) and the Veterans Administration (VA) help home buyers obtain low-interest, low-down-payment loans. VA loans are available to eligible veterans of the armed services. These government agencies do not actually lend the money. Instead, they help qualified buyers arrange for loans from regular lenders.

Typically, an agency guarantees repayment to the lender if the borrower defaults, or is unable to make payments. As a result, many government-guaranteed loans have lower interest rates. Although extra insurance fees may be added on to these loans, government-backed mortgages are a good deal for those who qualify for them.

Home Equity Loans

A second mortgage is also called a **home equity loan**, which is a loan based on the difference between the current market value of a home and the amount the borrower owes on the mortgage. To determine the amount of this type of loan, the financial institution will find out the current market value of a home and how much equity is in the property. Such loans can provide money for education, home improvements, or other purposes. However, some states limit the ways in which the money may be used.

Second mortgages are one source of extra cash for homeowners. However, taking out additional loans can keep a homeowner continually in debt. Also, if the borrower cannot make the payments on a second mortgage, the lender can take the home. For more information on home equity loans, see Chapter 19.

Refinancing

Many homeowners need extra money or want to reduce their monthly payments. These options are possible when they **refinance**, which is obtaining a new mortgage to replace an existing one. For example, Esther Aquino originally took out a fixed-rate mortgage at 11 percent interest, and then watched interest rates fall to 6 percent. Fortunately, she was able to refinance her home, and take out a new mortgage at the lower 6 percent interest rate. In Esther's case, her monthly payment decreased considerably.

Refinancing is not always a good choice. To refinance, a homeowner usually pays extra fees, which may reduce any savings from a small drop in interest rates. Moreover, refinancing may extend the life of a loan. In general, refinancing is an advantage when the interest rate drops two or more points below the current rate and when the owner plans to stay in his or her present home for at least two or more years.

STEP 5: Close the Transaction

What are closing costs?

The final step in the home-buying process is the **closing**, a meeting of the seller, the buyer, and the lender of funds, or representatives of each party, to complete the transaction. At the closing, documents are signed, last-minute details are settled, and money is paid. The seller and buyer must also pay a number of fees and charges, which are *closing costs*.

WebQuest

Your Own Home
Learn about different kinds of mortgages and how to qualify for one. Then learn how to negotiate the purchase of your first home.

@ To continue with Tasks 4 and 5 of your WebQuest project, visit **persfinance07.glencoe .com**.

Closing Costs

Most closing costs involve the legal details related to purchasing a home. For example, a title company researches the property to make sure that no disputes exist over its ownership or that there are no unpaid real estate taxes for the property. The title company also offers **title insurance**, a type of insurance that protects the buyer if problems with the title are found later.

Another typical closing cost is a fee for recording the **deed**, which is the official document transferring ownership from seller to buyer. Buyers also pay for private mortgage insurance, which protects the lender from any loss resulting from default on the loan. See **Figure 7.7** for a list of other common closing costs.

Escrow Account

After the closing, your lender might require that you deposit money into an escrow account. The money, usually held by the lender, is set aside to pay for taxes and insurance. The lender does not have to worry whether the borrower is paying these obligations because the money is available. See **Figure 7.8** for a list of home-buying issues.

Taxes and Insurance   Homeowners must pay property taxes and homeowners insurance in addition to their mortgage payments. In most states, property taxes generally cover the cost of public services, such as police and fire protection, schools, and street repair. Homeowners insurance protects the lender's investment in case of damage to the home from fire or other hazards.

Figure 7.7	Closing Costs	

	Cost Range	
Item	**Buyer**	**Seller**
Title search fee	$ 50 – $ 100	$ 300 – $ 900
Title insurance	$ 300 – $ 900	$ 50 – $1000
Attorney's fee	$ 50 – $1000	$ 100 – $ 500
Property survey	–	–
Appraisal fee	$ 100 – $ 350	–
Recording fees	$ 30 – $ 65	$ 35 – $ 65
Credit report	$ 35 – $ 75	–
Termite inspection	$ 100 – $ 250	–
Lender's origination fee	1–5% of loan	–
Real estate agent's commission	–	5–7% of purchase price
Insurance, taxes, and interest	varies	–

Costs Add Up   Closing costs add to the expense of buying a home.

For a loan amount of $100,000 with $3,500 in insurance, taxes, and interest, what could a buyer pay in closing costs, based on the figures in this chart?

Figure 7.8   **The Elements of Buying a Home**

It is important to consider these factors when making a home purchase:

- **Location** Consider both the surrounding community and the geographic region. The same home may vary greatly in cost depending on where it is located: in Kansas or California, on a busy highway or a quiet street, in a landscaped suburb or an urban neighborhood.

- **Down Payment** A large down payment reduces your mortgage costs, but how much can you afford to pay up front?

- **Mortgage Rates and Points** You will have to choose between a lower mortgage rate with points and a higher mortgage rate without points. You will also need to consider what type of mortgage to arrange. When you apply for the loan, be prepared to provide the lender with copies of your financial records and other relevant information.

- **Closing Costs** Settlement costs may range anywhere from 2 to 6 percent of the total amount you borrow. That is in addition to the down payment.

- **Monthly Payments** Your monthly payment for interest, principal, insurance, and taxes will be among your largest, most enduring expenses. Beware of buying a home that costs more than you can afford.

- **Maintenance Costs** Homes require a lot of repair and maintenance. Be sure to set aside funds for these necessities.

Think It Over

Buying a home is a complicated process.

What are some possible results of not thinking through all the elements listed above?

Selling a Home
What can an owner do to his or her home to get the best selling price?

As your needs change, you may decide to sell your home. You will have to get it ready for the market, set a price, and decide whether to sell it on your own or get professional help from a real estate agent.

Preparing a Home for Selling

The nicer your home looks, the faster it will sell at the price you want. Real estate salespeople recommend that homeowners make needed repairs and paint worn exterior and interior areas when preparing a home for selling. For example, Dora and Dennis Muldoon repainted several rooms, replaced some light fixtures, and changed the living room carpet before they put their house on the market. They kept the house as clean, neat, bright, and airy as possible while prospective buyers were visiting. They also made sure that the lawn was cut regularly and that their children did not leave toys in the yard. Their work paid off: They sold their home within a few months of listing their home.

A real estate agent will suggest to a seller ways to improve the "curb appeal" of a home, such as landscaping, to attract buyers. *What is the biggest disadvantage of using a real estate agent?*

Determining the Selling Price

Setting a price on a home can be difficult. A price that is too high may scare off potential buyers. Setting the price too low will result in lost profit. Some sellers will pay for an **appraisal**—an estimate of the current value of the property—and use that as a basis for a listing price. If you ever sell a home, find out whether the current market and demand for housing favors buyers or sellers. Then decide how quickly you need to sell your home and evaluate any improvements you have made to the property. Adding certain features—such as a deck or an extra bathroom—can increase a home's value.

Choosing a Real Estate Agent

Many sellers put the sale of their home into the hands of a licensed real estate agent who is affiliated with an agency. There is a wide choice of firms, from small local real estate agencies to nationally known companies. When choosing an agent, pick someone who knows your neighborhood and is eager to sell your home.

Real Estate Agent Services Real estate agents provide various services. They can help determine a selling price, attract buyers, show your home, and handle the financial aspects of the sale.

They are paid a commission, or fee, upon the sale of a home—usually 5 to 7 percent of the purchase price.

Sale by Owner

Each year about 10 percent of home sales are made directly by homeowners without the help of real estate agents. Selling your home yourself can save you thousands of dollars, but it will cost you time and energy. Advertising the home will be up to you. Showing the home to prospective buyers will also be your responsibility. Be sure to use the services of a lawyer or a title company to help you with the contract, closing, and other legal matters.

Making Choices

Your housing decisions will be affected by many factors, including your lifestyle and financial situation. By carefully reviewing your options, making educated decisions, and following the appropriate processes, you will make the best housing choice to suit your needs.

After You Read

REACT

With the information provided in this chapter, do you feel that you could make a wise decision about whether to rent or buy a home? Why or why not?

Section 7.3 Assessment

QUICK CHECK

1. What are five steps that make up the process of buying a home?
2. What costs are associated with buying a home?
3. What activities are associated with selling a home?

THINK CRITICALLY

4. State three reasons you should carefully inspect the property you plan to purchase.

USE COMMUNICATION SKILLS

5. **Owner Obligations** Imagine that you are a condominium owner attending a meeting of the condominium association. What should the association do about a homeowner who leaves garbage in the hallway? Should the association limit the use of the pool and tennis courts to owners?

Write About It Write a paragraph answering one of the questions.

SOLVE MONEY PROBLEMS

6. **Making an Offer** After several weeks of searching for a new home, Renée has found a house that seems to be in good shape and is located in a nice neighborhood. The listing price is $125,000, which is about $15,000 more than she wants to pay. She would like to make a lower bid, but the housing market is tight, and she worries that someone else may buy the house at the listing price. Renée wonders what she should do.

 Analyze Working in a small group, brainstorm some ideas about what factors Renée should consider in making a decision.

Chapter 7 Review & Activities

CHAPTER SUMMARY

- Renting tends to be less expensive than buying and offers more flexibility. Home ownership offers stability, financial benefits, and increased value over time.
- Renting a residence has the advantages of mobility, few maintenance responsibilities, and relatively low initial costs. Disadvantages include rent increases, few tax benefits, and restricted activities.
- The cost of renting is affected by the neighborhood, space, monthly rent, security deposit, and renters insurance.
- Advantages of owning a residence include stability, individual expression, tax benefits, and increased value.

- Disadvantages include financial risk, the possibility of value not increasing, limited mobility, and high expenses.
- When evaluating property, walk through the neighborhood, check the home exterior and interior, and get a home inspection.
- A down payment is needed to purchase a home. Then a buyer must get a long-term loan, or mortgage, to pay for the remaining purchase price. Closing costs must also be paid.
- To sell a home, decide whether to use a real estate agent, prepare the home, set a fair price, and keep the home neat and clean.

Communicating Key Terms

With a partner, role-play a real estate agent and a client discussing preparations for closing on a house. Write a script of the conversation you would have, using most of the terms below.

- mobility
- tenant
- landlord
- lease
- security deposit
- renters insurance
- equity
- escrow account

- private mortgage insurance (PMI)
- mortgage
- points
- amortization
- fixed-rate mortgage
- adjustable-rate mortgage (ARM)

- home equity loan
- refinance
- closing
- title insurance
- deed
- appraisal

Reviewing Key Concepts

1. **Evaluate** the various housing alternatives that are available.
2. **List** the advantages and disadvantages of renting.
3. **Identify** the costs of renting.
4. **List** the advantages and disadvantages of owning a residence.
5. **Explain** how to evaluate a property.
6. **Discuss** the financing involved in purchasing a home.
7. **Describe** a plan for selling a home.

Language Arts   Different life circumstances affect housing needs for people at different stage of their lives.
Write About It   Write a paragraph describing the housing needs of a 28-year-old married couple expecting a baby in six months, who have a combined annual income of $62,000. Compare their needs with those of a 23-year-old single person who is earning $36,000 a year.

Choosing Prices   Imagine that you want to purchase a home and you have narrowed your choice down to three different houses. The prices for the houses are: House #1—$165,000; House #2—$151,000; House #3—$172,000.

1. **Calculate** the monthly mortgage payment for each home, assuming that there will be a 10 percent down payment and a 30-year mortgage with a simple interest rate of 5.2 percent.
2. **Compute** by going to the Web site of a real estate company or bank to find current interest rates and monthly payments.

Connect with Math   Today it is possible to buy a home without making a down payment. This is called a 100 percent mortgage. It is available to people with good credit scores and usually requires private mortgage insurance and slightly higher interest on the overall loan.

1. **Research**   Use an Internet search engine to find a financial institution that offers 100 percent mortgages.
2. **Think Critically**   For whom would a 100 percent mortgage be a good deal?

Selling a Home   Your neighbors are thinking of selling their two-bedroom home in the suburbs and moving to a two-bedroom condominium. Help them make this decision.

 Log On   Use an Internet search engine to find local real estate Web sites. Answer these questions:

1. What is the average asking price of a two-bedroom home in your neighborhood or nearby?
2. Based on the prices you find, would you advise a neighbor to sell this type of home? Why or why not?

Newsclip: Low Interest Rates   Home prices have been on the rise since 2000, driven by low interest rates that make mortgages affordable.

 Log On   Go to persfinance07.glencoe.com and open Chapter 7. Learn more about the different types of mortgages available. How is buying a home different today? Write a list of answers.

WHAT'S YOUR FINANCIAL **ID?**

WHERE WOULD YOU LIKE TO LIVE?

There are many factors that will help you decide where to live. These factors may change over the next few years. As you look into your housing options, you will need to consider your lifestyle, family situation, finances, and future plans. Here is a quick quiz to test your preferences. Write your answers on a separate sheet of paper.

1. I do not care about having a yard.

True   False

2. My income varies right now.

True   False

3. I never want to own a house or a condominium.

True   False

4. I need to be able to move at any time.

True   False

5. I want to keep my expenses as low as possible.

True   False

6. I do not want to be responsible for repairs and upkeep.

True   False

7. I do not plan to have a family for a while.

True   False

Scoring: The more "true" answers you have, the better it is for you to rent an apartment and postpone house hunting until you are ready.

Your Financial Portfolio

Renting or Buying Your Home

Atul and Elena have saved enough money to buy a townhouse and have found one they like, but they need to consider how much it will actually cost to live there. The rent on their apartment is $700 a month ($8,400 a year), and the townhouse costs $85,000. They will need to consider any additional costs.

Atul and Elena's Dilemma

Rental Costs	
Annual rent payments	$8,400
Renters insurance	170
Total annual cost of renting	**$8,570**

Buying Costs	
Down payment (at 10%)	8,500
Annual mortgage payments	8,060
Property taxes (annual costs)	1,275
Mortgage insurance (annual premium)	536
Homeowners insurance (annual premium)	400
Estimated maintenance costs	850

Financial Benefits of Home Ownership	
Less: Tax savings for mortgage interest	−1,820
Less: Tax savings for property taxes	−357
Total cost of buying first year	**$17,444**
Less: one-time down payment	−8,500
Estimated annual appreciation (4%)*	−3,400
Total long-term annual cost of buying	**$5,544**

*Nationwide average; actual appreciation varies by geographic area and economic conditions.

Atul and Elena compared the annual costs of renting ($8,570) and buying ($5,544) and decided that it would be a good investment to buy the townhouse.

Compare

On a separate sheet of paper, compare renting versus buying your place of residence. Check a newspaper for a rental price for a two-bedroom apartment and a selling price for a two-bedroom house. Use those figures to complete your comparison.

Unit 2 LAB

Get a Financial Life!

Home Ownership

Overview

Carrie Houston finished her associate of arts degree at the local community college and is now working as a fashion designer for Outside Box Designs. Last year she married David Lanier, a high school computer science teacher and basketball coach. Carrie and David have many decisions to make as a married couple. One of their goals is to purchase a home within the next two years. Recently, Carrie and David met with a real estate agent and a banker. The real estate agent helped them think about the features and location they want for their future residence. The banker discussed mortgages and budgeting with the young couple. Both Carrie and David realize that they have a lot of research and planning ahead of them.

Resources & Tools

- Crayons, markers, colored pencils
- Internet (optional)
- Newspapers and real estate magazines
- Portfolio (ring binder or file folder)
- Public or school library
- Spreadsheet software (optional)
- Word processor

Procedures

STEP A **The Process**
Carrie and David's combined income is $85,000 a year. Their banker told them that the most they should spend for a home is 2.5 times their annual income.

1. Determine the maximum amount that Carrie and David should spend on their future home.
2. Write a list of the features in the home. Then write a two-paragraph description of their future home and draw a picture of it.
3. Using the newspaper, real estate magazines, or the Internet, find an ad or listing for a home in their price range. You might look in different regions of the country to find different price ranges. Clip or print the ad or listing.
4. Request an amortization table from a local bank, or find one on the Internet. Determine Carrie and David's monthly mortgage payment based on current interest rates.
5. Contact a homeowners insurance company and find out the cost of insuring the home.
6. Contact companies that provide electricity, gas, water, cable television, telephone, and trash pickup. Determine the installation fees, deposits, and monthly cost of each service for the home.
7. Using newspapers, catalogs, garage sale ads, the Internet, or other sources, furnish their home for $15,000. Provide a picture or a drawing of the items bought.
8. Prepare a budget for Carrie and David for their first year as homeowners. If possible, use a spreadsheet program.

STEP B Create Your Portfolio

As you work through the process, save the results so that you can refer, review, and refine. Use a ring binder or a file folder to create a portfolio of your work.

1. The title of the binder or folder should be "Home Ownership." Decorate the front of the binder or folder—and be creative.
2. Organize the results of Step A (2–8) in your binder or folder. If possible, use a word processor to ensure that your work is neat and easy to read.
3. Read a magazine article on one of the following topics: (1) buying your first home, (2) making home repairs, (3) decorating a home, or (4) landscaping a home. Present a summary of the article to the class.

STEP C Technical Writing and Reading

Many workplaces need employees who are skilled in technical writing and reading. Technical writing is the process of communicating technical information in writing, clearly and accurately. To practice technical writing, complete activity 1 or activity 2 (below). Activity 3 will allow you to practice technical reading.

1. When Carrie and David are ready to purchase their home, they will have to decide which lender to use to obtain a mortgage. Write a technical paper (one or two pages) outlining the steps Carrie and David must take to choose a mortgage.
2. Carrie and David have decided to acquire a credit card. Write a technical paper (one or two pages) outlining the steps Carrie and David must take to choose a credit card.
3. Exchange technical writing papers with another student. Read your classmate's paper and critique it for accuracy, completeness, punctuation, and grammar. Return each other's papers.

Unit 3

Investing Financial Resources

WebQuest Internet Project

Nest Egg

Everyone wants to look forward to the future with confidence. Knowing you can be financially secure helps to build that confidence. Savings and investments are keys to financial security. If you do not have the resources right now to save and invest, you can begin planning to start your nest egg. In this project, you will find investment experts and get their advice about how a young person can get ready to save and invest.

 Log on to persfinance07.glencoe.com. Begin by reading Task 1. Then continue on your WebQuest as you study Unit 3.

Section	8.1	9.3	10.4	11.1
Page	241	286	337	358

FINANCE FILE

The Best Homes for Rollover IRAs

When you go to work for an employer, you are not just getting a job but a retirement account as well. You will be stuck with the 401(k) that is offered, and you get no opportunity to shop around for more attractive investment options or services.

But when you leave your job—for another one or to retire—the situation changes. Chances are you will want to roll over the money in the 401(k) to an IRA that will probably become the most important source of your income throughout retirement.

"Anyone who is shopping to move a 401(k) should identify three or four options, and do a thorough analysis so they understand the fees," Doland [a financial advisor] recommends. One cost is fees for services, such as opening or closing an account, or account maintenance.

When you retire, you'll be making regular withdrawals from your IRA, so easy access to information and good service may be more important than before. Online account management is a great tool for keeping track of balances and withdrawals.

—By Ellen Hoffman

Write About It Why might having a 401(k) retirement account be important to someone who already has Social Security?

Log On To read the complete *BusinessWeek* article and do the *BusinessWeek* Extension activity to help you learn more about IRAs and other investment options, go to **persfinance07.glencoe.com**.

CHAPTER 8

Saving and Investing

 What You'll Learn

When you have completed this chapter, you will be able to:

Section 8.1
- Explain how to establish goals for a savings or investment program.
- Discuss ways to obtain funds for investing.
- Identify the factors that affect your investment choices.

Section 8.2
- Identify the main types of savings and investment alternatives.
- Explain the steps involved in developing a personal investment plan.

Section 8.3
- Describe your role in a personal investment program.
- Identify sources of financial information.

Reading Strategies

To get the most out of your reading:

Predict what you will learn in this chapter.

Relate what you read to your own life.

Question what you are reading to be sure you understand.

React to what you have read.

In the **Real** World . . .

Nellie Magdaleno has been working as a part-time florist. She opened a checking account for her regular expenses as well as a savings account to earn interest. However, she earns only pennies for each dollar she saves. So Nellie has been researching stocks, bonds, and mutual funds. She has found investment plans that will earn her more interest than a savings account. She is excited about finding a way to make her money work for her and hopes to save enough to invest in real estate one day.

Different types of investments are suitable for different personalities, situations, and stages of life.

As You Read   *Consider how your personality and goals will affect your choices for investment and savings plans.*

Investments

Q: After paying my bills, I do not have much money left over. I save any extra that I get. Since I do not have a lot of money, why should I even consider investing?

A: If inflation increases at a higher rate than your savings account return, you can lose purchasing power. To stay ahead of inflation and taxes, the money you set aside for long-term goals will need to earn more than the rates usually paid on savings accounts. Consider other investments that can earn a higher return.

Ask Yourself Besides investing some of your money, what are some other things that you could do to help you reach your long-term financial goals?

 Go to **persfinance07.glencoe.com** to complete the Standard & Poor's Financial Focus activity.

Preparing for a Savings or Investment Program

Establishing Your Financial Goals

Why are financial goals important to your future?

When you think about the future, do you picture yourself owning your own home, being the president of your own company, or retiring at age 50? You might want to travel or start a family. No matter how much you may want to have something, you will not acquire it if you cannot pay for it.

To gather the funds, you need to plan carefully—and have self-discipline along the way. If you are saving or investing to meet a goal that will make you happy and financially secure, the sacrifices you make will be worth it.

A savings or investment plan starts with a specific, measurable goal. For example, you may want to save $15,000 to make a down payment on a house five years after graduating from school. To reach that goal, a savings account provides safety but does not increase in value quickly. An investment may be safe or risky and increase in value slowly or quickly—or it may lose value.

You might also decide that you should begin saving money in an **emergency fund**—a savings account that you can access quickly to pay for unexpected expenses or emergencies. For example, if you had to pay for an unexpected car repair or if you lost your job, you could use the money you put away in your emergency fund.

Your Goals and Values

Your goals should correspond with your values. At one extreme, some people save or invest as much of each paycheck as possible. The satisfaction they get from fulfilling long-term financial goals is more important to them than spending a lot of money on something temporary, such as a weekend trip. At the other extreme, some people spend every cent they earn, and then run out of money before they receive their next paycheck.

Outlining Goals

It is probably wise to take a middle-of-the-road approach. You can spend money on some things you enjoy and still save enough for a savings or investment program. As you will learn, even a small amount of money saved or invested on a regular basis can add up to a large amount over time.

As you outline your financial goals, ask yourself these questions:

- How do I want to spend my money?
- How much money do I need to satisfy my goals?
- How will I get the money?
- How long will it take to save the money?
- How much risk am I willing to take when I invest?
- What conditions in the economy or in my life could change my investment goals?
- Are my goals reasonable, considering my circumstances or future circumstances?
- Am I willing to make sacrifices to save?
- What will happen if I do not meet my goals?

Performing a Financial Check-Up
How can you assess the health of your finances?

Before you think about investing for the future, you must take steps to be sure your personal finances are in good shape. Then you will be ready to move ahead with your financial plan. See **Figure 8.1** on page 240 for tips on how to perform your own financial check-up.

Money to Get Started
What are some sources of money to invest?

After you have set your goals and completed your financial check-up, you are almost ready to start saving or investing. But first you have to get the money. Here are a few ways to do that.

Pay Yourself First

People often save or invest money that is left over after they have paid all their other expenses, from monthly bills to video games. As you might guess, in many cases, nothing is left over. Here is a better approach:

1. Include the amount you want to save in your monthly expenses. Pay that amount first. Consider it as a bill that you owe to yourself.
2. Pay your monthly living expenses, such as rent and food.
3. Use money that is left over for personal pleasures, such as going to the movies or buying a new CD.

As You Read

RELATE

If you used the pay-yourself-first plan, how much would you be able to save each month?

Figure 8.1   **Your Financial Checkup**

Keeping your personal finances in order is an important step in meeting your long-term financial goals.

1 **Balance your budget.** Spend less money than you make; stay out of debt; and limit your credit card use. Eventually, the amount of cash remaining after you pay your bills will increase. You will be able to use that money to start a savings program.

2 **Have insurance.** When you are on your own, you should have enough insurance to cover losses from events such as a car accident, a medical emergency, or theft.

3 **Start an emergency fund.** Save money that you can access quickly to help you pay for unexpected situations, such as not being able to work. You should have enough money to cover living expenses for three to nine months.

4 **Have other sources of cash.** A source might be a line of credit with a financial institution or cash advance capability from a credit card company. Use it only for serious emergencies.

Employer-Sponsored Retirement Plans

If your employer offers a retirement plan, usually a 401(k) or 403(b) plan, you can take advantage of a ready-made investment program. Saving is simple because an amount you choose is deducted automatically from each paycheck. Many employers match part or all of the money you save. For example, for every dollar you contribute, your employer may put in 25 cents, 50 cents, or even a dollar, which would double your savings. In addition, money put in a retirement fund is not taxed until you withdraw it—usually at retirement age.

Starting an employer-sponsored or private retirement plan is an important step toward having financial security when you are older. Most people will need this retirement income in addition to Social Security as the Social Security system is revised. To learn more about retirement plans, read Chapter 15.

Elective Savings Programs

Some employers provide the option of having money automatically withheld from your paycheck and deposited in a standard savings account. On your own, you can also arrange with a mutual fund or brokerage firm to take a certain amount from your bank account every month and invest it. This is an easy way to save because you do not have to think about it. You may be less tempted to use the money if you never see it. An elective savings program is an excellent way to fund a traditional IRA or Roth IRA account.

Special Savings Effort

Another way to save is to set aside a specific time each year when you cut back sharply on what you spend and put the money you save in an investment fund.

Gifts, Inheritances, and Windfalls

During your lifetime, you might receive gifts of money, or you might inherit some money. You may also receive bonuses at work, tax refunds, and salary raises.

What would you do with that money? Often people choose to spend this extra money on something they could not afford under normal circumstances. Consider Jihwan's plan and whether you would make the same choice.

When Jihwan received his income tax refund, his friends suggested that this would be the perfect time to buy a big-screen television. Jihwan's friends were disappointed when he decided to put the money in a certificate of deposit that earned 6 percent interest. Jihwan did not mind watching television on his parents' 19-inch TV screen because his savings deposit was increasing. No one can make you save money to finance a savings or investment program. You have to choose to do it.

Nest Egg
Before you can save and invest, you have to pay your bills—every month! That means sticking to a budget. Learn about budgeting—why it is important, how to do it, and how to maintain it—and create a budget that reflects your needs today.

@ To continue with Task 2 of your Web-Quest project, visit **persfinance07.glencoe.com**.

The Value of Long-Term Investment Programs

Why should you invest in a long-term program?

Many people do not start investing because they have only a small amount of money. Others believe that they are too young to invest. However, having a small amount of money in a bank account should not stop you.

Remember that small amounts of money add up because of the *time value of money*. As you read in Chapter 1, the time value of money is the increase in an amount of money due to interest earned over time.

Figure 8.2 shows the growth of $2,000 during different time periods and at different rates of return. A rate of return is the percentage of increase in the value of your savings due to earned interest. Remember that you must continue to add money to your investments to see the growth that is represented in Figure 8.2.

Figure 8.2	Long-Term Investing and Growth

	Balance at End of Year					
Rate of Return	**1**	**5**	**10**	**20**	**30**	**40**
4%	$2,000	$10,832	$24,012	$59,556	$112,170	$190,052
5%	2,000	11,052	25,156	66,132	132,878	241,600
6%	2,000	11,274	26,362	73,572	158,116	309,520
7%	2,000	11,502	27,632	81,990	188,922	399,280
8%	2,000	11,734	28,974	91,524	226,560	518,120
9%	2,000	11,970	30,386	102,320	272,620	675,780
10%	2,000	12,210	31,874	114,550	328,980	885,180
11%	2,000	12,456	33,444	128,406	398,040	1,163,660
12%	2,000	12,706	35,098	144,104	482,660	1,534,180

Growing Wild The growth shown in this table at different rates of return assumes that you will invest $2,000 at the end of each year.

Why would you be willing to invest $2,000 a year for a long term?

Making Investment Decisions

What are the factors you should consider when choosing investments?

Once you know how much money you need to meet your goals, you then have to think about where to invest it. To make that decision, you need to understand the different risk factors. Also, you should consider each investment's potential for income and growth as well as its liquidity.

Safety and Risk

In the financial world, the words *safety* and *risk* have specific meanings. Safety means that the chance of losing your money in an investment is fairly small. Risk indicates that you cannot be certain about the profit of your investment. You can select investments that are very safe or very risky, or in between these extremes.

Generally, if you choose a safe investment, your rate of return will be low. On the other hand, a **speculative investment** is considered a high-risk investment that might earn a large profit in a short time. The disadvantage of a speculative investment is the possibility that at any time you could lose most or all of the money you invest. **Figure 8.3** categorizes each type of investment according to its safety record.

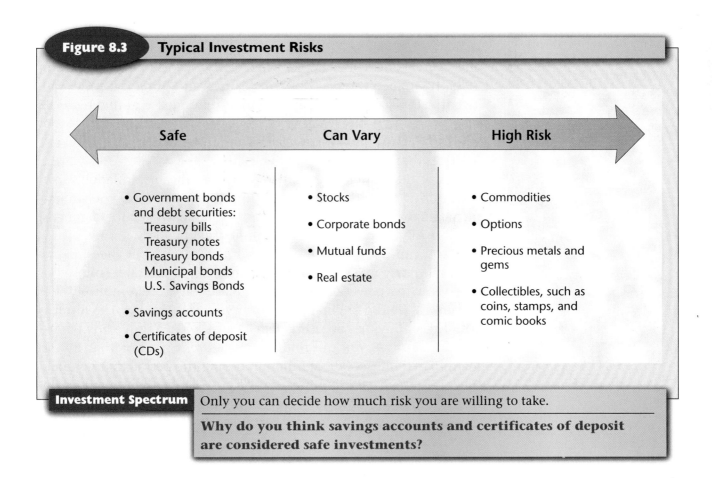

Figure 8.3 **Typical Investment Risks**

Safe	Can Vary	High Risk
• Government bonds and debt securities: Treasury bills Treasury notes Treasury bonds Municipal bonds U.S. Savings Bonds • Savings accounts • Certificates of deposit (CDs)	• Stocks • Corporate bonds • Mutual funds • Real estate	• Commodities • Options • Precious metals and gems • Collectibles, such as coins, stamps, and comic books

Investment Spectrum Only you can decide how much risk you are willing to take.

Why do you think savings accounts and certificates of deposit are considered safe investments?

One basic rule sums up the relationship between the factors of safety and risk: The potential return on any investment should be directly related to the risk you, the investor, take. Your attitude toward risk will vary according to your circumstances. For example, when you are young, you may be more willing to take risks because you have long-term investment goals. When you are older and close to retirement, you may decide to shift your investments from speculative to conservative investments to be sure that you will not lose your life savings.

Beginning investors may be afraid of the risk associated with some investments. However, it helps to remember that without risk, it is impossible to obtain returns that make investments grow. The key is to determine how much risk you are willing to take. Then choose quality investments that offer higher returns without an extremely high risk.

Five Components of Risk

Evaluate the overall risk factor of an investment by examining five different components of risk:

1. Inflation
2. Interest rate
3. Business failure
4. Financial market
5. Global investment

Inflation Risk Inflation is a persistent economic condition that affects everyone. For example, when Harry Majors opened his deli in 1985, he framed the first dollar he earned and hung it on the wall. Twenty years later, one of his customers reminded him that his 1985 dollar could now buy less than 50 cents' worth of salami. The loss of value to Harry's dollar was a result of inflation, which is a general rise in prices that affects everybody.

Investing your money can help you stay ahead of inflation. However, during periods of rapid inflation, the return from your investments might not keep up with the inflation rate. When that happens, you lose buying power, and your money will buy less.

You can calculate the effect of inflation on your investments. First, subtract your rate of interest from the inflation rate. This is your loss of buying power converted to a percentage. Then multiply that percentage by the original amount of your investment. The result is your loss of buying power in dollars. (See the **Go Figure** box.)

In addition, you can find out the current price of your investment, based on the rate of inflation during the period that you held the investment. Multiply the original price of the investment by the rate of inflation. Add that figure to the original price of the investment. The result is how much it would cost you to purchase the same investment today.

Some investments will protect you from inflation better than others. For example, over the period from 1926 to 2002, the compounded rate of return on common stocks adjusted for inflation was 7 percent. Concurrently, U.S. Treasury bills (T-bills) had an inflation-adjusted compounded rate of return of only 0.6 percent. During that time, common stocks provided a better protection against inflation than did T-bills.

Interest Rate Risk If you put money in an investment that gives you a fixed rate of return (stable rate), such as government or corporate bonds, the value of your investment will go down if interest rates go up. If you have to sell your bonds, you will get less than you originally paid.

To figure out the market price of a $1,000 bond if interest rates go up, divide one year of interest at a fixed rate of 8 percent by the new higher interest rate of 10 percent. (See the **Go Figure** box on page 246.) If you hold onto the bond until maturity, you will get your full $1,000 back, but you will receive only 8 percent annual interest.

 **FIGURE** | **FINANCIAL MATH**

INFLATION RATE AND INVESTMENTS

Synopsis: When prices and the cost of living rise in one year, your money will buy less and be worth less than it was during the prior year. For example, $500 this year will buy less than it did last year.

Example: Nina put $500 in a certificate of deposit for one year at 3 percent interest. The inflation rate during that year was 5 percent. How much of her buying power did she lose? How much money would she need at the end of the year to buy what she bought a year ago with $500?

A. Calculate the percentage of the loss of buying power:

Formula: Inflation Rate − Interest Rate = Loss-of-Buying-Power Percentage

Solution: 5% − 3% = 2% Loss of Buying Power

B. Calculate the loss of buying power in dollars:

Formula: Original Price of Investment × Loss of Buying Power Percentage = Loss of Buying Power in Dollars

Solution: $500 × 2% or .02 = $10

Nina lost $10.

C. Calculate how much it would cost to buy the same investment today:

Formula: (Original Price of Investment × Inflation Rate) + Original Price of Investment = Current Price of Investment

Solution: ($500 × 5% or .05) + $500 = $525

Nina would need $525 at the end of the year to buy what she bought a year ago with $500.

YOU FIGURE

A year ago, you worked part-time and put $1,000 in a savings account. The interest rate for one year was 6 percent. The inflation rate during that year was 4 percent. How much money would you need at the end of the year to buy what you bought a year ago with $1,000?

A BOND'S MARKET PRICE WHEN INTEREST RATES GO UP

Synopsis: A bond's interest earnings can be reduced if you sell it before the maturity date when bond rates are higher than those at time of purchase.

Example: You buy a $1,000 corporate bond that pays a fixed rate of 8 percent interest. You earn $80 a year ($1,000 × 8% or .08 = $80) until maturity. What price would you get if you sold it before the maturity date when bond rates were 10 percent?

Formula: $\dfrac{\text{Annual Interest Earned}}{\text{New Interest Rate}} = \text{Market Price}$

Solution: $\dfrac{\$80}{10\% \text{ or } .10} = \$800$

You would get $800, which equals a loss of $200. ($1,000 − $800 = $200).

YOU FIGURE

You buy a $1,500 corporate bond that pays a fixed rate of 8.5 percent interest. You earn $127.50 a year ($1,500 × .085 or 8.5% = $127.50) until maturity. What price would you get if you sold it before the maturity date when bond rates were 11 percent?

Academic Connection

LANGUAGE ARTS

It is commonly thought that choosing a foreign investment is more complicated than choosing a domestic one. In actuality, however, the process is much the same. When searching for a foreign mutual fund, for example, you should look for the characteristics you would look for in a domestic one, such as strong relative performance over time and reasonable expenses. *Research foreign investments and write a paragraph describing its benefits and its drawbacks.*

Business Failure Risk This type of risk applies to common stock, preferred stock, and corporate bonds. When you buy stocks or corporate bonds, you are investing in a particular company. You are betting that the company will succeed. However, it could fail, especially if the company is managed poorly. Even if the company offers a valuable product or service, positive response from customers is not guaranteed. Lower profits usually mean lower **dividends**, which are distributions of money, stock, or other property that a corporation pays to stockholders. If the company declares bankruptcy, your investment may become worthless. Your best protection is to do careful research on companies in which you might invest. Another good idea is to invest your money in more than one company.

Financial Market Risk Sometimes the prices of stocks, bonds, mutual funds, and other investments go up or down because of the overall state of financial markets. The value of a stock may decrease, even though a company is financially healthy. Factors that affect financial markets include social and political conditions. For example, the price of oil stocks may be affected by the political situation in the Middle East, where much of the world's oil supply is produced.

Global Investment Risk Today many investors are investing their money in stocks and bonds issued by companies in other countries. Because these types of investments may be risky, financial analysts advise small investors to invest in global mutual funds, instead of individual international stocks. Global mutual funds are offered by U.S. firms. These mutual funds specialize in companies that operate in another nation or region of the world. A mutual fund includes stocks or bonds from many companies and may offer more safety than one company's stocks or bonds.

A BOND'S MARKET PRICE WHEN INTEREST RATES GO DOWN

Synopsis: You may profit from selling a bond before maturity when bond interest rates are lower than those at time of purchase.

Example: Your $1,000 corporate bond pays a fixed rate of 8 percent interest, or $80 a year ($1,000 × 8% or .08 = $80). What price would you get if you sold it before maturity when bond rates were 6 percent?

Formula: $\dfrac{\text{Annual Interest Earned}}{\text{New Interest Rate}}$ = Market Price

Solution: $\dfrac{\$80}{6\% \text{ or } .06}$ = $1,333.33

You would receive $1,333.33, which equals a profit of $333.33 ($1,333.33 − $1,000 = $333.33).

YOU FIGURE

Your $1,200 corporate bond pays a fixed rate of 8.5 percent interest, or $102 a year ($1,200 × 8.5% or .085 = $102). What price would you get if you sold it before maturity when bond rates were 6 percent?

If you plan to invest in companies outside the United States, take these steps:

1. **Evaluate international investments as if they were U.S. investments:** Be aware that because of different accounting standards in other countries, it may be hard to discover the true financial condition of foreign companies.
2. **Consider the currency exchange rate:** This rate may affect the return on your investment, favorably or unfavorably. For example, if you buy stock in a French company, stock dividends will be paid to you in euros and then converted to dollars.

Also, keep in mind that the economic and political stability of a country can affect the value of your investment. It is risky to invest in stocks and bonds issued by individual companies in other countries. Only experienced investors should consider this option.

▼ **EXPLORING NEW WORLDS** When investing in global mutual funds, evaluate the choices carefully. *How does the currency exchange rate affect the return on an international investment?*

Investment Income

There are a variety of other types of investments for income. If you want a dependable source of income, you have several choices. The safest and most predictable investments include: savings accounts, certificates of deposit (CDs), U.S. Savings Bonds, and U.S. Treasury bills. With these programs, you know the interest rate and how much interest income you will receive on a specific date.

▲ TAKING CHANCES Only experts may be able to handle the risk of speculative investments. *Can you afford to lose money on a speculative investment?*

Other sources of investment income include government bonds, corporate bonds, preferred stocks, utility stocks, certain common stocks, annuities, and stable mutual funds. Before investing in stocks or corporate bonds, obtain information about the company's overall profits, its history of dividend payments, and its outlook for the future. Be sure to check out the costs associated with annuities before investing. See Chapters 9 and 10 for more information on stocks, bonds, and mutual funds.

Real estate rental property also offers income, but it is not guaranteed. For example, your profits from a rental property may be lower than expected if you have vacancies or expensive repairs. In addition, Real Estate Investment Trusts, or REITs, also offer income that is not guaranteed. These trusts are similar to mutual funds. See Chapter 11 for more information on real estate and other investments.

Speculative investments, such as commodities, options, precious metals and gems, and collectibles, offer little potential for income and are risky. These types of investments are more appropriate for investors who have expertise and experience in these markets.

Investment Growth

To investors, growth means that their investments will increase in value. The best opportunities for growth usually come from common stocks and growth stocks. A growth stock is a common stock issued by a corporation. This type of stock has the potential to earn above-average profits in comparison to other corporate stocks.

Growth companies usually reinvest their profits rather than pay dividends. **Retained earnings** are profits that a company reinvests, usually for expansion or to conduct research and development. Growth that is financed by retained earnings usually contributes to increasing the stock's value. Therefore, if you buy stock in a growth company, you may not receive immediate cash dividends, but you will benefit because your stock may increase in value.

Investment Liquidity

A final factor to consider when choosing investments is **investment liquidity**—the ability to buy or sell an investment quickly without substantially reducing its value. You may be able to sell some investments quickly, but market conditions or other factors may prevent you from regaining your original investment.

A passbook savings account is an example of a high-liquidity investment, because you can withdraw all your money immediately. A low-liquidity investment requires more time to sell your investment. An investment in real estate is usually a low-liquidity investment because finding a buyer takes time.

As You Read

QUESTION

If you want to buy a house in ten years, should you put your money in a CD or invest it in growth stocks? Why?

Section 8.1 Assessment

QUICK CHECK

1. What steps should you take when preparing to establish an investment program?
2. How can you obtain the money you need to start investing?
3. What factors might affect your investment choices?

THINK CRITICALLY

4. A friend wants to invest a $500 bonus she received. What would you advise?

USE COMMUNICATION SKILLS

5. **Risk Tolerance** Everyone has a different tolerance for risk. Some people will try anything once, including skydiving and white-water rafting. Others take every precaution to avoid danger.

Analyze With a small group of classmates, discuss the five components of risk. Decide which components of risk might affect every investor.

SOLVE MONEY PROBLEMS

6. **Preparing for Emergencies** Roya and Sashi are performing a financial check-up. They are trying to decide how much money to put into an emergency fund and what type of account to open. The couple has $3,000 in take-home pay a month and monthly living expenses of $2,600. They have a young child and a limited health insurance plan. They are worried about unexpected expenses.

Write About It Write a plan describing how much money Roya and Sashi should have in their emergency fund and what type of account they should choose for the fund.

Read to Learn
- How to identify the main types of savings and investment alternatives.
- How to explain the steps involved in developing a personal investment plan.

Main Idea
The more you know about different investment opportunities and the planning process, the better able you will be to select a savings or investment program that meets your needs.

Key Terms
- equity capital
- common stock
- preferred stock
- corporate bond
- government bond
- mutual fund
- diversification

Before You Read

PREDICT

Since stock investments can be risky, why do you think people choose them?

Savings and Investment Options

Types of Investments
How would you invest your money?

When you have your personal finances in order, an emergency fund, money for investments, and you know how much risk you can take, you can begin to research different types of investment alternatives: stocks, bonds, mutual funds, and real estate.

Stocks

A business that is owned by one person gets operating money from that one owner, who is the sole proprietor. In a partnership, the partners provide the money, or equity capital. **Equity capital** is money that a business gets from its owners in order to operate. A corporation gets its equity capital from its stockholders, who become owners when they buy shares of stock in the company. The two basic types of stock are common and preferred.

Common Stock **Common stock** is a unit of ownership of a company, and it entitles the owner, or stockholder, to voting privileges. Common stock can sometimes provide a source of income if the company pays dividends. Stock can provide growth profits if the dollar value of the stock increases. In addition, if the company "splits" its stock, or divides shares into a larger number of shares, the stockholder gains because he or she will get more shares. Most large corporations generate money they need by selling common stock.

Preferred Stock A corporation may also issue preferred stock. **Preferred stock** is a type of stock that gives the owner the advantage of receiving cash dividends before common stockholders receive cash dividends. This is important if a company is having financial problems. If a company fails, preferred stockholders receive dividends first and any assets that are left before common stockholders receive anything. Chapter 9 discusses other factors you should consider when buying common or preferred stock.

Stock can be an attractive investment because, as owners, stockholders share in the success of the company. However, you should consider several facts before you invest in stock.

1. A corporation does not have to repay you what you paid for the stock. If you want to sell your stock, another investor must buy your shares through a stockbroker.
2. The current value of your stock is partially determined by how much another investor is willing to pay for your shares.
3. The corporation does not have to pay dividends. If the company has a bad year or decides to reinvest earnings, the board of directors can vote to eliminate dividend payments.

As You Read

RELATE

Are you willing to invest your money in stock, or would you prefer to keep your money in a CD?

Corporate and Government Bonds

You may also consider investing in bonds. There are two types of bonds an investor can consider: a corporate bond and a government bond. A **corporate bond** is a corporation's written pledge to repay a specific amount of money, along with interest. A **government bond** is the written pledge of a government or a municipality, such as a city, to repay a specific sum of money with interest. When you buy a bond, you are lending money to a corporation or government entity for a period of time.

The Value of a Bond Two key factors affect the value of a bond: (1) whether the bond will be repaid at maturity and (2) whether the corporation or government entity will be able to pay interest until maturity. Maturity dates range from 1 to 30 years, and interest on bonds is usually paid every six months. You can keep a bond until maturity and then redeem it, or you can sell it to another investor. In either case, the value of the bond is closely tied to the ability of the corporation or government agency to repay the bond at maturity. If a corporation or government agency cannot pay the interest on its bonds, the value of those bonds will decrease. Some investors also make money on bonds by receiving regular interest payments until maturity.

▶ **PAYING UP** Government bonds offer a fixed rate of interest. *What are two key considerations for buying a government bond?*

Mutual Funds

A **mutual fund** is an investment in which investors pool their money to buy stocks, bonds, and other securities selected by professional managers who work for an investment company. Their knowledge is an advantage for inexperienced investors. If one of the fund stocks or other securities performs poorly, the loss can be offset by gains in another stock or security within the mutual fund. Chapter 10 provides information on types of funds.

Real Estate

The goal of real estate investing is to own property that increases in value so that you can sell it at a profit—or to receive rental income. When you invest in real estate, you need to find out if the property is priced as similar properties. You also need to know what financing is available and the cost of property taxes.

Before making a decision to purchase any property, ask the following questions: Why are the present owners selling? Is the property in good condition? What is the condition of other properties in the area? Is there a chance that the property will decrease in value?

When you sell real estate, consider these questions: Can you find an interested buyer? Can the buyer get financing to buy the property? Chapter 11 provides more information on real estate investments.

Careers in Finance

INVESTMENT ANALYST

Michelle Bondi
Robert Half Finance & Accounting

Michelle Bondi is fascinated with the world of finance. She studies and tracks the performance of financial market sectors, such as finance or construction. In addition to tracking the performance of individual stocks, Michelle studies the factors that affect them and compares the stocks' results with other similar stocks. She prepares internal and external reports on a stock's financial health on a daily basis or as requested. Investment analysts enjoy making connections between the news and economics, as well as finding patterns in the unpredictable world of finance.

SKILLS: Math, statistics, economics, and teamwork skills

PERSONAL TRAITS: Analytical, methodical, rigorous, self-starting, and up-to-date in current events

EDUCATION: High school diploma or equivalent; bachelor's degree in finance, accounting, economics, or business

ANALYZE Why would an investment analyst need to be aware of news and current events?

@ To learn more about career paths for investment analysts, visit **persfinance07.glencoe.com.**

Learn to identify and understand the standard financial documents you will use in the real world.

Investigate: A Savings Goals Worksheet

A savings goals worksheet contains this information:

- Your savings goal
- Amount you have
- Amount you need to achieve your goal
- Target date to goal

Your Motive: In order to make large purchases or achieve lofty financial goals, you need a savings plan. A savings plan will help you determine how much you need to reach your goals and how long it will take to achieve them.

Savings Goals Worksheet

Name: Susan Sharpe

Goals	Target Dates	Cost	Current Assets	Amount Still Needed	Years to Target Date	Amount to Save This Year
Down payment to purchase a house	2010	$30,000	$5,000	$25,000	5 years	$5,000
Buy a new car	2008	$22,000	$7,000	$15,000	3 years	$5,000
Save for retirement	2035	$500,000	$10,000	$490,000	30 years	$10,000

Key Points: A savings plan should be ambitious but not unrealistic. Do not try to set goals that you know you cannot reach. You should also reevaluate your savings plan at least once each year to make sure your savings plan is on track with your goals.

Find the Solutions

1. How much should Susan save to reach her goal?
2. What should Susan save this year to be on track to achieve her goals?
3. What assets other than savings might Susan use to help pay for a new car?
4. Why might Susan need to adjust her plan each year?
5. Susan's retirement savings plan calls for saving $10,000 each year for 30 years to save $300,000. However, she needs $490,000. What missing factor will enable Susan to achieve her savings goal?

Figure 8.4   **Possible Investments**

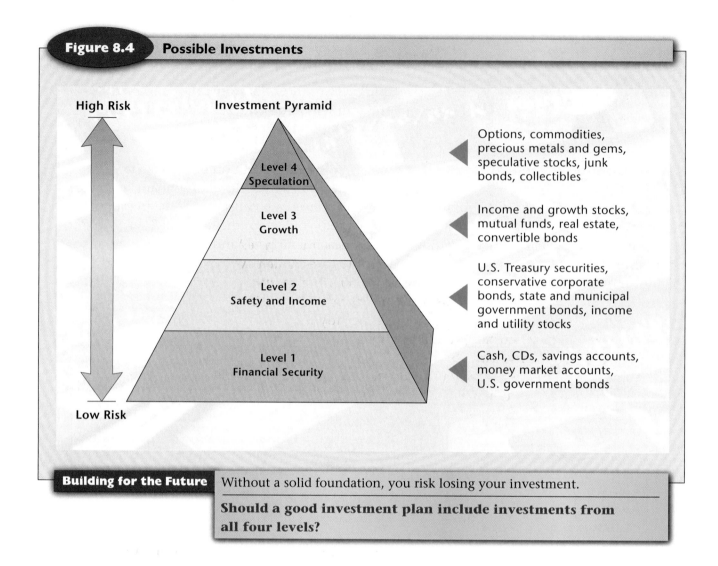

Investment Pyramid

High Risk

Level 4
Speculation
— Options, commodities, precious metals and gems, speculative stocks, junk bonds, collectibles

Level 3
Growth
— Income and growth stocks, mutual funds, real estate, convertible bonds

Level 2
Safety and Income
— U.S. Treasury securities, conservative corporate bonds, state and municipal government bonds, income and utility stocks

Level 1
Financial Security
— Cash, CDs, savings accounts, money market accounts, U.S. government bonds

Low Risk

Building for the Future   Without a solid foundation, you risk losing your investment.

Should a good investment plan include investments from all four levels?

Evaluating Investment Alternatives

How would you diversify your investments?

You have learned how safety, risk, income, growth, and liquidity affect investment choices. You have also examined different investment possibilities. Which ones would you choose?

As you make your choices, remember it is wise to diversify. **Diversification** is the process of spreading your assets among several different types of investments to reduce risk. You should avoid "putting all your eggs in one basket." Some financial advisers suggest that you think of your investment program as a pyramid, as illustrated in **Figure 8.4**. This strategy provides both financial growth and protection no matter what your age, circumstances, or level of financial knowledge. Level 1 provides a solid foundation with safe investments. Once that foundation is built, you may choose from the alternatives listed in Levels 2 and 3, which carry moderate risk. Because the investments in Level 4 are highly speculative, you may want to skip that level entirely.

Developing a Personal Investment Plan

How do you create an investment plan?

To be a successful investor, develop a plan and put it into action. Each person has different ideas and goals. Establish your investment goals first, and then continue to follow through. Often the follow-through is the most important component of a successful, long-range, personal investment plan. Follow a series of steps and begin earning money through investment.

Consider this case: Ginny is single and has recently started her first full-time job after graduation. Her monthly take-home pay (after deductions for taxes and other items) is $1,600. Her monthly expenses are $1,200. She has a surplus of $400 a month. She is using her surplus to set up an emergency fund. She recently received an inheritance of $5,000 when her grandfather died. She plans to use this money to fund her investments.

Figure 8.5 illustrates how Ginny developed her individual investment plan. Your plan may be quite different, but the steps will be the same.

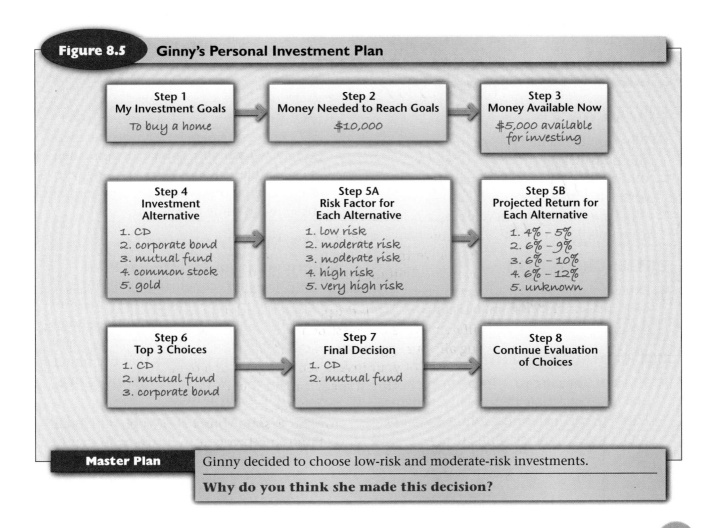

Figure 8.5 **Ginny's Personal Investment Plan**

Step 1
My Investment Goals
To buy a home

Step 2
Money Needed to Reach Goals
$10,000

Step 3
Money Available Now
$5,000 available for investing

Step 4
Investment Alternative
1. CD
2. corporate bond
3. mutual fund
4. common stock
5. gold

Step 5A
Risk Factor for Each Alternative
1. low risk
2. moderate risk
3. moderate risk
4. high risk
5. very high risk

Step 5B
Projected Return for Each Alternative
1. 4% – 5%
2. 6% – 9%
3. 6% – 10%
4. 6% – 12%
5. unknown

Step 6
Top 3 Choices
1. CD
2. mutual fund
3. corporate bond

Step 7
Final Decision
1. CD
2. mutual fund

Step 8
Continue Evaluation of Choices

Master Plan Ginny decided to choose low-risk and moderate-risk investments.

Why do you think she made this decision?

You may find these steps helpful to get started:

1. Establish investment goals.
2. Decide how much money you will need to reach those goals by a particular date.
3. Determine the amount of money you have to invest.
4. List all the investments you want to evaluate.
5. Evaluate the risks and potential return for each investment on your list.
6. Reduce your list of possible investments to a reasonable number.
7. Choose at least two investments so that you have some diversity. You may want to add more investments as the value of your holdings grows.
8. Because your investment goals may change as you go through life, recheck your investment program regularly. Remember that changes in the economy can affect your investments. For example, if interest rates on certificates of deposit are high, you might invest some of your money in a CD.

To develop your personal investment plan, establish your goals, and then follow through. If your goals are important to you, you will be willing to work to attain them.

Section 8.2 Assessment

QUICK CHECK

1. What are the main types of investment alternatives?
2. When choosing investment alternatives, why is it wise to diversify?
3. What are the steps in developing a personal investment plan?

THINK CRITICALLY

4. Explain why financial advisers suggest that your investment program be set up like a pyramid.

USE COMMUNICATION SKILLS

5. **Hidden Treasures?** Today many people purchase collectible items as investments. They buy baseball cards, commemorative coins, stuffed animals, and art.

Role-Play With a partner, role-play two financial advisors: one who explains why high-risk investments, such as collectibles, are not wise; and one who discusses why this type of investment is attractive to some people.

SOLVE MONEY PROBLEMS

6. **Developing an Investment Plan** Every day after school, Trent volunteers at his neighborhood community center. He helps the young children with their homework and organizes sports activities. Trent really believes in the work that the center is doing. He wants to invest some money to donate to the center.

Write About It Write a personal investment plan for Trent so that he can reach his goal.

Reducing Risk and Sources of Information

Financial Planners

What is the role of a financial planner?

When making your investment decisions, you may want to consult a **financial planner**, a specialist who is trained to offer specific financial help and advice.

There are two main factors to consider when deciding if you need a financial planner: (1) your income level and (2) your willingness to make your own financial decisions. If you make less than $45,000 a year, you may not need a planner's services.

Types of Financial Planners

Financial planners work for various insurance companies, investment companies, real estate agencies, and law firms. Some are self-employed. There are four main types of financial planners:

1. **Fee-only planners** charge an hourly rate from $75 to $200 or a flat fee, ranging from about $500 to several thousand dollars. They may also charge an annual fee ranging from 0.04 percent to 1 percent of the value of the investments they manage.
2. **Fee-offset planners** charge an hourly or annual fee, but they reduce, or offset, it with the commissions, or earnings, they make by buying or selling investments.
3. **Fee-and-commission planners** charge a fixed fee for a financial plan and earn commissions from the products they sell.
4. **Commission-only planners** earn all their money through the commissions they make on sales of insurance, mutual funds, and other investments.

When hiring a financial planner, find out the exact fees for specific services. Also discuss how and when the fees will be collected from you. There should be no hidden commission charges if the financial planner provides "fee only" services.

Focus on Reading

Read to Learn
- How to describe your role in a personal investment program.
- How to identify sources of financial information.

Main Idea

By becoming an informed investor, you will be able to reach your investment goals.

Key Terms
- financial planner
- tax-exempt income
- tax-deferred income
- capital gain
- capital loss
- prospectus

Before You Read

PREDICT

How might investing change your income tax reporting?

$avvy Saver

Giving Is Fun

1. Give whatever you can afford to your favorite charity.
2. Donate old clothes, toys, books, or eyeglasses instead of money.
3. Cash in your bottles and cans at a recycling center and give the money to charity.
4. Volunteer at a hospital, nursing home, animal shelter, or favorite charity.
5. Save $1 a week for a year, and make a donation to your favorite charity.

Selecting a Financial Planner

Look for a financial planner who will provide these basic services:

- Assess your current financial situation
- Offer a clearly written plan with investment recommendations
- Discuss the plan with you and answer questions
- Help you keep track of your progress
- Guide you to other financial experts and services as needed

You can find a financial planner by looking in the yellow pages, by contacting financial institutions, and by getting recommendations from friends, coworkers, or professional contacts. **Figure 8.6** suggests questions that you might ask a financial planner to help you make a decision.

Certification of Financial Planners

The requirements for becoming a financial planner vary from state to state. Some states require that financial planners pass an exam. Other states issue licenses to individual planners and planning companies. Some states have no regulations at all. The federal government requires that the Securities and Exchange Commission (SEC) monitor the largest financial planning companies.

A financial planner may have credentials, such as Certified Financial Planner (CFP) or Chartered Financial Consultant (ChFC). Not all planners are licensed, however. You should research and investigate any financial planner you might be considering.

Figure 8.6 **Selecting a Financial Planner**

When evaluating a financial planner, ask the following questions:

- What are your areas of expertise?
- Are you affiliated with a major financial services company, or do you work independently?
- Are you licensed or certified?
- What is your education and training?
- How is your fee determined? (Is this amount something I can afford?)
- Am I allowed a free initial consultation?
- May I see a sample of a written financial plan?
- May I contact some of your clients as references?
- Is financial planning your primary activity?

Research, Research This type of investigation takes time and effort.

Why do you think it is worthwhile?

Standard and Poor's publishes the globally recognized S&P 500® financial index. It also gathers financial statistics, information, and news, and analyzes this data for international businesses, governments, and individuals to help guide their financial decisions.

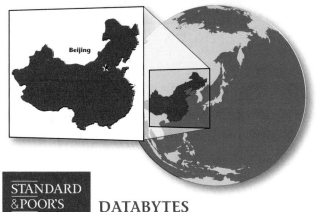

Beijing

CHINA

Though lagging behind the United States, China is catching up as the number one consumer of oil. The United States uses 20.5 million barrels of oil per day; China uses 6.3 barrels. By 2010, that number may double. The country's swelling population—the world's largest—and increasing affluence has stimulated a fuel-driven economy. Thousands of factories stretch across the country; car sales are up by 55 percent; and China's electric power grids are on overdrive. Once energy independent, the country imports half of

its oil. Soon China will be in serious competition with other oil-consuming nations for a dwindling supply of oil. Meanwhile, the country copes. In one city, shopping malls lowered their thermostats. In another, electricity was cut off four days a week to save on oil consumption.

STANDARD &POOR'S **DATABYTES**

Capital	Beijing
Population	1,288,679,000
Languages	Chinese (Mandarin), Cantonese, and other dialects and languages
Currency	yuan, or Renminbi
Gross Domestic Product (GDP)	$6.4 trillion (2003 est.)
GDP per capita	$5,000

Industry: Iron, steel, coal, machinery, armaments, textiles and apparel, petroleum, and cement

Agriculture: Rice, wheat, potatoes, sorghum, pork, and fish.

Exports: Machinery and equipment, textiles, apparel, footwear, toys, sporting goods, and mineral fuels

Natural Resources: Coal, iron ore, crude oil, mercury, tin, and hydropower

Think Globally
Would you buy stock in a Chinese electricity company? Why or why not?

Managing Your Investments
What should you do to manage your investments?

Most people do not have professional financial planners and need to learn how to manage their own finances. Managing your savings and investments requires ongoing attention. You can take an active role by taking these steps: Evaluate investments; monitor investments; keep accurate records; and consider tax consequences.

Evaluating Investments

Always research and evaluate before you invest so that you can make an informed decision. Suppose that you invest $2,000. With a 5 percent return the first year, you will earn $100. While your money is earning, you also need to continue to evaluate your current investment. Evaluate future investment opportunities as well.

Monitoring Your Investments

Many people forget to keep track of or monitor the value of their investments. Always keep track of the value of your stocks, bonds, or mutual funds by checking price quotations reported on the Internet, in newspapers, and on financial news programs. Keep a chart of the value of your investments to check their progress over time.

▶ **LOOKING AHEAD** Even if an investment company handles your money, always track and evaluate your investments on a regular basis. They will pay off for years to come. *What investment records should you keep?*

Keeping Accurate Records

Accurate recordkeeping helps you notice opportunities to increase your profits or reduce losses. It can also help you decide whether to put more money in a stock, bond, or other investment—or to sell a particular investment. Keep purchase records that list the cost of the investment and commissions or fees you have paid. Also keep the sources of information you used to evaluate an investment. With these records, you will know where to begin your research when it is time to reevaluate the investments you own.

Tax Considerations

It is your responsibility to determine how taxes may affect your investments. The city, state, and federal governments charge various amounts of tax to individuals and businesses for income they earn.

In general, investment income falls into three categories: tax-exempt, tax-deferred, and taxable. **Tax-exempt income** is income that is not taxed. For example, the interest you can receive from most state and municipal bonds is exempt from federal income tax. **Tax-deferred income** is income that is taxed at a later date. The most common type of tax-deferred income is earned from a traditional individual retirement account (IRA). When you withdraw earnings from your IRA, you must pay federal income tax. The 401(k) and 403(b) retirement plans offered by your employer or privately are also tax-deferred. Income from most other investments is taxable.

Dividends, Interest Income, and Rental Income You must report cash dividends on your tax return as ordinary income. You also have to pay tax on the interest from banks, credit unions, and savings and loan associations. In addition, interest you receive from bonds (unless tax-exempt), promissory notes, loans, and U.S. securities must be reported as income. Income from rental property is also taxable.

Capital Gains and Capital Losses A **capital gain** is the profit from the sale of assets such as stocks, bonds, or real estate. Capital gains are taxed according to how long you own an asset—over a short term or a long term.

Under current law, a short-term capital gain is profit you make when you sell an asset owned for 12 months or less. It is taxed as ordinary income. For example, if you are in the 15 percent tax bracket for general income taxes, you will also pay 15 percent tax on your short-term capital gains.

The profit from selling investments owned for more than 12 months is considered a long-term capital gain. Long-term capital gains are usually taxed at the rate of 5 to 15 percent. Investors in low tax brackets are taxed at only 5 percent. As of 2008, these investors pay no tax on long-term capital gains. Some personal property, such as collectibles, is taxed at a higher rate. Examples of collectible assets include rare books and stamp collections. You will learn more about collectibles in Chapter 11.

A Dollar a Day
Do you know that if you save a dollar a day—less than what you would spend on a soda and a candy bar—and save or invest it at 5 percent interest, in five years you will have more than $2,000? In ten years you will have $4,600! *How much would you have in 40 years?*

A **capital loss** is the sale of an investment for less than its purchase price. You can subtract up to $3,000 a year in capital losses from your ordinary income. If your losses are greater than $3,000, you can subtract the rest of the loss in later tax years.

Sources of Investment Information

Where can you find information about investments?

Because there is so much investment information available, both complex and basic, you need to be selective. The important thing is to be sure that the source of advice and information that you receive is accurate and reliable.

The Internet and Online Services

The Internet offers a wealth of information on investments with the click of a button. One of the best ways to find what you need is to use a search engine. Search engines are available through many Internet service providers (ISPs), including commercial Internet companies. Just type the key words for your topic into a search engine, and you will get a list of Web sites that provide information on that topic. Most large investment firms have Web sites where you can obtain a variety of information and services:

- Interest rates for certificates of deposit
- Prices of stocks, bonds, and other securities
- Advice on starting an investment program
- Trading of securities through online brokers

Newspapers and News Programs

The financial page of your metropolitan newspaper or *The Wall Street Journal* is another source of investment information that is easy to access. In addition, many radio and television stations broadcast investment market summaries and economic information as part of their regular news programs. Several television channels, such as CNN Fn (Financial), are also dedicated to financial news.

Business and Publications

Barron's, BusinessWeek, Forbes, Fortune, Harvard Business Review, and similar business publications provide general news about the economy as well as information about individual companies. Other publications cover specific industries. In addition, magazines, such as *Money, Consumer Reports, Smart Money,* and *Kiplinger's Personal Finance,* provide information and advice designed to improve your investment skills. In addition, national news magazines often feature stories on the economy and finance.

As You Read

QUESTION

How can you ensure that online sources of investment information are accurate and reliable?

▲ **IN THE KNOW** Keeping up with financial news helps you track your investments and may help you reach your goals. *Name at least three publications that could help you become a smart investor.*

Government Publications

The United States federal government is also an excellent resource of information—and much of it is free. *The Federal Reserve Bulletin,* published by the Federal Reserve System, and the *Survey of Current Business*, published by the Department of Commerce, are just two sources of useful financial information. You can read articles from both of these publications on the Internet.

Corporate Reports

As required by the federal government, any corporation selling new issues of securities must provide investors with a prospectus. A **prospectus** is a document that discloses information about a company's earnings, assets and liabilities, its products or services, a particular stock, and the qualifications of its management. All publicly owned corporations also send investors quarterly reports and annual reports that contain detailed financial data.

Statistical Averages

You can keep track of the value of your investments by following one or more recognized statistical averages, such as the Standard & Poor's 500 Stock Index or the Dow Jones Industrial Average. These averages are reported daily online and in newspapers. The average indicates whether the category it measures is increasing or decreasing in value. It will not pinpoint the value of a specific investment, but it will show the general direction of stocks, bonds, mutual funds, and other investments. **Figure 8.7** lists some of the most widely used statistical averages.

Figure 8.7   **Statistical Averages for Evaluating Investments**

Statistical Average	Type of Investment
Dow Jones Industrial Average	Stocks
Standard & Poor's 500 Stock Index	Stocks
Value Line Stock Index	Stocks
New York Stock Exchange Index	Stocks on New York Stock Exchange
American Stock Exchange Index	Stocks on American Stock Exchange
NASDAQ Composite Stock Index	Over-the-counter stocks
Lipper Mutual Funds Index	Mutual funds
Dow Jones Bond Average	Corporate bonds
The Wall Street Journal Consumer Rates Index	Interest and finance rates
New Residential Sales Index	Real estate
Dow Jones Spot Market Index	Commodities
Sotheby's Art Sales Index	Art/paintings
Linn's Trends of Stamp Values	Stamps

Trend Watchers   You can locate these statistical averages in the newspaper and on the Internet.

How do these averages affect investments?

Investor Services

Many stockbrokers and financial planners mail free newsletters to their clients. In addition, investor services, such as Moody's Investors Service, sell subscription newsletters that are available in print and on the Internet.

Five widely used and useful publications are:

- *Standard & Poor's Stock and Bond Guide*
- *Value Line Investment Survey*®
- *Handbook of Common Stocks* (information on companies)
- *Morningstar Mutual Funds*™
- *Wiesenberger Investment Companies Yearbook* (information on mutual funds)

In addition to these publications, securities exchanges provide information in print and on the Internet. They include the American Stock Exchange, the Chicago Mercantile Exchange, the New York Stock Exchange, and the NASDAQ market. All of these sources of financial information are most often used by professionals. Many individual private investors also refer to them to become well-informed when making investment decisions.

After You Read

REACT

Would it be useful to follow the Dow Jones Industrial Average and/or the Standard and Poor's 500 Stock Index before making investments? Why or why not?

Section 8.3 Assessment

QUICK CHECK

1. What is a financial planner's role in a personal financial program?
2. What is your role in your personal financial program?
3. What are some sources of financial information?

THINK CRITICALLY

4. Why do you think some people do not keep track of their investments? Give reasons why they should.

USE COMMUNICATION SKILLS

5. **Tax Considerations** Elliott is going to receive capital gains on some stock he just sold. He owned the stock for less than a year and made a profit of $200. He is in the 15 percent tax bracket.

Calculate How much will Elliott pay in capital gains tax on the profits from his stock sale?

SOLVE MONEY PROBLEMS

6. **Finding a Financial Planner** Helene has decided to hire a financial planner. She has to rely on ads and the yellow pages for names because she is new in town. She wants to meet with several people before choosing one.

Write About It Compile a list of specific questions that Helene should ask candidates when she interviews them.

Chapter 8 Review & Activities

CHAPTER SUMMARY

- Before investing, set financial goals that are compatible with your values.
- Obtain money to start investing by setting aside funds before you buy other things; by contributing to employer-sponsored retirement plans and savings programs; and by saving gifts of money and unexpected windfalls.
- An investment's safety or degree of risk, income potential, and liquidity are factors to consider before choosing an investment. Also, diversifying your investments is wise.
- Saving and investment alternatives include savings accounts, certificates of deposit, stocks, bonds, some annuities, mutual funds, and real estate.

- Steps in developing a personal investment plan include establishing goals, determining funds needed and funds available, evaluating investments in terms of risk and return, and choosing at least two investments.
- Check your investments for yourself, keep track of them, keep accurate records, and consider the tax consequences of buying and selling.
- A great deal of investment information is available on the Internet, in books, magazines, newspapers, government publications, as well as from individual corporations and investment companies.

Communicating Key Terms

You are a financial planner. One of your clients, who owns a medium-sized company with 75 employees, asks you to speak to her employees to encourage them to participate in the company 401(k) retirement savings plan. Use as many of the terms below as possible in writing your speech.

- emergency fund
- speculative investment
- dividends
- retained earnings
- investment liquidity
- equity capital

- common stock
- preferred stock
- corporate bond
- government bond
- mutual fund
- diversification

- financial planner
- tax-exempt income
- tax-deferred income
- capital gain
- capital loss
- prospectus

Reviewing Key Concepts

1. **Explain** why it is important to have a goal before making investments.
2. **Describe** sources of funds for investing.
3. **Describe** a demographic group that may not prefer investment risk. Describe another demographic group that may be more comfortable with a greater degree of risk.
4. **Compare** the main types of investment alternatives in terms of their risk and liquidity.
5. **Write** an investment plan for yourself.
6. **Describe** the role of the investor in the investment process.
7. **List** four specific sources of financial information.

Economics You should buy insurance and establish an emergency fund before you invest, and you should invest early.

Write About It Write several paragraphs explaining why you should take these steps before investing and how you can do both.

Investing Your Money You are evaluating two investments that each require $1,000. One is a municipal bond that pays 9 percent interest annually. The interest is exempt from federal and state taxes. The other is a corporate bond that pays 11 percent interest, but its earnings are subject to 20 percent capital gains tax if kept for less than 12 months, and 15 percent capital gains tax if kept for more than 12 months.

1. **Calculate** (a) Which bond provides the largest return? (b) Does the situation change if you need to sell the bond before 12 months?
2. **Compute** by using spreadsheet software to create scenarios about the circumstances under which each investment gives a bigger return.

Connect with Economics Risk associated with investments can be categorized as diversifiable risk and undiversifiable risk. This is one reason mutual funds are so popular—many investors' money is pooled and numerous stocks are purchased. Some of the risk is reduced because you buy a piece of so many different companies. Undiversifiable risks are those over which you have no control, such as the risks described in Section 8.1.

1. **Research** Use an Internet search engine or look in the newspaper or magazine to find descriptions of three mutual funds.
2. **Think Critically** Select one mutual fund of interest to you. Why did you select it?

401(k) Retirement Savings Many employers offer 401(k) retirement savings plans as an employee benefit. Many companies match a certain percentage of each employee's deposits in the plan.

Log On Use an Internet search engine to find Web sites of two companies you might be interested in working for in the future. Answer the following questions:

1. Do they offer 401(k) plans profit-sharing or other savings programs?
2. Do your relatives, neighbors, or friends participate in such plans? Why?

Newsclip: Less Savings Americans do not save as they once did. Weak savings mean fewer investments in the economy, and that contributes to slower economic growth.

Log On Go to persfinance07.glencoe.com and open Chapter 8. Learn more about the different types of investments. Write down what type of investment you would buy and explain why.

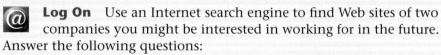

ARE YOU A RISK TAKER?

As a general rule, the greater the promised return on an investment, the greater the risk involved. Risk tolerance is your ability to ride the ups and downs of the market without panicking when the value of your investment goes down. This quiz will help you gauge your own risk tolerance. Answer the following questions on a separate sheet of paper:

1. Which best describes your feelings about investing?
   a. Better safe than sorry
   b. Moderation in all things
   c. Nothing ventured, nothing gained

2. Which is most important to you as an investor?
   a. You receive a steady income.
   b. You receive a steady income and growth.
   c. The price of your investments rises rapidly.

3. You won! Which prize would you pick?
   a. $4,000 in cash
   b. A 50 percent chance to win $10,000
   c. A 20 percent chance to win $100,000

4. The stocks you own have dropped 20 percent since the last quarter. What would you do?
   a. Sell the stocks to avoid losing more
   b. Keep the stocks and wait for their value to rebound
   c. Buy more stocks because they are cheaper now

5. The stocks you own have gone up 20 percent since the last quarter. What would you do?
   a. Sell the stocks and take the gains
   b. Keep the stocks and hope the price goes up higher
   c. Buy more stocks because the price may go up higher

6. Would you borrow money to take advantage of a good investment opportunity?
   a. Never   b. Maybe   c. Yes

7. How would you characterize yourself?
   a. I do not like to take risks.
   b. I am a moderate risk taker.
   c. I enjoy taking risks.

Give yourself one point for each question that you answered with "a."
Give yourself two points for each question that you answered with "b."
Give yourself three points for each question that you answered with "c."
If you scored 7–11 points, you're a conservative investor who prefers to minimize financial risks.
If you scored 12–16 points, you're a moderate risk taker.
If you scored 17–21 points, you're comfortable taking risks in pursuit of greater returns.

Source: "Five-Minute Quiz" from *Standard & Poor's Your Financial Future,* ©1996 by The McGraw-Hill Companies.

Your Financial Portfolio

Avoiding Future Shock

Mackenzie is already showing signs of being a great scholar at age three. At least that is what her dad, Jasper, thinks. He wants Mackenzie to be able to continue her education, so he has decided to start a college fund for her now. Jasper has $2,000 to start and has decided to invest $175 a month. He has developed an investment plan to reach his goal.

Jasper figures he has 15 years to invest and will invest in an aggressive stock mutual fund. He feels that the diversity of a mutual fund will be safer and give greater returns. Jasper has plenty of time to take a fair amount of risk and is comfortable that he will have Mackenzie's college money when she needs it.

Goal Tending		
Established goal:	College	
Amount of money needed:	$50,000	
Initial amount to invest:	$2,000	
Possible investment alternatives:	(1) savings account	(4) mutual fund
	(2) CD	(5) stock
	(3) money market account	
Risk factor for each alternative:	(1) low risk	(4) moderate risk
	(2) low risk	(5) high risk
	(3) low risk	
Expected return on each alternative:	(1) 1%–3%	(4) 6%–10%
	(2) 4%–5%	(5) 6%–12%
	(3) 4%–6%	
Top 3 choices:	(1) mutual fund	(3) CD
	(2) stock	
Final choice:	**mutual fund**	

Prepare

Choose a short-term or long-term financial goal you would like to reach. On a separate sheet of paper, prepare an investment plan for yourself using the same guidelines as shown above. Research some of the available investments and come up with your own investment alternatives. Explain the reasons for your final choice.

CHAPTER 9
Stocks

 ## What You'll Learn

When you have completed this chapter, you will be able to:

Section 9.1
- Explain the reasons for investing in common stock.
- Explain the reasons for investing in preferred stock.

Section 9.2
- Identify the types of stock investments.
- Identify sources of information to evaluate stock investments.
- Discuss the factors that affect stock prices.

Section 9.3
- Describe how stocks are bought and sold.
- Explain the trading strategies used by long-term investors and short-term investors.

Reading Strategies

To get the most out of your reading:

Predict what you will learn in this chapter.
Relate what you read to your own life.
Question what you are reading to be sure you understand.
React to what you have read.

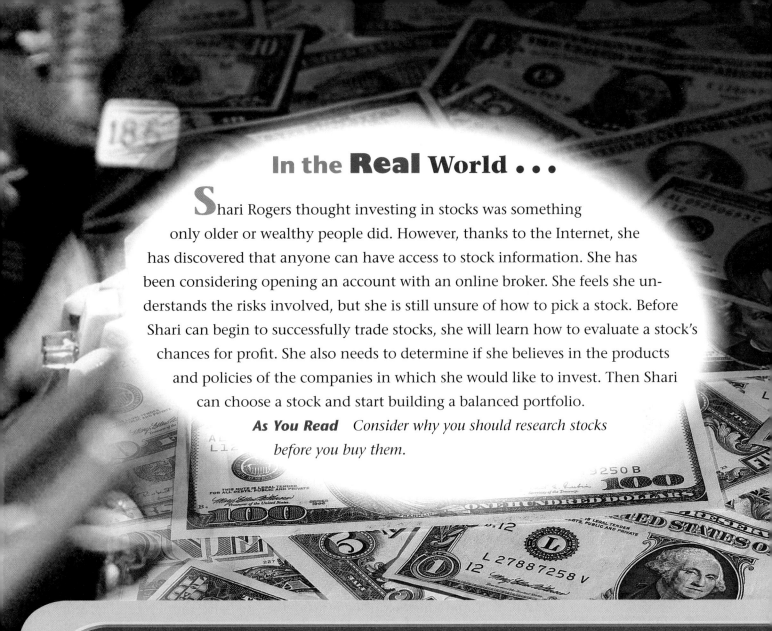

In the **Real** World . . .

Shari Rogers thought investing in stocks was something only older or wealthy people did. However, thanks to the Internet, she has discovered that anyone can have access to stock information. She has been considering opening an account with an online broker. She feels she understands the risks involved, but she is still unsure of how to pick a stock. Before Shari can begin to successfully trade stocks, she will learn how to evaluate a stock's chances for profit. She also needs to determine if she believes in the products and policies of the companies in which she would like to invest. Then Shari can choose a stock and start building a balanced portfolio.

As You Read *Consider why you should research stocks before you buy them.*

ASK STANDARD &POOR'S

Stock Certificates

Q: My parents gave me stock certificates for a graduation present. Is it a good idea to put them in a safe-deposit box and save them for retirement?

A: A safe-deposit box is a good way to store important documents, but a better option for stock certificates would be to place them in a brokerage account with a bank or brokerage firm. This will make it easier for you to buy or sell shares of these or other stocks. Also, you will receive statements showing the value of your shares and dividends.

Ask Yourself Why do you think it is easier to buy and sell shares of stock if you have a brokerage account?

 Go to **persfinance07.glencoe.com** to complete the Standard & Poor's Financial Focus activity.

Section 9.1

Section 9.1

Focus on Reading

Read to Learn
- How to explain the reasons for investing in common stock.
- How to explain the reasons for investing in preferred stock.

Main Idea
Recognizing the reasons for investing in common and preferred stock will enable you to make the best investments for your financial situation.

Key Terms
- securities
- private corporation
- public corporation
- par value

Before You Read
PREDICT

What do you think it means to own stock in a company?

Common and Preferred Stocks

Common Stock
Why do companies offer common stock?

Investors have a choice of **securities**, which are all of the investments—stocks, bonds, mutual funds, options, and commodities—that are bought and sold on the stock market.

When investors buy shares of stock in a company, the company uses that money to make and sell its products, fund its operations, and expand. If the company earns a profit, the stockholders (owners of shares of stock in the company) earn a return, or gain, on their investment. People buy and sell stocks for one reason: They want larger returns than they can get from more conservative investments, such as savings accounts or government bonds.

Before you invest your money in stock, it might help you to understand why corporations issue common stock.

Why Corporations Issue Common Stock

Companies issue common stock to raise money to start up their businesses and then to help pay for ongoing activities. A **private corporation**, or a closely held corporation, is a company that issues stock to a small group of people. A private corporation's stocks are not traded openly in stock markets. On the other hand, a **public corporation**, or publicly held corporation, is one that sells its shares openly in stock markets, where anyone can buy them. Some large corporations, such as AT&T, General Electric, Procter & Gamble, and General Motors, have thousands or even millions of stockholders.

A Form of Equity Because corporations do not have to repay the money a stockholder pays for stock, they are able to use that money to fund their ongoing activities. For the stockholder to make money on the stock, he or she sells the stock to another investor. The price is set according to how much the buyer is willing to pay. As the demand for a certain company's stock increases or decreases, the price goes up or down accordingly. News on expected sales revenues, earnings, company expansions, or mergers with other companies can make demand for the stock go up or down.

Dividends Not Mandatory It is up to the corporate board of directors, a group of individuals elected to make the major decisions for the corporation, to decide whether any profits will be paid to stockholders as dividends. Companies that are growing quickly might pay low or no dividends. They may decide to use profits to expand the company even further. Of course, any company's board of directors can reduce or even stop dividend payments when a corporation has a bad year.

Why Investors Purchase Common Stock

Most investors purchase common stock to make money in three different ways: They profit when they receive dividends, when the dollar value of their stock appreciates (increases), and when the stock splits and increases in dollar value.

Income from Dividends A corporation's board members do not have to pay dividends, but they do want to keep stockholders happy because those same stockholders are funding the corporation's business. As a result, board members often vote to pay dividends if possible, unless they decide to place the profits back into the company.

With a cash dividend, each common stockholder receives an equal amount per share. Most dividends are paid quarterly, or every three months. Some companies that have large increases in earnings might declare a special cash dividend at the end of the year. You might also receive a dividend of company stock—or of company products, though this is very unusual.

Appreciation of Stock Value If the market value of the stock increases, or appreciates, you must decide whether to sell your stock at the higher price or continue to hold on to it. If you sell, the difference between the price that you paid and the price at which you sell is your profit. Of course, if the value of the stock falls, then your return will be less than your original investment. **Figure 9.1** on page 274 provides tips for tracking your stock investment. If a company's board decides to place profits back into the company, it might reward its stockholders through dollar appreciation of stock value instead of dividends.

Increased Value from Stock Splits Your profits can also increase through a stock split. A stock split occurs when the shares of stock owned by existing stockholders are divided into a larger number of shares.

▲ **UNDERSTANDING STOCKS** Investors buy stocks in the hopes of earning a large return on their investments. *What causes the demand for stock to change?*

For example, in a two-for-one stock split, the corporation doubles the number of outstanding shares. Suppose that a corporation has 10,000 shares of stock valued at $50 a share. If the corporation splits its stock, the value of each share decreases to $25, but the number of outstanding shares increases to 20,000. If you owned 200 shares before the split, you would own 400 shares after it.

	Before	After
Shares issued	$10,000	$20,000
Value	50	25
Your shares	200	400
Your value	$10,000	$10,000

Why do corporations split their stock? Often the management believes that the stock should be trading within an ideal price range. If the market value is a lot higher than this range, a stock split brings the market value back into line. The lower price of stocks after they are split often attracts more investors. As a result, the price starts to rise again. The public wants to buy because of the belief that most corporations split their stock only when the company's financial future looks very good. Be aware that a stock's market value is not guaranteed to go up after a stock split.

Figure 9.1   **Tracking Your Stock Investments**

1. **Monitor.**
   Graph the dollar value of your stock on a daily or weekly basis.

2. **Watch the financials.**
   Continually evaluate the company's current sales and profits and those projected for the future. Compare its progress to the performance of other companies in the same industry. If it can not compete, sell.

3. **Track the products.**
   Poor-quality products or a lack of new or up-to-date products can make the value of a company's stock drop.

4. **Watch the economy.**
   The inflation rate, the state of the overall economy, and other economic factors can affect your company's stock price.

5. **Be patient.**
   If you think that you have bought into a good company, hang on. Over time, your investment will usually increase in value.

Evaluating Stocks   By keeping up with information about the companies that issue stock you own, you are more likely to increase the return on your investment.

Why is patience important in investing?

Voting Rights and Control of the Company In addition to the profit that stockholders may make on their investments, they are also given certain rights in return for the money they invest. For example, a corporation is required by law to hold a yearly meeting at which stockholders can vote on company business. Stockholders usually get one vote for each share they own.

Some states require that corporations offer existing stockholders a preemptive right. A preemptive right gives current stockholders the right to buy any new stock a corporation issues before its stock is offered to the public. By buying more shares, a stockholder can keep the same proportion of ownership in the company. This can be important when a corporation is small and control is critical.

Preferred Stock
Is preferred stock preferable?

You could buy preferred stock in addition to, or instead of, common stock. Remember from Chapter 8 that preferred stock gives the owner the advantage of receiving cash dividends before common stockholders receive any cash dividends. If a company is struggling financially, then the preferred stockholder might get the dividends.

Preferred stockholders should know the amount of the dividend they will receive. It is either a specific amount of money or a percentage of the par value of the stock. The **par value** is an assigned dollar value that is printed on a stock certificate. If the par value of a stock is $30 and the dividend rate is 5 percent, then the dollar amount of the dividend is $1.50 per share ($30 X 5% or .05 = $1.50). Unlike market value, par value does not change.

Why Corporations Issue Preferred Stock

Few corporations use preferred stock as a way of raising money. However, for some companies, it is another method of financing which may attract more conservative investors who do not want to buy common stock. Preferred stockholders receive limited voting rights, and they usually vote only if the corporation issuing the stock is in financial trouble.

Why Investors Purchase Preferred Stock

Preferred stock is considered a "middle investment." The yield on preferred stock is generally lower than the yield on corporate bonds but higher than the yield on common stock. Preferred stock is considered a safer investment than common stock, but not as safe as bonds. People who want a steady source of income often buy preferred stock. However, preferred stocks lack the potential for growth that common stocks offer. As a result, preferred stocks are not considered a good investment for most people.

As You Read

RELATE

Imagine that you own stock in a small Web design firm. Describe a situation where preemptive rights would benefit you.

TechByte

Playing Games One of the best ways to learn about how the stock market works without risking any of your money is to play a stock market simulation game. In a simulation game, players work in teams and create a stock portfolio using virtual money. Based on their research of market trends, economic conditions, and business news, the teams select and trade common or preferred stocks. Portfolios "earn" interest and "pay" commissions—and make and lose virtual money.

@ Read a review of stock market simulation games and list those you would like to play through **persfinance07.glencoe.com**.

As You Read

QUESTION

Why might it be rare for corporations to offer a participation feature to their stockholders?

To make preferred stocks more attractive to investors, some corporations may offer cumulative preferred stock, convertible preferred stock, or a participation feature.

Cumulative Preferred Stock Cumulative preferred stock is stock whose unpaid dividends build up and must be paid before any cash dividend is paid to the common stockholders. This means that if a corporation decides to omit one or more dividend payments to preferred stockholders, people who hold cumulative preferred stock will still receive those dividend payments during a later payment period.

Convertible Preferred Stock Convertible preferred stock is stock that can be exchanged for a specific number of shares of common stock. This feature provides an investor with the safety of preferred stock and the possibility of greater returns through conversion to common stock.

Participation Feature Some corporations offer a participation feature, which allows preferred stockholders to share in the corporation's earnings with the common stockholders. After a required dividend is paid to preferred stockholders and a stated dividend is paid to common stockholders, the remainder of earnings is shared by preferred and common stockholders. This feature is rare.

Section 9.1 Assessment

QUICK CHECK

1. Why do corporations issue common stock?
2. Why do investors purchase common stock?
3. Why do investors purchase preferred stock?

THINK CRITICALLY

4. Justify a corporation's decision to split its stock when the stock price has risen significantly.

USE COMMUNICATION SKILLS

5. **Part Owners** Investors purchase common stock as a way to increase their income. As stockholders, they earn the right to vote on company business.

Write About It Write a paragraph that tells why a stockholder might wish to exercise his or her voting rights.

SOLVE MONEY PROBLEMS

6. **Perks of Preferred Stock** Kwame's grandmother recently gave him 25 shares of preferred stock. Kwame would like to figure out the actual dollar amount of the dividend, which is a percentage of the par value of the stock.

Calculate According to the stock certificates that Kwame's grandmother gave to him, the par value of each share is $45 and the dividend rate is 6 percent. What is the total dollar amount that Kwame should receive each year?

Evaluating Stocks

Types of Stock Investments
How are stocks classified?

Financial professionals classify most stocks into the following categories: blue-chip stocks, income stocks, growth stocks, cyclical stocks, defensive stocks, large-cap stocks, small-cap stocks, and penny stocks.

Blue-Chip Stocks

A **blue-chip stock** is considered a safe investment that generally attracts conservative investors. These stocks are issued by the strongest and most respected companies, such as AT&T, General Electric, and Kellogg. If you are interested in a blue-chip stock, look for a company that shows leadership in an industry, a history of stable earnings, and consistency in the payment of dividends.

Income Stocks

An **income stock** pays higher-than-average dividends compared to other stock issues. The buyers of preferred stock are also attracted to this type of common stock because the dividends are predictable. Stocks issued by companies such as Bristol-Myers Squibb and Dow Chemical are classified as income stocks. This is also the type of stock issued by gas and electric companies.

Focus on Reading

Read to Learn
- How to identify the types of stock investments.
- How to identify sources of information to evaluate stock investments.
- How to discuss the factors that affect stock prices.

Main Idea
Knowing how to evaluate, buy, and sell stocks helps you increase the value of your investments.

Key Terms
- blue-chip stock
- income stock
- growth stock
- cyclical stock
- defensive stock
- large-cap stock
- capitalization
- small-cap stock
- penny stock
- bull market
- bear market
- current yield
- total return
- earnings per share
- price-earnings (PE) ratio

◀ CLASSIFYING STOCKS
This corporation issues blue-chip stocks. *Why do conservative investors like blue-chip stocks?*

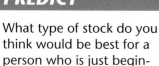

Growth Stocks

A **growth stock** is issued by a corporation whose potential earnings may be higher than the average earnings predicted for all the corporations in the country. Stocks issued by these corporations generally do not pay dividends. Look for signs that the company is engaged in activities that produce higher earnings and sales revenues: building new facilities; introducing new, high-quality products; or conducting recognized research and development. Growth companies in the early 2000s included Home Depot and Southwest Airlines.

Cyclical Stocks

A **cyclical stock** has a market value that tends to reflect the state of the economy. When the economy is improving, the market value of a cyclical stock usually goes up. During an economic decline, the market value of a cyclical stock may decrease. This is because the products and services of these companies are linked directly to the activities of a strong economy. Investors try to buy these stocks when they are still inexpensive, just before the economy starts to improve. Then they seek to sell them just before the economy declines. Stocks issued by Ford and Centex (a construction firm) are considered cyclical stocks.

Defensive Stocks

A **defensive stock** is a stock that remains stable during declines in the economy. The companies that issue such stocks have steady earnings and can continue dividend payments even in periods of economic decline. Many blue-chip stocks and income stocks, such as those issued by Procter & Gamble, are defensive stocks.

Large-Cap and Small-Cap Stocks

A **large-cap stock** is stock from a corporation that has issued a large number of shares of stock and has a large amount of *cap*italization. **Capitalization** is the total amount of stocks and bonds issued by a corporation. The stocks listed in the Dow Jones Industrial Averages, a stock indicator which measures the overall condition of the stock market, are typically large-cap stocks. These stocks appeal to conservative investors because they are considered secure.

STANDARD &POOR'S

Global Financial Landscape

Standard and Poor's publishes the globally recognized S&P 500® financial index. It also gathers financial statistics, information, and news, and analyzes this data for international businesses, governments, and individuals to help them guide their financial decisions.

UNITED KINGDOM

In 1698, the London Stock Exchange (LSE) got its start at Jonathan's Coffee House, located in London's bustling Change Alley. The founders created a simple list entitled "The Course of the Exchange and Other Things," which announced stock and commodity prices to the local traders. Today, more than 300 years later, the LSE lists more than 2,700 companies—from high profile to high tech—that are worth a total of over $2.7 billion. The LSE has become Europe's largest stock exchange and one of the world's most famous. It is headquartered close to where it originated, at the heart of London's financial district. Displayed on the stock exchange building's exterior is the LSE's coat of arms, which boasts the Latin motto *Dictum Meum Pactum,* which means "My Word is My Bond."

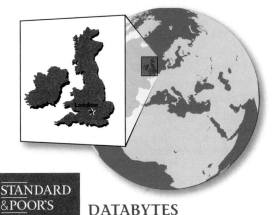

STANDARD &POOR'S DATABYTES

Capital	London
Population	59,200,000
Languages	English, Welsh, and Scottish form of Gaelic
Currency	British pound
Gross Domestic Product (GDP)	$1.66 trillion (2003 est.)
GDP per capita	$27,700

Industry: Tools, electric power equipment, automated equipment, railroad equipment, and shipbuilding

Agriculture: Cereals, oilseed, potatoes, vegetables, cattle, and fish

Exports: Manufactured goods, fuels, chemicals, food, beverages, and tobacco

Natural Resources: Coal, crude oil, natural gas, tin, limestone

Think Globally
Do you think the LSE lists large-cap stocks? Why or why not?

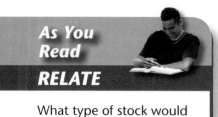

As You Read

RELATE

What type of stock would you buy? Why?

A **small-cap stock** is a stock issued by a company with a capitalization of $500 million or less. Since these stocks are issued by smaller, less-established companies, they are considered to be a higher investment risk.

Penny Stocks

A **penny stock** typically sells for less than $1 a share, although it can sell for as much as $10 a share. These stocks are issued by new companies or companies whose sales are very unsteady. The prices of these stocks can go up and down wildly. It is difficult to keep track of a penny stock's performance because information about them is hard to find. Penny stocks should be purchased only by investors who understand the risks.

Sources for Evaluating Stocks

How do you assess a stock investment?

There are many sources where you can find information about stocks before making investment decisions. Some sources include: newspapers, the Internet, stock advisory services, and corporate news publications.

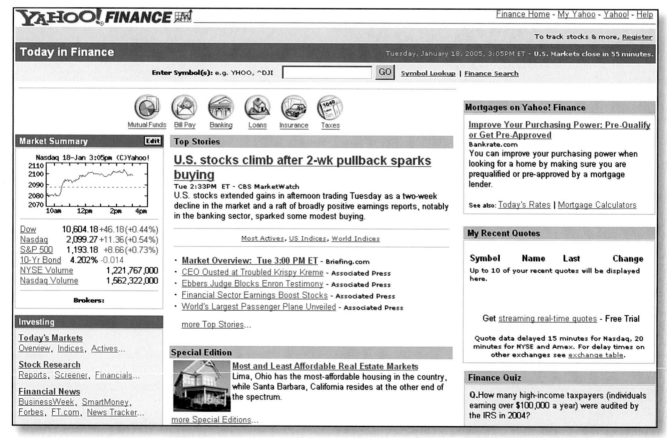

▲ **UTILIZING THE INTERNET** This search engine is one example of the many Web sites that can be used to find financial information. *What Web sites would help you find up-to-date information about a corporation's financial status?*

Newspapers

Most major newspapers have financial sections that contain information about stocks that are listed on major stock exchanges, such as the New York Stock Exchange (NYSE) and the American Stock Exchange (AMEX). Newspapers may also cover stocks of local interest. **Figure 9.2** illustrates the detailed information provided in *The Wall Street Journal* about common stock.

The Internet

Today most corporations have their own Web sites. The information may be more up to date and detailed than material from the corporation's printed publications.

You can also use search engines to find information about investing in stocks. Sites provide general financial news and specific information about a company and its stock's performance.

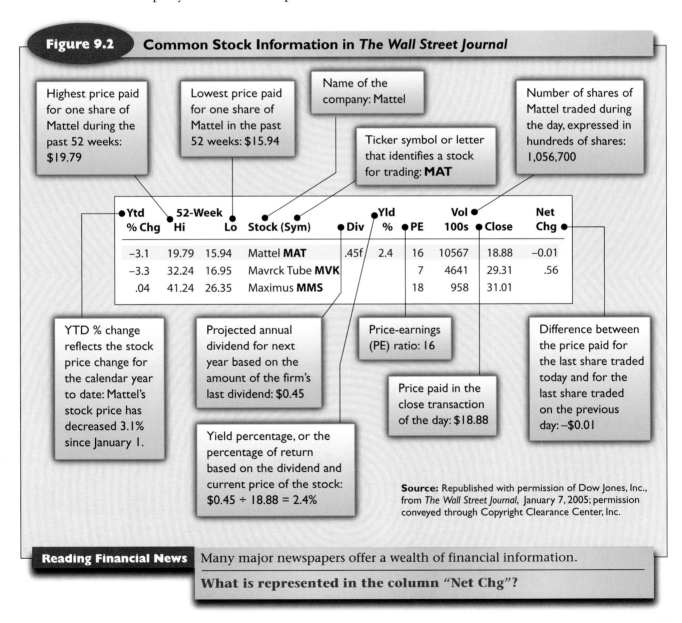

Figure 9.2 **Common Stock Information in *The Wall Street Journal***

Highest price paid for one share of Mattel during the past 52 weeks: $19.79

Lowest price paid for one share of Mattel in the past 52 weeks: $15.94

Name of the company: Mattel

Ticker symbol or letter that identifies a stock for trading: **MAT**

Number of shares of Mattel traded during the day, expressed in hundreds of shares: 1,056,700

Ytd % Chg	52-Week Hi	Lo	Stock (Sym)	Div	Yld %	PE	Vol 100s	Close	Net Chg
−3.1	19.79	15.94	Mattel **MAT**	.45f	2.4	16	10567	18.88	−0.01
−3.3	32.24	16.95	Mavrck Tube **MVK**			7	4641	29.31	.56
.04	41.24	26.35	Maximus **MMS**			18	958	31.01	

YTD % change reflects the stock price change for the calendar year to date: Mattel's stock price has decreased 3.1% since January 1.

Projected annual dividend for next year based on the amount of the firm's last dividend: $0.45

Yield percentage, or the percentage of return based on the dividend and current price of the stock: $0.45 ÷ 18.88 = 2.4%

Price-earnings (PE) ratio: 16

Price paid in the close transaction of the day: $18.88

Difference between the price paid for the last share traded today and for the last share traded on the previous day: −$0.01

Reading Financial News Many major newspapers offer a wealth of financial information.

What is represented in the column "Net Chg"?

Document Detective

Learn to identify and understand the standard financial documents you will use in the real world.

Investigate: A Stock Confirmation Report

A stock confirmation report contains the following information:

- Name and address of the stock owner
- Account number
- Name of the stock purchased or sold
- Price of the stock
- Number of shares held
- Commission and fees

Your Motive: When you buy or sell stock, you will receive a confirmation report that the purchase or sale has occurred. Be sure to check that the transaction was completed correctly. Check to see that the correct number of shares were purchased or sold, and that the fees for completing the transaction are reasonable.

Taylor Financial Services
175 Montrose Avenue
Cincinnati, OH 52549

Account Number: DR 199704

Hector Gonzales
3482 Mayfair Lane
Cincinnati, OH 52546

Trade date:	04/29/20––
Date processed:	04/29/20––
Payment Date:	05/04/20––

SOLD:

Quantity	Description	Price	Gross Amount	Commission	Fees	Total Amount
160	Analog Devices	$43.90	$7,024.00	$159.20	$5.42	$6,859.38

Key Points: When you own stock, there will be times when you want to sell or buy more. You may also want to purchase stocks from other companies as well. When you make these transactions, you will receive a stock confirmation report that will help you keep track of all your stock transactions.

Find the Solutions

1. Who performed the stock transaction?
2. Did Hector purchase or sell stock?
3. How many shares were involved in the transaction?
4. Why is there a difference between the gross amount and the total amount Hector received?
5. When will Hector be sent his money?

Stock Advisory Services

In addition to newspapers and the Internet, you can use stock advisory services to evaluate potential stock investments. Many stock advisory services, such as Moody's Investors Service, charge fees for their information, which can vary from simple alphabetic listings to detailed financial reports. As mentioned in Chapter 8, three widely used sources for information on companies' stock are *Standard & Poor's Stock and Bond Guide, Value Line Investment Survey,* and Mergent's *Handbook of Common Stocks.*

As shown in **Figure 9.3** on page 284, basic financial report from *Mergent's Handbook of Common Stocks* consists of six sections. One section contains information about stock prices and capitalization, earnings, and dividends. A background section, "Business," provides a detailed description of the company's major operations, such as the products they produce. A third section, "Recent Developments," offers current information about net income and sales revenue. A "Prospects" section describes the company's outlook, or prospects for the future. The "Annual Financial Data" section provides important statistics on the company for a specific length of time in the past. A final section lists information such as important officers in the corporation and the location of its headquarters.

As You Read

QUESTION

What are some sources for evaulating stock?

▲ **ONCE A YEAR** An annual report can provide a great deal of information for investors. *How can you get a copy of an annual report?*

Figure 9.3 **A Basic Financial Report**

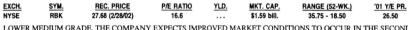

REEBOK INTERNATIONAL, LTD.

EXCH.	SYM.	REC. PRICE	P/E RATIO	YLD.	MKT. CAP.	RANGE (52-WK.)	'01 Y/E PR.
NYSE	RBK	27.68 (2/28/02)	16.6	...	$1.59 bill.	35.75 – 18.50	26.50

LOWER MEDIUM GRADE. THE COMPANY EXPECTS IMPROVED MARKET CONDITIONS TO OCCUR IN THE SECOND HALF OF 2002.

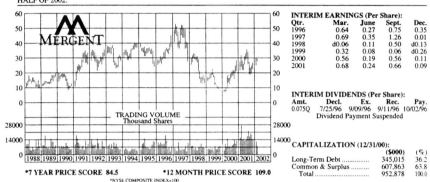

*7 YEAR PRICE SCORE 84.5   *12 MONTH PRICE SCORE 109.0
*NYSE COMPOSITE INDEX=100

INTERIM EARNINGS (Per Share):

Qtr.	Mar.	June	Sept.	Dec.
1996	0.64	0.27	0.75	0.35
1997	0.69	0.35	1.26	0.01
1998	d0.06	0.11	0.50	d0.13
1999	0.32	0.08	0.06	d0.26
2000	0.56	0.19	0.56	0.11
2001	0.68	0.24	0.66	0.09

INTERIM DIVIDENDS (Per Share):

Amt.	Decl.	Ex.	Rec.	Pay.
0.075Q	7/25/96	9/09/96	9/11/96	10/02/96

Dividend Payment Suspended

CAPITALIZATION (12/31/00):

	($000)	(%)
Long-Term Debt	345,015	36.2
Common & Surplus	607,863	63.8
Total	952,878	100.0

BUSINESS:

Reebok International, Ltd. is a worldwide company engaged primarily in the design and marketing of sports and fitness products, including footwear and apparel, as well as the design and marketing of footwear and apparel for casual use. The Company has four major brand groups. The Reebok Division designs, produces and markets sports, fitness and casual footwear, apparel and accessories under the REEBOK® brand. The Rockport Company designs, pro-duces and distributes specially-engineered comfort footwear for men and women worldwide under the ROCK-PORT® brand. Ralph Lauren Footwear Co., Inc., a subsidiary of the Company, is responsible for footwear and certain apparel sold under the RALPH LAUREN® and POLO SPORT® brands. The Greg Norman Division produces a range of men's apparel and accessories marketed under the GREG NORMAN name and logo.

RECENT DEVELOPMENTS:

For the year ended 12/31/01, net income grew 26.9% to $102.7 million from $80.9 million in the previous year. Net sales increased 4.5% to $2.99 billion versus $2.87 billion in the prior year. U.S. footwear sales rose to $930.5 million from $925.1 million a year earlier, while U.S. apparel sales climbed 68.1% to $395.1 million. International sales declined slightly to $1.17 billion versus $1.18 billion in 2000. Sales from the Rockport division fell 5.4% to $399.6 million. For the quarter ended 12/31/01, net income dropped 17.7% to $5.1 million from $6.2 million in the year-earlier period. Net sales rose 6.8% to $664.6 million versus $622.5 million the year before.

PROSPECTS:

RBK continues to experience weakness in footwear sales in the United States as retailers ordered less replacement inventory. However, U.S. apparel sales are being fueled by licensing deals with the NBA and the NFL. Looking ahead, RBK will introduce a new group of street-inspired products called Rbk. The new collection will be aimed at young male consumers. In addition, RBK intends to continue its focus on the young women's market and its Classic print campaign. Going forward, RBK expects earnings to rise in 2002, with the majority of the increase occurring in the second half as general economic and market conditions improve.

ANNUAL FINANCIAL DATA:

FISCAL YEAR	TOT. REVS. ($mill.)	NET INC. ($mill.)	TOT. ASSETS ($mill.)	OPER. PROFIT %	NET PROFIT %	RET. ON EQUITY %	RET. ON ASSETS %	CURR. RATIO	EARN. PER SH. $	CASH FL. PER SH. $	TANG. BK. VAL. $	DIV. PER SH. $	PRICE RANGE	AVG. P/E RATIO	AVG. YIELD %
p12/31/01	2,992.9	102.7							1.66			...	35.75 – 18.50	16.3	...
12/31/00	2,865.2	80.9	1,463.0	5.9	2.8	13.3	5.5	2.5	1.40	2.20	9.45	...	28.33 – 6.94	12.6	...
12/31/99	2,891.2	① 11.0	1,564.1	4.5	0.4	2.1	0.7	2.0	① 0.20	1.06	8.17	...	22.75 – 7.81	76.4	...
12/31/98	3,205.4	① 23.9	1,739.6	3.8	0.7	4.6	1.4	2.2	① 0.42	1.26	8.05	...	33.19 – 12.56	54.5	...
12/31/97	3,637.4	① 135.1	1,756.1	7.4	3.7	26.6	7.7	2.5	① 2.32	3.13	8.27	...	52.88 – 27.63	17.3	...
12/31/96	3,482.9	139.0	1,786.2	7.7	4.0	36.4	7.8	2.8	2.00	2.65	5.58	0.30	45.25 – 25.38	17.7	0.8
12/31/95	3,484.6	① 164.8	1,656.2	10.5	4.7	18.4	10.0	3.1	① 2.07	2.57	11.11	0.30	39.63 – 24.13	15.4	0.9
12/31/94	3,287.6	254.5	1,649.5	13.0	7.7	25.7	15.4	2.6	3.02	3.46	11.05	0.30	40.25 – 28.38	11.4	0.9
12/31/93	2,893.9	① 223.4	1,391.7	13.6	7.7	26.4	16.1	2.8	① 2.53	2.93	8.99	0.30	38.63 – 23.00	12.2	1.0
12/31/92	3,060.6	① 114.8	1,345.3	14.0	3.8	13.7	8.5	2.7	① 1.24	1.72	8.23	0.30	35.63 – 21.38	23.0	1.1

Statistics are as originally reported. ① Incl. non-recurr. chrg. 1999, $61.6 mill.; 1998, $35.0 mill.; 1997, $58.2 mill.; 1995, $72.1 mill.; 1993, $8.4 mill.; 1992, $155.0 mill.

OFFICERS:
P. B. Fireman, Chmn., C.E.O.
J. Margolis, Pres., C.O.O.
K. I. Watchmaker, Exec. V.P., C.F.O.
INVESTOR CONTACT: Neil Kerman, V.P., Finance, (781) 401-7152
PRINCIPAL OFFICE: 1895 J.W. Foster Boulevard, Canton, MA 02021

TELEPHONE NUMBER: (781) 401-5000
FAX: (781) 401-7402
WEB: www.reebok.com
NO. OF EMPLOYEES: 6,000 (approx.)
SHAREHOLDERS: 6,335
ANNUAL MEETING: In May
INCORPORATED: MA, July, 1979

INSTITUTIONAL HOLDINGS:
No. of Institutions: 204
Shares Held: 39,908,808
% Held: 67.8
INDUSTRY: Rubber and plastics footwear (SIC: 3021)
TRANSFER AGENT(S): American Stock Transfer & Trust Company, New York, NY

Source: *Handbook of Common Stocks,* © 2002 by Mergent, Inc. Reprinted by permission.

Up and Down

This financial report from Mergent's *Handbook of Common Stocks* provides information about Reebock International, Ltd.

What is reported in the lower section of the graph?

Corporate News Publications

Annual and quarterly reports offer a summary of a corporation's activities as well as detailed financial information. You do not have to be a stockholder to get an annual report. Simply call, write, or e-mail to request a copy from the company's headquarters. Financial publications such as *Barron's, BusinessWeek, Fortune, Kiplinger's Personal Finance, Money,* and *Smart Money* also provide information about specific companies.

Factors that Influence the Price of Stock

How would you determine whether your investment is increasing or decreasing in dollar value?

When you are deciding whether it is the right time to buy or sell a particular stock, you must first consider the overall condition of the stock market. A **bull market** is a market condition that occurs when investors are optimistic about the economy and buy stocks. Because of the greater demand for stock, the value of many stocks and the value of the stock market as a whole increases. A **bear market** is a market condition that occurs when investors are pessimistic about the economy and sell stocks. As a result of this decline in demand, the value of individual stocks and the stock market as a whole decreases.

Next you should consider the company's profits, losses, and other numerical measures of its financial situation.

▲ BULL AND BEAR MARKETS
Knowing the current market is important when you make decisions as an investor *How does a bull market affect stocks?*

Numerical Measures for a Corporation

Using numerical measures such as current yield, total return, earnings per share, and the price-earnings ratio is a good way to find out about the health of a corporation.

Current Yield   One of the most common calculations investors use to track the value of their investments is the current yield. **Current yield** is the annual dividend of an investment divided by the current market value. The current yield is expressed as a percentage. As a general rule, an increase in current yield is a healthy sign for any investment.

Total Return   The current yield calculation is useful, but you also need to know whether your investment is increasing or decreasing in dollar value. **Total return** is a calculation that includes the annual dividend as well as any increase or decrease in the original purchase price of the investment.

To calculate total return, add the current return on your investment to its capital gain. The current return is the total amount of dividends paid to you, based on the number of shares you own and how long you have held them. To figure out your current return, multiply your dividend amount per share by the number of shares and the length of time that you have held the shares.

Next determine your capital gain. As you learned in Chapter 8, capital gain is the profit you make from the sale of an asset, or the difference between the selling price and the purchase price. To compute capital gain, subtract the purchase price per share from the selling price per share. Then multiply that number by the number of shares held.

FINANCIAL MATH

CURRENT YIELD OF A STOCK INVESTMENT

Synopsis: Computing the current yield of your stocks will help you to determine the value of your investment.

Example: Suppose that Tanika purchases stock in EatGrapes.com. Assume that EatGrapes.com pays an annual dividend of $1.20 and is currently selling for $24 a share. What is Tanika's current yield?

Formula: $\dfrac{\text{Annual Dividend}}{\text{Current Market Value}} = \text{Current Yield}$

Solution: $\dfrac{\$1.20}{\$24.00} = 0.05 = 5\% \text{ or } .05$

Tanika's current yield would be 5 percent.

YOU FIGURE

If your stock pays an annual dividend of $.80 and is currently selling for $18 a share, what is your current yield?

TOTAL RETURN

Synopsis: Calculating the total return of your investment will let you know whether your investment is increasing or decreasing in value.

Example: Two years ago Mark bought 40 shares of Ferguson's Motor Company for $70 a share. The stock pays an annual dividend of $1.50. Mark is going to sell his stock at the current price of $120 a share. What would be the total return on his investment?

Formula:

Current Return + Capital Gain = Total Return

Solution:

A. Find the current return:

Dividend × Number of Shares × Years Held = Current Return

$1.50 × 40 × 2 = $120

The current return is $120.

B. Calculate the capital gain:

(Selling Price per Share − Purchase Price per Share)

× Number of Shares Held = Capital Gain

($120 - $70) × 40 = $2,000

The capital gain is $2,000

C. Find the total return:

Current return + Capital Gain = Total Return

$120 + $2,000 = $2,120

The total return on Mark's investment would be $2,120.

YOU FIGURE

If your current return on a stock is $60 and your capital gain is $1,280, what is your total return?

Once you have determined your current return and your capital gain, add those two figures to arrive at your total return.

In the **Go Figure** example, Mark's investment in Ferguson's Motor Company increased in value, so the total return was greater than the current return. For an investment that decreases in value, the total return will be less than the current return. The larger the dollar amount of the total return, the better.

Earnings Per Share Another measurement of a company's performance is **earnings per share**. Earnings per share are a corporation's net, or after-tax, earnings divided by the number of outstanding shares of common stock. This calculation measures the amount of corporate profit assigned to each share of common stock. This figure gives a stockholder an idea of a company's profitability. In general, an increase in earnings per share is a good sign for any corporation and its stockholders.

Price-Earnings Ratio The **price-earnings (PE) ratio** is the price of one share of stock divided by the corporation's earnings per share of stock over the last 12 months. This measurement is commonly used to compare the corporate earnings to the market price of a corporation's stock.

EARNINGS PER SHARE

Synopsis: Figuring out the earnings per share can help you find out a company's profits. This information can help you determine the general health of the company in which you are investing.

Example: EFG Corporation had net earnings of $800,000 last year. EFG had 100,000 outstanding shares of common stock. What were EFG's earnings per share?

Formula: $\dfrac{\text{Net Earnings}}{\text{Common Stock Outstanding}}$ = Earnings Per Share

Solution: $\dfrac{\$800,000}{100,000}$ = $8

The corporation's earnings per share were $8.

YOU FIGURE

You recently invested in an up-and-coming home improvement company and you want to know about the company's health. If the company had net earnings of $400,000 last year and had 80,000 outstanding shares of common stock, what were the company's net earnings per share?

The PE ratio is a key factor that serious investors as well as beginners can use to decide whether to invest in a stock. A low PE ratio indicates that a stock may be a good investment: The company has a lot of earnings when compared to the price of the stock. A high PE ratio tells you that it might be a poor investment. The company has little earnings when compared to the price of the stock.

Generally, you should study the PE ratio for a corporation over a period of time so that you can see a range. Although PE ratios vary by industry, they range between 5 and 35 for most corporations.

PRICE-EARNINGS RATIO

Synopsis: The price-earnings ratio is the most common measure of how expensive a stock is. Determining the price-earnings ratio can help you decide whether a stock is worth purchasing.

Example: EFG's stock is selling for $96 a share. EFG's earnings per share are $8. What is EFG's price-earnings ratio?

Formula: $\dfrac{\text{Market Price Per Share}}{\text{Earnings Per Share}}$ = Price-Earnings Ratio

Solution: $\dfrac{\$96}{\$8}$ = 12

The corporation's price-earnings ratio is 12.

YOU FIGURE

If a company's market price per share is $67 and its earnings per share is $6, what is the company's price-earning ratio?

Careers in Finance

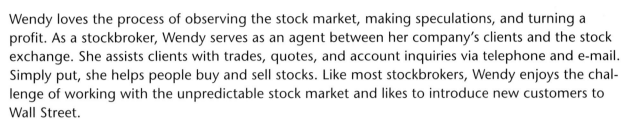

STOCKBROKER **Wendy Ross**
Scottrade

Wendy loves the process of observing the stock market, making speculations, and turning a profit. As a stockbroker, Wendy serves as an agent between her company's clients and the stock exchange. She assists clients with trades, quotes, and account inquiries via telephone and e-mail. Simply put, she helps people buy and sell stocks. Like most stockbrokers, Wendy enjoys the challenge of working with the unpredictable stock market and likes to introduce new customers to Wall Street.

SKILLS: Communication, math, customer-service, computer and data-entry, and multitasking skills

PERSONAL TRAITS: Organized, people oriented, able to travel 4 to 6 weeks per year, discreet, and positive

EDUCATION: Bachelor's degree in finance, business, or a related area or equivalent experience; current Series 7 and Series 63 licenses

ANALYZE The Internet enables individuals to trade their own stocks. What advantages might come from hiring a stockbroker instead of handling your stock trades yourself?

 To learn more about career paths for stockbrokers, visit **persfinance07.glencoe.com**.

Investment Theories
Which investment theory do you think makes the most sense?

Over the years theories have developed about ways to evaluate possible investments. Three investment theories dominate:

- The fundamental theory
- The technical theory
- The efficient market theory

The Fundamental Theory

The *fundamental theory* assumes that a stock's real value is determined by looking at the company's future earnings. If earnings are expected to increase in the future, then the stock's price should go up, too. People who believe in the fundamental theory also look at the financial strength of the company, the type of industry the company is in, its new products, and the state of the economy.

The Technical Theory

The *technical theory* is based on the idea that a stock's value is really determined by forces in the stock market itself. Technical theorists look at factors such as the number of stocks bought or sold over a certain period or the total number of shares traded.

The Efficient Market Theory

In the *efficient market theory,* sometimes called the random walk theory, the argument is that stock price movements are purely random. This theory declares that all investors have considered all of the available information on a stock as they make their decisions. Therefore, according to the efficient market theory, it is impossible for an investor to outperform the stock market average over a long period of time.

STANDARD & POOR'S

Put on Your Financial Planner's Cap

Your clients, Mayra and Bob, have $25,000 they want to invest. Bob is enthusiastic about investing in something that will make a quick return. Mayra does not want to jeopardize their savings. How should this couple invest their money?

Section 9.2 Assessment

QUICK CHECK

1. What are the different types of stock investments?
2. What are the sources that you might use to evaluate stock investments?
3. What numerical measures of corporations can be used to evaluate stock investments?

THINK CRITICALLY

4. Explain how the calculations that involve a company's earnings might help you to make a decision about buying or selling a particular stock.

USE MATH SKILLS

5. **Total Return** Two years ago, Andrei bought 100 shares of Snowland, a ski apparel company. The price of the stock is up $10 from the $20-a-share purchase price, and the stock even paid a dividend of $0.50 per share each year. Andrei wants to determine his total return on the stock.

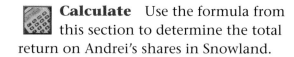

Calculate Use the formula from this section to determine the total return on Andrei's shares in Snowland.

SOLVE MONEY PROBLEMS

6. **Finding Stock Information** Sandy's mother works for Arf, a nationwide chain of dog kennels. She is receiving company stock as part of her employee retirement plan. She wants to track the stock's performance to see how her retirement nest egg is doing.

Write About It List two items in the stock reports in the financial section of the newspaper for Sandy's mother to review every week to get an idea of how the company's stock is doing. Write a paragraph explaining to Sandy why this information is useful and important to monitor.

Buying and Selling Stocks

Markets for Stocks

What are the markets for stocks?

To buy common or preferred stock, you usually have to go through a brokerage firm. In turn, the brokerage firm must buy the stock in the primary or secondary markets.

The Primary Markets

The primary market is a market in which investors purchase new security issues from a corporation through an investment bank or some other representative of the corporation. An investment bank is a financial firm that helps corporations to raise funds, usually by helping to sell new securities. The investors are commercial banks, insurance companies, pension funds, mutual funds, and the general public.

An initial public offering (IPO) occurs when a company sells stock to the general public for the first time. Companies use IPOs to fund new business start-ups or to finance new corporate growth and expansion. IPOs are considered a high-risk investment.

A corporation can also get financing through the primary market by selling directly to its current stockholders. By doing so, the corporation bypasses the investment bank, avoids any fees it might have had to pay, and therefore obtains financing at a lower cost.

The Secondary Markets

Once a company's stocks have been sold on the primary market, they can then be sold in the secondary market. The secondary market is a market for existing financial securities currently traded among investors.

Securities Exchanges A **securities exchange** is a marketplace where brokers who represent investors meet to buy and sell securities. Many securities issued by national corporations are first registered and then traded at either the NYSE or AMEX. There are also regional exchanges in San Francisco, Boston, Chicago, and other cities that trade stocks of companies in their respective regions. For example, American firms that do business abroad may also trade on the Tokyo, London, or Paris exchanges.

The NYSE is one of the largest securities exchanges in the world, listing more than 3,000 corporations with a total market value of about $16 trillion. Most of its 1,366 members, or seats, represent brokerage firms. In addition to meeting other requirements, a corporation must have a very large capitalization and trade many shares in order to be listed on the NYSE. Companies that cannot meet the NYSE requirements can use AMEX or regional exchanges.

Over-the-Counter Market Not all stocks are traded on organized exchanges. Several thousand companies trade their stock in the over-the-counter market. The **over-the-counter (OTC) market** is a network of dealers who buy and sell the stocks of corporations that are not listed on a securities exchange.

Most over-the-counter stocks are traded through NASDAQ (pronounced "NAZZ-dack"), an electronic marketplace for more than 4,000 different stocks. NASDAQ stands for the National Association of Securities Dealers Automated Quotation System. The association was established in 1939 to regulate the OTC. When you want to buy or sell a stock that trades on NASDAQ, such as Microsoft®, your brokerage firm sends your order in to the NASDAQ computer system. It shows up on a screen with all the other orders from people who want to buy or sell Microsoft. Then a NASDAQ dealer matches the orders of those who want to buy and those who want to sell Microsoft. Once a match is found, your order is completed.

Typically, NASDAQ handles trades for many forward-looking companies, many of which are fairly small. However, some very large companies such as Microsoft, Intel, and MCI are also traded on NASDAQ.

▲ **THE BIG BOARD** The New York Stock Exchange (NYSE) is one of the largest securities exchanges in the world. *What qualifications must a corporation have to be traded on the NYSE?*

How to Buy and Sell Stock
Why is it important to be directly involved in your investment program?

There are many decisions that you need to make before beginning to buy and sell stock. You must decide on a brokerage firm, an account executive, and on what type of order—market order, limit order, or stop order—you want to use to make your transaction.

Brokerage Firms

Today you can choose a full-service or discount brokerage firm or trade stocks online. The biggest difference is the amount of the commissions you will be charged when you buy or sell securities. A commission is a fee charged to an investor by a brokerage firm for the buying and/or selling of a security. Generally, full-service and discount brokerage firms charge higher commissions than online brokerage firms. Full-service firms usually charge the highest commissions in exchange for personalized service and free research information. However, there may be other differences among the types of firms.

First, consider the amount of research information that will be available to you and how much it costs. All of these firms offer excellent research materials, but you are more likely to pay extra for information if you choose a discount brokerage or online firm. Although most discount brokerage firms do not charge a lot of money for research reports, the fees can add up. Second, consider how much help you will need in order to make an investment decision. The full-service account executive may not have a lot of time to spend with each client, but you can expect him or her to answer questions and make recommendations.

Discount and online firms generally believe that you alone are in charge of your investment plan and that the most successful investors are totally involved in their programs. They usually have printed material or information on their Web sites to help you become a better investor.

▶ **ANOTHER WAY** More than 4,000 different stocks are traded on NASDAQ. *What market does NASDAQ serve?*

Account Executives

An account executive, or stockbroker, is a licensed individual who buys or sells securities, or stocks, for clients. Account executives usually work for brokerages.

Whether he or she is called an account executive or stockbroker, this person deals with all types of securities, not just stocks, and can handle your entire portfolio. A **portfolio** is a collection of all the securities held by an investor. Some account executives will take risks, while others are more conservative. When you are choosing an account executive, be sure that you can clearly describe your short- and long-term financial goals so that you will receive the best service for your needs.

Remember that account executives can make errors, so be sure to stay actively involved in decisions concerning your investments. Never let the stockbroker take action on your account without your permission. Brokerage firms are usually not responsible for financial losses that are the result of a recommendation by your account executive.

Be aware of a practice known as "churning." Churning occurs when an account executive does a lot of buying and selling of stocks within your portfolio to generate more commissions. Although churning is illegal, it is difficult to prove. Note that the value of your portfolio does not increase through churning; rather, it stays about the same.

Most traditional brokerage firms have a minimum commission that ranges from $25 to $55 for buying and selling stocks. However, commissions for online brokerage firms can be as low as $10. Additional fees based on the number of shares and the value of the stock can also be charged. On the floors of the exchanges, stocks are traded in round lots, which are 100 shares or multiples of 100 shares of a particular stock. An odd lot contains fewer than 100 shares of a stock.

▲ **YOUR BROKER** One of the biggest advantages of a full-service brokerage firm is personal attention from an account executive. *How can you protect your portfolio from a dishonest or incompetent account executive?*

Types of Orders

When you are ready to trade a stock, you will execute an order to buy or sell. Most investors do this either over the telephone or on the Internet. You can also go to a brokerage firm and place your order in person. The types of orders used to trade stocks include market orders, limit orders, and stop orders.

Market Orders A market order is a request to buy or sell a stock at the current market value. Because the stock market is essentially an auction, the account executive's representative will try to get the best price possible and make the transaction as soon as possible. **Figure 9.4** illustrates how a typical market order on the NYSE would be executed.

Figure 9.4   Trading Stock

Several steps are involved in trading stock on the New York Stock Exchange (NYSE).

1 Receiving an Order Your account executive receives your order to sell stock and relays the order electronically to the brokerage firm's representative at the stock exchange.

2 Signal to Floor Broker A clerk for the firm signals the transaction to a floor broker on the stock exchange floor.

3 Trading The floor broker goes to the trading post at which this stock is traded and trades with a floor broker (from another firm) who has an order to buy.

4 To the Ticker System The floor broker signals the transaction back to the clerk. Then a floor reporter—an employee of the NYSE—collects the information about the transaction and inputs it into the ticker system.

5 On the Board The sale appears on the price board, and a confirmation is relayed to your account executive, who notifies you of the completed transaction.

Stock Research

1. Choose a few companies whose products interest you.
2. Look up the stocks in the newspaper or on the Internet.
3. Watch how their prices change and graph their progress weekly.
4. Request and study an annual report from each company.
5. Research the companies in *Value Line Investment Survey.*

Note that every stock listed on the NYSE is traded at a computer-equipped trading post on the floor of the exchange. A computer monitor above the trading post indicates current price information for all stocks traded at each post.

Then each transaction is recorded, and the necessary information—the ticker symbol (the letters that identify a stock for trading), number of shares, and price—is transmitted through a communications network called the *ticker system.* The NYSE also uses the SuperDot system, which transmits orders electronically and can handle daily trading volumes of more than 2 billion shares.

Payment for stocks is generally required within three business days of the sale. About four to six weeks later, the broker sends a stock certificate (proof of ownership) to the purchaser. **Figure 9.5** shows a sample of a common stock certificate. However, the investor's brokerage firm can receive the certificate and hold it, which is convenient when it comes time to sell the stock. The phrase *left in the street name* is used to describe investor-owned securities held by a brokerage firm.

Limit Orders A limit order is a request to buy or sell a stock at a specified price. You agree to buy the stock at the best price up to a certain dollar amount. When you are selling, the limit order ensures that you will sell at the best price and not below a certain price.

Figure 9.5 **A Common Stock Certificate**

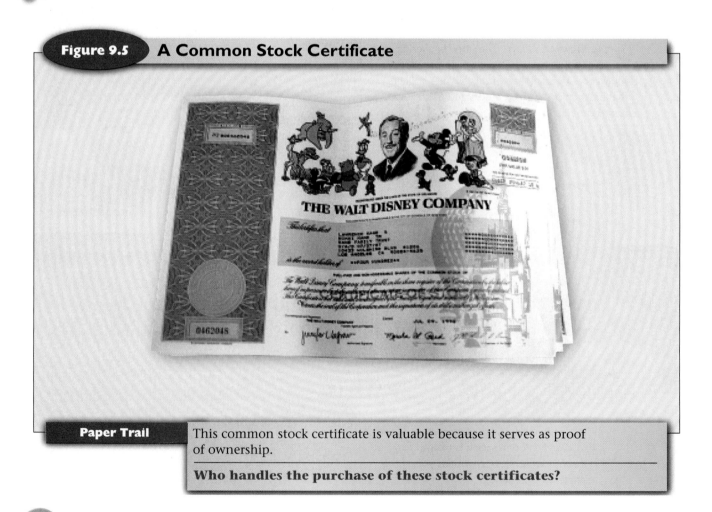

Paper Trail This common stock certificate is valuable because it serves as proof of ownership.

Who handles the purchase of these stock certificates?

For example, if you place a limit order to buy Kellogg common stock for $34 a share, the stock will not be purchased until the price drops to $34 or lower. If you place a limit order to sell a stock, the Kellogg stock will not be sold until the price rises to $34 or higher.

However, a limit order does not guarantee that the purchase or sale will be made when the desired price is reached. Limit orders are filled in the order in which they are received, so other investors may get orders filled before you do. If the price of Kellogg, for example, continues to rise while purchase orders ahead of yours are being filled, then when your turn comes, the price may reach $36, and you will miss the chance to buy the stock at $34.

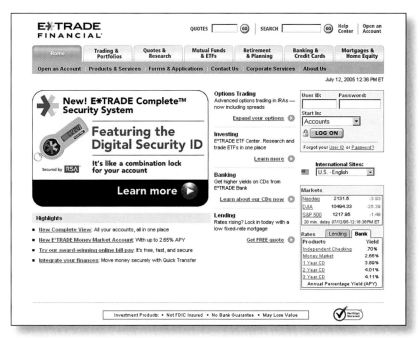

▲ **COMPUTERIZED TRANSACTIONS** Internet brokerage companies offer instant access to your account information and the ability to buy and sell online. *Why would having this be beneficial?*

Stop Orders   You can also place a stop order, which is used for selling stock. A stop order is a type of limit order to sell a particular stock at the next available opportunity when the market price reaches a specified amount. A stop order does not guarantee that your stock will be sold at the price you want, but it does guarantee that it will be sold at the next available opportunity. Both stop and limit orders can be good for a day, a week, a month, or until you cancel them.

Computerized Transactions

More and more people are using their computers to make securities transactions. To meet the demand for this service, discount brokerage firms and some full-service firms allow investors to trade online. You can use a software package or the brokerage's Web site to help you evaluate stocks, track your portfolio and monitor its value, and buy and sell securities online. Of course, you are still responsible for doing research and analyzing the information you get.

Investment Strategies
Which type of investment strategy would you use: long term or short term?

Once you purchase stock, the investment may be categorized as long term (held for ten years or more), or short term (held for one year or less). Generally, if you hold investments for at least a year, you are considered an investor. If you buy and sell investments within short periods of time, you are a speculator or a trader.

As You Read

QUESTION

What is the advantage of a dividend reinvestment plan?

Long-Term Techniques

Long-term techniques such as the buy-and-hold technique, dollar cost averaging, direct investment, and dividend reinvestment are used by all investors who are interested in avoiding losses in their investments.

Buy-and-Hold Technique   A typical long-term investing method is to buy stock and hold on to it for a number of years, often ten or more. During that time, you may get dividends, and the price of the stock may go up. The stock may also be split, which increases its value as well as number of shares owned.

Dollar Cost Averaging   With this method, you buy an equal dollar amount of the same stock at equal intervals. For example, suppose that you invested $2,000 in Johnson & Johnson common stock each year for a period of three years. When the price of the stock went up, your $2,000 purchased fewer shares, and when it went down, your $2,000 purchased more shares. This system protects investors from buying at high prices and selling at low prices. The price you pay for the stock averages out over time.

Direct Investment and Dividend Reinvestment Plans   A large number of companies sell their stock directly to investors. This plan lets you buy stock without going through your account executive at a brokerage firm and paying commissions. You have the same advantage of not paying fees with a dividend reinvestment plan, which automatically reinvests any dividends you earn by buying more shares of that stock with those earnings.

Short-Term Techniques

Investors sometimes use more speculative, short-term techniques. These methods are quite risky. Only investors who fully understand the risks should use techniques such as buying on margin and selling short.

Buying on Margin   When buying stock on margin, an investor borrows through a brokerage firm part of the money needed to purchase a stock. The Federal Reserve Board currently limits the margin requirement to 50 percent and $2,000, which means that you can borrow up to half of the purchase price as long as you have at least $2,000 in your brokerage account. Investors buy stock on margin in order to purchase more shares. If the shares go up in value, the investor makes more money. However, if the shares go down in value, the investor loses more money.

Selling Short   Your ability to make money buying and selling securities is related to how well you can predict what the stock is going to do—whether it will rise or fall in value. Normally you want to buy a stock that will go up in value, and this is called buying long. Of course, the value of stocks can decrease, too.

You can actually make money by selling short when the value of a stock appears as if it may go down. Selling short is selling a stock that has been borrowed from a brokerage firm and that must be replaced at a later date. You sell the stock you have borrowed today, knowing that you will have to buy the stock again at a later date. Here is how it is done:

1. Arrange to borrow a certain number of shares of a particular stock from a brokerage firm.
2. Sell the borrowed stock, assuming that it will drop in value in a reasonably short period of time.
3. Buy the stock at a lower price than the price it sold for in Step 2.
4. Use the stock you purchased in Step 3 to replace the stock that you borrowed from the brokerage firm in Step 1.

Remember that when you borrow the stock, it really belongs to someone else, so if a dividend is due, you must pay it. Eventually these dividends may absorb all the profits you make on the transaction. To make money, you have to predict correctly that the value of the stock will go down. If the value increases, you lose money.

After You Read

REACT

Using the information provided in this chapter, do you think you could develop an investment plan for yourself?

Section 9.3 Assessment

QUICK CHECK

1. What is the difference between the primary and secondary stock markets?
2. What are characteristics of full-service, discount, and online brokerage firms in terms of service and cost?
3. What are the trading techniques that are used by investors and speculators?

THINK CRITICALLY

4. Design a handout for students that explains the various long-term investment strategies.

USE COMMUNICATION SKILLS

5. **Short-Term Trading**   Some of your classmates are boasting that they can make a killing by trading stocks over a short period of time.

Present   Choose one of your favorite songs and create song lyrics for it that warn of the dangers of short-term trading methods. Be as specific about the methods as you can, noting why beginning investors could get "burned."

SOLVE MONEY PROBLEMS

6. **Using a Broker**   Bruce is a high school senior with a busy fall schedule. He saved enough money to start investing, but he has no time to monitor his investments or make decisions. He wants to let his account executive buy or sell stocks without bothering him.

Analyze   List and explain the dangers of Bruce's plan to let his account executive act without consulting him.

Chapter 9 Review & Activities

CHAPTER SUMMARY

- Investors choose common stock because stocks provide a greater potential return than bank savings accounts and government bonds.
- Investors choose preferred stocks because they are less risky than common stocks and because they provide a steady income in the form of dividends.
- Types of stock investments include blue-chip stocks, income stocks, growth stocks, cyclical stocks, defensive stocks, large- and small-cap stocks, and penny stocks.
- Information about stocks' risk can be found in newspapers, stock advisory services, corporate reports, and on the Internet.

- Factors affecting stock prices include general attitudes about current economic conditions and corporate performance.
- Stocks are bought and sold in primary markets, such as in an initial public offering (IPO), and in secondary markets, such as securities exchanges and the over-the-counter (OTC) market.
- Long-term investors buy and hold stocks, use dollar-cost averaging to smooth out the prices they pay for stocks they buy regularly, and reinvest their dividends and buy more stock directly from companies in which they have already invested to avoid stockbroker commissions. Short-term speculators use techniques such as buying stock on margin and selling short.

Communicating Key Terms

You have a client who owns a company with 75 employees. She asks you to describe the stock option offered to employees in the company's 401(k) retirement savings plan. Use as many of the terms below as possible to develop a presentation for these employees.

- securities
- private corporation
- public corporation
- par value
- blue-chip stock
- income stock
- growth stock
- cyclical stock

- defensive stock
- large-cap stock
- capitalization
- small-cap stock
- penny stock
- bull market
- bear market
- current yield

- total return
- earnings per share
- price-earnings (PE) ratio
- securities exchange
- over-the-counter (OTC) market
- portfolio

Reviewing Key Concepts

1. **Explain** why corporations prefer to issue common stock to raise funds for their operations.
2. **Explain** how cumulative preferred and convertible preferred stock offer advantages to investors.
3. **Describe** why a small-cap stock is more likely to be a growth stock rather than an income stock.
4. **Identify** the advantages and disadvantages of a stock advisory service to evaluate a stock.
5. **Describe** why the price-earnings ratio is a good measure of a stock investment.
6. **List** the differences among market order, limit order, and stop order.
7. **Identify** the tax advantages of long-term investment strategies.

Language Arts Sometimes the best career information comes from informational interviews with people working in the real world.

Write About It Interview a stockbroker and ask him or her questions about the background, education, training, and experience needed to work in that profession. Then write an article based on the interview for your school or class newsletter.

Buying and Selling Stocks You bought 200 shares of a stock at $17 per share in 2001. After 12 months, the stock doubled in value, and you sold 100 shares. Eighteen months later, the stock reached $60 and split. After another year, the stock is now selling at $52 a share.

1. **Calculate** (a) how much you received when you sold 100 shares in 2002; (b) your capital gain; (c) how many shares of this stock you own today; and (d) your gain on these shares.
2. **Compute** by using spreadsheet software to make these calculations.

Connect with Government The capital gains received on stock sales is considered income, and you have to pay taxes on it. To encourage people to invest and to hold on to those investments, the U.S. government taxes capital gains on investments held less than 12 months at the investor's regular tax rate, but capital gains on investments held longer are taxed at 15 percent—which for most people is less than the regular tax rate.

1. **Research** Use the Internet to find out more about why the government wants to encourage investors to hold on to their investments.
2. **Think Critically** How does the tax difference (15 percent tax rate versus regular tax rate) provide an incentive to people to invest in corporations, as opposed to corporate bonds or government bonds?

Institutional Investors Many investors buying stocks are not individuals, but institutions, such as retirement plans and mutual funds, which have extremely large amounts of money to buy and sell large blocks of stock.

Log On Use an Internet search engine to find Web sites of companies that manage such funds. One is TIAA-CREF, which manages the retirement funds of teachers in many states. Answer the following questions:

1. What types of investments do institutional investors make?
2. What can you say about their tolerance for risk?

Newsclip: Investor Concern Despite a growing economy, investor concern has decreased the popularity of stocks. However, quality stocks are usually sound even in shaky times.

 Log On Go to persfinance07.glencoe.com. Open Chapter 9. Learn about what affects stock prices and make a list of safe stocks.

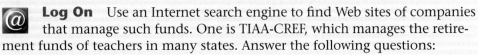

TAKING STOCK

Test your knowledge of stocks after you read the chapter. Write your answers on a separate sheet of paper. If you had the money, would you be ready to invest in stocks?

1. All stocks pay dividends.

True   False

2. Blue-chip stocks are generally a safe investment that attracts conservative investors.

True   False

3. A bull market occurs when ranchers take their cattle to the stockyards.

True   False

4. An initial public offering (IPO) occurs when a company first sells its products or services to the public.

True   False

5. The price-earnings (PE) ratio is the price of one share of stock divided by the stock's earnings per share.

True   False

6. A good way to learn about the financial health of a company is by reading its annual report.

True   False

7. An income statement shows a company's profits and losses.

True   False

8. The appeal of investing in high-risk stocks is the possibility of large returns.

True   False

Your Financial Portfolio

Investing in Stock

Rick would like to invest in the stock market. Before he invests any money, Rick is researching a company he thinks has potential. He picked eSongz, an online music store that lets you rent or purchase MP3 players and buy songs for them directly from its site. Along with the price of stock, he watches for any announcements or industry changes that may affect the stock.

Rick's Research

eSongz

Highest price paid per share during the past 52 weeks	$41.80
Lowest price paid per share in the past 52 weeks	$19.89
Current price paid per share	$35.35
Price-earnings (PE) ratio	20
Earnings per share	$1.78

Rick has studied eSongz' financial reports and also keeps tabs on its financial news reports. He believes eSongz will continue to be successful, but he plans to watch the stock a little longer before he makes his decision to invest.

Research

In your workbook or on a separate sheet of paper, choose a stock you would like to buy and research it. You can get information about a company in the financial section of major newspapers, the Internet, and from the companies themselves. You can also find information from *Standard & Poor's Stock and Bond Guide, Mergent's Handbook of Common Stocks,* or *Value Line Investment Survey.* What type of stock would you be interested in purchasing? Explain why. Do you think the company you chose to research would be a wise investment choice? Explain your answer.

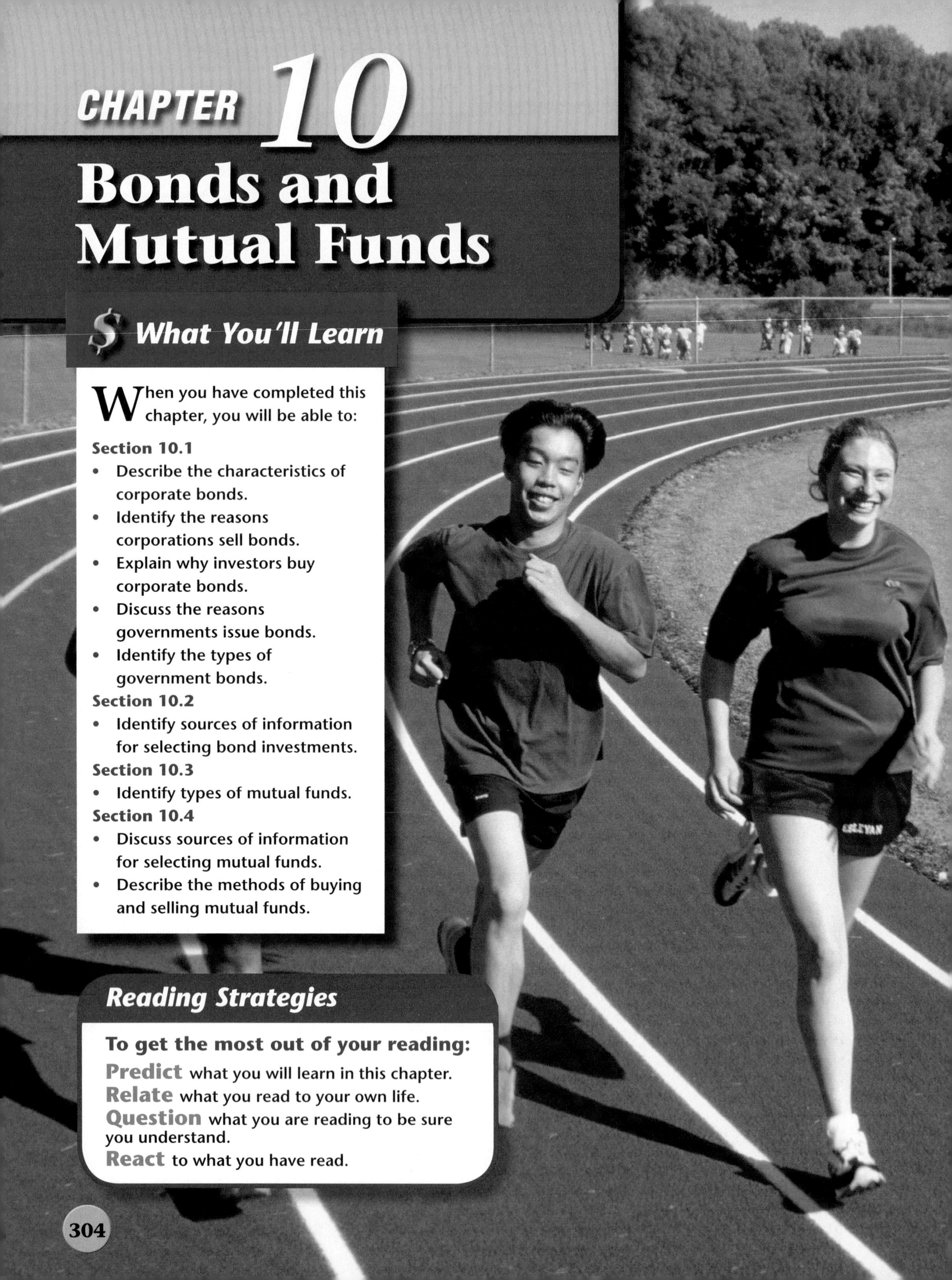

CHAPTER 10

Bonds and Mutual Funds

$ What You'll Learn

When you have completed this chapter, you will be able to:

Section 10.1
- Describe the characteristics of corporate bonds.
- Identify the reasons corporations sell bonds.
- Explain why investors buy corporate bonds.
- Discuss the reasons governments issue bonds.
- Identify the types of government bonds.

Section 10.2
- Identify sources of information for selecting bond investments.

Section 10.3
- Identify types of mutual funds.

Section 10.4
- Discuss sources of information for selecting mutual funds.
- Describe the methods of buying and selling mutual funds.

Reading Strategies

To get the most out of your reading:

Predict what you will learn in this chapter.
Relate what you read to your own life.
Question what you are reading to be sure you understand.
React to what you have read.

In the **Real** World . . .

When Julie Schmidt read her sample ballot, she noticed several government bond measures for everything from hiring new firefighters to building an elementary school. She was particularly interested in a bond measure that would pay for building an athletic facility and field at her former high school. She did not know much about government bonds, so she asked her local banker about them. The banker said they are almost risk-free as investments. She also learned that there are corporate bonds, which carry more risk but may earn more profit. So Julie decided to vote for the measure and invest in bonds.

As You Read   *Consider investment options such as bonds and mutual funds.*

ASK STANDARD &POOR'S

Mutual Funds

Q: I have about $50 a month to invest. What is a good investment choice for me?

A: Many mutual fund companies offer systematic investment programs in which you invest the same amount each month regardless of changes in the share price. As a result, your money buys more shares when prices are low and fewer shares when prices are high. Over time, this strategy can result in a lower average cost per share; however, it does not guarantee a profit or protect against a loss.

Ask Yourself Why is it a good idea to invest even a small amount of money each month?

 Go to **persfinance07.glencoe.com** to complete the Standard & Poor's Financial Focus activity.

Focus on Reading

Read to Learn

- How to describe the characteristics of corporate bonds.
- How to identify the reasons corporations sell bonds.
- How to explain why investors buy corporate bonds.
- How to discuss the reasons governments issue bonds.
- How to identify the types of government bonds.

Main Idea

Understanding bonds and why they are bought and sold will give you more choices to consider when investing your money.

Key Terms

- maturity date
- face value
- debenture
- mortgage bond
- convertible bond
- sinking fund
- serial bonds
- registered bond
- coupon bond
- bearer bond
- zero-coupon bond
- municipal bond

Corporate and Government Bonds

Corporate Bonds
What is a corporate bond?

When you buy a corporate bond, you are basically loaning money to a corporation. As discussed in Chapter 8, a corporate bond is a corporation's written pledge to repay a bondholder (the person who bought the bond) a specified amount of money with interest. **Figure 10.1** on page 313 shows an example of a typical corporate bond. The bond's interest rate, maturity date, and face value are stated on the bond. The **maturity date** is the date when a bond will be repaid. The **face value** is the dollar amount that the bondholder will receive at the bond's maturity. Typically, the face value of a corporate bond is $1,000. However, corporate bonds can have face values as high as $50,000.

Between the date when you buy a bond and the maturity date, the corporation pays you annual interest at the rate stated on the bond. Interest is usually paid semiannually (twice a year). By multiplying the face value by the interest rate, you can calculate how much interest you would earn each year.

At the maturity date, you cash in the bond and receive a check in the amount of the bond's face value. Maturity dates for bonds can range from 1 to 30 years. Maturities for corporate bonds are classified as short term (less than 5 years), intermediate term (5 to 15 years), and long term (more than 15 years).

Types of Corporate Bonds

There are several types of corporate bonds. These types include debentures, mortgage bonds, subordinated debentures, and convertible bonds.

Debentures Most corporate bonds are debentures. A **debenture** is a bond that is backed only by the reputation of the issuing corporation, rather than by its assets. Investors buy this type of bond because they believe that the company, or corporation, that issues them is on solid financial ground. Investors expect the company to repay the face value of the bond and make interest payments until the bond matures.

A BOND'S ANNUAL INTEREST

Synopsis: The interest on a bond is paid twice a year. By calculating the annual interest on your bond, you will be able to determine how much money you will earn on the bond each year.

Example: Suppose that you purchase a $1,000 Mobil Corporation bond. The interest rate for the bond is 8.5 percent (8.5%). How much annual interest would you earn on this bond?

Formula:

Face Value × Interest Rate = Annual Interest

Solution:

$1,000 × 8.5% or .085 = $85

You would receive interest of $85 a year from Mobil, paid in two installments of $42.50.

YOU FIGURE

If you purchased two $2,000 bonds that had an interest rate of 7 percent, how much annual interest would you earn?

Mortgage Bonds A bond issue occurs when a company makes available a quantity of bonds at one time. To make these bonds more appealing to conservative investors, a corporation may also issue mortgage bonds. A **mortgage bond,** sometimes referred to as a secured bond, is a bond that is backed by assets of a corporation. A mortgage bond is a safer investment than a debenture because it is backed by corporate assets. These assets, such as real estate or equipment, can be sold to repay the mortgage bondholders if the corporation fails to make good on its bonds. Though safer, mortgage bonds usually earn less interest than debentures because their risk to the investor is lower.

Subordinated Debentures A subordinated debenture is a type of unsecured bond that gives bondholders a claim to interest payments and assets of the corporation only after all other bondholders have been paid. Because subordinated debentures are more risky than other bonds, investors who buy them usually receive higher interest rates than other bondholders.

Convertible Bonds A **convertible bond** is a bond that an investor can trade for shares of the corporation's common stock. Because of the unique flexibility that it offers investors, the interest rate on a convertible bond is often 1 to 2 percent lower than interest rates on other types of corporate bonds.

Many bondholders choose not to convert their bonds into stock even when stock values are high. The reason for this is simple: As the market value of a company's common stock increases, the market value of the company's convertible bonds also increases. Bondholders benefit from this increase in value while keeping the relative safety of a bond and its interest income.

Before You Read

PREDICT

What do you think government bonds are?

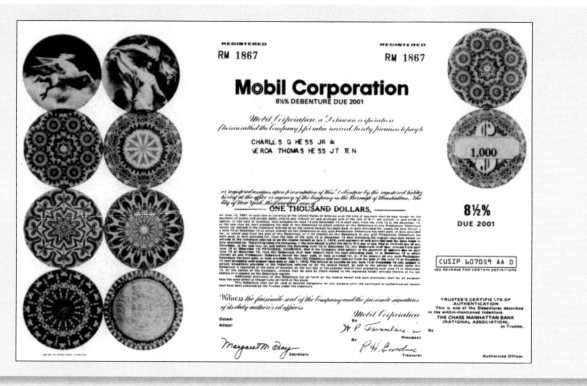

▲ A CORPORATE BOND
Mobil Corporation issued
this bond with an interest
rate of 8.5 percent. *What is
the face value of this bond?*

Methods Corporations Use to Repay Bonds

Today most corporate bonds are "callable," which means they have a call feature that allows a corporation to buy back bonds from bondholders before the maturity date. Corporations may get the money to call a bond by selling stock, by using profits, or by selling new bonds at a lower interest rate.

For example, suppose that Mobil Corporation issued bonds at 8.5 percent, but later, interest rates on comparable bonds dropped to 4.5 percent. Mobil Corporation might decide to call the bonds it had issued at 8.5 percent. By buying back those bonds early, Mobil would not have to pay bondholders interest at that high rate.

Premiums Usually, companies agree not to call their bonds for the first five to ten years after the bonds are issued. When they do call their bonds, they may have to pay bondholders a premium. A premium is an additional amount above the face value of the bond. The amount of the premium is stated in a *bond indenture*, which details all the conditions pertaining to a particular bond issue.

Sinking Funds A corporation may use one of two methods to make sure that it has enough funds to pay off a bond issue. First, the corporation may set up a sinking fund. A **sinking fund** is a fund to which a corporation makes deposits for the purpose of paying back a bond issue. If the bond indenture states that the corporation will deposit money in a sinking fund, the company will be able to repay its bonds.

Serial Bonds Second, a corporation may issue serial bonds. **Serial bonds** are bonds issued at the same time but which mature on different dates. For example, Seaside Productions issued $100 million of serial bonds for a 20-year period. None of the bonds matured during the first ten years. Therefore, during that time the company did not have to pay anything but the interest owed on the outstanding bonds. Instead, Seaside Productions used the funds raised by selling the bonds to grow its business. After that, only 10 percent of the bonds matured each year until all the bonds were retired at the end of 20 years. That allowed Seaside Productions to repay its bonds a few at a time instead of having to repay all $100 million at once.

As You Read

RELATE

Do you think that investing in corporate bonds would be a good way to reach your financial goals? Why?

Why Corporations Sell Bonds
What are a corporation's responsibilities to its stockholders and to its bondholders?

Corporations sell bonds to raise money when it is difficult or impossible to sell stock. Companies also often use bonds simply to finance regular business activities. Selling bonds can also reduce the amount of tax a corporation must pay because the interest paid to bondholders is tax-deductible.

A corporation may sell both bonds and stocks to help pay for its activities. However, the corporation's responsibility to investors is different for bonds and for stocks. Bondholders must be repaid at a future date for their investments. Stockholders do not have to be repaid. Companies are required to pay interest on bonds. They can choose whether to pay dividends to their stockholders. Finally, if a corporation files for bankruptcy, bondholders' claims to assets are paid before the claims of stockholders.

◄ **SECURE FOOTING** Mortgage bonds may be backed by a company's real estate, stock, or machinery and equipment. *Why would an investor want to buy a mortgage bond?*

Savings Mind-Set
It is exciting when you get a raise or finally pay off a loan. You know you have more money available. Be a smart saver—stick to your current budget and stash that newfound money in your savings or investment account. *If you received a $30 per week raise in net pay and were paid four times per month, how much "extra" money would you have in ten months from February to November? Would you save or invest that money? Why or why not?*

Why Investors Buy Corporate Bonds

Why are bonds considered safe investments?

Historically, stocks have resulted in greater profits than bonds. Why, then, should you consider investing in bonds? Many corporate and government bonds are safe investments. Some investors use corporate and government bonds to diversify their investment portfolios (all the securities held by an investor). Bonds offer you three other benefits:

- Most bonds provide interest income.
- Bonds may increase in value, depending on the bond market, overall interest rates in the economy, and the reputation and assets of the issuer.
- The face value of a bond is repaid when it reaches maturity.

Interest Income

Bondholders usually receive interest payments every six months. The dollar amount of annual interest is determined by multiplying the interest rate by the face value of the bond. The method used by a company to pay you interest depends on the type of corporate bond you purchase:

- Registered bond
- Coupon bond
- Bearer bond
- Zero-coupon bond

Registered Bonds   A **registered bond** is a bond registered in the owner's name by the company that issues the bond. This ensures that only the owner can collect money from the bond. Interest checks for registered bonds are mailed directly to the bondholder.

Coupon Bonds   A registered **coupon bond** is a bond that is registered in the owner's name for only the face value and not for interest. This type of bond comes with detachable coupons. Because the face value of the bond is registered, only the bond's owner can collect the face value. However, anyone who holds the coupons can collect the interest. To collect an interest payment on a registered coupon bond, you simply present one of the detachable coupons to the issuing corporation or to the appropriate bank or broker.

Bearer Bonds   A **bearer bond** is a bond that is not registered in the investor's name. As with registered coupon bonds, the owner of a bearer bond must present coupons in order to collect interest payments. Anyone who has physical possession of the bonds or their coupons can collect on them. A few bearer bonds are still in circulation, but they are no longer issued by corporations.

Zero-Coupon Bond A **zero-coupon bond** is a bond that does not produce interest payments. It is sold at a price far below its face value, but it is redeemed for its full face value at maturity. Because you buy it for less than its face value, you automatically make a profit when your zero-coupon bond is repaid.

Market Value of a Bond

Many beginning investors think that a $1,000 bond is always worth $1,000. Actually, the market value of a corporate bond may fluctuate before its maturity date. Usually, shifts in bond prices result from changes in overall interest rates in the economy.

For example, suppose that Vanessa has a bond with a 7.5 percent interest rate. If overall interest rates fall below 7.5 percent, Vanessa's bond will go up in market value because it earns more interest than bonds issued at the new lower rate. If overall interest rates rise above 7.5 percent, the market value of Vanessa's bond will fall because it earns less interest than bonds issued at the new, higher rate.

When a bond is selling for less than its face value, it is said to be selling at a *discount*. When a bond is selling for more than its face value, it is said to be selling at a *premium*. You can calculate a bond's approximate market value by using a formula that compares the bond's interest rate to that of similar new corporate bonds. (See **Go Figure** on page 312.) Find the dollar amount of the bond's annual interest by multiplying the face value by the annual interest rate. Then, compute the bond's approximate market value by dividing the dollar amount of annual interest by the interest rate of comparable new corporate bonds.

The market value of a bond may also be affected by the financial condition of the company that issues it. In addition, the law of supply and demand changes in the economy and can affect a bond's value.

As You Read

QUESTION

What type of investor would be interested in a zero-coupon bond?

◄ **REDEEMABLE COUPONS**
Registered coupon bonds come with detachable coupons. *How are the coupons used?*

APPROXIMATE MARKET VALUE OF A BOND

Synopsis: The market value of a bond can change many times before its maturity date. Calculating the approximate market value of a bond can help you determine what your bond will be worth at its maturity date.

Example: Shawn purchased a New York Telephone bond that pays 4.5 percent interest based on a face value of $1,000. Comparable new corporate bond issues are paying 7 percent. How much is Shawn's bond worth?

Formula:

$$\frac{\text{Dollar Amount of Annual Interest}}{\substack{\text{Interest Rate of Comparable} \\ \text{New Corporate Bonds}}} = \substack{\text{Approximate} \\ \text{Market Value}}$$

Solution:

A. Find the dollar amount of annual interest.

Face Value of Bond × Annual Interest Rate = Dollar Amount of Annual Interest

$1,000 × 4.5% or .045 = $45

The dollar amount of annual interest is $45.

B. Solve for approximate market value.

$$\frac{\text{Dollar Amount of Annual Interest}}{\substack{\text{Interest Rate of Comparable} \\ \text{New Corporate Bonds}}} = \substack{\text{Approximate} \\ \text{Market Value}}$$

$$\frac{\$45}{7\% \text{ or } .07} = \$642.86$$

The approximate market value of Shawn's New York Telephone bond is $642.86.

YOU FIGURE

You bought two $1,000 bonds, each with an interest rate of 5.5 percent. New corporate bonds being issued are paying 8 percent interest. What is the approximate market value of your bonds?

Repayment at Maturity

Corporate bonds are repaid at maturity. After you purchase a bond, you have two choices. You can keep the bond until its maturity date and then cash it in. You can also sell the bond at any time to another investor. In either case, the value of the bond is closely tied to the corporation's ability to repay it. Other investors will pay more money to get a quality bond that has solid prospects of repayment.

A Typical Bond Transaction
Where can you purchase corporate bonds?

Most bonds are sold through full-service brokerage firms, discount brokerage firms, or online. If you use a full-service brokerage firm, your account executive should provide information and advice about bond investments. If you use a discount brokerage firm or buy bonds online, you must do your own research and make your own decisions. However, you will probably pay a lower commission.

You can also buy corporate bonds directly from account executives or brokerage firms. If you buy or sell a bond through an account executive or brokerage firm, you should expect to pay a commission.

Purchasing in Primary and Secondary Markets

Bonds are purchased in the same way as stocks. Corporate bonds may be purchased in the primary or secondary markets. In the primary market, you purchase financial securities from an investment banker representing the corporation or government agency that issued them. In the secondary market, you trade financial securities with other investors. Corporate bonds issued by large companies are traded on the New York Bond Exchange and American Bond Exchange.

Sample Bond Transaction

Figure 10.1 shows an example of a bond transaction—Ms. Mansfield's Borden bond transaction. On October 8, 1995, Ms. Mansfield purchased an 8.375 percent corporate bond issued by Borden, Inc. She paid $680 for the bond plus a $10 commission ($680 + $10 = $690). On October 8, 2006, she sold it at its current market value of $1,030 minus a $10 commission ($1,030 − $10 = $1,020).

After paying commissions for buying and selling her Borden bond, Ms. Mansfield had a capital gain of $330 ($1,020 − $690 = $330). The market value of the bond increased because overall interest rates in the economy declined during the time she owned the bond. Borden also established a good business reputation during this period, making the bond more secure and, therefore, more valuable.

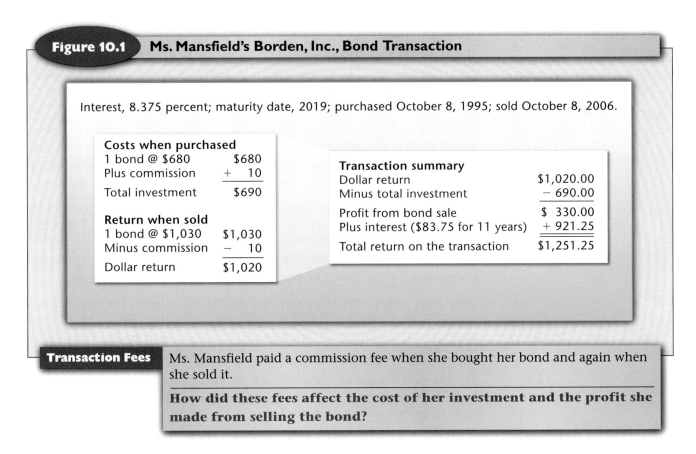

Figure 10.1   Ms. Mansfield's Borden, Inc., Bond Transaction

Interest, 8.375 percent; maturity date, 2019; purchased October 8, 1995; sold October 8, 2006.

Costs when purchased

1 bond @ $680	$680
Plus commission	+ 10
Total investment	$690

Return when sold

1 bond @ $1,030	$1,030
Minus commission	− 10
Dollar return	$1,020

Transaction summary

Dollar return	$1,020.00
Minus total investment	− 690.00
Profit from bond sale	$ 330.00
Plus interest ($83.75 for 11 years)	+ 921.25
Total return on the transaction	$1,251.25

Transaction Fees Ms. Mansfield paid a commission fee when she bought her bond and again when she sold it.

How did these fees affect the cost of her investment and the profit she made from selling the bond?

Ms. Mansfield also made money on her Borden bond by collecting interest payments. For each of the 11 years she owned the bond, Borden paid her $83.75 ($1,000 × 8.375% = $83.75) in interest. By the time she sold the bond, she had received interest payments totaling $921.25. These earnings, together with her $330 capital gain, added up to a total return of $1,251.25.

Government Bonds and Securities
Why does the government issue bonds and securities?

Like private corporations, the federal government as well as state and local governments issue bonds to help raise the money they need to operate.

The federal government sells bonds and other securities to help fund its regular activities and services, and to finance the national debt. U.S. government securities are considered to be almost risk-free. They are backed by the full faith and credit of the United States government. However, because they have a low risk of default, which means failure to pay debts, government bonds offer lower interest rates than corporate bonds.

Treasury Bills, Notes, and Bonds

The U.S. Department of the Treasury issues three basic types of securities: Treasury bills (T-bills), Treasury notes, and U.S. government savings bonds. Treasury bonds, another type of security, were sold by the Treasury Department until October 2001.

You can buy Treasury bills and Treasury notes online through Treasury Direct, which is a Web site operated by the Department of the Treasury. When you buy through Treasury Direct, you do not have to pay a commission. You can also buy these securities through banks or brokers, which charge a commission for their services. U.S. government savings bonds can also be purchased through Treasury Direct, commercial banks, savings and loan associations, or other financial institutions.

You can hold U.S. government securities until maturity or cash before the maturity date. You must pay federal income tax on interest you receive from these investments. However, state and local governments do not tax this income.

Treasury Bills Treasury bills are sold in units of $1,000. They may reach maturity in 4 weeks, 13 weeks, 26 weeks, or 52 weeks. T-bills are discounted securities. That means that the actual purchase price you pay when you buy a T-bill is less than the face value of the T-bill. On the maturity date, you receive the full face value of the T-bill. A T-bill held until maturity can be reinvested in another bill or can be paid to the owner.

DOLLAR AMOUNT OF RETURN ON A T-BILL

Synopsis: The purchase price of a Treasury bill is less than its full face value. By calculating the return you will receive at the T-bill's maturity date, you will be able to determine how much money you earned on your investment.

Example: Suppose that you buy a 52-week T-bill for $950. On the maturity date, you receive $1,000. What is the dollar amount of return on the T-bill?

Formula:

$$\text{Face Value} - \text{Purchase Price} = \text{Dollar Amount of Return}$$

Solution: $1,000 − $950 = $50

The dollar amount of return on your T-bill would be $50.

YOU FIGURE

The maturity date of your 13-week T-bill is coming up. If you paid $1,500 for a T-bill with a face value of $2,000, what is the dollar amount of your return?

To figure out the dollar amount of return on a T-bill, just subtract the purchase price of the T-bill from the face value.

After you have determined the dollar amount of return on your T-bill, you can calculate the rate of return by dividing the dollar amount of return by the purchase price. (See **Go Figure** on page 316.)

Treasury Notes   Treasury notes are issued in $1,000 units with a maturity of between one and ten years. Interest rates for Treasury notes are slightly higher than those for Treasury bills because investors must wait longer to get their money back.

Treasury Bonds   As mentioned earlier, the Treasury Department no longer issues Treasury bonds. However, many are still in existence and may be purchased in the secondary market through a broker or other financial institution.

Treasury bonds were issued in minimum units of $1,000 with maturities that ranged from 10 to 30 years. The most common maturity is 30 years. Because of the length of time to maturity, interest rates for Treasury bonds are usually higher than those for Treasury bills or Treasury notes.

Series EE Savings Bonds   As you learned in Chapter 5, the federal government also offers savings bonds called Series EE Savings Bonds. The purchase price for a Series EE bond is one-half of its face value. For example, a $100 bond costs $50. You can redeem a savings bond anytime from 6 months to 30 years after you purchase it. You receive the amount that you paid for it plus interest. Series EE bonds can accumulate interest for up to 30 years. The interest on Series EE bonds is not taxed by state or local governments. You do not pay federal taxes on the interest until you cash in the bond.

RATE OF RETURN ON A T-BILL

Synopsis: Calculating the rate of return on your T-bill will help you determine whether the T-bill is a good addition to your investment portfolio.

Example: The dollar amount of return on your T-bill is $50. What is the rate of return on the T-bill?

Formula:

Dollar Amount of Return ÷ Purchase Price = Rate of Return

Solution: $50 ÷ $950 = .0526 or 5.26%

The rate of return on your T-bill is 5.26 percent.

YOU FIGURE

If the dollar amount of return on your T-bill is $500 and you paid $1,500 for it, what is the rate of return on your T-bill?

Series I Savings Bonds The federal government offers other types of savings bonds, too. The most popular bonds, Series I bonds, are inflation-indexed. This means that Series I bonds pay a fixed interest rate that is lower than the rate of traditional savings bonds, but they also pay a variable rate that increases with inflation.

The inflation rate is measured by the Consumer Price Index, which measures the change in cost of a fixed group of products and services such as gasoline, food, and automobiles. The inflation rate for Series I bonds is recalculated twice a year. Series I bonds pay interest for up to 30 years. If you redeem the bond less than five years from the date purchased, there is a penalty of three months of earnings.

Bonds Issued by Federal Agencies
What are agency bonds?

In addition to the securities issued by the Department of the Treasury, bonds are issued by other federal agencies as well. Agency bonds, such as the participation certificates issued by the Federal National Mortgage Association (sometimes referred to as *Fannie Mae*) and the Government National Mortgage Association (sometimes referred to as *GinnieMae),* are almost completely risk-free. However, they offer a slightly higher interest rate than securities issued by the treasury department and have an average maturity of about 12 years. Generally, their minimum denomination is $25,000. Securities issues by federal agencies have maturities ranging from 1 year to 30 years, with an average life of about 12 years. You will learn more about these types of investments in Chapter 11, which discusses real estate and other investments.

TechByte

Security in an Uncertain Time Just like paper money, stock certificates, corporate bonds, and U.S. Treasury bills have value and can be counterfeited. Since 1877, the Bureau of Engraving and Printing (BEP) has been the sole maker of U.S. currency and other financial instruments, including U.S. Treasury bills, notes, and savings bonds. The BEP has been committed to advanced security for more than a century.

@ Read about how the Bureau of Engraving and Printing maintains a secure environment and describe the technology through **persfinance07.glencoe.com**.

▲ **TEAM EFFORT** State and local governments often finance major projects, such as schools, airports, and highways, by selling municipal bonds. *Where can you buy municipal bonds?*

Bonds Issued by State and Local Governments

What are the two classifications of municipal bonds?

A **municipal bond**, sometimes called a *muni,* is a security issued by a state or local government (town, city, or county) to pay for its ongoing activities. These bonds may also pay for major projects, such as the building of airports, schools, and highways. You can buy municipal bonds directly from the government that issues them or through an account executive.

State and local government securities are classified as either general obligation bonds or revenue bonds. A general obligation bond is a bond that is backed by the full faith and credit of the government that issued it. A revenue bond is a bond that is repaid from the income generated by the project it is designed to finance. For example, a municipal sports arena would generate profits that would repay the investors who bought the bond to build the arena.

Although these bonds are relatively safe, on rare occasions, governments have defaulted, or failed to repay, their bonds. If a government defaults, investors could lose millions of dollars.

Insured Municipal Bonds

If the risk of default worries you, you might consider buying insured municipal bonds. Some states offer to guarantee payments on these selected securities. Also, three large private insurers guarantee such bonds: MBIA, Inc.; the Financial Security Assurance Corporation; and the American Municipal Bond Assurance Corporation. Because of the reduced risk of default, insured municipal securities usually carry a slightly lower interest rate than uninsured bonds.

The interest on municipal bonds may be exempt from federal taxes. Tax-exempt status depends on how the funds generated by the bonds are used. Before you invest in a particular municipal bond, find out whether the interest that you will receive from it is taxable.

Like a corporate bond, a municipal bond may be callable by the government that issued it. In most cases, the municipality that issues the bond agrees not to call it for the first ten years. If your municipal bond is not called, you can hold the bond until the maturity date or sell it to another investor.

Section 10.1 Assessment

QUICK CHECK

1. What are three characteristics of bonds?
2. Why might the government or a company decide to issue bonds?
3. What are reasons investors buy bonds?

THINK CRITICALLY

4. Discuss ways in which securities issued by state and local governments are similar to corporate bonds.

USE COMMUNICATION SKILLS

5. **Comparing Bonds** You have decided to diversify your investment portfolio. To research, compare a type of corporate bond with a type of government security.

    Write About It Write one or two paragraphs making a case for both bonds. Then write a one-paragraph summary describing which investment you think would be best for diversifying your portfolio.

SOLVE MONEY PROBLEMS

6. **Personal and Financial Goals** The county in which Marie Kilbane lives is selling bonds to finance a new storm sewer system. Marie knows that the storm sewers need replacing because her street was flooded last week. At the same time, she knows that her county is not very stable financially. She is not sure that the bonds are a good investment.

    Analyze Use what you have learned about personal satisfaction and financial goals in previous chapters to help Marie decide what to do. Should she buy the bonds to help improve her community and her own personal living conditions, or should she invest her money in another way that has a better chance of helping her meet her financial goals? Explain your reasoning.

Investing in Bonds

Determining Investment Value

How do you determine the investment value of a bond?

Before you make a decision to include bonds in your investment portfolio, you must learn how to accurately determine the investment value of a bond. By understanding bond price quotations, researching various sources of information on bonds, checking bond ratings, and calculating the yield of your bond investment, you will be able to determine whether a bond is a good investment.

Bond Price Quotations

Before you buy or sell bonds, you should become familiar with bond price quotations. Not all local newspapers contain bond price quotations, but many metropolitan newspapers publish complete information on the subject. Two other valuable sources for bond information are *The Wall Street Journal* and *Barron's*.

In a bond price quotation, the price of a bond is given as a percentage of its face value. Remember that a bond's face value is usually $1,000. To find the current market value, or price, for a bond, you must multiply the face value ($1,000) by the price quotation given in the newspaper. For example, a price quoted as "84" means that the current market value is 84 percent of the face value. Therefore, the selling price is $840 ($1,000 × 84% = $840). Purchases and sales of bonds are reported in tables. (See **Figure 10.2** on page 320.)

For government bonds, most financial publications include two price quotations: the bid price and the asked price. The bid price is the amount a seller could receive for the bond. The asked price represents the amount a buyer could pay to purchase the bond. Newspaper bond sections also provide information about interest rates, maturity dates, and yields.

Sources of Information on Bonds

As a bondholder, you should always be aware of the financial stability of the issuer of your bonds. The most important questions are:

- Will the bond be repaid at maturity?
- Will you receive interest payments until maturity?

To help answer these questions, annual reports, the Internet, business magazines, and government reports are good resources.

Focus on Reading

Read to Learn
- How to identify sources of information for selecting bond investments.

Main Idea
Knowing how to read, analyze, and calculate bond information in newspapers and annual reports can help you make wise investments.

Key Terms
- investment-grade bonds
- yield

Before You Read

PREDICT

Do you think buying government bonds would free you from watching your investments?

Figure 10.2 Corporate Bond Information

Corporate Bonds

Monday, January 10, 2005

Forty most active fixed-coupon corporate bonds

COMPANY (TICKER)	COUPON	MATURITY	LAST PRICE	LAST YIELD	*EST SPREAD	UST	EST $ VOL (000's)
General Motors Acceptance (GM)	6.750	Dec 01, 2014	97.856	7.053	278	10	245,352
General Motors (GM)	8.375	Jul 15, 2033	101.029	8.280	346	30	242,397
General Motors Acceptance (GM)	5.625	May 15, 2009	98.754	5.953	222	5	111,727
Ford Motor Credit (F)	7.000	Oct 01, 2013	103.380	6.484	221	10	104,831
Encana Holdings Finance (ECACN)	5.800	May 01, 2014	106.151	4.965	67	10	96,000
Target (TGT)	5.875	Mar 01, 2012	109.037	4.385	10	10	95,148
General Motors Acceptance (GM)	6.875	Sep 15, 2011	100.858	6.711	298	5	94,355
General Electric (GE)	5.000	Feb 01, 2013	102.338	4.648	37	10	93,211

Look at the bond quotation highlighted above. Each column includes information about this bond. Reading from left to right:

Column 1: Company (Ticker)—The name of the issuing firm is Target. Its abbreviated name is TGT.

Column 2: Coupon—This bond's current yield, or return, based on today's market price is 5.875 percent.

Column 3: Maturity—The date this bond matures is March 1, 2012.

Column 4: Last Price—The current market price of this bond at the close of trading on this day was 109.037 percent of the bond's face value.

Column 8: Estimated $ Volume—On this day, 95,148,000 bonds of this issue were traded.

Source: Reprinted by permission of *The Wall Street Journal*, January 12, 2005; permission conveyed through Copyright Clearance Center, Inc.

Bond Values

Newspaper bond quotations indicate a bond's interest, yield, and price.

What was the last price of the Target (TGT) bond?

Annual Reports Annual reports provide detailed financial information about a company and its products, services, activities, goals, and future plans. You will also find news about the company's position in its industry and the industry's major trends. A typical annual report contains the following sections:

- Letter to stockholders from the chief executive officer
- Company highlights for the year
- Detailed company review for the year
- Financial statements
- Notes to financial statements
- Independent auditors' report
- List of directors and officers
- Investor information

To receive an annual report, call, e-mail, or write to the corporation's headquarters and request one. Many large companies have toll-free telephone numbers for customers. You may also find annual reports for major corporations on the Internet or in the reference section of some large libraries.

As you read an annual report, look for signs of financial strength or weakness and ask:

- Is the firm profitable?
- Are sales increasing?
- Are long-term liabilities increasing?
- How might the company's current activities and future plans affect its ability to repay bonds?

The Internet You can access a wealth of information about bond investments on the Internet. You will find answers to many of your questions on corporate Web sites, which typically offer information about the particular company's financial performance. Some sites even include financial information from past years, which allows you to compare one year's performance with another's.

Other sites are devoted to general information about bonds. However, some bond Web sites charge a fee for their research and recommendations.

When investing in bonds, you can use the Internet to obtain price information on specific bond issues to track investments. If you live in a small town or rural area without access to newspapers that provide bond coverage, the Internet can be a good source of current bond prices. You also might visit Web sites operated by Standard & Poor's or Moody's to obtain detailed information about both corporate and government bonds.

Once your research is completed, you can even use the Internet to purchase bonds, to monitor the value of your bonds, and to manage your investments. If you trade bonds online, you might pay lower commissions than you would if you used a full-service or discount brokerage firm.

Business Magazines Another way to research possible bond investments is by reading business magazines. They provide information about the overall economy and give detailed financial data about companies that issue bonds.

Government Reports and Research You can also consult reports and research published by the government to track the nation's economy. This information is available in printed form and on the Internet. If you want to buy U.S. Treasury bills or notes, or U.S. savings bonds, check Web sites run by the Federal Reserve System. In addition, you can review information from the Securities and Exchange Commission by accessing its Web site. State and local governments will also give you information about specific municipal bond issues upon request.

As You Read

RELATE

What section of an annual report would be most important for you to read? Why?

Academic Connection

GOVERNMENT

Federal, state, and local governments issue bonds to help raise money for various activities and to relieve debt. It is the job of the Bureau of the Public Debt, a division of the U.S. Department of the Treasury, to promote the sale of U.S. Savings Bonds. *Research the Bureau of the Public Debt and write a paragraph about its origins and duties.*

Figure 10.3 Bond Ratings

Quality	Moody's	Standard & Poor's	Description
High-grade	Aaa	AAA	Bonds that are judged to be of the best quality. They have the lowest risk and the most secure interest and principal payments.
	Aa	AA	Bonds that are judged to be of high quality by all standards. Protection of principal and interest payments is only slightly less than the best.
Medium-grade	A	A	Bonds that have many favorable investment attributes and adequate security.
	Baa	BBB	Bonds that are neither highly protected nor poorly secured.
Speculative	Ba	BB	Bonds that have some risky elements. Often their protection of principal and interest payment is very moderate.
	B	B	Bonds that lack the characteristics of a desirable investment. Investors cannot be sure that interest and principal will be paid in the future.
Default	Caa	CCC	Bonds that are of poor standing. They are currently unlikely to be repaid.
	Ca	CC	Bonds that are highly risky.
	C		Moody's lowest-rated class of bonds, considered the poorest investments.
		C	Standard & Poor's rating given to bonds whose issuers have filed for bankruptcy.
		D	Bond issues that are in default, or are failing to make payments.

Source: "Ratings Defintions," standardandpoors.com, March 18, 2003.

Know Your AAABC's Smart investors check a bond's rating before they buy.

Why are these ratings important to investors?

Bond Ratings

Before you invest in a particular corporate or municipal bond, you should check its rating. This rating will give you a good idea of the quality and risk associated with that bond. Bond issues are rated or evaluated by independent rating companies. These companies assign to each bond a rating based on the financial stability of its issuer.

Two of the best-known sources of bond ratings are *Moody's Bond Survey*, published by Moody's Investors Service, Inc., and *Standard & Poor's Stock and Bond Guide*, published by Standard & Poor's. Investors rely on this information when making investment decisions. You can also find bond ratings on the Internet, in financial magazines, and at your public library.

As you can see in **Figure 10.3,** bond ratings are generally categorized from AAA (the highest—the best) to D (the lowest—the worst). The top four categories (Moody's Aaa, Aa, A, and Baa and Standard & Poor's AAA, AA, A, and BBB) include investment-grade bonds. **Investment-grade bonds** are bonds that are issued by financially stable companies or municipalities. They are considered safe investments that will provide a predictable source of income.

Bonds in the next two categories (Moody's Ba and B and Standard & Poor's BB and B) are considered riskier, or speculative. Bonds in the C and D categories may be in default or cannot continue interest payments to bondholders.

U.S. government securities are usually not rated because they are basically risk-free. Long-term municipal bonds are rated in much the same way as corporate bonds. However, short-term municipal bonds are rated differently. Standard & Poor's rates municipal bonds that have maturity dates of three years or less with the following system:

- SP-1: Strong ability to pay face value and interest (Bonds with very safe characteristics get a plus (+) sign.)
- SP-2: Satisfactory ability to pay face value and interest
- SP-3: Doubtful ability to pay face value and interest

Yield of a Bond Investment

To determine the return that a particular bond may produce, investors calculate and track its yield. The **yield** is the rate of return, usually stated as a percentage, earned by an investor who holds a bond for a certain period of time.

GO FIGURE   **FINANCIAL MATH**

CURRENT YIELD OF A BOND INVESTMENT

Synopsis: Yield is the rate of return an investor earns. By calculating the current yield of a bond, you can determine the return on a bond.

Example: Suppose that you own a $1,000 AT&T corporate bond that pays 7.5 percent interest per year. This means that each year you will receive $75 in interest ($1,000 × 7.5% = $75). Assume that the current market value of the AT&T bond is $960. What is the current yield of your bond investment?

Formula:

$$\frac{\text{Dollar Amount of Annual Interest Income}}{\text{Current Market Value}} = \text{Current Yield of a Bond}$$

Solution: $\dfrac{\$75}{\$960} = 0.078$ or 7.8%

The current yield is 7.8 percent.

YOU FIGURE

You receive $120 in interest each year on your $2,000 corporate bond. What is the current yield of your bond?

Learn to identify and understand the standard financial documents you will use in the real world.

Investigate: A Mutual Fund Account Statement

A mutual fund account statement contains the following information:

- Name of the fund
- Account number
- Beginning and ending share balance
- Activity since the last statement

Your Motive: When you invest in a mutual fund, you need to monitor how effectively your investment is growing. Periodically, you may find it necessary to sell a mutual fund and place your money in another mutual fund that has a potential to grow faster.

President's Group
P.O. Box 605, Springfield, NY 12345

Tanya Sawyer
5744 Pioneer Trail, Harrison, UT 54321

Account number: 6875430001   Account statement: DECEMBER 31, 2005

JEFFERSON MUTUAL INVESTORS FUND

Trade Date	Description	Dollar Amount	Share Price	Shares This Transaction	Share Balance
10/1/05	Beginning share balance		$34.20		721.273
10/19/05	Income dividend	$104.58	$34.20	3.058	724.331
11/11/05	Income dividend	$105.03	$33.45	3.140	727.471
11/28/05	Direct investment	$1,000.00	$34.70	28.818	756.289
12/05/05	Direct investment	$700.00	$32.26	21.699	777.988
Ending share balance					777.988

Ending value as of 12/31/05 was $25,097.89

Key Points: An account statement for a mutual fund will list your contributions and any dividends your account has earned. It will also tell you how many shares of the mutual fund you own and what the value of each is on a given day.

Find the Solutions

1. How many shares did Tanya have at the beginning of the period?
2. How is the *Shares This Transaction* amount calculated?
3. Why is the share price different for each transaction?
4. How is the ending value calculated?
5. Did the value of Tanya's account grow or decline during this time period?

The simplest way to measure a bond's yield is to calculate its current yield. To find the current yield of a bond, divide the dollar amount of annual interest income by its current market value. (See **Go Figure** on page 323 for an example.)

This calculation lets you compare the yield on a bond investment with the yields of other investment alternatives such as savings accounts, certificates of deposit, common stocks, preferred stocks, and mutual funds. If the current market value is higher than the bond's face value, the current yield decreases. If the current market value is less than the bond's face value, the current yield increases. The higher the current yield, the better the return is for the investor.

Investors may also consider the yield to maturity of a bond. This calculation takes into account the relationship between a bond's maturity value, the time to maturity, the current price, and the dollar amount of interest. Like the current yield, the yield to maturity allows you to compare returns on a bond investment with other investments, which is another strategy to track and evaluate your investment finances.

As You Read

QUESTION

Why might an investor consider purchasing Ba, B, or BB bonds?

Section 10.2 Assessment

QUICK CHECK

1. What are three pieces of information about corporate bonds that you could find in the bond section of a newspaper?
2. What information in a company's annual report would be important to an investor who is interested in its corporate bonds?
3. How could you use the Internet to help you learn about investing in bonds?

THINK CRITICALLY

4. Identify two sources for bond ratings, and explain what a bond rating tells you about a bond.

USE MATH SKILLS

5. **Bond Quotations** Every day Elise looks at the bond section of The Wall Street Journal to see if she can get a good deal on a $1,000 bond and add it to her portfolio. This morning a price quotation of 98 for TechnoWiz, a telecommunications firm, caught her interest.

 Calculate Figure out the current market value of that bond.

SOLVE MONEY PROBLEMS

6. **Calculating Bond Yields** Tom and Rika Nagata plan to retire in ten years. In 2004, they purchased three bonds:

- Two 20-year AT&T corporate bonds, each with a face value of $1,000 and 7 percent annual interest. The purchase price was $830 each. The current market value is $910 each.

- A 30-year Coca-Cola corporate bond, with a face value of $1,000 and 8.5 percent annual interest. The purchase price was $1,050. The current market value is $1,020.

Calculate To plan ahead, Tom and Rika need to know the current yield on their bonds. Use the formula in this section to calculate the current yield on their bond investments.

Section 10.3

Focus on Reading

Read to Learn
- How to identify types of mutual funds.

Main Idea
Understanding the many kinds of mutual funds will help you decide which funds might be smart investments for you.

Key Terms
- closed-end fund
- open-end fund
- net asset value (NAV)
- load fund
- no-load fund

Before You Read

PREDICT

Based on its name, what do you think is the definition of a mutual fund?

Mutual Funds

Defining Mutual Funds
What are mutual funds?

Mutual funds are an excellent choice for many investors. A mutual fund is an investment alternative in which investors pool their money to buy stocks, bonds, and other securities based on the selections of professional managers who work for an investment company. By buying shares in a mutual fund, even an investor with limited resources can own part of an entire portfolio of diverse securities. These funds can also be used for retirement accounts, such as 401(k) and 403(b) plans, individual retirement accounts (IRAs), and Roth IRAs, which are discussed in Chapter 15.

Why Investors Buy Mutual Funds
What is a key benefit of purchasing a mutual fund?

One major reason for purchasing a mutual fund is professional management. Investment companies employ professional fund managers who try to pick the best securities for their mutual fund portfolios. However, this can lead some investors to become careless. Many mutual fund investors assume that their investments will increase in value. They might not research and evaluate funds carefully before they buy. They may also neglect to keep track of the performance of the funds they own. Even the best portfolio managers make mistakes. Therefore, wise investors should monitor and review their mutual funds regularly.

Another key reason for buying a mutual fund is diversification. Mutual funds include a variety of securities, which reduces the shareholders' risk. An occasional loss from one investment in a mutual fund is usually offset by gains from other investments in the same fund. Researching and tracking the right mutual fund can provide great results with less effort than it would take to maintain such a diverse portfolio on your own.

Because of these advantages, mutual funds have become extremely popular investments. In 1970, there were 361 mutual funds. By 2003, there were more than 8,300 mutual funds, and the combined assets owned by mutual funds in the United States were worth more than $6 trillion. In the month of April 2003 alone, investors poured more than $16.1 billion into mutual fund investments. Read the material in this section to see if mutual funds are right for you.

◄ GREAT TIP Mutual funds can be wise investments for people who have limited time and limited funds to invest. *Why might a mutual fund be a good choice for such an investor?*

Types of Mutual Funds
What is the difference between a closed-end and an open-end fund?

An investment company is a firm that invests the pooled funds of many investors in various securities. The firm receives fee for this service. Mutual funds managed by investment companies are classified as either closed-end funds or open-end funds.

Closed-End Funds

About 6 percent of all mutual funds are closed-end funds offered by investment companies. A **closed-end fund** is a mutual fund with a fixed number of shares that are issued by an investment company when the fund is first organized. After all the original shares have been sold, an investor can buy shares only from another investor. Shares of closed-end funds are traded (bought and sold) on the floors of stock exchanges or in the over-the-counter market. A special section of *The Wall Street Journal* provides information about closed-end funds.

Open-End Funds

Most mutual funds are open-end funds. An **open-end fund** is a mutual fund with an unlimited number of shares that are issued and redeemed by an investment company at the investors' request. Shares of open-end funds are bought and sold on any business day by contacting the investment company that manages the mutual fund.

NET ASSET VALUE

Synopsis: Investors can buy and sell shares in an open-end mutual fund at the net asset value (NAV). The net asset value is the amount that one share of a mutual fund is worth. Investors use the net asset value formula to assess the real worth of their portfolios and make buying decisions.

Example: Beth owns shares in the New American Frontiers Mutual Fund. The value of the fund's portfolio is $124 million, and its liabilities total $4 million. If this mutual fund has 6 million shares outstanding, what is the net asset value of each of Beth's shares?

Formula:

$$\frac{\text{Value of the Fund's Portfolio} - \text{Liabilities}}{\text{Number of Shares Outstanding}} = \text{Net Asset Value}$$

Solution:

$$\frac{\$124 \text{ million} - \$4 \text{ million}}{6 \text{ million shares}} = \$20 \text{ per share}$$

The net asset value of each of Beth's shares is $20.

YOU FIGURE

You own shares in an open-end mutual fund that has a portfolio value of $220 million. Its liabilities are $6 million, and it has 8 million shares outstanding. What is the net asset value of your shares?

Net Asset Value Investors are free to buy and sell shares at the net asset value. The **net asset value (NAV)** is the amount that one share of a mutual fund is worth. To calculate the net asset value of a mutual fund, subtract the fund's liabilities from the value of the fund's portfolio, and divide the result by the number of shares outstanding. Shares outstanding are the number of shares held by all the investors.

Services If you buy shares of an open-end fund from an investment company, you gain access to a wide variety of services. These services include payroll deduction programs, automatic reinvestment programs, and automatic withdrawal programs.

Load Funds

Before investing in any mutual fund, compare its cost or fees with the cost of other types of investments. Mutual funds are classified as either load funds or no-load funds. A **load fund** (sometimes referred to as an "A" fund) is a mutual fund for which you pay a commission every time you buy or sell shares. The commission, or sales charge, can be as high as 8.5 percent. The average load charge for mutual funds is between 3 and 5 percent. The supposed advantage of a load fund is that the fund's representatives, such as account executives and financial planners, will offer advice and guidance about when shares of the fund should be bought or sold.

No-Load Funds

A **no-load fund** is a mutual fund that has no commission fee. No-load funds do not charge commissions when you buy shares because they have no salespeople. No-load funds offer the same investment opportunities as load funds. If you have a choice between a load fund and a no-load fund, and both offer the same investment opportunities, choose the no-load fund.

Management Fees and Other Charges

The investment companies that sponsor mutual funds also charge management fees. This fee is a fixed percentage of the fund's asset value. The fees generally range from 0.5 to 1.25 percent of the fund's assets.

Instead of charging investors a fee when they purchase shares, some mutual funds charge a back-end load, which is a fee that is charged for withdrawing money from the fund. Fees range from 1 to 5 percent and are based on how long you own shares of the mutual fund. A back-end load is designed to discourage early withdrawals. A 12b-1 fee is a fee that an investment company charges to help pay for the marketing and advertising of a mutual fund. It is approximately 1 percent of a fund's assets per year.

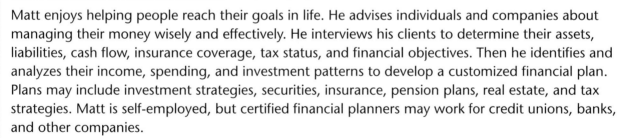

Careers in Finance

CERTIFIED FINANCIAL PLANNER **Matt Tucker**
Self-Employed

Matt enjoys helping people reach their goals in life. He advises individuals and companies about managing their money wisely and effectively. He interviews his clients to determine their assets, liabilities, cash flow, insurance coverage, tax status, and financial objectives. Then he identifies and analyzes their income, spending, and investment patterns to develop a customized financial plan. Plans may include investment strategies, securities, insurance, pension plans, real estate, and tax strategies. Matt is self-employed, but certified financial planners may work for credit unions, banks, and other companies.

SKILLS: Communication, math, economic, financial, and customer-service skills

PERSONAL TRAITS: Good listener, people-oriented, detail-oriented, trustworthy, discreet, honest, and tactful

EDUCATION: Bachelor's degree; Certified Financial Planner (CFP) or Chartered Financial Consultant (ChFC) designation

ANALYZE What sort of company might need help from a certified financial planner?

@ To learn more about career paths for certified financial planners, visit
persfinance07.glencoe.com.

WORLD-CLASS OPPORTUNITIES Investment firms that create international and global mutual funds are always looking for stocks in countries that are experiencing growth. *Why would an investor choose a fund that includes stocks from India or another such country?*

YOU SEE AN ANCIENT CULTURE. WE SEE MODERN HOMEOWNERS.

Templeton fund managers spot global investment opportunities others might miss.

TEMPLETON FUNDS In 1998, our fund managers recognized the investment opportunity presented by a mortgage company serving India's rapidly growing middle class. We purchased stock in the company, and our fund shareholders were able to get in on the ground floor of a dynamic housing boom.

Taking advantage of a global opportunity like this requires a unique perspective. One that comes from having offices in over 25 countries and on-the-ground analysts utilizing research techniques that have been honed for over 50 years. It's what's made Templeton a pioneer in global investing.

For more information on how Templeton's experience and expertise in global investing may benefit your clients' portfolio, call **1-800-FRANKLIN** or visit **franklintempleton.com**.

FRANKLIN TEMPLETON INVESTMENTS

< GAIN FROM OUR PERSPECTIVE® >

Courtesy of Franklin Templeton Investments. Copyright 2004–2005. Franklin Templeton Investments. All Rights Reserved.

As You Read

RELATE

Have you seen advertisements for mutual funds on television or the Internet? What information do these ads give you?

Categories of Mutual Funds
What are the three main groups of mutual funds?

The managers of mutual funds match their investment portfolios to the investment objectives of their customers. Usually a fund's objectives are clearly explained in its prospectus—a report that provides potential investors with detailed information about a company and its products, such as a particular mutual fund. It can be helpful to sort mutual funds into three main groups: stock mutual funds, bond mutual funds, and mixed mutual funds. Within each group, mutual funds may fall into one of many categories. Note that different sources of investment information may use different categories for the same mutual fund.

Stock Mutual Funds

Most mutual funds are part of the stock mutual funds group. Stock mutual funds are made up of stocks. These funds fall into 14 categories, which describe the fund objectives and types of stock.

Aggressive Growth Funds   Aggressive growth funds (sometimes called *capital appreciation funds*) seek to grow money rapidly by investing in stocks whose prices will increase greatly in a short period of time. Because the stocks are often risky, the market value of shares in this type of fund frequently swings between low and high.

Equity Income Funds   Equity income funds include stocks issued by companies with a long history of paying dividends. The major objective of these funds is to provide steady income. These funds are investment choices for conservative or retired investors.

Global Stock Funds   Global stock funds invest in stocks of companies throughout the world, including the United States. The managers of global funds are not restricted by national boundaries.

Growth Funds   Growth funds buy shares of companies expecting higher-than-average revenue and earnings growth. Growth funds tend to invest in larger, less risky companies that may pay some dividends. As a result, the market value of shares in a growth fund is more stable when compared to aggressive growth funds.

Growth and Income Funds   Growth and income funds purchase stocks that provide both a steady source of dividend income and the potential for growth. These funds are considered conservative because they invest in large, established companies.

Index Funds   Index funds include stocks of companies that are listed in an index such as Standard & Poor's 500 Stock Index. Fund managers select stocks issued by the companies that are included in the index. Thus, an index fund should provide about the same performance as the index. Index funds may have lower management fees.

International Funds   International funds include foreign stocks that are sold in securities markets throughout the world. That way, if the economy in one region or nation is in a decline, profits can still be earned in others. Such funds invest outside of the United States.

Large-Cap Funds   Large-cap funds generally invest in companies with market values greater than $8 billion. For most investors, a large-cap fund is a long-term holding used for retirement savings.

Mid-Cap Funds   Mid-cap funds include stocks of companies with total assets of at least $500 million. Mid-cap funds offer more security than small-cap funds and more growth potential.

Small-Cap Funds   Small-cap funds include shares of small, innovative companies with total assets of less than $500 million. They offer high growth potential but are riskier.

Micro-Cap Funds As the name suggests, micro-cap funds invest in the smallest companies. Micro-cap funds buy shares of companies with market values below $250 million. These funds tend to include start-up companies, takeover companies, or companies about to exploit new growing markets. With stocks this small, the risk is always extremely high, but the growth potential is exceptional.

Regional Funds Regional funds include stocks that are traded within one region of the world. Examples include the European region, the Latin American region, and the Pacific region.

Sector Funds Sector funds invest in companies within the same industry. Examples of sectors include health and biotechnology, science and technology, computers, and natural resources.

Utility Funds Utility funds include stocks of companies that provide utility services to their customers. Because these funds are generally safe and stable investments, they are often chosen by conservative investors, such as retired people.

Bond Mutual Funds

Mutual funds in the bond mutual funds group invest only in bonds. The bond fund categories are based on the type of bond the mutual funds purchase.

High-Yield (Junk) Bond Funds High-yield (junk) bond funds invest in high-yield, high-risk corporate bonds.

Insured Municipal Bond Funds Insured municipal bond funds include municipal bonds that provide tax-exempt income. An outside company insures them against the risk of default, or nonpayment.

Intermediate Corporate Bond Funds Intermediate corporate bond funds invest in investment-grade corporate bonds that have maturities between five and ten years.

Intermediate U.S. Bond Funds Intermediate U.S. bond funds include U.S. Treasury notes that have maturities between five and ten years.

Long-Term Corporate Bond Funds Long-term corporate bond funds buy investment-grade corporate bonds that have maturities of more than ten years.

Long-Term U.S. Bond Funds Long-term U.S. bond funds include U.S. Treasury bonds and zero-coupon bonds that have maturities of longer than ten years.

Municipal Bond Funds Municipal bond funds invest in municipal bonds that provide investors with tax-exempt interest income.

Short-Term Corporate Bond Funds Short-term corporate bond funds include investment-grade corporate bond issues that have maturities of between one and five years.

Short-Term U.S. Bond Funds Short-term U.S. bond funds invest in U.S. Treasury bills and some Treasury notes that have maturities of between one and five years.

Mixed Mutual Funds

Other mutual funds are part of a third group—mixed mutual funds. These funds invest in a mix of stocks and bonds or in various other types of securities. The funds fall into three categories: balanced funds, money-market funds, and stock/bond blend funds.

STANDARD &POOR'S

Global Financial Landscape

Standard and Poor's publishes the globally recognized S&P 500® financial index. It also gathers financial statistics, information, and news, and analyzes this data for international businesses, governments, and individuals to help them guide their financial decisions.

BRAZIL

Latin America is "Hot, hot, hot!" but it is not due to the climate. This enthusiastic description refers to the region's financial markets. Although stocks in a number of Latin countries have been riding high, Brazil has been the "darling of the investing public." Since the Brazilian president made a number of economic reforms in 2003, the stock market has soared. The easy money—over 100 percent return—may have been made already. Some stocks, however, still show promise. Brazil's Petrobras, a state-run oil giant, is a favorite, especially with the increasing cost of fuel. AmBev, the country's only Pepsi distributor, is another popular stock. For the more conservative investors, advisors suggest mutual funds as the safest way to go.

STANDARD &POOR'S **DATABYTES**

Capital	Brasilia
Population	176,464,000
Languages	Portuguese, Spanish, English, and French
Currency	real
Gross Domestic Product (GDP)	$1.38 trillion (2003 est.)
GDP per capita	$7,600

Industry: Textiles, shoes, chemicals, cement, lumber, and iron ore

Agriculture: Coffee, soybeans, wheat, rice, and beef

Exports: Transport equipment, iron ore, soybeans, footwear, and coffee

Natural Resources: Bauxite, gold, iron ore, manganese, and nickel

Think Globally
What type of mutual fund would include stocks from Brazilian companies? Would that fund be a good investment choice? Why or why not?

As You Read

QUESTION

Which of these investments, stock, bond, or mixed mutual funds, do you think would be a good investment? Why?

Balanced Funds   Balanced funds include both stocks and bonds to provide income while avoiding excessive risk. Often the percentage of stocks and bonds is stated in the fund's prospectus.

Money-Market Funds   Money-market funds invest in certificates of deposit, government securities, and other safe investments. It is relatively easy to withdraw money from a money-market fund.

Stock/Bond Blend Funds   Stock/bond blend funds invest in both stocks and bonds, enabling investors to diversify their holdings with a single fund.

Variety of Funds   A variety of mutual funds managed by one investment company is called a *family of funds*. Each mutual fund within the family has a different financial objective. For instance, one fund may be a short-term U.S. bond fund and a growth stock fund. Most investment companies make it easy for shareholders to switch among the mutual funds within a family. This allows investors to adjust their investments conveniently to suit their changing needs or to maximize their profits over time.

Section 10.3 Assessment

QUICK CHECK

1. What are the characteristics of closed-end mutual funds?
2. What is an open-end mutual fund?
3. What are three categories of funds that fall under the bond mutual fund group?

THINK CRITICALLY

4. Choose three categories of stock or bond funds in which you think you might like to invest. Explain why you think they are good investments.

USE MATH SKILLS

5. **Load Fund**   Noah is thinking about investing $1,000 in a global mutual fund. However, the fund is a load fund, which charges a commission of 8.5 percent. The investment company would deduct this fee from Noah's $1,000 before his money is invested in the fund.

Calculate and Advise   What is the dollar amount of the commission that Noah must pay the investment company to invest in this fund? Should he look for a no-load fund? Why or why not?

SOLVE MONEY PROBLEMS

6. **Fund Objectives**   Hilda wants to invest her savings in a mutual fund, but she is concerned about the risk of investing. She wants a fund that is stable and safe. Her friend Ana recommends that she consider utility funds and money-market funds. Her friend Jack says she should explore aggressive growth funds and high-yield (junk) bond funds.

Write About It   Review the characteristics of utility funds, money-market funds, aggressive growth funds, and high-yield (junk) bond funds. Write down a list of the objectives for these funds. Whose advice is best? Why?

Investing in Mutual Funds

Making an Informed Decision

What steps can you take to decide on mutual fund investments?

Which mutual funds are best for you? When should you buy or sell your shares? You will have to answer these questions for yourself. However, by considering your financial goals and consulting various sources of information on mutual funds, you will be able to determine the best approach for investing in mutual funds.

Considering Your Financial Goals

You can consider several questions when you are in the process of identifying your investment goals:

- How old are you?
- What is your family situation?
- How much risk do you want to take?
- How much money do you make now?
- How much money are you likely to make in the future?

After you have considered these factors and answered these questions, you can set your investment goals. Once you know your goals, find a mutual fund with investment objectives that match your own.

Information on Mutual Funds

You will find a great deal of information that can guide you through the decision-making process of buying or selling shares in a mutual fund. The main sources of information on mutual funds include:

- Newspapers
- Quotations
- Prospectuses
- Annual reports
- Financial publications
- Professional advice
- Internet

Newspapers   Metropolitan newspapers and financial newspapers, such as *The Wall Street Journal* and *Barron's*, provide a wealth of information.

Focus on Reading

Read to Learn
- How to discuss sources of information for selecting mutual funds.
- How to describe the methods of buying and selling mutual funds.

Main Idea
Knowing how to evaluate, buy, and sell mutual funds will enable you to invest wisely.

Key Term
- income dividends

Before You Read

PREDICT
What would be your definition of capital gain?

Figure 10.4 | **Mutual Fund Information in** *The Wall Street Journal*

How to Read the Monthly Performance Tables

Performance tables are provided by Lipper, Inc. These tables include all primary funds listed by NASDAQ. Bond performance numbers are preliminary. Though verified, the data cannot be guaranteed by Lipper or its data sources. Double-check with funds before investing.

Performance calculations assume reinvestment of all distributions and are after subtracting annual expenses. But figures do not reflect sales charges ("loads") or redemption fees.

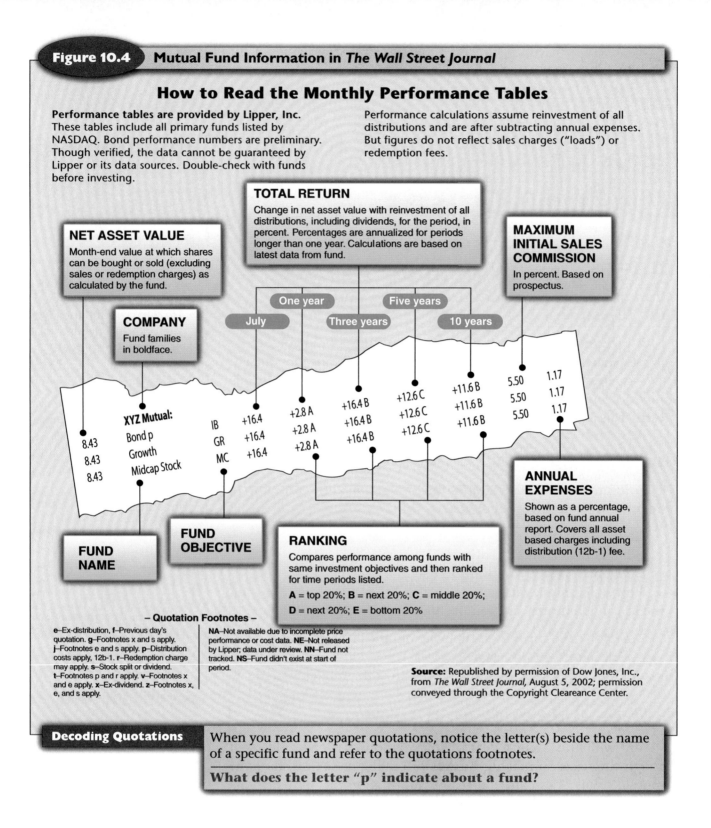

TOTAL RETURN
Change in net asset value with reinvestment of all distributions, including dividends, for the period, in percent. Percentages are annualized for periods longer than one year. Calculations are based on latest data from fund.

NET ASSET VALUE
Month-end value at which shares can be bought or sold (excluding sales or redemption charges) as calculated by the fund.

MAXIMUM INITIAL SALES COMMISSION
In percent. Based on prospectus.

COMPANY
Fund families in boldface.

One year • July • Three years • Five years • 10 years

XYZ Mutual:

8.43	Bond p	IB	+16.4	+2.8 A	+16.4 B	+12.6 C	+11.6 B	5.50	1.17
8.43	Growth	GR	+16.4	+2.8 A	+16.4 B	+12.6 C	+11.6 B	5.50	1.17
8.43	Midcap Stock	MC	+16.4	+2.8 A	+16.4 B	+12.6 C	+11.6 B	5.50	1.17

FUND NAME

FUND OBJECTIVE

ANNUAL EXPENSES
Shown as a percentage, based on fund annual report. Covers all asset based charges including distribution (12b-1) fee.

RANKING
Compares performance among funds with same investment objectives and then ranked for time periods listed.
A = top 20%; **B** = next 20%; **C** = middle 20%;
D = next 20%; **E** = bottom 20%

– Quotation Footnotes –

e–Ex-distribution. f–Previous day's quotation. g–Footnotes x and s apply. j–Footnotes e and s apply. p–Distribution costs apply, 12b-1. r–Redemption charge may apply. s–Stock split or dividend. t–Footnotes p and r apply. v–Footnotes x and e apply. x–Ex-dividend. z–Footnotes x, e, and s apply.

NA–Not available due to incomplete price performance or cost data. NE–Not released by Lipper; data under review. NN–Fund not tracked. NS–Fund didn't exist at start of period.

Decoding Quotations

When you read newspaper quotations, notice the letter(s) beside the name of a specific fund and refer to the quotations footnotes.

What does the letter "p" indicate about a fund?

Quotations As shown in **Figure 10.4,** mutual fund quotations contain information about a fund's net asset value, objective, performance, and cost. When you read mutual fund quotations, remember to note any letters beside the name of a specific fund. Then look up their meanings in the quotation footnotes.

Mutual Fund Prospectuses   After you have narrowed your search, check out the prospectuses of the mutual funds that most interest you. To get a copy of a prospectus, call, write, or e-mail the investment company that manages the mutual fund. Many investment companies have toll-free telephone numbers that you can find by calling the toll-free information number (1-800-555-1212). An investment company sponsoring a mutual fund must give a potential investor a prospectus when requested.

Read the prospectus completely before you invest. The prospectus summarizes the fund and lists any fees you will have to pay. The prospectus usually provides the following information:

- A description of the fund's objective
- The risk factor associated with the fund
- A fee table
- A description of the fund's past performance
- A description of the type of investments contained in the fund's portfolio
- Information about dividends, distributions, and taxes
- Information about the fund's management
- Information on limitations or requirements the fund must honor when choosing investments
- The process by which investors can buy or sell shares of the mutual fund
- A description of services provided to investors
- Fees for services
- Information about how often the fund's investment portfolio changes (sometimes referred to as *turnover ratio*)
- Information about how to open a mutual fund account

Mutual Fund Annual Reports   If you are a potential investor, you may request an annual report by mail, telephone, or by e-mail. When you become a shareholder, the investment company will automatically send you an annual report. Annual reports may also be posted on a company's Web site. A fund's annual report contains a letter from the president of the investment company, the fund manager, or both.

Do not forget the role of the fund manager in determining a fund's success. If a fund's present manager has been doing a good job for five years or longer, chances are that he or she will continue to perform well in the future.

The annual report contains detailed financial information about the fund's assets and liabilities. It also includes a statement of operations that describes expenses and day-to-day operating costs of the fund, a statement of changes in net assets, and a schedule of investments.

Finally, most annual reports include a letter from the fund's independent auditors. This letter backs up the accuracy of the information contained in the report.

Nest Egg
Have you ever pooled your money with friends or family to buy party supplies or donate to a charity? If you have, then you know something about mutual funds. In the world of investing and finance, a mutual fund contains a group of stocks, and you can buy a small piece of all of them by investing in the fund. Choosing a mutual fund that is right for you usually involves some careful research.

@ To continue with Task 4 of your Web-Quest project, visit persfi-nance07.glencoe.com.

Figure 10.5 **Mutual Fund Survey**

Equity Funds
MUTUAL FUND SCOREBOARD

How to use the tables

BUSINESSWEEK RATINGS Overall ratings are based on five-year, risk-adjusted returns. They are calculated by subtracting a fund's risk-of-loss factor (see RISK) from pretax total return. Category ratings are based on risk-adjusted returns of the funds in that category. The ratings;

A SUPERIOR	C– BELOW AVERAGE
B+ VERY GOOD	D POOR
B ABOVE AVERAGE	F VERY POOR
C AVERAGE	

These tables list A-rated funds. For others go to http://bwnt.businessweek.com/mutual_fund
MANAGEMENT CHANGES ⚑ indicates the fund's manager has held the job at least 10 years; a ⚐ indicates a change since Dec. 31, 2003.
S&P 500 COMPARISON The pretax total returns for the Standard & Poor's 500-stock index are as follows: 2004, 10.9%; three-year average (2002-2004), 3.6%; five-year average (2000-2004), –2.3%; 10-year average (1995-2004), 12.1%.
CATEGORY U.S. diversified funds are classified by market capitalization of the stocks in the portfolio and by the nature of those stocks.

If the average market cap is greater than $10 billion, the fund is large-cap; from $2 billion to $10 billion, mid-cap; less than $2 billion, small-cap. All-cap funds are those that don't follow a fixed-capitalization policy. Value funds are those whose stocks have price-to-earnings and price-to-book ratios lower than average for their market capitalizations. Growth funds have higher than average p-e and p-b ratios. Blend funds are those in which the ratios are about average. Hybrids mix stocks and bonds, and possibly other assets. World funds generally include U.S. stocks, foreign funds do not. Sector and regional funds are as indicated.

FUND/SYMBOL	OVERALL RATING	CATEGORY	RATING	SIZE		FEES		2004 RETURNS(%)		
	(COMPARES RISK-ADJUSTED PERFORMANCE OF EACH FUND AGAINST ALL FUNDS)	(COMPARES RISK-ADJUSTED PERFORMANCE OF EACH FUND AGAINST ALL FUNDS)		ASSETS $MIL	% CHG. 2003-2004	SALES CHARGE($)	EXPENSE RATIO(%)	PRE TAX	AFTER- TAX	YEILD
ABN AMRO MID CAP N CHTTX		**B+ Mid-cap Blend**	A	423.9	130	No load	1.34	18.9	18.3	0.0
ABN AMRO REAL ESTATE N ARFCX		**A Real Estate**	C	76.6	51	0.00*	1.37	33.4	32.2	1.9
ABA FIVE STAR LARGE CAP INSTITUTIONAL AFBEX		**C Large-cap Growth**	A	20.3	–1	No load	1.08	7.8	7.7.8	0.1
AFBA FIVE STAR USA GLOBAL INSTITUTIONAL AFGLX		**C Large-cap Growth**	A	40.0	1	No load	1.08	6.6	6.6	0.4
AIM ENERGY INV. FSTEX **(A)**		**A Natural Resources**	B	311.1	52	No load	1.76	36.6	36.6	0.0
AIM GOLD & PRECIOUS METALS INV. FGLDX **(b)** ⚐		**A Precious Metals**	C	117.8	–18	No load	1.93	–4.9	–5.0	1.1
AIM REAL ESTATE A IARAX		**A Real Estate**	B+	625.3	147	4.75	1.65	36.0	35.1	1.4
AEGIS VALUE AVALX		**A Small-cap Value**	B+	815.2	92	No load	1.50	13.5	12.7	0.0
AL FRANK VALUX		**A Mid-cap Value**	B+	244.0	103	0.00*	1.79	15.8	15.8	0.0
ALLIANCE BERNSTEIN REAL ESTATE INV. ADV. ARSYX		**A Real Estate**	B	159.3	56	No load	1.44	35.2	34.5	2.9

SALES CHARGE Many funds take this "load" out of the initial investment, and for ratings purposes, returns are reduced by these charges. Loads may be levied on withdrawls.

EXPENSE RATIO This counts expenses as a percentage of average net assets. Footnotes indicate a 12(b)-1 plan, which uses shareholder money for marketing. The average is 1.38%.

PRETAX TOTAL RETURN A fund's net gain to investors, including reinvestment of dividends and capital gains at month-end prices.

AFTERTAX TOAL RETURN Returns adjusted for U.S. taxes; treats all capital gains and long-term.

YIELD Income as a percent of net asset value.

TOP 10 STOCKS The percentage of fund assets that represents the 10 largest holdings. The higher the number, the more concentrated the fund, and the more dependent on the performance of a relatively small number of stocks.

Fund Scores

Every year *BusinessWeek* magazine publishes and rates equity funds based on performance and risk.

Besides ratings, what other types of information does this survey provide?

Financial Publications Financial magazines such as *Business-Week*, *Forbes*, *Kiplinger's Personal Finance*, and *Money* are sources of information about mutual funds. These publications provide annual surveys and rankings of mutual funds, such as the example from *BusinessWeek* magazine shown in **Figure 10.5.**

In addition to annual surveys, a number of mutual fund guide-books are available at bookstores or your local public library.

Figure 10.6 Morningstar Mutual Fund Research

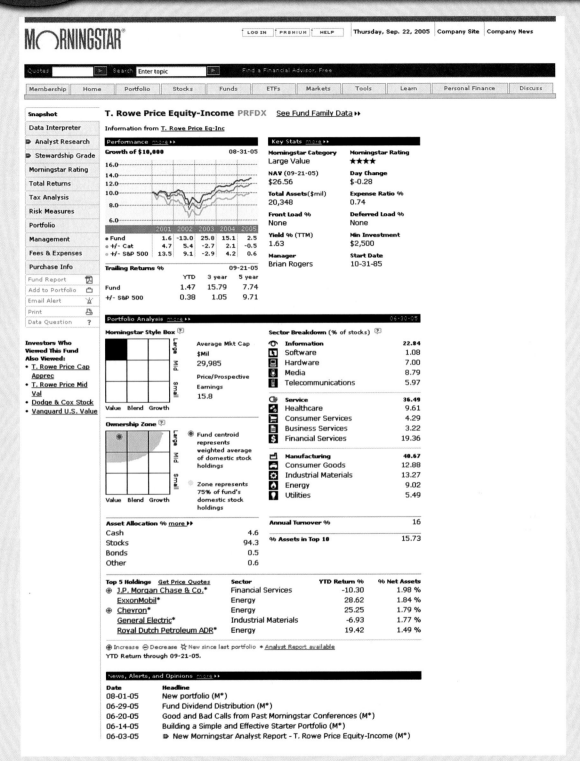

Online Information This report shows the type of information that Morningstar.com provides to an investor who is interested in the T. Rowe Price Equity Income Fund.

What can you learn by reading the section titled "Performance" at the top of the Web page?

As You Read

RELATE

Of the several listed resources available to research mutual funds, which two seem most important to you? Why?

Professional Advice Professional advisory services also provide detailed information on mutual funds (see **Figure 10.6**). Popular sources include Standard & Poor's, Lipper Analytical Services, Morningstar, Inc., Value Line, and Wiesenberger Investment Companies. In addition, various mutual fund newsletters provide financial information to subscribers for a fee. These publications are expensive, but you may be able to obtain copies of them from brokerage firms or public libraries.

Professional advisory services, such as Morningstar, also offer online research reports for mutual funds. Many investors find that the research reports provided by such companies are worth the fees they charge. The information is basically the same as that in the printed reports. However, the ability to obtain the information quickly can be a real advantage.

Internet Many investors research mutual fund investments on the Internet. You may access this information online by one of several methods. If you know the name or the four- or five-letter symbol for a fund, you may obtain current market values by using Web sites such as Yahoo! Finance. You can also get a price history and a profile.

Most investment companies that sponsor mutual funds have Web sites. These sites are another source of useful information. To obtain information, use a search engine, such as Google, and type in the name of the fund. You will find information regarding statistics about individual funds, procedures for opening an account, promotional literature, and investor services. However, investment companies want you to become a shareholder, and therefore, their Web-site material may read like a sales pitch. Look at the facts before you invest your money.

GO FIGURE   FINANCIAL MATH

CAPITAL GAIN

Synopsis: Capital gain is the amount by which a share's selling price exceeds its purchase price. Determining the capital gain that you will receive when you sell the shares of your mutual fund will tell you how much the return on your investment will be.

Example: Sani purchased shares in the Fidelity Stock Selector Fund at $17 per share. Two years later, Sani sold the shares at $19.50 per share. What was the capital gain per share on Sani's mutual fund?

Formula:

$$\text{Sales Price} - \text{Purchase Price} = \frac{\text{Capital Gain}}{\text{per Share}}$$

Solution: $19.50 − $17.00 = $2.50

The capital gain per share on Sani's mutual fund was $2.50.

YOU FIGURE

If you purchased mutual fund shares at $8.50 each and sold them for $11 per share, what would be your capital gain?

Return on Investment

What is the difference between a capital gain distribution and a capital gain?

As You Read

QUESTION

What factors influence the price of a fund's shares?

Whether you choose a closed-end fund or an open-end fund, the purpose of investing in a mutual fund is to receive income. As a mutual fund shareholder, you may gain income in one of three ways.

First, you may receive income dividends. **Income dividends** are the earnings a fund pays to shareholders. Second, you may earn capital gain distributions. Capital gain distributions are payments made to shareholders that result from the sale of securities in the fund's portfolio. Third, you may make a good return by buying shares at a low price and then selling them after the price increases.

When you sell shares in a mutual fund, the profit that results from an increase in value is referred to as a capital gain. As discussed in Chapter 8, a capital gain is the profit from the sale of an asset such as stocks, bonds, or real estate. Of course, if the price of a fund's shares goes down between the time of purchase and the time of sale, you lose money. Note the difference between a capital gain distribution and a capital gain. A capital gain distribution occurs when the fund sells securities within the fund's portfolio and distributes profits to shareholders. A capital gain occurs when the shareholder sells some of his or her shares in the mutual fund.

Taxes and Mutual Funds

How are mutual fund earnings taxed?

Income dividends, capital gain distributions, and capital gains are all taxable earnings. At the end of every year, investment companies and brokerage firms send each shareholder a statement detailing the income dividends and capital gain distributions he or she received. Usually, this information is provided on the IRS Form 1099DIV. However, the investor is responsible for maintaining clear and accurate records of the purchase and sale prices. The following are some general guidelines on how mutual fund transactions are taxed:

- Income dividends are reported along with all other dividend amounts you have received. They are taxed as regular income.
- Capital gain distributions are reported on your federal income tax return.
- Capital gains or losses that result from your selling shares in a mutual fund are reported on your federal income tax return.

You should be aware of two factors when you pay taxes on your mutual funds. First, almost all investment companies allow you to reinvest the capital gains distributions and income dividends you earn instead of receiving cash. These distributions are taxable and must be reported on your income tax return. Second, you decide when to sell your stocks or bonds.

▲ THE GOLDEN YEARS Many people use mutual funds to save for their retirement. *What is the advantage of starting to invest in a mutual fund at a young age?*

Thus, you can pick the tax year when you pay tax or deduct losses on these investments. Mutual funds, on the other hand, buy and sell securities on a regular basis during any 12-month period. Unlike investments that you manage, you have no control over when the mutual fund sells securities. Therefore, you have no control over when you are taxed on capital gain distributions.

Buying and Selling Mutual Funds
How do you buy and sell mutual funds to help you meet your financial goals?

The main reason for investing is the opportunity to make money on your investment. Mutual funds can provide investors with income dividends, capital gain distributions, and profits that result from their decision to sell their shares. Various purchase options and withdrawal options allow you to manage your mutual fund investments and profits to help you meet your financial goals.

Purchase Options

Before you buy shares in a fund, you will need to consider several different purchase options. As discussed earlier in this chapter, different types of funds are sold by different means. Closed-end funds are traded through stock exchanges, such as the New York Stock Exchange or in the over-the-counter market. You can purchase shares of an open-end fund from a brokerage firm or by contacting the investment company that sponsors the fund.

A wide variety of both no-load and load funds can also be bought from mutual fund supermarkets that are available through brokerage firms such as Charles Schwab and E*Trade. Mutual fund supermarkets offer at least two advantages. First, instead of dealing with several investment companies, you can make one toll-free phone call to buy or sell a large number of mutual funds. Second, you receive one statement from the brokerage firm instead of receiving a statement from each investment company. This statement provides the information that you need to monitor all of your investments in one place and in the same format.

When you buy shares in an open-end mutual fund from an investment company, you have several purchase options. You can choose a regular account transaction, a voluntary savings plan, a payroll deduction plan, a contractual savings plan, or a reinvestment plan.

Regular Account Transactions A regular account transaction is the most popular and least complicated way to buy shares. With this method you decide how much money to invest and when to invest it. Then you simply buy as many shares as possible.

Voluntary Savings Plans A voluntary savings plan lets you make smaller purchases than the minimum required by the regular account transaction. However, when you make your first purchase, you also must commit to making regular minimum purchases of the fund's shares. Such small monthly investments can be a great way to save for long-term objectives. For most voluntary savings plans, the minimum purchase ranges from $25 to $100.

Payroll Deduction Plans Most voluntary savings plans also offer payroll deduction plans. This means that with your approval, the investment company will deduct a certain amount from your paycheck each month and invest it in your mutual fund. Mutual fund savings plans can also be used to invest money that is contributed to tax-deferred 401(k) and 403(b) retirement plans or individual retirement accounts (IRAs).

Contractual Savings Plans Contractual savings plans require you to make regular purchases of shares over a specific period of time, usually 10 to 20 years. You will pay penalty fees if you do not make the required purchases. Financial experts and government agencies disapprove of contractual savings plans because many investors lose money with these plans.

After You Read

REACT

Which mutual fund purchasing plan do you think would be best for a young investor and for a retired investor? Why?

Reinvestment Plans You can also buy shares in an open-end fund by using the fund's reinvestment plan. With a reinvestment plan, your income dividends and capital gain distributions are automatically reinvested to buy additional shares of the fund. Most reinvestment plans allow shareholders to reinvest without having to pay additional sales charges or commissions. Reinvestment is a great way to add to your portfolio.

Withdrawal Options

If you choose to invest in mutual funds, you will also need to know how you can take your money out of a fund. You can sell shares of closed-end funds to another investor anytime you want on the stock exchange or in the over-the-counter market. Shares in an open-end fund can be sold to the investment company that sponsors the fund. In this case, provide proper notification, and the fund will send you a check for the net asset value of your shares. With some funds, you can write checks to withdraw money. If you have at least $5,000 worth of shares in a mutual fund, most funds will offer you four additional ways of withdrawing money.

Investment Period Withdrawal First, you may withdraw a certain amount each investment period until your fund has been exhausted. Typically, an investment period is three months, and most funds require investors to withdraw a minimum amount, usually $50, if the investor chooses to withdraw funds.

GO FIGURE FINANCIAL MATH

PERCENTAGE OF ASSET GROWTH WITHDRAWAL

Synopsis: Most mutual funds will allow an investor to withdraw a prearranged percentage of his or her investment's asset growth—or the amount that the investment has grown during a period.

Example: Marco invested $1,500 in a green energy mutual fund. This first period, his investment was reported to be worth $1,800. He is allowed to withdraw 60 percent of the asset growth per period. How much can he withdraw?

Formula:
Current Portfolio Value − Original Portfolio Value = Asset Growth

Asset Growth × Prearranged Percentage = Withdrawal Amount

Solution: $1,800 − $1,500 = $300

$300 × 60% or .60 = $180
Marco can withdraw $180.

YOU FIGURE

You invested $1,000 in a mutual fund specializing in cell-phone technology. During the first period, your portfolio has a value of $1,235. Your prearranged withdrawal percentage is 40 percent of net asset growth. How much can you withdraw?

Investment Period Liquidation A second option is to liquidate or "sell off" a certain number of shares each investment period. Of course the net asset value of shares in a fund varies from one period to the next. Therefore, the amount of money you receive will also vary.

Asset Growth Withdrawal A third choice lets you withdraw a prearranged percentage of your investment's asset growth, which is the amount by which your portfolio has increased in value. For example, suppose that you arrange to receive 60 percent of the asset growth of your portfolio. The asset growth of your portfolio was $800 in a particular investment period. For that period you will receive a check for $480 ($800 × 60% = $480). If the value of your portfolio does not increase, you receive no payment. Under this option, your principal (the amount of your original investment) remains untouched.

Dividend and Distribution Withdrawal A final option allows you to withdraw all income that results from income dividends and capital gains distributions earned during an investment period. Under this option, too, your principal remains untouched.

Section 10.4 Assessment

QUICK CHECK

1. What type of information does a mutual fund quotation provide to help you evaluate a fund?
2. What are three ways in which you can receive income from your mutual fund investments?
3. What are the withdrawal options that are available when selling shares in a mutual fund?

THINK CRITICALLY

4. Newspaper mutual fund quotations, financial magazines, and the Internet are three sources you might use to research a mutual fund that matches your financial goals. Decide which source you would use first, and explain why.

USE COMMUNICATION SKILLS

5. **Sales Pitch** Imagine that you are the professional manager of a large mutual fund. You are looking for investors to buy shares in your fund.

Present Prepare a flyer that will convince people to invest in your fund. Name your fund, and give as many reasons as possible why it would be a solid investment. Make your flyer appealing by using exciting language and by including pictures, charts, and graphs.

SOLVE MONEY PROBLEMS

6. **Purchase Options** Malia has invested in a mutual fund. She wants to add to her investment on a regular basis and is trying to decide which purchase option to use. Her mutual fund offers a voluntary savings plan, a contractual savings plan, and a reinvestment plan.

Analyze Analyze the advantages and disadvantages of the three purchase options available to Malia. Which purchase option would you suggest to her? Why?

CHAPTER SUMMARY

- Corporate bonds have the following characteristics: interest rates, maturity dates, and face values.
- Corporations sell bonds to raise funds for operations, expansions, or purchases.
- Investors buy bonds because they provide regular income, plus the principal must be repaid by maturity.
- Governments sell bonds for reasons similar to corporations: to fund regular activities and finance the national debt.
- Government bonds include Treasury bills, Treasury notes, and U.S. savings bonds (Series EE).

- Information on bonds is available in the financial press, corporate annual reports, bond rating reports, and online.
- Types of mutual funds include closed-end mutual funds, open-end mutual funds, load funds, and no-load funds.
- Mutual fund information is found in newspapers, annual reports, and financial publications, and through Web sites and advisors.
- Methods of buying and selling include regular account transactions, voluntary savings plans, payroll deduction plans, contractual savings plans, reinvestment plans, and withdrawal options.

Communicating Key Terms

You meet with employees who will retire in five years to discuss adding bonds to their 401(k) plans. Explain the benefits of bond investments, using as many of these key terms as possible.

- maturity date
- face value
- debenture
- mortgage bond
- convertible bond
- sinking fund
- serial bonds

- registered bond
- coupon bond
- bearer bond
- zero-coupon bond
- municipal bond
- investment-grade bonds
- yield

- closed-end fund
- open-end fund
- net asset value (NAV)
- load fund
- no-load fund
- income dividends

Reviewing Key Concepts

1. **Explain** the advantages of the call feature on bonds to corporations and to investors.
2. **Explain** why corporations may prefer to issue bonds to raise funds for their operations.
3. **Explain** how the market value of a bond is determined.
4. **List** three examples of reasons state and local governments might issue bonds.
5. **Describe** the characteristics of a municipal bond, including tax factors.
6. **Explain** the meaning of bond ratings and their impact on buying decisions.
7. **Describe** the characteristics of a closed-end, open-end, load, and no-load mutual fund.
8. **Describe** a mutual fund prospectus.
9. **Compare** the three ways you can purchase mutual funds.

History   Today mutual funds are very popular investment options. However, since their origin in 1924, they have fallen in and out of favor.

Write About It   Research and write a one-page essay on the history of mutual funds in the United States.

Bond Market Value   You own 12 20-year General Electric Capital Services corporate bonds with face values of $1,000. Their coupon rate is 7.5%. Their current yield is 5.2%.

1. **Calculate** (a) What is the current market value of one of these bonds? (b) Of the total investment? (c) If you do not have an immediate need for the cash, what would be your best course of action, sell and reinvest in some other security or hold?
2. **Compute** by using spreadsheet software to make and present these calculations.

Connect with Economics   You just inherited $4,000. You need to decide whether to invest this money in a mutual fund, pay down your credit card debt, or simply hold the money in an interest-bearing checking account to pay upcoming bills.

1. **Think Critically**   What is your current financial situation, and do you foresee a legitimate need for extra funds in the short term?
2. **Analyze**   What is the "health" of your emergency fund?

Mutual Fund Prospectus   The prospectus of a mutual fund is where you find out about the structure, fees, and "rules" of investing in the fund.

@ **Log On**   Use an Internet search engine and find Web sites of mutual fund companies, such as Fidelity and T. Rowe. Review at least one mutual fund's prospectus. Answer the following questions:

1. What are the investment orientation, risk tolerance, and goals of the managers of this fund?
2. Would you recommend this fund? Why or why not?

Newsclip: Reliable Bonds?   A bond fund is a mutual fund comprised mainly of bonds. These types of funds are usually safe investments with greater opportunity for returns.

@ **Log On**   Go to persfinance07.glencoe.com and open Chapter 10. Learn more about the different types of bond funds. Write a list of points you have learned about bond funds. Would you invest in a bond fund? Why or why not?

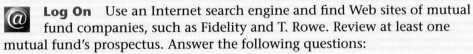

WHAT'S YOUR INVESTING IQ?

WHAT'S YOUR FINANCIAL ID?

The more you know about investing, the greater your chance for higher returns. Before you read this chapter, answer the questions below on a separate sheet of paper. After you have studied the chapter in class, take the quiz again to see how much you have learned.

1. Liquidity is the ability to _____.
   a. easily convert your financial resources into cash without a loss in value
   b. invest in any liquid substance
   c. transfer funds electronically

2. The least speculative investment listed below is _____.
   a. municipal bonds
   b. treasury bonds
   c. zero-coupon bonds

3. A mutual fund prospectus is _____.
   a. a possible date for Saturday night
   b. a report that provides potential investors with information about the fund
   c. a statement of your earnings

4. Federally tax-exempt interest can be earned on _____.
   a. an annuity
   b. a convertible bond
   c. a municipal bond

5. Investors buy junk bond funds because _____.
   a. of the possibility of a high yield
   b. municipalities always need to remove junk
   c. they usually resist fluctuations in the stock market

6. Mutual funds are popular because _____.
   a. they generally receive the highest (AAA) rating
   b. investors can choose which stocks are in their portfolio
   c. investors can acquire a diversified portfolio

Your Financial Portfolio

Evaluating Mutual Funds

Eric is looking at a mutual fund because it might earn a greater return than a CD. He used the following checklist as a way to evaluate the Pacific Sun Growth Fund, a stock mutual fund.

After evaluating Pacific Sun Growth Fund, Eric has decided that he likes the potential for a high return. He may go with the fund, even though he needs $1,000 to make his initial investment.

Pacific Sun Growth Fund

1. Name of mutual fund	**1.**	Pacific Sun Growth Fund
2. Mutual fund group and category	**2.**	Stock mutual fund/aggressive growth
3. Mutual fund's objective (Aggressive growth, moderate growth, income and safety, and income)	**3.**	Aggressive growth of capital
4. Yield in the last twelve months	**4.**	15%
5. Average return or yield for last five years	**5.**	11%
6. Average return or yield for last ten years	**6.**	18%
7. Load fees or redemption fees	**7.**	no fees
8. What is the minimum investment?	**8.**	$1,000
9. Is the fund closed to new investors?	**9.**	No
10. Morningstar rating (in stars and risk)	**10.**	Three-star rating and moderate risk

Research

Call an investment company for a prospectus of a mutual fund. You can also visit your local library and look in *Morningstar Mutual Funds* or the *Weisenberger Investment Companies Yearbook*. On a separate sheet of paper, fill in the information on the checklist to evaluate the fund.

CHAPTER 11

Real Estate and Other Investments

$ What You'll Learn

When you have completed this chapter, you will be able to:

Section 11.1
- Explain the different types of real estate investments.
- Discuss the advantages and disadvantages of real estate investments.

Section 11.2
- Identify the different types of precious metal and gem investments.
- Describe collectibles investments.
- Analyze the risks of investing in precious metals, gems, and collectibles.

Reading Strategies

To get the most out of your reading:

Predict what you will learn in this chapter.
Relate what you read to your own life.
Question what you are reading to be sure you understand.
React to what you have read.

In the **Real** World . . .

Erica Sato loves to visit thrift shops, where she looks for rare books and records that cannot be found on CDs. She has a knack for knowing what items are in demand and supplements her income by selling those things through online auctions. Erica also knows that old Disney® and Coca-Cola® items are coveted by collectors around the world. The Internet makes it easy for her to sell to people near and far, and she has built an excellent online reputation by sending items on time and in protective boxes. Collectibles can be a good investment, but Erica realizes they are more risky than other investments, so she wants to diversify her investments to include real estate and other alternatives.

As You Read *Why do you think collectibles are considered a risky investment?*

ASK STANDARD &POOR'S

Collecting

Q: Are collectible action figures a smart investment for retirement?

A: Although collecting can be an enjoyable and sometimes profitable pursuit, collectibles are not a mainstay of retirement planning. It would be best if you focused your retirement planning efforts on building a diversified portfolio that may include stock and bond investments. You could still use collectibles as a small part of your portfolio, but their returns are very unpredictable.

Ask Yourself Why are the returns on collectibles so unpredictable?

 Go to **persfinance07.glencoe.com** to complete the Standard & Poor's Financial Focus activity.

Focus on Reading

Read to Learn

- How to explain the different types of real estate investments.
- How to discuss the advantages and disadvantages of real estate investments.

Main Idea

Real estate investment opportunities vary widely. Consider the advantages and disadvantages of each type of investment opportunity.

Key Terms

- direct investment
- commercial property
- indirect investment
- syndicate
- participation certificate (PC)
- financial leverage

Before You Read

PREDICT

Why do you think so many Americans invest in real estate?

Real Estate Investment

Real Estate Investments

What is the difference between direct and indirect investment in real estate?

Real estate has always been a favorite investment for Americans. Unlike stocks and bonds, a piece of property is something you can see and touch and take pride in. However, if you are new to the real estate market, you may be confused by all the different choices you have.

Direct Real Estate Investments

Real estate investments can be direct or indirect. The owner of a **direct investment** holds legal title to the property he or she has purchased. Direct investments include single-family houses, duplexes, apartments, land, and commercial property.

A Home as an Investment   What is a home? Obviously, it is the place where you and your family live. However, owning a home can also be a good investment.

According to Mortgage Bankers Association of America, home ownership is most Americans' largest financial asset. In 2003, the market value of homes in the United States was nearly $12 trillion, which was 50 percent higher than five years earlier. Homeowners' equity, the value of a home less the amount owed on the money borrowed to purchase it, accounted for 30 percent of household wealth.

As discussed in Chapter 8, during periods of inflation, the purchasing power of your money declines. Investing your money can help you stay ahead of inflation. Owning a home is a good investment because, generally, home prices have risen steadily over the years, as shown in **Figure 11.1.** In fact, during the past 150 years, owning a home produced an average rate of return after inflation of about 2.5 percent. That is about the same rate of return you would expect from a bond.

Most homeowners have mortgages, which can provide certain tax benefits. Homeowners can report the interest charges on mortgage payments as well as property taxes as deductions on their income tax returns.

Vacation Homes   Second-home mortgages also provide tax benefits. For example, Kevin's parents own a vacation home on Fox Lake. It is a good investment because the family uses it year-round and never rents it out to others. According to the federal government, that qualifies it as a second home. Therefore, Kevin's parents can take advantage of certain tax deductions. If the parents rented out the home for more than 14 days each year, the government would consider it a rental property. As a result, any tax deductions would depend on whether Kevin's parents managed the property and on the size of their income.

Commercial Property   In addition to the vacation home on the lake, Kevin's parents also own commercial property. **Commercial property** is land and buildings that produce rental income. Kevin's parents own an apartment building that adds to their income. Other examples of commercial property include duplexes, hotels, office buildings, and stores. Most small investors favor duplexes, four-plexes, or small apartment buildings. Many investors start by purchasing a small commercial property. Then they buy larger properties as the equity in their original investment increases.

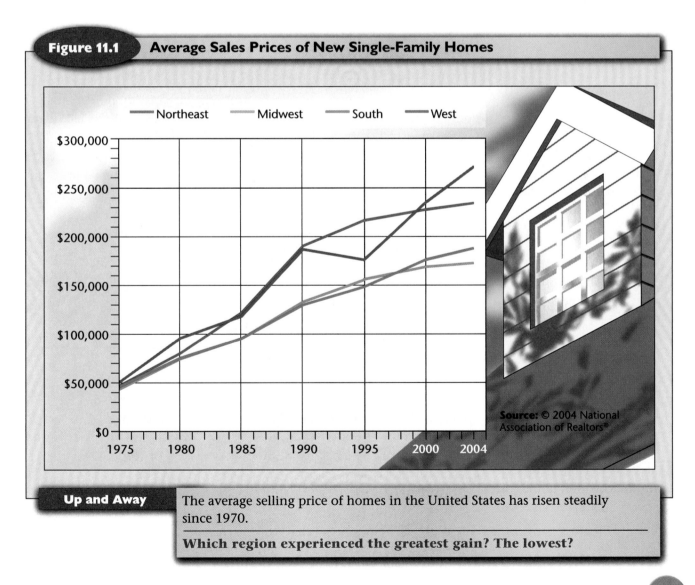

Figure 11.1   **Average Sales Prices of New Single-Family Homes**

Source: © 2004 National Association of Realtors®

Up and Away   The average selling price of homes in the United States has risen steadily since 1970.

Which region experienced the greatest gain? The lowest?

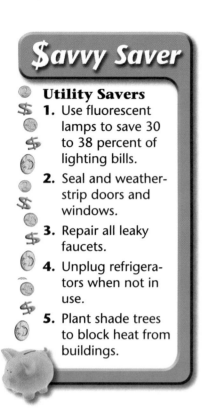
Land In 1986, Kevin's parents received quite a shock. Tax laws in the United States were rewritten so that many popular real estate investments, such as apartment buildings, lost some of their tax advantages. Owning commercial property became less appealing to some real estate investors. Many of these investors began investing in land that was ready to be developed.

Kevin's parents talked to an investment banker before they purchased land. She told them that while land investments often promise tremendous gains, they also pose enormous risks. If construction in general slowed or business activity declined, Kevin's parents might not be able to sell their property at a profit. Even worse, they might not be able to get the price that they had paid for it. Furthermore, the banker reminded them that unlike an apartment building, land in urban areas usually does not produce any income.

The banker also cautioned Kevin's parents about buying land and then dividing it into smaller lots to build single-family houses. They must be certain that water, sewers, and other utilities would be available. Otherwise, they would have to supply those services. The most common and least expensive way to obtain water and sewer service is to connect to existing services in a nearby city or town.

Indirect Real Estate Investments

Suppose that you want to invest in real estate, but you do not have enough money to purchase property on your own. The answer may be an indirect real estate investment. An **indirect investment** is an investment in which a trustee is appointed to hold legal title to the property on behalf of an investor or group of investors. Indirect investments include real estate syndicates, real estate investment trusts, high-risk mortgages, and participation certificates.

▶ **INVESTMENT IN LEISURE** A family vacation home can be part of a sensible investment strategy. *Why are vacation homes smart investments?*

Real Estate Syndicates or Limited Partnerships A **syndicate** is a temporary association of individuals or business firms organized to perform a task that requires a large amount of funds. A real estate syndicate invests in real estate. A syndicate may be organized as a corporation or as a trust. Most commonly, however, a syndicate is organized as a limited partnership.

Here is how a limited partnership works: A general partner, who takes complete responsibility for all of the partnership's liabilities, forms the partnership. The general partner then sells participation units, or shares, to a number of limited partners, or investors. Suppose that you decide to join the syndicate. As a limited partner, you are liable for only the amount of money you have invested, perhaps $5,000 or $10,000. This limited liability is an important condition of a real estate syndicate because the syndicate's mortgage debt may be more than your personal net worth or that of the other limited partners.

A real estate syndicate offers you and the other partners a variety of benefits. For example, if the syndicate purchases several types of property, your investment will be diversified. That is, you will be part owner of different types of property. In addition, the property owned by the syndicate is professionally managed. You do not need to care for it yourself.

At one time, people would join a real estate syndicate to create a tax shelter, which is a legal arrangement to take advantage of income tax deductions. However, the Tax Reform Act of 1986 limits the tax advantages available to syndicate investors. For example, investors can no longer use losses from their syndicate investments to offset, or reduce, their income from other sources. The 1986 law limits deductions for interest and for depreciation, which is the cost of general wear and tear. It also raised the tax on capital gains.

Real Estate Investment Trusts (REITs) Joshua's grandfather gave him $3,000 for graduation. Joshua would like to invest that money in real estate, but realizes that he cannot buy an apartment building or condominium for that much money. One real estate investment choice Joshua could consider is a real estate investment trust (REIT). A REIT works much like a mutual fund. Like mutual funds, REITs combine money from many investors. However, while mutual funds are investments in stocks, bonds, and other securities, REITs are investments of the investors' money in real estate or in construction or mortgage loans. Shares in REITs are traded on stock exchanges or on the over-the-counter market.

There are three types of REITs: equity, mortgage, and hybrid. If you choose an equity REIT, your money will be invested in properties. Choosing a mortgage REIT will put your money to work financing construction loans and mortgages on developed properties. If you want to combine the investment goals of equity and mortgage REITs, you can choose a hybrid REIT.

As You Read

RELATE

Do you know anyone who owns a home or invests in real estate?

Learn to identify and understand the standard financial documents you will use in the real world.

Investigate: A County Real Estate Valuation

A county real estate valuation contains the following information:

- Property parcel ID number
- Description of the property
- Appraised value
- Assessed value

Your Motive: Real estate property, such as a house or land, is taxed based on its value. The higher the value, the more taxes you pay to the local government. You will need to make sure that your property is valued correctly so that you do not pay excessive taxes.

Parcel Number:	30-05655
Owner:	Milo Lucky
Property Address:	6731 Williamsburg Circle
Legal Description:	Williamsburg Colony Phase C Lot 73
Land Description:	100 ft. by 200 ft.

Description of Primary Building(s)

Colonial frame 2.0 story 2,251 sq. ft. built about 1988 with 8 total rooms with 4 bedrooms with 2 bathrooms with 1 half bath with full basement with no attic with 0 car basement garage with 1 fireplace.

Description OBY Building(s) Value	Proposed 2007 Appraised Value		2007 Assessed Value	
WD1: Wood Deck $1,330	Land:	$42,900	Total:	$205,770
	Building(s):	$162,870	Land:	$15,020
	Total:	$205,770	Building(s):	$57,010
			Total:	$72,020

Key Points: The county government assesses the value of real estate property to determine how much tax should be paid for the property. County auditors review the value of recent real estate purchases and any improvements made to the property. The auditors then determine an appraised value for the property and an assessed value. The assessed value determines the amount of tax. Then a statement is sent to the property owner explaining the valuation.

Find the Solutions

1. What is the parcel ID number?
2. How many square feet of interior space does the building have?
3. What style is the building?
4. What is the appraised value of the wood deck?
5. What is the total square footage of the lot?

According to federal government regulations, REITs are required to:

- Distribute at least 90 percent of their net annual earnings to shareholders.
- Avoid investing in risky, short-term real estate holdings in the hope of selling them for quick profits.
- Hire independent real estate professionals to carry out certain management activities.
- Have at least 100 shareholders, with no more than half the shares owned by five or fewer people.

If you are interested in finding out more about REITs, you can contact the National Association of Real Estate Investment Trusts.

High-Risk Mortgages Some investors accept high risk in exchange for possible profits. For example, Mr. Moy is a wealthy investor who purchases high-risk mortgages and other debt contracts. Because he is wealthy, Mr. Moy is willing to take risks that financial institutions, such as banks and savings and loan associations, will not. For example, Mr. Moy might purchase the mortgage on a property that is not in demand because the title to the property may not be legally clear or insurable. Because of such risks, Mr. Moy and other similar investors might receive a high rate of return on their investments. Even though Mr. Moy is not guaranteed a high rate of return, he hopes that the demand for his property will increase so he will make a handsome profit in the future. On the other hand, if the demand does not increase, Mr. Moy may lose most or all of his investment.

Participation Certificates Unlike Mr. Moy, investors cannot afford to take such risks with their money. If you are looking for a risk-free real estate investment, then participation certificates might be a good choice for you. A **participation certificate (PC)** is an investment in a group of mortgages that have been purchased by a government agency. Because the investment is made in a group of mortgages, it is considered a mutual fund. You can buy participation certificates from these federal agencies:

- Government National Mortgage Association (Ginnie Mae)
- Federal Home Loan Mortgage Corporation (Freddie Mac)
- Federal National Mortgage Association (Fannie Mae)
- Student Loan Marketing Association (Sallie Mae)

▲ PART OF SOMETHING BIG Giant corporate complexes can cost millions of dollars to build and maintain. *Do you need to be extremely wealthy to invest in large commercial properties? Why or why not?*

As You Read

QUESTION

Why do people join limited partnerships and/or REITs?

A few states also issue participation certificates. You can purchase PCs from the State of New York Mortgage Agency (Sonny Mae) and the New England Education Loan Marketing Corporation (Nellie Mae).

Agencies with close ties to the federal government guarantee Maes and Macs. The PCs they issue are as secure as U.S. Treasury bonds and notes. You can invest as little as $1,000 to buy shares. Each month, you can receive a check for the principal and interest or reinvest the profits.

Real Estate Investment: Pros and Cons

What should you know when considering real estate investment?

Before you invest in real estate, you will want to weigh the advantages and disadvantages.

Advantages of Real Estate Investments

There are several advantages enjoyed by certain types of real estate investments:

Hedge Against Inflation When inflation rises, your purchasing power decreases. Both direct and indirect investments in areas such as real estate are wise because they provide some protection against inflation. Historically, real estate continues to increase in value or at least hold its value, thus protecting investors from declining purchasing power.

Easy Entry By making an indirect investment in a real estate syndicate, you can easily become a part owner of an apartment building or a shopping center. By combining your money with that of other investors, you can purchase commercial property.

Limited Financial Liability An indirect investment in a real estate syndicate allows you to be a limited partner. That means you are not liable, or responsible, for losses beyond your original investment. This advantage is important if the syndicate is investing in a risky venture.

Financial Leverage **Financial leverage** is the use of borrowed funds for direct investment purposes. By using borrowed money, you can purchase more expensive property. If property values and incomes are rising, this can be an advantage.

For example, suppose that Deborah buys a building for $100,000 with no borrowed funds. She then sells the building for $120,000. Deborah's $20,000 profit equals a 20 percent return on her $100,000 investment ($20,000 ÷ $100,000 = 0.20 or 20%).

On the other hand, suppose that Deborah invested just $10,000 of her own money and had a $90,000 mortgage with an interest rate of 8.5 percent. After three years, she sells the property for $120,000, with a profit of $7,721 ($20,000 profit − $12,279 in interest = $7,721). Her profit would represent a 77 percent return on her $10,000 investment ($7,721 ÷ $10,000 = 0.7721 or 77.21%).

WebQuest

Nest Egg
Is it a waste of time for a young person to think about investing in real estate? Buying a home is just for married couples, right? Not necessarily. You can make owning real estate a part of your plan for the future starting right now. Learn about the basic steps for investing in real estate.

To continue with Task 5 of your WebQuest project, visit persfinance07.glencoe.com.

Disadvantages of Real Estate Investments

Unfortunately, investors such as Deborah cannot be certain that their real estate investments will pay off. There are several possible disadvantages to real estate investments:

Illiquidity Real estate is an illiquid investment, which means that it cannot be easily converted into cash without a loss in value. It may take months or even years to sell commercial property or shares in a limited partnership.

Declining Property Values As discussed earlier, real estate investments usually offer some protection against inflation. However, when interest rates fall, or if the economy is in a decline, the value of real estate investments may decrease. If you own property, you may have to make the difficult decision to sell your property for less than you paid for it and accept a loss.

Lack of Diversification Because real estate is expensive, many investors can afford only one or two properties. Subsequently, it may be difficult to build a diversified real estate investment portfolio. Keep in mind, however, that REITs, PCs, and syndicates do offer various levels of diversification.

Careers in Finance

COMMERCIAL PROPERTY MANAGER   **Yvonne Inger**
Hartman Management

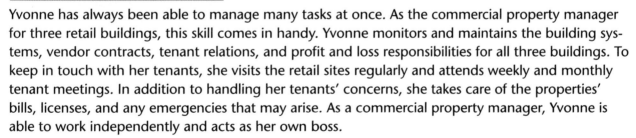

Yvonne has always been able to manage many tasks at once. As the commercial property manager for three retail buildings, this skill comes in handy. Yvonne monitors and maintains the building systems, vendor contracts, tenant relations, and profit and loss responsibilities for all three buildings. To keep in touch with her tenants, she visits the retail sites regularly and attends weekly and monthly tenant meetings. In addition to handling her tenants' concerns, she takes care of the properties' bills, licenses, and any emergencies that may arise. As a commercial property manager, Yvonne is able to work independently and acts as her own boss.

SKILLS: Communication, math, management, customer-service, organization, and time-management skills

PERSONAL TRAITS: Discretion, good judgment, and tactfulness

EDUCATION: Bachelor's degree or master's degree in business administration, finance, administration, or related fields

ANALYZE How might a skilled commercial property manager affect the value of the property?

@ To learn more about career paths for commercial property managers, visit persfinance07.glencoe.com.

Lack of a Tax Shelter   In the past, real estate syndicates were tax shelters for investors. However, the Tax Reform Act of 1986 eliminated that advantage. Syndicate investors cannot deduct real estate losses from the income they receive through other sources, such as wages, dividends, and interest.

Management Problems   When you invest in REITs, syndicates, or PCs, property management is provided as a part of your investment. When you invest in mortgages, property management is not an issue. However, when you buy your own properties, you must manage them. That means that you are responsible for such things as finding reliable tenants, replacing worn carpeting, and fixing the furnace. Property management can be a full-time job, and many investors are not willing to take on that much responsibility.

Investment Options

If you consider all the advantages and disadvantages of investing in real estate and you believe it is too risky or too complicated, you might consider other tangible investments. Gold and other precious metals, gems, and collectibles are options that some investors choose. However, these investments carry risk with the reward, as discussed in the next section.

Section 11.1 Assessment

QUICK CHECK

1. What are examples of direct and indirect real estate investments?
2. What are the advantages of indirect real estate investments?
3. What are the disadvantages of direct and indirect real estate investments?

THINK CRITICALLY

4. Identify some similarities and differences among syndicates, REITs, and PCs.

USE COMMUNICATION SKILLS

5. **Selling Participation Certificates**   PCs are considered risk-free investments. This makes them appealing to investors who are looking for protection against inflation but who do not have a lot of money to invest. How would you interest potential investors in these certificates?

Write About It   Write a persuasive ad that points out the advantages of participation certificates. Be sure to include information that highlights the risk-free nature of these investments.

SOLVE MONEY PROBLEMS

6. **Diversification**   Teresa has been working as an advertising copywriter for five years. She has been saving money and now has $10,000 to invest in real estate. Teresa wants to make sure that her real estate investments will be diversified, not too risky, and easy for her to manage.

Analyze   Give Teresa some advice about the different types of real estate investments that would best meet her investment goals.

Precious Metals, Gems, and Collectibles

Gold

Why do people invest in gold and other precious metals?

Precious metals include such valuable ores as gold, platinum, and silver. Many people invest their money in precious metals as a hedge, or protection, against inflation.

When Mark graduated from high school, his grandfather gave him a gold pocket watch. Ever since, Mark has been fascinated by gold and has wanted to own more of it. If you are interested in purchasing gold, you have several choices, as shown in **Figure 11.2** on page 362.

The price of gold rises when people believe that war, political unrest, or inflation may be just around the corner. As international tensions ease or the political situation stabilizes, the price of gold falls. In January 2005, the price of gold was about $425 per ounce. **Figure 11.3** on page 363 shows how the price of gold rose and fell from 1979 to 2003.

Silver, Platinum, Palladium, and Rhodium

What is one disadvantage of investing in a precious metal such as platinum?

Other precious metals that rise in value during times of political or economic trouble are silver, platinum, palladium, and rhodium. Silver prices have ranged from a historic low of 24.25 cents an ounce in 1932 to more than $50 an ounce in early 1980. In January 2005, the price of silver was about $6.80 an ounce.

Platinum, palladium, and rhodium, which are three lesser-known precious metals, are also popular investments. All of these metals have industrial uses, particularly in automobile production. In January 2005, platinum sold for about $877 an ounce, palladium for about $200 an ounce, and rhodium for about $1,300 an ounce.

Focus on Reading

Read to Learn

- How to identify the different types of precious metal and gem investments.
- How to describe collectibles investments.
- How to analyze the risks of investing in precious metals, gems, and collectibles.

Main Idea

Understanding the risks and rewards of investing in precious metals, gems, and collectibles will help you build a sound, diversified portfolio.

Key Terms

- precious metals
- precious gems
- collectibles

Before You Read

PREDICT

Do you think investments in precious metals, gems, or collectibles are risky or safe?

Figure 11.2   **Investing in Gold**

When the economy weakens or political unrest develops, some people believe that gold is the safest investment they can make. Investments in gold can take many forms.

1 **Bullion** You can purchase gold bullion, which is offered in bars and wafers, from dealers of precious metals and from banks. The seller's commission can range from 1 to 8 percent. If you do not store the gold with the dealer, you must have it reassayed (tested for quality) before you can resell it.

2 **Coins** Gold coins represent a simple way to invest in this precious metal. Most coin dealers require a minimum order of ten coins and will charge you a seller's commission of at least 2 percent.

3 **Stocks** You can diversify your investment portfolio by purchasing common stock in gold mining companies. When the economy is healthy, the price of gold stocks tends to fall while the value of other investments rises. When the economy falters so that traditional investments lose value, gold stocks tend to rise in value.

Storing precious metals can be tricky. Twenty thousand dollars' worth of gold, for example, is about the size of a thick paperback book. That same amount in silver weighs more than 200 pounds and could require several safe-deposit boxes for storage space.

In addition, remember that while stocks, bonds, and other interest-bearing investments are earning money for you, precious metals sit in vaults, earning nothing. In order to make a profit when you sell precious metals, you must correctly predict the behavior of the market and sell the metals when their value is higher than what you paid for them.

Precious Gems

What is one of the advantages of investing in precious gems?

When the Queen of England opens the British Parliament, she wears a crown and carries a scepter, both of which are covered with diamonds, rubies, sapphires, and other glittering gems. As soon as the ceremony is over, the royal ornaments are quickly locked up again in the Jewel House at the Tower of London.

Throughout world history people have valued the precious gems that lie below the earth's surface. **Precious gems** are rough mineral deposits (usually crystals) that are dug from the earth by miners and then cut and shaped into brilliant jewels. These gems include diamonds, sapphires, rubies, and emeralds. They appeal to investors because of their small size, ease of storage, great durability, and their potential as a protection against inflation.

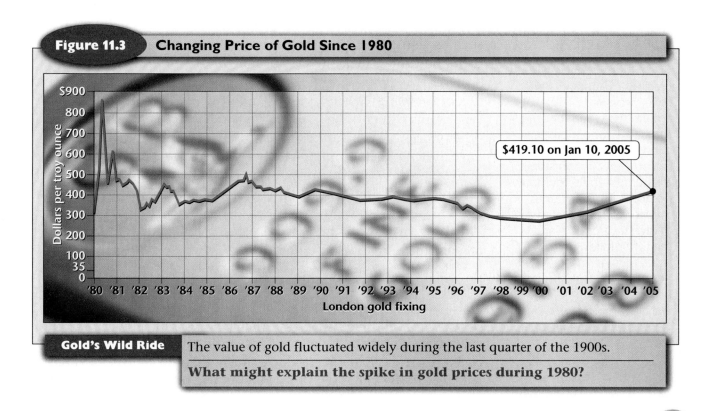

Figure 11.3   Changing Price of Gold Since 1980

$419.10 on Jan 10, 2005

London gold fixing

Gold's Wild Ride   The value of gold fluctuated widely during the last quarter of the 1900s.

What might explain the spike in gold prices during 1980?

▶ **CROWN JEWELS**

Throughout history, precious gems have been associated with royalty. *Why do you think diamonds, rubies, and other precious stones fascinate people?*

GEOGRAPHY

Precious metals and stones have fascinated people around the world for centuries. Billions of dollars change hands each year as valuable metals and stones are bought and sold. Many people invest in precious metals and stones as a way of diversifying their investment portfolios. *Print a world map and mark the places where gold, silver, platinum, diamonds, emeralds, and rubies are found. Use a color key to identify each precious metal and gem on the map.*

The inflation that occurred in the United States during the 1970s prompted investors to put more of their money into tangible assets such as gemstones. The result was a 40-fold increase in the price of diamonds. A few lucky investors made fortunes during that time.

Whether you are buying precious gems to store in a safe-deposit box or to wear as jewelry, keep in mind the risks associated with this type of investment. First, you cannot easily convert diamonds and other precious gems into cash. Also, as a beginning investor, you may have difficulty determining whether the gems you are purchasing are of high quality. Political unrest in gem-producing countries can affect supply and pricing. In addition, you will likely have to buy your gems at higher retail prices and sell them at lower wholesale prices. The difference is usually 10 to 15 percent and sometimes as high as 50 percent.

The best way to know exactly what you are getting in an expensive precious gem is to have the stone certified by an independent geological laboratory, such as the Gemological Institute of America. The certificate should list the stone's characteristics, including its weight, color, clarity, and quality of cut. The grading of gems, however, is not an exact science. Experiments have shown that the same stone submitted twice to the same laboratory may get two different ratings.

Despite the attraction of precious metals and gems, the investment risks are sizable. The primary risk is the great fluctuation in prices, which can be influenced by global, economic, financial, and political factors. For example, in 1980, world events caused the prices of precious metals and gems to shoot up. Investors bought gold for as much as $850 an ounce, and a one-carat diamond for $62,000.

As You Read

RELATE

Would you purchase precious metals? Why or why not?

Global Financial Landscape

STANDARD &POOR'S

Standard and Poor's publishes the globally recognized S&P 500® financial index. It also gathers financial statistics, information, and news, and analyzes this data for international businesses, governments, and individuals to help them guide their financial decisions.

SOUTH AFRICA

Diamonds, one of the oldest substances on Earth, are today's most popular gem. They were once used to guard against "evil spirits" but have since become a token of everlasting love. They are used to commemorate engagements, April birthdays, and 75th wedding anniversaries. Diamonds are mined in about 25 countries and on every continent but Europe and Antarctica.

One country that is well-known for its diamond mining is South Africa. Diamonds were discovered there in 1867. News spread quickly, and thousands of prospectors staked their claims and began to mine South Africa's diamond fields. This spurred economic growth in South Africa. Some of the world's most beautiful and famous diamonds were found in South Africa. In fact, the world's largest diamond was found in 1905 among the rich deposits of South Africa. It weighed 3,106.75 carats. When cut, the stone produced 105 gems, including the famous 530.20-carat "Star of Africa."

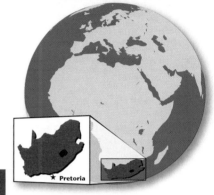

STANDARD &POOR'S

DATABYTES

Capital	Pretoria (administrative capital), Bloemfontein (judicial capital), and Capetown (legislative capital)
Population	44,024,000
Languages	Afrikaans, English, Ndebele, Pedi, Sotho, Swazi, Tsonga, Tswana, Venda, Xhosa, and Zulu
Currency	rand
Gross Domestic Product (GDP)	$456.7 billion (2003 est.)
GDP per capita	$10,700 (2003 est.)

Industry: Mining, automobile assembly, metalworking, and machinery

Agriculture: Corn, wheat, sugarcane, fruits, and beef

Exports: Gold, diamonds, platinum, other metals and minerals, and machinery and equipment

Natural Resources: Gold, diamonds, chromium, antimony, coal, and iron ore

Think Globally

With technology making it possible to manufacture imitation diamonds, do you think real diamonds will continue to be valued highly? Why or why not?

Collectibles

What are collectibles?

Collectibles are another type of investment. **Collectibles** include rare coins, works of art, antiques, stamps, rare books, comic books, sports memorabilia, rugs, ceramics, paintings, and other items that appeal to collectors and investors. Each of these items offers the knowledgeable collector or investor both pleasure and an opportunity for profit. Many collectors have been surprised to discover that items they bought for their own enjoyment have increased greatly in value while they owned them.

For example, when Hannah was a little girl, her Aunt Sylvia bought her two collectible dolls. As she grew up, Hannah received more dolls as gifts and also bought some of her own. She now has an extensive collection of over 100 different dolls. Although Hannah never really thought of her dolls as an investment, she recently discovered that several of them are worth $500 each, which is more than three times what she paid for them.

▲ **UNEXPECTED RICHES** Collecting can be an enjoyable and sometimes profitable pastime. *Are collectibles a wise investment?*

▲ **CYBER AUCTIONS** When buying or selling collectibles through online auction sites, do your research on quality and current values. *What are some advantages and disadvantages of collecting via the Internet?*

Collectibles on the Internet

Before the era of the World Wide Web, finding items to add to your collections could be very time-consuming. You would have to pore over collectors' trade magazines to research the value of items you wished to buy. Then you would have to go to shows, sometimes far away, where collectors met to buy and sell their merchandise.

That process has changed. The Internet has made buying and selling collectibles efficient and convenient, and the number of Web sites for collectors has exploded. In 1999, when Guernsey's Auction House offered Mark McGwire's 70th home run baseball to bidders, they opened the bidding process to online buyers as well. Although the baseball went to an anonymous telephone bidder (later known to be the famed comic book artist Todd McFarlane) for $3 million, the use of the Internet as an auction site was firmly established.

It is easy to see why the Internet appeals to collectors. As a buyer, you can search for items to add to your collection with a few keystrokes, and sellers can reach people all around the world. Prices are not necessarily lower on the Internet, but comparison shopping is easier, and most sites do not charge a buyer's commission.

Of course, collecting through the Internet has its drawbacks. As an online buyer, you cannot assess a dealer face-to-face or examine the objects for flaws or trademarks. Furthermore, fraud is an ever-present danger.

Common CENTS

Collectible Gifts
Suggest to your family and friends that you make gifts for each other instead of buying them for special days and holidays. You will all save money, and your gifts may become family heirlooms. *How much money do you think you could save each year by making gifts instead of buying them?*

Figure 11.4 | **Stocks for the Long Term**

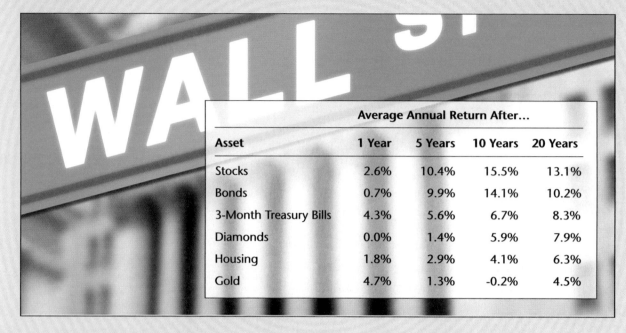

Asset	Average Annual Return After...			
	1 Year	5 Years	10 Years	20 Years
Stocks	2.6%	10.4%	15.5%	13.1%
Bonds	0.7%	9.9%	14.1%	10.2%
3-Month Treasury Bills	4.3%	5.6%	6.7%	8.3%
Diamonds	0.0%	1.4%	5.9%	7.9%
Housing	1.8%	2.9%	4.1%	6.3%
Gold	4.7%	1.3%	-0.2%	4.5%

Source: Sumner N. Levine, ed., *Business and Investment Almanac*, 1995 (Burr Ridge, IL: Richard D. Irwin, 1996), p. 249. © Sumner N. Levine, 1995.

Best Investments
According to this table, stocks and bonds offered investors the highest average annual return over the long term.

After one year, which asset provided the highest average annual return? After five years?

Let the Collector Beware

Collecting can be a satisfying hobby and a good investment. Nevertheless, a wise collector must always be alert for scams—on or off the Internet. For example, how do you know that the fielder's glove you bought was actually signed by Mickey Mantle? Could your Civil War–era postage stamps be counterfeit? Is that Barbie® doll, Lionel® locomotive, or Darth Vader™ action figure really as rare and valuable as you have been told?

When you trade collectibles, be aware that some online auction and exchange sites are more reliable than others. According to figures from Internet Fraud Watch, which is sponsored by the National Consumers League (NCL), 76 percent of the fraud complaints it received during the period between January and June of 2004 were related to online auctions. Consumers can report suspected Internet fraud by calling the NCL Fraud Hotline.

The safest way to steer clear of collectibles-related fraud is to learn everything you can about the items you collect and to buy and sell only with reputable dealers and auction Web sites.

As You Read

QUESTION

Take a mental inventory of your keepsakes and favorite possessions. Do you own any items that might be considered collectibles in the future?

Remember that collectibles do not offer interest or dividends. Also, you may have a hard time selling items at a good price on short notice. If your collection grows significantly in value, you will have to purchase insurance against damage and theft.

Planning Investments

How do you choose the best types of investments?

Investments such as stocks and bonds may not be very interesting or exciting, but as you can see in **Figure 11.4,** they have proven to be the most stable types of investments in the long run. Investing in collectibles may seem interesting, but it may not be the best way for you to achieve your financial goals.

Wise planning is the best way to get the most out of your investments. Be sure to research the types of investments that are available so you can make an informed decision. Weigh the advantages and disadvantages of each type of investment. Ask yourself how much risk and responsibility you are willing to assume. By taking these steps, you will be able to make a decision that is best for your financial future.

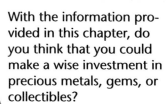

After You Read

REACT

With the information provided in this chapter, do you think that you could make a wise investment in precious metals, gems, or collectibles?

Section 11.2 Assessment

QUICK CHECK

1. What are the risks of investing in precious metals?
2. Why do precious gems appeal to investors?
3. How has the Internet increased the risks of investing in collectibles?

THINK CRITICALLY

4. Describe two different scenarios: one that causes the price of diamonds to rise and one that causes the price to fall.

USE MATH SKILLS

5. **Golden Investment** In 1978, Raul bought 50 ounces of gold for $1,750 as protection against rising inflation. He sold half the gold in 1980 at a price of $800 an ounce. Raul sold the other half in 1982 when the price was $400 an ounce.

Calculate What was Raul's profit in 1980 and in 1982? What would Raul's profit have been if he had sold all of his gold in 1980?

SOLVE MONEY PROBLEMS

6. **Evaluating an Inheritance** Samantha inherited a diamond-and-ruby necklace from her grandmother's estate. Unfortunately, the settings for the stones are damaged beyond repair. Samantha is trying to decide what to do with her inheritance.

Analyze Create a strategy that will help Samantha determine the value of her inheritance and how she might increase that value.

CHAPTER SUMMARY

- The owner of a direct investment in real estate directly holds the legal title to the residential or commercial property and is responsible for its maintenance and management. An indirect investment is similar to investing in mutual funds. A group of investors buys property, and legal title is held by a trustee. Real estate syndicates, limited partnerships, and real estate investment trusts (REITs) are examples of indirect investments.
- The advantages of investments (syndicates and REITs) in real estate are: use as a hedge against inflation, ease of entering the market, and limited liability.

Lack of liquidity and diversification, risk of declining property values, fewer tax incentives, and potential management problems are disadvantages.
- Precious metals include gold, silver, platinum, palladium, and rhodium. Precious gems include diamonds, sapphires, rubies, and emeralds.
- Collectibles include rare coins, works of art, antiques, stamps, rare books, comic books, sports memorabilia, rugs, ceramics, and other items.
- The value of precious metals and gems can fluctuate greatly, making them a risky investment. It is also difficult to predict the value of collectibles.

Communicating Key Terms

Your friend, Jeremiah, is the sole heir of a recently deceased relative. Jeremiah has discovered that his relative had invested in several REITs and Ginnie Mae certificates. Plus, Jeremiah found two diamond rings, as well as a collection of 40 Hummels, which are ceramic figurines made in Germany. Jeremiah asks your advice in determining which investments to keep and which to sell. Use the terms below to prepare your recommendations.

- direct investment
- commercial property
- indirect investment
- syndicate
- participation certificate (PC)

- financial leverage
- precious metals
- precious gems
- collectibles

Reviewing Key Concepts

1. **Compare and contrast** direct and indirect real estate investments.
2. **List** two advantages and two disadvantages of real estate investments.
3. **Describe** precious metal and gem investments and why they remain popular despite their speculative nature.
4. **Explain** what is meant by the term *collectible,* and give some examples of collectible items you or your family may own.
5. **Explain** why so many fraud complaints are related to online auctions.

ACADEMIC SKILLS

Communication Skills   A friend of yours tells you that his parents plan to pay for his college education by selling some family jewelry.
Write About It   Write a paragraph explaining why you might question this plan.

YOUR FINANCIAL FIGURES

Comparative Return   Imagine that you have $10,000 to invest. Use a newspaper, the Internet, or other source to select a mutual fund. Use the same source to find out how much gold you could buy for $10,000. Track the performance of these two investments for 30 days.

1. **Calculate** (a) the rate of return if you invested the $10,000 and sold the investment 30 days later. Disregard tax consequences or mutual fund withdrawal penalties. (b) How much return would you receive if you had put the money in a savings account with 4 percent interest?
2. **Compute** by using graphics or presentation software to show the two investments' performance.

REAL-WORLD Application

Connect with Economics   Your brother recently graduated from college and started his first job. He rents half a duplex, but the owner has put the building up for sale. Your brother thinks that purchasing the building would be a good investment for him. He asks for your opinion.

1. **Research**   Use the newspaper or search the Internet to find current prices for duplexes.
2. **Think Critically**   What are the positives and negatives of your brother buying the building? What factors need to be considered?

Internet CONNECTION

PBS Antiques Roadshow   The PBS television program, *Antiques Roadshow*, has generated enormous interest among viewers to find out the value of the furniture, art, jewelry, and collectibles they own.

 Log On   Go to persfinance07.glencoe.com for a link to the Web site of the *Antiques Roadshow* television program.

1. Click on "Follow the Stories" and select an area of interest and at least three stories from the *Antiques Roadshow*.
2. Summarize the stories you selected in one or two paragraphs. Add more information by using an Internet search engine to find out more about the area of interest you selected.

BusinessWeek ONLINE

Newsclip: A Piece of Childhood   Animation art, hand-painted images from which cartoons used to be made, is a popular collectible.

 Log On   Go to persfinance07.glencoe.com and open Chapter 11. Learn more about the different types of alternative investments, such as collectibles. Write a paragraph about the kinds of things you like to collect. Could any of them be valuable?

WHAT'S YOUR FINANCIAL ID?

ALL THAT GLITTERS

Whether you want to buy precious stones and metals as an investment, a gift, or for yourself, you will have the edge when you know what you are buying. Test your knowledge of gems and precious metals. Write your answers on a separate sheet of paper.

1. Precious stones generally have more commercial value than semiprecious stones. Some precious stones are (choose all that apply):

_____ garnet   _____ black onyx

_____ diamond   _____ amethyst

_____ turquoise   _____ opal

_____ pearl   _____ topaz

_____ ruby   _____ emerald

_____ sapphire

2. Rank these precious metals from 1 (most valuable per ounce) to 4 (least valuable):

_____ silver   _____ platinum

_____ gold   _____ copper

3. The word *brilliant* describes a diamond's _____.

_____ color   _____ clarity

_____ cut

4. When it comes to diamonds, the word *flawless* refers to _____.

_____ cut   _____ clarity

_____ color

5. All diamonds have a cubic crystal structure and are made primarily of _____.

_____ boron   _____ nitrogen

_____ carbon

Your Financial Portfolio

Collecting Treasures

Russell inherited three diamonds from his grandmother and needs to decide whether to keep them or sell them. He already had them evaluated for the "4 Cs"—clarity, color, cut, and carat weight—but not their actual dollar value. He took the diamonds and the evaluation papers to the Diamond Mart downtown.

A sales representative at the Diamond Mart appraised them. The four-carat diamond was the most valuable because it was beautifully cut in a marquise shape, and it also had good clarity, meaning it had few microscopic bits of other elements embedded in it. Its color, which was very close to the whitest end of the scale, also added to its value. The other two diamonds, a matched set of one-carat gems cut as round brilliants, were of a higher quality in clarity but more yellow. The appraiser told Russell that the three diamonds could be worth $5,000, but gem dealers would probably offer him about half that. He also told him that the Diamond Mart would not be interested in buying them.

Russell went to another store that had a sign, "We Buy Diamonds," but the most the store could offer was $2,350. Rather than settling for a price well below the actual worth of the diamonds, Russell decided to keep them in a safe-deposit box. By keeping them, he had the option of turning them into cash in the future, possibly selling them for more money. He also liked the idea of making them into jewelry someday. After researching his grandmother's diamonds, Russell is now interested in finding out more about other gems. One day he would like to start a gem collection.

Apply

On a separate sheet of paper, list five things you might enjoy collecting that will keep their value or possibly be worth more in the future. Choose one and describe why it appeals to you. Describe how an expert could appraise its value, using such criteria as age, quality, rarity, and popular demand. Why would this collectible be interesting for you to keep?

Do you think it would be a good or bad long-term investment? Explain why.

Unit 3 LAB

Get a Financial Life!

Investment Strategies

Overview

Carrie and David are about to celebrate their 36th birthdays. Carrie recently accepted a new position as a fashion design supervisor at a sportwear company. David is now an assistant principal at a high school specializing in technology and Internet applications. Through the years, they have saved money in traditional savings accounts and certificates of deposit. In addition, Carrie has invested money in a 401(k) plan at work. Because David has been working for the public school system, he has been investing in a 403(b) plan. Besides saving for retirement, Carrie and David realize that they will have to accumulate enough money to put their children, Eva and Jack, through college someday. Therefore, they would like to expand their investment strategies.

Resources & Tools

- Career development book
- Crayons, markers, colored pencils
- Internet (optional)
- Multimedia tools (videos, music, and so on)
- Portfolio (ring binder or file folder)
- Poster board
- Presentation software (optional)
- Public or school library
- Word processor

Procedures

STEP A **The Process** Imagine that you are a financial planner. Carrie and David have hired you to help them make investment decisions for their future. They have $25,000 in savings that they want to invest in stocks, bonds, mutual funds, and/or real estate.

1. Prepare a mock résumé for yourself as a financial planner. Showcase your experiences and qualifications so that Carrie and David will feel confident that they have hired an expert.

2. Recommend appropriate investment options for Carrie and David. To ensure a diverse portfolio, you must make at least three different recommendations.

3. Using the various sources of investment information (the financial section of a newspaper, business magazines, the Internet, investor services, and corporate reports), collect articles and other relevant information about the investment options that you will recommend. Your research should demonstrate to Carrie and David that your recommendations are sensible.

4. Contact a financial planner, investment counselor, banker, or accountant. Arrange for a time when you can either meet or speak on the phone to discuss the investment decisions you have made for Carrie and David. Prepare a report of your conversation.

STEP B Create Your Portfolio

As you work through the process, save the results so that you can refer, review, and refine. Create a professional-looking portfolio of investment recommendations that you will present to Carrie and David.

1. The first page should be a title page with the following information centered:
   - Investment Options
   - Presented to Carrie and David Lanier
   - By (Your Name)
2. Next include the résumé that you prepared.
3. Prepare a section in the portfolio for each investment option that you recommend. Include the recommendation and the research that supports your suggestion.
4. In the last section, include the report of the conversation you had with the financial expert you interviewed in Step A (4) on the previous page.

STEP C Teamwork

Teamwork is essential in today's workplace. Many companies are replacing the traditional management with self-managed work teams. Team members must be able to accept more responsibility, communicate effectively, and get along well with others.

Create a team of at least four classmates. Prepare a 15-minute seminar and present it to other members of your class or to other classes in the school. Organize your team in order to accomplish the following tasks in the best and most efficient way possible.

1. Choose one topic from Chapters 8–11 for your seminar.
2. Prepare an oral presentation, using presentation software, multimedia tools, posters, or other visuals.
3. Draft a written outline and relate the topics to financial planning for Carrie and David in the presentation.
4. Create handouts for the audience.
5. Prepare a pre-test and post-test for the audience. Compile the results in a graph.
6. Present the seminar to your class or to other classes in the school.

Protecting Your Finances

Internet Project

Avoiding Financial Fraud

You might experience financial trouble if you trust the wrong person or buy financial products from a disreputable company. You should plan for unforeseen problems. In this project, you will learn how to spot financial fraud and scams, and write a plan designed to help you protect your finances.

Log on to **persfinance07.glencoe.com**. Begin by reading Task 1. Then continue on your WebQuest as you study Unit 4.

Section	12.3	13.3	14.4	15.3
Page	392	432	467	510

FINANCE FILE

So What's the Plan?

Once you know how much you will need to retire, crafting a detailed map of your future financial moves is the next step. If you think you're too young to bother with a plan, remember that when it comes to building savings, time is on your side.

When I asked several financial planners how they work with clients who have figured out the amount of money they'll need in retirement, they said they start by compiling information on the client's financial status and potential retirement resources. Brewster [a planner] asks clients to provide up to 26 different types of documents, including investment- and retirement-account statements, tax returns, mortgage statement, insurance policies, and wills.

He raises such issues as whether the client has a realistic idea of future pension income. If the client were to switch jobs ten years before retirement, the final pension could end up being less than anticipated.

One of the findings [of the Retirement Confidence Survey was]: More than a quarter of those who feel "very confident" about their retirement prospects owe that peace of mind to "doing a good job of preparing financially."

— By Ellen Hoffman

Write About It How might financial planning protect you?

@ Log On To read the complete *BusinessWeek* article and do the *BusinessWeek* Extension activity to help you learn more about planning your finances for the present and future, go to **persfinance07.glencoe.com**.

CHAPTER *12*
Planning Your Tax Strategy

 What You'll Learn

When you have completed this chapter, you will be able to:

Section 12.1
- Discuss the importance of tax planning.
- Identify your taxable income.
- Explain deductions and tax credits.
- Explain the W-4 form.

Section 12.2
- Describe the types of federal income tax forms.

Section 12.3
- Identify tax strategies.

Reading Strategies

To get the most out of your reading:

Predict what you will learn in this chapter.

Relate what you read to your own life.

Question what you are reading to be sure you understand.

React to what you have read.

In the **Real** World . . .

Brigette Lindsey has just started her first job, and she is surprised at the amount of money that is taken out of her paycheck for taxes. In addition to federal tax, she has to pay state tax. Besides these payroll taxes, Brigette, like most people, also pays other taxes, such as sales tax and gasoline tax when she makes purchases. She has also learned that she must file income tax forms with the federal and state governments by April 15th of each year. The instructions for filing seem complicated. She is considering learning more about filing, buying a software program, or paying an accountant to do it. Brigette realizes that tax dollars fund civic activities, schools, libraries, and roads, but she would like to plan strategies to lower her taxes.

As You Read *Consider how income tax strategies could help you save money.*

Electronic Taxes

Q: I would like to file my income tax form electronically. Is it risky to file through the Internet?

A: If you are concerned about being charged late penalties if your tax return is not received by the IRS via the Internet, you can protect yourself by using filing services that offer a receipt, such as a confirmation number or e-mail confirmation.

Ask Yourself What would be the advantage of filing income tax forms electronically instead of by mail?

 Go to **persfinance07.glencoe.com** to complete the Standard & Poor's Financial Focus activity.

Income Tax Fundamentals

Focus on Reading

Read to Learn

- How to discuss the importance of tax planning.
- How to identify your taxable income.
- How to explain deductions and tax credits.
- How to explain the W-4 form.

Main Idea

Taxes are an important part of financial planning. There are several types of taxes and terms to know for preparing your tax return.

Key Terms

- tax liability
- estate tax
- inheritance tax
- income tax
- income tax return
- exclusion
- adjusted gross income
- taxable income
- tax deduction
- standard deduction
- itemized deduction
- exemption
- tax credit
- allowance

Taxes and You

Why are taxes so important?

Taxes are an everyday expense of life that allow your local, state, and federal governments to provide important services. Taxes pay the bills for those services such as Medicare, Medicaid, the military, the national debt, police and fire protection, public schools, road maintenance, parks, libraries, and safety inspection of foods, drugs, and other products.

You pay some type of tax every time you get a paycheck, buy a new CD, or fill up your car's gas tank. Each year the Tax Foundation, an independent public policy research group, determines how much of the year the average person works to pay taxes. In recent years, "Tax Freedom Day" came in early May. This means that from January 1 until early May, all the money you earn goes toward paying taxes.

Effective tax planning can help you to have money left after paying taxes and living expenses. Use several strategies to plan for taxes. First, find out how the current tax laws and regulations affect you. Second, maintain complete and accurate tax records. Third, learn how to make decisions that can reduce your **tax liability**, which is the total amount of taxes owed. If you follow these strategies, you will pay a fair share of taxes while taking advantage of tax benefits that allow you to owe less money.

Types of Taxes

What are the different types of taxes?

Throughout your life, you will pay different types of taxes in four major categories: purchases, property, wealth, and earnings.

Taxes on Purchases

You probably already pay sales tax each time you buy a product. These taxes are added to the prices of most products you purchase and are collected by state and local governments. Many states do not charge sales tax on food and medicine. Another type of sales tax is an *excise tax,* a tax on specific goods and services (such as gasoline, air travel, and telephone service) collected by federal and state governments.

Taxes on Property

Real estate property tax is a major source of income for local governments. This tax is based on the value of land and buildings. As the value of any real estate, such as a home, goes up, the amount of property tax may increase as well. In some areas of the country, state and local governments may assess taxes on the value of property, such as automobiles, boats, furniture, and farm equipment.

Taxes on Wealth

An **estate tax** is a federal tax collected on the value of a person's property at the time of his or her death. Unfortunately, that is not always the end of tax liability. States may collect an inheritance tax. An **inheritance tax** is a state tax collected on the property left by a person to his or her heir(s) in a will. Therefore, before heirs can claim their inheritance, they have to pay the inheritance tax.

Another type of federal tax on wealth is the gift tax. A gift tax is a tax collected on money or property valued at more than $11,000, given by one person to another in a single year. However, gifts of any amount that are designated for educational or medical expenses are not subject to gift taxes.

Before You Read

PREDICT

Why would planning a tax strategy be a good idea?

▲ **YOUR TAX DOLLARS** Public museums, parks, and roads are built and maintained with your taxes. *What other expenses are paid with tax funds?*

Taxes on Earnings

Income tax is the tax on wages, salaries, and self-employed earnings. Wages are payments received for hourly work, but salaries are payments received for weekly or monthly work, regardless of the number of hours worked. The personal income tax, or tax you pay on the income you receive, is the federal government's main source of revenue (money). Social Security funds are also collected as a tax. These funds finance retirement, disability, and life insurance benefits of the federal government's Social Security program. Current and future revisions to the Social Security program may affect amount of benefits.

STANDARD & POOR'S

Global Financial Landscape

Standard and Poor's publishes the globally recognized S&P 500® financial index. It also gathers financial statistics, information, and news, and analyzes this data for international businesses, governments, and individuals to help them guide their financial decisions.

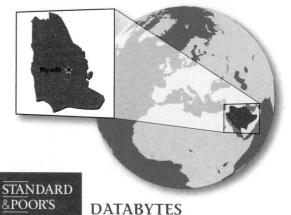

Riyadh

SAUDI ARABIA

Unlike U.S. citizens, Saudis are not required to pay income tax. They also do not pay local, regional, property, or most sales taxes. There is one exception. Saudi citizens must pay a religious tax called the *zagat*. The zagat amounts to an annual 2.5 percent of an individual's net worth. Before oil was discovered, when Saudi Arabia was a land of desert dwellers, the government survived with small taxes on

religious pilgrims and on tobacco. Although many people think that Saudi Arabia's oil wealth is responsible for its low tax status, scholars point to the independent nature of the population. The national attitude toward taxation might be summed up by the 1920s decree of the country's leaders: "Taxes, we have ruled, are completely illegal."

STANDARD & POOR'S

DATABYTES

Capital	Riyadh
Population	24,070,000
Languages	Arabic
Currency	Saudi riyal
Gross Domestic Product (GDP)	$286.2 billion (2003 est.)
GDP per capita	$10,500

Industry: Crude oil, petroleum, basic petrochemicals, and cement

Agriculture: Wheat, barley, tomatoes, melons, and mutton

Exports: Petroleum and petroleum products

Natural Resources: Crude oil, natural gas, iron ore, gold, and copper

Think Globally
Do you think the United States could operate under a similar taxation system? Why or why not?

The Internal Revenue Service (IRS) The Internal Revenue Service (IRS) is the federal agency that collects these taxes, or tax revenues. Headquartered in Washington, D.C., the IRS is an agency of the Department of the Treasury. The two primary missions of the IRS are to collect federal income taxes and to enforce the nation's tax laws.

Taxes on earnings are collected on a pay-as-you-earn basis. Your employer must withhold, or take out, Social Security and income tax payments from your paycheck and send the money to the IRS. If you are self-employed, own your own business, or are retired, you could be required to make your own estimated tax payments. When you complete your federal income tax return forms each year, you determine if you have paid too much or too little income tax. At that time you either pay more tax or you receive a refund from the IRS.

As You Read

RELATE

What kinds of taxes do you already pay?

Understanding Income Taxes
How do you determine how much tax you owe?

Every year millions of taxpayers in the United States prepare income tax returns and send their completed forms to the IRS by mail or through the Internet. An **income tax return** is a form, such as 1040 or 1040EZ, on which a taxpayer reports how much money he or she received from working and other sources and the exact taxes that are owed.

You determine the amount of tax you owe when filling out the returns. Then you compare that amount to the total income tax your employer withheld from your paychecks during the year. If the income tax you paid through your employer was greater than your tax liability, you will receive a refund. However, if your tax liability is greater than the tax you paid, you will need to pay the difference to the U.S. Treasury because you owe more taxes than were withheld.

Gross and Adjusted Gross Income

Most but not all income is subject to taxation. Gross income, or total income, can include one, two, or three main components:

1. **Earned income**—the money you receive for working, including wages, salary, commissions, fees, tips, bonuses, and self-employed earnings
2. **Interest income**—the interest that you receive from banks, credit unions, and savings and loan associations
3. **Dividend income**—the cash dividends that you receive from investments

Your gross income can also be affected by exclusions—amounts of income that do not have to be included in your gross income. An **exclusion** is also called tax-exempt income, or income that is not subject to taxes. For example, interest earned on most municipal bonds is exempt from federal income tax.

TechByte

Collecting Taxes
Helping federal, state, and local governments collect taxes is a growing market. Microsoft has partnered with several companies who have used Microsoft's technology to create tax collection software and integrated systems designed to be used by various government entities. For example, some programs help local municipalities collect property taxes, and others help government agencies distribute unemployment benefits and collect taxes from those employers who fund this program.

@ Read more about Microsoft's partnerships with tax collection software makers through **persfinance07 .glencoe.com**.

Another kind of income is tax-deferred income, or income that will be taxed at a later date. The earnings on an individual retirement account (IRA) are tax-deferred income. Although these earnings are credited to your account now, you do not have to pay tax on this money until you withdraw it from the account, usually at retirement.

You pay income tax on your adjusted gross income, not on your gross income. Your **adjusted gross income** is your gross income after calculating certain reductions. These reductions are called *adjustments* to income. They include items such as contributions to an IRA or student loan interest. The correct amount of your adjusted gross income is important because it is the basis for other tax calculations. (Note: If you have adjustments to income, you cannot use Form 1040EZ.)

Your Taxable Income

When you determine your adjusted gross income, you can figure out your **taxable income**. Your taxable income is your adjusted gross income less any allowable tax deductions and exemptions. Your income tax is calculated based on the amount of your taxable income.

Tax Deductions A **tax deduction** is an expense that you can subtract from your adjusted gross income to figure your taxable income. Every taxpayer receives at least the **standard deduction**, an amount of money set by the IRS that is not taxed. In 2004, a single person's standard deduction was $4,850. A married couple filing a joint tax return could deduct $9,700. People over age 65 or people who are blind are entitled to higher standard deductions.

You may qualify for other deductions that can reduce your taxable income. An **itemized deduction** is a specific expense, such as a medical expense, that you deduct from your adjusted gross income. You can take the standard deduction or itemize your deductions, but you cannot take both. You would take the standard deduction if it were greater than your total itemized deductions.

A few of the most common itemized deductions include:

▼ **MEDICAL DEDUCTIONS**
Medical expenses can help reduce the taxes you owe.
What are medical expenses?

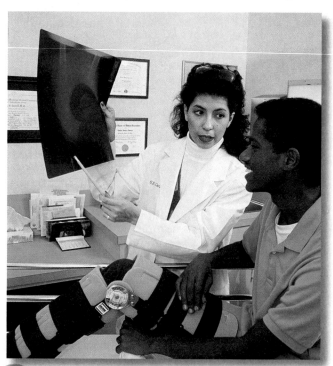

- **Medical and Dental Expenses** These include doctors' fees, prescription medications, hospital expenses, medical insurance premiums, eyeglasses, hearing aids, and medical travel that has not been reimbursed or paid by others, such as a health insurance provider. You can deduct only the amount of your medical and dental expenses that is more than 7.5 percent of your adjusted gross income (as of 2004). Therefore, if your adjusted gross income is $10,000, you can deduct only the amount of non-reimbursed medical and dental expenses that exceeds $750.

Figure 12.1 The Six-Rate System for Federal Income Taxes

Rate on Taxable Income	Single Taxpayers	Married Taxpayers
10%	Up to $7,000	Up to $14,000
15%	$7,000 – $28,400	$14,000 – $56,800
25%	$28,400 – $68,800	$56,800 – $114,650
28%	$68,800 – $143,500	$114,650 – $174,700
33%	$143,500 – $311,950	$174,700 – $311,950
35%	$311,950 and up	$311,950 and up

Tax Rates The six-rate system is an example of a progressive tax.

What do you think is meant by "progressive tax"?

- **Taxes** You can deduct state and local income tax, real estate property tax, and state and local personal property tax.
- **Interest** You can deduct home mortgage interest and home equity loan interest.
- **Contributions** You can deduct contributions of cash or property to qualified charities. If your contribution is more than 20 percent of your adjusted gross income, the deduction is subject to certain limitations.

You must keep records to document tax deductions. For more information about financial records, review Chapter 3.

Exemptions An **exemption** is a deduction from adjusted gross income for the taxpayer, the spouse, and qualified dependents. A dependent is someone you support financially, such as a child. To qualify as a dependent, a person must meet all of the following requirements:

1. A dependent must not earn more than a set amount unless he or she is under age 19 or is a full-time student under age 24.
2. He or she must be a specified relative or live in the home of the taxpayer who claims him or her on the tax return.
3. More than half of a dependent's support must be provided by the taxpayer who claims him or her on the tax return.
4. A dependent must meet certain citizenship requirements.

Calculating Your Tax

Once you know your taxable income, you can calculate how much income tax you owe. Most taxpayers use either a Tax Table or a Tax Rate Schedule to figure income tax. The Tax Rate Schedules are based on the six rates shown in **Figure 12.1.** The examples in this book use a Tax Table instead of Tax Rate Schedules.

Academic Connection

MATH

In states that charge sales tax, even people who live outside the state have to pay taxes on purchases they make within the state. This means that tourists who purchase items in a state that collects sales tax are helping to pay for the upkeep of the state. *If you live in a state that collects a sales tax of 6.25 percent, how much sales tax do you owe on a $125 purchase?*

As You Read

QUESTION

Why is it important for you to keep accurate and organized tax records?

Tax Credits   Your income tax may be reduced by a **tax credit**, which is an amount of money that can be subtracted directly from taxes you owe. A tax credit is different than a deduction. A tax deduction is an expense that you can subtract from your adjusted gross income. However, a tax credit results in a dollar-for-dollar reduction in the amount of taxes you owe. For example, suppose you owe $300 in taxes. If you can get a $100 tax credit, you can subtract that and owe only $200 ($300 − $100 = $200).

Lower-income workers can benefit from a tax credit called *earned income credit* (EIC). This federal tax credit is for people who work and whose taxable income is less than a certain amount. People who do not earn enough to owe federal income tax are also eligible for the EIC.

Making Tax Payments
How do you make income tax payments to the IRS?

You can pay your income taxes to the federal government in different ways: through estimated payments or payroll withholding payments. People who are self-employed may pay estimated taxes each quarter.

Payroll Withholding

When James Irving began his job at a company, his employer asked him to complete a W-4 form, or the Employee's Withholding Allowance Certificate. (See **Figure 12.2**). The amount of federal income tax an employer withholds, or deducts from your paycheck to send to the IRS, depends on the number of allowances you claim on a W-4 form. An **allowance** is an adjustment to the tax withheld from your paycheck, based on your marital status and whether you have dependents. An allowance can reduce the amount of income taxes your employer withholds.

Completing a W-4 Form   To fill out the W-4 form, follow these simple instructions:

1. Fill in your name and address.
2. Fill in your Social Security number.
3. Indicate whether you are single or married by checking the appropriate box.
4. Check the box if your last name is different from the name shown on your Social Security card.
5. Write the number of allowances you are claiming. To figure out how many allowances you can claim, complete the Personal Allowances Worksheet at the top of the W-4 form.
6. Indicate how much additional money, if any, you wish to have withheld.
7. If you meet the conditions listed on the form and indicate that you are exempt, or excused, from paying income tax, no income tax will be withheld.
8. Sign and date the form.

Figure 12.2 **The W-4 Form**

Personal Allowances Worksheet (Keep for your records.)

A Enter "1" for **yourself** if no one else can claim you as a dependent . . . . **A** _____

B Enter "1" if:
- You are single and have only one job; or
- You are married, have only one job, and your spouse does not work; or
- Your wages from a second job or your spouse's wages (or the total of both) are $1,000 or less. **B** _____

C Enter "1" for your **spouse**. But, you may choose to enter "-0-" if you are married and have either a working spouse or more than one job. (Entering "-0-" may help you avoid having too little tax withheld.) . . . . **C** _____

D Enter number of **dependents** (other than your spouse or yourself) you will claim on your tax return . . . . . **D** _____

E Enter "1" if you will file as **head of household** on your tax return (see conditions under **Head of household** above) . **E** _____

F Enter "1" if you have at least $1,500 of **child or dependent care expenses** for which you plan to claim a credit . . **F** _____
(**Note:** Do **not** include child support payments. See **Pub. 503,** Child and Dependent Care Expenses, for details.)

G **Child Tax Credit** (including additional child tax credit):
- If your total income will be between $15,000 and $42,000 ($20,000 and $65,000 if married), enter "1" for each eligible child plus **1 additional** if you have three to five eligible children or **2 additional** if you have six or more eligible children.
- If your total income will be between $42,000 and $80,000 ($65,000 and $115,000 if married), enter "1" if you have one or two eligible children, "2" if you have three eligible children, "3" if you have four eligible children, or "4" if you have five or more eligible children. **G** _____

H Add lines A through G and enter total here. **Note:** This may be different from the number of exemptions you claim on your tax return. ▶ **H** _____

For accuracy, complete all worksheets that apply.
- If you plan to **itemize or claim adjustments to income** and want to reduce your withholding, see the **Deductions and Adjustments Worksheet** on page 2.
- If you have **more than one job** or are **married and you and your spouse both work** and the combined earnings from all jobs exceed $35,000, see the **Two-Earner/Two-Job Worksheet** on page 2 to avoid having too little tax withheld.
- If **neither** of the above situations applies, **stop here** and enter the number from line H on line 5 of Form W-4 below.

- - - - - - - - - - - - - - - **Cut here and give Form W-4 to your employer. Keep the top part for your records.** - - - - - - - - - - - - - - -

Form **W-4**
Department of the Treasury
Internal Revenue Service

Employee's Withholding Allowance Certificate

▶ **For Privacy Act and Paperwork Reduction Act Notice, see page 2.**

OMB No. 1545-0010

20--

1 Type or print your first name and middle initial	Last name		**2** Your social security number
JAMES A.	IRVING		123 XX XXXX

Home address (number and street or rural route)	**3** ☐ Single ☐ Married ☐ Married, but withhold at higher Single rate.
23 CEDAR GLENN	**Note:** If married, but legally separated, or spouse is a nonresident alien, check the "Single" box.

City or town, state, and ZIP code	**4** If your last name differs from that shown on your social security card, check here. You must call 1-800-772-1213 for a new card. ▶ ☐
ARLINGTON, ILLINOIS 61312	

5 Total number of allowances you are claiming (from line **H** above **or** from the applicable worksheet on page 2) **5** 2

6 Additional amount, if any, you want withheld from each paycheck . . . . **6** $

7 I claim exemption from withholding for 20--, and I certify that I meet **both** of the following conditions for exemption:
- Last year I had a right to a refund of **all** Federal income tax withheld because I had **no** tax liability **and**
- This year I expect a refund of **all** Federal income tax withheld because I expect to have **no** tax liability.
If you meet both conditions, write "Exempt" here . . . . ▶ **7**

Under penalties of perjury, I certify that I am entitled to the number of withholding allowances claimed on this certificate, or I am entitled to claim exempt status.

Employee's signature
(Form is not valid unless you sign it.) ▶ *James A. Irving*   Date ▶ 1/3/20--

8 Employer's name and address (Employer: Complete lines 8 and 10 only if sending to the IRS.)	**9** Office code (optional)	**10** Employer identification number

Cat. No. 10220Q

Tax Withholding

The W-4 form allows employers to withhold federal income tax from their employees' paychecks.

How many allowances might you claim on your W-4 if you are married, you have only one job, and your spouse does not work?

Estimated Payments

Every summer John earns money by running his own landscaping business. How does he pay his taxes since he does not have an employer? Like other self-employed workers, John makes estimated payments to the government. These payments are due April 15th, June 15th, September 15th, and January 15th (the last payment is for the previous year). John's payments are based on his estimate of taxes due at the end of the year. Estimated payments must be at least equal to the taxes he owed last year or be at least 90 percent of the current year's taxes to avoid penalties for underpayment.

Claiming Allowances

Some employees claim fewer allowances on their W-4 forms than they actually have and, consequently, more tax money is withheld from their paychecks. Some employees claim no allowances. In both of these cases, employers withhold more money than is required from each paycheck. As a result, the employees look forward to receiving large refunds from the government when they file their tax returns. Claiming few or no allowances on their W-4 forms is one way to get that refund. They may view the extra tax withheld as a "forced savings account." However, as employees, they might use a payroll deduction plan for savings instead. They may be forgetting the opportunity cost of withholding excessive amounts of their money. These taxpayers may not realize that the extra deducted money is like providing an interest-free loan to the government. The government does not have to return that extra money for up to a year until tax returns are filed, usually by April 15th of each year. Wise taxpayers claim all the allowances to which they are entitled when preparing the W-4 form. That puts the money into their pockets.

Section 12.1 Assessment

QUICK CHECK

1. What is the relationship between taxes and personal financial planning?
2. What is your taxable income?
3. What are the steps to complete a W-4 form?

THINK CRITICALLY

4. Explain how deductions and tax credits affect the amount of income tax you pay.

USE MATH SKILLS

5. **Raising Funds**   As budget director for a small state, you must raise $350 million for emergency repairs to the state's bridges. You have several ways to fund the project. Your options include: place a sales tax of 5 percent on all purchases except food and prescription drugs; place a personal property tax on cars based on the purchase price and age of the vehicle; or place tolls of about $4 per round-trip for using each bridge.

Analyze   Weigh the pros and cons of each alternative and make a recommendation to the state.

SOLVE MONEY PROBLEMS

6. **Withholding**   Eric is single; he has no children or other dependents; and he is not claimed as a dependent on anyone else's tax return. He has only one job, as a manager at the local supermarket, and he earns $35,000 a year. Leland is married and has twin daughters whom he will claim as dependents. He works full-time at an architecture firm and also earns $35,000 a year.

Calculate   Using the Personal Allowances Worksheet on the W-4 form, determine who will have more money withheld from his paycheck, Eric or Leland.

Preparing an Income Tax Return

The W-2 Form

What information does the W-2 form provide?

Each year, when it is time for James to file his annual income tax return, his employer sends him a W-2 form, or the Wage and Tax Statement. This form lists his annual earnings and the amount withheld from his paychecks for federal income taxes, Social Security, and any applicable state and local income taxes. By law, your employer must send you this form by January 31st each year.

Understanding the Federal Income Tax Return

What should you know about the federal income tax return?

When you know how to compute your taxable income, you are ready to begin the yearly task of filling out your income tax return and sending it to the IRS. Before you begin, consider some basic information:

- Who must file
- Deadlines and penalties
- Tax forms

Who Must File?

Are you a citizen or a resident of the United States? Are you a U.S. citizen who resides in Puerto Rico? If so, then you are required to file a federal income tax return if your income is above a certain amount. That amount is based on your filing status and other factors, such as your age. For example, Kerry is a single person under the age of 65, and her gross annual income is more than $7,700. She is required to file an income tax return. Kerry would also be required to file an income tax return if she were a single person over age 65 and had a gross income of more than $8,850. Even if Kerry did not meet the filing requirements, she should still file a tax return to obtain a refund of the income tax withheld from her paycheck.

Focus on Reading

Read to Learn

- How to describe the types of federal income tax forms.

Main Idea

Special information and documents are needed to prepare income tax returns. You can choose one of three main federal tax return forms.

Key Term

- extension

Before You Read

PREDICT

What factors might determine whether you have to file income taxes?

These are the five filing status categories:

- **Single**—an individual who never married, or is divorced or legally separated with no dependents
- **Married, filing a joint return**— a husband and wife with combined income
- **Married, filing separate returns**—each spouse paying for his or her own tax
- **Head of household**—an unmarried individual or a surviving spouse who maintains a household, paying more than one-half of the costs for a child or other dependent relative
- **Qualifying widow or widower**—an individual whose spouse died within the last two years and who has a dependent

Deadlines and Penalties

You are required to file an income tax return each year by April 15th, unless that date falls on a Saturday or Sunday. In that case, you must file by the following Monday. If you have a refund owed to you, file your return as early as possible to avoid a long wait. You may have to pay financial penalties if you do not file on time, even if you are just one day late.

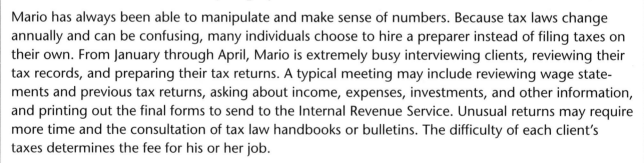

Careers in Finance

 **TAX PREPARER**   **Mario Cendreda**
Self-Employed

Mario has always been able to manipulate and make sense of numbers. Because tax laws change annually and can be confusing, many individuals choose to hire a preparer instead of filing taxes on their own. From January through April, Mario is extremely busy interviewing clients, reviewing their tax records, and preparing their tax returns. A typical meeting may include reviewing wage statements and previous tax returns, asking about income, expenses, investments, and other information, and printing out the final forms to send to the Internal Revenue Service. Unusual returns may require more time and the consultation of tax law handbooks or bulletins. The difficulty of each client's taxes determines the fee for his or her job.

SKILLS: Communication, mathematical, organizational, reasoning and problem-solving, and time-management skills

PERSONAL TRAITS: Detail oriented, good judgment, and tactful

EDUCATION: High school diploma or equivalent; college-level courses in economics, business, and computers; tax preparation training

ANALYZE   Why might a tax preparer require training every year?

@   To learn more about career paths for tax preparers, visit persfinance07.glencoe.com.

If you cannot meet the deadline, you can file Form 4868 by April 15th to receive a four-month **extension**, which is an extended deadline for *filing* an income tax return; but it does not delay your tax liability. When you submit Form 4868, you must also send a check for the estimated amount of the tax you may owe.

If you make quarterly estimated tax payments, they must be on time. If you underestimate the amount owed, you have to pay interest plus the amount you should have paid. Underpayment due to negligence or fraud can result in large penalties. Failing to file a required tax return is a serious violation of the tax code and can result in a substantial penalty.

The good news is that if you claim a refund several months or years late, perhaps because you discovered a calculation error or you did not take an allowable deduction, the IRS will pay you interest plus your refund. You must claim your refund and interest within three years of filing a return or within two years of paying the tax.

Choosing the Tax Form

The IRS offers about 400 tax forms and schedules. However, you have a choice of three basic forms: the short forms known as *Form 1040EZ* and *Form 1040A*, and the long form known as *Form 1040*.

Form 1040EZ   Form 1040EZ is the simplest tax form to complete. You may use this form if you meet the following qualifications:

- Your taxable income is less than $100,000.
- You are single or married (filing a joint tax return).
- You are under age 65.
- You claim no dependents.
- Your income consisted of only wages, salaries, and tips, and no more than $1,500 of taxable interest.
- You will not itemize deductions, claim any adjustments to income, or claim any tax credits.

For example, Yasmeen is a high school senior who works part time at a health clinic. She is single, earned less than the amount needed to file, and had only $11 in interest income last year. So, Yasmeen was able to use Form 1040EZ to obtain a tax refund.

Form 1040A   You may use this form if any of the following apply:

- You have less than $100,000 in taxable income.
- You have capital gains distributions but not capital gains or losses.
- You claim the standard deduction.
- You claim deductions for IRA contributions.
- You claim a tax credit for child and dependent care, education, earned income, adoption, or retirement savings contributions.
- You have deductions for IRA contributions, student loan interest, educator expenses, or higher education tuition and fees.
- You have no itemized deductions.

$avvy Saver

Advantages of 401(k) Plans

1. Many companies match up to 100 percent of your 401(k) savings.
2. You do not pay taxes on the money until you withdraw it.
3. Your contribution is automatically deducted from your paycheck.
4. You have several investment choices.
5. You can watch your money grow over the years.

Avoiding Financial Fraud

As a taxpayer, it is important to be very careful when choosing a professional to prepare your tax return. While most tax preparers are honest, and intend to provide good service to their clients, some are willing to file false information and take advantage of their clients for their own gain. Look for warning signs to help identify a fraudulent tax preparer.

@ To continue with Task 2 of your Web-Quest project, visit persfinance07.glencoe.com.

As You Read

RELATE

Have you filed income taxes yet? If not, do you consider yourself a tax-payer anyway? Why or why not?

Form 1040 Form 1040 is an expanded version of Form 1040A. It includes sections covering all types of income. You are required to use this form if your taxable income is more than $100,000, or if you have interest or dividends over a set limit, self-employment income, or income from the sale of property. Many taxpayers who earn less than $100,000 use this form and find Form 1040 offers tax advantages.

Itemize deductions on this form by using Schedule A. Deduct expenses, such as medical and dental expenses, home mortgage interest, and real estate property tax. These deductions will reduce your taxable income and, therefore, reduce the amount of tax you must pay.

Completing the Federal Income Tax Return

What do you need to complete the three main income tax forms?

Filling out a federal income tax return does not have to be difficult as long as you are prepared, have the correct documents and information, and understand the form you are using. Make a rough draft of your tax return before you complete a final draft.

Gathering Information and Documents

Being prepared at tax time means you have all the necessary documents. The following checklist of documents will help you complete a successful tax return:

- **Tax Forms and Instruction Booklets** Be sure that you have the most current forms and instruction booklets that contain the latest tax information. After you have filed your first tax return, the IRS will send these to you each year in January. If you need different or additional forms, you can download them from the Internal Revenue Service's Web site. You can also find them at some post offices, libraries, banks, and at your local IRS office.
- **Copies of Your Tax Returns** Have copies of your tax returns from previous years for reference—unless, of course, you are filing for the first time.
- **Your W-2 Form** You must attach a copy of your W-2 form to your tax return if you are filing by mail. If you worked for more than one employer during the tax year, you will receive more than one W-2.
- **Interest and Dividend Forms** You may also receive Form 1099-INT, which reports your interest income, (see **Figure 12.3**), and Form 1099-DIV, which reports your dividend income.

After you complete your returns, be sure to save copies of these forms and all supporting documents and paperwork in a safe place for at least six years.

Figure 12.3   The Interest Income Form

9292	☐ VOID	☐ CORRECTED		
PAYER'S name, street address, city, state, ZIP code, and telephone no.	Payer's RTN (optional)	OMB No. 1545-0112		
BAILEY'S BANK 1155 DARNESTOWN ROAD ARLINGTON, IL 61312		20—— **Interest Income** Form **1099-INT**		

PAYER'S Federal identification number 521283179	RECIPIENT'S identification number 123XXXXXX	1 Interest income not included in box 3 $ 45.00		**Copy A**
RECIPIENT'S name JAMES A. IRVING		2 Early withdrawal penalty $ .00	3 Interest on U.S. Savings Bonds and Treas. obligations $ .00	**For Internal Revenue Service Center** File with Form 1096.
Street address (including apt. no.) 23 CEDAR GLENN LANE		4 Federal income tax withheld $ .00	5 Investment expenses $ .00	For Privacy Act and Paperwork Reduction Act Notice and instructions for completing this form, see the
City, state, and ZIP code ARLINGTON, IL 61312		6 Foreign tax paid	7 Foreign country or U.S. possession	**20—— Instructions for Forms 1099, 1098, 5498, and W-2G.**
Account number (optional) 894-6210	2nd TIN Not. ☐	$ .00		

Form **1099-INT**   Cat. No. 14410K   Department of the Treasury - Internal Revenue Service

Do NOT Cut or Separate Forms on This Page — Do NOT Cut or Separate Forms on This Page

Interest Earned

You will receive a 1099-INT form from any institution that paid you interest over the year.

What box on the form indicates your interest income on a savings account?

Completing the Form 1040EZ

After you have collected all the necessary tax documents, it is time to begin filling out your tax return. Take a look at **Figure 12.4** on pages 394 and 395, which illustrates a sample tax return. Here is how James Irving would complete Form 1040EZ:

1. After printing his name, address, and Social Security number, James enters the total wages from his W-2 form on line 1 in the income section.

2. James earned $45 in interest on his savings account. (This was reported on Form 1099-INT.) He enters this amount on line 2.

3. James has nothing to report on line 3, so he leaves it blank.

4. James adds lines 1, 2, and 3 to get his adjusted gross income. He records it on line 4.

5. James's parents claim him as a dependent on their income tax return, so James uses the worksheet on the back of Form 1040EZ to calculate his maximum standard deduction. He enters $4,850 on line 5. (See Figure 12.4.)

6. He subtracts his deduction from his adjusted gross income and computes his taxable income: $5,445. He writes it on line 6.

7. On line 7, in the payments and tax section, James enters the amount of income tax that was withheld from his paychecks ($1,375) as reported on his W-2 form.

Figure 12.4 Form 1040EZ

Form **1040EZ**	Department of the Treasury—Internal Revenue Service **Income Tax Return for Single and Joint Filers With No Dependents** (99) **20--**		OMB No. 1545-0675

Label
(See page 11.)
Use the IRS label.
Otherwise, please print or type.

L A B E L   H E R E

Your first name and initial JAMES A.	Last name IRVING	Your social security number 123 : XX : XXXX
If a joint return, spouse's first name and initial	Last name	Spouse's social security number
Home address (number and street). If you have a P.O. box, see page 11. 23 CEDAR GLENN	Apt. no.	
City, town or post office, state, and ZIP code. If you have a foreign address, see page 11. ARLINGTON, ILLINOIS 61312		▲ **Important!** ▲ You **must** enter your SSN(s) above.

Presidential Election Campaign (page 11) ▶

Note. Checking "Yes" will not change your tax or reduce your refund.
Do you, or your spouse if a joint return, want $3 to go to this fund? . . . . . . ▶

	You	Spouse
	☐ Yes ☒ No	☐ Yes ☐ No

Income

Attach Form(s) W-2 here.
Enclose, but do not attach, any payment.

1	Wages, salaries, and tips. This should be shown in box 1 of your Form(s) W-2. Attach your Form(s) W-2.	1	10,250	00
2	Taxable interest. If the total is over $1,500, you cannot use Form 1040EZ.	2	45	00
3	Unemployment compensation and Alaska Permanent Fund dividends (see page 13).	3		
4	Add lines 1, 2, and 3. This is your **adjusted gross income.**	4	10,295	00

Note. You **must** check Yes or No.

5	Can your parents (or someone else) claim you on their return? **Yes.** ☒ Enter amount from worksheet on back. **No.** ☐ If **single,** enter $7,950. If **married filing jointly,** enter $15,900. See back for explanation.	5	4,850	00
6	Subtract line 5 from line 4. If line 5 is larger than line 4, enter -0-. This is your **taxable income.** ▶	6	5,445	00

Payments and tax

7	Federal income tax withheld from box 2 of your Form(s) W-2.	7	1,375	00
8a	**Earned income credit (EIC).**	8a		
b	Nontaxable combat pay election. 8b			
9	Add lines 7 and 8a. These are your **total payments.** ▶	9	1,375	00
10	**Tax.** Use the amount on **line 6 above** to find your tax in the tax table on pages 24–32 of the booklet. Then, enter the tax from the table on this line.	10	543	00

Refund
Have it directly deposited! See page 18 and fill in 11b, 11c, and 11d.

11a	If line 9 is larger than line 10, subtract line 10 from line 9. This is your **refund.** ▶	11a	832	00
▶ b	Routing number ▶ c Type: ☐ Checking ☐ Savings			
▶ d	Account number			

Amount you owe

12	If line 10 is larger than line 9, subtract line 9 from line 10. This is the **amount you owe.** For details on how to pay, see page 19. ▶	12		

Third party designee

Do you want to allow another person to discuss this return with the IRS (see page 19)? ☐ **Yes.** Complete the following. ☒ **No**

Designee's name ▶	Phone no. ▶ ( )	Personal identification number (PIN) ▶

Sign here
Joint return? See page 11.
Keep a copy for your records.

Under penalties of perjury, I declare that I have examined this return, and to the best of my knowledge and belief, it is true, correct, and accurately lists all amounts and sources of income I received during the tax year. Declaration of preparer (other than the taxpayer) is based on all information of which the preparer has any knowledge.

Your signature James A Irving	Date 2|2|--	Your occupation ASSISTANT MGR.	Daytime phone number (815)555-1941
Spouse's signature. If a joint return, **both** must sign.	Date	Spouse's occupation	

Paid preparer's use only

Preparer's signature ▶	Date	Check if self-employed ☐	Preparer's SSN or PTIN
Firm's name (or yours if self-employed), address, and ZIP code ▶		EIN	
		Phone no. ( )	

For Disclosure, Privacy Act, and Paperwork Reduction Act Notice, see page 23.   Cat. No. 11329W   Form **1040EZ** (20--)

Figure 12.4 **Form 1040EZ (continued)**

Form 1040EZ (20--)   Page **2**

Use this form if

- Your filing status is single or married filing jointly. If you are not sure about your filing status, see page 11.
- You (and your spouse if married filing jointly) were under age 65 and not blind at the end of 2004. If you were born on January 1, 1940, you are considered to be age 65 at the end of 2004.
- You do not claim any dependents. For information on dependents, use TeleTax topic 354 (see page 6).
- Your taxable income (line 6) is less than $100,000.
- You do not claim any adjustments to income. For information on adjustments to income, use TeleTax topics 451-458 (see page 6).
- The only tax credit you can claim is the earned income credit. For information on credits, use TeleTax topics 601-608 and 610 (see page 6).
- You had only wages, salaries, tips, taxable scholarship or fellowship grants, unemployment compensation, or Alaska Permanent Fund dividends, and your taxable interest was not over $1,500. But if you earned tips, including allocated tips, that are not included in box 5 and box 7 of your Form W-2, you may not be able to use Form 1040EZ (see page 12). If you are planning to use Form 1040EZ for a child who received Alaska Permanent Fund dividends, see page 13.
- You did not receive any advance earned income credit payments.
  If you cannot use this form, use TeleTax topic 352 (see page 6).

Filling in your return

For tips on how to avoid common mistakes, see page 20.

If you received a scholarship or fellowship grant or tax-exempt interest income, such as on municipal bonds, see the booklet before filling in the form. Also, see the booklet if you received a Form 1099-INT showing federal income tax withheld or if federal income tax was withheld from your unemployment compensation or Alaska Permanent Fund dividends.

Remember, you must report all wages, salaries, and tips even if you do not get a Form W-2 from your employer. You must also report all your taxable interest, including interest from banks, savings and loans, credit unions, etc., even if you do not get a Form 1099-INT.

Worksheet for dependents who checked "Yes" on line 5

(keep a copy for your records)

Use this worksheet to figure the amount to enter on line 5 if someone can claim you (or your spouse if married filing jointly) as a dependent, even if that person chooses not to do so. To find out if someone can claim you as a dependent, use TeleTax topic 354 (see page 6).

A. Amount, if any, from line 1 on front _____10,250_____
  + _____250.00_____ Enter total ▶ A. _____10,500.00_____
B. Minimum standard deduction . . . . B. _____800.00_____
C. Enter the **larger** of line A or line B here . . . . C. _____10,500.00_____
D. Maximum standard deduction. If **single,** enter $4,850; if **married filing jointly,** enter $9,700 . . . . D. _____4,850.00_____
E. Enter the **smaller** of line C or line D here. This is your standard deduction . . . . E. _____4,850.00_____
F. Exemption amount.
  - If single, enter -0-.
  - If married filing jointly and—
    —both you and your spouse can be claimed as dependents, enter -0-.
    —only one of you can be claimed as a dependent, enter $3,100. F. _____-0-_____
G. Add lines E and F. Enter the total here and on line 5 on the front . G. _____4,850.00_____

If you checked "No" on line 5 because no one can claim you (or your spouse if married filing jointly) as a dependent, enter on line 5 the amount shown below that applies to you.

- Single, enter $7,950. This is the total of your standard deduction ($4,850) and your exemption ($3,100).
- Married filing jointly, enter $15,900. This is the total of your standard deduction ($9,700), your exemption ($3,100), and your spouse's exemption ($3,100).

Mailing return

Mail your return by **April 15, 20--.** Use the envelope that came with your booklet. If you do not have that envelope or if you moved during the year, see the back cover for the address to use.

Form **1040EZ** (20--)

A Refund Option   James has a choice about how to receive his refund.

What are the purposes of lines 11b, c, and d?

As You Read

QUESTION

What could happen if your employer did not deduct federal income taxes from your paychecks?

Put on Your Financial Planner's Cap

STANDARD &POOR'S

If you were a financial planner, would you advise most of your clients to consult a CPA? Why or why not?

8. James cannot claim any earned income credit, so he leaves line 8 blank.

9. He adds lines 7 and 8 to find his total payments ($1,375). He enters this amount on line 9.

10. Now James finds out how much tax he owes. He knows from line 6 that his taxable income is $5,445. He checks the tax table in the Form 1040EZ instruction booklet (see **Figure 12.5**) and finds the column that says "If Form 1040EZ, line 6, is" and the row that corresponds with "At least" $5,400 "But less than" $5,450. Because he is single, he owes $543. He enters this amount on line 10.

11. James's employer withheld more tax than James owed. By subtracting his tax owed (line 10) from his tax withheld (line 9), James finds that the IRS owes him a refund of $832, which he enters on line 11a. If he fills in lines 11b, 11c, and 11d, he can have his refund deposited directly into his bank account. He leaves the lines blank so that he will receive a refund check.

12. He then signs and dates his income tax return and enters his occupation. James makes a photocopy of his tax return for his records, attaches his W-2 to the original tax return, and mails the completed return to the IRS.

Completing the Form 1040A

James used Form 1040EZ because his tax situation was uncomplicated. Some taxpayers, however, will benefit from using Form 1040A, shown in **Figure 12.6** on pages 398 and 399. Form 1040A enables taxpayers to claim deductions that will reduce the amount of tax they must pay.

GO FIGURE — FINANCIAL MATH

1040EZ TAX DUE

Synopsis: You can find out if you owe tax or if you will get a refund by using tax tables.

Example: Jacqui works part-time in a bookstore. Her year's adjusted gross income was $6,840. Her standard deduction is $4,850. She is using the tax table in **Figure 12.5**. How much is her tax?

Formula: Adjusted Gross Income − Standard Deduction = Taxable Income

Taxable Income bracket on Tax Table to find Tax Due

Solution: $10,840 − $4,850 = $5,990 Taxable Income

$5,959 to $6,000 for single person is $598 tax due.

YOU FIGURE

Your adjusted gross income is $9,438. If you are single, how much tax do you owe?

Figure 12.5 Sample Tax Table

20- - Tax Table

Example. Mr. Brown is single. His taxable income on line 6 of Form 1040EZ is $25,250. First, he finds the $26,250–26,600 income line. Next, he finds the "Single" column and reads down the column. The amount shown where the income line and filing status column meet → is $6,584. This is the tax amount he should enter on line 10 of Form 1040EZ.

At least	But less than	Single	Married filing jointly
		Your tax is—	
26,200	26,250	3,576	3,219
26,250	26,300	3,584	3,226
26,300	26,350	3,591	3,234
26,350	26,400	3,599	3,241

If Form 1040EZ, line 6, is—		And you are—		If Form 1040EZ, line 6, is—		And you are—		If Form 1040EZ, line 6, is—		And you are—		If Form 1040EZ, line 6, is—		And you are—	
At least	But less than	Single	Married filing jointly	At least	But less than	Single	Married filing jointly	At least	But less than	Single	Married filing jointly	At least	But less than	Single	Married filing jointly
		Your tax is—				Your tax is—				Your tax is—				Your tax is—	
3,000				**4,000**				**5,000**				**6,000**			
3,000	3,050	303	303	4,000	4,050	403	403	5,000	5,050	503	503	6,000	6,050	603	603
3,050	3,100	308	308	4,050	4,100	408	408	5,050	5,100	508	508	6,050	6,100	608	608
3,100	3,150	316	316	4,100	4,150	416	416	5,100	5,150	516	516	6,100	6,150	616	616
3,150	3,200	318	318	4,150	4,200	418	418	5,150	5,200	518	518	6,150	6,200	618	618
3,200	3,250	323	323	4,200	4,250	423	423	5,200	5,250	523	523	6,200	6,250	623	623
3,250	3,600	328	328	4,250	4,600	428	428	5,250	5,600	528	528	6,250	6,600	628	628
3,600	3,650	333	333	4,600	4,650	433	433	5,600	5,650	533	533	6,600	6,650	633	633
3,650	3,400	338	338	4,650	4,400	438	438	5,650	5,400	538	538	6,650	6,400	638	638
3,400	3,450	343	343	4,400	4,450	443	443	5,400	5,450	543	543	6,400	6,450	643	643
3,450	3,500	348	348	4,450	4,500	448	448	5,450	5,500	548	548	6,450	6,500	648	648
3,500	3,550	353	353	4,500	4,550	453	453	5,500	5,550	553	553	6,500	6,550	653	653
3,550	3,600	358	358	4,550	4,600	458	458	5,550	5,600	558	558	6,550	6,600	658	658
3,600	3,650	363	363	4,600	4,650	463	463	5,600	5,650	563	563	6,600	6,650	663	663
3,650	3,700	368	368	4,650	4,700	468	468	5,650	5,700	568	568	6,650	6,700	668	668
3,700	3,750	373	373	4,700	4,750	473	473	5,700	5,750	573	573	6,700	6,750	673	673
3,750	3,800	378	378	4,750	4,800	478	478	5,750	5,800	578	578	6,750	6,800	678	678
3,800	3,850	383	383	4,800	4,850	483	483	5,800	5,850	583	583	6,800	6,850	683	683
3,850	3,900	388	388	4,850	4,900	488	488	5,850	5,900	588	588	6,850	6,900	688	688
3,900	3,959	393	393	4,900	4,959	493	493	5,900	5,959	593	593	6,900	6,959	693	693
3,959	4,000	398	398	4,959	5,000	498	498	5,959	6,000	598	598	6,959	7,000	698	698

What If?

The tax table in the form 1040EZ instruction booklet tells you how much tax you owe, and thus it allows you to determine the refund you should receive, if any.

If James's Form 1040EZ, line 6, was at least $5,000 but less than $5,050, how much tax would he owe?

Filing Your Federal Income Tax Return

You may be able to file the return using one of several options. You can file the traditional paper return by filling out the forms and mailing them to the IRS. If you file electronically through the Internet, your return is transmitted directly to an IRS computer.

The IRS provides two ways for individuals to file electronically. First, you can use an authorized IRS e-file provider. With this method, either you or a tax professional would prepare your tax return. The tax professional would transmit it to the IRS. Second, you can file by using your personal computer and tax software. The IRS Web site provides information and instructions for preparing your own tax return via e-file.

Figure 12.6 Form 1040A

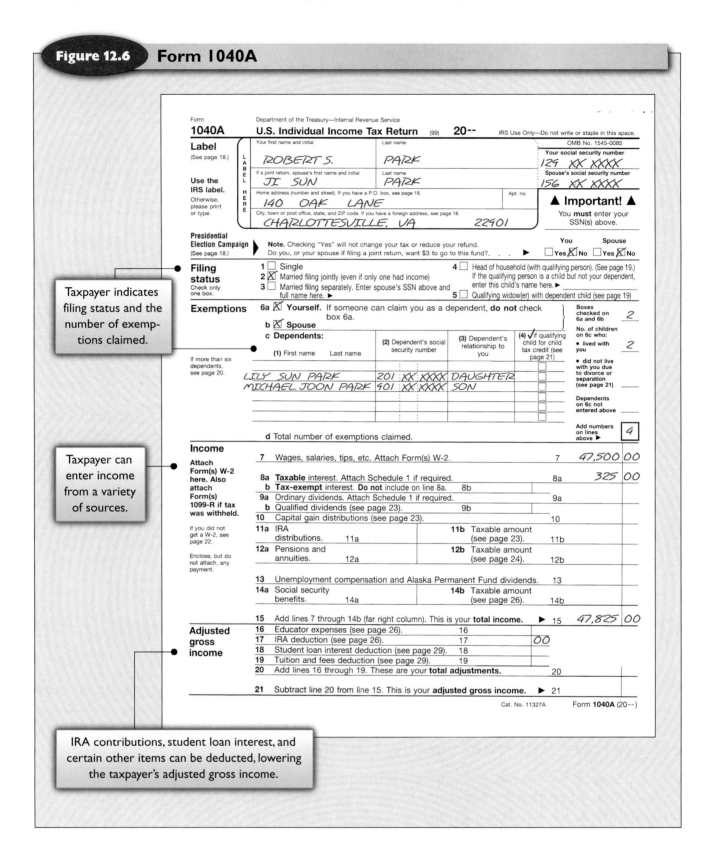

Taxpayer indicates filing status and the number of exemptions claimed.

Taxpayer can enter income from a variety of sources.

IRA contributions, student loan interest, and certain other items can be deducted, lowering the taxpayer's adjusted gross income.

Figure 12.6 Form 1040A (continued)

Form 1040A (20--)					Page **2**

Tax, credits, and payments

> Several types of tax credits, estimated tax payments, and withheld taxes add up to the total taxes.

22	Enter the amount from line 21 (adjusted gross income).		22	43,825 00
23a	Check if: ☐ You were born before January 2, 1940, ☐ Blind / ☐ Spouse was born before January 2, 1940, ☐ Blind } Total boxes checked ▶ 23a			
b	If you are married filing separately and your spouse itemizes deductions, see page 30 and check here ▶ 23b ☐			

Standard Deduction for—
- People who checked any box on line 23a or 23b **or** who can be claimed as a dependent, see page 31.
- All others:
Single or Married filing separately, $4,850
Married filing jointly or Qualifying widow(er), $9,700
Head of household, $7,150

24	Enter your **standard deduction** (see left margin).		24	9,700 00
25	Subtract line 24 from line 22. If line 24 is more than line 22, enter -0-.		25	34,125 00
26	If line 22 is $107,025 or less, multiply $3,100 by the total number of exemptions claimed on line 6d. If line 22 is over $107,025, see the worksheet on page 32.		26	12,400 00
27	Subtract line 26 from line 25. If line 26 is more than line 25, enter -0-. This is your **taxable income.** ▶		27	21,725 00
28	**Tax,** including any alternative minimum tax (see page 31).		28	2,544 00
29	Credit for child and dependent care expenses. Attach Schedule 2.	29		
30	Credit for the elderly or the disabled. Attach Schedule 3.	30		
31	Education credits. Attach Form 8863.	31		
32	Retirement savings contributions credit. Attach Form 8880.	32		
33	Child tax credit (see page 36).	33		
34	Adoption credit. Attach Form 8839.	34		
35	Add lines 29 through 34. These are your **total credits.**		35	—0—
36	Subtract line 35 from line 28. If line 35 is more than line 28, enter -0-.		36	
37	Advance earned income credit payments from Form(s) W-2.		37	
38	Add lines 36 and 37. This is your **total tax.** ▶		38	

If you have a qualifying child, attach Schedule EIC.

39	Federal income tax withheld from Forms W-2 and 1099.	39	4,550 00	
40	2004 estimated tax payments and amount applied from 2003 return.	40		
41a	**Earned income credit (EIC).**	41a		
b	Nontaxable combat pay election. 41b			
42	Additional child tax credit. Attach Form 8812.	42		
43	Add lines 39, 40, 41a, and 42. These are your **total payments.** ▶		43	4,550 00

Refund

Direct deposit? See page 50 and fill in 45b, 45c, and 45d.

44	If line 43 is more than line 38, subtract line 38 from line 43. This is the amount you **overpaid.**		44	2,006 00
45a	Amount of line 44 you want **refunded to you.** ▶		45a	2,006 00
▶ b	Routing number			
	▶ c Type: ☐ Checking ☐ Savings			
▶ d	Account number			
46	Amount of line 44 you want **applied to your 2005 estimated tax.**	46		

Amount you owe

47	**Amount you owe.** Subtract line 43 from line 38. For details on how to pay, see page 51. ▶	47		
48	Estimated tax penalty (see page 51).	48		

Third party designee

Do you want to allow another person to discuss this return with the IRS (see page 52)? ☐ **Yes.** Complete the following. ☒ No
Designee's name ▶   Phone no. ▶ ( )   Personal identification number (PIN)

Sign here

Under penalties of perjury, I declare that I have examined this return and accompanying schedules and statements, and to the best of my knowledge and belief, they are true, correct, and accurately list all amounts and sources of income I received during the tax year. Declaration of preparer (other than the taxpayer) is based on all information of which the preparer has any knowledge.

Joint return? See page 18. Keep a copy for your records.

Your signature *Robert S. Park* | Date 3/81-- | Your occupation LANDSCAPER | Daytime phone number 804 555-9394
Spouse's signature. If a joint return, **both** must sign. | Date 3/81-- | Spouse's occupation FLORIST

> If someone other than the taxpayer is paid to complete the form, he or she must also sign the form and provide additional information.

Paid preparer's use only

Preparer's signature | Date | Check if self-employed ☐ | Preparer's SSN or PTIN
Firm's name (or yours if self-employed), address, and ZIP code ▶ | | EIN | Phone no. ( )

Form **1040A** (20--)

Which Form?

You should fill out the tax form that best meets your needs.

Why would some people choose to file Form 1040 instead of Form 1040A?

Completing State Income Tax Returns

If you live in a state that levies income tax, you will have to complete a state income tax return. Only seven states do not have a state income tax:

- Alaska
- Florida
- Nevada
- South Dakota
- Texas
- Washington
- Wyoming

In most states the tax rate ranges from 1 to 10 percent and is based on your adjusted gross or taxable income reported on your federal tax return. States usually require their income tax returns to be filed at the same time as federal income tax returns. To find out more about state income tax forms and preparation, contact your state's department of revenue or tax board.

Section 12.2 Assessment

QUICK CHECK

1. Who must file a federal income tax return?
2. What are the three basic tax forms discussed in this section?
3. What documents do you need to begin to prepare your tax return?

THINK CRITICALLY

4. Briefly describe situations in which it would be advantageous to use Form 1040A instead of Form 1040EZ. When would you use Form 1040EZ?

USE MATH SKILLS

5. **A Taxing Question**   Last year, Shirley, a single college student, made $12,500 in total wages, salaries, and tips. She had $1,200 of federal income tax withheld. Her taxable interest was $59. No one was able to claim Shirley as a dependent on his or her tax return.

Calculate   Given the information above, use Form 1040EZ in Figure 12.4 on pages 394 and 395 and the corresponding tax table in Figure 12.5 on page 397 to determine whether Shirley will owe the government money or will obtain a refund. How much money will she owe, or how much will her refund be?

SOLVE MONEY PROBLEMS

6. **Planning for Tax Time**   Poor Fred. Tax time is drawing near, and he does not know how to begin to prepare his income tax return. He has piles of forms and other paperwork, but he just cannot figure out what to do with them. Fred needs help, and fast!

Write About It   Write instructions to Fred on the best way to prepare to file an income tax return. Tell him which forms are important and where he can go to get forms he needs.

Tax Assistance and Strategies

Tax Assistance
Is help available to prepare tax returns?

If your personal finances become more complex, your tax preparation will also become more complicated. All the rules and regulations can be confusing, but assistance is available. You will find many professionals and agencies willing to answer your questions and offer good advice. In addition, you can choose from a variety of software programs for tax preparation. A visit to a bookstore will uncover shelves of how-to books about tax planning and completing tax forms. Personal finance magazines also offer tax information. **Figure 12.7** on page 402 shows you some of the available options.

In addition, like all government agencies, the IRS is online. You can download forms and obtain important tax information and advice. You will find the same services at your local IRS office.

Tax Audits
What does it mean to be audited?

The IRS reviews all tax returns for completeness and accuracy. If your math is incorrect, the IRS will refigure your tax return and send you either a bill or a refund. In some cases, the IRS may audit your tax return and request additional information. A **tax audit** is a detailed examination of your tax return by the IRS. The IRS does periodic audits to determine whether taxpayers are paying all of their required taxes. The IRS does not discuss reasons for auditing returns; however, the agency may look for unusually large deductions or for deductions that you cannot claim.

If you receive an audit notice, you have the right to request time to prepare. You may also ask the IRS for clarification of items they are questioning. On the day of your audit, arrive on time for the appointment and bring only the documents that are relevant and consistent with the tax law. Be sure to answer the auditor's questions clearly, completely, and briefly. Maintain a positive attitude during the audit. If you prefer, your tax preparer, accountant, or lawyer may be present. If you have kept complete and accurate financial records, the audit should go smoothly.

Focus on Reading

Read to Learn
• How to identify tax strategies.

Main Idea
As your income and investments increase and your personal life changes, preparing your taxes may become more complex.

Key Term
• tax audit

Before You Read

PREDICT

Who do you think is an appropriate professional to hire for preparing your taxes?

As You Read

RELATE

Do you have a friend or relative who has been audited? What was his or her reaction?

Figure 12.7   Tax Assistance Is There for You

When you must file your income tax returns, take advantage of these tax assistance products and services.

1 IRS Web Site   Like all government agencies, the IRS is online. You can download forms and obtain important tax information and advice. You will find the same services at your local IRS office.

2 Books   Visit a bookstore to uncover shelves of how-to books about tax planning and completing tax forms. Personal finance magazines offer tax information as well.

3 Software   Tax preparation software is updated yearly to reflect changes in the tax laws.

4 Professionals   Tax professionals can help you with your tax preparation, answer questions, and determine if you are eligible for deductions and credits.

Planning Tax Strategies

What are some basic strategies to reduce the amount of tax you owe?

Smart taxpayers know how to legally minimize the amount of tax they have to pay. You must pay your fair share, but you do not have to pay more. Various strategies related to purchases, investments, and retirement help reduce the amount of tax you owe.

Consumer Purchasing Strategies

The buying decisions you make can affect the amount of taxes you pay. For example, if you purchase a house, the interest you pay on your mortgage and your real estate property taxes are deductible. You can also deduct the interest on a home equity loan. The IRS allows you to deduct the interest on home equity loans up to $100,000. Therefore, buying a home provides advantages that may reduce your income tax.

Some job-related expenses may also be deducted. Union dues, some travel and education expenses, business tools, and certain job-search expenses qualify. Only the portion of these expenses that exceeds 2 percent of your adjusted gross income is deductible. However, expenses related to finding your first job or obtaining work in a different field are not deductible.

Investment Decisions

Certain investment decisions may also reduce your income tax. Moreover, some investment decisions can increase your income—and lower your taxes. For example, the interest on municipal bonds is not usually taxed. Other investments may be tax-deferred, which means that the income is taxed at a later date.

As You Read

QUESTION

What are some job-related expenses that you can deduct from your taxes?

◄ **BUY TO SAVE** When purchasing products such as office supplies, you may be able to take tax deductions for business expenses. *What is one other type of expense that is deductible?*

Learn to identify and understand the standard financial documents you will use in the real world.

Investigate: Form W-2

A Form W-2 contains the following information:

- Employer's name and address
- Employee's name, address, and Social Security number
- Wages the employee earned
- Taxes withheld from earnings

Your Motive: The Form W-2 provides much of the information that you need to file your yearly federal income tax return. You must save this form and attach copies to your income tax return.

a Control number	22222	Void ☐	For Official Use Only ▶ OMB No. 1545-0008		
b Employer identification number (EIN) 26 - 8310024				1 Wages, tips, other compensation 86.411.75	2 Federal income tax withheld 21,880.59
c Employer's name, address, and ZIP code Group Transportation 37 Main Street Tampa, FL 33606				3 Social security wages 87,900.00	4 Social security tax withheld 5449.80
				5 Medicare wages and tips 88,775.00	6 Medicare tax withheld 1287.24
				7 Social security tips	8 Allocated tips
d Employee's social security number XXX - XX-7822				9 Advance EIC payment	10 Dependent care benefits
e Employee's first name and initial Theresa C. Last name Alvarez				11 Nonqualified plans	12a See instructions for box 12
1335 Smith Lane Tampa, FL 33605				13 Statutory employee ☐ Retirement plan ☐ Third-party sick pay ☐	12b
				14 Other	12c
					12d
f Employee's address and ZIP code					

15 State	Employer's state ID number	16 State wages, tips, etc.	17 State income tax	18 Local wages, tips, etc.	19 Local income tax	20 Locality name
FL	61 – 281517	86411.75	5326.50	88775.00	887.75	Tampa

Form **W-2** Wage and Tax Statement **20 - -**

Department of the Treasury—Internal Revenue Service

Copy A For Social Security Administration — Send this entire page with Form W-3 to the Social Security Administration; photocopies are **not** acceptable.

For Privacy Act and Paperwork Reduction Act Notice, see back of Copy D.

Cat. No. 10134D

Do Not Cut, Fold, or Staple Forms on This Page — Do Not Cut, Fold, or Staple Forms on This Page

Key Points: A Form W-2 is a document that employers are required to prepare and distribute to each employee and the IRS by the end of January each year. The form details the wages earned by the worker as well as all taxes withheld for the year. The Form W-2 is labeled and numbered to coincide with the IRS Form 1040 and Form 1040EZ income tax form.

Find the Solutions

1. What are Theresa's wages, tips, and other compensation for 2007?
2. How much was withheld from her wages for Social Security?
3. How much state income tax was withheld from her wages?
4. What is the employer's identification number?
5. What are Theresa's total Social Security wages?

Retirement Plans

Regardless of your age, whether you are 16 or 26, now is the time to start planning for your retirement. To encourage early planning, the government allows you to defer paying taxes on money that you invest in retirement plans. If you open an Individual Retirement Account (IRA) this year, the money you invest, up to a certain amount and under certain conditions, may qualify as a tax deduction. You do not have to pay any income tax on this money and the interest it earns until you withdraw it—perhaps 50 years from now!

Changing Your Tax Strategy

People pay taxes because they are required to do so by law. The government tries to find ways to minimize the taxes you owe without jeopardizing the important services it provides. This is one reason why the tax laws are always changing. Your tax strategies should change too. As the government allows new deductions or as deductible amounts change, you should review your financial plans to always take full advantage of new tax laws that may reduce the amount you pay.

After You Read
REACT

How does the government encourage early saving for retirement? Do you think starting to save for retirement when you are young is a good idea? Why?

Section 12.3 Assessment

QUICK CHECK

1. What are three sources of tax assistance?
2. How do purchasing decisions affect the amount of taxes you pay?
3. What types of investments might you make for tax purposes?

THINK CRITICALLY

4. Using what you have learned in this chapter, recommend several precautions that you might take to avoid a tax audit.

USE MATH SKILLS

5. **Personalized Tax Assistance**   Tax professionals can provide you with advice about how to minimize the amount of tax you have to pay and still pay a fair amount.

Role-Play   In pairs, role-play a tax professional and a client. The client should ask the tax professional for tax planning strategies. The tax professional should provide accurate and helpful answers to the client's questions.

SOLVE MONEY PROBLEMS

6. **Tax Audits**   Felicia cannot believe it. She has just heard from the IRS that she will be audited for the past two years. She has no idea why. Felicia does not know where to begin to prepare.

Write About It   Help Felicia put together a plan of action. Write a plan listing what she will need, whom she should consult, and how she should act.

CHAPTER SUMMARY

- Financial planning involves taxes because they reduce your take-home pay. Other financial decisions also affect the amount of taxes you pay.
- Your taxable income is earned income plus interest and dividend income minus exclusions, deductions, and exemptions.
- Tax deductions are expenses you are allowed to subtract from your adjusted gross income to arrive at your taxable income. The standard deduction is determined by the Internal Revenue Service. Tax credits are subtracted directly from the tax you owe.
- An employee fills out a W-4 form, which determines the tax withheld.

Preparing the W-4 form correctly ensures an employer will withhold the right amount of money owed to the IRS and state and local taxing authorities.

- Form 1040EZ is for filers with no dependents and less than a certain amount in taxable income. Form 1040A allows filers to claim deductions for IRA contributions and tax credits. Form 1040 must be filed if you are itemizing deductions and/or have more than a certain amount in taxable income.
- You can make strategic decisions that may reduce your tax liability, such as buying a home or saving money in an IRA.

Communicating Key Terms

Your family is hosting an exchange student from another country. He asks about the income tax system. Using the terms below, write an explanation of the ways people pay taxes in the U.S.

- tax liability
- estate tax
- inheritance tax
- income tax
- income tax return
- exclusion
- adjusted gross income
- taxable income
- tax deduction
- standard deduction
- itemized deduction
- exemption
- tax credit
- allowance
- extension
- tax audit

Reviewing Key Concepts

1. **Describe** how taxes have an impact on financial planning.
2. **Explain** how you determine your adjusted gross income and taxable income.
3. **Describe** why you should itemize deductions as opposed to taking the standard deduction.
4. **Identify** the factors to consider when filling out the W-4 form for your employer.
5. **Describe** the 1040EZ, 1040A, and 1040 income tax forms.
6. **List** some tax advantages of retirement investing.

ACADEMIC SKILLS

Civics/Government The rate or percentage at which the federal government taxes your income is determined by your tax bracket, which is your level of income. Each year, the tax brackets can change.

Write About It Research and write a paragraph explaining how the government decides the income tax rates and tax brackets for taxpayers.

YOUR FINANCIAL FIGURES

How Much Tax Do You Owe? Your gross earnings last year were $33,435, and your taxable interest income was $486. You also earned $3,766 on freelance projects, on which you have not paid any income tax. Last year, you contributed $512 to your company 401(k) retirement plan.

1. **Calculate** the tax you owe by using the six-rate system shown in Figure 12.1 on page 385.
2. **Compute** by using financial planning or tax software to determine your tax liability.

REAL-WORLD Application

Connect with Social Studies The U.S. government now excludes up to $1.5 million of an estate from tax. However, states vary in how they tax estates, whether they tax inheritances, and how much is excluded. New Jersey, for example, does not tax the inheritances of a deceased person's spouse and children but does tax other people who inherit.

1. **Research** Find out how your state taxes estates and inheritances.
2. **Write About It** Why do federal and state governments exclude parts of estates from taxation? What is your opinion about the variation in estate and inheritance taxes depending on the state where you die?

Internet CONNECTION

Charitable Contributions The IRS categorizes non-governmental organizations into various types. Organizations that qualify for 501c3 status are charitable, educational, and beneficial. Contributions to these organizations, including travel expenses in volunteering (but not time) are deductible.

Log On Go to persfinance07.glencoe.com for a link to the IRS Web site. Click on Charities and Non-Profits. Find out about the rules and limits on the deductibility of contributions. Answer these questions:

1. What records do you need to keep?
2. Where on your income tax return do you indicate these deductions?

BusinessWeek ONLINE

Newsclip: Tax Checkup Tax laws can change each year. Knowing the new rules can help you save money.

Log On Go to persfinance07.glencoe.com and open Chapter 12. Learn about the laws or tax updates during 2004. What do you need to know before filing your tax return from your summer job?

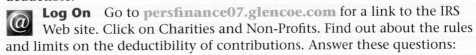

WHAT'S YOUR FINANCIAL ID?

TEST YOUR TAX FACTS

The more you know about the way tax laws relate to your personal finances, the easier it is to file your taxes. To test your knowledge of tax strategy, write the answer to these questions on a separate sheet of paper.

1. The tax-reporting requirement for cash tips is _____ .
   a. you need to report tips and pay taxes on them
   b. you do not need to report cash tips on your tax return
   c. your employer takes care of it

2. Besides saving your tax returns you need to keep all necessary paperwork and receipts for at least _____ .
   a. 1 year   b. 6 years   c. 20 years

3. Tax-deferred income is _____ .
   a. income that is not subject to tax
   b. income that has had all its fur removed
   c. income that will be taxed at a later date

4. Tax-exempt income is _____ .
   a. income that is not subject to tax
   b. income that you invest
   c. income that will be taxed at a later date

5. You would use the standard deduction instead of itemizing your deductions when _____ .
   a. itemized deductions are more than the standard deduction
   b. itemized deductions are less than the standard deduction
   c. line 32 on Schedule C exceeds the allowable limit of line 12 on Schedule E on Form 1040A

6. Estate tax is a _____ .
   a. tax on capital gains from selling a house
   b. tax on money withdrawn from a retirement account
   c. tax on the value of a person's property at the time of death

7. The person responsible for the contents of your tax return is _____ .
   a. your tax preparer
   b. your mom and dad
   c. you

8. If you itemize your deductions, you can deduct interest on _____ .
   a. credit cards
   b. mortgages, home equity, and student loans
   c. car loans

Your Financial Portfolio

Take It EZ

Using a photocopy of this form, complete your income tax return. Assume that your wages for the year were $13,220 and you earned $137 in interest. Your W-2 form shows that you had $1,003 in federal income tax withheld. Your parents cannot claim you on their income tax return. Find your tax using the tax table on page 397, and then calculate your refund or the amount you owe.

Form **1040EZ**	Department of the Treasury—Internal Revenue Service **Income Tax Return for Single and Joint Filers With No Dependents** (99) **20--**		OMB No. 1545-0675

Label (See page 11.) Use the IRS label. Otherwise, please print or type.

Your first name and initial	Last name	Your social security number
If a joint return, spouse's first name and initial	Last name	Spouse's social security number
Home address (number and street). If you have a P.O. box, see page 11.	Apt. no.	▲ **Important!** ▲ You **must** enter your SSN(s) above.
City, town or post office, state, and ZIP code. If you have a foreign address, see page 11.		

Presidential Election Campaign (page 11) ▶

Note. Checking "Yes" will not change your tax or reduce your refund.
Do you, or your spouse if a joint return, want $3 to go to this fund? . . . . . ▶

	You	Spouse
	☐Yes ☐No	☐Yes ☐No

Income
Attach Form(s) W-2 here.
Enclose, but do not attach, any payment.

1 Wages, salaries, and tips. This should be shown in box 1 of your Form(s) W-2. Attach your Form(s) W-2. — 1

2 Taxable interest. If the total is over $1,500, you cannot use Form 1040EZ. — 2

3 Unemployment compensation and Alaska Permanent Fund dividends (see page 13). — 3

4 Add lines 1, 2, and 3. This is your **adjusted gross income.** — 4

Note. You **must** check Yes or No.

5 Can your parents (or someone else) claim you on their return?
Yes. Enter amount from worksheet on back. **No.** If **single,** enter $7,950. If **married filing jointly,** enter $15,900. See back for explanation. — 5

6 Subtract line 5 from line 4. If line 5 is larger than line 4, enter -0-. This is your **taxable income.** ▶ 6

Payments and tax

7 Federal income tax withheld from box 2 of your Form(s) W-2. — 7

8a **Earned income credit (EIC).** — 8a

b Nontaxable combat pay election. — 8b

9 Add lines 7 and 8a. These are your **total payments.** ▶ 9

10 **Tax.** Use the amount on **line 6 above** to find your tax in the tax table on pages 24–32 of the booklet. Then, enter the tax from the table on this line. — 10

Refund
Have it directly deposited! See page 18 and fill in 11b, 11c, and 11d.

11a If line 9 is larger than line 10, subtract line 10 from line 9. This is your **refund.** ▶ 11a

▶ b Routing number _____ ▶ c Type: ☐ Checking ☐ Savings

▶ d Account number _____

Amount you owe

12 If line 10 is larger than line 9, subtract line 9 from line 10. This is the **amount you owe.** For details on how to pay, see page 19. ▶ 12

Third party designee

Do you want to allow another person to discuss this return with the IRS (see page 19)? ☐ **Yes.** Complete the following. ☐ **No**
Designee's name ▶ Phone no. ▶ ( ) Personal identification number (PIN) _____

Sign here
Joint return? See page 11.
Keep a copy for your records.

Under penalties of perjury, I declare that I have examined this return, and to the best of my knowledge and belief, it is true, correct, and accurately lists all amounts and sources of income I received during the tax year. Declaration of preparer (other than the taxpayer) is based on all information of which the preparer has any knowledge.

Your signature	Date	Your occupation	Daytime phone number ( )
Spouse's signature. If a joint return, **both** must sign.	Date	Spouse's occupation	

Paid preparer's use only

Preparer's signature ▶	Date	Check if self-employed ☐	Preparer's SSN or PTIN
Firm's name (or yours if self-employed), address, and ZIP code ▶		EIN :	
		Phone no. ( )	

For Disclosure, Privacy Act, and Paperwork Reduction Act Notice, see page 23. Cat. No. 11329W Form **1040EZ** (20--)

Home and Motor Vehicle Insurance

 What You'll Learn

When you have completed this chapter, you will be able to:

Section 13.1
- Identify types of risks and risk management methods.
- Explain how an insurance program can help manage risks.
- Describe the importance of property and liability insurance.

Section 13.2
- Identify the types of insurance coverage and policies available to homeowners and renters.
- Analyze the factors that influence the amount of coverage and cost of home insurance.

Section 13.3
- Identify the important types of motor vehicle insurance coverage.
- Explain factors that affect the cost of motor vehicle insurance.

Reading Strategies

To get the most out of your reading:

Predict what you will learn in this chapter.

Relate what you read to your own life.

Question what you are reading to be sure you understand.

React to what you have read.

In the **Real** World . . .

Josh Peterson just got his driver's license and bought a used car. According to state law, he was required to obtain auto insurance. Josh was alarmed by how much auto insurance cost—it was almost as much as his car payments. A month later, Josh became involved in his first traffic accident. Although no one was hurt and the damage to the cars was minimal, he was shocked to learn how much repairs cost. He was thankful he had auto insurance. Because Josh caused the accident, his auto insurance premiums would increase. His mother said they could shop around for an auto insurer with a better rate, but they would have to pay the higher rate for now.

As You Read *Consider why it is important to have insurance for protection.*

Insurance Rates

Q: My brother is 17 and has an excellent driving record. Why are his motor vehicle insurance rates higher than rates for females in his same age group?

A: Insurance rates are based on an analysis of accident statistics for all types of drivers. Since young men have a higher incidence of being involved in accidents than young women have, insurance rates for young men are more expensive. Some insurance companies offer discounts for young adults covered on a parent's policy.

Ask Yourself What can you do to ensure that your insurance rate stays as low as possible?

 Go to **persfinance07.glencoe.com** to complete the Standard & Poor's Financial Focus activity.

Insurance and Risk Management

Read to Learn

- How to identify types of risks and risk management methods.
- How to explain how an insurance program can help manage risks.
- How to describe the importance of property and liability insurance.

Main Idea

Recognizing the importance of insurance and knowing how to develop an insurance program can protect you from financial loss.

Key Terms

- insurance
- policy
- premium
- risk
- peril
- hazard
- negligence
- deductible
- liability

Before You Read

PREDICT

What do you think are the benefits of having a good insurance program?

What Is Insurance?

Why is it important to have insurance?

Insurance is protection against possible financial loss. Since you cannot predict the future, you never know when something bad might happen to you or your property. Insurance allows you to be prepared for the worst. It provides protection against many risks, such as unexpected property loss, illness, and injury. Although many kinds of insurance exist, they all have several characteristics in common. For example, they give you peace of mind, and they protect you from financial loss when trouble strikes.

An insurance company, or insurer, is a risk-sharing business that agrees to pay for losses that may happen to someone it insures. A person joins the risk-sharing group by purchasing a contract known as a **policy**. The purchaser of the policy is called a policyholder. Under the policy, the insurance company agrees to take on the risk of the policyholder. In return, the policyholder pays the company a **premium**, which is a fee for insurance. The protection provided by the terms of an insurance policy is known as *coverage,* and the person protected by the policy is known as the *insured.*

Types of Risks

What are the most common types of risks?

Risk, peril, and *hazard* are important terms in insurance. In everyday use, these terms have almost the same meanings. In the insurance business, however, each word has a distinct and special meaning.

Risk is the chance of loss or injury. You face risks every day. For example, if you cross the street, there is some danger that a motor vehicle might hit you. If you own property, there is risk that it will be lost, stolen, damaged, or destroyed.

In the insurance business, risk refers to the fact that no one can predict trouble. This means that an insurance company is taking a chance every time it issues a policy. Insurance companies frequently refer to the insured person or property as *the risk.*

Peril is anything that may possibly cause a loss. It is the reason that someone takes out insurance. People buy policies for protection against a wide range of perils, including fire, windstorms, explosions, robbery, and accidents.

Hazard is anything that increases the likelihood of loss through peril. For example, defective electrical wiring in a house is a hazard that increases the chance that a fire will start.

The most common risks are personal risks, property risks, and liability risks. Personal risks involve loss of income or life due to illness, disability, old age, or unemployment. Property risks include losses to property caused by perils, such as fire or theft, and hazards. Liability risks involve losses caused by negligence that leads to injury or property damage. **Negligence** is the failure to take ordinary or reasonable care to prevent accidents from happening. If a homeowner does not clear the ice from the front steps of her house, for example, he or she creates a liability risk because visitors could fall on the ice.

Personal risks, property risks, and liability risks are types of pure, or insurable, risk. The insurance company will have to pay only if some event that the insurance covers actually happens. Pure risks are accidental and unintentional. Although no one can predict whether a pure risk will occur, it is possible to predict how much it will cost if it does.

A speculative risk is a risk that carries a chance of either loss or gain. Starting a small business that may or may not succeed is an example of speculative risk. Speculative risks are not insurable.

As You Read

RELATE

Do you have any insurance now? If so, what kind?

Risk-Management Methods
Why is risk management important?

Risk management is an organized plan for protecting yourself, your family, and your property. It helps reduce financial losses caused by destructive events. Risk management is a long-range planning process. Your risk-management needs will change at various points in your life. If you understand how to manage risks, you can provide better protection for yourself and your family. **Figure 13.1** on page 415 summarizes various risks and effective ways of managing them.

Most people think of risk management as buying insurance. However, insurance is not the only way of dealing with risk.

Risk Avoidance

You can avoid the risk of a traffic accident by not driving to work. A car manufacturer can avoid the risk of product failure by not introducing new cars. These are both examples of risk avoidance. They are ways to avoid risks, but they involve serious trade-offs. You might have to give up your job if you cannot get there by driving a car. The car manufacturer might lose business to competitors who take the risk of producing exciting new cars.

In some cases, though, risk avoidance is practical. For example, by taking precautions in high-crime areas, you might avoid the risk of being robbed. By installing a security system in your car, you might avoid the risk of having it stolen.

Risk Reduction

You cannot avoid risks completely. However, you can decrease the likelihood that they will cause you harm. For example, you can reduce the risk of injury in a car accident by wearing a seat belt. You can reduce the risk of developing lung cancer by not smoking. By installing fire extinguishers in your home, you can reduce the damage that could be caused by a fire. In addition, you can lower your risk of illness by eating properly and exercising regularly.

▲ **REDUCING RISKS** Taking steps to protect yourself and your property from harm can reduce your risk of financial loss. *Besides wearing your seat belt, what are some other ways of reducing risks when you are driving?*

Risk Assumption

Risk assumption means taking on responsibility for the negative results of a risk. It makes sense to assume a risk if you know that the possible loss will be small. It also makes sense when you have taken all the precautions you can to avoid or reduce the risk.

When insurance coverage for a particular item is expensive, it may not be worth insuring. For instance, older cars are generally worth less than new cars. So even if an accident happens and the car is wrecked, you may be better off financially by not paying for the insurance coverage since the car was not worth much anyway.

Self-insurance is another option for risk assumption. By setting up your own special fund, perhaps from savings, you can cover the cost of loss. Self-insurance does not eliminate risks, but it does provide a way of covering losses as an alternative to an insurance policy. Some people self-insure because they cannot obtain insurance from an insurance company.

Risk Shifting

The most common method of dealing with risk is to shift it, which means to transfer it to an insurance company. In exchange for the fee you pay, the insurance company agrees to pay for your losses.

Most types of insurance policies include deductibles. Deductibles are a combination of risk assumption and risk shifting. A **deductible** is the set amount that the policyholder must pay per loss on an insurance policy. For example, if a falling tree damages your car, you may have to pay $200 toward the repairs. Your insurance company will pay the rest.

Planning an Insurance Program
What factors will affect your insurance goals?

Your personal insurance program should change along with your needs and goals. For example, Kirk and Luanne are a young married couple. The following four steps outline how they will plan their insurance program to meet their needs and goals.

STEP 1: Set Insurance Goals

Kirk and Luanne's main goal should be to minimize personal, property, and liability risks. They also need to decide how they will cover costs resulting from a potential loss. Income, age, family size, lifestyle, experience, and responsibilities are important factors in determining the goals they set. The insurance that they buy must reflect those goals.

Kirk and Luanne should try to come up with a basic risk-management plan that achieves the following goals:

- Reduces possible loss of income caused by premature death, illness, accident, or unemployment
- Reduces possible loss of property caused by perils, such as fire or theft, or hazards
- Reduces possible loss of income, savings, and property caused by personal negligence

Figure 13.1   Risks and Risk Management Strategies

Personal Events	Risks Financial Impact	Strategies for Reducing Financial Impact
Disability	• Loss of income • Increased expenses	• Savings and investments • Disability insurance
Death	• Loss of income	• Life insurance • Estate planning
Property Loss	• Catastrophic storm damage to property • Repair or replacement • Cost of theft	• Property repair and upkeep • Motor vehicle insurance • Homeowners insurance • Flood or earthquake insurance
Liability	• Claims and settlement costs • Lawsuits and legal expenses • Loss of personal assets and income	• Maintaining property • Homeowners insurance • Auto insurance

Risky Business   Risk management strategies help reduce the financial impact of various risks.

Can you think of other strategies that would apply to the risks mentioned in the chart?

Step 2: Develop a Plan

Planning is a way of taking control of your life instead of just letting life happen to you. Kirk and Luanne need to determine what risks they face and what risks they can afford to take. They also have to determine what resources can help them reduce the damage that could be caused by serious risks.

Furthermore, they need to know what kind of insurance is available. The cost of different kinds of insurance and the way the costs vary among companies will be key factors in their plan. Finally, this couple needs to research the record of reliability of different insurance companies.

Kirk and Luanne must ask four questions as they develop their risk-management plan:

- What do they need to insure?
- For how much should they insure it?
- What kind of insurance should they buy?
- Which insurance company should they choose?

Step 3: Put Your Plan into Action

After they have developed their plan, Kirk and Luanne need to follow through by putting it into action. During this process they might discover that they do not have enough insurance protection. If that is the case, they could purchase additional coverage or change the kind of coverage they have. Another alternative would be to adjust their budget to cover the cost of additional insurance. Finally, Kirk and Luanne might expand their savings or investment programs and use those funds in the case of an emergency.

The best risk-management plans will be flexible enough to allow Kirk and Luanne to respond to changing life situations. Their goal should be to create an insurance program that can grow or shrink as their protection needs change.

Step 4: Review Your Results

You should take time to review a risk-management plan every two or three years, or whenever family circumstances change.

For example, Kirk and Luanne have been satisfied with the coverage provided by their insurance policies. However, when the couple bought a house six months ago, it was time for them to review their insurance plan. With the new house, the risks became much greater. After all, what would happen if a fire destroyed part of their home?

The needs of a couple who rent an apartment differ from the needs of a couple who own a house. Both couples face similar risks, but their financial responsibilities differ greatly. When you are developing or reviewing a risk-management plan, ask yourself if you are providing the financial resources you will need to protect yourself, your family, if you have one, and your property.

Property and Liability Insurance in Your Financial Plan

Why is it important to include property and liability insurance in a financial plan?

Major natural disasters have caused catastrophic amounts of property loss in the United States and other parts of the world. In 2004, the damage caused by Hurricane Charley resulted in $6.8 billion in insurance claims in the state of Florida alone. Insurance claims are requests for payment to cover financial losses. Without the money they received from their insurance, the people affected by the hurricane may not have been able to make repairs to their homes.

Most people spend a great deal of money on their houses, vehicles, furniture, clothing, and other personal property. Therefore, protecting these items from loss is extremely important. Each year homeowners and renters in the United States lose billions of dollars from more than 3 million burglaries, 500,000 fires, and 200,000 cases of damage from other perils. The cost of injuries and property damage caused by vehicles is also enormous. By including property and liability insurance in your financial plan, you can help protect yourself from such financial loss.

Think of the price you pay for insurance as an investment in the protection of your most valuable possessions. Although the cost of such insurance may seem high, the financial losses against which it protects could be much higher.

There are two main types of risks related to your home and your car or other vehicle. One is the risk of damage to or loss of your property. The second type of risk involves your responsibility for injuries to other people or damage to their property.

▼ **DISASTROUS RESULTS** Events such as hurricanes and tornados can cause widespread devastation. *What can you do to protect your property against natural disasters?*

Property Damage or Loss

Property owners face two basic types of risks. The first is physical damage caused by perils such as fire, wind, and flooding. These perils can damage or destroy your property. For example, a windstorm might cause a large tree branch to smash the windshield of your car. As a result, you would have to find another way to get around while it was being repaired.

The second type of risk that property owners face is loss or damage caused by criminal behavior, such as robbery, burglary, vandalism, and arson. Insurance can help you protect yourself from loss of or damage to your property.

As You Read

QUESTION

Why do most people want to have their cars, homes, and personal property insured?

Liability

Liability is legal responsibility for the financial cost of another person's losses or injuries. You can be judged legally responsible even if the injury or damage was not your fault. For example, suppose that Terry falls and gets hurt while playing in her friend Lisa's yard. Terry's family may be able to sue Lisa's parents even though Lisa's parents did nothing wrong. Similarly, suppose that Sanjay accidentally damages a valuable painting while helping Ed move some of his furniture. Ed may take legal action against Sanjay to pay for the cost of the painting.

Usually, if you are found liable (or legally responsible) in a situation, it is because negligence on your part caused the mishap. Examples of such negligence include letting young children swim in a pool without supervision or cluttering a staircase with things that could cause someone to slip and fall, and become injured.

Section 13.1 Assessment

QUICK CHECK

1. What are the three main types of insurable risks?
2. How can developing an insurance program help you manage risk?
3. Why are property and liability insurance necessary to protect a homeowner from financial loss?

THINK CRITICALLY

4. "Insurance is a waste of money. If and when you suffer a financial loss because of an accident or some other event, you can pay for it from your savings account." Do you agree or disagree with this statement? Explain your position.

USE COMMUNICATION SKILLS

5. **My Favorite Things** Make a list of your most valuable possessions. Consider new and used items that may have collectible value. Also consider how much it would cost to replace your valuable possessions.

Write About It Write a paragraph discussing the personal and financial consequences of having the items on your list lost, stolen, damaged, or destroyed. Also explain the effect of having the items insured in the event of loss.

SOLVE MONEY PROBLEMS

6. **Paying for Insurance Protection** Hans has recently purchased a fully restored 1957 Chevy. The car cost $35,000, but for Hans, the price was worth it. The best price he can find for insurance is $2,500 per year. He is thinking about cutting corners on his insurance coverage to save money. However, he knows he would be taking a risk by doing so.

Calculate Help Hans solve his problem by comparing the cost of his insurance with the cost of his vehicle. Is it worth the insurance expense to protect his prized vehicle, or is it too much to spend to insure what is, after all, just a car?

Home and Property Insurance

Homeowners Insurance Coverage

What does a homeowners insurance policy cover?

Insuring your residence and its contents is absolutely necessary to protect your investment. **Homeowners insurance** is coverage that provides protection for your residence and its associated financial risks, such as damage to personal property and injuries to others.

A homeowners policy provides coverage for the following:

- The home, building, or any other structures on the property
- Additional living expenses
- Personal property
- Personal liability and related coverages
- Specialized coverages

Buildings and Other Structures

The main purpose of homeowners insurance is to protect you against financial loss in case your home is damaged or destroyed. Detached structures on your property, such as a garage and tool shed, are also covered under a homeowners insurance policy. In fact, the insurance coverage even includes trees, shrubs, and other plants, which are landscaping.

Additional Living Expenses

If a fire or other event damages your home, additional living expense coverage pays for you to stay somewhere else. For example, you may need to stay in a motel or rent an apartment while your home is being repaired or rebuilt. These extra living expenses will be paid for by your insurance. Some policies limit additional living expense coverage to 10 to 20 percent of the home's total coverage amount. They may also limit the payment period to a maximum of six to nine months. Other policies may pay additional living expenses for up to a year.

Personal Property

Household belongings, such as furniture, appliances, and clothing, are covered by the personal property portion of a homeowners insurance policy up to a portion of the insured value of the home. That portion is usually 55, 70, or 75 percent. For example, a home insured for $80,000 might have $56,000 (70 percent) worth of coverage for household belongings.

Personal property coverage typically includes limits for the theft of certain items, such as $1,000 for jewelry. It also provides protection against the loss or damage of articles that you take with you when you are away from home. For example, items you take on vacation or use at school are usually covered up to the policy limit. Personal property coverage even extends to property that you rent, such as a rug cleaner, while it is in your possession.

Most homeowners policies also include optional coverage for personal computers, including stored data, up to a certain limit. Your insurance agent can determine whether the computer equipment is covered against data loss as well as damage from spilled drinks or power surges.

Household Inventories If something does happen to your personal property, you must prove how much it was worth and that it belonged to you. To make the process easier, you can create a household inventory. A household inventory is a list or other documentation of personal belongings, with purchase dates and cost information. You can get a form for an inventory from an insurance agent. **Figure 13.2** provides a list of items you might include if you decide to compile your own household inventory. For items of special value, you should have receipts, serial numbers, brand names, model names, and proof of value.

In addition, keep a video recording or photographs of your home and its contents with your inventory list. Make sure that closet and storage area doors are photographed open. On the backs of the photographs, indicate the date and the value of the objects pictured. Update your inventory, photos, and related documents on a regular basis. Keep a copy of each document in a secure location, such as a safe-deposit box.

Additional Property Insurance If you own valuable items, such as expensive musical instruments, or need added protection for computers and related equipment, you can purchase a personal property floater. A **personal property floater** is additional property insurance that covers the damage or loss of a specific item of high value. The insurance company will require a detailed description of the item and its worth. You will also need to have the item appraised, or evaluated, by an expert from time to time to make sure that its value has not changed. In addition, keep photographs of valuable items as well as descriptions, receipts, and appraisals.

As You Read

RELATE

Do you own something you think should be insured separately from your parents' homeowners insurance?

Figure 13.2 **Household Inventory**

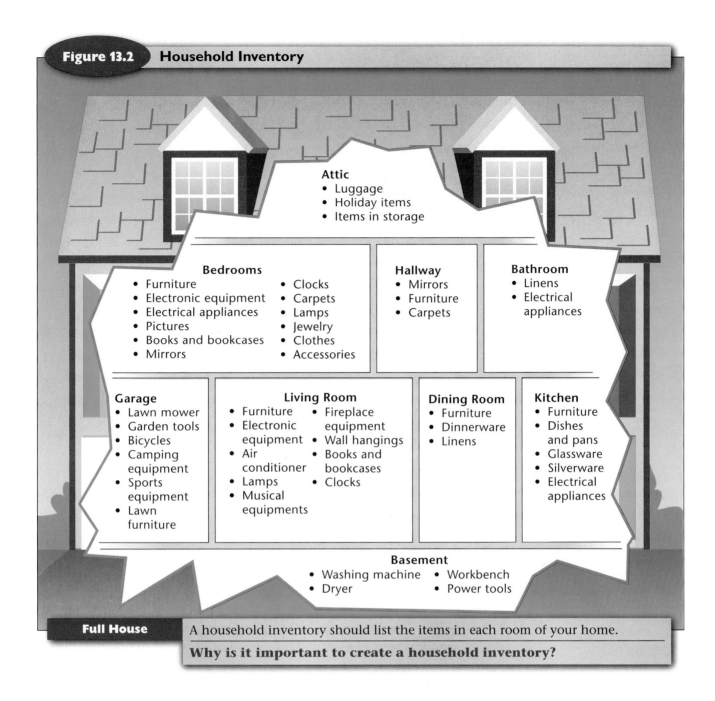

Attic
- Luggage
- Holiday items
- Items in storage

Bedrooms
- Furniture
- Electronic equipment
- Electrical appliances
- Pictures
- Books and bookcases
- Mirrors
- Clocks
- Carpets
- Lamps
- Jewelry
- Clothes
- Accessories

Hallway
- Mirrors
- Furniture
- Carpets

Bathroom
- Linens
- Electrical appliances

Garage
- Lawn mower
- Garden tools
- Bicycles
- Camping equipment
- Sports equipment
- Lawn furniture

Living Room
- Furniture
- Electronic equipment
- Air conditioner
- Lamps
- Musical equipments
- Fireplace equipment
- Wall hangings
- Books and bookcases
- Clocks

Dining Room
- Furniture
- Dinnerware
- Linens

Kitchen
- Furniture
- Dishes and pans
- Glassware
- Silverware
- Electrical appliances

Basement
- Washing machine
- Dryer
- Workbench
- Power tools

Full House A household inventory should list the items in each room of your home.

Why is it important to create a household inventory?

Personal Liability and Related Coverages

Every day people face the risk of financial loss due to injuries to other people or their property. For example, a guest could fall on a patch of ice on the steps to your home and break his arm. A spark from the barbecue in your backyard could start a fire that damages a neighbor's roof, or your son or daughter could accidentally break an antique lamp while playing at a neighbor's house.

In these situations, you could be held responsible for paying for the damage. The personal liability portion of a homeowners policy protects you and members of your family if others, except regular employees, sue you for injuries they suffer or for damage to their property. This coverage includes the cost of legal defense.

▲ ADDITIONAL PROTECTION
The purchase of a valuable item such as a high-quality musical instrument is a major investment. *Why would a person who buys an expensive piano get a personal property floater for it?*

Amounts of Coverage Most homeowners policies provide basic personal liability coverage of $100,000, but often that is not enough. An umbrella policy, also called a *personal catastrophe policy,* supplements basic personal liability coverage. This added protection covers all kinds of personal injury claims. For example, an umbrella policy will cover you if someone sues you for saying or writing something negative or untrue, damaging his or her reputation.

Extended liability policies are useful for wealthy people and for businesses. The policies are sold in amounts of $1 million or more. If you are a business owner, you may need other types of liability coverage as well.

Medical payments coverage pays the costs of minor accidental injuries to visitors on your property. It also covers minor injuries caused by you, members of your family, or even your pets, away from home. Settlements under medical payments coverage are made without determining who was at fault. This makes it fast and easy for the insurance company to process small claims, generally up to $5,000. If the injury is more serious, the personal liability portion of the homeowners policy covers it. Medical payments coverage does not cover injury to you or the other people who live in your home.

If you or a family member should accidentally damage another person's property, the supplementary coverage of homeowners insurance will pay for it. This protection is usually limited to $500 or $1,000. Again, payments are made regardless of fault. If the damage is more expensive, however, it is handled under the personal liability coverage.

Specialized Coverages

Homeowners insurance usually does not cover losses from floods and earthquakes. If you lived in an area that had frequent floods or earthquakes, you would need to purchase special coverage. In some places the National Flood Insurance Program, run by the federal government, makes flood insurance available. This protection is separate from a homeowners policy. An insurance agent or the Federal Emergency Management Agency (FEMA) of the Federal Insurance Administration can give you additional information about this coverage.

STANDARD &POOR'S

Global Financial Landscape

Standard and Poor's publishes the globally recognized S&P 500® financial index. It also gathers financial statistics, information, and news, and analyzes this data for international businesses, governments, and individuals to help them guide their financial decisions.

GERMANY

Sometimes called the "Motherland of the Automotive Industry," Germany is one of the world's leading car manufacturers. From the luxurious Mercedes-Benz to the sleek and sporty Porsche to the unique and practical Volkswagen Beetle, Germans design cars that turn heads. In fact, the German-made Volkswagen Beetle has been called the "most popular vehicle of all time."

The German economy has experienced ups and downs, but car manufacturing has remained one of its cornerstones. The industry pulls in over $90 million in sales within the country and over $145 billion from other countries. The United States, with its fondness for status cars, is Germany's number one foreign market.

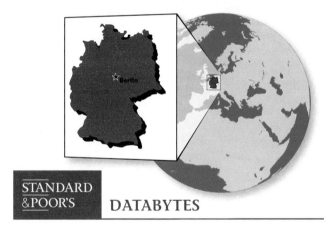

STANDARD &POOR'S DATABYTES

Capital	Berlin
Population	82,621,000
Languages	German
Currency	euro
Gross Domestic Product (GDP)	$2.27 trillion (2003 est.)
GDP per capita	$27,600

Industry: Iron, steel, coal, cement, chemicals, machinery, vehicles, machine tools, and electronics

Agriculture: Potatoes, wheat, barley, sugar beets, and cattle

Exports: Machinery, vehicles, chemicals, metals, foodstuffs, and textiles

Natural Resources: Iron ore, coal, potash, and timber

Think Globally
Automobile insurance is higher for someone who owns a sports car such as a Porsche. Why?

You may be able to get earthquake or flood insurance as an endorsement (addition of coverage) to a homeowners policy or through a state-run insurance program. The most serious earthquakes occur in the Pacific Coast region. However, earthquakes can happen in other regions, too. If you purchase a home in an area that has a high risk of earthquakes or floods, you may have to buy insurance for those risks.

Renters Insurance
Why is it important for a renter to get renters insurance?

For people who rent, home insurance coverages include personal property protection, additional living expenses coverage, and personal liability and related coverages. Renters insurance does not provide coverage on the building or other structures.

The most important part of renters insurance is the protection it provides for personal property. Many renters believe that they are covered under their landlords' policies. However, that is true only when the landlord is liable for damage. For example, if bad wiring causes a fire and damages a tenant's property, the tenant may be able to collect money from the landlord. Renters insurance is relatively inexpensive and provides protection similar to homeowners insurance.

Home Insurance Policy Forms
What coverage is offered by each type of policy form?

Home insurance policies are available in several forms. The forms provide different combinations of coverage. Some forms are not available in all areas.

The basic form (HO-1) protects against perils such as fire, lightning, windstorms, hail, volcanic eruptions, explosions, smoke, theft, vandalism, glass breakage, and riots. The broad form (HO-2) covers an even wider range of perils, including falling objects and damage from ice, snow, or sleet.

The special form (HO-3) covers all basic- and broad-form risks, plus any other risks except those specifically excluded from the policy. Common exclusions are flood, earthquake, war, and nuclear accidents. Personal property is covered for the risks listed in the policy.

The tenants' form (HO-4) protects the personal property of renters against the risks listed in the policy. It does not include coverage on the building or other structures.

The comprehensive form (HO-5) expands the coverage of the HO-3. The HO-5 includes endorsements for replacement-cost coverage on contents and guaranteed replacement-cost coverage on buildings.

Condominium owners insurance (HO-6) protects personal property and any additions or improvements made to the living unit. These might include bookshelves, electrical fixtures, wallpaper, or carpeting. The condominium association purchases insurance on the building and other structures.

Manufactured housing units and mobile homes usually qualify for insurance coverage with conventional policies. However, some mobile homes may need special policies with higher rates that are dependent on the home's location and the way it is attached to the ground. Mobile home insurance is quite expensive: A $50,000 mobile home can cost as much to insure as a $150,000 house.

Though some risks are not covered by home insurance (see **Figure 13.3**), home insurance policies do include coverage for addtional costs:

- Credit card fraud, check forgery, and counterfeit money
- Removal of damaged property
- Emergency removal of property to protect it from damage
- Temporary repairs after a loss to prevent further damage
- Fire department charges in areas with such fees

How Much Coverage Do You Need?
What is the actual cash value method?

You can get the best insurance value by choosing the right amount of coverage and knowing the factors that affect insurance costs. Your insurance should be based on the amount of money you would need to rebuild or repair your house, not the amount you paid for it. As construction costs rise, you should increase the amount of coverage. In fact, today most insurance policies automatically increase coverage each year as construction costs rise.

Figure 13.3	Not Everything Is Covered

Certain personal property is not covered by homeowners insurance:

- Items insured separately, such as jewelry, furs, boats, or expensive electronic equipment
- Animals or fish
- Motorized vehicles not licensed for road use, except those used for home maintenance
- Sound devices used in motor vehicles, such as radios and CD players

- Aircraft and parts
- Property belonging to tenants
- Property contained in a rental apartment
- Property rented by the homeowner to other people
- Business property

Coverage Exclusions Separate coverage may be available for personal property that is not covered by a homeowners insurance policy.

Give an example of another type of policy that would cover one of the items listed here.

▶ **CLAIM SETTLEMENTS**
Insurance companies use two different methods for settling insurance claims. *If your television is damaged in a fire, how will you be reimbursed for the television under the actual cash value method? Under the replacement value method?*

As You Read

QUESTION

Which policy would most likely pay you more if your home burned down?

In the past, many homeowners' policies insured a building for only 80 percent of the replacement value. If the building were destroyed, the homeowner would have to pay for part of the cost of replacing it, which could be expensive. Today most companies recommend full coverage.

If you are borrowing money to buy a home, the lender will require that you have property insurance. The amount of insurance on your home determines the coverage on your personal belongings. Coverage for personal belongings is usually between 55 and 75 percent of the amount of insurance you have on your home.

Insurance companies base claim settlements on one of two methods. Under the **actual cash value** method, the payment you receive is based on the replacement cost of an item minus depreciation. Depreciation is the loss of value of an item as it gets older. This means you would receive less for a five-year-old bicycle than what you originally paid for it.

Under the **replacement value** method for settling claims, you receive the full cost of repairing or replacing an item. Depreciation is not considered. Many companies limit the replacement cost to 400 percent of the item's actual cash value. Replacement value coverage is more expensive than actual cash value coverage.

Home Insurance Cost Factors
Why do the location and type of construction of your home affect your home insurance costs?

The cost of your home insurance will depend on several factors, such as the location of the home and the type of structure and construction materials used. The amount of coverage and type of policy you choose will also affect the cost of your home insurance. Furthermore, different insurance companies offer different rates.

Location of Home

The location of your home affects your insurance rates. Insurance companies offer lower rates to people whose homes are close to a water supply or fire hydrant—or are located in an area that has a good fire department. Rates are higher in areas where crime is common. People living in regions that experience severe weather, such as tornadoes and hurricanes, may pay more for insurance.

Type of Structure

The type of structure and its construction influence the price of insurance coverage. A brick house, for example, will usually cost less to insure than a similar structure made of wood. However, earthquake coverage is more expensive for a brick house than for a wooden dwelling because a wooden house is more likely to survive an earthquake. Also, an older house may be more expensive to restore to its original condition. That means that it will cost more to insure.

Price, Coverage Amount, Policy Type

The purchase price of a house directly affects how much you pay for insurance. Therefore, it costs more to insure a $300,000 home than a $100,000 home. Also, the type of policy you choose and the amount of coverage you select affect the amount of premium you pay.

◄ LOWER YOUR PREMIUM Fires can cause costly damage to property and personal possessions. *Why might insurance companies offer discounts to people who have homes with composite roofs instead of wood roofs?*

Careers in Finance

Rita Young

21st Century Insurance

Rita likes to help people when disasters strike. As an insurance claims adjuster, she is responsible for investigating complex homeowner claims by interviewing, inspecting, and securing documentation from insured clients, claimants, and witnesses. She evaluates the extent of damage to property and determines the value of claims. Helping clients is one of her favorite parts of her job. She provides a high level of customer service when she reviews policies with her clients and investigates claims-coverage questions.

SKILLS: Interpersonal, problem-solving, negotiating; mathematical skills; comprehensive knowledge of codes, home construction, repair techniques, and legal terminology

PERSONAL TRAITS: Organizational ability and tactfulness

EDUCATION: High school diploma or equivalent; bachelor's degree in business, insurance, or related area; certified Associate of Claims

ANALYZE Why might an insurance claims adjuster be expected to work on weekends or holidays?

 To learn more about career paths for insurance claims adjusters, visit **persfinance07.glencoe.com**.

The deductible amount listed on the policy also affects the cost of insurance. If you increase the amount of the deductible, the premium will be lower because the company will pay out less in claims. The most common deductible amount is $250. Raising the deductible from $250 to $500 or $1,000 can reduce the premium you pay by 15 percent or more.

Home Insurance Discounts

Most companies offer discounts if a homeowner takes action to reduce risks to a home. Your premium may be lower if you have smoke detectors or a fire extinguisher. If your home has dead-bolt locks and alarm systems, which make it harder for thieves to get in, insurance costs may be lower.

Company Differences

A homeowner can save up to 25 percent on homeowners insurance by comparing rates from several companies. Some insurance agents work for only one company. Others are independent agents who represent several different companies.

Do not select a company on the basis of price alone. Also consider service and coverage. Not all companies settle claims in the same way.

For example, suppose that all of the homes on Evergreen Terrace are hit on one side by large hailstones. They all have the same kind of siding. Unfortunately, the homeowners discover that this type of siding is no longer available. So all the siding on all the houses will need to be replaced. Some insurance companies will pay to replace all the siding. Others will pay only to replace the damaged parts.

State insurance commissions and consumer organizations can give you information about different insurance companies. *Consumer Reports*, a magazine that provides unbiased information on a variety of goods and services, rates insurance companies on a regular basis.

Section 13.2 Assessment

QUICK CHECK

1. What are six home insurance policy forms and their coverages?
2. What type of coverage does a personal property floater provide?
3. How can the location of a home affect insurance costs?

THINK CRITICALLY

4. Describe at least two situations in which personal liability coverage might be required.

USE MATH SKILLS

5. **Insurance Coverage** Homeowners insurance covers your personal possessions up to a percentage of the insured value of your home. When Carolina's house burned down, she lost household items worth a total of $25,000. Her house was insured for $80,000, and her homeowners policy provided coverage for personal belongings up to 55 percent of the insured value of the house.

Calculate Determine how much insurance coverage Carolina's policy provides for her personal possessions and whether she will receive payment for all the items destroyed in the fire.

SOLVE MONEY PROBLEMS

6. **Analyzing Insurance Costs** Kara and Adam Gottlieb are in the process of buying their first home. After months of shopping, they have narrowed down their choices to two. One is an older house near a river, where flooding occurs occasionally. The other is a newer house that is located farther from the river. They need to know how much homeowners insurance will cost for each house before making a final decision.

Analyze Given this information, make your best educated guess about which house would be less expensive to insure.

Focus on Reading

Read to Learn

- How to identify important types of motor vehicle insurance coverage.
- How to explain factors that affect the cost of motor vehicle insurance.

Main Idea

Various types of motor vehicle insurance offer different coverages. A variety of factors affect the cost of insurance.

Key Terms

- bodily injury liability
- uninsured motorist's protection
- property damage liability
- collision
- no-fault system
- assigned risk pool

Before You Read

PREDICT

Do you think your driving record affects your car insurance rates? Why?

Motor Vehicle Insurance

Motor vehicle accidents cost more than $150 billion in lost wages and medical bills every year. They can destroy people's lives physically, financially, and emotionally. Buying insurance cannot eliminate the pain and suffering that vehicle accidents cause. However, insurance can reduce the financial impact.

Every state in the United States has a financial responsibility law, which is a law that requires a driver to prove he or she can pay for damage or injury caused by an automobile accident if he or she is at fault. As of 2003, more than 45 states had laws requiring people to carry motor vehicle insurance. When injuries and property damage occur in an accident, the driver(s) is required to file a report with the state. In the remaining states, most people buy motor vehicle insurance by choice. Very few people have the money they would need to meet the financial responsibility requirements on their own.

The coverage provided by motor vehicle insurance falls into two categories: protection for bodily injury and protection for property damage. (See **Figure 13.4.**)

Motor Vehicle Bodily Injury Coverages

Who is covered by bodily injury liability insurance?

Most of the money that motor vehicle insurance companies pay out in claims goes for legal expenses, medical expenses, and other costs that arise when someone is injured. The main types of bodily injury coverages are:

- Bodily injury liability
- Medical payments
- Uninsured motorist's protection

Bodily Injury Liability

Bodily injury liability is insurance that covers physical injuries caused by a vehicle accident for which you are responsible. If pedestrians, people in other vehicles, or passengers in your vehicle are injured or killed, bodily injury liability coverage pays for expenses related to the crash.

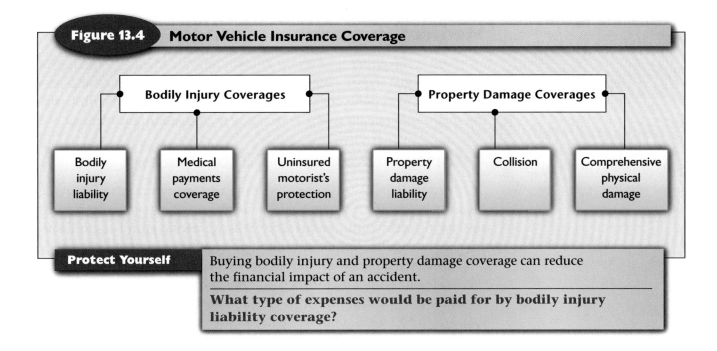

Figure 13.4 **Motor Vehicle Insurance Coverage**

Bodily Injury Coverages

- Bodily injury liability
- Medical payments coverage
- Uninsured motorist's protection

Property Damage Coverages

- Property damage liability
- Collision
- Comprehensive physical damage

Protect Yourself Buying bodily injury and property damage coverage can reduce the financial impact of an accident.

What type of expenses would be paid for by bodily injury liability coverage?

Liability coverage is usually expressed by three numbers, such as 100/300/50. These amounts represent thousands of dollars of coverage. The first two numbers refer to bodily injury coverage. In the 100/300/50 example, $100,000 is the maximum amount that the insurance company will pay for the injuries of any one person in any one accident. The second number, $300,000, is the maximum amount the company will pay for all injured parties (two or more) in any one accident. The third number, $50,000, indicates the limit for payment for damage to the property of others. (See **Figure 13.5.**)

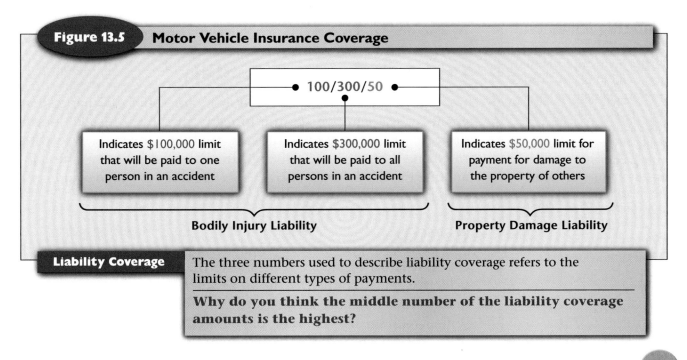

Figure 13.5 **Motor Vehicle Insurance Coverage**

100/300/50

- Indicates $100,000 limit that will be paid to one person in an accident
- Indicates $300,000 limit that will be paid to all persons in an accident
- Indicates $50,000 limit for payment for damage to the property of others

Bodily Injury Liability

Property Damage Liability

Liability Coverage The three numbers used to describe liability coverage refers to the limits on different types of payments.

Why do you think the middle number of the liability coverage amounts is the highest?

Medical Payments Coverage

Medical payments coverage is insurance for medical expenses of anyone injured in your vehicle, including you. This coverage also provides medical benefits for you and members of your family while riding in another person's vehicle or if any of you are hit by a vehicle.

Uninsured Motorist's Protection

Unfortunately, you cannot assume that everyone who is driving has auto insurance. You can guard yourself and your passengers against the risk of getting into an accident with someone who has no insurance by having uninsured motorist's protection.

Uninsured motorist's protection is insurance that covers you and your family members if you are involved in an accident with an uninsured or hit-and-run driver. In most states it does not cover damage to the vehicle itself. Penalties for driving without insurance vary by state, but they generally include stiff fines and the suspension of driving privileges.

Motor Vehicle Property Damage Coverages
What does comprehensive physical insurance cover?

One afternoon, during a summer storm, Carrie was driving home from her job as a hostess at a pancake house. The rain was torrential, and she could not see very well. As a result, she did not realize that the car in front of her had stopped to make a left turn, and she hit the car. The crash totaled Carrie's new car. Fortunately, she had purchased insurance with property damage coverage. Property damage coverage protects you from financial loss if you damage someone else's property or if your vehicle is damaged. It includes property damage liability, collision, and comprehensive physical damage.

Property Damage Liability

Property damage liability is motor vehicle insurance that applies when you damage the property of others. In addition, it protects you when you are driving another person's vehicle with the owner's permission. Although the damaged property is usually another car, the coverage also extends to buildings and to equipment such as street signs and telephone poles.

Collision

Collision insurance is insurance that covers damage to your vehicle when it is involved in an accident. You collect money no matter who is at fault. However, the amount that you can collect is limited to the actual cash value of your vehicle at the time of the accident. So keep a record of your car's condition and value.

As You Read
RELATE

Does your state require car owners to carry motor vehicle insurance? If so, what type?

Web Quest

Avoiding Financial Fraud
As the owner of a vehicle, you need to protect your investment with an insurance policy that covers the variety of risks that vehicle owners face. But if you become the victim of an automobile insurance fraud scheme, you may pay dearly—even with your life. Be aware of the different types of automobile insurance scams.

@ To continue with Task 3 of your WebQuest project, visit **persfinance07.glencoe.com**.

Comprehensive Physical Damage

Comprehensive physical damage insurance protects you if your vehicle is damaged in a non-accident situation. It covers your vehicle against risks such as fire, theft, falling objects, vandalism, hail, floods, tornadoes, earthquakes, and avalanches.

No-Fault Insurance
Why are some states adopting the no-fault system?

To reduce the time and cost of settling vehicle injury cases, some states are trying a number of alternatives, including the no-fault system. The **no-fault system** is an arrangement whereby drivers who are involved in accidents collect money from their own insurance companies. It does not matter who caused the accident. Each company pays the insured up to the limits of his or her coverage. No-fault systems and coverages vary by state.

Other Coverages
When is wage loss insurance required?

Several other kinds of motor vehicle insurance are available. For example, rental reimbursement coverage pays for a rental car if your vehicle is stolen or is being repaired. Wage-loss insurance pays for any salary or income you might have lost due to being injured in a vehicle accident. States that have adopted a no-fault insurance system usually require auto owners to carry wage-loss insurance. It is available by choice in other states.

Emergency road service coverage pays for mechanical assistance in the event that your vehicle breaks down. This can be helpful on long trips or during bad weather. If necessary, you can get your vehicle towed to a service station. However, once your vehicle arrives at the repair shop, you are responsible for paying the bill. If you belong to an automobile club, your membership may include towing coverage. If that is the case, paying for emergency road service coverage could be a waste of money.

Motor Vehicle Insurance Costs
Why is bodily injury liability coverage of 100/300 recommended?

Motor vehicle insurance is not cheap. The average household spends more than $1,000 for motor vehicle insurance yearly. The premiums are related to the amount of claims that insurance companies pay out each year.

Frank is a high school junior who recently got his license. At his part-time job, he earns minimum wage. Frank's situation provides an example of what to consider to get the best insurance value—amount of coverage, insurance premium factors, and ways to reduce insurance premiums.

As You Read
QUESTION

What kind(s) of vehicle insurance would you need if you knocked over your neighbor's mailbox with your car *and* the neighbor was injured by the falling mailbox?

TechByte

Reducing Car Insurance Costs High auto-theft rates lead to high auto insurance rates. Australia has one of the highest auto-theft rates in the world—twice that of the United States. Scientists there have developed a high-tech solution to keep insurance rates down. Tiny microdots called "DataDots" are laser-etched with vehicle identification numbers and spray-glued on engines and most other parts. This makes it difficult to resell stolen cars and parts.

@ Read more about DataDot technology and list other uses for this technological advance through persfinance07 .glencoe.com.

Amount of Coverage

The amount that Frank will pay for insurance depends on the amount of coverage he requires. He needs enough coverage to protect himself legally and financially.

Legal Concerns   As discussed earlier, most people who are involved in motor vehicle accidents cannot afford to pay an expensive court settlement with their own money. For this reason, most drivers buy liability insurance.

Many basic insurance policies provide 10/20 coverage for bodily injury liability. However, some accident victims have been awarded millions of dollars in bodily injury cases; therefore, coverage of 100/300 is usually recommended.

Property Values   Just as medical expenses amounts of and legal settlements have increased, so has the cost of vehicles. Therefore, Frank should consider a policy with a limit of $50,000 or even $100,000 for property damage liability.

Motor Vehicle Insurance Premium Factors

Vehicle type, rating territory, and driver classification are three other factors that influence insurance costs.

Vehicle Type The year, make, and model of a vehicle affect insurance costs. High-priced vehicles and vehicles that have expensive replacement parts and complicated repairs cost more to insure. Also, premiums can be higher for those vehicle makes and models that are frequently stolen.

Rating Territory   In most states the rating territory, or owner's place of residence, is used to determine the vehicle insurance premium. Different locations have different costs. For example, accidents and incidents of theft occur less frequently in rural areas. Your insurance would probably cost less than if you lived in a large city.

▲ RATE QUOTES Shopping around for the best auto insurance rate can save you money in the long run. *What are some factors that may affect the rates offered by different companies?*

Document Detective

Investigate: An Auto Insurance Declaration

The declaration lists this information:

- Policy identification number
- Time period of insurance policy
- Amount of insurance coverage
- Premium amount

Your Motive: In most states the law requires that you insure your automobile. To protect yourself from financial loss, it is important to know exactly what your auto insurance covers and how much it will cost.

The Premier Global Insurance Company Auto Declarations

Policy Number   A02 0076215
Policy Period: From 12/27/2007 To 12/27/2008
                     12:01 Standard Time at the Address of the Named Injured

Coverages and Limits of Liability

Coverages	Vehicle 1		Vehicle 2	
	Limit	Premium	Limit	Premium
A Bodily Injury and Property Damage		$265.00		$339.00
Each Accident	$1,000,000		$1,000,000	
B Medical Payments	$5,000	$9.00	$5,000	$11.00
C Uninsured Motorists Bodily Injury		$76.00		$76.00
Each Accident	$1,000,000		$1,000,000	
D Damage to Your Auto Other Than Collision		$63.00		$126.00
Actual Cash Value Less Deductible	$500.00		$500.00	
Collision		$155.00		$271.00
Actual Cash Value Less Deductible	$500.00		$500.00	

Additional Coverages

Transportation Expense		Included		Included
Per Day/Maximum	$20/$600		$20/$600	
Towing and Labor Costs		$10.00		$10.00
Each Disablement	$50		$50	
Theft Coverage - Electronic Tapes, Records & Discs				
GAP Coverage				
Total		**$578.00**		**$833.00**

Key Points: An auto insurance declaration details what is covered by the policy. It states what the policy will pay in the event of an accident. This includes damage to the car(s) and injury to people. The declaration also explains how the premium is determined.

Find the Solutions

1. What is the policy identification number?
2. What is the bodily injury payment limit?
3. How much will the policy pay for transportation expenses, such as renting a car?
4. How many vehicles are covered by this policy?
5. What is the cost of this policy?

The first Predict question in this chapter asked what you thought the benefits of a good insurance program might be. How would you revise your answer after reading the chapter?

Driver Classification Driver classification is based on age, sex, marital status, driving record, and driving habits. In general, young drivers (under 25) and elderly drivers (over 70) have more frequent and more serious accidents. As a result, these groups pay higher premiums. Because Frank is under 25, he may have to pay a standard higher rate. Your driving record will also influence how much you pay for insurance premiums. If you have accidents or receive traffic tickets, your rates will increase.

The cost and number of claims that you file with your insurance company also affect your premium. If you file expensive claims, your rates will increase. If you have too many claims, your insurance company may cancel your policy, and it will be difficult to get coverage from another company. To deal with this problem, every state has an **assigned risk pool**, which is a group of people who cannot get motor vehicle insurance who are assigned to each insurance company operating in the state. These policyholders pay several times the normal rates. If they establish a good driving record, they can reapply for insurance at regular rates.

Reducing Vehicle Insurance Premiums

Two ways in which Frank can reduce his vehicle insurance costs are by comparing companies and by taking advantage of discounts.

Comparing Companies Rates and services vary among motor vehicle insurance companies. Even among companies in the same area, premiums can vary by as much as 100 percent. Frank should compare the services and rates of local insurance agents. Most states publish this type of information. Furthermore, Frank can check a company's reputation with sources such as *Consumer Reports* or his state insurance department.

▶ **DRIVER CLASSIFICATION**
A driver's age affects the price of insurance premiums. *Who is likely to pay more for insurance—teenagers or parents? Why?*

Premium Discounts   The best way for Frank to keep his rates down is to maintain a good driving record by avoiding accidents and traffic tickets. In addition, most insurance companies offer various types of discounts.

Because Frank is under 25, he can qualify for reduced rates by taking a driver training program or maintaining good grades in school. In addition, installing security devices in his vehicle will decrease the chance of theft and lower Frank's insurance costs. Being a nonsmoker can qualify him for lower motor vehicle insurance premiums as well. Discounts are also offered for insuring two or more vehicles with the same company. Increasing the amounts of deductibles will also lead to a lower premium. For example, an older car may not be worth the cost of carrying collision and comprehensive coverage.

No matter what coverage you choose, motor vehicle insurance is a valuable and mandatory protection to include in any personal finance plan.

Common CENTS

Student Discounts
Many places, such as theaters, zoos, and museums, offer discount prices to students. You can also get discounts for buses and subways, movies, and cultural and sporting events. Be sure to ask before paying full price. *Why do you think businesses offer discounts to students?*

Section 13.3 Assessment

QUICK CHECK

1. What are three main types of motor vehicle insurance that cover bodily injuries?
2. What is the difference between collision and comprehensive physical damage coverages?
3. Why do some insurance companies offer discounts to drivers who install security devices in their vehicles?

THINK CRITICALLY

4. Explain some ways you might reduce motor vehicle insurance premiums.

USE COMMUNICATION SKILLS

5. **Drinking and Driving**   Alcohol use is a factor in more than 60 percent of all traffic accidents. Interview classmates, parents, and others to get their views on what can be done to reduce alcohol-related traffic incidents. Consider contacting an organization such as MADD (Mothers Against Drunk Driving) for information.

Present   You have probably seen or heard public service announcements urging people not to drink and drive. Use what you have learned to create your own public service announcement. It may be in the form of a radio or television script. If possible, get some friends to help you produce your spot, using audio or video recording equipment.

SOLVE MONEY PROBLEMS

6. **Cost of Motor Vehicle Insurance**   Malcolm wants to buy an expensive sport-utility vehicle. However, his mechanic has warned him that the replacement parts for the vehicle that he wants are costly. His friend Ishiro is on a tight budget and does not have a car. He is considering buying a car that has low maintenance costs. Malcolm and Ishiro live in the same neighborhood. Malcolm has never had a traffic accident, but he received one traffic ticket last year. Ishiro's driving record is perfect.

Analyze   Who will have a lower car insurance rate? Why?

Chapter 13 Review & Activities

CHAPTER SUMMARY

- Risk is the probability of loss or injury; peril is something that may cause a loss; hazards increase the probability of loss; and negligence is failing to take reasonable care to prevent accidents. Risk avoidance, risk reduction, risk assumption, and risk shifting are ways of managing risk.
- Insurance involves the risk management method of shifting risk: In exchange for fees, the insurance pays for losses.
- Property insurance protects from losses resulting from natural causes, fire, and criminal activity. Liability insurance covers legal responsibility for the cost of losses to others.
- Homeowners insurance covers the building, living expenses, personal property, and personal liability.

- Renters insurance covers personal possessions, living expenses, and personal liability.
- Factors affecting the cost of homeowners insurance are home location, structural type, coverage amount and policy type, discounts, and differences among insurance companies.
- The types of motor vehicle insurance include bodily injury liability, medical payments coverage, uninsured motorist's protection, property damage liability, collision, and comprehensive physical damage coverage.
- Factors affecting the cost of motor vehicle insurance include the amount of coverage, type of vehicle, rating territory, and driver classification.

Communicating Key Terms

Your older brother is preparing to take the state test for an insurance license. Help him review the following terms by making up fill-in-the-blank sentences that define each term.

- insurance
- policy
- premium
- risk
- peril
- hazard
- negligence
- deductible

- liability
- homeowners insurance
- personal property floater
- medical payments coverage
- actual cash value
- replacement value
- bodily injury liability

- uninsured motorist's protection
- property damage liability
- collision
- no-fault system
- assigned risk pool

Reviewing Key Concepts

1. **Identify** each type of risk and list the four methods of managing risk.
2. **Describe** how insurance uses different risk management methods to reduce risk.
3. **Explain** how property and liability insurance protect.
4. **Identify** reasons that home mortgage lenders require homeowners insurance.
5. **Explain** the difference between actual cash value and replacement value.
6. **List** advantages and disadvantages of the no-fault insurance system.
7. **Discuss** why lenders require drivers to carry bodily injury and property damage coverage.

ACADEMIC SKILLS

Geography   Prices for insurance vary in different areas of the United States. For example, auto insurance may be less expensive in rural areas.

Research   Look at a map of the United States. Find your town or city, Los Angeles, Chicago, Dallas, and Orlando. Research the population and average cost of auto insurance in each of these cities. Compare the cost to the population of each city. Is there a connection? If so, explain.

YOUR FINANCIAL FIGURES

Insurance Deductibles   The annual premium for a 2,500 square foot home in a medium-sized Midwestern city was $628 in 2005—with discounts for a home security system, a good claims record, and the combination of home and auto insurance policies. Replacement cost for the dwelling is estimated at $237,000, and the current deductible is $1,000. The insurance company offered to reduce the premium by $73 if the policyholder agreed to increase the deductible to 1 percent of the replacement cost.

1. **Calculate** the new premium amount and new deductible amount.
2. **Compute** by using the Internet to locate and compare homeowners premium and coverage information from five insurance companies.

REAL-WORLD Application

Connect with Ethics and Social Studies   Laws and penalties for driving under the influence (DUI) are extremely strict in many states. Furthermore, the number of motor vehicle accidents involving young drivers has increased and become more serious, resulting in more deaths and injuries.

1. **Research**   Access the Web site of your state's department of motor vehicles for the laws and penalties for DUI. Also check in your local newspaper for recent accidents involving young drivers.
2. **Think Critically**   Why are DUI penalties so stringent? Do you think the higher insurance premiums charged to younger drivers are "fair"? Why?

Internet CONNECTION

Risk Assessment   Actuaries determine the costs and risks involved with insuring people's property. Actuaries are experts in evaluating the likelihood of future events. They design creative ways to reduce the likelihood of undesirable events and decrease the impact of undesirable events that occur.

@ **Log On**   Go to the Web sites of insurance companies and the Society of Actuaries to find out factors that affect the cost of homeowners insurance. Answer the following questions:

1. Should any of these factors influence decisions when buying a home?
2. How can homeowners premiums be reduced?

BusinessWeek ONLINE

Newsclip: Higher Rates   Car insurance companies charge higher rates for male teenagers than female teenagers.

@ **Log On**   Go to persfinance07.glencoe.com and open Chapter 13. Learn about why insurance companies raise rates for males and not females. Write a list of reasons for this practice.

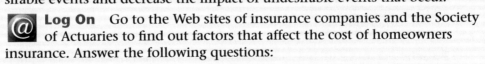

VEHICLE INSURANCE QUIZ

When you insure your vehicle, you will need to make decisions about the insurance you carry. Test your knowledge about motor vehicle insurance by answering questions on a separate sheet of paper.

1. Liability coverage pays for _____.
   a. theft, fire, vandalism, or other damages not related to an accident
   b. the accident-related cost of repairing or replacing your vehicle
   c. damage or injury for which you are responsible

2. Collision coverage pays for _____.
   a. theft, fire, vandalism, or other damages not related to an accident
   b. the accident-related cost of repairing or replacing your vehicle
   c. damage or injury for which you are responsible

3. Comprehensive coverage pays for _____.
   a. theft, fire, vandalism, or other damages not related to an accident
   b. the accident-related cost of repairing or replacing your vehicle
   c. all the items that passengers lose in the backseat of your vehicle

4. If you are in an accident, your vehicle insurance medical coverage handles _____.
   a. only people injured in your vehicle
   b. anyone injured
   c. only people injured who were not in your vehicle

5. A higher deductible results in _____.
   a. a higher premium
   b. a lower premium
   c. tax savings

6. Speeding tickets or accidents may result in _____.
   a. a higher premium
   b. a lower premium
   c. migraine headaches

7. Safety features such as antitheft devices and automatic seat belts may result in a _____.
   a. higher premium
   b. lower premium
   c. higher resale value

8. Taking driver education classes may result in a _____.
   a. higher premium
   b. lower premium
   c. later curfew

Your Financial Portfolio

The Price of Car Insurance

Before Mario bought the car he wanted, he needed to be sure he could afford the insurance for it. In this example he chose low liability, uninsured motorist coverage, and high deductibles to keep his insurance payments as low as possible. Clearly, Insurer B offered a lower price for the same coverage.

Investigating Insurance Companies

	Insurer A	Insurer B
Bodily Injury Coverage:		
Bodily injury liability $50,000 each person; $100,000 each accident	$472	$358
Uninsured motorist's protection	208	84
Medical payments coverage $2,000 each person	48	46
Property Damage Coverage:		
Property damage liability $50,000 each accident	182	178
Collision with $500 deductible	562	372
Comprehensive physical damage with $500 deductible	263	202
Car Rental:	40	32
Discounts: good driver, air bags, garage parking	(165)	
Annual Total	**$1,610**	**$1,272**

Research

Identify a make, model, and year of a vehicle you might like to own. Research two insurance companies and get prices using this example. You can get their rates by telephone. Many companies also have Web sites. On a separate sheet of paper, record your findings. How do they compare? Which company would you choose and why?

CHAPTER *14*
Health, Disability, and Life Insurance

 ## What You'll Learn

When you have completed this chapter, you will be able to:

Section 14.1
- Explain the importance of health insurance in financial planning.
- Analyze costs and benefits of various health insurance.

Section 14.2
- Differentiate between private and government health care plans.

Section 14.3
- Explain the importance of disability insurance in financial planning.
- Describe different sources of disability income.

Section 14.4
- Describe various types of life insurance coverage.
- Identify the key provisions in a life insurance policy.

Reading Strategies

To get the most out of your reading:

Predict what you will learn in this chapter.
Relate what you read to your own life.
Question what you are reading to be sure you understand.
React to what you have read.

In the **Real** World . . .

Upon graduating from college, Sharon Lewis discovered that she was no longer covered by her parents' health insurance. When she found out what the monthly premium would be if she purchased her own policy, she decided to do without one. She said, "I'm healthy, and I get plenty of exercise skiing. I haven't needed to visit the doctor in years." Then she got in an accident. Rushing out of her apartment one morning, she tripped and fell, injuring her ankle. When she went to the emergency room, she was shocked to learn how much the visit would cost. A follow-up visit would be an additional expense. Health, disability, and life insurance are important for even the healthiest person.

As You Read *Consider the importance of having health insurance when you need it.*

ASK STANDARD & POOR'S

Health Care Costs

Q: I am a high school student. Why should I be concerned about my future health care costs now?

A: Your health care costs, now and in the future, can be affected by your personal health habits. Many health problems result from poor habits, such as lack of exercise or inadequate diet, and may take years to develop. By establishing good habits now, you can reduce the likelihood of future health problems and related expenses.

Ask Yourself What good habits can you establish now that will help you ensure that your health care costs will stay low in the future?

 Go to **persfinance07.glencoe.com** to complete the Standard & Poor's Financial Focus activity.

Read to Learn

- How to explain the importance of health insurance in financial planning.
- How to analyze costs and benefits of various health insurance.

Main Idea

Knowing how to determine the type of health insurance plan that you need can help you meet your financial goals even when dealing with unexpected medical costs.

Key Terms

- health insurance
- coinsurance
- stop-loss
- co-payment

Before You Read

PREDICT

What does major medical expense insurance cover?

Health Insurance and Financial Planning

What Is Health Insurance?

Why is it important for healthy people to have health insurance?

Health insurance is a form of protection that eases the financial burden people may experience as a result of illness or injury. You pay a premium, or fee, to the insurer. In return, the company pays most of your medical costs. Plans vary, but some of the things that they might cover are hospital stays, doctors' visits, medications, and sometimes vision and dental care.

Health insurance includes both medical expense insurance and disability income insurance. *Medical expense insurance* typically pays only the actual medical costs. *Disability income insurance* provides payments to make up for some of the income of a person who cannot work as a result of injury or illness. In this chapter the term "health insurance" generally refers to medical expense insurance.

Health insurance plans can be purchased as several different plans: group health insurance, individual health insurance, and COBRA.

Group Health Insurance

Most people who have health insurance are covered under group plans. Typically, these plans are employer sponsored. This means that an employer offers the plans and usually pays some or all of the premiums. Other organizations, such as labor unions and professional associations, also offer group plans. Group insurance plans cover you and your immediate family. The Health Insurance Portability and Accountability Act of 1996 set new federal standards to ensure that workers will not lose their health insurance if they change jobs. For example, a parent with a sick child can move from one group health plan to another plan without a lapse in coverage. Moreover, the parent will not have to pay more for coverage than other employees do.

The cost of group insurance is fairly low because many people are insured under the same policy, which is a contract with a risk-sharing group or insurance company. However, group insurance plans vary in the amount of protection that they provide. For example, some plans limit the amount that they will pay for hospital stays and surgical procedures.

Coordination of Benefits If your plan does not cover all your health insurance needs, you have some options. If you are married, you may be able to take advantage of a coordination of benefits (COB) provision, which is included in most group insurance plans. This provision allows you to combine the benefits from more than one insurance plan. The benefits received from all plans are limited to 100 percent of all allowable medical expenses. For example, a couple could use benefits from the wife's group plan and from the husband's group plan up to 100 percent. If this type of provision is not available to you, or if you are single, you can get added protection by buying individual health insurance.

Individual Health Insurance

Some people may not be offered an employer-sponsored group insurance plan. Some may not have access to one because they are self-employed. Others are simply dissatisfied with the coverage that their group plans provide. In these cases, individual health insurance may be the answer. You can buy individual health insurance directly from the company of your choice. Plans usually cover you as an individual or as a family. Individual plans can be adapted to meet your own needs. You should comparison shop, however, because rates can vary between companies.

COBRA

The Consolidated Omnibus Budget Reconciliation Act of 1986, known as *COBRA*, allows an employee who loses his or her job to keep the former employer's group coverage for a set period of time. For example, Hakeem had a group insurance plan through his employer, but he was laid off. He wondered how he would be able to get medical coverage until he found a new job. Fortunately for Hakeem, COBRA allowed him to keep coverage for a while. He had to pay the premiums himself, but the coverage was not canceled. When he found a new job, he was then able to switch to the new employer's group plan with no break in coverage.

Not everyone qualifies for COBRA. You have to work for a private company or a state or local government to be eligible for the benefits.

Types of Health Insurance Coverage

Why do you think basic health insurance and major medical insurance are often offered together?

Several types of health insurance coverage are available, either through a group plan or through individual purchase. Some benefits are included in nearly every health insurance plan; other benefits are less common.

As You Read

RELATE

Imagine and describe a situation in which a young, healthy person would need health insurance.

Basic Health Insurance Coverage

Basic health insurance coverage includes hospital expense coverage, surgical expense coverage, and physician expense coverage.

Hospital Expense Hospital expense coverage pays for some or all of the daily costs of room and board during a hospital stay. Routine nursing care, minor medical supplies, and the use of other hospital facilities are covered as well. For example, covered expenses would include anesthesia, dressings, related X-rays, and the use of an operating room.

Most policies set a maximum amount they will pay for each day you are in the hospital. They may also limit the number of days they will cover. As you may remember from Chapter 13, many policies may also require a deductible.

Surgical Expense Surgical expense coverage pays all or part of the surgeon's fees for an operation, whether it is done in the hospital or in the doctor's office. Policies often have a list of the services that they cover, which specifies the maximum payment for each type of operation. For example, a policy might allow $500 for an appendectomy. If the entire surgeon's bill is not covered, the policyholder has to pay the difference. People often buy surgical expense coverage in combination with hospital expense coverage.

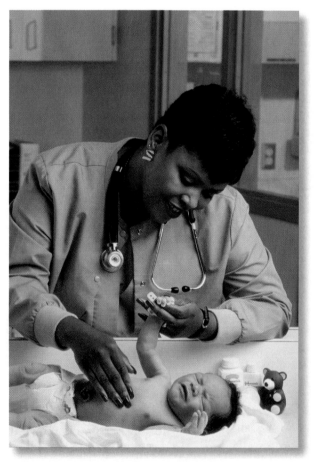

▼ MATERNITY WARD The medical costs of childbirth can be high. *What related costs might be paid by hospital expense coverage?*

Physician Expense Physician expense coverage meets some or all of the costs of physician care that do not involve surgery. It covers treatment by a physician in a hospital, a doctor's office, or even the patient's home. Plans may cover routine doctor visits, X-rays, and lab tests. Like surgical expense, physician expense includes maximum benefits for specific services. Physician expense coverage is usually combined with surgical and hospital coverage in a basic health insurance package.

Major Medical Expense Insurance

Most people find that basic health insurance meets their usual needs. The cost of a serious illness or accident, however, can quickly go beyond the amounts that basic health insurance will pay. For example, Chen had to have emergency surgery, which meant an operation, a two-week hospital stay, a number of lab tests, and several follow-up visits. He was shocked to discover that his basic health insurance paid less than half of the total bill, leaving him with debts of more than $10,000.

Major medical expense insurance would have better protected Chen. This coverage pays the large costs involved in long hospital stays and multiple surgeries. In other words, it takes up where basic health insurance coverage leaves off. Almost every type of care and treatment prescribed by a physician, in or out of a hospital, is covered by this type of plan. Maximum benefits can range from $5,000 to over $1 million per illness per year.

As You Read

QUESTION

Why do you think major medical expense insurance is expensive?

Coinsurance   Of course, this type of coverage is not inexpensive. To keep premiums lower, most major medical plans require a deductible. Some plans also include a coinsurance provision. **Coinsurance** is the percentage of the medical expenses the policyholder must pay in addition to the deductible amount. Many policies require policyholders to pay 20 or 25 percent of expenses after they have paid the deductible.

For example, Ariana's policy includes an $800 deductible and a coinsurance provision requiring her to pay 20 percent of all bills. If her bills total $3,800, the insurance company will first exclude $800 from coverage, which is Ariana's deductible. It will then pay 80 percent of the remaining $3,000, which would total $2,400. Therefore, Ariana's total costs are $1,400 ($800 for the deductible and $600 for the coinsurance).

Stop-Loss Provisions   Some major medical policies contain a stop-loss provision. **Stop-loss** is a provision that requires the policyholder to pay all costs up to a certain amount, after which the insurance company pays 100 percent of the remaining expenses covered in the policy. Typically, the policyholder will pay between $3,000 and $5,000 in out-of-pocket expenses before the coverage begins.

Comprehensive Major Medical   Major medical expense insurance may be offered as part of a single policy that includes basic health insurance coverage, or it can be bought separately. *Comprehensive major medical insurance* is a type of complete health insurance that helps pay hospital, surgical, medical, and other bills. It has a very low deductible, usually $200 to $300. Many major medical policies set limits on the benefits they will pay for certain expenses, such as surgery and hospital room and board.

Hospital Indemnity Policies

A hospital indemnity policy pays benefits when you are hospitalized. Unlike most of the other plans mentioned, however, these policies do not directly cover medical costs. Instead, you are paid in cash, which you can spend on medical or nonmedical expenses as you choose. Hospital indemnity policies are used as a supplement to—not a replacement for—basic health insurance or major medical insurance policies. The average person who buys such a policy, however, usually pays much more in premiums than he or she receives in payments.

Common CENTS

Fitness Fun
Expensive exercise clothes may look good, but they usually do not improve your workout. If you cannot afford to pay to join a health club, you can get your exercise by walking or jogging in your neighborhood or at your school's track. All you need is a good pair of athletic shoes. *How can staying fit save you money?*

Dental Expense Insurance

Dental expense insurance provides policyholders reimbursement for the expenses of dental services and supplies. It encourages preventive dental care because it pays for maintenance care. The coverage normally provides for oral examinations, X-rays, cleanings, fillings, extractions, oral surgery, dentures, and braces. However, some dental expense policies do not cover X-rays and cleanings. As with other insurance plans, dental insurance may have a deductible and a coinsurance provision, stating that the policyholder pays from 20 to 50 percent of the dental expenses after the deductible.

STANDARD &POOR'S

Global Financial Landscape

Standard and Poor's publishes the globally recognized S&P 500® financial index. It also gathers financial statistics, information, and news, and analyzes this data for international businesses, governments, and individuals to help them guide their financial decisions.

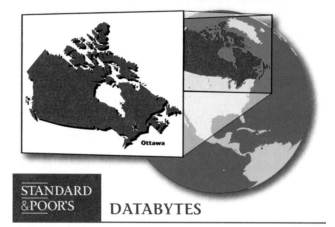

CANADA

When faced with the frustrations of finding affordable health care and insurance, Americans often think Canadians have the solution. Canada offers its citizens free doctor's visits, free hospital care, and free surgery. Children receive some dental work for free, and people over the age of 65 receive free prescription drugs. Taxes, which make up about 9 percent of the country's gross domestic product (GDP), cover these health care costs.

Though the Canadian health care system provides many benefits, it has a down side. Some Canadian patients complain of overcrowding, a shortage of medical staff, outdated equipment, and long waits for treatment. Citizens are prohibited from hiring private health services in Canada, but they can travel outside the country for care. Ironically, many Canadians have come to the United States for health care.

STANDARD &POOR'S DATABYTES

Capital	Ottawa
Population	31,630,000
Language	English and French
Currency	Canadian dollar
Gross Domestic Product (GDP)	$957.7 billion (2003 est.)
GDP per capita	$29,700

Industry: Transportation equipment, chemicals, processed and unprocessed minerals, and food products

Agriculture: Wheat, barley, oilseed, tobacco, dairy products, forest products, and fish

Exports: Motor vehicles and parts, industrial machinery, aircraft, telecommunications equipment, chemicals, timber, and crude petroleum

Think Globally
Why do you think medical costs have increased?

Vision Care Insurance

Many insurance companies offer vision care insurance as part of group plans. Vision care insurance may cover eye examinations, glasses, contact lenses, eye surgery, and the treatment of eye diseases.

Dread Disease Policies

Dread disease, trip accident, death insurance, and cancer policies are usually sold through the mail, in newspapers, and magazines. These policies play upon unrealistic fears, and they are illegal in many states. They only cover very specific conditions, which are already fully covered under a major medical plan.

Long-Term Care Insurance

Long-term care insurance provides coverage for the expense of daily help that you may need if you become seriously ill or disabled and are unable to care for yourself. It covers a lengthy stay in a nursing home and help at home with daily activities such as dressing, bathing, and household chores. Annual premiums range from $900 up to $15,000, depending on age and the amount of coverage.

Major Provisions in a Health Insurance Policy

What are the benefits and limits of the major provisions in a health insurance policy?

Although all health insurance policies have certain provisions in common, you must be sure that you understand what your own policy covers. What are the benefits? What are the limits? The following provisions are included in most health insurance policies:

- **Eligibility** This provision defines the people covered by the policy. That usually includes the policyholder, a spouse, and children up to a certain age.
- **Assigned Benefits** You are reimbursed for payments when you submit your bills and claim forms. When you assign benefits, you let your insurer make direct payments to your doctor or hospital.
- **Internal Limits** A policy with internal limits sets specific levels of repayment for certain services. Even if your hospital room costs $400 a day, you will not be able to get more than $250 if an internal limit specifies that maximum.
- **Co-payment** A **co-payment** is a flat fee that you pay every time you receive a covered service. The fee is usually between $5 and $20, and the insurer pays the balance of the cost of the service. This is different from coinsurance, which is the percentage of your medical costs for which you are responsible after paying your deductible.

- **Service Benefits**   Policies with this provision list coverage in terms of services, not dollar amounts. For example, you are entitled to X-rays, instead of $40 worth of X-rays per visit. Service benefits provisions are always preferable to dollar amount coverage because the insurer pays all of the costs for a particular service.
- **Benefit Limits**   This provision defines a maximum benefit, either in terms of a dollar amount or in terms of number of days spent in the hospital.
- **Exclusions and Limitations**   This provision specifies services that the policy does not cover. That may include preexisting conditions (conditions diagnosed before the insurance plan took effect), cosmetic surgery, and more.
- **Guaranteed Renewable**   With this provision, the insurer cannot cancel the policy unless you fail to pay the premiums. It also forbids insurers from raising your premiums unless they raise all premiums for all members of your group.
- **Cancellation and Termination**   This provision explains the circumstances under which the insurer can cancel your coverage. It also explains how you can convert your group insurance policy into an individual insurance policy.

Choosing Coverage
What type of health insurance coverage should you choose?

▼ SHARING THE COST
All health insurance policies have certain provisions in common.
What is a co-payment?

Now that you are familiar with the available types of health insurance and some of their major provisions, how do you choose one? The type of coverage you choose will be affected by the amount you can afford to spend on the premiums and the level of benefits that you feel you want and need. It may also be affected by the kind of coverage your employer offers, if you are covered through your employer.

You can buy basic health coverage, major medical coverage, or both basic and major medical coverage. Any of these three choices will take care of at least some of your medical expenses. Ideally, you should get a basic plan and a major medical supplement. Another option is to purchase a comprehensive major medical policy that combines the value of both plans in a single policy. See **Figure 14.1** for a description of the basic features you should look for in a health insurance plan. You should also consider the trade-offs of the various benefits.

Health Insurance Trade-Offs

Different health insurance policies may offer very different benefits. As you decide which insurance plan to buy, you should consider the following trade-offs.

Reimbursement Versus Indemnity   A reimbursement policy pays you back for actual expenses. An indemnity policy pays specified amounts, regardless of how much the actual expenses may cost.

For example, Katie and Seth were both charged $200 for an office visit to the same specialist. Katie's reimbursement policy has a deductible of $300. Once she has met the deductible, the policy will cover the full cost of subsequent visits. Seth's indemnity policy will pay him only $125, which is what his plan provides for each visit to any specialist.

Internal Limits Versus Aggregate Limits   A policy with internal limits covers only a fixed amount for an expense, such as the daily cost of room and board during a hospital stay. A policy with aggregate limits may limit only the total amount of coverage (the maximum dollar amount paid for all benefits in a year), such as $1 million in major expense benefits, or it may have no limits.

Deductibles and Coinsurance   The cost of a health insurance policy is affected by the size of the deductible, which is the set amount that the policyholder must pay toward medical expenses before the insurance company pays benefits. It can also be affected by the terms of the coinsurance provision.

Figure 14.1   Health Insurance Must-Haves

A health insurance plan should:

- Offer basic coverage for hospital and doctor bills.

- Provide at least 120 days' hospital room and board in full.

- Provide at least a $1 million lifetime maximum for each family member.

- Pay at least 80 percent for out-of-hospital expenses after a yearly deductible of $500 per person or $1,000 per family.

- Impose no unreasonable exclusions.

- Limit your out-of-pocket expenses to no more than $3,000 to $5,000 a year, excluding dental, vision care, and prescription costs.

Essential Coverage   Health insurance plans vary greatly, but all plans should have some basic features.

Would you add anything to this list of must-haves?

Out-of-Pocket Limits   Some policies limit the amount of money you must pay for the deductible and coinsurance. After you have reached that limit, the insurance company covers 100 percent of any additional expenses. Having out-of-pocket limits may help you lower your financial risk, but those limits may also increase the price of your premiums.

Benefits Based on Reasonable and Customary Charges   Some policies consider the average fee for a service in a particular geographical area. They then use that average amount to set a limit on payments to policyholders. If the standard cost of a certain procedure is $1,500 in your part of the country, then your policy will not pay more than that amount.

Section 14.1 Assessment

QUICK CHECK

1. Why is it important to include health insurance in your financial planning?
2. What are benefits provided by hospital expense coverage, surgical expense coverage, and physician expense coverage?
3. What are the trade-offs between reimbursement and indemnity?

THINK CRITICALLY

4. Explain why it is necessary for insurance companies to place limits on the amount of costs they will cover.

USE COMMUNICATION SKILLS

5. **Benefits of Insurance**   Your 25-year-old sister never gets sick and leads an active, healthy life. She sees no reason to buy health insurance and calls the premiums a waste of money.

   Role-Play   With a partner, role-play a response to your sister's argument. Explain why she might benefit from health insurance regardless of her current situation.

SOLVE MONEY PROBLEMS

6. **Choosing an Insurance Plan**   Richard is 35, single, and in reasonably good health. He works for a construction company that offers three health insurance plans. The first has a lifetime benefit of $1 million for all covered expenses, an annual deductible of $500, and a 15 percent coinsurance provision up to the first $2,000 in covered charges. The second requires a monthly premium of $50 and sets a $500,000 lifetime limit on benefits, has no annual deductible, and requires a $15 co-payment per office visit. The third has an annual deductible of $250 and a 25 percent coinsurance provision up to the first $1,500 in covered charges, with a lifetime limit on benefits of $700,000.

   Analyze   Help Richard determine which of these three plans makes the most sense for his particular situation. Be prepared to defend your reasoning.

Private and Government Plans

Private Health Care Plans
What is the difference between an HMO and a PPO?

Most health insurance in the United States is provided by private organizations rather than by the government. Private health care plans may be offered by a number of sources: private insurance companies; hospital and medical service plans; health maintenance organizations; preferred provider organizations; home health care agencies; and employer self-funded health plans.

Private Insurance Companies

Several hundred private insurance companies are in the health insurance business. They provide mostly group health plans to employers, who in turn offer them to their employees as an employment benefit. Premiums may be fully or partially paid by the employer, with the employee paying any remainder. These policies typically pay for medical costs by sending payments directly to the doctor, hospital, or lab that provides the services.

Hospital and Medical Service Plans

Blue Cross and Blue Shield are statewide organizations similar to private health insurance companies. Each state has Blue Cross and Blue Shield. **Blue Cross** is an insurance company that provides hospital care benefits. **Blue Shield** is an insurance company that provides benefits for surgical and medical services performed by physicians. The "Blues" provide health insurance to millions of Americans.

Managed Care

According to a recent industry survey, 23 percent of employed Americans are enrolled in some form of managed care, due to rising health care costs. **Managed care** refers to prepaid health plans that provide comprehensive health care to their members. Managed care is designed to control the cost of health care services by controlling how they are used. Managed care is offered by health maintenance organizations, preferred provider organizations, and point-of-service plans.

Focus on Reading

Read to Learn
- How to differentiate between private and government health care plans.

Main Idea
Understanding plans offered by private companies and by the government will help you choose the plan that best meets your physical and financial needs now and as you get older.

Key Terms
- Blue Cross
- Blue Shield
- managed care
- health maintenance organization (HMO)
- preferred provider organization (PPO)
- point-of-service (POS) plan
- Medicare
- Medicaid

Before You Read

PREDICT

What is the difference between insurance provided by private organizations and insurance provided by the government?

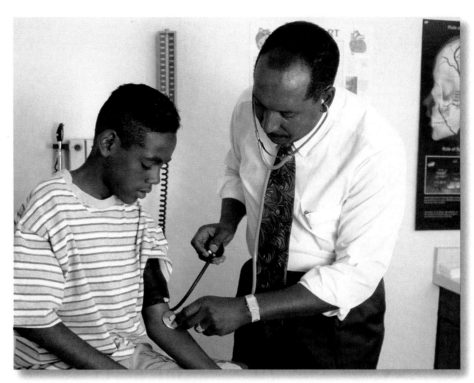

▲ **PROMOTING HEALTH** HMOs are based on the idea that preventive services will minimize future medical problems. *What kinds of preventive services do HMOs cover?*

Health Maintenance Organizations One managed-care option is a **health maintenance organization (HMO)**, which is a health insurance plan that directly employs or contracts with selected, or preapproved, physicians and other medical professionals to provide health care services in exchange for a fixed, prepaid monthly premium. HMOs are an alternative to basic health insurance and major medical expense insurance.

HMOs are based on the idea that preventive services will minimize future medical problems. Therefore, these plans typically cover routine immunizations and checkups, screening programs, and diagnostic tests. They also provide customers with coverage for surgery, hospitalization, and emergency care. If you have an HMO, you usually pay a small co-payment for each covered service, such as a doctor's office visit. Supplemental services may include vision care and prescription services, which are typically available for an additional fee.

When you first enroll in an HMO, you must choose a plan physician from a list of doctors provided by the HMO. This physician provides or arranges for all your health care services. If you receive care from a physician outside your HMO's approved physician list, you are responsible for the cost of the service. The only exception to this rule is in the case of a medical emergency. If you experience a sudden illness or injury that would threaten your life or health if not treated immediately, you may go to the nearest emergency room. All other care must be provided by hospitals and doctors under contract with the HMO.

HMOs are not for everyone. Many HMO customers complain that their HMO denies them necessary care. Others feel restricted by the limited choice of doctors.

Here are some tips on using and choosing an HMO. Because HMOs require you to use only certain doctors, you should make sure that those doctors are near your home or place of work. You should also be able to change doctors easily if you do not like your first choice. Second opinions should always be available at the HMO's expense, and you should be able to appeal any case in which the HMO denies care. Finally, look at the costs and benefits—whether you will incur out-of-pocket expenses or co-payments and what services the plan will provide.

Preferred Provider Organizations A variation on the HMO is a **preferred provider organization (PPO)**, which is a group of doctors and hospitals that agree to provide specified medical services to members at prearranged fees. PPOs offer these discounted services to employees either directly or indirectly through an insurance company. The premiums for PPOs are slightly higher than the premiums for HMOs.

PPO plan members often pay no deductibles but may have minimal co-payments. While HMOs require members to receive care from HMO providers only, PPOs allow members greater flexibility. Members can either visit a preferred provider (a physician selected from a pre-approved list) or go to their own physicians. Patients who decide to use their own doctors do not lose coverage as they would with an HMO. However, they must pay deductibles and larger co-payments.

Point-of-Service (POS) Plan A **point-of-service (POS) plan** combines features of both HMOs and PPOs. POS plans use a network of participating physicians and medical professionals who have contracted to provide services for certain fees. As with an HMO, you choose a plan physician who manages your care and controls referrals to specialists. As long as you receive care from a pre-approved provider, you pay little or nothing, just as you would with an HMO. However, you are allowed to seek care outside the network at a higher charge, as with a PPO.

Home Health Care Agencies

Rising hospital costs, new medical technology, and the increasing number of elderly people have helped make home care one of the fastest-growing areas of the health care industry. Home health care consists of home health care agencies; home care aide organizations; and hospices, which are facilities and organizations that provide care for the terminally ill. These providers offer medical care in a home setting in agreement with a medical order, often at a fraction of the cost charged by hospitals for similar services.

STANDARD &POOR'S

Put on Your Financial Planner's Cap

You just started your first full-time job, working for a company that provides both an HMO and a POS plan. Which health insurance plan would best fit your financial situation?

As You Read

RELATE

Would you choose an HMO, PPO, or POS? Why?

Employer Self-Funded Health Plans

Some companies choose to self-insure. The company runs its own insurance plan, collecting premiums from employees and paying medical benefits as needed. However, these companies must cover any costs that exceed the income from premiums. Unfortunately, some corporations do not have the financial assets necessary to cover these situations, which can cause a financial disaster for the company and its employees.

Government Health Care Programs

Who benefits most from government health care programs?

The health insurance coverages discussed so far are normally purchased through private companies. Some consumers, however, are eligible for health insurance coverage under programs offered by federal and state governments. The federal program is Medicare, and the federal and state program is Medicaid.

Medicare

Perhaps the best-known government program is Medicare. **Medicare** is a federally funded health insurance program available mainly to people over 65 and to people with certain disabilities. Medicare has two parts: hospital insurance (Part A) and medical insurance (Part B).

Medicare Part A is funded by part of the Social Security payroll tax. Part A helps pay for inpatient hospital care, inpatient care in a skilled nursing facility, home health care, and hospice care. Program participants pay a single annual deductible.

Part B helps pay for doctors' services and a variety of other medical services and supplies not covered, or not fully covered, by Part A. Part B has a deductible and a 20 percent coinsurance provision. Medicare medical insurance is a supplemental program paid for by individuals who feel that they need additional coverage. A regular monthly premium is charged. The federal government matches this amount.

Medicare Finances Medicare is at risk financially. Health care costs continue to grow, and the population of senior citizens in the United States is increasing. This situation puts Medicare in danger of running out of funds. According to projections made in 2004, the program will be bankrupt by the year 2019 if no changes are made.

The Balanced Budget Act of 1997 created the additional program, Medicare 1 Choice. This program allows many Medicare members to choose a managed care plan in addition to their Medicare coverage. For some additional costs, members can receive greater benefits.

As You Read

QUESTION

How might the projected shortfall in Medicare funds affect the future of government health care programs?

▲ **LIVING WELL** The Medicare health program covers more people over the age of 65 than ever because of the increasing population of senior citizens. *What services do Medicare Parts A and B cover?*

What Is Not Covered by Medicare? Medicare effectively covers many medical costs, but there are some medical expenses that Medicare will not cover at all. These expenses include certain types of skilled or long-term nursing care, out-of-hospital prescription drugs, routine checkups, dental care, and most immunizations. Medicare also limits the types of services it will cover and the amount it will pay for those services. If a doctor does not accept Medicare's approved amount as payment in full, the patient is responsible for paying the difference.

Medigap People who are eligible for Medicare and who would like to have more coverage may buy Medigap insurance. Medigap insurance supplements Medicare by filling the gap between Medicare payments and medical costs not covered by Medicare. It is offered by private companies.

Medicaid

The other well-known government health program is **Medicaid**, a medical assistance program offered to certain low-income individuals and families. Medicaid is administered by the individual states, but it is financed by a combination of state and federal funds. Unlike Medicare, Medicaid coverage is so comprehensive that people with Medicaid do not need supplemental insurance. Typical Medicaid benefits include:

- Physicians' services
- Inpatient hospital services
- Outpatient hospital services
- Lab services
- Skilled nursing and home health services
- Prescription drugs
- Eyeglasses
- Preventive care for people under 21

Careers in Finance

INSURANCE AGENT | Alicia Hopkins
Farmer's Insurance

Alicia is an excellent salesperson who cares about her clients. She sells insurance policies to individuals, families, business firms, and other groups to protect them from future financial loss due to injury, illness, death, property damage, or theft. Alicia interviews prospective clients to obtain data about their financial resources and needs, as well as the physical condition of the person or property to be insured. She then works out an insurance program suited to that customer, explains the program's costs and benefits, and writes a policy. Alicia follows up regularly with her client so she can handle any changes and renewals to his or her policy. Alicia, like all insurance agents, is always on the look-out for new clients.

SKILLS: Sales, communication, legal and financial awareness, mathematical, and time-management skills

PERSONAL TRAITS: Diligent, self-confident, outgoing, tactful, and good judgment

EDUCATION: High school diploma or equivalent; a license from the State Department of Insurance; pre-licensing and continuing education

ANALYZE Why might it be helpful for an insurance agent to be active in civic or social organizations?

 To learn more about career paths for insurance agents, visit persfinance07.glencoe.com.

Government Consumer Health Information Web Sites

The Department of Health and Human Services operates more than 60 Web sites that contain a wealth of reliable information related to health and medicine.

Healthfinder Healthfinder includes links to over a thousand Web pages operated by government and nonprofit organizations. It lists topics according to subject.

MedlinePlus MedlinePlus is the world's largest Internet collection of published medical information. It was originally designed for health professionals and researchers, but it is also valuable for students and others who are interested in health care and medical issues.

NIH Health Information The National Institutes of Health (NIH) operates a Web site that can direct you to the consumer health information in NIH publications and on the Internet.

FDA The Food and Drug Administration (FDA), a federal consumer protection agency, provides a Web site with information about the safety of various foods, drugs, cosmetics, and medical devices.

Section 14.2 Assessment

QUICK CHECK

1. What types of coverage are provided by Blue Cross and Blue Shield?
2. What are the differences between an HMO and a PPO?
3. What is the difference between Medicare and Medicaid?

THINK CRITICALLY

4. Identify the benefits and drawbacks to membership in an HMO.

USE MATH SKILLS

5. **PPOs** Last month Rose was involved in a car accident and was rushed to the emergency room. After receiving stitches for a facial wound and treatment for a broken finger, she was released from the hospital.

Calculate Under Rose's PPO, emergency room care at a network hospital is 80 percent covered after the member has met a $300 annual deductible. Assume that Rose went to a hospital within her PPO network. Her total emergency room bill was $850. What amount did Rose have to pay? What amount did the PPO cover?

SOLVE MONEY PROBLEMS

6. **HMOs** Your Aunt Alice will be 65. She pays $200 a month for an HMO she does not like. She will be eligible for Medicare and is wondering if she should drop the HMO coverage at that time.

Analyze With a partner, discuss Aunt Alice's alternative and if she should drop her HMO coverage.

Disability Insurance

Disability Income

Why is it important to have disability insurance?

Before disability insurance existed, people who were ill often lost more money from missed paychecks than from paying medical bills. Disability income insurance was set up to protect against such loss of income. **Disability income insurance** provides regular cash income when an employee is unable to work due to pregnancy, a non-work-related accident, or an illness. It protects your earning power, which is your most valuable resource. This kind of coverage is very common today, and several hundred insurance companies offer it.

The exact definition of the word *disability* varies from insurer to insurer. Some insurers will pay you when you are unable to work at your regular job. Other insurers will pay only if you are so ill or badly hurt that you cannot work at any job. A violinist with a hand injury, for example, might have trouble doing his or her regular work but might be able to perform a range of other jobs. A good disability income insurance plan pays you if you cannot work at your regular job. A good plan will also pay partial benefits if you are able to work only part-time.

Many people make the mistake of ignoring disability insurance, not realizing that it is very important to have. A disability can cause even greater financial problems than death because disabled persons lose their earning power but still have to pay for their living expenses. In addition, they often face huge costs for the medical treatment and special care that their disabilities require.

Sources of Disability Income

Before you buy disability income insurance from a private insurance company, remember that you may already have some form of this insurance. This coverage may be available through worker's compensation if you are injured on the job. Disability benefits may also be available through your employer or through Social Security in case of a long-term disability.

Worker's Compensation If your disability is the result of an accident or illness that occurred on the job, you may be eligible to receive worker's compensation benefits. The amount of benefits will depend on your salary and your work history.

Employer Many employers provide disability income insurance through group insurance plans. In most cases, your employer will pay part or all of the cost of such insurance. Some policies may only provide continued wages for several months, while others will provide long-term protection.

Social Security Social Security may be best known as a source of retirement income, but it also provides disability benefits. If you are a worker who pays into the Social Security system, you are eligible for Social Security funds if you become disabled. How much you get depends on your salary and the number of years you have been paying into Social Security. Your dependents also qualify for certain benefits. However, Social Security has very strict rules. Workers are considered disabled if they have a physical or mental condition that prevents them from working for at least 12 months, or if they have a condition that may result in death. Benefits start at the sixth full month the person is disabled. They stay in effect as long as the disability lasts.

Private Income Insurance Programs Privately owned insurance companies offer many policies to protect people from loss of income resulting from illness or disability. Disability income insurance gives weekly or monthly cash payments to people who cannot work due to illness or accident. The amount paid is usually 40 to 60 percent of a person's normal income. Some plans pay as much as 75 percent.

As You Read

RELATE

Do Social Security disability benefits provide enough coverage for you to feel comfortable about your financial future if you were to become disabled? Why or why not?

◄ACCIDENTS HAPPEN
Disability income insurance can be very important because it provides funds if you are unable to work due to illness or injury. *How would disability income insurance help a dancer who broke a leg in a surfing accident?*

Disability Insurance Trade-Offs

When you purchase health or disability insurance, you must make certain trade-offs when you decide among different private disability insurance policies. You should consider several factors as you look for a plan.

Waiting or Elimination Period   Your benefits will not begin the day you become disabled. You will have to wait between one and six months before you can begin collecting. This span of time is called a waiting, or elimination, period. Usually a policy with a longer elimination period charges lower premiums.

Duration of Benefits   Every policy names a specified period during which benefits will be paid. Some policies are valid for only a few years. Others are automatically canceled when you turn 65. Still others continue to make payments for life. You should look for a policy that pays benefits for life. If a policy stops payments when the policyholder is age 65, then having a permanent disability could be a major financial burden.

Amount of Benefits   You should aim for a benefit amount that, when added to other sources of income, will equal 70 to 80 percent of your take-home pay. Of course, greater benefits cost more money.

▶ **HIGH RISK** Your chances of becoming disabled are greater in professions that involve physical risk. *What program would provide disability income for a construction worker who is injured on the job?*

Accident and Sickness Coverage Some disability policies pay only for accidents. However, accidents are not the only cause of disability, so coverage for sickness is also important.

Guaranteed Renewability If your health becomes poor, your disability insurer may try to cancel your coverage. Look for a plan that guarantees coverage as long as you continue to pay your premiums. Some plans may even suspend premiums if you become disabled.

As You Read

QUESTION

What are the disability insurance trade-offs?

Your Disability Income Needs

How do you determine your disability income needs?

After you find out what your benefits would be from the numerous public and private sources, you should determine whether those benefits would meet your disability income needs. Ideally, you want to replace all the income you otherwise would have earned. This money should enable you to pay your day-to-day expenses while you are recovering. You will not have work-related expenses, and your taxes will be lower during the time that you are disabled. In some cases, you may not have to pay various taxes at all.

Section 14.3 Assessment

QUICK CHECK

1. Why is disability income insurance important in personal financial planning?
2. What are the four main sources of disability income?
3. What are two trade-offs that you might have to make when choosing among different private disability insurance policies.

THINK CRITICALLY

4. Describe at least two situations for which a person might need disability income insurance.

USE COMMUNICATION SKILLS

5. **Earning Power** Many people who insure their houses, cars, and other property fail to insure their most valuable resource—their earning power.

Write About It Imagine that you are a health columnist for a newsletter aimed at people in the entertainment industry, such as dancers, actors, writers, and musicians. Explain why these artists should make sure that they are adequately covered by disability insurance.

SOLVE MONEY PROBLEMS

6. **Choosing Plans** Your next-door neighbor has about nine months' salary saved up. He is 58, has no dependents, and plans to retire in seven years. He has just changed jobs. He now works in the office of a road-building company where he has a choice of disability insurance plans.

Analyze What features should your neighbor be looking for in a disability income insurance plan?

Section 14.4

Focus on Reading

Read to Learn
- How to describe various types of life insurance coverage.
- How to identify the key provisions in a life insurance policy.

Main Idea
Making decisions about life insurance and choosing the right policy takes time, research, and careful thought.

Key Terms
- beneficiary (insurance)
- term insurance
- whole life insurance
- cash value
- endowment

Before You Read
PREDICT

Who do you think would need life insurance most, a 65-year-old widower with grown children or a single mother with three young children?

Life Insurance

What Is Life Insurance?

Why is it important to include life insurance in your financial planning?

When you buy life insurance, you are making a contract with the company issuing the policy. You agree to pay a certain amount of money—the premium—periodically. In return, the company agrees to pay a death benefit, or a stated sum of money upon your death, to your beneficiary. A **beneficiary** is a person named to receive the benefits from an insurance policy.

The Purpose of Life Insurance

Buying life insurance can help you protect the people who depend upon you from financial losses caused by your death. Those people could include a spouse, children, an aging parent, or a business partner. Life insurance benefits may be used to:

- Pay off a home mortgage or other debts at the time of death.
- Provide lump-sum payments as an endowment for children when they reach a certain age.
- Provide an education or income for children.
- Make charitable donations after death.
- Provide a retirement income.
- Accumulate savings.
- Establish a regular income for survivors.
- Set up an estate plan.
- Pay estate and death taxes.

The Principle of Life Insurance

No one can say with any certainty how long a particular person will live. However, insurance companies are able to make some educated guesses. Over the years they have compiled tables that show an estimate of how long people live. Using these tables, the companies make a rough guess about a person's life span and set the price of insurance premiums for him or her accordingly. The sooner a person is likely to die, the higher the premium he or she will pay to have life insurance. For example, life insurance will cost more for a 65-year-old woman than for a 25-year-old woman.

How Long Will You Live?

If history is any guide, you will live longer than your ancestors lived. In 1900, the life expectancy of an American male was 46.3 years, and it was 48.3 years for an American female. In contrast, by the year 2000, the life expectancy increased to 74 years for men and 80 years for women. **Figure 14.2** shows an estimate of how many years a person can be expected to live today. This type of table guides insurance companies when they set prices. For example, a 30-year-old woman can be expected to live another 50.6 years. That does not mean that she has a high probability of dying at age 80.6. This just means that 50.6 is the average number of additional years a 30-year-old woman may expect to live.

Do You Need Life Insurance?

Before you buy life insurance, you will have to decide whether you need it at all. Generally, if your death would cause financial hardship for somebody, then life insurance is a wise purchase. Households with children usually have the greatest need for life insurance. Single people who live alone or with their parents, however, usually have little or no need for life insurance unless they have a great deal of debt or want to provide for their parents or a friend, relative, or charity.

Figure 14.2 **Life Expectancy Table**

Age	Both Sexes	Male	Female	Age	Both Sexes	Male	Female
0	76.9	74.1	79.5	45	34.4	32.2	36.3
1	76.4	73.7	79.0	50	30.0	27.9	31.8
5	72.5	69.8	75.1	55	25.7	23.8	27.4
10	67.6	64.9	70.1	60	21.6	19.9	23.1
15	62.6	59.9	65.2	65	17.9	16.3	19.2
20	57.8	55.2	60.3	70	14.4	13.0	15.5
25	53.1	50.6	55.4	75	11.3	10.1	12.1
30	48.3	45.9	50.6	80	8.6	7.6	9.1
35	43.6	41.3	45.8	85	6.3	5.6	6.7
40	38.9	36.7	41.0				

The Average Life This type of table helps insurance companies determine insurance premiums.

Use the table to find the average number of additional years a 15-year-old male and female were expected to live, based on the statistics gathered by the U.S. government as of 2000.

Types of Life Insurance Policies

When do you think it is most important to have life insurance?

You can purchase life insurance from two types of life insurance companies: stock life insurance companies, which are owned by shareholders, and mutual life insurance companies, which are owned by their policyholders. About 95 percent of life insurance companies in the United States are stock companies. Insurance policies can be divided into two types: term insurance and whole life insurance.

Term Insurance

Term insurance, which is sometimes called *temporary life insurance*, is insurance that provides protection against loss of life for only a specified term, or period of time. A term insurance policy pays a benefit only if you die during the period it covers, which may be 1, 5, 10, or 20 years, or up to age 70. If you stop paying the premiums, your coverage stops. Term insurance is often the best value for most consumers. You need life insurance coverage most while you are raising children. As your children become independent and your assets increase, you can reduce your coverage. Term insurance comes in many different forms.

Renewable Term   The coverage of term insurance ends at the conclusion of the term, but you can continue it for another term, such as five years, if you have a renewable option. However, the premium will increase because you will be older. It also usually has an age limit, which means you cannot renew your coverage after you reach a certain age.

Multiyear Level Term   A multiyear level term, or straight term, policy guarantees that you will pay the same premium for the duration of your policy.

◄ COMING TO TERMS Many experts say that term insurance is best for most people—especially growing families. *Name the types of term insurance policies that are available.*

Conversion Term This type of policy allows you to change from term to permanent coverage. This change will require a higher premium.

Decreasing Term Term insurance is also available in a form that pays less to the beneficiary as time passes. The premiums are usually the same over the entire period of coverage. The insurance period you select might depend on your age or on how long you want to be covered. For example, if you have a mortgage on a house, you might buy a 25-year decreasing term policy as a way to make sure that the debt could be paid if you died. The coverage would decrease as the balance on the loan decreased.

Whole Life Insurance

The other major type of life insurance is known as whole life insurance (also called a straight life policy, a cash value policy, or an ordinary life policy). **Whole life insurance** is a permanent policy for which you pay a specified premium each year for the rest of your life. The insurance company pays your beneficiary a stated sum when you die. The amount of your premium depends mostly on the age at which you purchase the insurance.

Whole life insurance can also serve as an investment. Part of each premium you pay is set aside in a savings account. When and if you cancel the policy, you are entitled to the accumulated savings, which is known as the **cash value**. Whole life policies are popular because they provide both a death benefit and a savings component. You can also borrow from your cash value if necessary, although you must pay interest on the loan. Cash value policies may make sense for people who intend to keep the policies for the long term or for people who want a more structured way to save. However, the Consumer Federation of America Insurance Group suggests that you explore other savings and investment strategies before investing your money in a permanent policy.

The premium on a term insurance policy will increase each time you renew your insurance. In contrast, whole life policies have higher annual premiums at first, but the payment amount remains the same for the rest of your life. Several types of whole life policies have been developed to meet the needs of different customers. These include the limited payment policy, the variable life policy, the adjustable life policy, and universal life insurance.

Limited Payment Policy Limited payment policies charge premiums for only a certain length of time, usually 20 or 30 years or until the insured reaches a certain age. At the end of this time, the policy is "paid up" and the policyholder remains insured for life. When the policyholder dies, the beneficiary receives the full death benefit. The annual premiums are higher for limited payment policies because the premiums have to be paid within a shorter period of time.

Avoiding Financial Fraud

Choosing the right type of life insurance policy can be complicated. There are many options available, and it can be difficult to sort out the details to decide what is best. Another complicating factor is that con artists may try to defraud you. Learn some of the do's and don'ts of choosing life insurance and avoiding fraud.

@ To continue with Task 4 of your WebQuest project, visit **persfinance07.glencoe.com**.

As You Read

QUESTION

What are the risks and benefits associated with variable life insurance?

Variable Life Policy   With a variable life policy, premium payments are fixed. As with a cash value policy, part of the premium is placed into a separate account; this money is invested in a stock, bond, or money market fund. The death benefit is guaranteed, but the cash value of the benefit can vary considerably according to the ups and downs of the stock market. Your death benefit can also increase if the earnings of that separate fund increase.

Adjustable Life Policy   An adjustable life policy allows you to change your coverage as your needs change. For example, if you want to increase or decrease your death benefit, you can change either the premium payments or the period of coverage.

Universal Life   Universal life insurance is essentially a term policy with a cash value. Part of your premium goes into an investment account that grows and earns interest. You are able to borrow or withdraw your cash value.

Other Types of Life Insurance Policies

Other types of life insurance policies include group life insurance, credit life insurance, and endowment life insurance.

Group Life Insurance   Group life insurance is a variation of term insurance. It covers a large number of people under a single policy. The people included in the group do not need medical examinations to get coverage. Group insurance is usually offered by employers, who pay part or all of the costs for their employees. It may also be offered by professional organizations, which allow members to obtain coverage. However, it can be more expensive than similar term policies.

Credit Life Insurance   Credit life insurance pays off debts, such as auto loans or mortgages, in the event that you die before they are paid in full. These types of policies are not the best buy for the protection they offer. Decreasing term insurance is a better option.

Endowment Life Insurance   **Endowment** is life insurance that provides coverage for a specific period of time and pays a sum of money to the policyholder if he or she is living at the end of the endowment period. If the policyholder dies before that time, the beneficiary receives the money.

Key Provisions in a Life Insurance Policy

Why should you consider adding provisions to your life insurance policy?

Study the provisions in your policy carefully and be sure to update the necessary information as changes in your life occur. The following features are the most common provisions found in life insurance policies.

Document Detective

Learn to identify and understand the standard financial documents you will use in the real world.

Investigate: A Life Insurance Policy Statement

A life insurance policy statement contains the following information:

- Policy identification number
- Name of insured
- Death benefit amount
- Cash value
- Cost of the premium

Your Motive: If a person who holds a life insurance policy dies, the people who depended upon that policyholder can be protected from financial losses by the life insurance policy. By obtaining a life insurance policy, you are ensuring that your loved ones, who are your beneficiaries, will not be stuck with your debts.

GHL GENERAL HOME LIFE

Policy Anniversary Statement

Juan Ramirez
21 First Street
Smithville, Florida 55523

Policy number:	2–615–879
Date prepared:	May 18, 20--
Insured:	Juan Ramirez
Plan name:	Whole Life
Face amount:	$36,364
Premium:	$41.87 monthly
Issued:	June 23, 2003
Paid to:	June 23, 2016

This policy will provide the following benefits up to June 23, 2016, assuming premiums are paid to that date and no other changes occur.

	DEATH BENEFIT	CASH VALUE
Basic policy	$36,364.00	$4,253
Paid-up additions	$81.39	$7.82
Option term	$63,554.61	0.00
TOTAL	**$100,000.00**	**$4,260.82**

Key Points: A life insurance policy provides a predetermined payment that the insurance company will make in the event of the death of the policy owner. This amount is called the death benefit. In addition, the policy also accumulates a cash value over time as the holder of the policy pays premiums. If the owner chooses to cancel the policy before death, he or she will receive the policy's cash value.

Find the Solutions

1. What is the yearly cost of this policy?
2. When was this policy issued or started?
3. How much will the policy pay upon Juan's death?
4. When does Juan's insurance coverage expire?
5. If Juan decides to cancel this policy, how much will the insurance company pay him?

Beneficiary Designation

You decide who receives the benefits of your life insurance policy. The beneficiary could be your spouse, your child, or your business partner, for example. You can also name *contingent beneficiaries*, those who will receive the money if your primary beneficiary dies before or at the same time as you do. You will need to update your list of beneficiaries as your needs change.

Incontestability Clause

The incontestability clause says that the insurer cannot cancel the policy if it has been in force for a specified period, usually two years. After that time the policy is considered valid during the lifetime of the insured. The incontestability clause protects the beneficiaries from financial loss in the event that the insurance company refuses to meet the terms of the policy.

Suicide Clause

Many insurance policies state that in the first two years of coverage, beneficiaries of someone who dies by suicide receive only the amount of the premiums paid. After two years from the date of death, beneficiaries may receive the full value of death benefits. However, some insurance policies will not provide benefits at all if a policyholder dies by suicide.

Riders to Life Insurance Policies

An insurance company can change the conditions of an insurance policy by adding a rider to it. A rider is a document attached to a policy that changes its terms by adding or excluding specified conditions or altering its benefits. Examples of riders include a waiver of premium disability benefit, an accidental death benefit, and a guaranteed insurability option.

Waiver of Premium Disability Benefit   One type of rider is a waiver of premium disability benefit. This clause allows a policyholder to stop paying premiums if he or she is totally and permanently disabled before reaching a certain age, usually 60. The insurance company will continue to pay the premiums at its own expense so that the policy remains in force.

Accidental Death Benefit   Another typical rider to life insurance policies is an accidental death benefit, sometimes called *double indemnity*. Double indemnity pays twice the value of the policy if the insured is killed in an accident. Again, the accident must occur before a certain age, generally 60 or 65. Experts counsel against adding this rider to your coverage. The benefit is expensive, and your chances of dying in an accident are slim.

Guaranteed Insurability Option A third important rider is a guaranteed insurability option. This rider allows you to buy a specified additional amount of life insurance at certain intervals without undergoing medical exams. This is a good option for people who anticipate needing more life insurance in the future.

Cost of Living Protection This special rider is designed to help prevent inflation from eroding, or reducing, the purchasing power of the protection that your policy provides. A *loss, reduction,* or *erosion of purchasing power* refers to the effect that inflation has on a fixed amount of money. As inflation increases the costs of goods and services, that fixed amount of money will not buy as much in the future as it does today.

Insurance Needs

Before you buy any type of insurance, you should always consider a number of factors, such as your source of income, financial responsibilities, savings, and net worth. As your life situation and goals change, you need to regularly evaluate your insurance needs to determine if you have the right kind of coverage to support your personal financial plan.

After You Read

REACT

Using the information provided in this chapter, what insurance plans would you choose to meet both your health and financial needs?

Section 14.4 Assessment

QUICK CHECK

1. What is the purpose of life insurance?
2. What are the differences between term and whole life insurance?
3. What are the key provisions in a life insurance policy?

THINK CRITICALLY

4. "Term insurance is often the best value for most consumers." Do you agree or disagree with this statement? Support your argument.

USE MATH SKILLS

5. **Life Expectancy** Review the life expectancy tables in Figure 14.2 on page 465.

   Present Show the life expectancy at various ages for both genders on a line graph. Add number of years lived to number of years expected to remain.

For example, at age 50, life expectancy for males and females is 80 years (50 + 30 = 80). What trends do you notice in your line graph?

SOLVE MONEY PROBLEMS

6. **Life Insurance Comparisons** Jon is a 27-year-old single man with no children. He has a younger sister who has a developmental disability. Both his parents are living, though neither parent is in good health. Jon has an auto loan, a $50,000 mortgage on his condominium, and no consumer debt.

   Analyze Is Jon a good candidate for life insurance? If so, what kind and how much life insurance should he buy? In a small group, discuss Jon's situation and his needs to determine his ideal life insurance policy.

CHAPTER SUMMARY

- Health insurance is important for financial planning because it can help protect against the financial burden of illness or injury.
- Health insurance policies have certain similarities but can differ in terms of reimbursement versus indemnity, internal limits versus aggregate limits, deductibles and coinsurance, and out-of-pocket limits.
- Private health care plans are offered by private insurance companies, hospital and medical service plans, health maintenance organizations, preferred provider organizations, home health care agencies, and employer self-funded health plans. Government health care programs are Medicare and Medicaid.

- Disability insurance provides regular cash income for people who are unable to work due to pregnancy, a non-work-related accident, or illness.
- Sources of disability income are workers' compensation, an employer, Social Security, and private disability insurance.
- Types of life insurance policies include term insurance, whole life insurance, group life insurance, credit life insurance, and endowment life insurance.
- The key provisions in a life insurance policy include naming a beneficiary, an incontestability clause, a suicide clause, and policy riders.

Communicating Key Terms

Choose your ideal benefits package for a job and include health and life insurance. Using the terms below, write instructions for what insurance you want your employer to buy for you.

- health insurance
- coinsurance
- stop-loss
- co-payment
- Blue Cross
- Blue Shield
- managed care

- health maintenance organization (HMO)
- preferred provider organization (PPO)
- point-of-service (POS) plan
- Medicare
- Medicaid

- disability income insurance
- beneficiary (insurance)
- term insurance
- whole life insurance
- cash value
- endowment

Reviewing Key Concepts

1. **Explain** how increasing co-payments and deductibles affects premium rates.
2. **Discuss** basic health insurance coverage and major medical expense insurance.
3. **Compare** government health care programs and those offered by private companies.
4. **Explain** the importance of disability insurance in financial planning.
5. **Describe** the advantages of worker's compensation.
6. **Identify** the types of term and whole life insurance.
7. **Explain** the key provisions of life insurance.

Social Studies   Hector Ramirez and Walter Chan are both shopping for life insurance policies. Hector and his wife just bought a car. Walter, his wife, and four children just moved into a new $150,000 home. Hector and Walter have narrowed their choices to either decreasing term insurance or credit life insurance.

Write About It   Which type of insurance should each person choose? Provide a list of reasons for each of your choices.

Heath Insurance Premiums   Because you are self-employed, you started buying individual health insurance nine years ago at a cost of $579 per quarter. Now the quarterly premium is $806.

1. **Calculate** what your annual premium was nine years ago and what it is today. What was the percentage increase over those nine years?
2. **Compute** by using an Internet search engine to locate information on health insurance premiums and coverage from five insurance companies. Compare and contrast the offers using spreadsheet software.

Connect with Economics and Law   Many companies that once sold just life insurance have "reinvented" themselves as financial services companies. Many of these firms promote themselves as "one-stop shops" for all your financial service needs.

1. **Research**   Access the Web site of your state's insurance regulatory agency and find out what requirements insurance agents must meet to be able to sell other financial products, such as mutual funds.
2. **Think Critically**   What are the pros and cons of buying financial products from an insurance company versus a stockbroker?

Buying Insurance on the Internet   You may not need to purchase life insurance right now, but it is a good idea to know how much a policy will cost so that you will be able to plan your finances accordingly.

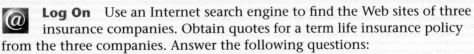

Log On   Use an Internet search engine to find the Web sites of three insurance companies. Obtain quotes for a term life insurance policy from the three companies. Answer the following questions:

1. What forms of term life insurance do these companies offer?
2. Choose one form of term life insurance offered by all three companies and determine which company's policy you feel is the best deal for you. Explain why you would choose that policy.

Newsclip: More Choices   A health savings account (HSA) is a plan that allows employees to save for medical expenses in a tax-free account.

Log On   Go to persfinance07.glencoe.com and open Chapter 14. Learn more about HSAs. Write a paragraph about how HSAs might affect your future. Would you sign up for an HSA?

INSURANCE FACTS AND FICTION

Insurance may not be a big issue for you now, but when you are no longer covered under your parents' or guardian's policies or you start full-time employment, you will need to know your options. Here is an opportunity to test your knowledge. Write your answers to the following questions on a separate sheet of paper.

1. Health insurance is only available as a benefit from an employer.

True   False

2. You can continue your health insurance even if you leave a job.

True   False

3. A co-payment is the small amount you pay for a doctor's visit or a prescription.

True   False

4. In general the younger you are, the less expensive life insurance is.

True   False

5. Life insurance can also be used as an investment for retirement.

True   False

6. Life insurance companies can cancel policies if you develop a serious illness after you are insured.

True   False

7. You can collect life insurance benefits before you die.

True   False

8. The amount of disability insurance you can buy is based on a percentage of your total income.

True   False

Your Financial Portfolio

Comparing Life Insurance

Sean Richards is investigating the cost of life insurance. He is 28 years old, married, and has two children. Sean contacted two reputable insurance companies and based his comparison on $100,000 worth of insurance.

Type of Policy	Company A	Company B
20-year decreasing term insurance $100,000		
Monthly premium	$14.00	$8.25
Total premiums for 20 years	$3,360.00	$1,980.00
Cash value in 20 years	none	none
Whole life insurance (limited payment) $100,000		
Monthly premium	$82.00	$62.60
Total premiums for 20 years	$19,280.00	$15,024.00
Cash value in 20 years	$25,000.00	$21,243.00

Sean chose the 20-year decreasing term insurance because of the low cost, even though he cannot convert it into cash at a future date. He purchased his policy with Company B.

Compare

On a separate sheet of paper, follow Sean's chart to compare life insurance rates. Using the Internet, or by visiting, calling, or writing, get quotes from two different insurance companies. Base the quote on (1) a 20-year decreasing term insurance policy for $100,000 and (2) a whole life (limited payment) insurance policy for $100,000. Use your own age.

CHAPTER 15

Retirement and Estate Planning

 What You'll Learn

When you have completed this chapter, you will be able to:

Section 15.1
- Explain the importance of retirement planning.
- Identify retirement living costs and housing needs.

Section 15.2
- Describe the role of Social Security in planning for retirement.
- Discuss the benefits offered by employer pension plans.
- Explain various personal retirement plans.

Section 15.3
- Identify various types of wills.
- Discuss several types of trusts.
- Describe common characteristics of estates.
- Identify the types of taxes that affect estates.

Reading Strategies

To get the most out of your reading:

Predict what you will learn in this chapter.

Relate what you read to your own life.

Question what you are reading to be sure you understand.

React to what you have read.

In the **Real** World . . .

Every summer, Shelly Garfield visits her grandparents, who live in a retirement community designed with swimming pools and recreation rooms. Her grandparents decided to move there after Shelly's grandmother broke her hip. They liked the idea of having a full medical staff on duty. Shelly's grandparents had saved enough money so they could afford to move there. As the elderly population increases, Social Security, Medicare, and pensions will be stretched, and may not cover many retirees' total expenses. Shelly is a high school senior, but it is not too early for her to start thinking about retirement. By estimating retirement costs and housing needs now, she can save for retirement on her own terms.

As You Read *Consider why it is wise to begin a retirement plan early.*

ASK STANDARD &POOR'S

Will Power

Q: My parents do not have a lot of money, so is it really that important for them to write up a will?

A: Even if your parents do not have a lot of money, they should have a will. If they die without a will, their state of residence will step in and control how their estate is distributed. It costs somewhere between $200 and $350 to have an attorney draft a will. The peace of mind it will provide your parents will be worth the cost.

Ask Yourself If you had to write up a will right now, how would you want your possessions and money distributed?

 Go to **persfinance07.glencoe.com** to complete the Standard & Poor's Financial Focus activity.

Focus on Reading

Read to Learn

- How to explain the importance of retirement planning.
- How to identify retirement living costs and housing needs.

Main Idea

Estimating your retirement living costs and housing needs will enable you to save or invest enough money to live comfortably during retirement.

Key Term

- assisted-living facility (ALF)

Before You Read

PREDICT

When do you think you should begin planning for your retirement?

Retirement Planning

Planning for Retirement

What factors should you consider when planning for retirement?

A recent poll from Harris Interactive reported that 95 percent of people ages 55 to 64 years old plan to do at least some work after they have retired. Another survey reported that future retirees expected to continue to learn, try news things, and pursue new hobbies and interests. Someday, when you retire, you too may desire an active life.

Your retirement years may seem a long way off right now. You are still in high school, and after you graduate, you will probably work for many years. However, it is never too early to start planning for retirement. Planning can help you cope with sudden changes that may occur in your life, and it can give you a sense of control over your future. Planning can also help make the retirement years more comfortable.

If you have not done any research on the subject of retirement, you may have some misconceptions about the "golden years." Here are some myths about retirement:

- You have plenty of time to start saving for retirement.
- Saving a small amount of money will not help.
- You will spend less money when you retire.
- Your retirement will last about 15 years.
- You can depend on Social Security and a company pension plan to pay your basic living expenses.
- Your pension benefits will increase to keep pace with inflation.
- Your employer's health insurance plan and Medicare will cover all your medical expenses.

Some of these statements may have been true in the past, but they are no longer true today. You may live for many years after you retire. If you want your retirement to be a happy and comfortable time of your life, you will need enough money to suit your lifestyle. That is why you should start planning and saving as early as possible. It is never too late to start saving for retirement, but the sooner you start, the better off you will be.

Suppose that you want to have at least $1 million when you retire at age 65. If you start saving at age 25, you can meet that goal by putting about $127 per month into investment funds that grow at a rate of about 11 percent each year. If you wait to begin saving until age 50, the monthly amount to achieve that goal skyrockets to $2,244.

Setting Long-Range Goals

As you think about your retirement years, consider your long-range goals. What does retirement mean to you? Maybe it will be a time to stop working and to relax. Perhaps you imagine traveling the world, developing a hobby, or starting a second career. Ask yourself: Where do you want to live after you retire? What type of lifestyle would you like to have? Then analyze your current financial situation to determine what you need to do to reach your long-range goals.

As You Read

RELATE

Imagine what you would like to do when you retire. What are three financial goals for that time?

Conducting a Financial Analysis

The checklist in **Figure 15.1** is an example of how you might analyze your financial assets and liabilities. As you learned in Chapter 3, an asset is any item of value that you own, including cash, property, personal possessions, and investments. This includes cash in checking and savings accounts, a house, a car, a television, and so on. It also includes the current value of any stocks, bonds, other investments, life insurance policies, and pension funds.

Your liabilities are the debts you owe, including the balance on an automobile loan, credit card balances, other loans, and unpaid taxes. If you subtract your liabilities from your assets, you get your net worth. Ideally, your net worth should increase each year.

Figure 15.1   **Assets, Liabilities, and Net Worth**

Assets:		Liabilities:	
Cash:		Current unpaid bills	$ 600
Checking account	$ 800	Home mortgage	
Savings account	4,500	(remaining balance)	9,700
Investments:		Auto loan	1,200
U.S. Savings Bonds		Property taxes	1,100
(current cash-in value)	5,000	Home improvement loan	3,700
Stocks, mutual funds	4,500	Total liabilities	$16,300
Life insurance:			
Cash value, accumulated			
dividends	10,000		
Company pension rights:			
Accrued pension benefit	20,000	**Net worth:**	
Property:			
House (resale value)	50,000	Assets − Liabilities = Net Worth	
Furniture and appliances	8,000	$108,800 − $16,300 = $92,500	
Collections and jewelry	2,000		
Automobile	3,000		
Other:			
Loan to brother	1,000		
Gross assets	$108,800		

Calculating Net Worth   Assets are everything that you own, while liabilities are everything you owe.
How can you determine your net worth?

▲ **LIVING THE GOOD LIFE** When you retire you may not be able to afford to take lavish vacations or buy many expensive items. *What are some of the decisions you will have to make now to ensure a comfortable retirement?*

Reviewing Assets

Review your assets on a regular basis. You may need to make adjustments in your saving, spending, and investments to stay on track with your goal. As you review your assets, consider the following factors: housing, life insurance, savings, and investments. Each asset will have an important effect on your retirement income.

Housing   A house can be your most valuable asset. However, if you buy a home with large mortgage payments, you may be unable to save money for retirement. In that case, you might consider buying a smaller, less expensive place to live. A smaller house is usually easier and less expensive to maintain. You can use the money you save by having lower payments to increase your retirement fund.

Life Insurance   At some point in the future, you might buy life insurance to provide for your loved ones. If you have children, life insurance can provide financial support in case you die while they are still young. As you near retirement, though, your children will probably be self-sufficient. When that time comes, you might reduce your premium payments by decreasing your life insurance coverage. This would give you extra money for living expenses or investments.

As You Read

QUESTION

Does planning for your retirement alter today's investment strategies?

Other Investments When you review your assets, also evaluate any other investments you have. When you originally chose those investments, you may have been more interested in making your money grow over time than in getting a quick return. When you are ready to retire, you may want to use the income from those investments to cover living expenses.

Retirement Living Expenses
What living expenses should you consider when planning for retirement?

When planning for retirement, estimate how much money you will need to live comfortably during your retirement years. You cannot predict exactly how much money you will need, but you can estimate the expense of your basic needs. To do this, think about how your spending patterns and living situation might change.

For example, when you are retired, you may spend more money on recreation, health insurance, and medical care than you will as a young adult. At the same time, you may spend less money on transportation and clothing. Your federal income taxes may be lower as well. Also, some income from various retirement plans may be taxed at a lower rate or not at all. **Figure 15.2** provides an example of retirement expenses.

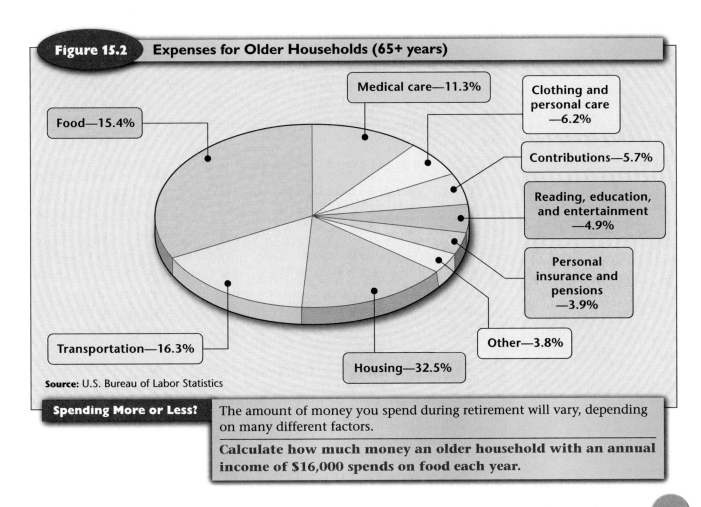

Figure 15.2 **Expenses for Older Households (65+ years)**

Medical care—11.3%

Clothing and personal care —6.2%

Food—15.4%

Contributions—5.7%

Reading, education, and entertainment —4.9%

Personal insurance and pensions —3.9%

Transportation—16.3%

Other—3.8%

Housing—32.5%

Source: U.S. Bureau of Labor Statistics

Spending More or Less? The amount of money you spend during retirement will vary, depending on many different factors.

Calculate how much money an older household with an annual income of $16,000 spends on food each year.

Figure 15.3 **Inflation Over Time**

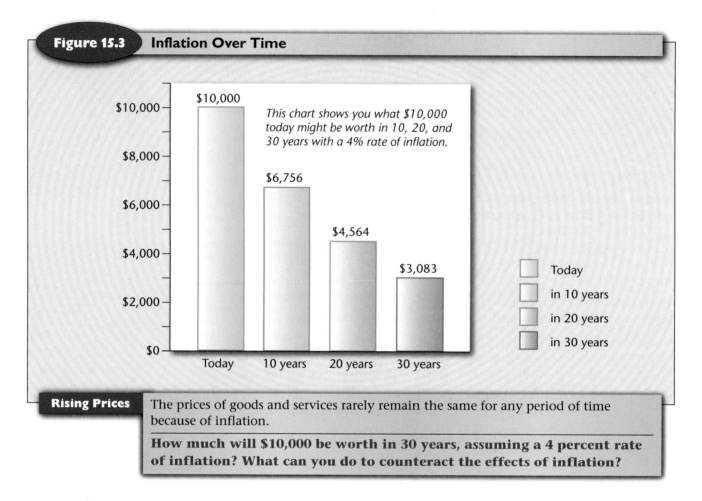

$10,000

This chart shows you what $10,000 today might be worth in 10, 20, and 30 years with a 4% rate of inflation.

$10,000 —

$8,000 —

$6,000 —

$6,756

$4,000 —

$4,564

$2,000 —

$3,083

$0 —

Today   10 years   20 years   30 years

☐ Today
☐ in 10 years
☐ in 20 years
☐ in 30 years

Rising Prices The prices of goods and services rarely remain the same for any period of time because of inflation.

How much will $10,000 be worth in 30 years, assuming a 4 percent rate of inflation? What can you do to counteract the effects of inflation?

Remember to take inflation into account. Estimate high when calculating how much the prices of goods and services will rise by the time you retire. (See **Figure 15.3.**) Even a 3 percent rate of inflation will cause prices to double every 24 years. Also, plan for emergencies as you consider future retirement living expenses.

Retirement Housing
What factors should you consider regarding housing needs during retirement?

The place where you live can have a significant impact on your financial needs. In the years before retirement, use vacations to explore areas and cities where you might want to settle. If you find a place you like, go there at different times of the year. That way, you will be able to experience the climate and environment. Meet people who live in the area and learn about activities, transportation, and taxes.

Retirement Relocation Pitfalls

Consider the downside of moving to a new location. People sometimes find themselves stuck in a place they really do not like. Some retirees find they miss their children, grandchildren, and friends and relatives left behind. Other retired people move to the location of their dreams and discover they have made a mistake financially.

Researching Locations Here are some tips from specialists on how to research taxes and other costs before moving to a new area:

- Contact the local chamber of commerce for details on area property taxes and the local economy.
- Contact the state tax department to research income, sales, inheritance taxes, and exemptions for retirees.
- Read the Sunday edition of the local newspaper of the town or city you are considering.
- Check with local utility companies to estimate energy costs.
- Visit the area in different seasons and talk to local residents about the cost of living there.
- If you plan to buy a home, take time and rent a home first.

Types of Housing

Even if you do not move to a new location, housing needs may change during retirement. Many retirees want a home that is easy and inexpensive to maintain, such as a smaller house, a condominium, or an apartment. Having access to public transportation, stores, and recreation areas is also important. **Figure 15.4** presents several housing options.

Careers in Finance

ESTATE ADMINISTRATOR   **Paul Francisco**
Choate, Hall & Stewart

Paul has very strong organizational and communication skills, which are essential in his work as an estate administrator. Under the direction of the attorney responsible for estate administration, Paul handles all phases of estate execution. He determines and informs the parties of procedural and tax deadlines and ensures compliance with the deadlines. He also calculates debts, expenses, taxes, and cash needs. In his role as an estate administrator, Paul may need to develop and implement steps to uncover and reconcile conflicts between beneficiaries or family members.

SKILLS: Writing, communication, organizational, problem-solving, analytical, and multitasking skills

PERSONAL TRAITS: Discreet, good judgment, likes working with people and numbers, tactful, and quick thinking

EDUCATION: High school diploma or equivalent; bachelor's degree in finance or related field or equivalent work experience

ANALYZE How might planning for retirement affect your will?

@ To learn more about career paths for estate administrators, visit *persfinance07.glencoe.com*.

Figure 15.4 Retirement Housing Options

Housing options for retirement are based on personal, financial, and medical factors. The goal of most retirees is to have comfortable and affordable housing that meets their particular needs.

1 **Most retired people** decide to remain where they are and continue living in their own homes.

2 **Living with grown children** and young grandchildren can be a choice for some elderly retired people and their families.

3 **For retired people with disabilities,** a universal design home built with special features, such as extra-wide doors, lower appliances, and automatic faucets, can be both appealing and practical. These homes help people with disabilities to maintain their independence.

A great majority of people prefer to grow old in their own homes in their own communities. Recognizing this trend, building suppliers offer everything from lever door handles to faucets that turn on automatically when you put your hand beneath the spout. Remodeling to accommodate aging homeowners is creating a demand for these products. In addition, contractors are building universal design homes from scratch that can accommodate people who use wheelchairs and walkers or those who simply want more convenience.

Many elderly people move into assisted-living facilities during their retirement years. An **assisted-living facility (ALF)** is a residence complex that provides personal and medical services for the elderly. Assisted-living facilities offer everything from minimal services to full, continuous nursing care. They may vary greatly in quality, but ALFs are increasingly popular with elderly retirees, some of whom are no longer able to live alone and care for themselves.

Section 15.1 Assessment

QUICK CHECK

1. What are several reasons that early retirement planning is important?
2. What factors should you consider when estimating your retirement living expenses?
3. What are some features and benefits of an assisted-living facility?

THINK CRITICALLY

4. Imagine that you are 20 years away from retirement and you are thinking of spending a large portion of your income to purchase an expensive home. Discuss the advantages and disadvantages of this plan.

USE COMMUNICATION SKILLS

5. **Free at Last!** Enrique and his wife, Maribel, have both been working at the same company for almost 35 years and are nearing retirement. They have been looking forward to the time when they will be free to do almost anything they want. They already have a long list of places they would like to visit, things they would like to do, and ways they would like to spend their time after they retire.

Present Imagine the type of life you would like to have when you retire. Combine pictures and words to create a collage that expresses your thoughts and feelings about your retirement dreams.

SOLVE MONEY PROBLEMS

6. **Changing Lifestyles** Jeff and Maureen McBride have been retired for a couple of years. Although their income is lower than when they were working, they continue to live as they did before retirement. They have a three-bedroom house in New Jersey. Twice a year, they travel to California to visit their children and grandchildren. Unfortunately, they now find themselves in a financial pinch. They need to cut back on their expenses and have a plan to live more economically without giving up many of the activities they enjoy.

Analyze Help Jeff and Maureen by discussing various options they might have for saving money.

Focus on Reading

Read to Learn
- How to describe the role of Social Security in planning for retirement.
- How to discuss the benefits offered by employer pension plans.
- How to explain various personal retirement plans.

Main Idea
Various types of retirement plans are suited to different financial situations and personal needs.

Key Terms
- defined-contribution plan
- 401(k) plan
- vesting
- defined-benefit plan
- individual retirement account (IRA)
- Keogh plan
- annuity (insurance)
- heirs

Before You Read

PREDICT

Besides Social Security, what other retirement plans might be available?

Planning Retirement Income

Public Pension Plans
Who receives benefits under Social Security?

You learned in Chapter 2 that a pension plan is a retirement plan that is funded, at least in part, by an employer. Public pension plans are established by states and municipalities. Social Security is a public pension plan established by the United States government in 1935. The government agency that manages the program is called the Social Security Administration.

Social Security

Social Security is an important source of retirement income for many Americans. The program covers 97 percent of all workers, and almost one out of every six Americans currently collects some form of Social Security benefit. Social Security is a package of protection that provides benefits to retirees, survivors, and disabled persons. You should not rely on Social Security to cover all of your retirement expenses. Social Security was not designed to provide 100 percent of retirement income. In addition, current and future revisions to the program may reduce retirement benefits in years to come.

Who Is Eligible   The amount of Social Security retirement benefits you receive is based on your earnings over the years. The more you earn, the greater your benefits will be, up to a maximum amount.

Each year the Social Security Administration will send you a history of your earnings and an estimate of your future monthly benefits. The statement includes an estimate, in today's dollars, of how much you would get each month if you retired at different ages. For example, your statement might list benefits for retirement at age 62, 67, and 70, based on the year you were born, your earnings to date, and your projected future earnings.

To qualify for retirement benefits, you must earn a certain number of credits. These credits are based on the length of time you work and pay Social Security tax, or contributions, on your earnings. Your credits are calculated on a quarterly basis. The number of quarters needed to qualify depends on your year of birth. For example, people born after 1928 need at least 40 quarters to qualify for benefits.

Dependent Eligibility Certain dependents of a worker may also receive benefits under the Social Security program. They include a spouse age 62 or older; unmarried children under 18 (or under 19 if they are full-time students no higher than grade 12); and unmarried individuals with disabilities aged 18 or older. Widows and widowers can receive Social Security benefits before age 62.

Social Security Retirement Benefits Most people can begin collecting Social Security retirement benefits at age 62. However, the monthly amount at age 62 is less than it would be if the person waited until full retirement age. This initial amount becomes the permanent base amount.

In the past people could receive full retirement benefits at age 65. However, the full retirement age is being increased in gradual steps. For people born in 1960 and later, the full retirement age is 67. If you postpone applying for benefits when you are eligible, your monthly payment amount will increase slightly for each year you wait, but only up to age 70.

Social Security Information For more information about Social Security, you can visit the Social Security Web site. It provides access to forms and publications and gives links to other valuable information. To learn more about the taxability of Social Security benefits, contact the Internal Revenue Service (IRS) and ask for Publication 554, Older Americans' Tax Guide, and Publication 915, Social Security and Equivalent Railroad Retirement Benefits. These publications can also be found on the IRS Web site.

As You Read

RELATE

If you currently hold a job, look at a recent paycheck stub. Are you paying into Social Security?

▲ **SOCIAL SECURITY BENEFITS** Social Security is an important source of income for many retired people. *How are Social Security benefits calculated?*

Other Public Pension Plans

Besides Social Security, the federal government provides other special retirement plans for federal government workers and railroad employees. These employees are not covered by Social Security. The Veterans Administration provides pensions for survivors of people who died while serving in the armed forces. It also offers disability pensions for eligible veterans. In addition, many state and local governments provide retirement plans for their employees.

Employer Pension Plans
What is one of the benefits of having an employer pension plan?

Another possible source of retirement income is an employer pension plan offered by the company for which you work. With this type of plan, your employer contributes to your retirement benefits, and sometimes you contribute, too. These contributions and their earnings remain tax-deferred until you withdraw them during retirement.

Private employer pension plans vary. If the company you work for offers one, find out what benefits you will receive and when you will become eligible to receive those benefits. Most employer plans are one of two basic types: defined-contribution plans or defined-benefit plans.

Defined-Contribution Plan

A **defined-contribution plan**, sometimes called an individual account plan, is an individual account for each employee. The employer contributes a specific amount to the account annually. This type of retirement plan does not guarantee any particular benefit. When you retire and become eligible for benefits, you receive the total amount of funds (including investment earnings) that is in your account. Several types of defined-contribution plans exist.

Money-Purchase Plans With a money-purchase plan, your employer promises to set aside a certain amount of money for you each year. That amount may be a percentage of your earnings.

Stock Bonus Plans Under a stock bonus plan, your employer's contribution is used to buy stock in the company for you. The stock is held in trust until you retire. Then you can keep your shares or sell them.

Profit-Sharing Plans Under a profit-sharing plan, your employer's contribution depends on the company's profits each year.

401(k) Plans A **401(k) plan**, or salary-reduction plan, is a type of retirement savings plan funded by a portion of your salary that is deducted from your gross paycheck and placed in a special account. Many employers match their employees' 401(k) contributions up to a specific dollar amount or percentage of salary.

The funds in 401(k) plans can be invested in stocks, bonds, and mutual funds. As a result, you can accumulate a significant amount of money in this type of account if you begin contributing to it early in your career. In addition, the money that accumulates in your 401(k) plan is tax-deferred, which means that you do not have to pay taxes on it until you withdraw it.

403(b) Plans If you are employed by a tax-exempt institution, such as a hospital or a nonprofit organization, the salary-reduction plan is called a Section 403(b) plan. The funds in this plan are also tax-deferred. The 401(k) and 403(b) plans are known as tax-sheltered annuity (TSA) plans. The amount that can be contributed each year to 401(k) and 403(b) plans is limited by law, as is the amount of contributions to other types of defined-contribution plans.

Vesting Employee contributions to a pension plan belong to you, the employee, regardless of the amount of time that you are with a particular employer. But what happens to the contributions that the employer has made to your account if you change jobs and move to another company? One of the most important aspects of these plans is vesting. **Vesting** is the right of an employee to keep the company's contributions from company-sponsored plans, such as pensions, even if the employee no longer works for that employer. Vesting occurs at different points in time, depending on company policy. After a certain number of years with a company, you become fully vested, or entitled to receive 100 percent of the company's contributions to the plan on your behalf. Under some plans, vesting may occur in stages. For example, you might become eligible to receive 20 percent of your benefits after three years and gain another 20 percent each year until you are fully vested.

Defined-Benefit Plan

A **defined-benefit plan** is a retirement plan that specifies the benefits an employee will receive at retirement age, based on total earnings and years on the job. The plan does not specify how much the employer must contribute each year. Instead, your employer's contributions are based on how much money the fund will need for each participant in the plan who retires. If the fund is inadequate, the employer will have to make additional contributions.

Moving to Another Plan

Some pension plans allow "portability," which means that you can carry earned benefits from one pension plan to another when you change jobs. Workers are also protected by the Employee Retirement Income Security Act of 1974 (ERISA), which sets minimum standards for pension plans. Under this act, the federal government insures part of the payments promised by defined-benefit plans.

\$avvy Saver

Making the Most of a 401(k) Plan
1. Begin contributing as soon as your company allows.
2. Contribute the maximum amount.
3. Learn as much as you can about the investment options offered.
4. Review your investments periodically.
5. Make adjustments to your investments as needed.

Personal Retirement Plans

What is the biggest benefit of an IRA?

In addition to public and employer retirement plans, many people choose to set up personal retirement plans. Such plans are especially important to self-employed people and other workers who are not covered by employer pension plans. Among the most popular personal retirement plans are individual retirement accounts (IRAs) and Keogh accounts.

Individual Retirement Accounts

An **individual retirement account (IRA)** is a special account in which a person saves a portion of income for retirement. **Figure 15.5** on page 492 summarizes the various types of IRAs.

Regular IRA A regular IRA, which is a traditional or classic IRA, allows you to make annual contributions until age 70½. In the year 2004, you could contribute up to $3,000 per year. From 2005 to 2007, the limit was set at $4,000. From 2008 and on, you can contribute up to $5,000 per year. Depending on your tax filing status and income, the contribution may be fully or partially tax-deductible. The tax deductibility of a traditional IRA also depends on whether you belong to an employer-provided retirement plan.

Roth IRA Annual contributions to a Roth IRA are not tax-deductible, but the earnings are tax-free. You may contribute the same amounts as allowed for a regular IRA if you are a single taxpayer with an adjusted gross income (AGI) of less than $95,000. For married couples, the combined AGI must be less than $150,000.

You can continue to make annual contributions to a Roth IRA even after age 70½. If you have a Roth IRA, you can withdraw money from the account without paying taxes or penalities after five years if you are at least 59½ years old or if you are using the money to help buy your first home. You may convert a regular IRA to a Roth IRA. Depending on your situation, one type of account may be better for you than the other.

Simplified Employee Pension (SEP) Plan A Simplified Employee Pension (SEP) plan, also known as a *SEP-IRA*, is an individual retirement account that is ideal for small businesses or for self-employed individuals. For a small-business SEP-IRA, each employee sets up an IRA account at a bank or other financial institution. Then the employer makes an annual contribution up to a maximum set by law. The employees' contributions, which can vary from year to year, are fully tax-deductible, and earnings are tax-deferred. The SEP-IRA for a self-employed individual works much the same way. An individual could contribute up to $42,000 a year in 2005. The limits increase yearly until 2010.

Spousal IRA You can make contributions to a Spousal IRA on behalf of your nonworking spouse if you file a joint tax return. The contributions are the same as for the traditional and Roth IRAs. This contribution may be fully or partially tax-deductible.

Rollover IRA A rollover IRA is a traditional IRA that allows roll over, or transfer of, all or a portion of your taxable distribution from one retirement plan to another IRA without paying taxes on it.

Global Financial Landscape

STANDARD &POOR'S

Standard and Poor's publishes the globally recognized S&P 500® financial index. It also gathers financial statistics, information, and news, and analyzes this data for international businesses, governments, and individuals to help them guide their financial decisions.

MEXICO

According to the U.S. Embassy, a growing number of American citizens are finding Mexico an attractive place to spend their golden years. Americans are drawn to Mexico's warm climate, easygoing lifestyle, and lower cost of living. Since the average Social Security benefit is only about $1,000 a month, many retirees cannot afford to stay in the United States. In Mexico, however, they can live comfortably. San Miguel is a favorite place for many of the older generation. The city is designated as a national monument and offers culture, fine restaurants, and an easy drive to the warm waters of the Gulf of Mexico.

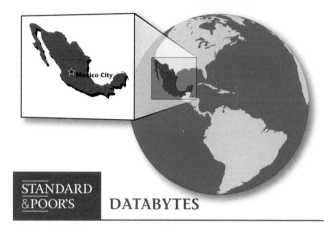

STANDARD &POOR'S DATABYTES

Capital	Mexico City
Population	106,202,903
Languages	Spanish, Mayan, and Nahuatl
Currency	Mexican peso
Gross Domestic Product (GDP)	$1.006 trillion
GDP per capita	$9,600

Industry: Food and beverages, tobacco, chemicals, iron and steel, petroleum, mining, textiles, clothing, motor vehicles, consumer durables, and tourism

Agriculture: Corn, wheat, soybeans, rice, beans, cotton, coffee, fruit, tomatoes, beef, poultry, dairy products, and wood products

Exports: Manufactured goods, oil and oil products, silver, fruits, vegetables, coffee, and cotton

Natural Resources: Petroleum, silver, copper, gold, lead, zinc, natural gas, and timber

Think Globally
What services needed by retirees might be lacking in a foreign country?

Figure 15.5 Types of IRAs

Type of IRA	IRA Features
Regular IRA	• Tax-deferred interest and earnings • Annual limit on individual contributions • Limited eligibility for tax-deductible contributions • Contributions do not reduce current taxes
Roth IRA	• Tax-deferred interest and earnings • Annual limit on individual contributions • Withdrawals are tax-free in specific cases • Contributions do not reduce current taxes
Simplified Employee Pension Plan (SEP-IRA)	• "Pay yourself first" payroll reduction contributions • Pre-tax contributions • Tax-deferred interest and earnings
Spousal IRA	• Tax-deferred interest and earnings • Both working spouse and nonworking spouse can contribute up to the annual limit • Limited eligibility for tax-deductible contributions • Contributions do not reduce current taxes
Rollover IRA	• Traditional IRA that accepts rollovers of all or a portion of your taxable distribution from a retirement plan • You can roll over to a Roth IRA
Education IRA	• Tax-deferred interest and earnings • 10% early withdrawal penalty is waived when money is used for higher-education expenses • Annual limit on individual contributions • Contributions do not reduce current taxes

Planning Ahead

IRAs can be a good way to save money for retirement.

What are the features of the Education IRA?

Education IRA An Education IRA, also known as a *Coverdell Education Savings Account,* is a special IRA with certain restrictions. It allows individuals to contribute up to $2,000 per year toward the education of any individual under age 18. The contributions are not tax-deductible, but they do provide tax-free distributions for education expenses.

Even if you are covered by another type of pension plan, you can make IRA contributions that are not tax-deductible. All of the income your IRA earns will compound, tax-deferred, until you begin making withdrawals. Remember, the biggest benefit of an IRA lies in its tax-deferred earnings growth. (See **Figure 15.6.**)

IRA Withdrawals When you retire, you can withdraw the money from your IRA by one of several methods. You can take out all of the money at one time, but the entire amount will be taxed as income. If you decide to withdraw the money from your IRA in installments, you will have to pay tax only on the amount that you withdraw. You might also place the money that you withdraw in an annuity that guarantees payments over your lifetime. See the discussion on annuities later in this section for further information about this option.

Keogh Plans

A **Keogh plan**, which is also an H.R.10 plan or a self-employed retirement plan, is a retirement plan specially designed for self-employed people and their employees. Keogh plans have various restrictions, including limits on the amount of annual tax-deductible contributions you can make. You should get professional tax advice before using this type of personal retirement plan.

Limits on Retirement Plans
When must you begin to withdraw your money?

With the exception of Roth IRAs, you cannot keep money in most tax-deferred retirement plans forever. When you retire, or by age 70½ at the latest, you must begin to receive "minimum lifetime distributions." These are withdrawals from the funds you have accumulated through your plan. The amount of the distributions, or withdrawals, is based on your life expectancy at the time the distributions begin. If you do not withdraw the minimum distributions from a retirement account, the IRS will charge you a penalty.

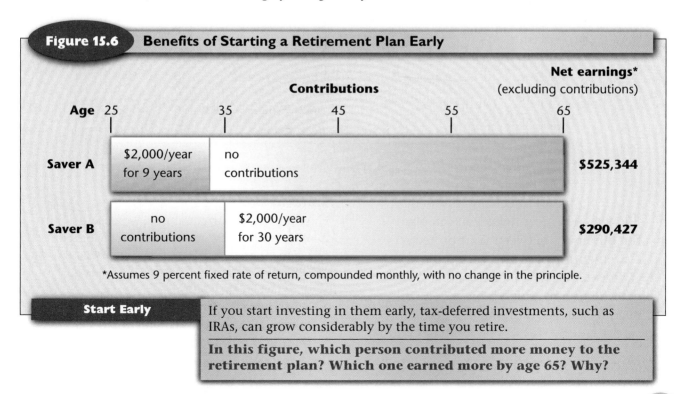

Figure 15.6 **Benefits of Starting a Retirement Plan Early**

		Contributions			Net earnings* (excluding contributions)
Age	25	35	45	55	65
Saver A	$2,000/year for 9 years	no contributions			$525,344
Saver B	no contributions	$2,000/year for 30 years			$290,427

*Assumes 9 percent fixed rate of return, compounded monthly, with no change in the principle.

Start Early If you start investing in them early, tax-deferred investments, such as IRAs, can grow considerably by the time you retire.

In this figure, which person contributed more money to the retirement plan? Which one earned more by age 65? Why?

Document Detective

Learn to identify and understand the standard financial documents you will use in the real world.

Investigate: A Projected Retirement Budget Worksheet

A projected retirement budget worksheet contains the following information:

- Your current annual income and projected income
- Your current annual expenses and projected expenses

Your Motive: The best time to plan for your retirement is when you are young. You will need to save money each month during your working career to provide you with enough money to live on when you stop working.

Projected Retirement Budget Worksheet —Robert & Emily Rathcliff

Annual Income	Current	Retirement	Annual Expenses	Current	Retirement
Wages	$85,000	$0	Mortgage/rent	$27,600	$0
Pension	0	12,000	Real estate taxes	4,500	7,500
Social Security	0	19,200	Homeowner's insurance	1,200	2,000
Rental income	0	0	Income and Social Security taxes	29,750	13,750
IRAs	0	14,000	Contributions to savings	5,000	1,000
Annuities	0	5,000	Utilities	450	750
Bond interest	0	0	Food	1,000	650
Stock dividends	0	2,300	Medical expenses insurance	750	3,500
Mutual fund dividends	0	3,210	Life insurance	850	0
Money market interest	250	0	Vehicle payments	1,500	750
Other	0	0	Vehicle insurance	1,400	800
Total Income	**$85,250**	**$55,710**	Vehicle maintenance and gasoline	2,500	1,500
			Charitable contributions	1,000	1,000
			Gifts	1,500	1,000
			Travel/entertainment	5,000	15,000
			Loans/credit cards	1,200	500
			Other	0	0
			Total Expenses	**$85,200**	**$49,700**
			Total Income Minus Expenses	$50	$6,010

Key Points: A Projected Retirement Budget Worksheet helps you calculate the difference between your projected retirement income and your projected expenses. This worksheet will help you determine how much money you will need to save for retirement years.

Find the Solutions
1. What are the current annual expenses?
2. Why would they not list a mortgage or rent payment as an expense in retirement?
3. Why might food and vehicle expenses go down when they retire?
4. Why might the Rathcliffs not have a life insurance expense in retirement?
5. Do they have enough projected income?

Annuities

Why do people purchase annuities in addition to other retirement plans?

What do you do if you have funded your 401(k), 403(b), Keogh, or profit-sharing plans up to the allowable limits and you want to put away more money for retirement? The answer may be an annuity. An **annuity** is a contract purchased from an insurance company that guarantees a future fixed or variable payment to the purchaser for a certain number of years or for life.

You might also want to purchase an annuity with the money you receive from an IRA or company pension. You can buy an annuity to supplement the income you will receive from these other types of retirement plans. You can choose to purchase an annuity that has a single payment or installment payments. You will also need to decide whether you want the insurance company to send the income from your annuity to you immediately or begin sending it to you at a later date. The payments you receive from an annuity are taxed as ordinary income. However, the interest you earn from the annuity accumulates tax-free until payments begin.

Academic Connection
LANGUAGE ARTS

Employer pension plans can be beneficial not only to employees but to employers as well. For example, employers may receive a tax credit for part of the costs of starting up a retirement plan. They may also receive a tax deduction for any plan contributions they make. *Write an essay explaining why a retirement plan is beneficial to employers and how that benefits employees.*

It's swim or swim.

GUARANTEED INCOME FOR LIFE When you retire, you're not about to sit on the sidelines. Your MetLife advisor can show you how you can continue to do the things you love with an annuity that offers you a safe and secure income. So you'll enjoy financial freedom to explore all life still has to offer. For more information, **call 1-800-MetLife or visit metlife.com**

have you met life today?®

MetLife®

◄ **GOLDEN TIME** With continuing revisions in the Social Security system, many people are thinking ahead and making arrangements for supplemental income in their golden years. *What advantage does an annuity offer?*

Types of Annuities

Annuities may be fixed or variable. Fixed annuities provide a certain amount of income for life. Variable annuities provide payments guaranteed above a minimum amount, depending on the rate of return on your investment. Either way, the rate of return on an annuity is usually tied to overall interest rates.

Immediate Annuities People approaching retirement age can purchase immediate annuities. These annuities provide income payments at once. They are usually purchased with a lump-sum payment. When you are 65, you may no longer need all of your life insurance coverage—especially if you have grown children. You may decide to convert the cash value of your insurance policy into a lump-sum payment for an immediate annuity.

Deferred Annuities With deferred annuities, income payments start at some future date. Meanwhile, interest accumulates on the money you deposit. Younger people often buy such annuities to save money toward retirement. A deferred annuity purchased with a lump-sum payment is known as a *single-premium deferred annuity*. A "premium" is the payment you make. These annuities are popular because of the greater potential for tax-free growth. If you are buying a deferred annuity on an installment basis, you may want one that allows flexible premiums, or payments. That means that your contributions can vary from year to year.

Costs of Annuities

There are various choices regarding the type of annuity and the annuity income it will generate. The costs, fees, and other features of annuities differ from policy to policy, so you should discuss all of the possible options with an insurance agent. Ask about charges, fees, and interest-rate guarantees. Also, be sure to check the financial health of the insurance company that offers the annuity.

Living on Retirement Income
What are some things you can do to stretch retirement income farther?

As you plan for retirement, you will estimate a budget or spending plan. When the time to retire arrives, however, you may find that your expenses are higher than you had expected. If that is the case, you will have to make some adjustments.

First, make sure that you are getting all the income to which you are entitled. Are there other programs or benefits for which you might qualify? You will also need to think about any assets or valuables you might be able to convert to cash or into other sources of income.

Common CENTS

Time to Save
Saving money in a savings or retirement account is the simplest way to build assets for retirement. Starting to save while you are young may even allow early retirement. However, if you have 30 or 40 years until retirement, every year without saving can subtract from one to five years off retirement. *At what age will you want to retire?*

In addition, retirees can re-examine the trade-off between spending and saving. For example, instead of taking an expensive vacation, they can take advantage of free and low-cost recreation opportunities, such as public parks, museums, libraries, and fairs, which are enjoyable options. Retirees can also receive special discounts at movie theaters, restaurants, stores, and more.

Working During Retirement

Retirees can use their skills and time instead of spending money. Some people decide to work part-time after they retire. Some even take new full-time jobs. Many people prefer to keep active and pursue new careers. Work can provide a person with a greater sense of usefulness, involvement, and self-worth. It is also a good source of supplementary retirement income.

▲ **RETIREMENT INCOME** The income needed during retirement can come from various sources. *What are some possible sources of income you might find?*

Using Your Nest Egg

When should you take money out of your "nest egg," or savings, during retirement? The answer depends on your financial circumstances, your age, and how much you want to leave to your heirs. Your **heirs** are the people who will have the legal right to your assets when you die. Your savings may be large enough to allow you to live comfortably on just the interest earned by your savings. On the other hand, you may need to make regular withdrawals to help finance your retirement. However, do so with caution.

If you dip into your retirement funds, you should consider: how long your savings will last if you make regular withdrawals? For example, if you have $10,000 in savings that earns 5.5 percent interest, compounded quarterly, you could take out $68 every month for 20 years before reducing those savings to zero. Whatever your situation, you should try to conserve your retirement fund to make it last.

Section 15.2 Assessment

QUICK CHECK

1. What are the eligibility requirements to receive Social Security retirement benefits?
2. What is the difference between defined-contribution plans and defined-benefit plans?
3. What is the difference between regular IRAs and Roth IRAs?

THINK CRITICALLY

4. Describe the trade-offs that you would need to consider if you reached retirement age and realized that your expenses were higher than you could afford.

USE MATH SKILLS

5. **Growing a Nest Egg** When Jamal graduated from college recently, his parents gave him $1,000 and told him to use it wisely. Jamal decided to use the money to start a retirement account. After doing some research about different options, he put the entire amount into a tax-deferred IRA that pays 11 percent interest, compounded annually.

Calculate How much money will Jamal have in his IRA at the end of ten years, assuming that the interest rate remains the same and that he does not deposit any additional money? Show your calculations in the form of a chart.

SOLVE MONEY PROBLEMS

6. **Making Decisions** Mike Johnson has worked for the same company for 45 years. Now, at age 67, he is about to retire. When he does, he will be entitled to receive the $600,000 that has accumulated in his 401(k) plan. Now Mike has to decide what to do with the money. If he manages it wisely, it can help make his retirement years comfortable and rewarding.

Analyze Use what you have learned in this section to help Mike decide what to do with his 401(k) funds. Consider the options available to him, such as rollover IRAs and annuities. Explain why your recommendation would make the best use of Mike's money.

Estate Planning and Taxes

The Importance of Estate Planning

Why is it important to have an estate plan?

Many people think of estates as belonging only to the rich or elderly. However, the fact is that everyone has an estate. An **estate** is all property and assets owned by an individual or group. During your working years, your financial goal is to build your estate by acquiring and accumulating money for your current and future needs. However, as you grow older, your point of view will change. Instead of working to acquire assets, you will start to think about what will happen to your hard-earned wealth after you die. In most cases, people want to pass that wealth along to their loved ones. That is why estate planning becomes important.

What Is Estate Planning?

Estate planning is the process of creating a detailed plan for managing personal assets to make the most of them while you are alive and to ensure that they are distributed wisely after your death. It is not pleasant to think about your own death, but doing so is a necessary part of estate planning. Without a good estate plan, the assets you accumulate during your lifetime might be greatly reduced by various taxes when you die.

Estate planning is an essential part of retirement planning and financial planning. It has two stages. The first stage involves building your estate through savings, investments, and insurance. The second stage consists of making sure that your estate will be distributed as you wish at the time of your death. If you get married, your estate planning should take into account the needs of your spouse and children, if you have any. If you are single, your financial affairs should be in order for your beneficiaries. A **beneficiary (estate)** is a person who is named to receive a portion of someone's estate.

When you die, your surviving spouse, children, relatives, and/or friends will face a period of grief. One or more of these people will probably be responsible for settling your affairs. This will be a difficult time, and so your estate plan should be clear and well-organized.

Otherwise, the people you have left behind may encounter problems settling your estate, and your intentions may not be carried out according to your wishes. One way to avoid these problems is to make sure that important documents are accessible, understandable, and legal.

Legal Documents

An estate plan involves various legal documents such as a **will**, which is a legal declaration of a person's wishes regarding disposal of his or her estate after death. When you die, the person who is responsible for handling your affairs will need access to your will and other important documents. The documents must be reviewed and verified before your heirs can receive the money and other assets to which they are entitled. If no one can find the necessary documents, your heirs may experience difficult delays. They could even lose a portion of their inheritance as a result. You should collect and organize various important papers:

▲ **ASSETS AND POSSESSIONS** Most people have various assets and possessions that make up their estate. *What does your estate consist of at this point in your life?*

- Birth certificates for you, your spouse, and your children
- Marriage certificates and divorce papers
- Legal name changes (especially important for protecting adopted children)
- Military service records
- Social Security documents
- Veteran's documents
- Insurance policies
- Transfer records of joint bank accounts
- Safe-deposit box records
- Automobile registrations
- Titles to stock and bond certificates

Have several copies of the documents needed for processing insurance claims and settling your estate. In some cases, children whose parents have died may need to have documents proving their parents' births and marriage and/or divorce. Surviving spouses, children, and other heirs may also be required to show proof of death in the form of a death certificate.

Wills

Why is a will such an important document?

One of the most important documents that every adult should have is a written will. If you die **intestate**—which is the status of not having a valid will—your legal state of residence will step in and control the distribution of your estate without regard for your wishes. Make sure that you have a written will. An attorney with estate planning experience can draft a will, which can help your heirs avoid many difficulties. Legal fees for drafting a will vary with the size of an estate and particular family situation. A standard will costs between $200 and $500.

Types of Wills

You have several options in preparing a will. The four basic types of wills are the simple will, the traditional marital share will, the exemption trust will, and the stated dollar amount will. The differences among the types of wills can affect how your estate will be taxed.

All types of wills usually designate a beneficiary, the person who is named to receive a portion or all of an estate after your death. A beneficiary can be a spouse, relative, friend, or organization. In the following discussions, the beneficiary will be referred to as the *spouse*.

Simple Will   A simple will leaves everything to the spouse. Such a will is generally sufficient for people with small estates. However, for a large or complex estate, a simple will may not meet objectives. This type of will may also result in higher overall taxation, since everything left to the spouse will be taxed as part of his or her estate.

Traditional Marital Share Will   The traditional marital share will leaves one-half of the adjusted gross estate (the total value of the estate minus debts and costs) to the spouse. The other half of the estate may go to children or other heirs. It can also be held in trust for the family. A **trust** is an arrangement in which a designated person known as a *trustee* manages assets for the benefit of someone else. A trust can provide a spouse with a lifelong income and would not be taxed at his or her death.

Exemption Trust Will   With an exemption trust will, all assets go to the spouse except for a certain amount, which goes into a trust. This amount, plus any interest it earns, can provide the spouse with lifelong income that will not be taxed. In 2004 and 2005, the tax exemption amount was $1.5 million. That amount increased to $2 million for the years 2006 through 2008. In 2009, the amount increases to $3.5 million. The tax-free aspect of this type of will may become important if property values increase considerably. This type of will is beneficial for large estates.

Stated Dollar Amount Will The stated dollar amount will allows you to pass on to your spouse any amount that satisfies your family's financial goals. For tax purposes, you could pass on the exempted amount of $1.5 million (in 2004 and 2005). However, you might decide to pass on a stated amount related to your family's future income needs or related to the value of personal items.

State law may dictate how much you must leave to your spouse. Most states require that the spouse receive a certain amount, usually one-half or one-third of the value of an estate. States also have laws regarding when and how portions of an estate must pass to beneficiaries.

The stated dollar amount will has one major drawback. Suppose that you leave specific dollar amounts to your listed heirs and the balance to your spouse. Although these amounts may be fair and reasonable when the will is drafted, they can soon become outdated. What if the value of the estate decreases because of a business problem or a drop in the stock market? That decrease will not affect heirs who are left specific dollar amounts, but it will affect the value of your spouse's inheritance. For this reason, most experts recommend using percentages rather than specific amounts.

▲ **PEACE OF MIND** Preparing a will can make things easier for your family and can ensure that your estate is distributed according to your wishes. *What would happen if an adult were to die without preparing a will?*

Wills and Probate

The type of will that is best for your particular needs depends on many factors, including the size of your estate, inflation, your age, and your objectives. No matter what type of will you choose, it is best to avoid probate. **Probate** is the legal procedure of proving that a will is valid or invalid. It is also the process by which your estate is managed and distributed after your death, according to the provisions of your will. A special probate court validates wills and makes sure that your debts are paid. You should avoid probate because it is expensive, lengthy, and public. As you will read later in this chapter, a living trust avoids probate and is also less expensive, quicker, and private.

As You Read

RELATE

What situations might motivate you to change your will?

Formats of Wills

Wills may be either holographic or formal. A *holographic will* is a handwritten will that you prepare yourself. It should be written, dated, and signed entirely in your own handwriting. No printed or typed information should appear on its pages. Some states do not recognize holographic wills as legal.

A *formal will* is usually prepared with the help of an attorney. It may be typed, or it may be a preprinted form that you fill out. You must sign the will in front of two witnesses; neither witness can be a beneficiary named in the will. Witnesses must sign in front of you.

A *statutory will* is prepared on a preprinted form, which is available from lawyers, office-supply stores, and some stationery stores. There are serious risks in using preprinted forms to prepare your will. The form may include provisions that are not in the best interests of your heirs. If you change the preprinted wording, part or all of the will may be declared invalid. Furthermore, the form may not remain up-to-date with current laws regarding wills. For these reasons, it is best to seek a lawyer's advice when you prepare your will.

Writing Your Will

Writing a will allows you to express exactly how you want your property to be distributed to your heirs. It is the only way to make sure that all of your property will end up where you want it. Some guidelines for writing a will include:

1. Work closely with your spouse or partner to prepare your will.
2. Write your will to conform to your current wishes.
3. Do not choose a beneficiary as a witness.
4. Consider signing prenuptial agreement if you are remarrying.
5. Consider using percentages instead of dollar amounts.
6. If you are married, your spouse should also write a will.
7. Be flexible.
8. Keep your original will in a safe place and a copy at home.
9. If you alter your will, prepare a new one or add a codicil.
10. Select an executor who is willing to do the needed tasks.

Selecting an Executor   An **executor** is a person who is willing and able to perform the tasks involved in carrying out a will. These tasks include preparing an inventory of assets, collecting any money due, and paying off debts. An executor must also prepare and file all income and estate tax returns. In addition, he or she will be responsible for making decisions about selling or reinvesting assets to pay off debts and provide income for your family while the estate is being settled. Finally, an executor must distribute the estate and make a final accounting to beneficiaries and to the probate court. An executor can be a family member, a friend, an attorney, an accountant, or the trust department of a bank. You may also name a beneficiary as the executor. State law sets fees for executors. If you do not name an executor in your will, the court will appoint one. Naming your own executor eliminates that possibility and helps prevent unnecessary delay in the distribution of your property. It will also minimize estate taxes and settlement costs.

Selecting a Guardian   If you have children, your will should name a guardian to care for them in the event that you and your spouse die at the same time and the children cannot care for themselves. A **guardian** is the person who accepts the responsibility of caring for the children of the deceased and managing an estate for the children until they reach a certain age. Many states require a guardian to post a bond (several hundred dollars) with the probate court. The bonding company will reimburse the minor's estate the amount of the bond if the guardian uses the minor's property for his or her own gain. When you name a guardian for your children, choose someone you know who loves them and shares your beliefs about raising children. Of course, the person must also be capable and willing to accept the responsibilities associated with the role of being a parent.

Altering or Rewriting Your Will   There may be times when you wish to change the provisions of your will because of changes in your life or in the law. After you have made a will, review it frequently so that it remains current. Here are some reasons to review your will:

- You have moved to a new state that has different laws.
- You have sold property that is mentioned in the will.
- The size and composition of your estate have changed.
- You have married, divorced, or remarried.
- Potential heirs have died, or new ones have been born.

Do not make any written changes on the pages of an existing will. Additions, deletions, or erasures on a will that has been signed and witnessed can invalidate the will. If you want to make only a few minor changes, adding a codicil may be the best choice. A **codicil** is a document that explains, adds, or deletes provisions in an existing will. To be valid, it must meet the legal requirements for a will. If you want to make major changes in your will, or if you have already added a codicil, it is best to prepare a new will. In the new will, be sure to include a clause that revokes, or cancels, all earlier wills and codicils.

A Living Will

Why is it important to have a living will?

At some point in your life, you may become physically or mentally disabled and unable to act on your own behalf. If that happens, a living will can help ensure that you will be cared for according to your wishes. A **living will** is a legal document in which you state if you want to be kept alive by artificial means if you become terminally ill and are unable to make such a decision. Many states recognize living wills. **Figure 15.7** illustrates a typical living will. Sign and date the document before two witnesses. Review your living will from time to time to update your decisions.

Figure 15.7   A Living Will

Living Will Declaration

Declaration made this _____ day of _____ (month, year)

I, _____, being of sound mind, willfully and voluntarily make known my desire that my dying shall not be artificially prolonged under the circumstances set forth below, do hereby declare: if at any time I should have an incurable injury, disease, or illness regarded as a terminal condition by my physician and if my physician has determined that the application of life-sustaining procedures would serve only to artificially prolong the dying process and that my death will occur whether or not life-sustaining procedures are utilized, I direct that such procedures be withheld or withdrawn and that I be permitted to die with only the administration of medication or the performance of any medical procedure deemed necessary to provide me with comfort care.

In the absence of my ability to give directions regarding the use of such life-sustaining procedures, it is my intention that this declaration shall be honored by my family and physician as the final expression of my legal right to refuse medical or surgical treatment and accept the consequences from such refusal. I understand the full import of this declaration, and I am emotionally and mentally competent to make this declaration.

Signed _____

City, County, and State of Residence_____

The declarant has been personally known to me, and I believe him or her to be of sound mind.

Witness_____

Witness_____

Making Choices   A living will ensures that a person's preference about medical care is honored if he or she becomes terminally ill or falls into a coma.

What is the basic purpose of a living wills?

You might consider writing a living will when you draw up a traditional will. Most lawyers will prepare a living will at no cost if they are already preparing a traditional will or your estate plan. You can also get the necessary forms for a living will from nonprofit groups such as Aging With Dignity.

Power of Attorney

A **power of attorney** is a legal document that authorizes someone to act on your behalf. If you become seriously ill or injured, you will probably need someone to take care of your needs and personal affairs. This can be done through a power of attorney.

You can assign a power of attorney to anyone you choose. You can give that person power to carry out only certain actions or transactions, or you may allow the person to act on your behalf in all matters, including your living will.

Letter of Last Instruction

In addition to a traditional will and a living will, it is a good idea to prepare a letter of last instruction. This document is not legally binding, but it can provide heirs with important information. It should contain preferences for funeral arrangements as well as the names of the people who are to be informed of the death. With a letter of last instruction, you can also let people know the locations of your bank accounts, safe-deposit box, and other important items.

Trusts
Why is it important that trusts avoid probate?

Basically, a trust is a legal arrangement that helps manage the assets of your estate for your benefit or that of your beneficiaries. The creator of the trust is called the *trustor,* or *grantor.* The trust is administered by the trustee, which can be a person or an institution, such as a bank. A bank charges a small fee for its services in administering a trust. The fee is usually based on the value of the assets in the trust.

Individual circumstances determine whether it makes sense to establish a trust. Some of the common reasons for setting up a trust are to:

- Reduce or provide for payment of estate taxes.
- Avoid probate and transfer your assets immediately to your beneficiaries.
- Free yourself from managing your assets while you receive a regular income from the trust.
- Provide income for a surviving spouse or other beneficiary.
- Ensure that your property serves a desired purpose after your death.

▲ **IN WHOM WE TRUST** For some people, setting up a trust is an effective way to organize and manage an estate. *What are some of the main reasons to establish a trust?*

Types of Trusts

There are many types of trusts, including a credit-shelter trust, a disclaimer trust, a living trust, and a testamentary trust. Choose the type of trust that is most appropriate for your situation. An estate attorney can advise you about the right type of trust for your needs.

Trusts can be either revocable or irrevocable. A *revocable trust* is one in which you have the right to end the trust or change its terms during your lifetime. Revocable trusts avoid the lengthy process of probate, but they do not protect assets from federal or state estate taxes. An *irrevocable trust* is one that cannot be changed or ended. Irrevocable trusts avoid probate and help reduce estate taxes. However, by law you cannot remove any assets from an irrevocable trust, even if you need them at some later point in your life.

Credit-Shelter Trust A credit-shelter trust is a trust that enables the spouse of a deceased person to avoid paying federal taxes on a certain amount of assets left to him or her as part of an estate. As of 2004, the exemption amount was $1.5 million. It increased to $2 million in 2006 and continues to increase to $3.5 million in 2009. As the most common estate-planning trust, the credit-shelter trust has many other names: bypass trust, residuary trust, A/B trust, exemption equivalent trust, and family trust. A single person does not need to set up a credit-shelter trust because assets passing to someone other than a spouse automatically qualify for the estate exemption amount.

Disclaimer Trust A disclaimer trust is appropriate for couples who do not have enough assets to need a credit-shelter trust but who may in the future. With a disclaimer trust, the surviving spouse is left everything, but he or she has the right to disclaim, or deny, some portion of the estate. Anything that is disclaimed goes into a credit-shelter trust. This approach allows the surviving spouse to protect wealth from estate taxes.

Living Trust A living trust, also known as an *inter vivos trust,* is a property management arrangement that you establish. It allows you, as trustor, to receive benefits during your lifetime. To set up a living trust, you simply transfer some of your assets to a trustee. Then you give the trustee instructions for managing the trust while you are alive as well as after your death. A living trust has several advantages:

- It ensures privacy. A will is a public record; however, a trust is not a public record.
- The assets held in trust avoid probate at your death. This eliminates probate costs and delays.
- It is advantageous if you own property in more than one state.
- It enables you to review your trustee's performance and make changes if necessary.
- It can relieve you of management responsibilities.
- It is less likely than a will to create arguments between heirs upon your death.
- It can guide your family and doctors to follow your wishes if you become terminally ill or if you become unable to make your own decisions.

Setting up a living trust costs more money than creating a will. However, depending on your particular circumstances, a living trust can be a good estate planning option.

Testamentary Trust A testamentary trust is established by your will and becomes effective upon your death. Such a trust can be valuable if your beneficiaries are inexperienced in financial matters. It may also be the best option if you expect your estate taxes will be high. A testamentary trust provides many of the same advantages as a living trust.

Your Estate

How does the type of joint ownership affect the distribution of an estate?

As you learned earlier in this chapter, your estate consists of everything you own. Therefore, an important step in estate planning is taking inventory of your assets. Do not forget to include in your inventory jointly owned property, life insurance policies, employee retirement benefits, money owed to you by others, and all of your personal possessions.

Some states are known as *community-property states*. Community property is any money earned by either spouse during the marriage and any property or possessions purchased with that money. It does not include assets received as gifts or through inheritances. In community-property states, each spouse owns 50 percent of the property. Thus, half of the couple's assets are included in each spouse's estate.

In non-community-property states, property is included in the estate of the spouse who owns it. The way you own property can make a significant tax difference.

Joint Ownership

Joint ownership of property between spouses is very common. Joint ownership may also exist between parents and children or other relatives. Joint ownership may help avoid probate and inheritance taxes in some states. However, it does not avoid federal estate taxes. It may, in fact, increase the amount of federal estate taxes.

There are three types of joint ownership, each of which has different tax and estate-planning consequences.

1. You and your spouse may own property as "joint tenants with the right of survivorship."
   - The property is considered to be owned 50–50 for estate tax purposes and will automatically pass to one spouse at the other's death.
   - No estate tax is paid at the first death. However, when the surviving spouse dies, more estate taxes may be due than with a traditional marital share will.
2. You and your spouse may own property as "tenants in common."
   - Each individual is considered to own a certain share of property for tax purposes, and only your share is included in your estate.
   - Your share does not go to the other tenant in common at your death. Instead, it is included in your probate estate, and you decide who gets it.
   - Gift and estate taxes do not apply to property that belongs to spouses.
3. Married couples may own property under the form of "tenancy by the entirety."
   - Both spouses own the property.
   - When one spouse dies, the other gets the property automatically.
   - Neither spouse may sell the property without the consent of the other.

Joint ownership is a poor substitute for a will because it provides less control over how property is distributed and taxed after death. State laws govern the types and effects of joint ownership. An attorney should be consulted on these matters.

WebQuest

Avoiding Financial Fraud

Many people with assets protect their heirs from estate problems by setting up trust funds. However, since trusts are so popular, trust preparation is a service targeted by a number of sophisticated con-artists. Learn how to avoid estate-planning fraud.

 To continue with Task 5 of your WebQuest project, visit persfinance07.glencoe.com.

After You Read

REACT

Has the information in this chapter convinced you to start your retirement planning sooner than you may have originally planned? Why or why not?

Life Insurance and Employee Benefits

If you have life insurance, the benefits of that insurance will be counted among the assets in your estate. Life insurance benefits are free of income tax, and they do not go through probate. They are also partially exempt from most state inheritance taxes. However, they are subject to federal estate taxes under certain circumstances, such as when you change beneficiaries, surrender the policy for cash, or make loans on the policy.

Death benefits from qualified employer pension plans or Keogh plans are usually excluded from an estate. One exception is if the benefits are payable to the estate. Another exception is if the beneficiary chooses a special provision for averaging income tax in lump-sum distributions.

Lifetime Gifts and Trusts

You may give part of your estate as a gift or set up a trust for your spouse or a child. Under certain conditions, such gifts and trusts are not included as part of your estate upon your death. However, if you keep any control or use of the gift or trust, it remains part of your estate and is subject to taxes. For example, if you transfer title of your home to a child but continue to live in it, the value of the home is taxed as part of your estate. Similarly, if you put property in a trust but keep some control over the income or principal, the property is included in your estate even though you may not be able to obtain it yourself.

Taxes and Estate Planning
Which government, state or federal, imposes inheritance taxes?

Federal and state governments impose various types of taxes that you must consider in estate planning. The four major types of taxes are estate taxes, estate and trust federal income taxes, inheritance taxes, and gift taxes.

Estate Taxes

An estate tax is a federal tax collected on the value of a person's property at the time of his or her death. The tax is based on the fair market value of the deceased person's investments, property, and bank accounts, less an exempt amount.

As of 2006, the exempt amount was $2 million. This means that the "first" $2 million is not used to compute the estate tax. Only the amount in excess of $2 million can be considered. The exempt amount is $3.5 million in 2009. The tax rate applied to the remaining amount is 48 percent. With careful planning, federal estate taxes can be avoided for estates over $2 million.

Estate and Trust Federal Income Taxes

In addition to the federal estate tax return, owners of estates and certain trusts must file federal income tax returns with the IRS. Taxable income for estates and trusts is computed in the same manner as taxable income for individuals. Taxes must be paid quarterly on both trusts and estates.

Inheritance Taxes

Your heirs might have to pay a tax for the right to acquire the property that they have inherited. An inheritance tax is a tax collected on the property left by a person in his or her will.

Only state governments impose inheritance taxes. Most states collect an inheritance tax, but state laws differ widely as to exemptions and rates of taxation. A reasonable range for state inheritance taxes would be 4 to 10 percent of whatever the heir receives.

Gift Taxes

Both the federal and state governments impose a gift tax, a tax collected on money or property valued at more than $11,000 given by one person to another in a single year. One way to reduce the tax liability of your estate is to reduce the size of the estate while you are alive by giving away portions of it as gifts. You are free to make such gifts to your spouse, children, or anyone else at any time. However, when doing this, be careful that you do not give away assets that you may need in your retirement.

According to federal law, you may give up to $11,000 per person per year free of any gift tax. A married couple may give up to $22,000 per person per year without paying the tax. Gifts that exceed those amounts are subject to the tax. Gift tax rates are currently the same as estate tax rates, and they are called *unified transfer tax rates*. However, gifts might be considered as part of your estate and be taxed if they were given within three years of your death. Many states have other gift tax laws as well.

Paying the Tax

After doing everything possible to reduce your estate taxes, you may still find that taxes are due. In that case, you will have to think about the best way to help your heirs pay the taxes. The federal estate tax is due nine months after a death. State taxes, probate costs, debts, and other expenses are also usually due within that same period. These costs might result in a real financial problem for your survivors. Finding enough cash to pay taxes, debts, and other costs without causing financial hardship can be very difficult.

There are a number of ways this problem can be handled.

1. Obtain life insurance. A life insurance policy may be the best way to provide your heirs with the tax-free cash that they will need to settle your estate.
2. Save enough cash ahead of time to pay taxes and expenses when they are due. However, the cash may be subject to income tax during your lifetime and also subject to estate tax at your death.

3. Your heirs could sell assets to pay taxes. However, this could result in the loss of important sources of income.
4. Your heirs might borrow money. However, it is unusual to find a commercial lender that will lend money to pay taxes. Besides, borrowing money only prolongs the problem and adds interest costs in the process.

◀ FOR LIFE Considering the expense of estate taxes can mean more money or assets for your family or heirs. *What are at least two sources of funds to pay for taxes and debts when settling an estate?*

5. If your family members or beneficiaries can show they have a reasonable cause, the IRS may allow them to make deferred or installment payments on taxes that are due. However, like borrowing, making payments may prolong the problem.

Planning for the Future

Estate planning is essential not only to ensure that your assets are distributed in the way you choose, but also to make sure that your loved ones are not left with difficult or costly problems.

Planning for your estate and taxes as well as writing a will are just a few of the steps you can take to have a secure financial future for yourself and others. In addition, planning and saving for your own retirement will help ensure that your needs are met in your later years. Remember that the trade-offs, decisions, and goals that you make for yourself today affect your personal finances, which will continue to affect your life now and in the future.

Section 15.3 Assessment

QUICK CHECK

1. What are the four basic types of wills?
2. What is a credit-shelter trust, a disclaimer trust, and a living trust?
3. What are several strategies that you might use to arrange for paying estate taxes?

THINK CRITICALLY

4. Which format of a will—holographic or formal—is the best from a legal point of view? Why?

USE MATH SKILLS

5. Too Much Money Joel and Rachel Simon are both retired. They have been married for 50 years and have amassed an estate worth $2.4 million. If either of them dies between the years 2006 and 2008, the surviving spouse can receive $2 million tax-free. The amount over that exemption will be subject to federal estate tax. The couple has no trusts or other types of tax-sheltered assets.

Analyze If Joel or Rachel dies in between 2006 and 2008, how much federal estate tax would the surviving spouse have to pay, assuming that the estate is taxed at the 48 percent rate?

SOLVE MONEY PROBLEMS

6. Cost versus Satisfaction Irving and Irma Lansing are making plans for the distribution of their assets after they die. They have wills, but they want to make sure that they are using the right type of will to maximize the benefits for the surviving spouse and their four grown children. The estimated value of their estate is currently $1.4 million. However, most of their assets are in high-risk stocks, which can vary greatly in value depending on economic conditions and the stock market.

Write About It Help Irving and Irma by writing a summary of the benefits and drawbacks of the four main types of wills. Identify which type would be best for them.

CHAPTER SUMMARY

- The sooner you start planning and saving for retirement, the faster your assets will accumulate.
- Estimating your living expenses is the first step of retirement planning. Housing needs will depend on your desires and your health.
- Social Security provides a regular monthly income payment but is not meant to cover all retirement expenses.
- Employer pension plans include two types: A defined-contribution plan is an individual account for each employee into which an employer contributes a specific annual amount; a defined-benefit plan specifies benefits based on total earnings and years on the job.

- Personal retirement accounts include regular IRAs, Roth IRAs, SEP plans, Spousal IRAs, Rollover IRAs, Education IRAs, and Keogh plans.
- The various types of wills include simple wills, traditional marital share wills, exemption trust wills, and stated dollar amount wills.
- The several types of trusts include credit-shelter trusts, disclaimer trusts, living trusts, and testamentary trusts.
- One common characteristic of many estates is joint ownership of property between spouses.
- Estates are taxed with estate taxes, estate and trust federal income taxes, inheritance taxes, and gift taxes.

Communicating Key Terms

Imagine you are a financial planner for a company. Prepare text for a PowerPoint presentation using as many of these terms as possible to introduce the employees to estate planning.

- assisted-living facility (ALF)
- defined-contribution plan
- 401(k) plan
- vesting
- defined-benefit plan
- individual retirement account (IRA)
- Keogh plan

- annuity (insurance)
- heirs
- estate
- estate planning
- beneficiary (estate)
- will
- intestate

- trust
- probate
- executor
- guardian
- codicil
- living will
- power of attorney

Reviewing Key Concepts

1. **Identify** three ways expenses decrease at retirement.
2. **Describe** alternative living and housing arrangements for retirement.
3. **Identify** two reasons Social Security should not be a primary source of retirement funds.
4. **Define** employer-sponsored defined-contribution plans and defined-benefit plans.
5. **Explain** the advantages of the Roth IRA over a regular IRA.
6. **Explain** why creating a living will is an important part of estate planning.
7. **Describe** the major advantages of trusts.
8. **Explain** what it means to be an executor of an estate.
9. **List** some estate planning methods to reduce inheritance taxes.

ACADEMIC SKILLS

Science   The need for retirement planning is greater in the 21st century because more people are living longer lives.

Research   Find out the life expectancy for people born in the United States in each decade of the 20th century: 1900, 1910, 1920, 1930, 1940, 1950, 1960, 1970, 1980, 1990, and 2000. Then find out how long someone born today is expected to live. Make a timeline illustrating the life spans. Then list several reasons why people are living longer lives.

YOUR FINANCIAL FIGURES

Cost of Living in Retirement   Pretend you are in your late 60s. With careful planning, you have about $35,000 per year for living expenses after taxes. Find a Web site that compares the cost of living in different cities.

1. **Calculate** how much you would need if you lived in U.S. cities that are attractive to retirees, such as West Palm Beach, Florida; Phoenix, Arizona; and Dallas, Texas.
2. **Compute** by using spreadsheet or presentation software to develop charts and/or graphs comparing the cost of living in different cities.

REAL-WORLD Application

Connect with Economics and Social Studies   Because of longer life expectancies and declining birth rates, fewer workers are currently paying into the Social Security system than previously, and more people are in retirement for more years.

1. **Research**   Find out what the American Association of Retired Persons (AARP) thinks about Social Security and various ideas to reform it.
2. **Think Critically**   Is it "fair" for younger workers to fund current retirees' benefits? Do you believe you will receive Social Security benefits when you retire? Why or why not?

Internet CONNECTION

Wills and Trusts   You need a lawyer to help you draw up wills and trusts. However, you can minimize the amount of time a lawyer will have to spend preparing the will or trust by organizing your documents and doing some research on your own first.

 Log On   Use an Internet search engine to find Web sites showing sample will and trust documents. Answer the following questions:

1. Under what circumstances is a trust essential? Do you need one currently?
2. What are some of your state's requirements for a will or trust to be valid?

BusinessWeek ONLINE

Newsclip: Social Security Reform   Social Security reform has been highly debated in the news for years. Many politicians aim to change the system.

Log On   Go to persfinance07.glencoe.com and open Chapter 15. Learn more about retirement saving options. Write a list of ways to help save seniors from financial hardships. Also write a list of ways to help younger people prepare for retirement.

WHAT'S YOUR
FINANCIAL
ID?

WHAT IS YOUR PERSONALITY?

Part of the fun of planning a successful future is considering your personal preferences. The closer you can match your activities with your personality, the more likely you are to enjoy your life. Read through the following list and write your top three characteristics on a separate sheet of paper.

____ **1.** I am steady and reliable.

____ **2.** I tend to think a lot.

____ **3.** I enjoy being by myself.

____ **4.** I almost always plan before I do something.

____ **5.** I am very emotional.

____ **6.** I love being the center of attention.

____ **7.** I enjoy drama.

____ **8.** I like to express what I feel.

____ **9.** I am always ready to get up and go.

____ **10.** I like to participate in high-action sports.

____ **11.** I am happiest when doing physical activities.

____ **12.** I find it hard to keep still.

Thinker: If all of your selections were from numbers 1–4, consider activities that use your ability to think.

Heartfelt/Feeler/Enthusiast: If all of your selections were from numbers 5–8, you are probably happiest when doing something that gives you an emotional lift.

Doer: If all of your selections were from numbers 9–12, you enjoy being active.

Adapter: If your selections were from more than one of the three sections (1–4, 5–8, or 9–12), you are versatile and could choose activities that require thinking, involve emotions, or are active.

Continue to think about the different aspects of your personality and consider what types of activities you like to do. Thinking about these things now will help you better plan for your retirement years.

Your Financial Portfolio

Saving for Retirement

Henri has become eligible to participate in his company's 403(b) program. He can invest from 2 to 15 percent of his salary, which is $20,000 a year. The company matches the first 5 percent at a rate of 50 percent, or 50 cents for every dollar he invests. Henri has decided to save 5 percent of his salary. Based on the current investment return of 10 percent compounded annually, Henri has calculated how much he would be able to save over 10 years, including company-matching contributions.

	Contributions	Interest	Total
Henri's contribution of 5 percent of his $20,000 salary	$1,000/year	10%	
Company contribution matching 50 percent of 5 percent of his salary	$500/year		
1st Year	$1,500	$150.00	$1,650.00
2nd Year	1,500	315.00	3,465.00
3rd Year	1,500	496.50	5,461.50
4th Year	1,500	696.15	7,657.65
5th Year	1,500	915.77	10,073.42
6th Year	1,500	1,157.34	12,730.76
7th Year	1,500	1,423.08	15,653.84
8th Year	1,500	1,715.38	18,869.22
9th Year	1,500	2,036.92	22,406.14
10th Year	1,500	2,390.61	26,296.75
Total	**$15,000**	**$11,296.75**	**$26,296.75**

Calculate

On a separate sheet of paper, calculate how much you would have in ten years if you saved $2,000 a year at an annual interest rate of 10 percent, with the company contributing $500 a year.

Unit 4 LAB

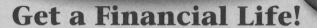

Get a Financial Life!

Making Retirement Plans

Overview

Carrie and David have been working and saving for their retirement for many years. Soon it will become a reality. They are looking forward to spending time with their future grandchildren, developing hobbies, traveling, volunteering, and maybe even working part-time, without having to worry about earning full-time wages. Their goal is to retire within the next five years. They need to develop a clear and organized plan for how they will spend their days, how much money their activities will cost, and where they will live.

Resources & Tools

- Internet (optional)
- Math textbook (for reference)
- Portfolio (ring binder or file folder)
- Public or school library
- Word processor

Procedures

STEP A **Step A The Process**
If you were Carrie or David, how would you spend your retirement years?

1. Write a short story (one or two pages) describing how Carrie and David will spend their retirement years. Where will they live? Will they travel? Will they work? Do they have hobbies? Use your creativity and imagination.

2. Research long-term care insurance. Then help Carrie and David decide whether they should purchase it or invest their money in another way.

3. Watch a movie or TV show about people who are retired or nearing retirement age. You might rent a video or DVD of *Grumpy Old Men, Cocoon, Space Cowboys*, or a more recent film. Make a list of the hobbies and activities of the characters. Write one or two paragraphs comparing the characters' hobbies and activities to those of people you know who are teens or young adults.

4. In 2004, about 12 percent of the American population was 65 or older. By 2050, that number will increase to 21 percent. Many of these Americans are or will be living in retirement communities, assisted-living facilities, or nursing homes. As a service project, plan an activity for a group of senior citizens in your community. You might develop a craft project, a music festival, or a game day. Use your imagination. Then contact a local center and ask if you can present your activity there.

STEP B — Create Your Portfolio

As you work through the process, save the results so that you can refer, review, and refine. Create a portfolio to showcase the information you collected in Step A.

1. Include your short story about Carrie and David's retirement years.
2. Present your recommendations and reasoning on whether or not Carrie and David should purchase long-term care insurance.
3. Write a summary of the movie or TV show you watched. Include the list of hobbies and activities you created and the comparison paragraph you wrote.
4. Present your plan for the senior citizens' activity. If you are able to implement it, survey the participants to find out if they enjoyed the activity. Ask how you might improve it for another time.

STEP C — Mathematics

Math skills are essential for managing your own finances and planning for retirement. Also, employers look for employees who have math skills. Adding, subtracting, multiplying, dividing, working with fractions and decimals, and using algebra are the basic math skills used in the workplace.

1. Create ten word problems using basic math skills to solve financial problems from this unit. For example: David's employer matches David's contributions to his 401(k) retirement savings plan. If David contributes $250 per month to the plan, how many years must David continue to save to accumulate $90,000 without interest? ($250 + $250 = $500; $500 × 12 = $6,000; $90,000 ÷ $6,000 = 15 years)
2. Form groups of three, and as a team, solve the word problems.
3. Compile the problems and their answers into a classroom notebook. Label the notebook "Math Problems in Personal Finance." If possible, categorize the problems according to the skill (adding, subtracting, fractions, and so on).

Appendix: Math Skills Builder

WRITING NUMBERS AS WORDS AND ROUNDING NUMBERS

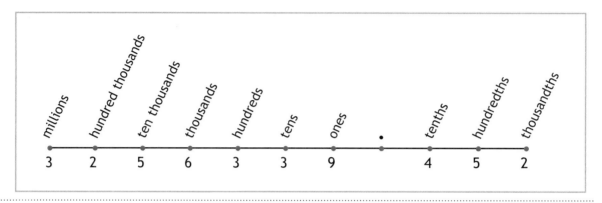

The place-value chart shows the value of each digit in the number 3,256,339.452. The place-value chart can help you write numbers.

EXAMPLE

482
  8.557
$39.45

SOLUTION

four hundred eighty-two
eight and five hundred fifty-seven thousandths
thirty-nine and forty-five hundredths dollars
or thirty-nine and $^{45}/_{100}$ dollars

Place value is also used in rounding numbers. If the digit to the right of the place value you want to round is 5 or more, round up by adding 1 to the number in the place value. Then change all the digits to the right of the place value to zeros. If the number is 4 or less, round down by changing all the numbers to the right of the place value to zeros.

EXAMPLE   Round 4765 to the nearest hundred.

SOLUTION

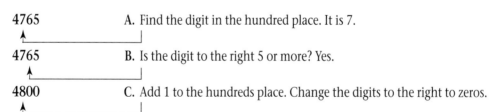

4765   A. Find the digit in the hundred place. It is 7.

4765   B. Is the digit to the right 5 or more? Yes.

4800   C. Add 1 to the hundreds place. Change the digits to the right to zeros.

EXAMPLE   Round 0.843 to the nearest tenth.

SOLUTION

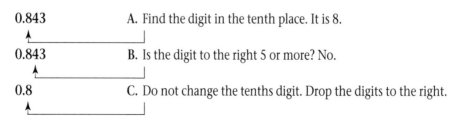

0.843   A. Find the digit in the tenth place. It is 8.

0.843   B. Is the digit to the right 5 or more? No.

0.8   C. Do not change the tenths digit. Drop the digits to the right.

WRITING NUMBERS AS WORDS AND ROUNDING NUMBERS

Dollar and cents amounts are often rounded to the nearest cent, or the hundredths place.

EXAMPLE $26.7443   **SOLUTION** $26.74
              $683.1582 $683.16

PROBLEMS

Write as numbers.
1. three thousand four hundred ninety-nine
2. one hundred eleven and $^{32}/_{100}$ dollars
3. two hundred six and eighty-eight thousandths

Write in word form.
4. 572
5. 2.897
6. $325.10

Round to the nearest place value shown.
7. ten thousand   327,975
8. thousand   816,777
9. hundred   26,312
10. ten   6336

11. one   28.91
12. tenth   86.379
13. hundredth   5.5787

Round 23,793,611 to the place value shown.
14. millions
15. ten millions
16. thousands
17. hundreds
18. ten thousands
19. hundred thousands

Round to the nearest place value shown.
20. cent $87.2671
21. ten cents $213.432
22. one dollar $671.98

23. ten dollars $5,982
24. hundred dollars $12,785

APPLICATIONS

25. As an accountant for the advertising agency of Phillips & Phillips, Marcia Strasser writes many checks. Write each check amount in words.
    a. $27.83
    b. $121. 77
    c. $569.14
    d. $8,721. 65

26. Juan Sanchez, an inventory clerk for a lumber yard, often rounds inventory figures for easier handling. Round the number from the inventory list to the nearest ten.
    a. grade 1 oak   519 ft.
    b. grade 2 oak   795 ft.
    c. grade 1 pine   323 ft.
    d. grade 2 pine   477 ft.

ADDING AND SUBTRACTING DECIMALS

When adding decimals, write the addition problem in vertical form. Be sure to line up the decimal points. When adding amounts with different numbers of decimal places, write zeros in the empty decimal places.

EXAMPLE $15.27 + 16.39 + 36.19$

SOLUTION
```
  15.27
  16.39
+36.19
  67.85
```

EXAMPLE $58.2 + 3.97 + 8 + 123.796$

SOLUTION
```
   58.2            58.200
    3.97            3.970
    8.              8.000
+123.796        +123.796
                 193.966
```

When subtracting decimals, write the subtraction problem in vertical form. Be sure to line up the decimal points. When subtracting amounts with different numbers of decimal places, write zeros in the empty decimal places.

EXAMPLE $78.63 - 42.41$

SOLUTION
```
  78.63
-42.41
  36.22
```

EXAMPLE $149.9 - 28.37$

SOLUTION
```
 149.9           149.90
-28.37          -28.37
                121.53
```

Adding and subtracting amounts of money is just like adding and subtracting decimals. The decimal point separates the dollars and cents. Remember to put a dollar sign in the total.

EXAMPLE $74.99 + 8.76

SOLUTION
```
 $74.99
 +8.76
 $ 83.75
```

EXAMPLE $750 - 43.29

SOLUTION
```
 $750.00
 -43.29
 $706.71
```

PROBLEMS

1.
```
 19.87
 32.24
+27.55
```

2.
```
 4.377
 6.829
+2.707
```

3.
```
   8.3
  12.78
+322.437
```

4.
```
  46.65
   3.5
+125.397
```

5.
```
$  2.77
  35.96
 +10.37
```

6. $22.19 + 47.75 + 13.88 + 19.85$
7. $0.78 + 9.82 + 36.242 + 37.4$
8. $6.7 + 27.81 + 653.47 + 5.5$
9. $54.32 + 0.37 + 2.5 + 0.797$
10. $6.22 + $53.19 + $ .33 + 7.85
11. $4.78 + $12.50 + $22 + 17.10

12.
```
 3.75
-2.18
```

13.
```
 376.55
-27.42
```

14.
```
 468.47
-233.55
```

15.
```
 367.05
-219.87
```

16.
```
$363.27
-79.14
```

17. $547.7 - 127.6$
18. $76.99 - 3.87$
19. $695.13 - 428.1$
20. $3076 - 2205.50$
21. $\$300 - \$5.75$
22. $\$445.19 - \$175.76$

APPLICATIONS Complete the sales receipts by finding the subtotals and the totals.

23.

Date 6/1/--	Auth. No. 86430	Identification	Clerk DL	Reg./Dept.	☑ Take ❑ Send
Qty	Class	Description	Price	Amount	
1		dress		77	98
1		jacket		85	99
2		hosiery	12.99 ea	25	98

a. Freight charges will be included with your invoice at the time of shipping. You will be billed the published rates from UPS, US Postal Service.

CUSTOMER SIGNATURE x _Shelley Turner_

b. Sales Slip

Subtotal	?	
Tax	13	30
Total	?	

24.

Date 3/14/--	Auth. No. 42	Identification	Clerk JR	Reg./Dept.	☑ Take ❑ Send
Qty	Class	Description	Price	Amount	
1		couch		599	95
1 pr		draperies		279	88

a. Freight charges will be included with your invoice at the time of shipping. You will be billed the published rates from UPS, US Postal Service.

CUSTOMER SIGNATURE x _Betty Clark_

b. Sales Slip

Subtotal	?	
Tax	57	19
Total	?	

Complete the bank deposit slips by finding the subtotals and the total deposits.

25.

		DOLLARS	CENTS
CASH	CURRENCY	72	00
	COINS		
CHECKS	LIST SEPARATELY 95-76	413	12
	98-11	25	00
	95-13	211	10
a.	SUBTOTAL	?	
↻	LESS CASH RECEIVED	50	00
b.	TOTAL DEPOSIT	?	

a.
b.

26.

		DOLLARS	CENTS
CASH	CURRENCY	23	00
	COINS	7	44
CHECKS	LIST SEPARATELY 85-76	175	66
	88-11	23	33
		12	87
a.	SUBTOTAL	?	
↻	LESS CASH RECEIVED	75	00
b.	TOTAL DEPOSIT	?	

a.
b.

27.

		DOLLARS	CENTS
CASH	CURRENCY		
	COINS	4	75
CHECKS	LIST SEPARATELY 57-12	25	95
	57-10	38	11
	SUBTOTAL	?	
↻	LESS CASH RECEIVED	25	00
	TOTAL DEPOSIT	?	

a.
b.

28. You are a cashier at a coffee shop. Compute the correct change for each of the following orders.

	Customer's Order	Customer Gives You	Change
a.	$8.76	$10.00	
b.	$12.94	$15.00	
c.	$9.30	$10.50	
d.	$16.11	$20.00	
e.	$5.57	$5.75	
f.	$22.02	$25.00	
g.	$7.12	$7.15	
h.	$3.33	$5.00	
i.	$28.04	$30.04	
j.	$6.12	$10.25	

MULTIPLYING AND DIVIDING DECIMALS

When multiplying decimals, multiply as if the decimal numbers were whole numbers. Then count the total number of decimal places in the factors. This number will be the number of decimal places in the product.

EXAMPLE

$$18.7 \leftarrow \text{factor}$$
$$\underline{\times 0.34} \leftarrow \text{factor}$$
$$748$$
$$\underline{561}$$
$$6358 \leftarrow \text{product}$$

SOLUTION

$$18.7 \leftarrow 1 \text{ decimal place}$$
$$\underline{\times 0.34} \leftarrow + 2 \text{ decimal places}$$
$$748$$
$$\underline{561}$$
$$6.358 \leftarrow 3 \text{ decimal places}$$

If the product does not have enough digits to place the decimal in the correct position, you will need to write zeros. Start at the right of the product in counting the decimal places and write zeros at the left.

EXAMPLE

$$0.63$$
$$\underline{\times 0.05}$$
$$315$$

SOLUTION

$$0.63 \leftarrow 2 \text{ decimal places}$$
$$\underline{\times 0.05} \leftarrow + 2 \text{ decimal places}$$
$$0.0315 \leftarrow 4 \text{ decimal places}$$

When multiplying amounts of money, round the answer to the nearest cent. Remember to put a dollar sign in the answer.

EXAMPLE

$$\$2.25$$
$$\underline{\times 1.5}$$
$$3.375$$

SOLUTION

$$\$ 2.25 \leftarrow 2 \text{ places}$$
$$\underline{\times 1.5} \leftarrow + 1 \text{ place}$$
$$\$3.375 \leftarrow 3 \text{ places}$$

$$\$2.25 \times 1.5 = \$3.375$$
$$= \$3.38$$
rounded to the nearest cent

When multiplying by 10, 100, or 1000, count the number of zeros. Then move the decimal point to the right the same number of spaces.

EXAMPLE

$$8.32 \times 100$$

SOLUTION

$$8.32 \times 100 = 8.32 = 832 \quad$$ 100 has 2 zeros; move decimal 2 places.

PROBLEMS

1.
$$18.3$$
$$\underline{\times 2.5}$$

2.
$$27.5$$
$$\underline{\times 8.2}$$

3.
$$56.8$$
$$\underline{\times 0.33}$$

4.
$$88.1$$
$$\underline{\times 0.23}$$

5.
$$0.57$$
$$\underline{\times 0.14}$$

6.
$$0.88$$
$$\underline{\times 0.07}$$

7.
$$0.93$$
$$\underline{\times 0.04}$$

8.
$$0.323$$
$$\underline{\times 0.005}$$

9. $\$17.85 \times 15.5 = \$276.675 =$

10. $\$25.24 \times 6.3 = \$159.012 =$

11. $\$18.15 \times 6.5 = \$117.975 =$

12. $\$14.98 \times 8.7 = \$130.326 =$

13. $33.8 \times 10 =$

14. $55.399 \times 100 =$

15. $0.518 \times 1000 =$

16. $532.788 \times 10,000 =$

APPLICATION

17. Below are partial payroll records for Fanciful Flowers. Complete the records by calculating gross earnings (hourly rate x hours worked), Social Security tax (gross earnings × 0.062), Medicare tax (gross earnings × 0.0145), federal income tax (gross earnings × 0.15), and state income tax (gross earnings × 0.045). Round each deduction to the nearest cent. Find the total deductions and subtract from gross earnings to find the net pay.

	Employee	Hourly Rate	Number of Hours	Gross Earnings	Social Security Tax	Medicare Tax	Federal Inc. Tax	State Inc. Tax	Total Deductions	Net Pay
a.	M. Smith	$8.25	24							
b.	R. Nash	$9.15	33							
c.	C. Young	$7.75	15							
d.	D. Cha	$9.15	30							

When dividing decimals, if there is a decimal point in the divisor, you must move it to the right to make the divisor a whole number. Move the decimal point in the dividend to the right the same number of places you moved the decimal point in the divisor. Then divide as with whole numbers.

$$\text{divisor} \quad 6\,\overline{)840} \quad \begin{array}{l} \overset{140}{} \quad \text{quotient} \\ \quad \text{dividend} \end{array}$$

EXAMPLE

$3.44\,\overline{)15.5488}$

SOLUTION

$3.44\,\overline{)15.5488}$

$$\begin{array}{r} 4.52 \\ 344\,\overline{)1554.88} \\ -1376 \\ \hline 1788 \\ -1720 \\ \hline 688 \\ -688 \\ \hline \end{array}$$

Add zeros to the right of the decimal point in the dividend if needed.

EXAMPLE

$0.42\,\overline{)0.147}$

SOLUTION

$0.42\,\overline{)0.147}$

$$\begin{array}{r} 0.35 \\ 42\,\overline{)14.70} \quad \text{zero added} \\ -126 \\ \hline 210 \\ -210 \\ \hline \end{array}$$

When the dividend is an amount of money, remember to place the dollar sign in the quotient and round the answer to the nearest cent.

EXAMPLE

$48\,\overline{)\$95.12}$

SOLUTION

$$48\,\overline{)\$95.120}^{\,\$1.981}$$

$\$95.12 \div 48 = \$1.98$ rounded to the nearest cent.

MULTIPLYING AND DIVIDING DECIMALS

When dividing by 10, 100, or 1000, count the number of zeros in 10, 100, or 1000 and move the decimal point to the left the same number of places.

EXAMPLE

15,213.7 ÷ 1000

SOLUTION

15,213.7 ÷ 1000 = 15213.7   1000 has 3 zeros;
= 15.2137   move decimal 3 places

PROBLEMS

Round to the nearest hundredth or the nearest cent.

18. $2.7\overline{)11.61}$

19. $1.3\overline{)7.67}$

20. $6.2\overline{)44.02}$

21. $0.3\overline{)1.62}$

22. $.05\overline{)1.47}$

23. $.04\overline{)28.4}$

24. $8.3\overline{)46.99}$

25. $3.4\overline{)178.3}$

26. $88\overline{)\$356.68}$

27. $45\overline{)\$42.79}$

28. $15\overline{)\$87.32}$

29. $14.1\overline{)7.823}$

APPLICATIONS

30. Your family is looking into buying a late model, used vehicle. Calculate (to the nearest tenth) the gas mileage for the following types of vehicles.

	Type of Vehicle	Miles	Gallons of Fuel	Miles per Gallon
a.	Subcompact	631	17.8	
b.	4-door sedan	471.4	16.6	
c.	Minivan	405.1	18.2	
d.	Compact	512.2	15.7	
e.	SUV	298.1	23.2	

FRACTION TO DECIMAL, DECIMAL TO FRACTION

Any fraction can be renamed as a decimal and any decimal can be renamed as a fraction. To rename a fraction as a decimal, use division. Think of the fraction bar in the fraction as meaning "divide by." For example, $5/8$ means "5 divided by 8." After the 5, write a decimal point and as many zeros as are needed. Then divide by 8.

EXAMPLE Change $3/8$ to a decimal.

SOLUTION

$$3/8 \rightarrow 8 \overline{)3.000} \quad \begin{array}{r} 0.375 \\ \hline 3.000 \\ -24 \\ \hline 60 \\ -56 \\ \hline 40 \\ -40 \end{array}$$

EXAMPLE Change $1/5$ to a decimal.

SOLUTION

$$1/5 \rightarrow 5 \overline{)1.0} \quad \begin{array}{r} 0.2 \\ \hline 1.0 \\ -10 \end{array}$$

If a fraction does not divide evenly, divide to one more decimal place than you are rounding to.

EXAMPLE Change $5/7$ to a decimal rounded to the nearest hundredth. (Divide to the thousandths place.)

SOLUTION

$$5/7 \rightarrow 7 \overline{)5.000} \quad \begin{array}{r} 0.714 = 0.71 \\ \hline 5.000 \\ -49 \\ \hline 10 \\ -7 \\ \hline 30 \\ -28 \\ \hline 2 \end{array}$$

EXAMPLE Change $2/7$ to a decimal rounded to the nearest thousandth. (Divide to the ten thousandths place.)

SOLUTION

$$2/7 \rightarrow 7 \overline{)2.0000} \quad \begin{array}{r} 0.2857 = 0.286 \\ \hline 2.0000 \\ -14 \\ \hline 60 \\ -56 \\ \hline 40 \\ -35 \\ \hline 50 \\ -49 \\ \hline 1 \end{array}$$

To rename a decimal as a fraction, name the place value of the digit at the far right. This is the denominator of the fraction.

$$0.83 = {}^{83}/_{100}$$

3 is in the hundredths place, so the denominator is 100.

$$0.007 = {}^{7}/_{1000}$$

7 is in the thousandths place, so the denominator is 1000.

Note that the number of zeros in the denominator is the same as the number of places to the right of the decimal point. The fraction should always be written in lowest terms.

$$0.25 = {}^{25}/_{100} = {}^{1}/_{4}$$

$$3.375 = 3 \, {}^{375}/_{1000} = 3 \, {}^{3}/_{8}$$

FRACTION TO DECIMAL, DECIMAL TO FRACTION

Change the fractions to decimals. Round to the nearest thousandth.

1. $^2/_5$ 2. $^5/_6$ 3. $^4/_9$ 4. $^7/_{10}$
5. $^9/_{25}$ 6. $^{115}/_{200}$ 7. $^1/_7$ 8. $^{13}/_{40}$
9. $^4/_{15}$ 10. $^5/_{12}$ 11. $^{11}/_{16}$ 12. $^1/_4$

Change the fractions to decimals. Round to the nearest hundredth.

13. $^1/_8$ 14. $^5/_9$ 15. $^{33}/_{35}$ 16. $^{12}/_{25}$
17. $^7/_{20}$ 18. $^2/_{25}$ 19. $^{15}/_{16}$ 20. $^2/_9$
21. $^3/_7$ 22. $^3/_4$ 23. $^1/_6$ 24. $^{31}/_{32}$

Change the decimals to fractions reduced to lowest terms.

25. 0.275   26. 0.3   27. 0.15   28. 0.8
29. 1.125   30. 0.117   31. 0.32   32. 2.5
33. 44.755   34. 0.005   35. 5.545   36. 0.2

37. In the past, stock prices were quoted as dollars and fractions of a dollar. Change the stock prices to dollars and cents. Round to the nearest cent.

Stock	Price
a. AdobeSy	$61\,^5/_{16}$
b. AirTran	$4\,^{15}/_{32}$
c. CNET	$50\,^3/_4$
d. ETrade	$20\,^1/_4$
e. Omnipoint	$112\,^5/_8$
f. Qualcomm	$142\,^1/_{16}$
g. WebLink	$17\,^{13}/_{16}$
h. Winstar	$70\,^{23}/_{32}$

38. Individual bowling averages in the Southern Community League are carried to the nearest hundredth. Convert the decimals to fractions reduced to the lowest terms.

Name	Average
a. B. Taylor	220.13
b. J. Scott	217.02
c. T. Anfinson	216.97
d. G. Ingram	212.08
e. D. Ingram	210.50
f. B. Jordan	209.25
g. G. Maddux	207.88
h. A. Jones	205.15

PERCENT TO DECIMAL, DECIMAL TO PERCENT

Percent is an abbreviation of the Latin words *per centum*, meaning "by the hundred." So percent means "divide by 100." A percent can be written as a decimal. To change a percent to a decimal, first write the percent as a fraction with a denominator of 100, then divide by 100.

EXAMPLE Change 31% to a decimal.

SOLUTION $31\% = {}^{31}/_{100} = 0.31$

EXAMPLE Change 17.3% to a decimal.

SOLUTION $17.3\% = {}^{17.3}/_{100} = 0.173$

When dividing by 100, you can just move the decimal point two places to the left. When you write a percent as a decimal, you are moving the decimal point two places to the left and dropping the percent sign (%). If necessary, use zero as a placeholder.

EXAMPLE

A. 31%

B. 7%

SOLUTION

$31\% = 31. = 0.31$ ◀——— Drop % sign.
——— Move decimal 2 places.

$7\% = 07. = 0.07$ ——— Insert a zero as a placeholder.

To write a decimal as a percent, move the decimal point two places to the right and add a percent sign (%).

EXAMPLE

A. 0.31

B. 0.07

C. 2.5

D. 0.008

SOLUTION

$0.31 = 0.31 = 31\%$ ◀ Add % sign.
——— Move decimal 2 places.

$0.07 = 0.07 = 7\%$

$2.5 = 2.50 = 250\%$

$0.008 = 0.008 = 0.8\%$

PROBLEMS

Write as decimals.

1. 35%
2. 22%
3. 68%
4. 30%

5. 49.2%
6. 88.7%
7. 11.5%
8. 92.9%

9. 322%
10. 526%
11. 663%
12. 275%

13. 9%
14. 5%
15. 4%
16. 12%

17. 7.03%
18. 9.02%
19. 2.0725%
20. 3.0843%

Write as percents.

21. 0.75
22. 0.17
23. 0.44
24. 0.26

25. 0.06   26. 0.07   27. 0.01   28. 0.02

29. 0.003   30. 0.009   31. 0.0045   32. 0.0029

33. 3.12   34. 4.14   35. 6.007   36. 5.000

37. 0.1   38. 0.5   39. 325.5   40. 0.2015

APPLICATIONS

41. The percent changes in retail sales were reported as a decimal in the October issue of *Retail Monthly* magazine. Change the decimals to percents.

	Retail Sales	
	Month	Change
a.	February	0.012
b.	March	0.006
c.	April	0.013
d.	May	0.038
e.	June	0.043
f.	July	0.011
g.	August	0.022

42. The commission rate schedule for a stockbroker is shown. Change the percents to decimals.

	Commission Rate Schedule	
	Dollar Amount	% of Dollar Amount
a.	$0 – $2,499	2.3%, minimum $30
b.	$2,500 – $4,999	2.0%, minimum $42
c.	$5,000 – $9,999	1.5%, minimum $65
d.	$10,000 – $14,999	1.1%, minimum $110
e.	$15,000 – $24,999	0.9%, minimum $135
f.	$25,000 – $49,999	0.6%, minimum $175
	$50,000 and above	negotiated

43. During the National Basketball Association season, the teams had these won–lost records. The Pct. column shows the percent of games won, expressed as a decimal. Change the decimals to percents.

EASTERN CONFERENCE
Atlantic Division

	W	L	Pct.	GB
a. Miami	28	16	.636	-
b. New York	27	17	.614	1
c. Philadelphia	25	21	.543	4
d. Boston	21	25	.457	8
e. Orlando	21	26	.447	8½
f. New Jersey	17	29	.370	12
g. Washington	15	31	.326	14

WESTERN CONFERENCE
Midwest Division

	W	L	Pct.	GB
p. San Antonio	30	16	.652	-
q. Utah	27	17	.614	2
r. Minnesota	25	18	.581	3½
s. Denver	21	22	.488	7½
t. Houston	19	27	.413	11
u. Dallas	18	27	.400	11½
v. Vancouver	12	32	.273	17

Central Division

	W	L	Pct.	GB
h. Indiana	29	15	.659	-
i. Milwaukee	26	21	.553	4½
j. Charlotte	24	20	.545	5
k. Toronto	24	20	.545	5
l. Detroit	22	23	.489	7ᵗ
m. Cleveland	19	26	.422	10½
n. Atlanta	17	26	.395	11½
o. Chicago	9	34	.209	19½

Pacific Division

	W	L	Pct.	GB
w. L.A. Lakers	34	11	.756	-
x. Portland	34	11	.756	-
y. Sacramento	28	16	.636	5½
z. Seattle	29	18	.617	6
aa. Phoenix	26	18	.591	7½
ab. Golden State	11	32	.256	22
ac. L.A. Clippers	11	34	.244	23

44. How many teams have won more than 75% of their games? _____
Who are they? _____

45. How many teams have won more than 50% of their games? _____

46. How many have won less than 30% of their games? _____

FINDING A PERCENTAGE

Finding a percentage means finding a percent of a number. To find a percent of a number, you change the percent to a decimal, then multiply it by the number.

EXAMPLE   30% of 90 is what number?

SOLUTION $30\% \times 90 = n$ — In mathematics, *of* means "times" and *is* means "equals."
— Let n stand for the unknown number.

$0.30 \times 90 = n$ Change the percent to a decimal.

$27 = n$ Multiply.

30% of $90 = 27$ Write the answer.

EXAMPLE   The delivery charge is 8% of the selling price of $145.00. Find the delivery charge.

EXAMPLE   The student had 95% correct out of 80 questions. How many answers were correct?

SOLUTION
$8\% \times \$145.00 = n$
$0.08 \times \$145.00 = n$
$\$11.60 = n$
$8\% \times \$145.00 = \$11.60$ delivery charge

SOLUTION
$95\% \times 80 = n$
$0.95 \times 80 = n$
$76 = n$
$95\% \times 80 = 76$ correct

PROBLEMS

Find the percentage.

1. 25% of 60
2. 45% of 80
3. 40% of 30
4. 33% of 112

5. 58% of 420
6. 50% of 422
7. 3% of 100
8. 2% of 247

9. 110% of 65
10. 7% of 785
11. 1% of 819
12. 4% of 19.5

13. 185% of 95
14. 200% of 720
15. 135% of 860
16. 120% of 3.35

17. 4.5% of 50
18. 1.25% of 300
19. 33.3% of 80
20. 67.2% of 365

Round the answer to the nearest cent.

21. 7% of $35.78
22. 6.5% of $80
23. 10% of $93.20
24. 5.5% of $135

25. 4.25% of $65.00
26. 2.75% of $115
27. 125% of $98
28. 7.5% of $150

29. 0.3% of $450
30. 0.15% of $125
31. 8.2% of $19.89
32. 5.25% of $110.15

FINDING A PERCENTAGE

33. The following items appeared in a sales flyer for a major department store. Calculate the amount saved from the regular price as well as the sale price for each item. Round to the nearest cent.

	Amount Saved	Sale Price
a. Save 25% on juniors knit shirts. Reg. $18.		
b. Save 30% on women's dresses. Reg. $69.99		
c. Save 20% on men's shoes. Reg. $135.		
d. Save 25% on all nursery cribs. Reg. $119.99		
e. Save 25% on all boxed jewelry sets. Reg. $19.99		
f. Save 30% on family athletic shoes. Reg. $59.99		

34. Student Sean Hu received these test scores. How many answers were correct on each test?

	Subject	Test Score	Number of Items	Correct Answers
a.	Math	90%	80	
b.	English	70%	90	
c.	Science	80%	110	
d.	Spanish	90%	50	
e.	Government	85%	100	

35. Sales taxes are found by multiplying the tax rate times the selling price of the item. The total purchase price is the selling price plus the sales tax. Find the sales tax and total purchase price for each selling price. Round to the nearest cent.

	Selling Price	Tax Rate	Sales Tax	Total Purchase Price
a.	$14.78	4%		
b.	$22.50	5%		
c.	$3.88	6%		
d.	$95.85	6.5%		
e.	$212.00	7.25%		
f.	$85.06	8.25%		
g.	$199.99	7.455%		

Glossary

A

actual cash value a method of insurance claim settlement in which the payment the insured receives is based on the replacement cost of an item minus depreciation (p. 426)

adjustable-rate mortgage (ARM) a mortgage with an interest rate that increases or decreases during the life of the loan, also known as a "variable-payment mortgage" (p. 222)

adjusted gross income gross income after certain reductions are calculated (p. 384)

allowance an adjustment to the tax withheld from your paycheck, based on your marital status and whether you have dependents (p. 386)

amortization the reduction of a loan balance through payments made over a period of time (p. 221)

annual percentage rate (APR) the cost of credit on a yearly basis, expressed as a percentage (p. 163)

annual percentage yield (APY) the amount of interest that a $100 deposit would earn, after compounding, for one year (p. 137)

annuity a series of equal regular deposits to a savings account (p. 22)

annuity (insurance) a contract purchased from an insurance company that guarantees a future fixed or variable payment to the purchaser for a certain number of years or for life (p. 495)

appraisal an estimate of the current value of the property (p. 226)

aptitudes the natural abilities people possess (p. 34)

arbitration a process whereby a conflict between a customer and a business is resolved by an impartial third party whose decision is legally binding (p. 108)

assets items of value that an individual or company owns, including cash, property, personal possessions, and investments (p. 65)

assigned risk pool a group of people who cannot get motor vehicle insurance (p. 436)

assisted-living facility (ALF) a residence complex that provides personal and medical services for the elderly (p. 485)

automated teller machine (ATM) a computer terminal that allows a withdrawal of cash from an account (p. 126)

B

bank reconciliation a report that accounts for the differences between the bank statement and your checkbook balance (p. 145)

bankruptcy a legal process in which some or all of the assets of a debtor are distributed among the creditors because the debtor is unable to pay his or her debts (p. 188)

bear market market condition that occurs when investors are pessimistic about the economy and sell stocks (p. 285)

bearer bond a bond that is not registered in the investor's name (p. 310)

beneficiary (estate) a person who is named to receive a portion of someone's estate (p. 499)

beneficiary (insurance) a person named to receive the benefits from an insurance policy (p. 464)

Blue Cross an insurance company that provides hospital care benefits (p. 453)

Blue Shield an insurance company that provides benefits for surgical and medical services performed by physicians (p. 453)

blue-chip stock a safe investment that generally attracts conservative investors, usually stocks issued by the strongest and most respected companies (p. 277)

bodily injury liability insurance that covers physical injuries caused by a vehicle accident for which you were responsible (p. 430)

budget a plan for using money to meet wants and needs (p. 74)

budget variance the difference between the budgeted amount and the actual amount that you spend (p. 77)

bull market market condition that occurs when investors are optimistic about the economy and buy stocks (p. 285)

C

cafeteria-style employee benefits programs that allow workers to choose the benefits that best meet their personal needs (p. 49)

capital gain profit from the sale of assets such as stocks, bonds, or real estate (p. 261)

capital loss the sale of an investment for less than its purchase price (p. 262)

capitalization the total amount of stocks and bonds issued by a corporation (p. 279)

career a commitment to work in a field that you find interesting and fulfilling (p. 32)

cash flow the money that goes into and out of your wallet and bank accounts (p. 70)

cash value in a whole life policy, the accumulated savings to which you are entitled when and if you cancel the policy (p. 467)

certificate of deposit (CD) a savings alternative in which money is left on deposit for a stated period of time to earn a specific rate of return (p. 132)

class-action suit a legal action on behalf of all the people who have suffered the same injustice(p. 110)

closed-end credit credit as a one-time loan that you will pay back over a specified period of time in payments of equal amounts (p. 157)

closed-end fund a mutual fund with a fixed number of shares that are issued by an investment company when the fund is first organized (p. 327)

closing a meeting of the seller, the buyer, and the lender of funds, or representatives of each party, to complete the transaction (p. 223)

codicil a document that explains, adds, or deletes provisions in an existing will (p. 504)

coinsurance the percentage of the medical expenses the policyholder must pay in addition to the deductible amount (p. 447)

collateral a form of security to help guarantee that the creditor will be repaid (p. 166)

collectibles items that appeal to collectors and investors, including rare coins, works of art, antiques, stamps, rare books, comic books, sports memorabilia, rugs, ceramics, and paintings (p. 366)

collision insurance that covers damage to your vehicle when it is involved in an accident (p. 432)

commercial bank a for-profit institution that offers a full range of financial services, including checking, savings, and lending (p. 129)

commercial property land and buildings that produce rental income (p. 353)

common stock a unit of ownership of a company that entitles the owner, or stockholder, to voting privileges (p. 250)

compounding the process in which interest is earned on both the principal—the original amount you deposited—and on any previously earned interest (p. 136)

consumer a person who purchases and uses goods or services (p. 17)

consumer credit the use of credit for personal needs (p. 154)

consumer price index (CPI) a measure of the changes in prices for commonly purchased goods and services in the United States (p. 77)

convertible bond a bond that an investor can trade for shares of the corporation's common stock (p. 307)

cooperative a nonprofit organization owned and operated by its members for the purpose of saving money on the purchase of goods and services (p. 99)

cooperative education a program that allows students to enhance classroom learning with part-time work related to their majors and interests (p. 41)

co-payment a flat fee that you pay every time you receive a covered service (p. 449)

corporate bond a corporation's written pledge to repay a specific amount of money, along with interest (p. 251)

cosigning agreeing to be responsible for another person's loan payments if that person fails to make them (p. 182)

coupon bond a bond that is registered in the owner's name for the face value only and not for interest (p. 310)

cover letter a personal letter you present along with your résumé (p. 45)

credit an arrangement to receive cash, goods, or services now and pay for them in the future (p. 154)

credit rating a measure of a person's ability and willingness to make credit payments on time (p. 170)

credit union a nonprofit financial institution that is owned by its members and organized for their benefit (p. 130)

creditor an entity, such as a financial institution, merchant, or individual, that lends money (p. 154)

current yield the annual dividend of an investment divided by the current market value (p. 286)

cyclical stock stock with a market value that tends to reflect the state of the economy (p. 278)

D

debenture a bond that is backed only by the reputation of the issuing corporation, rather than by its assets (p. 306)

debit card a cash card that allows you to withdraw money or pay for purchases from your checking or savings account (p. 126)

deductible the set amount that a policyholder must pay per loss on an insurance policy (p. 414)

deed the official document transferring ownership from seller to buyer (p. 224)

defensive stock stock that remains stable during declines in the economy (p. 278)

deficit the financial situation that occurs when more money is spent than is earned or received (p. 72)

defined-benefit plan a retirement plan that specifies the benefits an employee will receive at retirement age, based on total earnings and years on the job (p. 489)

defined-contribution plan an individual retirement account for each employee, also called an "individual account plan" (p. 488)

demand the amount of goods and services people are willing to buy (p. 14)

demographic trends tendencies of people grouped by age, gender, ethnicity, education, or income that change over time (p. 37)

direct deposit an automatic deposit of net pay to an employee's designated bank account (p. 125)

direct investment real estate investment in which the owner holds legal title to the property he or she has purchased (p. 352)

disability income insurance coverage that provides regular cash income when you are unable to work due to a pregnancy, non-work-related accident, or illness (p. 460)

discretionary income the money left after paying for the essentials, such as food, clothing, shelter, transportation, and medication (p. 71)

diversification the process of spreading your assets among several different types of investments to reduce risk (p. 254)

dividends distributions of money, stock, or other property that a corporation pays to stockholders (p. 246)

down payment a portion of the total cost of an item that must be paid at the time of purchase (p. 96)

E

earnings per share a corporation's net, or after-tax, earnings divided by the number of outstanding shares of common stock (p. 287)

economics the study of the decisions that go into making, distributing, and using goods and services (p. 14)

economy the ways in which people make, distribute, and use their goods and services (p. 14)

emergency fund a savings account you can access quickly to pay for unexpected expenses or emergencies (p. 238)

endorsement the signature of the payee, the party to whom the check has been written (p. 144)

endowment life insurance that provides coverage for a specific period of time and pays a sum of money to the policyholder if he or she is living at the end of the endowment period (p. 468)

equity the value of the home less the amount still owed on the money borrowed to purchase it (p. 209)

equity capital money that a business gets from its owners in order to operate (p. 250)

escrow account an account where money is held in trust until it can be delivered to a designated party (p. 217)

estate all property and assets owned by an individual or group (p. 499)

estate planning the process of creating a detailed plan for managing personal assets to make the most of them while you are alive and to ensure that they are distributed wisely after your death (p. 499)

estate tax a federal tax collected on the value of a person's property at the time of his or her death (p. 381)

exclusion income that is not subject to taxes, also called "tax-exempt income" (p. 383)

executor a person who is willing and able to perform the tasks involved in carrying out a will (p. 504)

exemption a deduction from adjusted gross income for the taxpayer, the spouse, and qualified dependents (p. 385)

extension an extended deadline for filing an income tax return (p. 391)

F

face value the dollar amount that the bondholder will receive at the bond's maturity (p. 306)

Federal Reserve System the central banking organization of the United States (p. 16)

finance charge the total dollar amount you pay to use credit (p. 160)

financial leverage the use of borrowed funds for direct investment purposes (p. 358)

financial planner a specialist who is trained to offer specific financial help and advice (p. 257)

fixed-rate mortgage a mortgage with a fixed interest rate and a fixed schedule of payments, also called a "conventional mortgage" (p. 221)

401(k) plan a type of retirement savings plan funded by a portion of your salary that is deducted from your gross paycheck and placed in a special account, also called a "salary-reduction plan" (p. 488)

fraud dishonest business practices that are meant to deceive, trick, or gain an unfair advantage (p. 104)

future value the amount your original deposit will be worth in the future based on earning a specific interest rate over a specific period of time (p. 21)

G

geographic trends tendencies of people moving from one area of the country to another as financial centers shift location (p. 37)

goals things you want to accomplish (p. 6)

good a physical item that is produced and can be weighed or measured (p. 11)

government bond the written pledge of a government or a municipality, such as a city, to repay a specific sum of money with interest (p. 251)

grace period a time period during which no finance charges will be added to your account (p. 160)

growth stock stock issued by a corporation whose potential earnings may be higher than the average earnings predicted for all the corporations in the country (p. 278)

guardian the person who accepts the responsibility of caring for the children of the deceased and managing an estate for the children until they reach a certain age (p. 504)

H

hazard anything that increases the likelihood of loss through peril (p. 413)

health insurance a form of protection that eases the financial burden people may experience as a result of illness or injury (p. 444)

health maintenance organization (HMO) a health insurance plan that directly employs or contracts with selected, or preapproved, physicians and other medical professionals to provide health care services in exchange for a fixed, prepaid monthly premium (p. 454)

heirs the people who will have the legal right to your assets when you die (p. 498)

home equity loan a loan based on the difference between the current market value of a home and the amount the borrower owes on the mortgage (p. 223)

homeowners insurance coverage that provides protection for your residence and its associated financial risks (p. 419)

I

impulse buying purchasing items on the spur of the moment (p. 99)

income cash inflow, or the money you receive (p. 70)

income dividends the earnings a fund pays to shareholders (p. 341)

income stock stock that pays higher-than-average dividends compared to other stock issues (p. 277)

income tax tax on wages, salaries, and self-employed earnings (p. 382)

income tax return a form, such as 1040 or 1040EZ, on which a taxpayer reports how much money he or she received from working and other sources and the exact taxes that are owed (p. 383)

indirect investment a real estate investment in which a trustee is appointed to hold legal title to the property on behalf of an investor or group of investors (p. 354)

individual retirement account (IRA) a special account in which a person sets aside a portion of income for retirement (p. 490)

inflation rise in the level of prices for goods and services over time (p. 16)

informational interview a meeting with someone who works in your area of interest who can provide you with practical information about a career or company of interest (p. 43)

inheritance tax a state tax collected on the property left by a person to his or her heir(s) in a will (p. 381)

insolvency a financial state that occurs if liabilities are greater than assets (p. 69)

insurance protection against possible financial loss (p. 412)

interest the price that is paid for the use of another's money (p. 17)

interest inventories tests that help you identify the activities you enjoy the most (p. 34)

internship a position in which a person receives training by working with people who are experienced in a particular field (p. 41)

intestate a status of not having a valid will (p. 501)

investment liquidity the ability to buy or sell an investment quickly without substantially reducing its value (p. 249)

investment-grade bonds bonds that are issued by financially stable companies or municipalities (p. 323)

itemized deduction a specific expense, such as a medical expense, that you deduct from your adjusted gross income (p. 384)

J

job work you do mainly to earn money (p. 32)

K

Keogh plan a retirement plan specially designed for self-employed people and their employees, also known as an "H.R.10 plan" or a "self-employed retirement plan" (p. 493)

L

landlord the person who owns the property that is rented (p. 202)

large-cap stock stock of a corporation that has issued a large number of shares of stock and has a large amount of capitalization (p. 279)

lease a legal document that defines the conditions of the rental agreement between the tenant and the landlord (p. 205)

legal aid society a network of community law offices that provide free or low-cost legal assistance (p. 111)

liabilities the debts you owe (p. 68)

liability legal responsibility for the financial cost of another person's losses or injuries (p. 418)

line of credit the maximum amount of money a creditor will allow a credit user to borrow (p. 157)

liquid assets cash and items that can be quickly converted to cash (p. 67)

liquidity the ability to easily convert financial assets into cash without loss in value (p. 9)

living will a legal document in which you state if you want to be kept alive by artificial means if you become terminally ill and are unable to make such a decision (p. 505)

load fund a mutual fund for which you pay a commission every time you buy or sell shares (p. 328)

M

managed care prepaid health plans that provide comprehensive health care to their members (p. 453)

market value the price at which property would sell (p. 67)

maturity date the date when a bond will be repaid (p. 306)

mediation the attempt by a neutral third party to resolve a conflict between a customer and a business through discussion and negotiation (p. 108)

Medicaid a medical assistance program for certain low-income individuals and families (p. 458)

medical payments coverage insurance that pays the costs of minor accidental injuries to visitors on your property (p. 422)

Medicare a federally-funded health insurance program for people over 65 and people with certain disabilities (p. 456)

mentor an experienced employee who serves as a teacher and counselor for a less-experienced person (p. 52)

minimum monthly payment the smallest amount you can pay and remain a borrower in good standing (p. 168)

mobility the ability to move easily from place to place (p. 198)

money management planning how to get the most from your money (p. 60)

money market account a savings account that requires a minimum balance and earns interest that varies from month to month (p. 134)

mortgage a long-term loan extended to someone who buys property (p. 218)

mortgage bond a bond that is backed by assets of the corporation, also called a "secured bond" (p. 307)

municipal bond a security issued by a state or local government (town, city, or county) to pay for its ongoing activities (p. 317)

mutual fund an investment in which investors pool their money to buy stocks, bonds, or other securities selected by professional managers who work for an investment company (p. 252)

N

negligence the failure to take ordinary or reasonable care to prevent accidents from happening (p. 413)

net asset value (NAV) the amount one share of a mutual fund is worth (p. 328)

net income the income you receive (take-home pay, allowance, gifts, and interest) (p. 162)

net worth the difference between the amount that you own and the debts that you owe (p. 65)

networking making and using contacts to get job information and advice (p. 43)

no-fault system a system of insurance in which drivers who are involved in accidents collect money from their own insurance companies (p. 433)

no-load fund a mutual fund that has no commission fee (p. 329)

O

open dating a labeling method that indicates the freshness, or shelf life, of a perishable product, such as milk or bread (p. 100)

open-end credit credit as a loan with a certain limit on the amount of money you can borrow for a variety of goods and services (p. 157)

open-end fund a mutual fund with an unlimited number of shares that are issued and redeemed by an investment company at the investors' request (p. 327)

opportunity cost what is given up when making one choice instead of another (p. 8)

overdraft protection an automatic loan made to an account if the balance will not cover checks written (p. 141)

over-the-counter (OTC) market a network of dealers who buy and sell the stocks of corporations that are not listed on a securities exchange (p. 292)

P

par value an assigned dollar value that is printed on a stock certificate (p. 275)

participation certificate (PC) an investment in a group of mortgages that have been purchased by a government agency (p. 357)

penny stock stock that typically sells for less than $1 a share, although it can sell for as much as $10 a share (p. 280)

pension plan a retirement plan that is funded at least in part by an employer (p. 49)

peril anything that may possibly cause a loss (p. 413)

personal balance sheet also a net worth statement, a financial statement that lists items of value owned, debts owed, and a person's net worth (p. 65)

personal financial planning arranging to spend, save, and invest money to live comfortably, have financial security, and achieve goals (p. 6)

personal financial statement a document that provides information about an individual's current financial position and presents a summary of income and spending (p. 65)

personal property floater additional property insurance that covers the damage or loss of a specific item of high value (p. 420)

point-of-sale transaction a purchase by a debit card of a good or service at a retail store, a restaurant, or elsewhere (p. 127)

point-of-service (POS) plan a health insurance plan that combines features of both HMOs and PPOs (p. 455)

points extra charges that must be paid by the buyer to the lender in order to get a lower interest rate (p. 219)

policy a contract between an insurance company and a person by which that person joins a risk-sharing group (p. 412)

portfolio a collection of all the securities held by an investor (p. 294)

potential earning power the amount of money you may earn over time (p. 33)

power of attorney a legal document that authorizes someone to act on your behalf (p. 506)

precious gems rough mineral deposits (usually crystals) that are dug from the earth by miners and then cut and shaped into brilliant jewels (p. 363)

precious metals valuable ores such as gold, platinum, and silver (p. 361)

preferred provider organization (PPO) a group of doctors and hospitals that agree to provide specified medical services to members at prearranged fees (p. 455)

preferred stock a type of stock that gives the owner the advantage of receiving cash dividends before common stockholders receive cash dividends (p. 250)

premium the fee a policyholder pays for insurance (p. 412)

present value the amount of money you would need to deposit now in order to have a desired amount in the future (p. 22)

price-earnings (PE) ratio the price of one share of stock divided by a corporation's earnings per share of stock over the last 12 months (p. 287)

principal the original amount of money you deposit (p. 20)

private corporation a company that issues stock to a small group of people, also called a "closely held corporation" (p. 272)

private mortgage insurance (PMI) a special policy that protects the lender in case the buyer cannot make payments or cannot make them on time (p. 218)

probate the legal procedure of proving that a will is valid or invalid (p. 503)

property damage liability motor vehicle insurance that applies when you damage the property of others (p. 432)

prospectus a document that discloses information about a company's earnings, assets and liabilities, its products or services, a particular stock, and the qualifications of its management (p. 263)

public corporation a company that sells its shares openly in stock markets, where anyone can buy them, also called a "publicly held corporation" (p. 272)

R

rate of return the percentage of increase in the value of your savings from earned interest (p. 135)

real estate land and any structures that are on it, such as a house or other building, that a person or family owns (p. 67)

rebate a partial refund of the price of a product (p. 100)

refinance obtaining a new mortgage to replace an existing one (p. 223)

registered bond a bond registered in the owner's name by the company that issues the bond (p. 310)

renters insurance a type of insurance that covers the loss of a tenant's personal property as a result of damage or theft (p. 208)

replacement value a method for settling claims in which the insured receives the full cost of repairing or replacing an item (p. 426)

résumé one- or two-page summary of your education, training, work experience, and qualifications (p. 45)

retained earnings profits that a company reinvests (p. 249)

risk the chance of loss or injury (p. 412)

S

safe-deposit box a small, secure storage compartment that you can rent in a bank (p. 63)

savings and loan association (S&L) a financial institution that traditionally specialized in savings accounts and mortgage loans but now offers many of the same services as commercial banks (p. 130)

securities all the investments that are bought and sold on the stock market, including stocks, bonds, mutual funds, options, and commodities (p. 272)

securities exchange a marketplace where brokers who represent investors meet to buy and sell securities (p. 291)

security deposit an amount of money paid to the owner of the property by a tenant to guard against any financial loss or damage that the tenant might cause (p. 208)

serial bonds bonds issued at the same time but that mature on different dates (p. 309)

service a task that a person or a machine performs for you (p. 11)

service contract a separately purchased agreement by the manufacturer or distributor to cover the costs of repairing an item (p. 103)

service industries businesses that provide services for a fee (p. 39)

simple interest the interest computed only on the principal, the amount that you borrow (p. 167)

sinking fund a fund to which a corporation makes deposits for the purpose of paying back a bond issue (p. 308)

small claims court a court that deals with legal disputes that involve amounts below a certain limit (p. 109)

small-cap stock stock issued by a company with a capitalization of $500 million or less (p. 280)

speculative investment a high-risk investment that might earn a large profit in a short time (p. 243)

standard deduction an amount of money set by the IRS that is not taxed (p. 384)

standard of living a measure of quality of life based on the amounts and kinds of goods and services a person can buy (p. 32)

stop-loss an insurance policy provision that requires the policyholder to pay all costs up to a certain amount, after which the insurance company pays 100 percent of the remaining expenses covered in the policy (p. 447)

stop-payment order a request that a bank or other financial institution not cash a particular check (p. 143)

supply the amount of goods and services available for sale (p. 14)

surplus extra money that can be spent or saved, depending on a person's financial goals and values (p. 72)

syndicate a temporary association of individuals or business firms organized to perform a task that requires a large amount of funds (p. 355)

T

take-home pay the amount of income left after taxes and other deductions are taken out of your gross pay (p. 71)

tax audit a detailed examination of your tax return by the IRS (p. 401)

tax credit an amount of money that can be subtracted directly from taxes you owe (p. 386)

tax deduction an expense that you can subtract from your adjusted gross income to figure your taxable income (p. 384)

tax liability the total amount of taxes owed (p. 380)

taxable income adjusted gross income less any allowable tax deductions and exemptions (p. 384)

tax-deferred income income that is taxed at a later date (p. 261)

tax-exempt income income that is not taxed (p. 261)

tenant a person who pays for the right to live in a residence owned by someone else (p. 202)

term insurance insurance that provides protection against loss of life for only a specified term, or period of time, also called "temporary life insurance" (p. 466)

time value of money the increase of an amount of money due to earned interest or dividends (p. 19)

title insurance a type of insurance that protects the property buyer in case problems with the title are found later (p. 224)

total return a calculation that includes the annual dividend as well as any increase or decrease in the original purchase price of an investment (p. 286)

trends developments that mark changes in a particular area (p. 32)

trust an arrangement in which a designated person known as a "trustee" manages assets for the benefit of someone else (p. 501)

U

uninsured motorist's protection insurance that covers you and your family members if you are involved in an accident with an uninsured or hit-and-run driver (p. 432)

unit pricing the use of a standard unit of measurement to compare the prices of packages that are different sizes (p. 100)

V

values beliefs and principles you consider important, correct, and desirable (p. 7)

vesting the right of an employee to keep the company's contributions from company-sponsored plans, such as pensions, even if the employee no longer works for that employer (p. 489)

W

warranty a written guarantee from the manufacturer or distributor that states the conditions under which the product can be returned, replaced, or repaired (p. 101)

wealth an abundance of valuable material possessions or resources (p. 65)

whole life insurance a permanent policy for which you pay a specified premium each year for the rest of your life (p. 467)

will a legal declaration of a person's wishes regarding disposal of his or her estate after death (p. 500)

Y

yield the rate of return, usually stated as a percentage, earned by an investor who holds a bond for a certain period of time (p. 323)

Z

zero-coupon bond a bond that does not produce interest (p. 311)

Index

S

Travel and entertainment (T&E)
    card, 160–161
Travelers check, 146
Treasury Direct, 314
Treasury notes, 314–6315
Trends, 32
Triplex, 211
Trust, 506–508
    defined, 501
    importance of avoiding probate,
        506
    types of, 507–508
Trustor, 506
Truth in Lending Act, 164, 168, 183
Truth in Savings law, 137
TSA. *See* Tax-sheltered annuity (TSA)
TSA. *See* Transferable Skills Analysis
    (TSA)
Turnover ratio, 337
21st Century Act, 127, 141

U

Unemployment, 17
Unified transfer tax rate, 512
Uninsured motorist's protection, 432
United Kingdom, 279
United States Secret Service, 75
Unit pricing, 100–101
Universal life insurance, 468
Up-front cash, 166
U.S. Bankruptcy Act of 1978, 190
U.S. Better Business Bureau, 108
U.S. Department of Commerce, 263
U.S. Department of Housing and
    Urban Development (HUD), 201
U.S. Savings Bond, 133–135, 247, 321
U.S. Secret Service, 182
U.S. Treasury bills (T-bills), 245, 247,
    321
    defined, 314
    dollar amount of return on, 315
    rate of return on, 316
U.S. Treasury bonds, 314–316, 321,
    358
U.S. Treasury notes, 315–316, 321,
    358
Utilities, 208
Utility fund, 332
Utility stock, 248

V

VA. *See* Veterans Administration (VA)
Vacation home, 353
Value Line, 340
Value Line Investment Survey, 283
Value Line Stock Index, 264–265
Value of a bond, 251
Values
    defined, 7
    life situations and, 14
Variable expenses, 71, 75–77
Variable interest rate, 166
Variable life policy, 467–468
Vesting, 489
Veterans Administration (VA),
    222–223, 488
Vision care insurance, 449
Voluntary savings plan, 343
Volunteering, 40–41, 506
Voting rights, 275

W

Wage and Tax Statement. *See* IRS
    Form W-2
Wage loss insurance, 433
Waiver of premium disability
    benefit, 470
Wall Street Journal, The, 43, 262, 264,
    281, 319
Want, defined, 7
Warehouse, 98
Warranty, 101–103
Wealth
    defined, 65
    taxes on, 381
Whole life insurance, 467–468
Wiesenberger Investment
    Companies, 340
*Wiesenberger Investment Companies
    Yearbook,* 265
Will(s)
    altering and rewriting, 504
    defined, 500
    format of, 503
    importance of, 501
    living, 505–506
    and probate, 503
    types of, 501–502
    writing your, 503–504

Windfall, 241
Withdrawal options, 344
Work culture, 48
Work environment, 47–48
Worker's compensation, 460

Y

Yield, 323, 325

Z

Zero-coupon bond, 311
Zoning laws, local, 215

Features Index

AFP/Corbis 309; AbleStock/Royalty Free 181ml; age fotostock/SuperStock 293, 295br, 427; Alan Abramowitz/Getty Images 426; Erik Aeder/SuperStock 461; Bruce Ayers/Getty Images 110, 450; Bill Bachman/PhotoEdit 38, 240mc; David Ball/ Getty Images 366; Paul Barton/Corbis 176, 181mr, 381; Randa Bishop/Image State 80; Ed Bock/Corbis 216b, 240b; Cleve Bryant/PhotoEdit 317; Jeffrey Burke/Image State/Royalty Free 78b; Jeffrey Burke/Imagestate xi, 350, TM157; Paul Chesley/Getty Images 497; Steve Chenn/Corbis 446; Stephen Chernin/Getty Images 295t; Gianni Cigolini/Image Bank 362t; Kindra Clineff/Index Stock 128r; Stewart Cohen/Getty Images 96; Comstock Images/Alamy/Royalty Free 128l; Comstock Images/Getty Images/Royalty Free 51; Corbis/Royalty-Free viii(b), xiii(b), xiv(m), 153, 196, 476, 507, 653, TM113, TM199; Philip James Corwin/Corbis xii(t), 378, TM167; Will Crocker/ Image Bank 362m; Jim Cummins/Getty Images 457, 487; Robert E. Daemmrich/Getty Images 384; Patrick De Wilde/Imagestate 365; Tony Demin/Imagestate xiii(t), 442, TM187; Digital Vision/Getty Images/Royalty Free 164, 502; Melanie Einzig/Getty Images 285; Myrleen Ferguson/PhotoEdit 36bl; Fisher/Hatcher/Getty Images 210; Peter M. Fisher/Corbis 156; Tony Freeman/PhotoEdit 93; Getty Images 9l; Getty Images/Royalty Free ix, 240br, 236, TM125; Martyn Goddard/Corbis 187; Larry Dale Gordon/ Getty Images 484br; Jeff Greenberg/PhotoEdit 41, 125, 278; Nick Gunderson/Getty Images 462; Charles Gupton/Corbis 422; Will Hart/PhotoEdit 33; Chip Henderson/Getty Images 48; Hemera.com 153b, 154t, 155, 156b; Maria Hesse/ Imagestate 402tl; Jeremy Hoare/Life File/Getty Images 448; Jack Hollingsworth/Corbis 714; Tony Hopewell/Getty Images 179; Dave G. Houser/Corbis v(t), 30, TM61; Richard Hutchins/PhotoEdit 226; Image State 20, 140; Imagestate/ Royalty Free 204, 295mr; Index Stock 234-235, TM122; iStock 161, 163; Mark Junak/Getty Images 24; Wolfgang Kaehler/Corbis 382; Reed Kaestner/Imagestate 511; Zigy Kalunzny/Getty Images 480; Bonnie Kamin/PhotoEdit 129r, 273; Helen King/Corbis 181bl; Jutta Klee/Corbis 181tr; Michael Krasowitz/Getty Images 78tr; Frederic Lucano/Getty Images 8m; Court Mast/Getty Images 169; Masterfile/Royalty Free 374-375, TM123; Francis G. Mayer/Corbis 364; Joe McBride/Corbis 118-119, TM88; Patti McConville/Getty Images xii(b), 410, TM177; Medioimages/Imagestate 333, 423; Cathy Melloan Resources/PhotoEdit 211; Benn Mitchell/Image Bank 362b; Antonio Mo/Getty Images 357; Christopher J. Morris/Corbis 277; Roy Morsch/Corbis 2-3 TM50; John Neubauer/PhotoEdit 251; Michael Newman/ PhotoEdit 44, 92r, 99, 134, 402b, 403; Chris Noble/Getty Images 248; Roy Ooms/Masterfile 234-235, TM89; Lisa Peardon/Getty Images 414; Jose Luis Pelaez, Inc./Corbis 9r, 116-117, TM51, 129l, 294; Photos.com/Royalty Free 167, 169; Pictor/Imagestate 279; Pluriel Phototheque/SuperStock 216t; Frank Polich/Reuters/Corbis 417; Todd Powell/Index Stock vii(b),120, TM91; Michael Prince/Corbis 08l; Patrick Ramsey/Imagestate 454; Reuters Newmedia, Inc/Corbis 295bl, 295tl; Reuters/Corbis x(t), 270, TM135; Mark Richards/PhotoEdit 402m; Jon Riley/Getty Images 9m, 36t, 311; Elena Rooraid/ PhotoEdit 217m; David Rosenberg/Getty Images 263; Galen Rowell/Corbis 15; Norbert Schaefer/Corbis 61; Jed & Kaory Share/Getty Images 126; H. Sitton/Corbis 146; George Shelley/Corbis 376-377, TM164; Ariel Skelley/ Corbis 105, 129r, 219, 466; Don Smetzer/Getty Images v, 4, TM53; Lee Snider/Corbis 334; Bill Stanton/Imagestate x(b), 304, TM145; Tom Stewart/Corbis vi(b), 58, 159, 36tl, 518-519, TM71, TM165; Mark Stone/Getty Images 251; Stockbyte Platinum/Alamy 82; Superstock Inc./SuperStock 220; The Cover Story/Corbis 247; ThinkStock/Royalty Free vii(t), 88, TM81; ThinkStock/SuperStock/Royalty Free 354; Bob Torrez/Getty Images 216m; Pablo Corral Vega/Corbis 106; Victoria Blackie/Getty Images 484l; Steve Vider/Imagestate 259, 491; Alana Wesley White/PhotoEdit viii(t), 152, TM101; Dana White/PhotoEdit 67; Matthew Wiley/Masterfile 512; David Young Wolff/PhotoEdit 7, 36br, 240tr, 342, 484tr, 500; Mei Yan/Masterfile 92l.